Risk-Based Approach to Secure Cloud Migration

Minakshi
King Khalid University, Saudi Arabia

Tarun Kumar
Galgotias University, India

IGI Global
Scientific Publishing
Publishing Tomorrow's Research Today

Vice President of Editorial Melissa Wagner
Director of Acquisitions Mikaela Felty
Director of Book Development Jocelynn Hessler
Production Manager Mike Brehm
Cover Design Phillip Shickler

Published in the United States of America by
IGI Global Scientific Publishing
701 East Chocolate Avenue
Hershey, PA, 17033, USA
Tel: 717-533-8845
Fax: 717-533-7115
Website: https://www.igi-global.com E-mail: cust@igi-global.com

Library of Congress Cataloging-in-Publication Data

LCCN: 2024053531 (CIP Data Pending)
ISBN: 979-8-3693-7137-4
EISBN: 979-8-3693-7139-8
British Cataloguing in Publication Data
A Cataloguing in Publication record for this book is available from the British Library.

Table of Contents

Detailed Table of Contents

In recent times the adoption of advanced technology has been increasing in the general masses. Hence the amount of data being produced in an average smart city has increased by many times. This leads to high latency and low reliability issues in the traditional cloud computing paradigm. Therefore, stagnating the functionality of the cities as a whole and thus the practice of edge computing may bring about a positive change. The decentralizing computing resources decreases the reliance on traditional cloud computing. This minimizes latency and optimizes data processing. Distributed deep learning in central and edge cloud systems reduces latency. Intelligent offloading improves service quality in smart cities, and machine learning enhances mobile edge computing. In this work, suggestions for reducing the cost for handling the smart cities are discussed. These findings and discussions can be the stepping stones towards the future. A future where smart cities can be operated with less hassle and better cost management.

The exponential growth of cloud computing has increased concerns over data security and privacy for organizations and individuals. Traditional security mechanisms often fail to provide robust protection against emerging threats. This review paper explores the integration of blockchain technology to enhance cloud data security and encryption. Blockchain's decentralized, immutable, and transparent nature offers a promising solution to vulnerabilities in centralized cloud architectures. The paper discusses blockchain's fundamental principles and their application in securing cloud data. It also reviews current research and case studies on the practical implementation and benefits of blockchain in cloud security. Challenges and future directions in merging blockchain and cloud data security are identified and analyzed. This comprehensive review aims to demonstrate how blockchain can revolutionize cloud data security, providing a trustworthy framework for data protection in the digital age.

Cloud computing is an advanced technology that provides access to different services via the internet. These services include applications such as servers, networking, data storage, databases, and software. For this reason, this technology is very popular for institutions and individuals for many reasons such as cost, production, efficiency and speed.In this study, data replication is discussed in order to solve security breaches in cloud computing technologies. Data replication is the process of making one or more backup copies of a database or other data store, in whole or in part. The primary benefit of data replication is to ensure the availability of data recovery and functional critical applications in disaster situations. In such a case, if the primary data source is damaged, a copy of that data source can be created. In addition, transactional consistency is ensured so that data is up-to-date and consistent. Data replication tools can lighten the IT burden of creating and managing enterprise-wide data replication operations. Thus, data loss in cloud computing is reduced.

This article highlights the significance of database encryption and offers an extensive examination of various encryption techniques that have been proposed. With data security being a top priority for governments, companies, and organizations, the need to protect databases from cyberattacks is imperative. Over the years, numerous encryption schemes have been developed to safeguard databases from unauthorized access. Cloud storage is crucial for remote data storage, but many establishments are concerned about the security of their files when they are sent to the cloud. To maintain the integrity of stored data, data encryption techniques are necessary. While businesses once believed that cloud providers could manage all their data securely, it has become evident that cloud providers cannot always honor such commitments when responding to government information requests. This study emphasizes the importance of database encryption and provides a comprehensive overview of various encryption techniques.

Cloud infrastructure has improved corporate scalability and cost-efficiency, but it has also increased security vulnerabilities. Strong security mechanisms are needed to secure sensitive data and comply with regulations as cloud computing grows. This study compares the CSA Cloud Controls Matrix, NIST Cloud Computing Security Framework, and ISO/IEC 27017 cloud security frameworks. It examines their pros, cons, and suitability for multi-tenancy, encryption, and regulatory compliance. Organisations may use the paper's best practices to create complete cloud security strategies that mitigate evolving risks, scale, and comply with regulations. This analysis shows how organisations may negotiate the difficult security landscape by combining frameworks to protect their cloud systems. The findings show that the dynamic cloud ecosystem requires a coordinated strategy to modern security concerns.

In todays digital world, organizations are growing rapidly leveraging Cloud Infrastructure. However Data breach is one of the top concerns in the cloud realm. With poorly defined access control mechanisms threat actors gain unauthorized access to sensitive data leading to financial loss, brand damage to organizations. IAM is a preventive access control framework that consists of various tools, technologies and processes to build access policies around the protected asset to minimize the impact of cyber attack. This chapter will cover fundamentals of IAM, opportunities and challenges of IAM in the cloud, and effective access management strategies. This chapter will deep dive into some of the key IAM components including multi-factor authentication (MFA), identity federation, policy-based access control and identity providers. APIs are essential for cloud service communication. This chapter will include real world case studies involving IAM solutions in cloud, latest trends and emerging technologies that shape up today's cloud landscape.

In the modern digital age, Cloud security is among the primary problems. Cloud security is a collection of procedures and technology meant to mitigate threats to an organization's security from the inside as well as the outside. Cloud security is essential for organisations as they progress with their modernisation strategy and include cloud-based tools and services into their infrastructure. "cloud migration" and "digital transformation" have gained widespread usage in commercial settings in recent years. This article offers an overview of cloud computing security benefits and uses, as well as a description of the major requirements in cloud computing, security essential technologies, standards, and regulations, etc. This chapter makes the case that the alterations to the aforementioned elements will bring about a technological revolution in the information security industry.

In the fast-evolving world of cloud computing, we have to ensure that systems run seamlessly even in the presence of challenges. Load balancing serves as a vital protector by offering fault tolerance and high availability, efficiently allocating workloads across multiple resources rather than merely distributing traffic. Traditional load balancing models reduce the risk of component overload failures but struggle to handle the unique challenges of cloud environments, such as dynamic workloads and unpredictable failures. In this paper, we presented the rise of advanced solutions and their power to overcome the drawbacks of conventional load balancing methods. Advanced methods improve fault tolerance and high availability by considering server status and workload nature, going beyond traditional traffic splitting techniques. The research enhances the understanding of load balancing and parallel scheduling in the cloud, focusing on security and resilience. As a result, we have demonstrated the significant role played by self-adaptive and intelligent load balancing approaches.

Today's increasingly frequent and costly cyber threats underscore the importance of securing machine learning (ML), which can automate reactions to identified risks and decrease the time needed to counteract possible assaults. Steps like separating infected systems and launching predetermined security procedures fall under this category. Machine learning algorithms sift through mountains of data, searching for irregularities that indicate potential security risks. Unusual user activity, malware,

Preface

The exponential growth of cloud computing has fundamentally transformed modern digital infrastructure, offering unprecedented capabilities in data processing, storage, and resource management. Yet, this technological evolution introduces complex security vulnerabilities that span from edge computing environments to smart grid systems. In this landscape of emerging cyber threats, implementing comprehensive security measures across distributed architectures has become mission critical. With this book, *Risk-Based Approach to Secure Cloud Migration,* we present an in-depth examination of how cutting-edge technologies - from blockchain and distributed deep learning to intelligent load balancing and multifactor authentication - can be strategically integrated to create resilient cloud security frameworks, addressing the multifaceted challenges faced by organizations in protecting their cloud resources and sensitive data.

As editors, we bring diverse perspectives from our academic and professional experiences. Minakshi from King Khalid University, Saudi Arabia; and Tarun Kumar from Galgotias University, India, have collaborated to curate this book as an authoritative resource for both practitioners and researchers. It is evident that the integration of diverse technologies - from edge computing and blockchain to multifactor authentication and serverless architecture - creates a robust foundation for modern cloud security, enabling organizations to build resilient and secure digital infrastructures while maintaining operational efficiency.

The primary objective of this book is to explore the intricate landscape of cloud computing security, from edge computing solutions to advanced authentication mechanisms and load balancing strategies. The chapters examine the convergence of emerging technologies like blockchain, distributed deep learning, and machine learning with traditional cloud infrastructure to address modern security challenges. Each chapter has been carefully structured to provide in-depth insights into:

- The evolution of cloud security frameworks spanning various environments - smart cities, cyber-physical systems, and smart grids - with emphasis on data replication, encryption, and identity management solutions.
- The integration of advanced technologies like serverless computing, multi-factor authentication, and ML-based intrusion detection systems for countering cyber threats.
- The optimization of cloud resources via intelligent load balancing, access controls, and security frameworks (CSA, NIST, ISO/IEC 27017) for efficiency and compliance.

To bridge the gap between theory and practice, the book showcases practical applications across diverse domains, from smart cities using edge computing to network operators migrating infrastructure to the cloud. Through examples of Identity Management, load balancing, and authentication systems, the text illustrates real-world security solutions, demonstrating how organizations balance robust protection with operational efficiency.

CHAPTER OVERVIEW

Chapter 1: Chapter 1 discusses the growing challenges faced by smart cities due to increased data generation and the limitations of traditional cloud computing, such as high latency and low reliability. It advocates for edge computing as a solution, emphasizing its ability to decentralize data processing, reduce latency, and enhance service quality. The chapter explores how distributed deep learning and intelligent offloading can optimize resource management in smart cities, ultimately aiming for improved operational efficiency and cost-effectiveness in urban environments.

Chapter 2: Chapter 2 explores the intersection of cloud computing and blockchain technology, emphasizing their potential to enhance security and efficiency. Cloud computing offers flexible, scalable services for various industries, while blockchain provides decentralized, secure data management. The chapter discusses the benefits of cloud storage, including cost savings and accessibility, alongside challenges like reliability and compliance. It highlights how blockchain's immutable audit trails and encryption methods can address cloud security concerns, making it a transformative force in protecting data integrity and privacy in cloud environments.

Chapter 3: Chapter 3 discusses the growing importance of cloud computing and data replication in ensuring data security. As data production increases, users prefer online platforms for efficient access and management. Data replication, which involves backing up data across multiple locations, enhances confidentiality, integrity, and availability. The chapter highlights various replication methods and tools, such as Oracle GoldenGate and DBMoto, while addressing challenges like transfer delays. Emphasizing the need for robust security measures, it concludes that both cloud service providers and users must prioritize data protection strategies to mitigate risks.

Chapter 4: In an increasingly digital world, database security is crucial as users share sensitive information online. This chapter emphasizes the importance of encrypting data before storage to protect against unauthorized access and potential misuse by intruders. It discusses the rapid growth of cloud computing and the need for robust security measures to safeguard user data during transit and at rest. Key challenges include ensuring data integrity, confidentiality, and addressing risks associated with virtualization and multi-tenancy in cloud environments.

Chapter 5: explores the critical need for robust cloud security frameworks in response to the increasing reliance on cloud computing across various sectors. It highlights the vulnerabilities associated with cloud environments, such as data breaches and misconfigurations, which necessitate effective security measures. The chapter compares three prominent frameworks: the Cloud Security Alliance's Cloud Controls Matrix, NIST's Cloud Computing Security Framework, and ISO/IEC 27017. Each framework offers unique strengths and challenges, emphasizing the importance of selecting a suitable model to enhance organizational security strategies against evolving threats in the cloud ecosystem.

Chapter 6: This chapter discusses the importance of security in Cyber-Physical Systems (CPS) and highlights the role of machine learning in enhancing intrusion detection systems (IDS). It emphasizes the vulnerabilities of CPS, particularly regarding network attacks that can disrupt control software and physical systems. The chapter introduces the EMHDL-AD technique, which utilizes deep learning for effective attack detection, achieving high accuracy rates in various datasets. The integration of advanced algorithms shows promise for improving CPS security across multiple industries.

Chapter 7: Cloud computing is increasingly vital for enterprises, yet it faces significant security challenges. Traditional security measures are inadequate against evolving threats, necessitating advanced techniques for protecting data and resources. Key vulnerabilities include insider attacks, hacking, and misconfigured services, which can lead to data breaches that compromise sensitive information. Organizations must implement robust security strategies, including encryption, access controls, and continuous monitoring, to mitigate risks. As cloud environments grow, maintaining data integrity and user trust remains paramount for service providers and clients alike.

Chapter 8: Securing cloud resources is critical for businesses as they increasingly shift operations online, exposing them to cyber threats and compliance risks. Data breaches can lead to significant damage, including customer dissatisfaction and legal repercussions. Implementing Identity and Access Management (IAM) is essential for controlling access, ensuring compliance with regulations like GDPR and HIPAA, and mitigating risks. Challenges in implementation in IAM include integration complexities and identity duplication. Best practices involve using Role-Based Access Control (RBAC), multi-factor authentication (MFA), and automation to enhance security while maintaining operational efficiency.

Chapter 9: Cloud computing is transforming IT by offering scalable, flexible resources managed remotely, enhancing efficiency and collaboration. However, security remains a critical concern, as organizations face risks like data breaches and unauthorized access. Major cloud service providers invest in robust security measures, yet vulnerabilities persist due to the dynamic nature of cloud environments. The future of cloud computing hinges on addressing these security challenges while leveraging its advantages, such as cost-effectiveness and rapid innovation, to drive business growth and adaptability.

Chapter 10: Load balancing is crucial in cloud computing for ensuring fault tolerance and high availability. It intelligently distributes workloads across multiple servers to prevent overload and maintain performance during dynamic conditions. Traditional models face challenges in handling unpredictable failures, leading to the development of advanced algorithms that enhance resource allocation and system resilience. This paper explores these innovative approaches, emphasizing the importance of self-adaptive load balancing methods that optimize server utilization while safeguarding against downtime, thus improving overall service reliability in cloud environments.

Chapter 11: This chapter emphasizes the critical role of multifactor authentication (MFA) in enhancing cybersecurity amidst rising cyber threats. It discusses how machine learning algorithms can identify security risks by analyzing user behavior patterns, thereby automating responses to potential attacks. Despite the effectiveness of MFA in preventing unauthorized access, its adoption remains low, especially among smaller organizations. The chapter highlights the need for robust security measures, including compliance with data protection regulations and addressing privacy concerns, to strengthen MFA systems against evolving cyber threats.

Chapter 12: This chapter discusses the transformative impact of cloud computing on business operations, emphasizing its advantages such as scalability, flexibility, and cost-efficiency. However, it also highlights significant security challenges that arise with cloud adoption, including data breaches and regulatory compliance issues. The chapter advocates for a comprehensive security framework that incorporates technological solutions and strategic management practices. Key concepts like the CIA triad and Zero Trust Architecture are explored, alongside the shared responsibility model, to enhance cloud security. It concludes by addressing future trends and best practices for organizations transitioning to cloud environments.

Chapter 13: Focusing on Cloud computing, originating in the 1950s and gaining momentum in the 1990s, revolutionizes how organizations manage data and resources by providing scalable, on-demand access to computing power over the internet. It encompasses various service models, including Infrastructure as a Service (IaaS), Platform as a Service (PaaS), and Software as a Service (SaaS), which enhance flexibility and reduce costs. Key benefits include improved collaboration, automatic updates, and cost efficiency. However, challenges such as security concerns, reliance on internet connectivity, and compliance with regulations like GDPR and HIPAA must be addressed for successful implementation.

Chapter 14: This chapter discusses serverless computing in cloud environments, its benefits, and security challenges. It explains how serverless architecture allows users to build applications without managing physical infrastructure, making it cost-effective and reducing operational complexity. The text covers various security threats including SQL injection, MAC spoofing, and cross-site scripting. It emphasizes the importance of robust security measures, particularly for data protection, and discusses emerging solutions like RFID technology and information-centric security approaches. The chapter concludes by highlighting the need for unified security standards to increase user trust in cloud architecture.

Chapter 15: The chapter discusses cloud computing security challenges and their solutions. It examines major security issues including data breaches, data loss, insecure APIs, cloud misconfigurations, and multi-cloud sprawl problems. The text emphasizes how traditional security approaches are inadequate for cloud environments and highlights the importance of encryption, multi-factor authentication, automated security tools, and proper identity management. It also stresses the shared responsibility between cloud service providers and customers in maintaining security, while noting that cloud security is crucial for business growth and organizational development.

Chapter 16: The chapter discusses cloud security challenges in smart grid environments and introduces the Cloud Transfer Methodology for Smart Grid (CTMS). While cloud solutions offer robust computing platforms and cost benefits, they present significant security concerns, especially for critical infrastructure like smart grids. The study examines various security aspects, including risk assessment, disaster recovery, and incident response procedures. It presents case studies of distribution network operators migrating to cloud systems and emphasizes the need for comprehensive security documentation and automated processes for secure cloud migration.

This publication is intended for a broad audience, including cloud security professionals, students, researchers, academicians, faculty members, cloud architects, IT managers, decision-makers, and regulatory compliance experts. By addressing the multifaceted challenges of cloud security, we aim to provide actionable insights and strategies that resonate with readers at all levels of expertise.

The integration of edge computing, blockchain, and machine learning marks a pivotal shift in cloud security approaches. From smart cities to cyber-physical systems, these technologies create a robust defense against emerging threats. Through comprehensive analysis of data replication, encryption, and serverless computing to smart grid security, this book provides a roadmap for building resilient cloud infrastructures. It equips professionals and researchers with essential knowledge to tackle tomorrow's security challenges while maintaining operational efficiency.

We extend our heartfelt gratitude to the contributors whose expertise and dedication have enriched this publication. It is our hope that this book will serve as a valuable resource for organizations and individuals seeking to navigate the complexities of cloud security with confidence and competence.

Minakshi
King Khalid University, Saudi Arabia

Tarun Kumar
Galgotias University, India

Chapter 1
A Critical Analysis on Edge Computing in Smart City Applications

Nikhil Kumar Chaudhary
https://orcid.org/0009-0003-0972-4814
School of Computer Engineering, KIIT University, Bhubaneswar, India

Archisha Verma
https://orcid.org/0009-0008-7031-6576
School of Computer Engineering, KIIT University, Bhubaneswar, India

Ashutosh Rath
https://orcid.org/0009-0009-6065-5256
School of Computer Engineering, KIIT University, Bhubaneswar, India

Sandali Dev Sinha
https://orcid.org/0009-0007-0953-1771
School of Computer Engineering, KIIT University, Bhubaneswar, India

Garvit Babbar
https://orcid.org/0009-0001-0953-9980
School of Computer Engineering, KIIT University, Bhubaneswar, India

Hitesh Mohapatra
https://orcid.org/0000-0001-8100-4860
School of Computer Engineering, KIIT University, Bhubaneswar, India

ABSTRACT

In recent times the adoption of advanced technology has been increasing in the general masses. Hence the amount of data being produced in an average smart city has increased by many times. This leads to high latency and low reliability issues in the traditional cloud computing paradigm. Therefore, stagnating the functionality of the cities as a whole and thus the practice of edge computing may bring about a positive change. The decentralizing computing resources decreases the reliance on traditional cloud computing. This minimizes latency and optimizes data processing. Distributed deep learning in central and edge cloud systems reduces latency. Intelligent offloading improves service quality in smart cities, and machine learning enhances mobile edge computing. In this work, suggestions for reducing the cost

DOI: 10.4018/979-8-3693-7137-4.ch001

for handling the smart cities are discussed. These findings and discussions can be the stepping stones towards the future. A future where smart cities can be operated with less hassle and better cost management.

1. INTRODUCTION

In the last few years, the world has witnessed a shift towards urbanization, a shift that surely does not intend to slow down in the coming years. However, it brings along with it some challenges that need to be dealt with to support the improved quality of life desired by many (Albino et al., 2015). The emerging concept of smart cities, which strives to convert the world into an intelligent ecosystem can prove to be useful in the society's quest to tackle (Das et al., 2024), or at the very least reduce challenges which includes increased population and resource management that one encounters in the face of urbanization and the constant demand for a more progressive lifestyle. The whole aim of smart cities is to capitalize on information and communication technologies to support urban development and at the same time make headway towards a more refined quality of life for us humans. Smart cities use the combined knowledge and power of Internet of Things (IoT) with intelligent infrastructure and data analytics to not only support efficient resource management and elevated public service but to also provide a sturdy and viable urban environment. Smart cities essentially integrate various urban systems and services from transportation, utilities, public safety to healthcare and cleanliness, these are data driven cities that collect vast amounts of data from the various sensors and IoT devices, these cities gain knowledgeable insights into urban trends, patterns, and issues, allowing policymakers to make informed and data-driven decisions and optimize resource allocation (Diener, n.d.). These cities also often prioritize sustainability by promoting eco-friendly practices such as energy efficiency, waste reduction, renewable energy adoption, and sustainable transportation solutions to minimize environmental impact and address climate change challenges (Gali & Mahamkali, 2022). Smart cities often include the engagement of citizens through digital platforms and applications including social media. They also cultivate the innovation ecosystems by fostering partnerships between government agencies, academia, business, startups, and community organizations to develop and deploy cutting-edge technologies and solutions that address urban challenges (Hough, 2009), they also improve greatly on the quality of life in general. While smart cities can prove to be very beneficial in our pursuit of a better life, they still have very specific requirements that the cloud must adhere to for producing productive and effective results. Smart city applications require high-bandwidth, low latency as well as the ability of cloud to work in real-time (Khan et al., 2020).

These needs, however, may not be fulfilled to the extent required under the usual operations of cloud. The conventional approach to cloud computing is not always efficient in terms of adaptability and scalability. Cloud computing introduces latency issues; the data centers are often centralized, real-time applications such as traffic management or emergency response systems are often impacted by this, delays in data transmission between sensors or devices and the cloud can also hinder responsiveness (Komninos et al., 2012). It also lacks in its ability to deliver services as well as results in a dynamic environment which is a key requirement for sustaining smart city applications. Hence there is a need for an alternative approach, one that is more agile and follows a flexible technological framework.

In recent years, Edge Computing, a method that combines data processing and computation by bringing it closer to the source of data generation, has revealed itself to be a fantastic approach with great potential, the utilization and exploration of which can greatly and efficiently assist in our quest to make this transformation (Kumar et al., 2024). Edge Computing is a promising approach that provides an efficient solution to the shortcomings of traditional cloud computing. The limitations posed by the usual cloud computing approach holds back Smart City Applications from reaching their full potential. These limitations are, however, tackled by spreading-out computing power and processing data closer to its source. This renewed approach of data processing addresses issues of latency, resource and energy management, scalability, adaptability, privacy and security faced due to centralized cloud computing (Lv et al., 2021). Edge Computing is what we as a society or civilization can use to ease the burden on the cloud computing architecture for the increasing amount of the data that has been produced by the general public because of the adoption of Internet of Things (IoT) enabled devices that interact with the surroundings and keep on updating the inflow and outflow of data, because there is only so much amount of hardware a cloud vendor could purchase to store the ridiculous amounts of data. The amount of data produced is so high that the cloud vendors have to face a lot of trouble to handle the performance of the systems.

Figure 1. Hierarchy representing Edge Computing with respect to Fog and cloud Computing

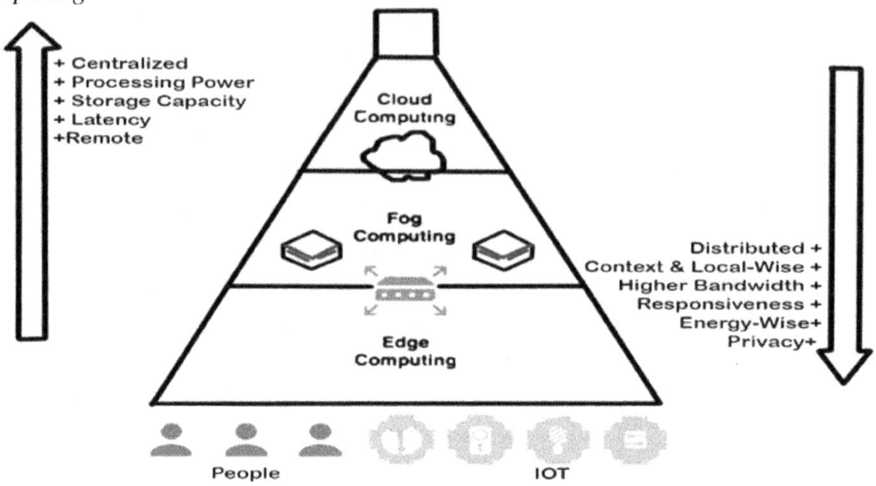

Figure 1 shows us the way edge computing interacts with the surroundings. The distribution is more so the burden of the data handling is less and privacy is more along with performance and consistent response. Edge computing is, hence, a worthy solution to the challenges faced by smart city applications in the endeavor to achieve a dynamic and efficient smart city environment.

2. LITERATURE REVIEW

The technology involved in edge computing is not entirely new but the attention and traction that it has been getting is very new due to the increase in the demand for better processing speeds and lower latency. There are several ways in which edge computing can be utilized in a smart city environment proposed by curious and esteemed researchers. In this critical analysis paper, we will be going over some of the proposed approaches and discuss the problem they encountered and how they approached the solution (Mohapatra, 2021). We will also look at the difficulties faced by them and how they found a way around such roadblocks. In the introduction we mention the difficulties faced in smart cities for cloud computing, however, the very first paper we analyze, proposes a way to collaborate edge computing and cloud computing for smart city applications in IoT devices with the help of deep learning (Mohapatra & Mishra, 2024), with the increase in the number of mobile devices, and computers that are to be handled by the limited CPU processing capability, disk capacity, energy efficiency, and ecological awareness, also the more complicated tasks like OCR(Optical Character Recognition), facial detection, and AR(Augmented Reality), are impractical for local processing, and then to add the increasing number of IoT devices which are delay-sensitive the computation and communication cost can increase drastically. The paper formalizes the MEC (Mobile Edge Computing) and MCC (Mobile Cloud Computing) hybrid task placement issue as a problem of optimizing several contrasting objectives simultaneously to minimize the combined utility of the system and the assignment of the network capacity or bandwidth for each mobile phone mutually, and introduces a capable and practical offloading structure equipped with smart decision-making abilities. Also, it develops a DDTO (Distributed Deep learning-driven Task Offloading) algorithm, which employs multiple parallel deep neural networks to generate offloading decisions over the mobile devices, edge cloud server, and central cloud server efficiently and effectively. Experiments are conducted under many different circumstances for the optimal assessment of the competence of DDTO algorithm. The proposed DDTO algorithm outclasses and outperforms the several other schemes and algorithms used for offloading that are designed without the mutual integration of MCC and MEC (Mohapatra & Rath, 2019).

This system model is built upon a hierarchical structure consisting of multiple mobile devices, edge cloud servers, and a central cloud. Computational tasks are distributed based on network conditions and the complexity of the tasks (Mohapatra & Rath, 2020). For instance, data-intensive tasks are directed to edge servers to ensure low latency, while tasks requiring heavy computation are offloaded to the central cloud, which offers greater processing power. This approach effectively minimizes delays, alleviates load bottlenecks, and enhances fault tolerance (Mohapatra & Rath, 2021). The system operates through three computing models. The first is local computing, which allows basic tasks to be handled directly on mobile devices but is limited by battery life. The second model is edge computing, which utilizes wireless technologies such as Wi-Fi or Bluetooth, offering proximity-based processing that significantly reduces latency. Lastly, central cloud computing provides the highest computational power, though it comes with time and energy costs that are calculated mathematically. Each of these models incurs unique energy consumption and execution time costs. The computational prowess of the three models is often given as:

$$f_m < f_e < f_{c,} \tag{1}$$

The symbol (f_m) representing computational power of local mobile devices, model based on edge computing (f_e) and model based on the central cloud computing(f_c), respectively. The paper proposes a function with the purpose to minimize both the time required for execution(T) and the consumption of energy(E) of all the tasks in the mobile devices:

$$\Phi(wl, d, bw) = \xi \times E + (1 - \xi) \times T \tag{2}$$

where $wl = \{wl_{(n,m)} \mid n \in N, m \in NT\}$, $bw = \{bw_n \mid n \in N\}$, $d = \{d^1_{(n,m)}, d^2_{(n,m)} \mid n \in N, m \in NT\}$, NT is the number of tasks and N is the number of mobile devices. ξ is a parameter whose value ranges between 0 and 1 i.e. $0 \leq \xi \leq 1$, it is a parameter used for weighting and it symbolizes the degree of importance of the execution time and consumption of energy, the user requirements can be taken into account which can influence the weighted cost model accordingly. To stress on improving the speed and overall performance, the values of ξ must be less than 0.5; while to emphasize on reducing consumption of the energy, the value of the parameter ξ must be greater than 0.5. Time of execution is only considered when $\xi = 0$, and consumption of energy of the mobile devices is only taken into account when $\xi = 1$. Hence, the paper tries to minimize the time and energy utilized by the mobile devices so that the remaining energy can be used for other tasks involving IoT devices and delay-sensitive devices. Now, the recommended solution of the paper is based on designing a DDTO algorithm and it suggests the DDTO algorithm for MEC and MCC, which relies on several concurrent deep neural networks (DNNs). The users' tasks or workloads (*wl*) are given by the target is to make the most optimal offloading decision

$$\mathrm{wl} = [\mathrm{wl}_{(1,1)}, \mathrm{wl}_{(1,2)}, \ldots, \mathrm{wl}_{(N,M)}] \tag{3}$$

$$d = [d^1_{(1,1)}, d^2_{(1,2)}, d^1_{(1,2)}, \ldots, d^1_{(N,M)}, d^2_{(N,M)}] \tag{4}$$

Assumption is made that the number of tasks is same for all the users so that the application can be split into different multiple tasks and the workloads of any additional tasks can just be treated as zero. Moreover, due to the lack of predefined optimal decisions in the input data, this problem transforms into a challenging unsupervised learning problem without any straightforward solutions. As a result, the paper proposes an approach to determine the offloading decisions and turn this problem into a supervised learning problem, which are relatively easier to solve. It regards the workloads *wl* as the input to the neural networks and the optimal offloading decisions *d* as the output. Crucially, it saves the workloads *wl*, the best decisions *d*, and the minimum value of the function *Q(wl,d)* in a database collectively. This data is then used to train multiple concurrent DNNs later, which then creates fresh data to refresh the database which still has the old data stored in it originally. This procedure allows the updating of the database and also the training of the deep neural networks to correctly address the NP-hard problem. For the generation of the best decisions for offloading the mean squared error(μ) function is used to keep a check on the error and as a result to minimize the loss function that is being used in deep learning, it is expressed as:

$$\mu = \frac{1}{n} \sum_{t=1}^{n} (logits_t - outputs_t)^2 \tag{5}$$

Where, the label is denoted by *logits* and the predicted value by *outputs*. Since the elements of the decisions are in binary form, the value of logits can either be 0 or 1. It is rather simple to prove that the value of logits will be 1 if that of the output is larger than 0.5, and 0 otherwise. This is the process of minimization of the function μ, indicating that the model has the highest precision and accuracy (Panda et al., 2024). Once the optimal landing decision, denoted as d^*, is identified, the corresponding data are prepared for training in the database. It includes the workload *wl*, the optimal decision d^*, and the cost of the process $\Phi(wl,d^*)$. Database capacity is limited and can be set to any chosen size. It works on a round-robin basis, which means that when capacity is reached, the oldest cases are replaced by new ones. Moreover, all deep neural networks (DNNs) are trained using labeled data sets. However, training an entire DNN with the entire labeled dataset from the database would be too time-consuming. Instead, each DNN receives a shared database to randomly select some data sets for training. System performance is constantly improved by constantly updating the database, ensuring high accuracy of the new data. Because this situation poses a classification challenge, cross-entropy that has been chosen as the loss function for analysis can be expressed as:

$$L(\lambda_k) = -d^T \log f_\lambda k(wl) - (1 - d^T) \log(1 - f_{\lambda k}(wl)) \tag{6}$$

In this context, the parameter λ_k represents the specifications of the Deep Neural Network (DNN). To minimize the cross-entropy loss, the gradient descent method adjusts all the DNN parameters. After the training phase, the testing phase generates offloading decisions as logits, while the database is updated in real-time. Convergence is reached when the process approaches a specific value, known as the extremum. The minimum value of the function $\Phi(wl, d)$, obtained during offloading decision-making, is labelled as Φ_1. If a random data batch is selected from the database and the process is repeated, a new optimal value of $\Phi(wl, d)$, called (Φ_2), is found. The ratio $\rho 1$ can be calculated as:

$$\rho 1 = \frac{min(\Phi 1, \Phi 2)}{max(\Phi 1, \Phi 2)} \tag{7}$$

ρ1 shows the convergence achieved by the DDTO algorithm. The extremum should not be treated as the true minima or maxima value, therefore, all cases are enumerated to find the true minima value of *Φ(wl, x)* written as Φ^*_1 and compare the result of this ratio with our ideal value Φ^*_2. Φ^*_1. The ideal offloading decision is determined by using a greedy algorithm that meticulously evaluates all possible combinations. This process can be time-consuming. The ratio of the minimum value to the optimal value is then calculated and defined as ρ2. This metric can be expressed as:

$$\rho 2 = \frac{\Phi 1^*}{\Phi 2^*} \tag{8}$$

where, zero < ρ_2 ≤ unity, indicates how close the solution found by our algorithm comes to the true optimal solution achieved by the greedy algorithm. ρ_2 = 1 indicates that the ideal solution has been found which is also called the *relative optimality* (Komninos et al., 2012). Komninos et al. (2012) has introduced a novel DDTO algorithm which diverges from traditional distributed deep learning methods by utilizing a dual-cloud system, comprising both a central and an edge cloud. This algorithm balances energy usage and processing time within a combined MCC and MEC offloading framework by recording offloading decisions, workload and system usage data in a database. At the same time, it also enhances the performance of many DNNs in parallel by training them with a set of classified data (Pomp et al., 2022). In summary DDTO algorithm assesses whether to process tasks locally or to offload them to either central or edge cloud considering both the options.

In recent years, the idea of smart cities has garnered immense interest from technologists, architects and civilians alike. Incorporating information and communication technologies (ICTs) into the infrastructure of urban cities can introduce efficient and secure ways of life in urban areas (Priyadarshi et al., 2024). But, as cities grow into vast and complex ecosystems of interconnected devices, systems and networks, managing the extensive data generated by cameras, sensors and smart devices can prove to be quite challenging. Even though cloud computing, along with several conventional computing models, has greatly impacted the conversation around and implementation of computational and storage needs in urban domains, it still proves to be lacking with respect to the real-time processing requirements of smart cities. These limitations of traditional and centralized computing have become even more apparent with rapid population growth. As conventional computing paradigms have evolved, their evolution has proved to be instrumental to modern technology. A gradual progression from conventional computing paradigms to contemporary paradigms and to ultimately transformative computing paradigms comprises the evolution of 'edge computing'. Looking chronologically at the development of computing models to gain insights into the functionalities, advantages, potential and underlying structural components of each model by evaluating them through six key factors - scalability, flexibility, cost optimizations, automation, latency and mobility support - can help us understand just how essential edge computing can prove to the conception and realization of smart cities (Rauf et al., 2024).

As conventional computational models scale the globe, Edge Computing has become an innovative approach to decentralize resources near to where data originates or is consumed. This approach improves context awareness, security, resource usage and provides for mobility and thus is well suited for addressing inherent problems associated with conventional compute. The paper (Sharma et al., 2024) focuses on Edge Computing framework in smart cities by presenting evolution of Edge Computing, its applications and issues. It presents innovative use-cases like self-driven vehicle accident reporting, smart fire alarm, as well as defines the role of Edge computing for transforming rescue services and smart environment.

Edge Computing plays a crucial role in enhancing smart systems across various sectors. In smart transportation, it improves device-to-device communication and performance, benefiting areas like smart tourism. Augmented Reality relies on Edge Computing for lightweight security and low latency, while smart healthcare uses it with federal learning to secure data. Smart grids leverage it for security and privacy. By evaluating sectors such as transportation, AR, healthcare, grids, farming, and buildings, Edge Computing is shown to boost efficiency, real-time processing, and address latency, security, and interoperability challenges. Future ongoing research is therefore needed to improve on the intelligence, the robustness and sustainability of smart cities (Singh & Pant, 2024). IT departments are increasingly adopting edge computing for efficient data storage and real-time processing, driving demand for this technology. However, its application presents challenges. This paper reviews recent studies on edge computing, covering resource control, intelligence, security, and sustainability. It evaluates literature on achieving smart city goals and offers solutions to problems faced by researchers and practitioners. The future of edge computing in smart cities looks promising, with network slicing enabling the connection of thousands of sensors and devices for instant analytics. Real-time services, low latency, and improved QoS will be supported by SDN and NFV, boosting profitability through infrastructure slicing. The third literature that we take a look at is the paper titled An Edge Computing-enhanced Internet of Things Framework for Privacy-preserving in Smart City (Song et al., 2019) that is focused about the problems that can occur while using IOT devices to plan smart cities, there can a huge amount of data to be managed efficiently where we can face two issues such as:

1. Heterogenous and fulfilling diversity amongst IoT technologies in various devices

2. Privacy-focused and prevention of unintentional disclosure of very sensitive data

The challenges of heterogeneity and privacy in IoT devices are often handled inefficiently with a single privacy rule for all, while heterogeneity is addressed separately. The proposed ontology data model aims to solve this by integrating privacy and heterogeneity into the architectural design of network margins, enhancing smart city effectiveness. It includes an ontology for IoT devices and privacy rules, along with a method to determine when device privacy is needed. This solution, validated for smart cities, leverages edge computing for faster processing and an ontology server to handle privacy-preserving operations (Venugopal & Jagadeesh, 2024).

The ontology data storage model harmonizes smart city device information and privacy properties to address heterogeneity issues, including changes in privacy behavior. Devices like cameras, speed, tilt, and temperature sensors gather data, while privacy is maintained by sending the device ID and its ontology to the server. The server tracks the privacy rule's lifetime for each device, updating it as needed. When the lifetime expires, ownership is randomly reassigned to deceive threats, and a new privacy rule is generated (Yu et al., 2020). The IoT device then uses this rule to transmit data to the ontology server at the network edge, which sends it to the cloud for further analysis. Future research will determine the best privacy rule for each device type. The proposed ontology server solution for IoT device privacy is assessed by representing devices as bulbs and privacy rules as colors with lifetimes managed on the network edge server. Upon expiration, device ownership and privacy rules are randomly changed to prevent data misuse. The server's CPU usage, which remains below 9%, makes this solution viable for large-scale smart cities. However, scalability remains a challenge with many interconnected devices. This dynamic privacy management approach addresses network heterogeneity and enhances traditional methods for high data flow. While the solution ensures near real-time privacy management, scalability and further optimization, such as using machine learning, remain areas for future research.

The second paper that we review in the subsequent part of this study is titled Intelligent Offloading for Collaborative Smart City Services in Edge Computing and aimed at enhancing the Quality of Experience (QoE) for smart city encompassing the IoT and collaborative services. The Edge Computing model is flexible when it comes to implementation but raises questions about security. Real world challenges such as increasing efficiency of energy use, distribution load, response time etc still remain. To mitigate these challenges, an Intelligent Offloading Method (IOM) is presented in the current research. In this model, response time consists of waiting time, transmission time and execution time, where waiting time is obtained with the help of $M/M/Z/\infty/\infty$ queuing model and rest from the aspects as mentioned in

(Hough, 2009). The total gives the system's response time The time response of a system is defined as the time it takes for the system to respond to an input.

$$\tau^{tot}_{n,j}=\tau^{qu}+\tau^{ex}_{n,j}+\tau^{tr}_{n,j} \tag{9}$$

Where, $\tau^{tot}_{n,j}$ - Response time of the service, τ^{qu} - Average waiting time, τ^{ex}_{nj} - Execution time, $\tau^{tr}_{n,j}$ - Transmission time

The overall energy power of unloading the service to the Edge Node (EN) is generated by considering the sum of the energy consumption incurred by the time taken for the terminal to propagate and the energy consumed while executing other services in the edge node.

$$\varepsilon^{tot}_{n,j}=\varepsilon^{tr}_{n}+\varepsilon^{ex}_{n,j} \tag{10}$$

Where, $\varepsilon^{tot}_{n,j}$ - Total energy power, ε^{tr}_{n} - Energy consumed during terminal propagation, $\varepsilon^{ex}_{n,j}$ -Energy consumed by execution of service. The services are meant to be propagated to varied edge nodes for obtaining execution. Where, ov_j - occupied VMs, av - average occupied VMs

$$\mathrm{lb} = \frac{1}{J}\sum_{j=1}^{J} (\mathrm{ov}_j - \mathrm{av})^2 \tag{11}$$

From the above-mentioned models, the major issue of offloading services in edge computing is developed as min τ, min ε, min lb. Privacy entropy and the security provided during the offloading process have a direct relationship. Where, *S(s)* - Privacy entropy value, *S* - Entropy value, s_{n-} Service.

$$\mathrm{S(s)} = \frac{1}{N}\sum_{n=1}^{N} \mathrm{S(s_n)} \tag{12}$$

The IOM utilizes the Ant Colony Optimization (ACO) algorithm to solve problems efficiently by defining edge node layouts and improving ant performance through a cyclic value function. The ACO algorithm selects the best service offloading approach by considering the pheromone concentration at each node, where higher pheromone levels increase the probability of selection. Edge nodes are encoded, and ants recommend offloading strategies based on response time, power consumption, and load-sharing factors. Pheromone release and decay guide subsequent ants, and the optimal path discovered by the ants updates the pheromone matrix (Hough, 2009). The method is compared with First Fit (FF), Next Fit (NF), and a Benchmark algorithm for smart city service delivery through edge computing. NF ranks Nametrons by computational capacity, while FF offloads services to the first available edge node. The Benchmark method randomly assigns services to edge nodes.

IOM maintains high edge node occupancy, outperforming FF and NF in resource utilization, though the Benchmark method occupies most nodes.

- Second, Energy Consumption: NF consumes the most energy, particularly during uploading. FF and IOM have similar, lower energy consumption rates.
- Third, Transmission Time: NF takes the longest, lacking propagation awareness, while FF also lags due to unoptimized offloading. Benchmark minimizes transmission time through random offloading, reducing losses.
- Fourth, Execution Time: Both NF and FF struggle to reduce execution time—NF sends services to the previous EN, and FF overlooks execution time reduction. IOM excels in minimizing execution time, outperforming Benchmark.
- Fifth, Response Time: IOM completes services faster due to its reduced execution time.
- Sixth, Load Balance: IOM ensures balanced load by keeping most edge nodes occupied, as does Benchmark, unlike NF and FF, which leave some nodes underutilized, causing higher load variance for smaller services.
- Finally, Privacy Entropy: IOM leads slightly, showing linear growth in privacy entropy, indicating better security during offloading compared to the other algorithms.

The proposed article mainly proposes a method, named IOM, to simultaneously optimize four important metrics during service offloading. IOM contributes to achieving the tradeoffs among minimizing the time taken for response by services, optimizing the consumed energy, and balancing the load while providing the assurance of preserving privacy during the offloading of services. Comparing it with the other three algorithms, that is, NF, FF and Benchmark, IOM maintains a constant streak of performing better, proving its effectiveness and efficiency. However, IOM does not show any significant improvement when it comes to privacy entropy. The performance measure for all the methods in providing security during the offloading process remains more or less the same. The next step could be to have a practical implementation of the Intelligent Offloading Method in real life, focusing on more definite details.

The final paper that we look at is titled Intelligent edge computing based on machine learning for smart city. With growing numbers of smart devices, the amount of data generated is huge. The data generated is dispersed and generally selfish in nature, i.e., they don't want to collaborate for reasons like privacy etc. For this reason, collecting and performing calculations over all of the produced data is tedious. To tackle such problems Mobile Edge Computing (MEC) can be taken into consideration. The resources around MEC servers can be further used for collaborative computing to get better performance. Mobile Edge Computing (MEC) is a network architecture which enables cloud computing capabilities and services at the edge of a network, close to where data is generated or used. MEC reduces the latency, bandwidth and cost of data transmission by storing and processing data locally, rather than sending it to a centralized cloud server. Traditional wireless networks cannot handle this ever growing and unrelated data, for that reason, computing such data can be done in a cloud platform which provides a high-end resource-rich environment to handle such complex tasks. Now comparing this with MEC devices, MEC servers perform computations really better than cloud computing, which has more limitations on how much computing power it can use. With this immense data, distributed machine learning repositories seem promising. So, machine learning in distributed task scheduling algorithms and distributed device coordination algorithms can be applied to increase the MEC system's computational efficiency.

ADMM (Alternating Direction Method of Multipliers) tries solving complex optimization problems by decomposing them into smaller subproblems with individual objective functions. A constraint linking these sub-problems is managed through an additional penalty term that is included in the objective function, incentivizing their agreement. The algorithm minimizes each sub-problem objective function while updating a dual variable controlling the penalty term in every iteration. This process drives convergence to the optimal solution by simultaneously addressing the sub-problems and the overarching constraint. In edge computing, distributed task scheduling plays an important function in coordinating tasks across numerous edge devices. But the selfish devices pose a challenge, as they may not collaborate with the central MEC server. To solve this problem, a distributed task scheduling model where an MEC server interacts with "N" edge devices can be used. Each device offers limited computing power and data, and can execute one task at a time. The model incentivizes devices to participate by negotiating task allocations, that aims to maximize collaborative effort while accounting for network latency and server limitations (Albino et al., 2015). This system benefits from its distributed nature, potentially adapting to large-scale deployments and ensuring stable performance.

To optimize task scheduling in edge computing for machine learning, a novel two-layer optimization approach fusing Stackelberg game theory and ADMM is taken into consideration. Here the MEC server incentivizes edge devices to collaborate. Crucially, this method iterates through internal and external loops. In case of internal loop, using ADMM, the server analyses the device provided scheduling policies to find the optimal solution matching with its objective. In the case of the external loop, the server updates incentive parameters based on the current state, ensuring it matches with its own objective function. By employing sequential updates and coordinated variables, the algorithm ensures convergence to the optimal solution without oscillation. This innovative combination of Stackelberg game theory and ADMM holds promise for enhanced machine learning performance in distributed edge computing scenarios (Sharma et al., 2024). How the limitations of existing machine learning algorithms for distributed and scalable optimization in edge computing scenarios can be tackled is shown in this research work. The LASSO regression model can be taken into consideration as traditional models like stochastic gradient descent suffer from slow convergence and randomness. The model utilizes data collected by numerous IoT devices that are connected through the MEC technology, at the same time, resolving challenges like limited server resources and privacy problems (Mohapatra, 2021). This model aims to overcome such limitations and achieve efficient storing of large-scale data by enabling distributed processing and centralized coordination. This can also improve privacy protection to some extent. By employing the simulation function of the Stackelberg game strategy which is based on ADMM, i.e., and a simulation function, i.e., as naive method (ω = specific value), observations show that the naive method can't converge rapidly before 100 epochs whereas the Stackelberg game method based on ADMM can successfully converge rapidly.

$$\Gamma_i^k = \nabla_{xi}(-\alpha_i x_i^k T + \beta_i E_i) \tag{13}$$

$$\Gamma_i^{k+1} = \Gamma_i^k \pm \omega \tag{14}$$

The change rate could be seen faster and more accurately, which concluded that the geely function which is used in the Stackelberg game algorithm based on ADMM's performs way better than other simulation functions (Mohapatra, 2021). The leader objective function value is the lowest when $\in_0 = 10^{-5}$, so it is fixed as a stopping condition in other experiments. It is observed, when followers number increases the leader objective function value decreases. It shows why this algorithm can be used to enable a large number of IoT devices in large-scale network scenarios. Observations show that edge computing faces difficulties in processing complex data (Mohapatra, 2021). It is observed that the algorithm shows visible convergence after 20 epochs at its best and after 150 epochs at its worst. For the centralized algorithm the fastest one needs 600 epochs whereas the slowest one uses 800 epochs. This shows the ADMM based distributed algorithm is way better than the centralized algorithm. It is seen that no matter how many IoT devices are connected, the proposed algorithm can achieve desired target values under any circumstances. The Mean Square Error for the ADMM based distributed algorithm is found to be 0.01 always whereas that of a centralized algorithm is observed to be 0.981 always. According to these results, the prior algorithm can attain the optimal state.

This research uses machine learning to enhance Mobile Edge Computing (MEC) performance, focusing on distributed task scheduling for mobile devices. Building upon existing models, they propose two novel algorithms. The first one being Stackelberg game-based scheduling, this achieves fast convergence and stability in large networks, potentially improving MEC efficiency. Secondly, Distributed coordination algorithm, ensures rapid convergence and near-optimal performance in intelligent edge computing while preserving data diversity and guaranteeing scalability. These algorithms promise to improve MEC intelligence and advance IoT technology. However, limitations exist, such as focusing on single MEC servers. Future work could expand upon this research by considering multi-server scenarios and delving deeper into specific applications in big data, IoT, and AI. This is not all of the research that has been done on this topic of edge computing helping in the smart city applications, but nonetheless these are some of the most promising and state of the art researches that need to be praised at all corners of the research world.

3. PROPOSED STUDY

3.1. Research Gap

The DDTO algorithm used in this research (Wu et al., 2020) is really efficient but it has some disadvantages as well. It struggles to train models with high-dimensional datasets where the number of features or input variables is quite larger than the number of observations. In case of too many features, it might overfit the training data making the model poorly generalized to unseen examples. It involves complex mathematical operations and optimization techniques so understanding the inner workings and interpreting the model can be challenging. As it is computationally intensive, training high-dimensional data may require a good number of computational resources. It assumes features are independent, which might not hold true in the real world.

Lately, focus and deployments of edge computing for smart city scenarios have been emerging. However, very limited work has been done in terms of studying the issues that surround the practical integration of edge computing in such settings. As much as previous research expositions the value of such systems, few of them focus on the ways of deploying such applications, integration problems, the degree to which these solutions can upscale, or the best way to maximize the use of these applications. Other research areas which have been left uncovered include socio-technical and policy, security and privacy, and resources. Thus, to close these research gaps and provide essential insights for stakeholders, further empirical research oriented to improving smart cities' resilience and efficiency based on edge computing is needed (Asim et al., 2023).

The third paper (Gheisari et al., 2020) focuses on <1> bringing diversity among IoT devices, and <2> protecting privacy or safeguarding against accidental exposure of confidential data and it achieves better results from research prior to this particular research although there are some shortcomings of the research too. As there are diverse IoT devices, deploying the proposed ontology, and implementing dynamic privacy-preserving methods could pose challenges in terms of system complexity and interoperability. The proposed solution requires substantial computational resources, especially for managing ontologies and dynamically adjusting privacy behaviors of IoT devices. This could lead to increased infrastructure costs and resource utilization, particularly in large-scale smart city deployments. Introducing additional layers of abstraction, such as ontologies and dynamic privacy-preserving methods, may reduce existing security risks but pose new security risks including potential vulnerabilities in the system that could be exploited by malicious actors to compromise the privacy and security of IoT devices and data within the smart city infrastructure. While edge computing offers benefits such as real-time processing and reduced latency, its dependencies on edge nodes and networks poses reliability issues, network congestion, and limited processing capabilities at the edge could affect the performance and scalability of the proposed solution.

The Intelligent Offloading Method in the fourth paper (Xu et al., 2020), focuses on the use of Ant Colony Optimization (ACO) technique for rapid determination of solution. Still, ACO has its drawbacks, for example, in cases when multiple local optima are present the function does not converge to the global maximum in many cases. Its dependence on pheromone trails and local decision making can bring it to premature stabilization with poor solutions. ACO is relatively time-consuming for large-scale problems, while the time and space requirement increases with the number of ants and iterations for ACO and thus unsuitable for real-time applications. ACO also performs less well if changes are made in dynamic environments which need adjustments. Thus, probably, other non-parametric algorithms are more suitable for certain problems.

This element is inherited from the MEC model discussed in the previous paper (Lv et al., 2024), where storage requirements are high and so is the cost for employing enhanced infrastructures; security issues are expected given the size of the data. The ADMM Stackelger game algorithm, like the straight up ADMM, introduces interaction levels among the agents where there are extra overhead, high latency and higher cost. The central controller is principal, agents are the respondents, yet it is challenging to implement appropriate motivating factors which in turn influence the rate of convergence. It also has the problem of being unable to scale as organizing more agents scales up the level of difficulty. The algorithm for the distributed device system, using ADMM, as proposed in (Lv et al., 2024), also has these problems. Even though it performs well in large scale optimization, the drawback is that it heavily communicates. The changes in one MEC server are considered and the multiple MEC servers with different scheduling policies are examined as the potential research topic for future works.

3.2. Critical Analysis

The first paper (Wu et al., 2020) proposes DDTO algorithm for distributed deep learning in a system with central and edge clouds, the second (Khan et al., 2020) is just a review paper for the effective assistance while integrating edge computing to foster robust smart cities. The third paper (Gheisari et al., 2020) highlights Ontology, Edge computing, IoT and Cloud computing to improve abstraction and security compared to traditional models. The fourth paper (Xu et al., 2020) proposes an intelligent offloading method adopting the ACO (Ant Colony Optimization) improving the edge utility and the last paper (Lv et al., 2021) proposes an MEC (Mobile Edge Computing) model that use Stackelberg game algorithm based on ADMM and Distributed device system algorithm to achieve better convergence and to get near optimal results. In this research paper we have done critical analysis of five different research papers. The following table below shows the comparison between all the analyzed papers discussing the feature, topic, key findings, strengths and weaknesses observed in each of the research papers.

Table.1 illustrates the comparison among papers. Table.2 presents the performance comparison among existing cloud techniques from paper 2. Table 3 presents the performance comparison among existing cloud techniques from paper 3. Table 4 presents the performance comparison among existing cloud techniques from paper 4. Table 5 presents the performance comparison among existing cloud techniques from paper 5. Table 6 presents the performance comparison among existing cloud techniques from paper 6.

Table 1. Comparison table for Paper 1

Feature	(Wu et al., 2020)	(Khan et al., 2020)	(Gheisari et al., 2020)	(Xu et al., 2020	(Lv et al., 2024)
Topic	DDTO Algorithm for Offloading Decisions	Comprehensive Overview of Edge Computing	Ontology Server Solution for Privacy	Intelligent Offloading Method (IOM)	Existing Offloading Models vs New Models
Key Findings	High accuracy, reduced complexity for offloading	Evolution, advances, challenges, case studies, future prospects of edge computing	Advantages in dynamic privacy, heterogeneity, scalability/ efficiency	Better resource utilization, transmission time, service response time compared to others	Existing models perform worse in all aspects compared to new models
Strengths	Improves offloading decisions and reduces complexity	Provides broad understanding of edge computing	Efficient privacy control and data handling	Outperforms existing models in resource management and task execution	New models achieve significant improvements
Weaknesses	Not compared with other specific offloading algorithms	Lacks in-depth analysis of specific technologies	Limited security mechanisms, scalability concerns with many devices	No significant improvement in privacy compared to existing models	Existing models underperform in all aspects

Table 2. Comparison table for Paper 2

Feature	DDTO Algorithm	Local-Only Scheme	Edge Cloud Computing	MCC (Mobile Cloud Computing)
Accuracy	High (Near-optimal offloading)	N/A	N/A	N/A
Computational Complexity	Low (Reduced by 63% compared to Local-Only)	High	Moderate	High
Latency	Low	High	Moderate	Moderate
Bandwidth	High	Moderate	Moderate	High
Network Congestion	Effectively Managed	High	Moderate	High
Computing Power	High (Suitable for Smart City IoT demands)	Low	Moderate	Moderate

Table 3. Comparison Table for Paper 3

Features	Edge Computing	Fog Computing	Cloud Computing
Latency	Low	Moderate	High
Bandwidth	Moderate to high	Moderate to high	High
Accuracy	Moderate	Moderate	High
Computing Power	High	Moderate	High
Deployment Flexibility	High	Moderate	Limited
Scalability	Scalable	Scalable	Scalable

Table 4. Comparison Table for Paper 4

Features	Heterogeneity Among IoT Devices	Privacy-Preserving Methods
System Complexity	High	High
Interoperability	Challenges due to diverse IoT devices	Challenging due to dynamic privacy-preserving methods
Computational Resources	Substantial requirement	Substantial requirement
Resource Utilization	High	High
Security Risks	Reduced existing risks, but potential for new vulnerabilities	Potential for new vulnerabilities
Scalability	Potentially affected	Potentially affected

Table 5. Comparison Table for Paper 5

Feature	Intelligent Offloading Method (IOM)	Next Fit (NF)	First Fit (FF)	Benchmark
Occupied ENs	High	Low	Low	High
Energy Consumption	Moderate	High	Moderate	N/A
Transmission Time	Low	High	High	N/A
Execution Time	Low	N/A	N/A	Moderate
Service Response Time	Low	N/A	N/A	N/A
Privacy Entropy	High (Slight lead)	N/A	N/A	N/A

Table 6. Comparison Table for Paper 6

Features	MEC Model	ADMM Stackelberg Algorithm	Distributed Device System Algorithm
Storage Capacity	High requirement	N/A	N/A
Security concerns	High	N/A	N/A
Communication overhead	N/A	High	High
Latency	N/A	High	High
Resource Consumption	N/A	High	High
Scalability	Limited	Limited	Limited

3.3. Comparative Analysis of Existing Work

From the comparative analysis of the first paper (Wu et al., 2020), it is found that the DDTO algorithm is capable of producing nearly perfect decisions for task offloading in edge and cloud computing settings with improved accuracy. It achieves superior performance and lowers computational complexity more effectively when contrasted with alternative offloading methods. Studies indicate that the DDTO approach can enhance computational complexity by 63% over methods that only utilize local resources. It solves the challenges faced by centralized service mode and access bandwidth of MCC and provides low latency, high bandwidth and effectively manages network congestion. Compared to edge cloud computing, DDTO has high computing power that can satisfy the requirements of smart city IoT applications. Considering that edge computing has become a domain of interest for many researchers, the existence of various detailed analyses and theses is not unusual. However, the paper distinguishes itself through its scope and coverage, presenting a comprehensive overview of the evolution of edge computing, recent advances, research challenges, case studies as well as future prospects.

The incorporation of the critical evaluation as well as comparative analysis of existing and emerging technologies in context of edge computing for smart cities, practical insights through case studies, evaluation of existing approaches and the identification of research gaps ensures that the paper offers a detailed and penetrative examination of the topic as a whole. This is found from the comparative analysis of the next paper (Khan et al., 2020). In the following paper (Gheisari et al., 2020), the comparison of the proposed ontology server solution shows advantages in dynamic privacy rules, heterogeneity resolution, and efficiency compared to traditional approach to privacy preserving. But it has the drawback of scalability as the number of devices increases and does not have strong security features (Gheisari et al., 2020).

Thus, researchers and practitioners can evaluate the applicability of the proposed conceptualization for specific smart city implementations, and determine tangible possibilities for its enhancement. Despite the fact that the solution is scalable by computational cost, performance could deteriorate as the number of IoT devices increases. In fact, it needs more means to meet security issue; despite increasing privacy as a benefit and it may require further protection against potential threats (Gheisari et al., 2020).

In the next paper (Xu et al., 2020), we compare the Intelligent Offloading Method (IOM) with three existing models: The four algorithms suggested are: Benchmark, Next Fit (NF), and First Fit (FF) algorithms in the following six factors. First, for the EN occupancy the picture is as follows: IOM and Benchmark have a higher rate than both NF and FF. Looking at the energy consumption, the NF consumes the highest energy because its upload period is the largest followed by FF and IOM. They also have the longest transmission time of all the pathways out of the CNS, along with FF. As expected, IOM excels during the execution time and Benchmark has the best result with random offloading (Das et al., 2024). IOM comparing with Ant Colony Optimization cuts service response time and therefore time taken to complete the operation. Relating to privacy entropy I would say that IOM has a slight advantage but the gap is not very big. A prior paper (Lv et al., 2024) illustrates that these models significantly enhance the performance over the existing algorithms such as ADMM-based Stackelberg game algorithm with fast convergence and stability; distributed algorithm for minimizing data diversity loss in intelligent edge computing.

3.4. Finds From Comparative Analysis

The findings from the first paper (Wu et al., 2020) are, it proposes the DDTO algorithm for distributed deep learning in a system combining central and edge clouds. DDTO uses both energy consumption as well as execution time while deciding which task to run. The algorithm is trained with the data which includes system consumption, workload, and the offloading decisions for those workloads. It was found that this algorithm is more efficient and accurate than the previous methods which can also be improved by including more factors and creating a platform to evaluate its performance in real world scenarios. Blockchain and metadata technologies can be incorporated to address security issues, environment adaptability, and portability challenges in the future. This research (Khan et al., 2020) examines the use of edge computing in smart cities. Cloud computing's delays make edge computing's real-time processing power attractive for these applications. The study explores the development of edge computing, the relevant technologies, and its advantages (Rauf et al., 2024). It also details recent advances, proposes a classification system for edge computing in smart cities, and identifies key requirements for its successful implementation. Real-world examples and open research challenges are also discussed. Overall, the research highlights the promise of edge computing for smart cities while acknowledging the challenges that need to be addressed.

The findings from the next research (Gheisari et al., 2020) are, computational cost can be reduced down to 9.0 percent, suggesting that the solution will impose a relatively low overhead on the system, implying that the solution can manage large-scale, complex non-static projects like smart cities integrated with ontology server which enhances security and abstraction over traditional privacy-preserving methods. The paper (Xu et al., 2020) proposes a new method IOM to improvise collaborative smart city services. The current challenges that exist with previous models are slow response time and poor quality of service (QoS). IOM uses edge computing to address limitations of city terminals. This method is aimed to reduce response time, workload distribution, energy consumption and to protect user privacy at the same time. The research demonstrates the effectiveness in simulations. The research from the last paper (Lv et al., 2021) focuses on improving MEC (Mobile Edge Computing) performance using machine learning. By using 2 algorithms namely, Stackelberg Game Algorithm based on ADMM based algorithm, Stackelberg Game, which achieves fast convergence and stability in large networks and another ADMM based algorithm, Distributed Device System, that achieves nearly perfect results in intelligent edge computing.

4. LIMITATION AND FUTURE SCOPE

Edge Computing indeed offers a lot of advantages, but there are some limitations that come along with it. The DDTO algorithm, first (Wu et al., 2020) paper lacks real-world testing and hence might require more factors for decision making. The second (Khan et al., 2020) paper mostly deals with the potential of edge computing, however, more research on certain applications would increase the understanding of the computing technique. There is a need for the implementation of the suggested privacy solution in the third (Gheisari et al., 2020) paper in real life. In the case of the Intelligent Offloading Method (IOM) mentioned in the fourth (Xu et al., 2020) paper, there is a need for validation in smart city pilots. And lastly, numerous detailed algorithm comparisons would help in understanding machine learning exploration, as mentioned in the fifth (Lv et al., 2024) paper. Overall, putting emphasis on security and scalability would enable edge computing to help reach its peak potential in smart cities.

The future of edge computing in smart cities is surely very bright and has a lot of potential. The first (Wu et al., 2020) paper which comprises the DDTO algorithm can be improved by including certain factors like security and network bandwidth for more nuanced decision making. In addition to this, working on real-world testing platforms will confirm its effectiveness. For optimizing the performance of use cases mentioned in the second (Khan et al., 2020) paper, emphasis can be laid on certain domains like traffic management and environmental monitoring. The third (Gheisari et al., 2020) paper provides a privacy preserving solution which can be improvised by integrating it with already existing platforms which will not only help learn its interoperability but also contribute in identifying the possible challenges in a functioning ecosystem. The IOM method as suggested in the fourth (Xu et al., 2020) paper can be implemented in pilot projects of smart city environments. On doing so, the effectiveness and unexpected issues associated with the method can be observed and evaluated. And lastly, comparisons with certain approaches like deep reinforcement learning can help discover the most efficient solution for diverse MEC scenarios within smart cities, as discussed in the fifth (Lv et al., 2024) paper. Working on the analyzed limitations would result in discovering the actual potential of smart cities. Prioritizing factors like security and scalability will help develop efficient systems that would capture the true essence of edge computing.

5. CONCLUSION

Research on distributed deep learning and edge computing has a lot of potential for building smarter cities. This detailed analysis used five key papers to dive deep into these areas. The first (Wu et al., 2020) paper proposes the DDTO algorithm for distributed deep learning in central-edge cloud systems. DDTO effectively manages both energy consumption and execution time and incorporating a self-learning algorithm could dynamically adjust these weights based on real time conditions making task allocation more efficient. The second (Khan et al., 2020) paper observes the advantages of edge computing in smart cities. Its exploration in relevant technologies and recent developments provide valuable insight. However, developing a simulation framework tailored to specific smart city applications (e.g., traffic management, waste collection) would enable researchers to evaluate the performance of different edge computing architectures in those scenarios. The third (Gheisari et al., 2020) paper focuses on ontology matching which is a privacy preserving technology ensuring data security in smart cities. The proposed solution in this paper (Gheisari et al., 2020) reduces computational cost significantly that makes it suitable for large scale deployments. Integrating this with existing smart city platforms and experimenting on real world applications would be a valuable step in the future. The fourth (Xu et al., 2020) paper proposes the IOM method for collaborative smart city services solving existing limitations like slow response time and poor quality of service (QoS). The simulations show its effectiveness, implementing the same in the real-world smart city pilot project is crucial. The last (Lv et al., 2021) paper explores machine learning for improving Mobile Edge Computing (MEC) performance. The paper evaluates two algorithms but doesn't compare them with alternative methods like deep reinforcement learning. Including such comparisons would be beneficial for identifying the most efficient solution for different MEC scenarios within smart cities. By incorporating these suggestions, researchers can enhance and refine the presented solutions. This will result in robust and efficient distributed deep learning and edge computing systems leading to smarter and more efficient cities.

REFERENCES

Albino, V., Berardi, U., & Dangelico, R. M. (2015). Smart cities: Definitions, dimensions, performance, and initiatives. *Journal of Urban Technology*, 22(1), 3–21. DOI: 10.1080/10630732.2014.942092

Asim, M., Junhong, C., Wenyin, L., & Abd El-Latif, A. A. (2023). Artificial intelligence-based secure edge computing systems for IoTDs and smart cities: A survey. *EAI/Springer Innovations in Communication and Computing*, 155-173. DOI: 10.1007/978-3-031-51097-7_13

Das, A., Nanda, P., Jain, R., Saini, T., Bhaskar, S., & Mohapatra, H. (2024). Security considerations of SDN networks during DDoS attacks in load balancing. *Advances in Human and Social Aspects of Technology*, 123–140. DOI: 10.4018/979-8-3693-9235-5.ch007

Diener, E. Assessing subjective well-being: Progress and opportunities. *Social Indicators Research Series*, 26, 421–475. DOI: 10.1007/1-4020-3742-2_16

Gali, M., & Mahamkali, A. (2022). A distributed deep Meta learning based task offloading framework for smart city Internet of things with edge-cloud computing. *Journal of Internet Services and Information Security*, 12(4), 224–237. DOI: 10.58346/JISIS.2022.I4.016

Gheisari, M., Wang, G., & Chen, S. (2020). An edge computing-enhanced Internet of things framework for privacy-preserving in smart city. *Computers & Electrical Engineering*, 81, 106504. DOI: 10.1016/j.compeleceng.2019.106504

Hough, S. (2009). Elizabeth MacKinlay (ed.): Ageing, disability and spirituality: Addressing the challenge of disability in later life. *Sexuality and Disability, 27*(1), 65-66. DOI: 10.1007/s11195-009-9109-0

Khan, L. U., Alsenwi, M., Yaqoob, I., Imran, M., Han, Z., & Hong, C. S. (2020). Resource optimized federated learning-enabled cognitive Internet of things for smart industries. *IEEE Access : Practical Innovations, Open Solutions*, 8, 168854–168864. DOI: 10.1109/ACCESS.2020.3023940

Khan, L. U., Yaqoob, I., Tran, N. H., Kazmi, S. M., Dang, T. N., & Hong, C. S. (2020). Edge-computing-Enabled smart cities: A comprehensive survey. *IEEE Internet of Things Journal*, 7(10), 10200–10232. DOI: 10.1109/JIOT.2020.2987070

Komninos, N., Pallot, M., & Schaffers, H. (2012). Special issue on smart cities and the future internet in Europe. *Journal of the Knowledge Economy*, 4(2), 119–134. DOI: 10.1007/s13132-012-0083-x

Kumar, A., Bag, A., Anand, A., Saha, S., Mohapatra, H., & Kolhar, M. (2024). Examining healthcare services utilizing cloud technology in intelligent urban environments. *Advances in Healthcare Information Systems and Administration*, 77–98. DOI: 10.4018/979-8-3693-7225-8.ch004

Lv, Z., Chen, D., Lou, R., & Wang, Q. (2021). Retracted: Intelligent edge computing based on machine learning for smart city. *Future Generation Computer Systems*, 115, 90–99. DOI: 10.1016/j.future.2020.08.037

Lv, Z., Chen, D., Lou, R., & Wang, Q. (2024). Retraction notice to "Intelligent edge computing based on machine learning for smart city" [Future generation computer systems 115 (2020) 90–99]. *Future Generation Computer Systems*, 158, 569. DOI: 10.1016/j.future.2024.04.045

Mohapatra, H. (2021). Socio-technical challenges in the implementation of smart city. *2021 International Conference on Innovation and Intelligence for Informatics, Computing, and Technologies (3ICT)*, 57-62. https://doi.org/DOI: 10.1109/3ICT53449.2021.9581905

Mohapatra, H., & Mishra, S. R. (2024). Unlocking insights: Exploring data analytics and AI tool performance across industries. *Studies in Big Data*, 265-288. DOI: 10.1007/978-981-97-0448-4_13

Mohapatra, H., & Rath, A. K. (2019). Detection and avoidance of water loss through municipality taps in India by using smart taps and ICT. *IET Wireless Sensor Systems*, 9(6), 447–457. DOI: 10.1049/iet-wss.2019.0081

Mohapatra, H., & Rath, A. K. (2020). Nub less sensor based smart water tap for preventing water loss at public stand posts. *2020 IEEE Microwave Theory and Techniques in Wireless Communications (MTTW)*, 145-150. DOI: 10.1109/MTTW51045.2020.9244926

Mohapatra, H., & Rath, A. K. (2021). A fault tolerant routing scheme for advanced metering infrastructure: An approach towards smart grid. *Cluster Computing*, 24(3), 2193–2211. DOI: 10.1007/s10586-021-03255-x

Panda, A. K., Lenka, A. A., Mohapatra, A., Rath, B. K., Parida, A. A., & Mohapatra, H. (2024). Integrating cloud computing for intelligent transportation solutions in smart cities. *Advances in Civil and Industrial Engineering*, 121–142. DOI: 10.4018/979-8-3693-6695-0.ch005

Pomp, A., Burgdorf, A., Paulus, A., & Meisen, T. (2022). Towards unlocking the potential of the Internet of things for the skilled crafts. *Proceedings of the 24th International Conference on Enterprise Information Systems*, 203-210. DOI: 10.5220/0011066100003179

Priyadarshi, S., Subudhi, S., Kumar, S., Bhardwaj, D., & Mohapatra, H. (2024). Analysis on enhancing urban mobility with IoT-integrated parking solutions. *Advances in Civil and Industrial Engineering*, •••, 143–172. DOI: 10.4018/979-8-3693-6695-0.ch006

Rauf, A., Guru, A., & Mohapatra, H. (2024). Exploring the social model of smart home devices. *Advances in Human and Social Aspects of Technology*, 233–256. DOI: 10.4018/979-8-3693-9235-5.ch012

Sharma, A., Anand, N., Mukherjee, S., Kumar, S., Kumar, S., & Mohapatra, H. (2024). Analyzing territorial variations in the implementation of IoT-based smart homes. *Advances in Electronic Government, Digital Divide, and Regional Development*, 305–334. DOI: 10.4018/979-8-3693-6854-1.ch010

Singh, R. K., & Pant, V. (2024). Cyber security concerns in social media and online interactions. *Advances in Human and Social Aspects of Technology*, 273–288. DOI: 10.4018/979-8-3693-9235-5.ch014

Song, Z., Li, Z., & Chen, X. (2019). Local differential privacy preserving mechanism for multi-attribute data in mobile Crowdsensing with edge computing. *2019 IEEE International Conference on Smart Internet of Things (SmartIoT)*, 283-290. https://doi.org/DOI: 10.1109/SmartIoT.2019.00050

Venugopal, K., & Jagadeesh, B. (2024). Theoretical insights into user security and privacy in social media environments. *Advances in Human and Social Aspects of Technology*, 289–312. DOI: 10.4018/979-8-3693-9235-5.ch015

Wu, H., Zhang, Z., Guan, C., Wolter, K., & Xu, M. (2020). Collaborate edge and cloud computing with distributed deep learning for smart city Internet of things. *IEEE Internet of Things Journal*, 7(9), 8099–8110. DOI: 10.1109/JIOT.2020.2996784

Xu, X., Huang, Q., Yin, X., Abbasi, M., Khosravi, M. R., & Qi, L. (2020). Intelligent offloading for collaborative smart city services in edge computing. *IEEE Internet of Things Journal*, 7(9), 7919–7927. DOI: 10.1109/JIOT.2020.3000871

Yu, D., Cheng, X., Dressler, F., Kowalski, D. R., & Lv, W. (2020). Guest editorial: Special issue on high-confidence city IoT for collaborative smart city services. *IEEE Internet of Things Journal*, 7(9), 7848–7850. DOI: 10.1109/JIOT.2020.3021495

Chapter 2
Cloud Data Security and Encryption Using Blockchain

Garima Mathur
https://orcid.org/0000-0002-8841-3920
Sagar Institute of Science and Technology, India

Pankaj Savita
https://orcid.org/0000-0002-2447-6244
Sagar Institute of Science and Technology, India

Sachin Murarka
https://orcid.org/0009-0002-0409-262X
Sanjeev Agrawal Global Educational (SAGE) University, India

ABSTRACT

The exponential growth of cloud computing has increased concerns over data security and privacy for organizations and individuals. Traditional security mechanisms often fail to provide robust protection against emerging threats. This review paper explores the integration of blockchain technology to enhance cloud data security and encryption. Blockchain's decentralized, immutable, and transparent nature offers a promising solution to vulnerabilities in centralized cloud architectures. The paper discusses blockchain's fundamental principles and their application in securing cloud data. It also reviews current research and case studies on the practical implementation and benefits of blockchain in cloud security. Challenges and future directions in merging blockchain and cloud data security are identified and analyzed. This comprehensive review aims to demonstrate how blockchain can revolutionize cloud data security, providing a trustworthy framework for data

DOI: 10.4018/979-8-3693-7137-4.ch002

protection in the digital age.

INTRODUCTION

Technological advancement and Internet-based services have led to the development of cloud computing. It offers computation and storage as its two primary service models (Omurgonulsen et al., 2021). All cloud computing services require high-performance cloud storage to meet customer requests. Thus, one of the crucial elements of the cloud computing system is cloud storage, because these services save on infrastructure and maintenance costs, for many small-scale businesses and individuals like them. Cloud storage makes it simple for multiple people to view and share data. Within the cloud computing paradigm, one of the untrusted entities is the cloud server (CS). The user no longer has physical control over the data once it has been outsourced on CS and stored at any data center. There is no method for cloud users to verify that this data is correctly outsourced.

Applications of blockchain technology contribute to immutable audit trails, data integrity, decentralized identity management, and other areas that can greatly improve cloud security (Aste et al., 2017). Organizations must, however, carefully consider if the technology fits their unique use cases and deal with any implementation-related issues. Blockchain's contribution to strengthening and increasing cloud security is expected to gain significance as long as it remains a major focus.

Cloud computing has blown up the software tech sector with its amazing benefits. Globally, businesses use cloud computing for disaster recovery, software development and testing, data backup and storage, and other purposes. Cloud computing is being used by numerous other industries, including healthcare, automotive, and retail, to provide cutting-edge solutions. Its applications are not just restricted to the IT and software sectors. Cloud computing is not without its restrictions, though. Herein lies the role of blockchain technology, another game-changing innovation.

Blockchain's decentralized, transparent, and secure features make it a popular choice for various industrial applications among millions of organizations. However, combining blockchain technology with cloud computing can further transform several sectors.

Blockchain provides improved decentralization, network security, and data privacy; cloud computing enables great flexibility and scalability. Therefore, blockchain technology and cloud computing have enormous potential to produce novel solutions, especially when combined with a distributed cloud like Ridge Cloud. This chapter will give a comprehensive overview of blockchain technology in cloud computing, including blockchain security, blockchain cloud platform, and associated ideas.

Figure 1. Basics of Blockchain

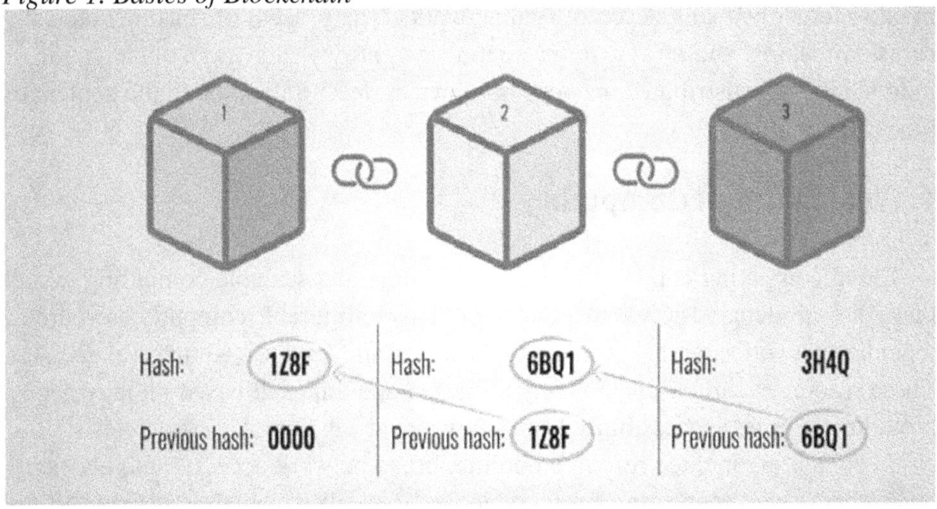

Blockchain is a kind of distributed database where data is stored digitally in chunks and then linked together using cryptography. In blockchain, blocks serve as basic information containers that store encrypted data.

A block is made up of various parts, like the block body and header. Every block in the chain contains the recorded data as seen in Figure 1, a cryptographic hash of the preceding block, and a timestamp indicating the precise moment the block was added to the chain. Since blocks can only hold so much data, when they are filled, they are closed and connected to the previously filled block to form a data chain. Next, any fresh information is added to a freshly formed block on the blockchain. A new block cannot be produced until the previous block (and the data within it) has been confirmed.

Another name for blockchain is distributed ledger technology, or DLT. because it tracks digital assets, logs transactions, and saves them. Various transactions are placed in each block, and once a transaction occurs, it is recorded in the ledger of each participant.

The records of a transaction can only be distributed via a blockchain system; they cannot be copied or moved. A block becomes very difficult to remove or modify after it is accepted by the blockchain's chain. This implies that it is very difficult to change or remove transaction records from the blockchain. Furthermore, since blockchain generates a series of blocks, hackers can't compromise a blockchain system without altering every block. Blockchain thereby removes fraud and lowers security and privacy issues.

Blockchain technology reduces the requirement for individuals to have faith in one another by using decentralized networks. The process of shifting authority, decision-making, and power from a centralized entity—such as an organization or individual—to a distributed network is known as decentralization in the context of blockchain.

1. What is Cloud Computing

Cloud computing can be defined as a flexible and scalable computing model that offers on-demand access to a shared pool of configurable computing resources, including networks, servers, storage, applications, and services (Kumar et al., 2024a). These resources can be dynamically allocated and adjusted based on user needs, providing seamless accessibility from anywhere at any time. Key characteristics of cloud computing include resource pooling, broad network access, rapid elasticity, on-demand self-service, and measurable services, all of which contribute to the efficient and automated management of computing resources with minimal direct human interaction (Omurgonulsen et al., 2021). Figure 2 gives essential characteristics of cloud computing.

Figure 2. Essential characteristics of cloud computing

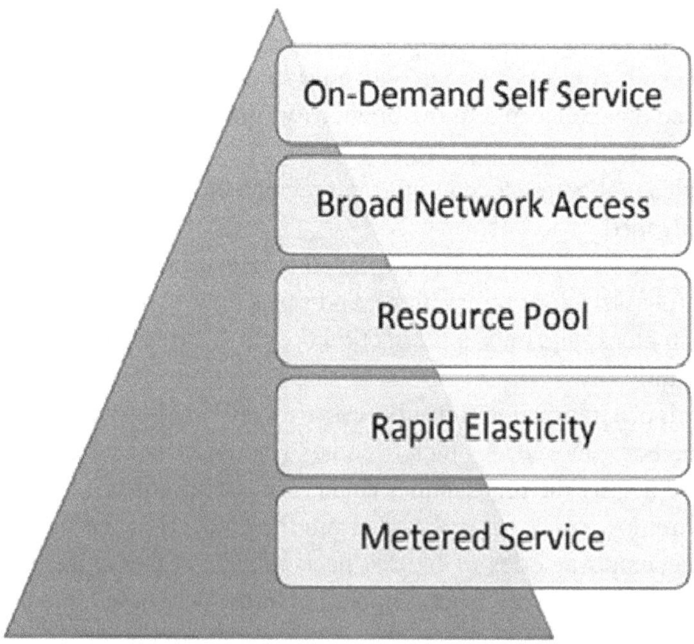

In cloud computing, the operational efficiency and flexibility of the model are driven by its service and deployment models. Deployment models define how cloud resources are accessed and managed, dividing cloud environments into four key types:

First is Public Cloud, which offers services over the public internet. Next is the private cloud, which is dedicated to a single organization for enhanced control and security. Third is the Hybrid Cloud, which combines both public and private clouds for a balanced approach; Lastly, the Community Cloud is shared among organizations with similar needs and concerns.

On the other hand, service models serve as the foundation of cloud computing by offering customers a variety of resources. These fall into three main categories: The first is Infrastructure-as-a-Service, or IaaS, which offers online access to virtualized computer resources. The second is Platform-as-a-Service (PaaS), which provides platforms for the users to create, execute, and manage applications without having to deal with the problem of creating and maintaining the underlying infrastructure. Software-as-a-Service (SaaS), which distributes software applications online through a subscription model, is the third service. When combined, these models provide cost-effective, scalable, and adaptable cloud solutions that can be customized to satisfy a range of business requirements.

Figure 3. Architecture of cloud computing

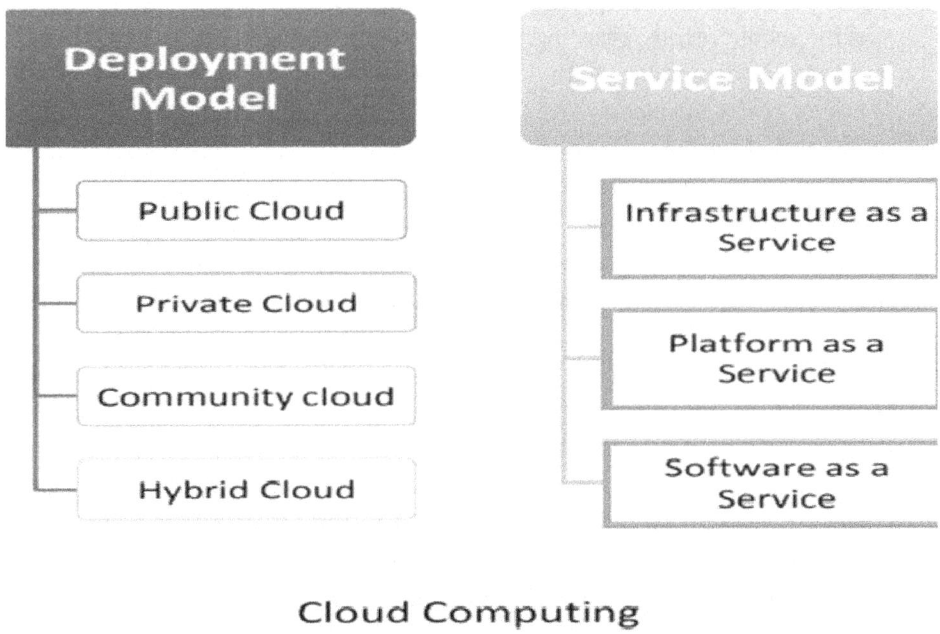

In Cloud Computing Environment, data must be stored in data center which is located in various region to provide IT infrastructure services like servers, storage, and networking. Data can be access, manage and monitored by organisation from any location. These organisations are using various services of different cloud environment to secure data and responsible for data governance with pay as you go service. So, this leads cost optimisation and resource optimisation to increase customer retention. Therefore, now a days Organisations provide maximum benefits to their customers and users.

2. Challenges and Opportunities in Cloud Computing

a) *Reliability:* Cloud services are expected to be available 24/7 to users. However, there are instances where servers stop providing services due to maintenance or other time constraints. Modern cloud users anticipate enhanced services, established standards, and best practices from cloud providers. Cloud servers, like traditional resident servers, also experience downtime and depend heavily on the cloud service provider. This dependency can lead to users being locked into a specific provider, posing potential business risks.

b) *Compliance:* Accessing, storing, and using data in the cloud is subject to numerous regulations that require regular reporting and audit trails. Some customers have specific requirements regarding the data centers managed by cloud providers, necessitating compliance with these requirements.

c) *Service Level Agreements (SLAs):* Cloud services are governed by SLAs that allow multiple instances of an application to be replicated across different servers based on priority needs. Lower-priority applications may be minimized or shut down by the cloud provider. The primary challenge for cloud users is evaluating SLAs with vendors, as most vendors draft SLAs that favor themselves, offering minimal assurances on data protection, outage handling, and pricing structures. Users must carefully review these terms before signing contracts with providers.

d) *Cloud Data Management: Managing data in the cloud is a significant research issue due to the massive,* often unstructured, or semi-structured nature of cloud data. Service providers depend on infrastructure providers for complete data security, as they cannot directly access the physical security systems of data centers. Even with virtual machines, providers can set security conditions remotely, without always knowing if they are securely implemented. Infrastructure providers need to ensure terms like auditability, which attests to the security settings of applications, and confidentiality, which secures data access and transfer. Confidentiality can be maintained using encryption methods, and auditability can be ensured through remote checking techniques. However, because virtual machines can move around often, remote checking may not always be a practical solution.

3. Overview of Cloud Computing Security

Cloud computing offers many benefits, including the ability to scale easily, adapt to different needs, and save costs. However, it also comes with serious security challenges, like the risk of data breaches, insider threats, and weaknesses in the cloud's systems. Cloud computing has grown thanks to progress in technologies like grid computing, distributed computing, parallel computing, utility computing, and simulation. These technologies provide features like high scalability, virtualization, advanced data storage, and strong computing power, all while being affordable and dependable.

Although cloud computing has many benefits, security is still a big concern and slows down its wider use (Kumar et al., 2024b). The main worries are making sure services are always available and keeping data private and safe. To handle these security challenges, a mix of traditional and modern methods is needed to protect the whole cloud system. Cloud computing can improve security by letting service providers take care of data protection, but these providers must ensure that the data stored in their systems is secure.

Several leading companies, such as Google, IBM, Microsoft, Amazon, VMware, and EMC, provide cloud computing platforms, each emphasizing the importance of security in their offerings. Since cloud systems operate over the internet, they inherit many of the security challenges associated with online environments, like those encountered in traditional computing. A significant concern is the protection of personal user data within the cloud, which can introduce new security challenges (Harshavardhan et al., 2018). Beyond security, trust in cloud services is a critical factor, influenced by elements such as automation, management practices, human factors, operational processes, and policies. One specific security challenge in cloud computing is the application of encryption techniques within security protocols.

In today's digital age, where cloud computing underpins most business operations, ensuring the security of data and transactions in the cloud is more critical than ever. Cyberattacks and data breaches are ongoing threats, pushing organizations to find new ways to improve cloud security. One promising solution is blockchain technology, which can help make cloud systems more secure and trustworthy.

OVERVIEW OF BLOCKCHAIN TECHNOLOGY

1. Introduction to Blockchain Technology?

Blockchain is an online platform for safely storing and exchanging data. Initially, it was simply designed to solve the issues related to cryptocurrencies like Bitcoin. With tremendous outcomes, blockchain technology was turned out to be milestone for another domain as well as digital market.

Architecture of blockchain, as it names concern, governing data into small chunks called "blocks" followed by other blocks like linked as a chain. Each blocks contain special code, called "hash" to provide security between the blocks. So, it prohibited data by malware attacks (Aste, T. et al., 2017). The blockchain is deployed throughout the cluster connected with different network, known as a peer-to-peer network, leads to avoid centralized location related issues (Sleiman et al., 2015). As blockchain technology also known as to provide secured and reliable characteristics, ensures only authorized user can access the data by using asymmetric cryptography. It uses pair of keys called public and private, which works together to lock and unlock data. (Aumasson, 2017). Figure 4 illustrates the complete blockchain process.

Blockchain technology gives immense characteristic like data immutability. That simply means unauthorized user couldn't alter or malpractices with the data or organizational accounts. So, this technology prevents all types of attack by its supremacy service like cryptography hash. By this, most of the organisation uses this service for their payment gateway as well. Basically, hashing is the process to give fixed length data string from arbitrary format. So, it benefits various crypto-currencies like bitcoin by fixed length string outcomes. Blockchain uses SHA 256 encryption techniques to generate hash values (Wanga et al., 2019).

Immutability, transparency and security are the main three key characteristics of blockchain which brought revolution in the field of data governance like users or customer can securely migrate, view or store their data anywhere anytime.

2. Blockchain-Based Encryption Techniques

Blockchain technology uses different type of encryption methods which strong enough to provide security to data in cloud environment. This type of encryption technique well defined in following section as how it provides security to data.

a) Symmetric and Asymmetric Encryption

Symmetric Encryption

As security is main concern to prevent data breaches. So, Symmetric encryption provides security to big data by using single secrete key technique, which means, to encrypting and decrypting the huge volume of data with single key. So, it reduces the key challenges of big data after increasing the velocity of it. Authorised users can easily decrypt data with the same key. For achieving this aspects, symmetric encryption technique uses algorithm like Advanced Encryption Standard (AES) and Data Encryption Standard (DES). Normally, encryption techniques used before storing the data itself, thereafter data can securely be shared by using asymmetric technique.

Asymmetric Encryption

Unlike Symmetric encryption technique, Asymmetric encryption uses two keys called private key and public key simultaneously. Like, for encryption public key is used and for decryption private key is used. The basic difference between both the key is, public key can be shared to any users openly while to decrypt the data private key remains restricted. In blockchain technology, this technique uses widely to ensure security and integrity of data that only authorised user can decrypt the data having its private key.

b) Hybrid Encryption

Hybrid encryption is a method that combines both symmetric and asymmetric encryption techniques to balance efficiency and security. In this approach, data is first encrypted using a symmetric key, which is faster and efficient for handling large data volumes. Then, the symmetric key itself is encrypted using the recipient's asymmetric public key, ensuring secure key distribution. This method leverages the speed of symmetric encryption for managing data and the robust security of asymmetric encryption for sharing keys. In blockchain applications, hybrid encryption ensures that data is encrypted efficiently while also being securely transmitted, making it particularly valuable for secure data sharing and transactions.

c) Homomorphic Encryption

As of latency and throughput are always a key concern in big data era. Like, to reduce the latency and increase the throughput in blockchain environment, Homomorphic encryption is used. By this encryption technique data can be extract, processed and load without decrypting it. So, data remains secured while ETL governance. This technique is widely used in blockchain technology and provide robust and secured solution to client. For example, any client can query their data without any decryption key or knowing insight of the data.

d) Attribute-Based Encryption (ABE)

During the encryption, users restricted by particular access policies that actually satisfy by attributes of the users, is a method of Attribute-Based Encryption (ABE). So, user access to the encrypted data only granted if and only if user policies is predefined or aligned with their attributes. Also, in this technique, owner permission may not be required for data sharing once it has been encrypted. As users are restricted to their attributes, they have assigned to particular role to enhance access management in blockchain technology.

e) Secure Hash Algorithms

In blockchain technology, data integrity is also a key concern to increase trust system in market. So, secure hash algorithms verify authentication of data securely. It uses SHA-256 algorithm, which is well known algorithm for secure hash algorithm family. To ensure data integrity as well as security, it generates 256- bit hash value from input data. This algorithm proves milestone to blockchain in market which is widely used in network like bitcoin. For example, Data-driven technology for bitcoin depends upon blockchain technology in which each blocks having SHA-256 hash of their previous blocks. It also connects blocks securely and also ensures integrity between blocks for end-to-end blockchain technology.

Moreover, SHA -3, the latest algorithm used by SHA family, is reduces advance challenges of security. It provides robustness and to prevent collision attacks. Now a days SHA-3 is widely used by blockchain technology due to its highly recommended as comparison to SHA-256. Also, to maintain more trust and secure environment, Both SHA-256 and SHA-3 used simultaneously by blockchain technology. So, together they address more data integrity and security in blockchain environment.

f) Zero-Knowledge Proofs (ZKPs)

Using cryptography technique in blockchain environment give more success to reduce big data challenges. ZKF are one of best cryptography technique to allowing source to prove itself to destination with a statement which is not actual or with confidentiality of insights. Even though, verification has been enabled, it has been ensured that data is sensitive and its integrity should not be compromised. Apart from this, there are two more types, which is also used widely called zk-SNARKs

(Zero-Knowledge Succinct Non-Interactive Arguments of Knowledge) & zk-STARKs (Zero-Knowledge Scalable Transparent Arguments of Knowledge). To minimized computational resources and communication overhead zk-SNARKs is used where as to emphasize scalability and transparency zk-STARKs is used.

So, ZKPs play vital role to provide data security and data integrity in blockchain technology. With this, verification of transaction automated to reduce any data leakage vulnerability, which ensures confidentiality and integrity. For example, it improves security to private transactions, in which insights remain confidential and also secure voting system, where voters have right to preserve their information to whom they voted. ZKPs enables privacy preserving operations which play crucial roles in blockchain technology.

g) Confidential Transactions
  - Description: A technique used to hide the amount of cryptocurrency being transacted. It ensures that transaction details are only visible to the parties involved.
  - Technology: Pedersen Commitments, Ring Signatures.
  - Importance in Blockchain: It enhance transaction privacy used in blockchain environment like Monero and ensures validation of transaction. So, user's account remains confidentially in every aspect.

h) Differential Privacy
  - Description: A method to ensure that aggregate data analysis does not compromise individual data privacy.
  - Application in Blockchain: Ensures that data analytics on blockchain data can be performed without compromising the privacy of individuals whose data is included in the analysis.

3. Benefits of Blockchain

Using the technology of blockchain-based cloud computing has several advantages, some of which include:

- **Improved Security:** The immense security of blockchain technology is one of its biggest benefits. Blockchain replaces centralized data storage by storing data in ledgers throughout a network of computers. Because of the decentralized architecture, hackers have a very difficult time breaking into the system and altering data. Furthermore, it is practically impossible to conduct fraud because every transaction is checked and validated by the network before being added to the ledger.

- **Enhanced Efficiency:** Blockchain technology is used to increase a cloud-based system's capacity. As blockchain technology prevents individuals like translators and broker due to its distributed database capability. Which results increasing in transaction speed and overall efficiency.
- **Increased Scalability:** Ethereum is decentralized open source blockchain platform which is highly scalable and operates as a distributed database system. This platform has capability to scale-up more resources in case of more traffic. For example, Client uses a cloud platform which can simply scale or improve their performance with Ethereum platform.
- **Better Traceability:** For tracking and monitoring the sensitive data blockchain technology uses cloud base platform to keep their real time records for every transaction. This importance of blockchain technology play vital role in health and finance domain where data is more sensitive to keep their records securely. Data are handling and monitoring very carefully by tracking each transaction. So, Client can ensure their data security and data integrity.
- **Reduced Cost:** Blockchain provides automation in technology to reduce administrative cost as compare to traditional system. It simply replaces the need of mediator or pipelining processes.
- **Easy to Program Models:** In case of data migration to the cloud, blockchain technology provides easy to program model. Companies may leverage more straightforward, cloud-compatible programming methods. When moving to the cloud, can save costs and time.
- **Enhanced Interoperability:** The capacity of various systems and apps to cooperate is known as interoperability. Blockchain can facilitate interoperability by standardizing data formats. As a result, several systems can communicate and share data according to a standard.

4. Enterprise Cloud Computing Problems addressed by Blockchain Technology (with examples)

Cloud computing safety, confidentiality of information, scalability, and interoperability are some of the major issues. All of these problems may be resolved by blockchain technology's decentralized structure. Below are some instances of how blockchain applications for cloud storage might benefit various businesses.

- **Medical security:** Medical security breaches were identified on a daily average of 2.05 in 2023, according to data from the HIPAA Journal. Due to its centralized data storage, the healthcare sector is a popular target for hackers because it handles sensitive patient data. Encrypting and decentralizing patient data is one way that a blockchain-based healthcare application can help reduce these dangers (Mathur, G. et al., 2024; Pandey, A. et al., 2024; & Goyal, S., 2024). Hackers find it harder to access and alter sensitive data on these kinds of systems as a result. Medical diagnoses, treatments, and procedures can be securely recorded using blockchain technology. This would facilitate the tracking of a patient's medical history and guard against mistakes or fraud (Kaur et al., 2018).

- **Banking:** In Banking domain, Security is key issues for big data. It has been seen since many years, that due to data breaches, banking sector losses increases day by day. But since Blockchain comes in a picture, which give immense relief to this sector helping data security and provide real time protection. It uses digital signature for an instance to confirm user identity. So, Blockchain prevents fraud and malware practices to data.
- **Supply Chain:** Supply chains produce important data, which must be properly maintained. Blockchain applications can improve data management in the supply chain and guarantee product authenticity. For instance, blockchain technology would allow us to follow a product's whole route from the maker to the store, reducing the chance of counterfeiting.

Blockchain technology can also aid in supply chain optimization by eliminating the demand for paper paperwork. Here are some instances of how blockchain technology can be used to solve issues with enterprise cloud computing. This technology has many other applications in other sectors.

5. Enhancing Cloud Security with Blockchain Technology (Zhu et al., 2018)

- **Immutability**: Blockchain's best defining features is its immutability, which ensures that once data is entered, it cannot be modified or erased without collective agreement from the network. This characteristic of blockchain can create permanent audit monitoring of all processing unit in cloud environment. Data access, data migration or any data accesses are safely replicated in blockchain environment. It keeps this technology trustworthy to every user or client.
- **Data Security:** As discussed, earlier section, blockchain technology uses cryptography hashes for every block that generates unique codes to safety of data. So, with cloud environment blockchain play immense role to provide security as well. Somehow, any unauthorized user tries to access the data, then it will trigger the notification to the admin team.
- **Identity management:** As cloud environment has already IAM service to secure login and authorization, blockchain also added security for login and

access to cloud environment. So, user can safely migrate their data anytime anywhere.

- **Security Rule Automation:** As blockchain technology also provides Automation as discussed earlier with having smart contracts just a digital agreement written in code (Murthy et al., 2020). With this, any client & user can access or utilize any cloud services with their authorization credential.
- **Supply Chain Security**: Through blockchain technology, it is necessary to protect software supply chain from virus or malware in Cloud Environment. By establishing an open, unchangeable record of software and updates, blockchain can be used to confirm the legitimacy and source of upgrades.
- **Zero Trust Security:** Zero Trust security concepts can coexist with blockchain. Blockchain-based access and identity administration guarantees that only authorized and verified entities can access cloud resources by never assuming anything and by continuously verifying everything.

Blockchain technology may have its roots in cloud computing technologies. Blockchain implementations can benefit greatly from cloud security settings because blockchain networks can operate there. Due to their security protection mechanisms, blockchain and the cloud are both immune to cybercrime.

Blockchain technology is generally seen as an incorruptible technology since it is gaining momentum in a variety of fields. Blockchain technology can help with several security-related problems in cloud environments. Because of the blockchain's consensus mechanism, every transaction data is preserved and difficult to erase. In addition, it becomes more difficult for the hacker to alter the transaction data. This implies that the more blockchain nodes there are, the harder it is to change the data.

There is a cost associated with this blockchain-based approach to the security and legal issues around the cloud forensic dilemma. Large-scale blockchain ledger distribution increases the cost of performance. Although these technologies offer benefits to enterprises, they also present significant obstacles (Mathur, 2023).

The main advantages of cloud computing are associated with increased operational efficiency. The advantages of blockchain emphasize security more. Blockchain guarantees transaction traceability and data privacy, but it can also result in higher performance costs in cloud computing environments. Blockchain offers a novel means of exchanging knowledge from other sources that one does not already have to have faith in an entity or individual.

ROLE OF BLOCKCHAIN BASED CLOUD COMPUTING

Blockchain technology can be used in cloud computing to build a distributed system of nodes that exchange information and computational capacity. So, Organisations can simultaneously use anyone of cluster to avoiding single or centralized source. So, relying on distributed computer system means independent of any one organisation.

System must design to have High availability, Scalability, and higher security. So, Blockchain technology provides such services. Therefore, client uses this technology to develop advanced application that support cloud-based architecture as well (Zhu et al., 2018). Thereafter, this automation system leads to develop decentralized file repository that is more secure.

The uses of Blockchain in cloud computing as a cloud service or cloud of things. Basically, Cloud of things is integration of cloud computing and internet of things which covers data storage, extraction, loading or analytics. It just also integrates data comes from various domain like automobile to industrial machinery, household goods, smart wearable technologies. Due to cloud computing's immense capability of computational power, flexibility or scalability, Blockchain easily relates cloud of things for data driven. By 2029, according to study there will be 28 billion IoT devices in use.

Blockchain technology in cloud computing can easily promote organisation for better managing and secured any data. Whatever data has collected by IoT devices may securely integrated to the cloud environment and stored through blockchain technology. In addition, most Internet of Things devices have a finite amount of storage.

1. Blockchain vs Cloud: A detailed comparison

Every cloud infrastructure built on blockchain has a copy of the blockchain stored on each node. Every time a new transaction is added to the blockchain, the new data is updated on all nodes within the network. This makes it possible to manage and store the data in a decentralized, transparent, and safe manner. The blockchain cloud has the power to completely transform data management as well. It might be used for anything from tracing the origin of food to storing medical information.

Figure 4. Centralized Vs Decentralized

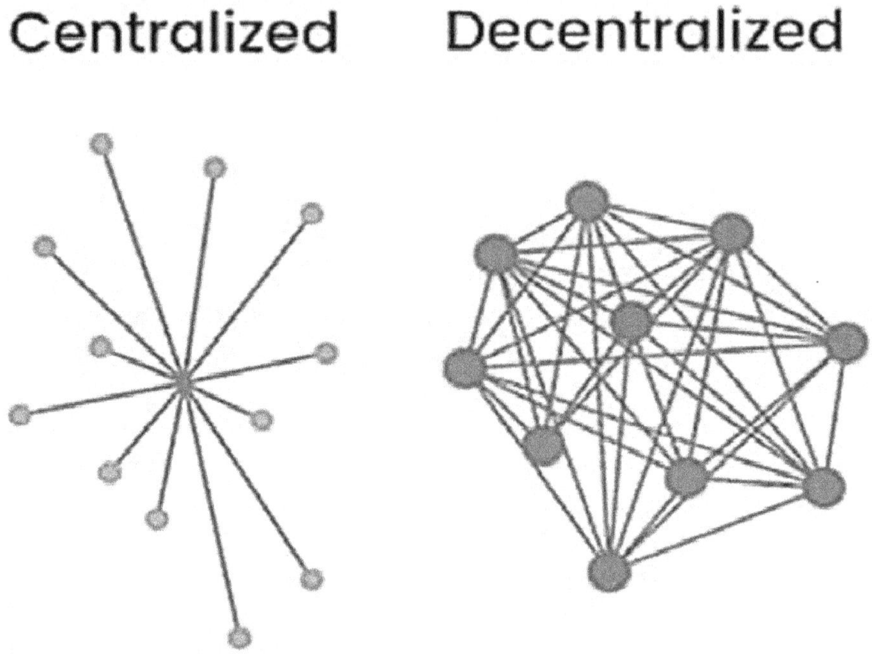

Blockchain technology and cloud computing are very distinct from one another (figure 4). Nonetheless, they each have special advantages that can be combined to produce a complete solution that benefits businesses. A method for storing and accessing data and apps online is provided by cloud computing. Enterprises of various sizes can make use of this adaptable and expandable solution (Tapas et al., 2019).

Alternatively, distributed databases are maintained on a growing list of records through the use of blockchain technology. Blocks are the name for these records. With cryptography, they are connected. As discussed earlier as well, blockchain technology is continuously utilizing to immutable account for cryptocurrency exchanges, there are various technology with different factors as follows:

- Data Access: Both cloud computing and blockchain allow users to access data online. Cloud platforms depend upon different data center, while blockchain techniques uses encryption and hashing to data security.
- Costs: Cloud computing uses pay as you go services, but sometime it may costly while providing end to end services for complete data governance but due to blockchain cost may be optimised.

- Data Consistency: In cloud computing, authorised user can easily modify or update data with having specific roles. But in blockchain once data is encrypted, it cannot be altered. It assures accuracy of data.
- Data Protection: Cloud computing and blockchain both are offering data protection algorithm in various ways. Like in security concern cloud computing uses IAM roles or active directory for encryption and regular monitoring, while blockchain's uses SHA crypto algorithm to avoid data breaches.
- Speed: Cloud computing much better performance as comparison with blockchain in case speed. Like, to process big data, cloud computing gives quick processing result, but blockchain is slightly slow, reason behind this is, it requires validation step for transactions.
- Security Issues: As comparison with security, blockchain's decentralised design provides more security as cloud platform combining with its crypto hashing and validation methods. Most of the organisation faced lots of cloud security issue and attacks like phishing attacks gives more vulnerability reveals by 2023 survey report.

This is wrong to say that blockchain technology cannot breakable or cloud platform is not secure. It's important to keep in mind, too, that while blockchain has remained mostly unhacked, the cloud has recently faced criticism for security lapses. Although blockchain technology and cloud computing share many characteristics, they also differ significantly. When discussing blockchain vs. cloud-based computing, there are several differences between the two technologies.

The architecture of normal cloud computing is centralized, but blockchain cloud design completely depends on decentralization. One more distinction between blockchain and cloud computing is the ease with which data may be stored online with cloud services. However, blockchain technology makes use of a variety of encryption-based mechanisms. Additionally, it stores data in specialized databases. Blockchain security is combined with cloud convenience when cloud providers integrate blockchain technology with their tech stack.

Blockchain provides significantly better security than the cloud, which is another obvious distinction when considering blockchain vs. cloud or blockchain vs. cloud storage. Blockchain-based cloud storage prevents data and information from being changed, in contrast to regular cloud storage where data can be edited. Finally, while cloud computing is more susceptible to attackers and data breaches, the blockchain eliminates data tampering.

Storage, virtual computers, networking, and other necessary resources are provided by third-party providers via the internet under the Infrastructure as a Service (IaaS) cloud service model. Users are solely accountable for handling the management of their data, including handling data recovery in the event of a loss. They must also install and manage the apps and operating systems that are used with the supplied infrastructure.

Cloud computing service models and Blockchain IaaS are similar to standard IaaS, but offer additional security and decentralization benefits. In a Blockchain IaaS configuration, the unused processing capacity of CPUs and GPUs inside a decentralized network can be utilized, providing consumers with additional computing resources on demand. Blockchain technology and cloud computing together may offer businesses a better, more secure option.

2. *Challenges of Blockchain based Cloud Storage Applications*

Blockchain shows a lot of potential in cloud computing, but it also faces some challenges when used in cloud storage, such as:

- **New and Evolving Technology**: Blockchain is still a developing technology, and there aren't many providers offering solutions or services yet. This limited availability can make it hard for organizations to find a system that fits their specific needs. For example, A healthcare organisation may struggle with blockchain solution due to its privacy rule is very strict, may not meet its security requirements.
- **Complication and its Use**: Sometime deployment of blockchain technology may be complicated. For example, in organisation, it is tough or extensive training for employees in blockchain for storage and security. So, it is difficult to manage complexity of the system.

3. The Necessity of Blockchain based Cloud Computing

The infrastructure of Cloud of Things (CoT) and traditional cloud computing faces several risks and limitations. Blockchain technology presents a promising solution to overcome these challenges. The main issues include:

- **Limited Control Over Data:** In traditional cloud computing, users have restricted control over their data, processes, and code once they are uploaded to cloud servers.
- **Less Transparency**: Users unable to understand insight of cloud operation that how it carried out, due to this they are fully depended on cloud providers for data handling. Which lead trust issues between user and cloud provider in terms of privacy and security.

- **Centralized Communication Models:** CoT relies on centralized communication models, it is difficult to scale processing units and extend IoT networks for big deployments.

So, blockchain-based cloud computing network may reduce these risks with implementing encryption method into the network using blockchain technology also called Blockchain as a Service (BaaS). It provides variety of services like smart contracts, User transaction verification, blockchain-based cloud storage which helps to enable IoT applications. Figure 5 shows Architecture blockchain-based cloud network.

Figure 5. Blockchain-based Cloud

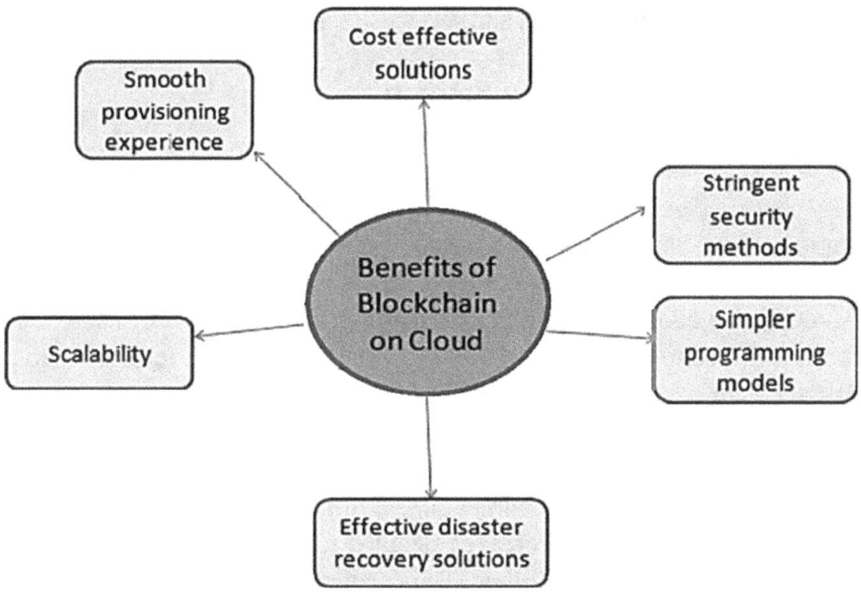

Blockchain technology provides various features that can improve systems related with the Cloud of Things (CoT) and cloud solutions. The key benefits of extracting blockchain into edge and cloud computing are:

Decentralization: Addressing Challenges in CoT Systems

CoT (Cloud of Things) systems often face the challenge of depending on a centralized server for data governance and decision making. A failure in the data center can lead to system- failure and potential data loss. Additionally, centralized servers are more vulnerable to cyberattacks, posing significant security risks.

Data should be distributed in multiple replicas across the network of nodes, this architecture only possible by using blockchain based cloud computing.

If single node goes down then other system of various server still in operational mode by the decentralized approach of blockchain. Also, by distributed replica of data in storage system, it reduces the chance of data loss and enable fast disaster recovery. Blockchain gives highly benefits to different industries like logistics, where real time tracking system is always in active mode, apart from this it also increases supports and monitoring to goods and services.

Improved Cloud Security and Storage

For sensitive data like video recordings and voice data are very much need security concern So, in traditional cloud platform it is big challenge to maintain. If data is breaches then it would be big loss. So, blockchain-based decentralized cloud storage system ensures security for reducing this risk by distributing data into encrypted blocks and connecting them using a hashing algorithm. These chunks are then replicated to different multiple decentralized nodes in the cluster to give strong data security.

To ensuring protection against data breaches or malware practices, only authorized user can access with same keys for encryption and decryption the data. So, it leads blockchain based cloud computing a strongly dependable technology for security framework solution. Moreover, detailed record of storage, data integrity, data security, tampering prevention etc all are maintained by blockchain technology. These decentralized storage solutions are not only secure but also efficient, scalable, and cost-effective, offering unlimited storage capacity.

4. Research Questions

Can Blockchain Replace Cloud Computing?

- What are the current trends indicating about the potential for blockchain to replace cloud computing?
- Why is it unlikely that blockchain will completely replace cloud computing?

How Can Blockchain and Cloud Computing Complement Each Other?

- How blockchain strengthen the security of data stored on cloud computing platforms?
- How does the blockchain technology contributes to the robustness and resilience of cloud-based applications? Explain its decentralized concept?

What is the strength for Integrating Blockchain with Cloud Computing?

- What new opportunities can arise from the integration of blockchain and cloud computing that were not possible before?
- What are the most compelling aspects of combining these two technologies?

What Competency are Needed to Manage and Develop These Technologies?

- What expertise is required for professionals to effectively manage, operate, and develop blockchain and cloud computing technologies?
- How can talent marketplaces like Revelo support companies in finding pre-vetted remote tech talent with the necessary skills and experience?

EXISTING WORK DONE ON BLOCKCHAIN-BASED CLOUD STORAGE SYSTEM

To improvement of security, decentralization and data integrity, blockchain based cloud storage system proves milestone in the market. This literature survey concludes studies about blockchain-enabled cloud storage systems, examining key areas such as security, privacy, performance, and associated challenges. This also explain about emerging trends and gaps in the current research. Also gives valuable identification for future work.

1. Introduction to Cloud Computing and Blockchain Technology

To achieve scalability, on-demand access to shared resources for computing, data migration, storage, processing and overall data governance cloud computing has been introduced. Challenges were still concern for traditional cloud platform such as data security, privacy concerns, and reliance on centralized control (Murthy et al., 2020). Cloud computing is providing scalable, on-demand access to distributed computing resources, transformed data storage and management. Blockchain technology, offers a trust solution to these issues with its decentralized and tamper-resistant account.

Blockchain based cloud computing system improves the data security & privacy, reliability on cloud computing. This research work also defines how blockchain addresses challenges to provide like data integrity and data security. So, blockchain reduces risks of inherent in centralized infrastructure by its immense characteristics of decentralization. (Al Shinwan et al., 2022).This integration optimized the emerging trends through efficient cloud-based systems.

2. Security Enhancements through Blockchain Integration

A key focus of research is leveraging blockchain technology to enhance security in cloud storage systems, as traditional cloud models are prone to risks such as unauthorized access and data breaches. Blockchain's cryptographic methods, including encryption and digital signatures, provide robust mechanisms for securing cloud-stored data (Sharma et al., 2020).

Researchers have investigated blockchain's potential to establish decentralized storage networks, where data is distributed across multiple nodes. This decentralized architecture suddenly reduces the likelihood of system-wide compromises. Furthermore, blockchain's transparent and immutable ledger enables quick detection and traceability of unauthorized modifications (Al Shinwan et al., 2022).

Despite its security advantages, integrating blockchain with cloud storage presents new challenges, such as performance bottlenecks from slower transaction speeds and limited scalability. Current research is actively addressing these issues by exploring innovative strategies to enhance the efficiency of blockchain-based cloud systems (Murthy et al., 2020).

3. Privacy Concerns and Blockchain Solutions

Privacy is a persistent challenge in cloud computing, as users must often entrust third-party providers with sensitive personal data. Blockchain addresses this issue by enabling users to retain control over their data. Its decentralized architecture removes the reliance on centralized entities, while smart contracts enforce privacy policies and ensure that data access is both conditional and transparent (Macrinici et al., 2018).

Research has extensively explored blockchain's potential to enhance data privacy in cloud systems. One promising approach involves creating encrypted, decentralized storage platforms where data access is protected by cryptographic keys. This ensures that even if a cloud provider is compromised, unauthorized parties cannot access sensitive user data (Haber and Stornetta, 1990).

However, balancing privacy with factors such as accessibility and performance present significant challenges. Blockchain's emphasis on privacy can increase system complexity and operational costs, potentially impeding widespread adoption. Addressing these trade-offs remains a focus of ongoing research to optimize privacy in blockchain-integrated cloud systems.

4. Blockchain-as-a-Service (BaaS) and Cloud Integration

The emergence of Blockchain-as-a-Service (BaaS) platforms has played a pivotal role in integrating blockchain technology with cloud computing. Prominent cloud providers such as AWS, Microsoft Azure, and IBM offer BaaS solutions, enabling businesses to leverage blockchain technology without the need to develop or maintain complex infrastructure (Zheng et al., 2019).

BaaS platforms provide essential tools for building and managing blockchain applications, enhancing the security, transparency, and efficiency of cloud-based services. By utilizing scalable cloud infrastructures, these platforms address some of the scalability limitations typically associated with blockchain systems. Moreover, BaaS lowers the barriers to blockchain adoption, making it accessible to a wide range of industries.

Despite these benefits, reliance on centralized cloud providers for blockchain services raises concerns about undermining blockchain's decentralization, creating a potential paradox. Current research focuses on mitigating this issue, exploring methods to preserve blockchain's core principles of decentralization and security within BaaS platforms (Xie et al., 2020).

5. Real-world applications and Case Studies

Real-world applications of blockchain-based cloud storage illustrate its potential to solve specific challenges across various industries. Suddenly, in chain management, blockchain enhances traceability and transparency by creating tamper-proof records of transactions. This satisfy that all stakeholders have access to accurate and reliable data as goods progress through the supply chain (Dursun et al., 2022).

In the healthcare sector, blockchain is proposed as a secure solution for storing and sharing electronic health records (EHRs). Research shows that blockchain can improve privacy and security for patient data, empowering patients with more control while ensuring that only authorized healthcare providers can access the information. These applications showcase blockchain's versatility in tackling industry-specific challenges.

However, real-world implementations also reveal challenges, such as the need for seamless interoperability with existing systems and the potential increase in complexity and costs. Addressing these obstacles is crucial to fully realizing blockchain's potential in cloud computing.

6. Challenges and Limitations in Blockchain-Based Cloud Storage

While integrating blockchain with cloud storage brings many advantages, it also introduces several significant challenges. One of the key issues is scalability. Public blockchain networks often face performance limitations as transaction volumes grow, leading to slower processing speeds and increased costs, especially for large-scale cloud systems.

Another challenge is the complexity of implementing and managing blockchain solutions. Many organizations lack the necessary expertise to integrate blockchain effectively into their existing cloud infrastructures. This knowledge gap can result in higher implementation costs and operational difficulties, potentially deterring the adoption of blockchain-based cloud systems (Tapas et al., 2019).

Legal and regulatory concerns also present substantial barriers. Issues such as data sovereignty, compliance with international data protection laws, and the legal recognition of smart contracts are complex and require thorough examination. Addressing these challenges is crucial to ensuring the legal and ethical sustainability of blockchain-powered cloud solutions.

7. Research Gaps

For future work, various prospectives is still remains for research gap in blockchain-based cloud storage. To handling the use of on demand cloud platform in large scale blockchain technology gives scalable solution. Sharding, sidechains and hybrid models are still the main concern for researchers and they exploring these technologies to overcome scalability challenges. Moreover, Energy consumption is still a main concern for blockchain technology. For this proof of concept (PoC) is still going on about energy efficiency in cloud computing. But still Proof of Stake (PoS) and Proof of Authority (PoA) gives energy efficient options apart from using in large scale, means more work to do with large scale.

Legal and regulatory issues still a key concern for research gap. So, more challenges like data sovereignty, cross-region data center compliance with data protection laws, and the enforceability of smart contracts across jurisdictions must be shorted out for better communication between regions. So, blockchain play vital role to solve such challenges in cloud computing after integration of both.

Now, integration between different blockchain platform is also a key concern for research. As blockchain is involving more and more, it enables better communication and data migration between different servers. It is jus more efficient for data governance system with full potential while achieving interoperability of blockchain-based cloud storage.

Latest challenge comes in a picture is to maintain balance between privacy and security benefits. Blockchain enhances privacy and security benefits, but it increases complexity and reduced efficiency of the system. To increase effectiveness of cloud storage system, optimisation of trade-offs must develop in future research.

CONCLUSION AND FUTURE SCOPE

To enhance solution for data security and privacy challenges, blockchain based cloud computing technology is play vital role. To provide strong protection against the various vulnerability in traditional cloud systems, blockchain immense characteristics like decentralized, immutable, and transparent gives perfect solution. This study has also brief about data confidentiality, integrity, and availability are successfully achieved through blockchain-based encryption techniques and protocols. This case studies meets with real world as well and analyses various research findings like blockchain can play key role to enhance cloud data security, providing a more robust and reliable architecture.

Future Scope

However, research in every aspect never goes end like enhancing cloud data security so, blockchain technology requiring further research and innovation:

- **Scalability**: To manage big data challenges with 5 V's and storage needs large cloud storage system, there is need of scalability without compromising performance or efficiency.
- **Interoperability**: To provide automated solution for various challenges, research should focus on interoperability like establishing standards and protocols to different blockchain platforms and cloud storage system.
- **Energy Efficiency**: Energy efficient consensus mechanism and optimisation with blockchain protocols must be offer proof of concept during deployment in cloud environments. So, those who are utilizing proof of concept consensus, are called energy-intensive.
- **Regulatory Compliance**: Compliance with data protection laws and industry standard must meet for smooth optimisation between blockchain and cloud.

So, research smoothly focused on solution for various challenges and blockchain's benefits with regulatory requirements.

- **Hybrid Approaches**: Cloud security demands various innovative solutions, blockchain completes their promise with emerging technologies like artificial intelligence (AI) and the Internet of Things (IoT). So, hybrid models approach explores to enhance security and efficiency with same technologies.
- **User Privacy**: To achieve user privacy is vital challenge, also having a balance between user privacy and blockchain characteristics unlocks the challenges. So, focusing on zero-knowledge proofs and secure multi-party computation are play vital role to fight with such challenges.
- **Real-World Applications**: Organizational use cases and ongoing projects in cloud environment is play very important role. By this, researchers can study valuable insights about all characteristics to do best practices for deploying blockchain-based cloud computing.

REFERENCES

Al Shinwan, M., Shdefat, A., Mostafa, N., Al Sokkar, A., Alsarhan, T., & Almajali, D. (2022). Integrated cloud computing and blockchain systems: A review. International Journal of Data and Network Science.

Aste, T., Tasca, P., & Di Matteo, T. (2017). Blockchain technologies: The foreseeable impact on society and industry. *Computer*, 50(9), 18–28. DOI: 10.1109/MC.2017.3571064

Aumasson, J. (2017). *Serious cryptography: A practical introduction to modern encryption*. No Starch Press.

Dursun, T., Birinci, F., Alptekin, B., Sertkaya, I., Hasekioglu, O., Tunaboylu, B., & Zaim, S. (2022). Blockchain technology for supply chain management. In *Studies in Big Data*. Springer.

Haber, S., & Stornetta, W. S. (1990). How to time-stamp a digital document. In *Conference on the Theory and Application of Cryptography* (pp. 437-455).

Harshavardhan, A., Vijayakumar, T., & Mugunthan, S. R. (2018). Blockchain technology in cloud computing to overcome security vulnerabilities. In 2018 2nd International Conference on I-SMAC (pp. 408-414). IEEE. DOI: 10.1109/I-SMAC.2018.8653690

Kaur, H., Alam, M. A., Jameel, R., Mourya, A. K., & Chang, V. (2018). A proposed solution and future direction for blockchain-based heterogeneous medicare data in the cloud environment. *Journal of Medical Systems*, 42(8), 156. DOI: 10.1007/s10916-018-1007-5 PMID: 29987560

Khan, M. A., & Salah, K. (2018). IoT security: Review, blockchain solutions, and open challenges. *Future Generation Computer Systems*, 82, 395–411. DOI: 10.1016/j.future.2017.11.022

Kumar, T., Kumar, P., & Namasudra, S. (2024). Secure access control of cloud data using DNA computing. In 5th IEEE International Conference on Computing, Power and Communication Technologies (IC2PCT) (pp. 1996-2001). IEEE. DOI: 10.1109/IC2PCT60090.2024.10486550

Kumar, T., Kumar, P., & Namasudra, S. (2024). A DNA-based authentication system for securing cloud data storage and transactions. In 2024 11th International Conference on Computing for Sustainable Global Development (INDIACom) (pp. 1692-1698). IEEE.

Macrinici, D., Cartofeanu, C., & Gao, S. (2018). Smart contract applications within blockchain technology: A systematic mapping study. *Telematics and Informatics*, 35(8), 2337–2354. DOI: 10.1016/j.tele.2018.10.004

Mathur, G. (2023). GANACHE: A robust framework for efficient and secure storage of data on private Ethereum blockchains. *Research Square*. DOI: 10.21203/rs.3.rs-3495549/v1

Mathur, G., Pandey, A., & Goyal, S. (2024). A review on blockchain for DNA sequence: Security issues, application in DNA classification, challenges and future trends. *Multimedia Tools and Applications*, 83(2), 5813–5835. DOI: 10.1007/s11042-023-15857-1 PMID: 37362738

Murthy, C. V. N. U. B., Shri, M. L., Kadry, S., & Lim, S. (2020). Blockchain-based cloud computing: Architecture and research challenges. *IEEE Access : Practical Innovations, Open Solutions*, 8, 205190–205205. DOI: 10.1109/ACCESS.2020.3036812

Murthy, C. V. N. U. B., Shri, M. L., Kadry, S., & Lim, S. (2020). Blockchain-Based Cloud Computing: Architecture and Research Challenges. *IEEE Access : Practical Innovations, Open Solutions*, 8, 205190–205205. DOI: 10.1109/ACCESS.2020.3036812

Omurgonulsen, M., Ibis, M., Kazançoğlu, Y., & Singla, P. (2021). Cloud computing: A systematic literature review and future agenda. *Journal of Global Information Management*, 29(6), 1–25. DOI: 10.4018/JGIM.20211101.oa40

Roehrs, A., da Costa, C. A., & da Rosa Righi, R. (2017). OmniPHR: A distributed architecture model to integrate personal health records. *Journal of Biomedical Informatics*, 71, 70–81. DOI: 10.1016/j.jbi.2017.05.012 PMID: 28545835

Sharma, P., Jindal, R., & Borah, M. (2020). Blockchain technology for cloud storage: A systematic literature review. *ACM Computing Surveys*, 53(4), 1–32. Advance online publication. DOI: 10.1145/3403954

Sleiman, M. D., Lauf, A. P., & Yampolskiy, R. (2015). Bitcoin message: Data insertion on a proof-of-work cryptocurrency system. In *International Conference on Cyberworlds (CW)* (pp. 332-336). IEEE. DOI: 10.1109/CW.2015.56

Tapas, N., Merlino, G., Longo, F., & Puliafito, A. (2019). Blockchain-based publicly verifiable cloud storage. In *IEEE International Conference on Smart Computing (SMARTCOMP)* (pp. 381-386). DOI: 10.1109/SMARTCOMP.2019.00076

Wang, L., Shen, X., Li, J., Shao, J., & Yang, Y. (2019). Cryptographic primitives in blockchains. *Journal of Network and Computer Applications*, 127, 43–58. DOI: 10.1016/j.jnca.2018.11.003

Xie, S., Zheng, Z., Chen, W., Wu, J., Dai, H. N., & Imran, M. (2020). Blockchain for cloud exchange: A survey. *Computers & Electrical Engineering*, 81, 106526. DOI: 10.1016/j.compeleceng.2019.106526

Zheng, W., Zheng, Z., Chen, X., Dai, K., Li, P., & Chen, R. (2019). NutBaaS: A blockchain-as-a-service platform. *IEEE Access : Practical Innovations, Open Solutions*, 7, 134422–134433. DOI: 10.1109/ACCESS.2019.2941905

Zheng, Z., Xie, S., Dai, H., Chen, X., & Wang, H. (2017). An overview of blockchain technology: Architecture, consensus, and future trends. In IEEE International Congress on Big Data (BigData Congress) (pp. 557-564). IEEE.

Zhu, H., Wang, Y., Hei, X., Ji, W., & Zhang, L. (2018). A blockchain-based decentralized cloud resource scheduling architecture. In *International Conference on Network and Network Applications (NaNA)* (pp. 324-329). DOI: 10.1109/NANA.2018.8648712

Chapter 3
Data Security With Replication for Cloud Computing

Mecit Yüzkat
https://orcid.org/0000-0003-4808-5181
Faculty of Engineering and Architecture, Department of Software Engineering, Muş Alparslan University, Turkey & Health Institutes of Türkiye (TUSEB), Istanbul, Turkey

Çiğdem Bakır
https://orcid.org/0000-0001-8482-2412
Faculty of Engineering, Department of Software Engineering, Dumlupinar University, Kütahya, Turkey

ABSTRACT

Cloud computing is an advanced technology that provides access to different services via the internet. These services include applications such as servers, networking, data storage, databases, and software. For this reason, this technology is very popular for institutions and individuals for many reasons such as cost, production, efficiency and speed.In this study, data replication is discussed in order to solve security breaches in cloud computing technologies. Data replication is the process of making one or more backup copies of a database or other data store, in whole or in part. The primary benefit of data replication is to ensure the availability of data recovery and functional critical applications in disaster situations. In such a case, if the primary data source is damaged, a copy of that data source can be created. In addition, transactional consistency is ensured so that data is up-to-date and consistent. Data replication tools can lighten the IT burden of creating and managing enterprise-wide data replication operations. Thus, data loss in cloud computing is reduced.

DOI: 10.4018/979-8-3693-7137-4.ch003

INTRODUCTION

Nowadays, the size and variety of data produced is increasing rapidly. People prefer platforms where they can access online rather than physical storage devices, so that the access to this increasing data is more efficient and secure. Cloud computing, which enables storage, backup and data control-management via remote internet, meets these needs of people. When the cloud is mentioned, it can be briefly called the transfer of computer resources to virtual networks and platforms. The content of data and applications that can be stored in the cloud may contain information that may have low security concerns, as well as very sensitive data (social security numbers, medical records, private personal information or government data). It is important to know the methods to be used to ensure the security of these data and applications (Al_Hachemi, 2022). In this study, it is mentioned how to ensure the confidentiality, integrity and availability of the cloud with data replication. In order to help the content of the study, other articles on the subject were examined and data replication on platforms with cloud features and the protection of individuals or companies' shares, private information, applications and the benefits it provides to the user are shown.

Data replication is the backup of the data accumulated in the environment during the process, or a certain part of it, in more than one location (Mansouri et al., 2021) . It is the process of transferring all the transactions made by all users in the system to another source without causing any inconsistency. In this system, data moves according to the wishes of the person and two different users can perform their duties without interfering with each other's work. In short, data replication is the ability of data to move freely without creating confusion in the internet environment. In this way, all transactions are replicated and the update is performed simultaneously on all the replicated data.

Data replication is not a static backup of data. It ensures replication of transactions, such that backups are in a consistently updated state and synchronized with the source (Miloudi et al., 2021). There are different methods of performing replication operations, depending on the specific availability requirements for the data. Problems with data replication can result from data transfer delays or service interruptions. Commercial data replication products attempt to mitigate business risk due to replication errors or failures.

There are various data replication tools used today. For example; Oracle GoldenGate is a comprehensive tool that enables data replication between both Oracle and non-Oracle data stores. Another example of real-time data replication, DBMoto, provides fast data transfer between databases.

Data replication ensures that data is securely protected in different environments. It provides a fast and accurate return on queries performed on the database. It allows authorized users to access the data. This increases usability in all transactions. High performance is provided. However, despite all these positive aspects, data replication can create complex structures by requiring additional storage areas because it copies a lot of data. For this reason, it may require more cost.

Rapidly increasing data and applications have increased the usage rate of cloud platforms a lot compared to previous years. The security of data stored in the cloud is important for many people. In this study, the importance of data replication for data security in cloud computing is emphasized. It also demonstrates how the three key elements of cloud security (availability, integrity and confidentiality) are ensured by data replication. In this study, data security methods have been shown with some definitions and examples, and it has been concluded that it would be beneficial for the individual or corporate environment to use cloud platforms to use these methods. Emphasizing that businesses providing cloud computing services and customers using this service should pay great attention to security for both parties, some methods are included.

The objectives achieved in this study are given below:

- To emphasize how important data replication is in terms of ensuring data security and getting fast response.
- To explain how to guarantee accessibility, integrity and confidentiality.
- To show how cloud security is provided by data replication methods.
- To define and explain with examples the data security methods used in cloud platforms.
- To explain how using data security methods will be beneficial for individual or corporate environments.
- To emphasize that cloud service providers and users should give importance to appropriate methods to ensure security for both parties.

RELATED WORKS

Within the scope of this study, different scientific publications on data replication in cloud computing in recent years have been examined and the results of these studies are given in detail below:

Based on the rapid development of big data and cloud technology in recent years, there has been an increasing demand to process and analyze data produced and stored in geographically dispersed data centers. However, collecting data and performing calculations in a single data center is becoming increasingly. Convolbo et al., with the DRASH (Data Replication Awake Timer) method they developed in their work, used data replication to prevent unnecessary data transfer in a job planning and increase overall system performance (Convolbo et al., 2016). As a result of the evaluations using simulations with realistic workloads, they found that the DRASH method outperforms other existing approaches. DRASH performed significantly better in average job completion time than other available methods. They also achieved further improvement under high data duplication factors.

Reliable access to data is the cornerstone of many information technology services. High availability, low operating cost, and data consistency often create significant challenges in data replication research. Usman et al., have examined a strategy called "semantic data replication" (SDR) in their work (Usman et al., 2017). SDR aims to develop a structure with low cost and high processing capacity. In addition, it makes the replication process more efficient with the previous data offered by this space. The use of data encoding schemes contributes significantly to SDR by speeding up read and write operations, as well as providing consistent access to the state of the replicated object during read operations.

When outsourcing data in the cloud information system, high security measures are required as it can be modified. This can affect the performance of the cloud due to the longer data acquisition time. The time of data acquisition should be taken into account when implementing security measures. Salunkhe et al. sought to solve both problems by deploying them on cloud (Salunkhe and Patil, 2016). File fragments are copied to cloud nodes to improve retrieval time.

In a structured P2P network, to ensure high availability of data, pieces of data are usually replicated from one node to other neighboring nodes. However, in P2P networks with some heterogeneous configurations, neighboring nodes may not always be geographically close to each other. Therefore, permanent loss of some data may be inevitable in case of some local disasters. Wang et al. suggested a different data replication method for heterogeneous structural P2P networks. This has greatly reduced the complexity of not only maintaining large-scale local disaster data items, but also data migration whenever nodes enter and exit the network, that is, when new nodes are added to the system or when nodes leave the system (Wang et al., 2019).

Data duplication and synchronization techniques have recently attracted the attention of researchers working in this field. The security of data transmitted during replication must be ensured. The protocol is one of the ways to ensure security before sending information to an external copy site. When comparing the two existing protocol types, TCP or UDP. The first factor behind this is that UDP does not use many authentication messages. UDP is the preferred option when bandwidth is limited. In their study, Soyjaudah et al. discussed the reliability of the UDP protocol when measuring packets in sending packets of different lengths. During the data copying process, it is questioned whether the UDP protocol can be preferred as the transmission method. Maximum Transmission Unit size has been adjusted to have minimal packet loss (Soyjaudah et al., 2016).

Mansouri developed an adaptive replication strategy model in cloud computing in order to increase data availability, provide fast data processing time and reliability (Mansouri, 2016). In the author's work, if all the replicated data and requests are correct and distributed, the replication process realizes the successful processing time in cloud computing. This convenient processing time is however much more complex for large-scale, dynamic and virtualized data centers. For this reason, in the study, cost-effective replication process and adaptive data replication strategy that will minimize application and work times has been proposed for very large data centers. The proposed model consists of five stages such as average service time, calculation of failure probability, load variance, delay and storage usage. In the study, data replication has been done in a logical way and a recommendation model has been presented that will enable the replacement of newly created copies depending on the use of the files. Using this model CloudSim simulator, the number of accesses is evaluated according to the replication size and the results are presented. This proposed model was compared with the ARS, DRSP, CIR and CDRM algorithms used in the literature in the simulation environment, and the results were interpreted.

Data replication algorithms are divided into static and dynamic. In static replication, replication is predetermined and well defined. In dynamic replication, on the other hand, the replication process is automatically identified and duplicates are automatically deleted according to changing access patterns. Both of these data replication algorithms are classified by grouping them into distributed and centralized algorithms. Sun et al. developed a dynamic data replication model in order to ensure data security and data availability among users in cloud computing environments. By increasing the usability, this model reduces the false copying process and error rate that occurs during data replication, thus ensuring a highly effective and efficient interaction between users. In the study, it was aimed to reduce the waiting time of the users and to increase the data access speed with data replication (Sun et al., 2012). Duplications created on data centers with dynamic data replication are mathematically formulated. Execution time and cloud computing bandwidth are minimized. The trigger times of missing copies and duplication processes were calculated. Copies are conveniently placed within the data nodes, and when a certain threshold value is passed, data replication operations are triggered. In addition, the applicability of this study is presented with an experimental study and the obtained data are shown comparatively.

Lin et al. have proposed a QoS (different quality of service) based data replication model and minimum-cost maximum-flow (MCMF) models in order to scale the increasing data in cloud computing and to prevent changes in the errors that occur in the data. The main idea behind this model is intuitive QoS-based replication. In addition, this study has been developed to solve the flow problem in networks for systems with very dense data. With this proposed greedy algorithm, data replication cost is reduced and QoS-based data replication is performed securely without causing data loss. With the MCMF algorithm used in this study, the polynomial analysis time and the computation time of data replication are reduced. In addition, since cloud computing systems contain many nodes, node aggregation techniques have been proposed to reduce these nodes and increase performance (Lin et al., 2013). QoS has increased the heterogeneity of devices in cloud computing for secure and accurate data replication. Data replication compatible with QoS has been taken into account. The MCMF algorithm is proposed to best solve the QADR problem. The computational complexity that occurs during data replication is tried to be solved. Node combinations are used for very large data.

CLOUD COMPUTING

Cloud computing is explained as a service model used for information technologies and services, which requires low-scale management and can be accessed flexibly when needed (Tamimi et al., 2019,) Horrow et al., 2012). To make a general definition on the basis of this definition, cloud computing is based on the principle of using the required storage areas and processing unit power as much as needed, as well as allowing remote access of data in a controlled manner, where infrastructure and applications are processed independently from each other, and capacity usage is flexible. It is a type of informatics where, thanks to its structure, it can be increased or decreased rapidly, the use of resources can be easily controlled and reported. Cloud computing resources are shown in Figure 1. Access is provided from many devices and applications such as computers, laptops, smartphones, servers, etc. with internet connection.

Figure 1. Cloud Computing Source

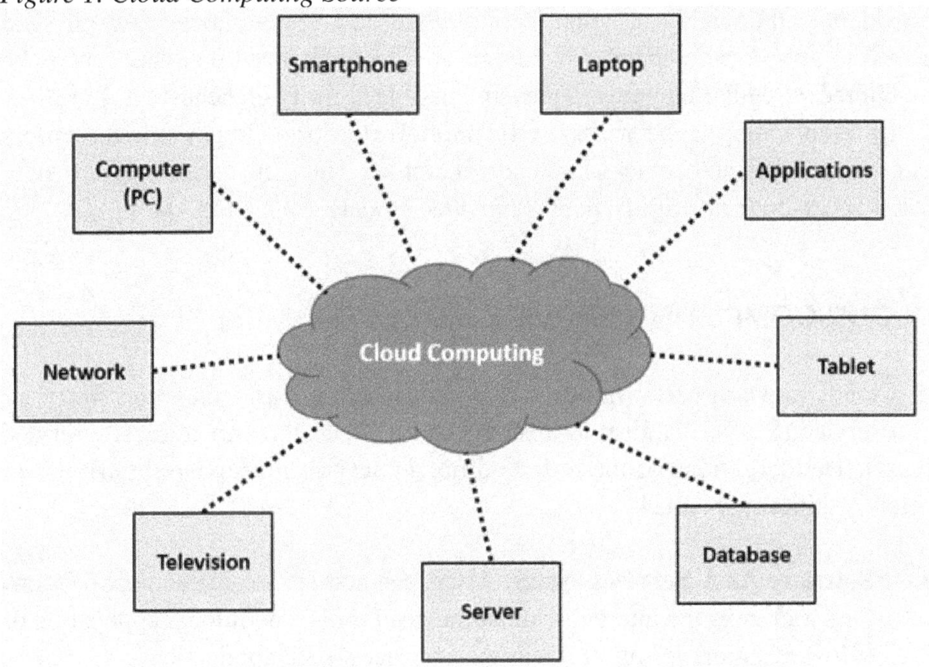

In order to save resources, reduce costs, and increase efficiency, cloud service providers usually store data from multiple customers on the same server without separating them (Haghighat et al., 2015, Srivastava and Khan, 2018).

In order to ensure the security of data in cloud computing, the data security measures discussed in this study can be divided into three main categories: accessibility, integrity, and confidentiality. For example, encryption ensures the confidentiality, availability, and integrity of data by preventing unauthorized access. Similarly, backups help ensure data integrity, while firewalls ensure confidentiality and access control (Tahirkheli et al., 2021, Yu et al., 2010).

Security concerns associated with cloud computing cover the security issues faced by cloud service providers, customers using cloud platforms, and organizations hosting applications or storing data on these platforms (Shirgaonkar et al., 2022). The cloud service provider must assure its customers that its infrastructure is secure and that its applications as well as the data stored therein are protected. On the other hand, customers must take the necessary measures to protect their data and applications by using strong passwords and authentication methods (Cai et al., 2019).

When a company or individual chooses to store their data or applications in a public cloud environment, they lose physical access to the servers where this data is stored. This can make sensitive information, in particular, more vulnerable to external attacks (Liu et al., 2011). For this reason, it is very important for cloud service providers to thoroughly question employees in data centers about their physical access to servers beforehand. In addition, it is recommended that data centers be monitored at regular intervals to prevent possible security breaches.

Data replication has been proposed to minimize the loss of important data of users as a result of possible attacks in cloud computing. Thus, in case of data invasion, users' access to their original data is provided by data replication.

CLOUD COMPUTING SERVICE MODELS

Cloud computing service models are divided into three basic categories: Software as a service (SaaS), Platform as a service (PaaS), and Infrastructure as a service (IaaS). The definitions of these three different service models are briefly given below (Fatima et al., 2024):

- **Software As A Services (SaaS)**: Users can access the data and applications they want over the internet without the need for any additional application or software. Examples of this are e-mail services, ERP applications.
- **Platform As A Services (PaaS):** In this service model, users can run applications they create. By renting a Java platform on Windows, users can create Java applications. In short, with this service model, many users can develop and present applications on the same project. This service model includes the entire technological infrastructure.
- **Infrastructure As A Services (IaaS):** Users provide their own network equipment, processors and applications through physical servers that are available. Users rent these physical servers according to their wishes and make the payment as much as they want. Users can use this service model in applications that require huge processor performance, such as big data applications. Users retain the right to access the applications and operating system on these physical servers. All updates are the responsibility of the user.

Cloud computing service models are the combination of some services by service providers according to the needs of the customers. Suggesting a suitable cloud service model for that user is of great importance for the success of the services of the people who will use the cloud. When the traditional information technology (Traditional IT) concept and cloud technology service models are compared, they all have different authorizations and shares. Figure 2 shows which services are managed by whom.

Figure 2. Cloud Computing Service Models

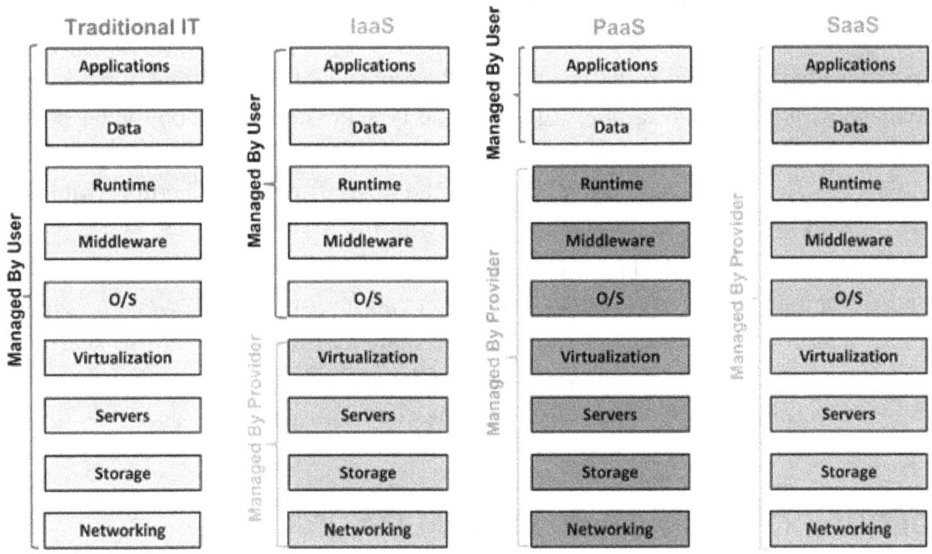

CLOUD COMPUTING INSTALLATION MODELS

Cloud services during the installation of cloud platforms; It can be classified into four groups as Public Cloud, Private Cloud, Hybrid Cloud and Community Cloud (Merseedi and Zeebaree, 2024).

Public Cloud: This cloud deployment model is delivered and managed to customers through servers in internet networks. In addition, this installation model includes the basic structure of the cloud system. It is for all users and users pay as much as they use. Cloud services are provided by resources or services connected to a data center. Although institutions and organizations do not transfer their applications to the public cloud due to security vulnerabilities, users can make their applications more usable thanks to the public cloud. For example, institutions and organizations can adapt applications such as data that cannot be kept confidential, web, e-mail, virtual document sharing in the public cloud more easily. For such reasons, public cloud has advantages such as ease of use, flexibility, scalability, cost and reliability.

Private Cloud: This cloud model is built on data centers housed within the scope of a business or organization. It is a very old and frequently used classic model. Institutions undertake all operations, from infrastructure to software, to maintenance and management of systems. Private cloud provides more control, flexibility and energy efficiency than other cloud models. But aside from these benefits, it doesn't scale as well as the public cloud model.

Hybrid Cloud: Hybrid Cloud; It uses public and private cloud options together. In order for this model to be successful, the transfer of applications must have a management strategy. Examples of this cloud type are configuration management, budgeting, security, change display, and error catching. The advantages of hybrid clouds are flexibility, scalability, security and cost efficiency. The disadvantages are networking problems and security compatibility.

Community Cloud: The community cloud is the cloud model that caters to users with common needs, and customers and organizations jointly use their data sources, goals, and policies. It includes two or more installation models. It also shares IT resources among users and makes them available for common use. For example, the E-Government application is built on the community cloud.

CLOUD COMPUTING AND VIRTUALIZATION

When it comes to cloud computing, the first concept that comes to mind is the concept of virtualization. Virtualization concept; It is called leaving the physical structure to virtual machines. In other words, creating a virtual system with the simulation method in the hypervisor or Linux phase of a physical structure is called virtualization.

The name of the software used to create a virtual system and to increase the functionality of the hardware is called Hypervisor. The hypervisor enables the aggregation of multiple virtual machines on a single piece of hardware in terms of task. IBM first developed native hypervisors in the 1960s.

Virtualization categories can be listed as six items as follows (Rehan, 2024):

1. Network Virtualization: It allows working with less hardware and more virtual network setup. It enables the creation of virtual networks by establishing bridges between systems. Such networks can provide end-to-end service.
2. Server Virtualization: It is the most commonly used virtualization method. It is intended to aggregate multiple servers on only one physical server.
3. Desktop Virtualization: It enables computers to be virtualized so that users can connect with remote access. The computer is virtualized and the user can access this server via a network.
4. Application Virtualization: Application virtualization allows applications to run as if they were installed on the device by running them through the server layer without the need to install them on devices.

5. Storage Virtualization: Storage virtualization is performed by combining multiple data storage devices and managing them from a common management interface. Thanks to this common interface, the management factor is facilitated and system complexity is reduced. Thus, special powers are given to individuals.

DATA REPLICATION

Companies have to ensure the security of customer data in order to determine the customer portfolio and to meet the needs of the customers. In particular, the inappropriate use of data, the ignorance of individuals about information security threats, the weakness of risk taking and the emergence of information security risks that can be considered difficult to compensate. Confidentiality, integrity and accessibility are the basic concepts that need to be emphasized in order to ensure security in cloud computing (Alimjon, 2022).

There are many security risks to data that needs to be stored and backed up in the cloud. These risks can be divided into two groups: traditional and innovative threats. Traditional threats include eavesdropping on network traffic, illegal attacks, denial of service attacks, and side-channel attacks, while specific threats associated with cloud computing include vulnerabilities in virtualization systems and misuse of cloud services. One of the most commonly used methods to ensure data security in cloud technologies is data replication (Mealha et al., 2019).

Data replication, which can be defined as the process of copying data from a central database, means keeping data in more than one location. In this system, data is stored the same in all locations without any inconsistency. In data replication, different systems are preferred according to the needs of the institutions. For example, a system that many people want to access may not be able to handle this load. In this case, the data copied by data replication is shared on different servers, thus increasing both speed and data accessibility (Boru et al., 2015). Data in one center can be copied or reproduced in another database. All users see data the same way. Or, the user who updates the data in one center sees the data in the other center in the same way. There is no inconsistency in the data. Operations such as editing and deletion performed on records in a replicated database are also reflected in other databases. For this reason, solutions such as temporary deletion are used in database replication applications. Soft deletion means marking data as deleted so that it can be restored if needed. Such data is not truly deleted and continues to be left in the database. Only administrators can see the temporarily deleted data. Since all deleted data will continue to be stored in the database in this method, the system in question may create a serious data load in the long run and therefore server costs due to the need for additional storage unit. Data replication operations performed in databases are shown in Figure 3. The data owned by more than one user is saved through a single server and then duplicated and stored in multiple databases. Thus, in case of data loss that users may experience in the future, a solution is produced for their problems thanks to the copied databases.

Figure 3. Data replication

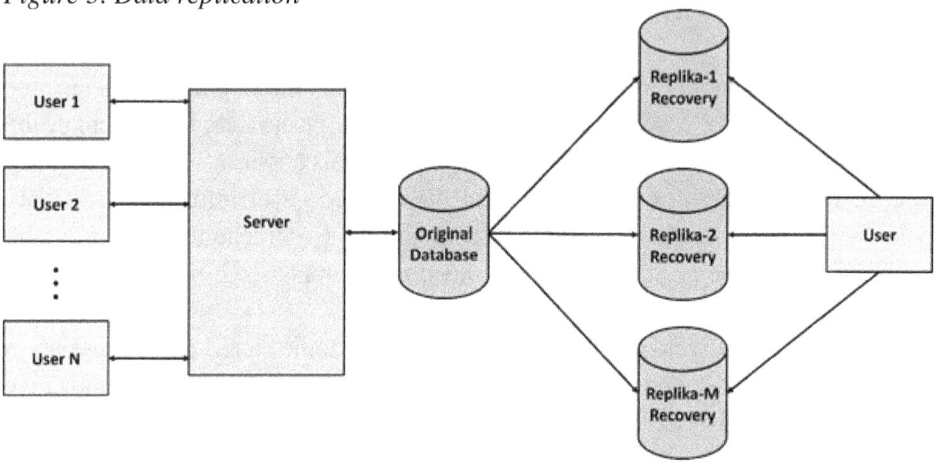

Data is kept in multiple sources, copied. A failure in the central database does not cause data loss. Multiple users can operate on the same data. With database replication, multiple users can work with the same data over databases. Thus, it becomes possible to carry out the work of a change to be made in the central database in other databases. The data on which the transaction is made is seen in an updated form in the database. Thus, secure data sharing is ensured (Silva et al., 2016).

Data Replication Strategies

Data replication strategies play a critical role in ensuring data security and availability in cloud environments. These strategies vary by use case, and each addresses challenges such as data consistency, conflict resolution, and latency in different ways. This section will cover strategies such as synchronous and asynchronous replication, eventual consistency, and majority-based replication (Taleb et al., 2024).

Synchronous Replication: Synchronous data replication ensures that data is updated instantly with all copies. This method is used in applications that require high data consistency. For example, it is preferred for instant data updates in the financial services and healthcare sectors. However, it can create problems such as high performance requirements and network congestion.

Asynchronous Replication: Asynchronous replication ensures that data is copied at specific intervals or when a transaction is completed. This strategy is typically used in distributed systems with low latency requirements. Asynchronous replication provides data replication with low bandwidth, but it can create data inconsistencies and conflicts.

Eventual Consistency: Eventual consistency is associated with asynchronous replication strategies and ensures that data is consistent over time. In this model, data is eventually updated across all copies, but this process is not instantaneous. It is widely used in use cases such as web applications and big data analytics.

Quorum-based replication: Majority-based replication requires data to be valid across most copies. This method ensures high availability and data consistency in distributed systems. However, latency can occur due to network failures or congestion, and data conflicts can occur.

Data Consistency and Conflict Resolution: Data replication strategies present various challenges in terms of data consistency and conflict resolution. In asynchronous replication, data inconsistencies and user conflicts can occur. These conflicts are usually resolved at the application level, and the user is notified about data accuracy.

Latency Issues: Since synchronous data replication requires systems to be kept in sync at all times, network delays and performance issues can occur. Modern research is developing new algorithms and protocols to minimize these delays. Delay-aware replication protocols offer solutions to manage network congestion.

As a result, data replication strategies play an important role in cloud security. However, challenges such as data consistency, conflict resolution, and latency issues can impact the effectiveness of these strategies. Modern research is developing new solutions to overcome these problems.

CLOUD COMPUTING SECURITY MODELS

Data security elements in cloud computing are shown in Figure 4. These security elements include: Data protection, privacy, accessibility and access control, integrity, identity verification and management, personal security, physical security measures, cloud application/network layer and penetration testing.

Figure 4. Cloud Computing Security

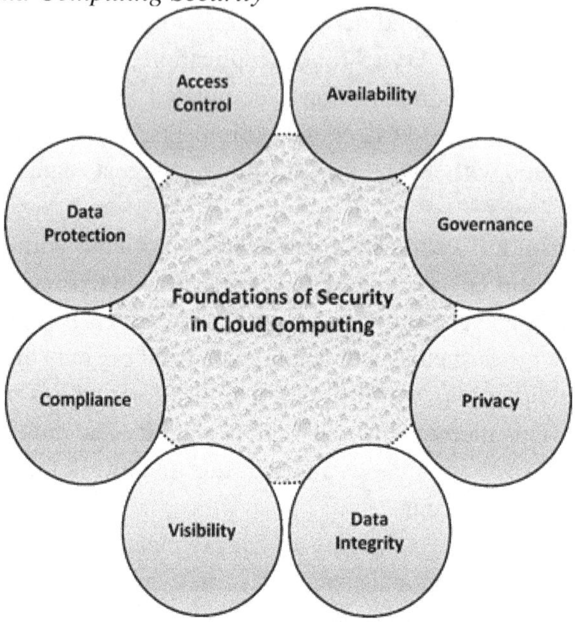

Data Protection: The processing of data has accelerated with the developments in application software and internet. Inappropriate use of these developments that make people's life easier, the fact that individuals do not have enough information about information security threats, etc. have brought about problems related to data security. The security of digital data is gaining importance today in order to protect data in electronic environment such as copyrights and ethics, privacy, security and encryption. Information security was defined as three different concepts by ISACA (Lin and Chen, 2009) in 2009; It is shown as ensuring the confidentiality, integrity and accessibility of information at any time. These defined privacy, integrity and accessibility issues are the basic concepts that should be emphasized in order to ensure security in cloud computing.

Privacy

Data privacy means that data is only available to authorized individuals and that unauthorized individuals are prevented from accessing it. Privacy ensures that sensitive information, in particular, can only be viewed by those with appropriate access permissions. Privacy in cloud technologies is critical to protecting users' personal data. In cloud systems, data is usually stored on remote servers and can be managed by cloud service providers and third parties. This can cause users to lose control over their data and risk it falling into the wrong hands (Younis et al., 2014).

Security measures such as encryption, data isolation, authentication and access control are used to protect privacy. Encryption ensures that data is only accessed by authorized users, thus reducing the risk of data leaks and misuse. In addition, data isolation and virtual separation methods are applied to provide more control over data owners. This ensures that a user's data is kept separate from other users' data. Cloud service providers must also protect their customers' personal information within legal and ethical limits by complying with privacy regulations (such as GDPR) in data processing processes. As a result, privacy in cloud technologies should be ensured not only by technical measures, but also by legal and administrative control mechanisms.

Accessibility and Access Control

Accessibility can restrict access to their data as they wish, in order to externally participate in the cloud system (Sujitha and Selvi, 2024). Accessibility can also be defined to as usability. Ensures the right amount of leave is given to the right people. While legitimate users can be authorized by the data owner to access the data, other people cannot gain unauthorized access to the data as they are not authorized to access them. However, applying granular access control to external data is often requested by individuals, ie different users need to be offered different access privileges according to different pieces of data. Unauthorized access should be strictly prohibited, but in some cases, access for users' use should be allowed and monitored at the same time by providing administrative savings (Younis et al., 2014).

Integrity

Data integrity is a concept that ensures that data is protected accurately, consistently and completely (Goswami et al., 2024). Owners of data or applications always want their data to be stored accurately and reliably in a cloud. This means that data should not be accessed, altered, intentionally deleted, or maliciously generated. If any undesired operation corrupts or deletes data, the cloud service owner should be able to detect it. If some external data is corrupted or lost, the data must be retrievable. Security policies should be designed to protect data not only against malicious attacks but also against unintentional changes. An example of an integrity-encompassing security audit is the automatic backup of data.

Identity Management

Identity Management System (IDM) is a software system used to identify, authenticate, track and control the identities of users in an organization. As part of the identity management process, cloud service providers can integrate their customers' identity management systems with their own infrastructure or offer their own identity management solutions using methods such as federated identity, Single Sign-On (SSO) technology, and biometric-based authentication systems (Charanya and Aramudhan, 2016) SSO refers to a user's ability to log in with a single user ID and password to access more than one system they need. Cloud identity provides cloud-based and cross-institutional biometric authentication while protecting users' privacy. It matches the confidential information provided by users with their biometric data and stores this data in an encrypted form. Using searchable encryption techniques, the cloud service provider or potential data attackers are prevented from accessing sensitive data or the content of individual queries, and biometric authentication is performed in the encrypted field (Yang et al., 2023).

Physical Security

Cloud service providers (Amazon, Azure, Oracle, IBM, etc.) protect IT hardware (routers, servers, cables, etc.) from threats such as unauthorized access, tampering, theft, fire and flooding (Peter, 2011).

Personnel Security

Data security concerns related to cloud services are addressed in pre- and post-hiring processes for IT and other employees. These processes include security screenings, assessing potential candidates, creating security awareness, training programs, and proactive security measures.

Cloud Application/Network Layer and Penetration Testing

In short, penetration testing is to attack the system in order to understand the existence of any problem in the system. This is also called a penetration test (Jangra and Rana, 2024). It is very important to understand what is being asked when performing the test. Network layer testing refers to tests involving interconnected systems throughout the local network, as well as internal or external connections.

Penetration Test

Penetration testing is a security test performed by simulating an attacker in order to detect security vulnerabilities. Because the cloud platform is a shared environment with multiple businesses leasing services, step-by-step penetration test participation rules must be followed. If the aforementioned usage policies are violated, this will result in the complete termination of the cloud service (Meghanathan, 2013).

Common Cloud Security Issues and Data Replication's Contribution to Them

This study has discussed in detail the common cloud security issues and how data replication techniques address these issues (Rambabu and Govardhan, 2024). Cloud security faces many challenges, especially in data protection, access control, data integrity, and privacy. Therefore, data replication stands out as an important tool to reduce these security threats in cloud environments.

The first problem is data loss and access interruptions. In cloud environments, data loss or service interruptions can lead to users not being able to access their data. This can occur due to service providers' infrastructure failures, natural disasters, or attacks. Data replication minimizes the risk of data loss by ensuring that data is copied to multiple locations. In this way, data is always accessible and can be recovered quickly in the event of a possible data loss.

The second problem is related to data privacy and unauthorized access. In cloud environments, data is accessible to users and third parties, which poses a major threat to data privacy and security. Data replication enables data to be stored in various locations, allowing only authorized users to access data. This process, when supported by data backup and access management strategies, increases confidentiality and prevents unauthorized access. Another common security issue is data integrity. In cloud environments, data manipulation or incorrect processing can compromise data integrity. Data replication is used to ensure data consistency. Replicated data helps detect and retrieve erroneous data, ensuring data accuracy.

Comparison of Data Replication Techniques with Other Security Measures

Data replication offers a stronger security solution when considered together with other security measures commonly used in cloud security. For example, encryption is used to ensure that data can only be read by authorized persons. Encryption ensures the security of data in transmission, but does not guarantee the physical security of data. Data replication, on the other hand, allows data to be stored in multiple locations and facilitates data recovery in the event of a possible data loss. In this context, encryption and data replication are complementary methods (Akbar et al., 2024).

Another important security measure is intrusion detection systems (IDS). IDS is a technique used to detect security threats in cloud environments. However, IDS only detects threats and is generally limited in preventing damage. Data replication comes into play at this point as a measure that directly prevents data loss. Replicated data provides backup against attacks and offers a rapid recovery opportunity in case of data damage. IDS ensures that threats are detected, but data replication helps prevent possible damage in advance.

Securing cloud environments is a complex process because it requires dealing with different security threats and threat actors. Data replication offers an effective countermeasure against these security threats. However, relying on this technique alone is not enough. When used together with other security measures such as encryption and intrusion detection systems, data replication creates a more robust and flexible approach to securing the cloud. Therefore, it is necessary to adopt a multi-layered security strategy to ensure cloud security. In conclusion, data replication is an important tool to increase security in cloud environments, but it is not enough on its own. Integrating data replication techniques with other security measures such as encryption and intrusion detection systems will help manage the complexity of securing cloud environments more effectively.

CONCLUSION

As a result of the widespread use of the Internet and the rapid increase in information, the importance of information technologies has increased. The basis of the concept of cloud computing, which is one of the information technology concepts that has been heard a lot recently, is based on the internet. One of the biggest advantages of using the cloud is that the device performance and features of the users who will access the cloud are not important. The person can connect to the cloud platform at any time he wants and from any location, provided that he has internet access. At the beginning of its advantages is to connect to the internet from anywhere, but integration with the internet also brings a disadvantage. If the user does not have internet access, they will not be able to access the cloud platform.

It is necessary to take some security measures to protect the data and applications transferred to the cloud platform and to prevent unwanted situations. Since cloud platforms work with a system open to internet access, they are open to attacks that may come from the internet. While ensuring the security of transferred and stored data, the important point is not only to protect the data and applications against external attacks, but also to ensure the integrity of the data, to prevent unwanted data loss, and to reach the desired response in the system in terms of data security.

Institutions and companies have turned to cloud technologies in order to increase business continuity and obtain reliable and efficient resources and have grown rapidly. However, in proportion to this growth, some problems such as data breaches and data leakage have arisen due to the continuous use of cloud technologies. In order to prevent these possible disaster scenarios, replication services have emerged, which have made significant progress in establishing the systemic infrastructure. This replication process is performed by storing data on remote virtual servers at certain time intervals. Replication services, which are an ideal solution for institutions, also reduce the need for hardware and labor and improve the performance of institutions. The fact that the replication service can be performed at short intervals, fast action in recovery scenarios and other features make cloud replication services an important cloud computing service in the digital age.

REFERENCES

Akbar, M., Ahmad, I., Mirza, M., Ali, M., & Barmavatu, P. (2024). Enhanced authentication for de-duplication of big data on cloud storage system using machine learning approach. *Cluster Computing*, 27(3), 3683–3702. DOI: 10.1007/s10586-023-04171-y

Al Hachemi, S. A. G. A. (2022). Cloud Computing Services with Minimal Redundancy, Storage, and Effective Processing Capabilities. *Texas Journal of Engineering and Technology*, 9, 143–149.

Alimjon, D. (2022). Problems of data replication in distribution systems. *ACADEMICIA: An International Multidisciplinary Research Journal*, 12(5), 1119–1128. DOI: 10.5958/2249-7137.2022.00585.7

Boru, D., Kliazovich, D., Granelli, F., Bouvry, P., & Zomaya, A. Y. (2015). Energy-efficient data replication in cloud computing datacenters. *Cluster Computing*, 18(1), 385–402. DOI: 10.1007/s10586-014-0404-x

Cai, F., Zhu, N., He, J., Mu, P., Li, W., & Yu, Y. (2019). Survey of access control models and technologies for cloud computing. *Cluster Computing*, 22(3), 6111–6122. DOI: 10.1007/s10586-018-1850-7

Charanya, R., & Aramudhan, M. (2016, February). Survey on access control issues in cloud computing. In *2016 International Conference on Emerging Trends in Engineering, Technology and Science (ICETETS)* (pp. 1-4). IEEE. DOI: 10.1109/ICETETS.2016.7603014

Convolbo, M. W., ... "DRASH: A Data Replication-Aware Scheduler in Geo-Distributed Data Centers." Cloud Computing Technology and Science (CloudCom), 2016 IEEE International Conference on. IEEE, 2016. DOI: 10.1109/CloudCom.2016.0056

Fatima, E., Sumra, I. A., & Naveed, R. (2024). A Comprehensive Survey on Security Threats and Challenges in Cloud Computing Models (SaaS, PaaS and IaaS). *Journal of Computing & Biomedical Informatics*, 7(01), 537–544.

Goswami, P., Faujdar, N., Debnath, S., Khan, A. K., & Singh, G. (2024). Investigation on storage level data integrity strategies in cloud computing: Classification, security obstructions, challenges and vulnerability. *Journal of Cloud Computing (Heidelberg, Germany)*, 13(1), 45. DOI: 10.1186/s13677-024-00605-z

Haghighat, M., Zonouz, S., & Abdel-Mottaleb, M. (2015, November). CloudID: Trustworthy cloud-based and cross-enterprise biometric identification. *Expert Systems with Applications*, 42(21), 7905–7916. DOI: 10.1016/j.eswa.2015.06.025

Horrow, S., & Sardana, A. (2012, August). Identity management framework for cloud based internet of things. In *Proceedings of the First International Conference on Security of Internet of Things* (pp. 200-203). DOI: 10.1145/2490428.2490456

Jangra, N., & Rana, R. P. S. (2024, June). Perception To Application Layer: A Critical Review On Vulnerability Assessment Of Iot Device. In 2024 15th International Conference on Computing Communication and Networking Technologies (ICCCNT) (pp. 1-11). IEEE. DOI: 10.1109/ICCCNT61001.2024.10725063

Lin, C., & Chen, L. C. (2009, June). Development of an Interdisciplinary Information Technology Auditing Program. In 13th Colloquium for Information Systems Security Education, Seattle, WA.

Lin, J. W., Chen, C. H., & Chang, J. M. (2013). QoS-aware data replication for data-intensive applications in cloud computing systems. *IEEE Transactions on Cloud Computing*, 1(1), 101–115. DOI: 10.1109/TCC.2013.1

Liu, F., Tong, J., Mao, J., Bohn, R., Messina, J., Badger, L., & Leaf, D. (2011). NIST cloud computing reference architecture. NIST special publication, 500(2011), 1-28.

Mansouri, N. (2016). Adaptive data replication strategy in cloud computing for performance improvement. *Frontiers of Computer Science*, 10(5), 925–935. DOI: 10.1007/s11704-016-5182-6

Mansouri, N., Javidi, M. M., & Zade, B. M. H. (2021). Hierarchical data replication strategy to improve performance in cloud computing. *Frontiers of Computer Science*, 15(2), 1–17. DOI: 10.1007/s11704-019-9099-8

Mealha, D., Preguiça, N., Gomes, M. C., & Leitão, J. (2019, March). Data replication on the cloud/edge. In *Proceedings of the 6th Workshop on Principles and Practice of Consistency for Distributed Data* (pp. 1-7).

Meghanathan, N. (2013). Review of access control models for cloud computing. *Computer Science & Information Science*, 3(1), 77–85. DOI: 10.5121/csit.2013.3508

Merseedi, K. J., & Zeebaree, S. R. (2024). The cloud architectures for distributed multi-cloud computing: A review of hybrid and federated cloud environment. *Indonesian Journal of Computer Science*, 13(2). Advance online publication. DOI: 10.33022/ijcs.v13i2.3811

Miloudi, I. E., Yagoubi, B., & Bellounar, F. Z. (2021, October). A Survey of Dynamic Replication Strategies in Cloud Computing Systems. In *2021 International Conference on Networking and Advanced Systems (ICNAS)* (pp. 1-6). IEEE. DOI: 10.1109/ICNAS53565.2021.9628963

Peter,(2011). The NIST Definition of Cloud Computing, National Institute of Standards and Technology, U.S. Department of Commerce, Special Publication 800-145, United States.

Rambabu, D., & Govardhan, A. (2024). Survey on data replication in cloud systems. *Web Intell.*, 22(1), 83–109. DOI: 10.3233/WEB-230087

Rehan, H. (2024). Revolutionizing America's Cloud Computing the Pivotal Role of AI in Driving Innovation and Security. Journal of Artificial Intelligence General science (JAIGS) ISSN: 3006-4023, 2(1), 239-240.

Salunkhe, S. D., & Patil, D. (2016, August). Division and replication for data with public auditing scheme for cloud storage. In *2016 International Conference on Computing Communication Control and automation (ICCUBEA)* (pp. 1-5). IEEE. DOI: 10.1109/ICCUBEA.2016.7859985

Shirgaonkar, M., Shinde, A., Sankpal, P., & Gutte, V. (2022, March). Cloud Computing Security using Cryptographic Algorithms. In *2022 6th International Conference on Computing Methodologies and Communication (ICCMC)* (pp. 31-37). IEEE. DOI: 10.1109/ICCMC53470.2022.9753711

Silva, G. H. G., Holanda, M., & Araujo, A. (2016, June). Data replication policy in a cloud computing environment. In *2016 11th Iberian conference on information systems and technologies (CISTI)* (pp. 1-6). IEEE.

Soyjaudah, K. M. S., Catherine, P. C., & Coonjah, I. (2016, April). Evaluation of UDP tunnel for data replication in data centers and cloud environment. In 2016 international conference on computing, communication and automation (ICCCA) (pp. 1217-1221). IEEE.

Srivastava, P., & Khan, R. (2018). A review paper on cloud computing. *International Journal of Advanced Research in Computer Science and Software Engineering*, 8(6), 17–20. DOI: 10.23956/ijarcsse.v8i6.711

Sujitha, S. J., & Selvi, P. T. (2024, May). Ensuring Access Control Reliability and Security of Lightweight Blockchain-Based IOT Cloud-Based Electronic Medical Records Sharing. In *2024 International Conference on Advances in Computing, Communication and Applied Informatics (ACCAI)* (pp. 1-5). IEEE. DOI: 10.1109/ACCAI61061.2024.10602256

Sun, D. W., Chang, G. R., Gao, S., Jin, L. Z., & Wang, X. W. (2012). Modeling a dynamic data replication strategy to increase system availability in cloud computing environments. *Journal of Computer Science and Technology*, 27(2), 256–272. DOI: 10.1007/s11390-012-1221-4

Tahirkheli, A. I., Shiraz, M., Hayat, B., Idrees, M., Sajid, A., Ullah, R., Ayub, N., & Kim, K. I. (2021). A survey on modern cloud computing security over smart city networks: Threats, vulnerabilities, consequences, countermeasures, and challenges. *Electronics (Basel)*, 10(15), 1811. DOI: 10.3390/electronics10151811

Taleb, Y., McGehee, K., Yan, N., Wang, S., Müller, S. C., & Samuels, A. (2024, June). Amazon MemoryDB: A fast and durable memory-first cloud database. In *Companion of the 2024 International Conference on Management of Data* (pp. 309-320). DOI: 10.1145/3626246.3653380

Tamimi, A. A., Dawood, R., & Sadaqa, L. (2019, April). Disaster recovery techniques in cloud computing. In *2019 IEEE Jordan International Joint Conference on Electrical Engineering and Information Technology (JEEIT)* (pp. 845-850). IEEE. DOI: 10.1109/JEEIT.2019.8717450

Usman, A., Schadek, R., & Theel, O. (2017, January). A Novel Highly Available Data Replication Strategy exploiting Data Semantics, Coding Techniques and Prior At-Hand Knowledge. In 2017 IEEE 22nd Pacific Rim International Symposium on Dependable Computing (PRDC) (pp. 301-310). IEEE.

Wang, Y., Qiu, X., Zhang, C., Mi, W., Li, L., & Ji, Y. (2009, September). Effective data replication in heterogeneous structured P2P networks. In 2009 5th International Conference on Wireless Communications, Networking and Mobile Computing (pp. 1-4). IEEE.

Yang, J., Chen, Y. L., Por, L. Y., & Ku, C. S. (2023). A systematic literature review of information security in chatbots. *Applied Sciences (Basel, Switzerland)*, 13(11), 6355. DOI: 10.3390/app13116355

Younis, Y. A., Kifayat, K., & Merabti, M. (2014). An access control model for cloud computing. *Journal of Information Security and Applications*, 19(1), 45–60. DOI: 10.1016/j.jisa.2014.04.003

Yu, S., Wang, C., Ren, K., & Lou, W. (2010, March). *Achieving secure, scalable, and fine-grained data access control in cloud computing. In 2010 Proceedings IEEE INFOCOM*. Ieee.

Chapter 4
Database Security and Study of Data Encryption Methods in Cloud Storage

Komal Tahiliani
https://orcid.org/0009-0006-1872-7314
Sagar Institute of Science and Technology, India

Vasima Khan
https://orcid.org/0000-0002-6903-9910
Sagar Institute of Science and Technology, India

ABSTRACT

This article highlights the significance of database encryption and offers an extensive examination of various encryption techniques that have been proposed. With data security being a top priority for governments, companies, and organizations, the need to protect databases from cyberattacks is imperative. Over the years, numerous encryption schemes have been developed to safeguard databases from unauthorized access. Cloud storage is crucial for remote data storage, but many establishments are concerned about the security of their files when they are sent to the cloud. To maintain the integrity of stored data, data encryption techniques are necessary. While businesses once believed that cloud providers could manage all their data securely, it has become evident that cloud providers cannot always honor such commitments when responding to government information requests. This study emphasizes the importance of database encryption and provides a comprehensive overview of various encryption techniques.

DOI: 10.4018/979-8-3693-7137-4.ch004

INTRODUCTION TO DATABASE SECURITY

In today's ever changing innovative world, gadgets have turned out to be an integral part of our routine work. Online activities have become an important part of our daily routine, from accessing social media to online digital payments . These have made our lives easier, and we fully rely on them in numerous ways. However, it is important to make a note that as we can use different online options and facilities, we are actually feeding our private and confidential info in various databases among different websites & multiple applications. The data is vulnerable to infringement threats, and therefore, its security is of utmost importance to prevent any misusing of data (Baraani-Dastjerdi et al., 1996).

Cloud storage is a service that permits users to store, manage, and to have back up of their data over a network. One crucial and important aspect of securing this data is by encrypting it before it is saved in these websites.

Could you just explain why it is mandatory and important to encrypt data before storing it in a database? While authorization and authentication can restrict access to a certain extent, if an intruder access the database, they could potentially misuse the data. By encrypting all the info before saving it in the database, however, even if the hacker gains access, they will not be able to misuse the data. This article aims to highlight the significance and use of database encryption & provide an evaluation of various encryption methodology.

In recent years, Cloud Computing has experienced rapid progress. Cloud Computing provides users via the Internet with a variety of means such as computing power, computing platforms, and applications. FEAR Cloud developers in current markets scenarios are Amazon, Google, and many more. With rise in number of entities using Cloud resources, it becomes imperative and mandatory to safeguard the data of different users. One of the essential and main obstacles facing Cloud Computing is just to safeguard, secure and transform user data. Defined below the two main stages in which your data resides in the Cloud: first is when the data is transiting and secondly when the data is resting, where it should be more secure. The two main scenarios illustrated below helps us to understand deeply the safety and privacy in data in the Cloud.

Figure 1 shown below narrates a situation in which a connection is seen between a local network & a Cloud system network .In some portion of the network, data gets removed via the local network and is put in the network of Cloud, but all the pivotal data is stored in the network itself.. However, in some instances, the Cloud can access some information which can be found on the network, at the time of this access, there is a likelihood of unlawful access to local resources. We describe typical network security problems where info can face active as well as passive attacks. Active attacks include muddying, repeated attacks, alterations of data and service rejection. attacks which are Passive usually include traffic analysis. These attacks are normally to occur/arise typically when the information flow departs or exits the client-side network for the Cloud network.

Figure 1. Unauthorized access of information

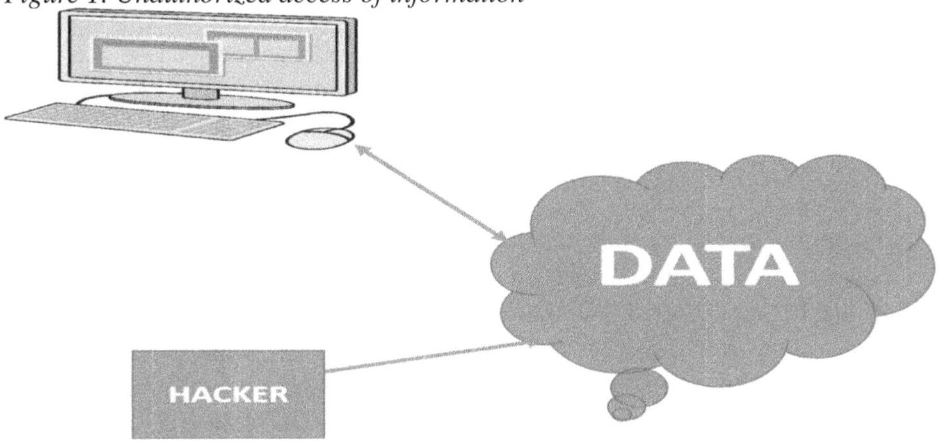

Figure shows the situation in which local network data set resides in the Cloud, where the local network and the lawful & genuine users can physically access all this data in the Cloud. At the moment, there is one ability for unwanted and unauthorized persons/ users to access all data in the Cloud. In this Location, virtual machines are being allotted and assigned to all the Cloud users. These cars have Valid login credentials. However, these identifiers can be misused and hacked. Also, Data can also be accessed indirectly. When it comes to this field of study, most technical research articles have adopted conventional survey techniques. Few reports have given an innovative and suggested idea of a security model. However, there is minimal work that has taken ideas into account by various Cloud Computing security experts. This study provides the reader with an precise image of the security processes which is followed by various Cloud Computing entities during recent times. There are very less articles to emphasize on security techniques for specific applications. Our research brings deep understanding into this size and also foreseen threats of future that Cloud Computing is likely to face and solutions to these threats.

1. ESSENTIAL FEATURES OF CLOUD COMPUTING

Any Model based on cloud computing is defined by 5 important and core characteristics:

1. **Self-Service**: This characteristic contemplates that users can independently & provisionally compile computing resources like server access-time & storage, automatically as and when required, without interacting with the provider.
2. **Broad Network Access**: All Resources can be accessible to a network and are accessed through a standardized mechanism, thereby allowing use of different client platforms, including mobiles, tablets, laptops etc.
3. **Pooling of Resources**: The cloud side provider's resources can be shared in between many users using a multi-tenant model, along with all resources dynamically allocated based on their need. This model depicts a level of location autonomy, where users normally do not control or know the exact location of all the resources but can easily identify locations preferences at a broader level, like region or even data centers. Some Examples of such things may include, power of processing, memory usage, storage & also bandwidth of the network.
4. **Rapid Elasticity**: We know that Cloud services can rapidly scale up or even can scale down depending on requirement, giving the impression of infinite resources available for allocation at any particular point of time.
5. **Measured Service**: Cloud based systems can supervise monitor & optimize its resource usage through metering, thereby providing a pay-per-use model. This usually enables limpidity in usage for both the provider and user, along with the resources, for example storage, processing power, and active accounts being tracked and reported.

1.1 DEFINITION AND KEY CONCEPTS

As the trust on cloud computing eventually continues to grow, thereby assuring the privacy security and protection of data has become a prime concern. Cloud security comprises a broad spectrum of technical concepts and technologies, all policies, & designed controls to save data, and structure in cloud computing situations. The escalating demand of cloud computing has introduced a variety of challenges relating to privacy and security as given by various studies . In fact, security concerns are normally quoted as the primary obstacle enterprises from fully embracing cloud services.

A detailed data security framework has been proposed significantly for cloud computing networks (Pandey et al., 2013). Furthermore, Kifayat & Younis have conducted a profound and deep survey on securing cloud computing, with a deep focus on its application to critical infrastructure (Younis & Kifayat, 2013). In this context of privacy, the study experiments both tangible and intangible threats, focusing key issues in data security like as ensuring the data security, securing data from unrecognized access, and guaranteeing the availability of data.

1.2 SECURITY GOALS

Securing the information in cloud computing is far much essential task than just the encryption technique. The need for securing data primarily depends on 3 service models: PaaS, IaaS, and SaaS. There are 2 types of data normally pose to threaten the security aspect in clouds: one is Data, which is at Rest, which typically depicts the data must be handled in the cloud, and next Data which is in process, which usually understands data that are now in transit. The secrecy, data privacy and data integrity are based on the type, basic behavior of data protection techniques/ mechanisms, and procedures.

a) As per our belief, Integrity of data is one of the pivotal elements of a system. Generally, data and its integrity shows the securing data from unauthorized access, modification, fabrication or deletion. By adjusting and maintaining an entity's permission and right to particular enterprise and resources guarantees that valuable and important data and its services provided are not at all harmed, disorganized, or even stolen. Integrity can easily be achieved using a alone system .

Data integrity is nothing but a system which is updated or organized through various database transactions, constraints which is normally under completed by using a database management system (DBMS). Transactions must follow Atomicity, Consistency,, Durability & Isolation (ACID) properties to guarantee data integrity. Most of the databases support ACID transactions to store and secure the integrity and privacy of data. Authorization is mainly used to limit data access. This is that kind of approach by which any system will find the access level through an authorized person .Integrity mainly protects data integrity in cloud-based systems. Data should not be changed by unknown and unrecognized users. Data integrity is the premise of services provided by cloud computing .

b) confidentiality of data is utmost important factor for people to save personal or secret data on the cloud. Authentication strategies were broadly used to make sure that data is confidential. Access control issues, Data confidentiality, and authentication in cloud computing can be addressed by just enhancing trustworthiness and cloud reliability . The major issue is actually the highlighting of the data in the above-stated stages.

c)Data at Rest(DAR):Data which is under rest means the data including the backup storage and live data. As stated above, it is usually difficult for entities to prevent data at rest only if they are just going to maintain a personal cloud because actually, they do not have access to the data. However, this problem can be solved by just maintaining a personal or a private cloud with proper mechanisms.

d) Data in Transit:Data which is in under transit means data that are moving through the cloud. These data of cloud could be in the structure of a file or can be stored in the cloud. When the data is loaded to the cloud, at that time the data which is uploaded is called data in transit. Data which is under transit can be too delicate, sensitive, such as passwords and its usernames, and can be surely encrypted .Moreover encrypted data are also in transit (Shen et al., 2010).

Figure 2 shows that Data in transit are many times more prone to risk than data which is at rest due to transition from one location to another. (See Fig 2). There are several and many different methods in which software can drop on any of the info and at times can modify the data on its way before it reaches the desired location . One of the appropriate techniques for making it secure or protecting data in transit is the method of encryption.

Figure 2. Data at rest and transit

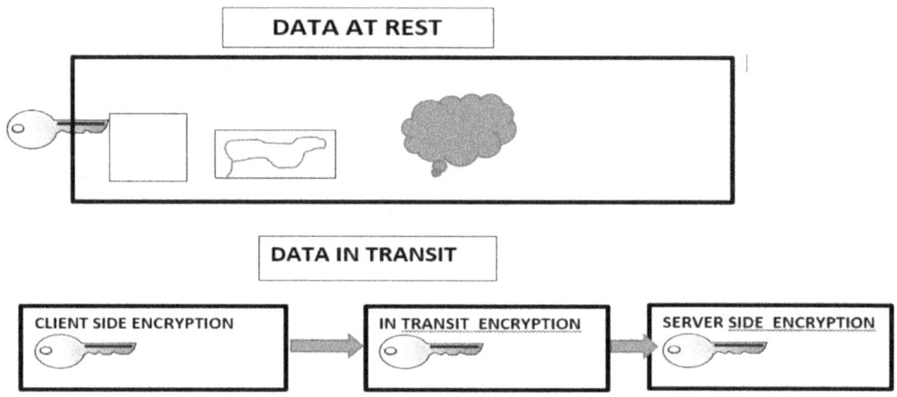

1.3 SECURITY IN CLOUD COMPUTING

Figure 3 below clearly shows the statistical graph which basically presents findings from a survey organized by the (IDC) ie International Data Corporation in August month of 2008, which involves specifically IT professionals and business executives . The survey is focused and emphasizes on identifying the key challenges that impact the performance of cloud computing, with security depicting as the most significant concern.

During a session at the Brookings policy titled "Cloud Computing for Business and Society," additional insights showcases from counsel Brad Smith from a survey commissioned under Microsoft in year 2010 of month January . The results revealed that 58% of the crowd and 86% of leaders were enthusiastic regarding the capacity of cloud computing. However, over 90% of respondents expressed serious concerns regarding the private integrity, securing data in the cloud.

Both surveys show that security remains the primary challenge affecting the performance and adoption of cloud computing.

Figure 3. Client concerns on Cloud computing issues

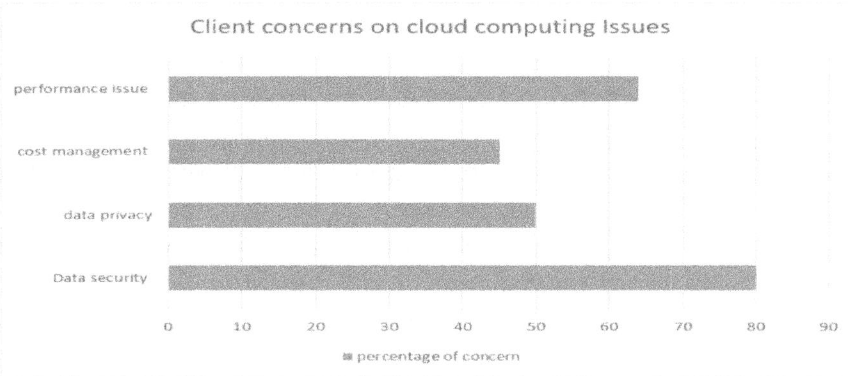

2. SECURITY CONCERNS AND RISKS IN CLOUD COMPUTING

In the category of cloud computing enormous risks & security issues are in association with its data. Although, this study discusses the public cloud storage, virtualization, which are basically related to the security of data in cloud computing (Velumadhava Rao & Selvamani, 2015).

2.1 Virtualization

Virtualization is nothing but a method or technique wherein a operational OS is captured in yet another OS to basically use all the material of the OS to the fullest. A unique function known as hyper-visor which is needed to execute a guest OS as a virtual device of a host (Pandey et al., 2013) (Rivest et al., 1978). Virtualization is nothing but a foundation component of cloud which is helping in producing the moral values of CC. but, even virtualization is not devoid of risking data in cloud computing. One probable risk factor is at stake a hyper-visor itself. A hyper-visor may be a main target if it is acting as a vulnerable. If a hyper-visor is compromising, the whole system can be shut down or collapse and compromising and hence the data (AlZain et al., 2011). Yet Another risk factor with virtualizing is concerned with re-allocation & allocation of its resources. If the operation data is saved and written in memory, and it is not mentioned before reallocating memory for VM, then there is a scope for data exposed to the VM which may be unwanted or undesirable (Ram & Sreenivaasan, 2010). The best possible solution to the above-mentioned issues is better planning and strategy for using virtualization. Resources should be properly implemented, and data must be properly well authorized before the re-allocation of all the resources.

2.2 Public storage

Storing data in any public cloud space is the yet other security issue or problem in cloud computing. Usually clouds implement all storage concepts, which are interesting target for hackers. Resources for storage are really a complicated one that have usually hardware and s/w coding and could cause data if a minute or slight changes arises in the cloud (Kardaş et al., 2013). To avoid and overcome such risks, it is normally advised to have a personal private cloud, if possible, for extreme delicate data. Multifarious Sharing access or multitenancy is also considered as one of the major risks to data in cloud computing (Delettre et al., 2011). It is a threat not to a single person but also to multi users. In these situations, always there is a risk of private data leaking to other people. Multi-tenancy could be too risky as one fault or error within the system may allow other hackers to use all remaining data . These are some problems and issues that we can take care of by meticulously authorizing the users before they can use the data. There are so many authentication methods which are in use to remove multi-tenancy problems in cloud computing. Multiplicity is also one of the most important effects of information in accounting. Since multiple users use shared computer resources such as CPU storage, it affects many users. In such cases, there is anytime a risk that personal information will be inadvertently disclosed to other users. Multitasking could be incredibly hazardous.

2.3 Unauthorized access

SaaS & PaaS systems have the capacity to deploy services in demand and which is mostly needed by using various service tools. Whereas they also introduce the potential for unauthorized use. Organizations are left vulnerable when services and features are provisioned or used without Information technology and computer science knowledge. Employees who access cloud based data using various devices such as computers, laptops, tablet PC can sometimes deploy remote security. This raises concerns on cloud security for renowned business specially when employees are insincere and careless.

The speed of transition of authorities will be decided by the cloud storage services used, like IaaS and SaaS. PaaS and full privacy can lead to various business, privacy, and security vulnerabilities. Security breaches, data duplication, and improper controls can adjust the privacy of cloud data as well as to reduce the accuracy of security controls. These risks could be prevented by installing security systems that monitor data & also identifies unusual user behavior. The most common cloud security issue organizations faces is lack of visibility (Rajawat & Gaur, 2014).

Cloud infrastructure networks are prone to system failures due to their intricacy and trust in third-party support. Security vulnerabilities can be cracked by hackers, allowing them to destroy sensitive data. Insecure systems, shared memory, and tools can serve as entry points for malicious attacks and large-scale data breaches (Agha et al., 2022).

The ease of data sharing in clouds is a significant advantage, but it also poses significant risks. Data theft, deletion, and leakage are major concerns. When data is stored in cloud storage, it can be easily shared with others, either intentionally or unintentionally, through public URLs. (Han et al., 2012).Moreover, technologies can scan the website just for insecure cloud distributions, posing a security risk.

As cloud computing becomes increasingly popular, the rate of account hijacking is growing rapidly. Employees can access their accounts from various devices, allowing hackers to steal easily all sensitive data stored in the cloud. Moreover, hackers can even alter or delete this data. Reused passwords and programming errors are additional vulnerabilities that can be exploited/used by attackers, thereby allowing them access to sensitive information.

3. DATABASE SECURITY IN CLOUD STORAGE

As entities increasingly embark on data for storage solutions, securing that data is of prime concern. Cloud storage offers various benefits, which includes size, efficiency, and availability. However, it also brings with it many security risks which can affect and compromise the confidentiality & integrity of stored data. Deeply Understanding the threats is important to implement effective security measures to protect information.

3.1 CLOUD STORAGE AND ITS SECURITY THREATS

Types of Security Threats

a)Un-authorized access

Unauthorized access usually occurs when individuals access data without requisite prior permissions. This can lead to weak authentication mechanisms, weak access controls, or insider threats. Once done, attackers can steal, modify or delete sensitive information.

b)Data breach

Data breaches usually occur when pivotal and sensitive data is accessed, stolen, or compromised without permission and authorization. Cloud Storage data breaches can happen in many ways:

- **Insider Threats**: These threats occur when authorized personnel deliberately /intentionally or unintentionally compromise cloud storage security.
- **Data Encryption Weaknesses**: Weakness in data encryption can just allow unauthorized access to sensitive data.
- **Cloud Storage Provider Vulnerabilities**: Vulnerabilities in cloud storage provider systems may allow unauthorized access to sensitive data.

c)Loss of data

Data loss usually occurs when data is deleted, corrupted, or becomes inaccessible. Cloud storage data loss can happen in several ways:

- **Accidental Deletion**: This can occur when users or administrators mistakenly delete files or folders.
- **Data Corruption**: Data corruption can occur when data is modified or corrupted during transmission or storage.
- **Cloud Storage Provider Outages**: Outages by cloud storage providers can make data inaccessible.

d)Insider threats

Insider threats may include malicious actions by insiders /employees or other trusted individuals with access to the cloud storage environment. These insiders can misuse their access rights to steal or modify data for individual profit or to destroy the organization.

Malware and ransomware attacks can affect cloud storage environments, encrypted data & can demand a random payment against it . These attacks can interrupt business tasks/work and cause significant financial losses.

e)Denials of Service (DoS) attacks.

This type of attacks comprises overwhelming clouds storage resource with traffic in order to make them unavailable. This can happen in several ways:

- **Traffic Flooding**: Traffic flooding includes sending large amounts of traffic to cloud storage resources to overwhelm them.
- **Resource Exhaustion**: Resource exhaustion means consuming all available resources (e.g. CPU, memory) to make cloud storage resources unavailable.

f) Man in the Middle (MitM) attacks.

These attacks involve interpreting communication among two parties in order to steal sensitive information. Cloud storage MitM attacks can occur in several ways:

- **SSL/TLS Weaknesses**: Weaknesses in SSL/TLS encryption can permit MitM attacks to occur.
- **Malware**: Malware is used to intercept communication between cloud storage users and providers.

g) Bad configurations

Misconfigurations of cloud storage settings can create vulnerabilities that attackers exploit. Common misconfigurations may include unencrypted data storage, and exposed endpoints.

It is imperative to have fair understanding of these security threats so as to ensure protection of your cloud storage environment. By practicing strong security measures, organizations can mitigate these risks and guarantees the protection of their valuable data.

3.2 EXAMPLES OF BREACHES IN CLOUD STORAGE

Some notable examples of security breaches in cloud storage include:

- **Dropbox Breach**: A Dropbox employee's password may hacked, allowing unauthorized access to a Dropbox account.

- **Apple iCloud Breach**: A vulnerability permits hackers to access sensitive data, including celebrity photos.
- **Amazon S3 Breach**: This allowed unauthorized access to crucial data, involving Security numbers & credit card information.

These examples emphasize the usage and value of practicing robust security methods to save cloud storage resources.

3.3 DATABASE SECURITY MEASURES

Measures designed for database security are designed to protect databases from unrecognized access, destruction, usage, updation. These measures are categorized into many types:

1. Access Control

These security measures ensure that permitted authorized personnel should have access to the database which includes:

- **Authentication**: cross-checking and verifying the identity of each user and ensuring that they are who they claim to be.
- **Authorization**: Granting or denying/rejecting access rights to database resources based on user identity and privileges.
- **Managing Account**: Managing user accounts, including creation, modifying, and deleting accounts.

2. Data Encryption

Measures for data encryption protects data from unwanted access by converting it into an unreadable format. This may include:

- **Encryption using Symmetric Key**: same key could be used for both methods ie decryption as well as encryption .
- **Asymmetric Key Encryption**: Making use of keys, one for decryption and another for encryption.
- **Hashing**: Conversion of data into a string of characters, thereby making it possible to reverse-engineer the actual data.

3. Network Security

Network security protects the database from unauthorized access via the network. This may include:

- **Firewalls**: Blocking unauthorized access to the database by restricting incoming and outgoing network traffic.
- **Virtual Private Networks**: Encrypting data transmitted over the network to prevent eavesdropping and interception.
- **Intrusion Detection and:** Supervising networks traffics for signs of unauthorized access

4. Logging and auditing

These measures usually track & record database activity in order to detect & respond to security incidents. This includes:

- **Audit Trails**: This includes recording all database activity, user actions and system events.
- **Log Analysis**: This comprises of analyzing audit trails to detect security incidents and identify trends.
- **Alerting and Notification**: Alerts administrators and security personnel regarding potential security incidents.

5. Recovery and Backup

Backup and recovery measures ensure that data is protected from loss or corruption. This may include:

- **Data Backup**: Creating multiple or many copies of data to ensure and guarantee business continuity in data loss or corruption.
- **Data Recovery**: Restoring data from backups in the account of data lost or data corruption.
- **Recovery of Disaster**: This includes ensuring business continuity on account of a disaster or major outage.

6. Physical Security

Physical security measures make sure to protect/secure the database from physical threats, like unauthorized authentication to the data center . This includes:

- **Access Control**: Controlling or restricting access to the server room.
- **Surveillance**: Means Monitoring / supervising the data center for signs of unauthorized access.
- **Environmental Controls**: This ensures that the server room and data center is protected from environmental hazards or issues, such as flooding or fire.

7. Patch Management

Patch management measures make sure that the database and related systems are up-to-mark with the security protocols. This will include:

- **Patch Assessment**: To identify vulnerabilities and determining the need for patches.
- **Patch Deployment**: To Deploy and implement patches to the database and other related systems.
- **Patch Verification**: to Verify that patches have been successfully deployed and implemented and are properly functioning .

Applying these database security measures and procedures, any organization can protect their databases from restricted access, disclosure, hacking, destruction and modification.

3.4 DATABASE SECURITY MODELS IN CLOUD

Security Model Implementation Typically cloud deployments are managed internally (Private Cloud) or through third party & for some logical reasons they are deployed as a private-public cloud . "Community Cloud" is the 4th category of cloud deployment model, where the infrastructure is distributed across multiple entities and accessible by a specific organization. The NIST i.e. National Institute of Standards and Technology has proposed 4 main concepts for cloud development: including hybrid cloud, private cloud, public cloud. Figure 4 below describes the different types of cloud models of deployment .

In private cloud systems, the organization can manage the infrastructure, both physically and virtually, or outsource it to third parties. Security in the home infrastructure can be controlled and does not require additional trust mechanisms. A personal cloud is used by any organization, and all of the infrastructure of cloud are available only within the organization. This could be too risky and expensive (Kashukeevetal.,2020).

In a public cloud model, a 3rd -party service provider offers cloud services that are on a basis of pay as you go method, allowing users to take advantage of economies of scale, flexible short-term usage, and optimized resource utilization. However, ensuring the secure use of shared public cloud resources can be more complex in comparison to private clouds. As a result, public clouds are better suited for applications that are less sensitive or vulnerable to security risks (Sharma, 2022).

The hybrid cloud model offers a balanced approach for integrating different implementation models, enabling seamless portability of data & services while minimizing vulnerabilities. Although it reduces threats, integration points between different cloud models remain potential weak spots. By combining the benefits of various cloud types, such as public & private clouds, hybrid clouds provide maximum flexibility and a wide range of data distribution options. Also, they are managed and monitored from a single, unified platform.

Cloud Community is simply a cloud which typically permits computer and to be used through a cluster of various industries to show the info. It is naturally organized and monitored by numerous entities in the community.

Figure 4. Cloud Computing Deployment models

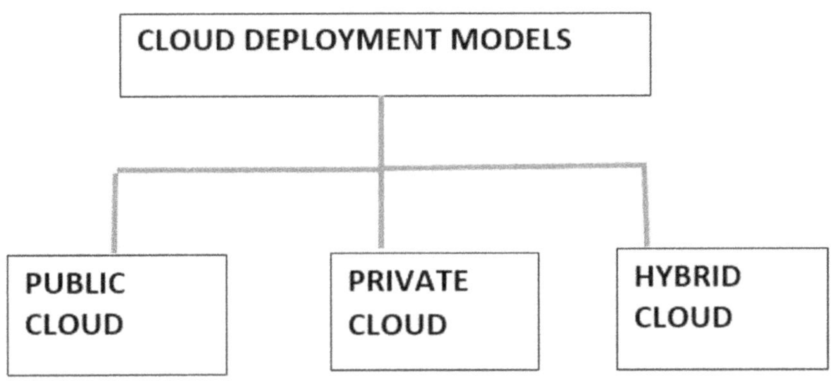

3.5 SECURITY IN SERVICE DELIVERY MODELS

As a usual practice Cloud service developers offer 3 deliveries that are the IaaS, Platform as a service which is known as PaaS, and SaaS, which are alternatively known as distribution and provision models. Figure 5 Shows various cloud service models.

The Infrastructure segment caters users with the underlying infrastructure for their cloud based operations including the core components and software that communicates with them. This comprises of servers, networks, other storage systems (Singh,2016).

PaaS is a deployment framework that developers need to develop and deploy their applications. However some authors have a view that Paas and Iaas are of same category. Meanwhile web providers offers some proprietary development languages and APIs (Chauhan & Shiaeles, 2023).

Software as a service is accessed via the network through the users like colleagues, any employees, all managers (Chauhan & Shiaeles, 2023).

Figure 5. cloud service models

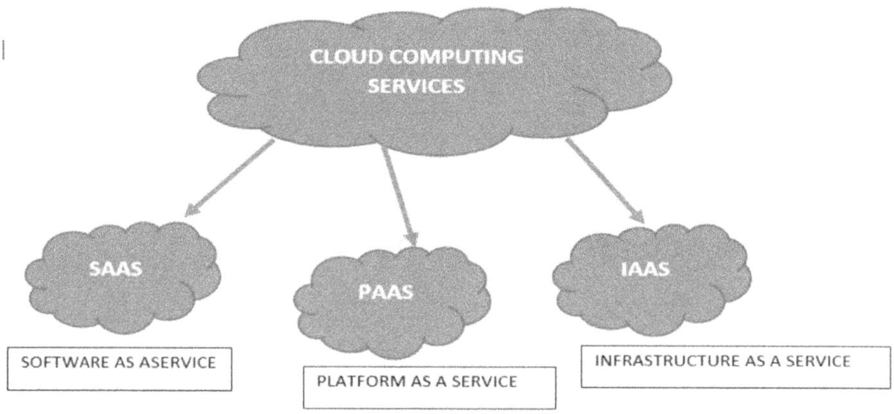

3.6 MANAGING CLOUD SECURITY

To effectively manage cloud security, it is essential to follow five key principles:

1. **Network Segmentation**: Implementing a robust zoning strategy is pivotal for keeping instances, containers, applications, and entire systems separated (Rajawat & Gaur, 2014). This isolation prevents movement during any attack and restricts unauthorized access among systems by an actor.
2. **Access Controls based on clouds**: Every aspect of cloud computing should be regulated by control panel. Since all services such as databases could be deployed independently, it is mandatory to implement and enforce strict access controls. This applies to all virtual infrastructure, operating systems, applications, and

monitoring tools. Adopting a least-privilege security model, where access is fully restricted unless explicitly needed, is recommended. Additionally, resources should not be publicly accessible unless absolutely necessary, and any exposed resources should be securely protected.

3. **Cloud Computing Multitenancy**: Although multi-tenancy provides scalability and various advantages, it also poses multiple risks such as data leakage and unchartered territories/ boundaries (e.g., during reporting or data export) (Agha et al., 2022). Implementing stringent use controls in a scenario & clearly defining boundaries for policy for any accounts is mandatory.
4. **Cloud Access Management**: Given that cloud resources are not under your direct control, managing privileged access becomes crucial.. Hence one is required to supervise privileged accessing to all cloud resources & prepare for disaster recovery and potential access failures (Wood & Pereira, 2010). On-premise practices such as password management & accounts of administrator need to be mirrored in the cloud. However, cloud administrator rights should be carefully managed to avoid negating the benefits of accessing control lists. Priority should be based on role, properly delegated, and monitored closely to ensure appropriate use.
5. **Vulnerabilities and Cloud Computing Threats**: This principle aligns closely with on-premise implementations but often involves the use of agents and other integration technologies to identify vulnerabilities. Once vulnerabilities are detected, they should be prioritized based on threat intelligence and addressed promptly. This basic cybersecurity practice is vital, regardless of the computing environment, to maintain robust security hygiene.

1.4 DATA ENCRYPTION

4.1 INTRODUCTION

In today's ever changing world, data security is supreme. Governments, corporates, and other entities have suffered noteworthy financial losses because of the actions of malicious attackers & hackers . Over the years, many encryption schemes were deployed to protect databases from numerous types of intrusions. Given that data is the lifeblood of one and all organization, there is a critical requirement and demand to securely store the data which is generated daily to ensure recovery in the event of an attack. Cloud storage provides a solution or conclusion for remote data storage, but many establishments are only worried about the security of these files when they are transmitted to the cloud (Zhang et.al,2010). They are concerned about their files being exposed or compromised by different actors, as occurred in history. The techniques are essential and crucial to maintain the confidentiality of data.

Commonly not all corporate data needs to be encrypted, and access requirements may vary among users. In order to ensure data protection, businesses must establish protocols and regulations to individually identify which information requires encryption and which can be safely saved in plain text. So, Segregation of data using Software as a service application that simply encrypt data inside the applications can effectively protect important data. Additionally, data protection should not negatively impact business processes.

Data that may require encryption can even exist in 3 different states, but protecting data at rest is crucial and important . The prudent approach and method is to encrypt sensitive data at creation, ensuring protection when stored in a data center.

In the past, many businesses blindly relied upon cloud providers to manage and secure all their data properly, thereby relying on contracts, controls, and even conducted audits to mitigate security risks. Nonetheless over a period of time evidently it has come to notice that cloud providers will not always uphold these commitments, especially when replying to statutory requests information. This article hence discusses the scope of database and its encryption and provides an depth picture and feedback of different encryption techniques.

In the current scenario, majority of the tasks in the nature of social networking to digital payments are managed by computer/gadgets. Notwithstanding the efficacy and convenient nature of the services offered by these gadgets it is imperative to store our personal, private and sensitive data in websites. This data is vulnerable to threats, making its protection a top priority to prevent misuse. (Baraani-Dastjerdi et al., 2022).

Cloud Storage is nothing but a type of a system where data is properly authenticated, stored, maintained, and backed up. These services are available to users over a network, which is mainly the internet. Most Important method of securing this data is making use of data encryption which is actually storing data and other related information in the databases of the websites.

4.2 ENCRYPTING THE DATA-NEED OF AN HOUR

The basic requirement of data encryption beforehand storing it in a database is to ensure restriction/stopping the usage of data could provide help to a great extent, but what if in case the hacker gets into the database (Cherry & Larock, 2011). The hacker, upon gaining all rights and access to all the database, can mis handle it as per his choice, so here data encryption ie first saving it in database arises into picture. If the info is encrypted before saving it, even with access to the database the hacker cannot make undue use of the data. So, the main goal of the matter is to discuss the role of database encryption and making an in deep review or study of many encryption techniques.

4.3 DATA ENCRYPTION

We know Database encryption typically involves encrypting data stored within a database . This crucial strategy aims to protect and save the data's content from unrecognized access and misuse. The core concept is that if an intruder gains access/rights to the database, they will be unable to exploit or fetch the encrypted data.

As illustrated in Figure 6, the database encryption and decryption process operates/functions as follows- the plaintext or data intended for storage is first converted into ciphertext using a specific algorithm and key. This encrypted data (which is ciphertext) is then stored in the database. When a user is interested in retrieving the data, this ciphertext is decrypted into plaintext using the same algorithm and the key, making the original data accessible to any user. Database Encryption can only be done in 2 ways (Albugmi et al., 2016).

Figure 6. Data encryption and Decryption process

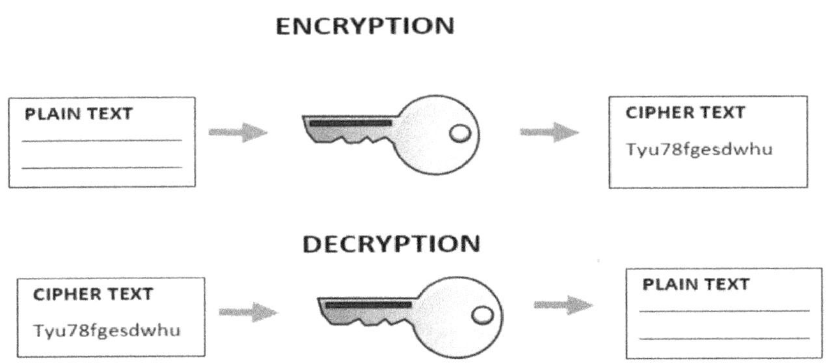

4.3.1 Encryption

The process of encryption is wherein a plain simple text is being converted to text using a key, then using this same key you can even decrypt the cipher text to plain text (Younis & Kifayat, 2013). This Encryption can be performed through many algorithms.. Most importantly and widely used algorithms are RC2, DES, AES128, AES 256 . Figure 7 below shows a simple encryption process (Han et al., 2012).

4.3.2 Hashing

Hashing is nothing but a 1-way procedure in which any text is being converted into hashed (which is encrypted form). Once the data is hashed through a Hash Function it couldn't be changed again to Text (Han et al., 2012). Normally this procedure is used for password encryption, when we want to log in, the password entered is hacked using hash function and then we need to first match with the password already fed into the database which is previously in encrypted form, if it matches the user will get access and is allowed to use it else it displays the message of not valid username and passcode . Mostly used Hash Functions used are SHA-1,SHA-2,MD5, etc. Figure 7 shows the working of hashing (Shaikh & Haider, 2011).

Figure 7. Encryption and Hashing

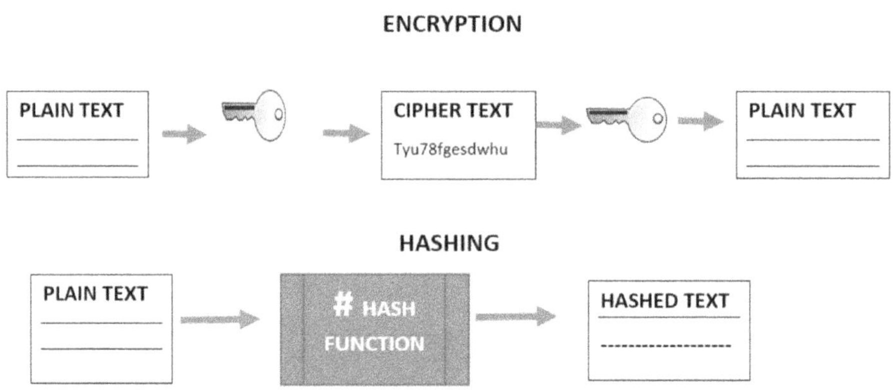

4.4 ENCRYPTION METHODS IN CLOUD STORAGE

Encryption is an important aspect of security in cloud storage as it makes sure that every time the data is being protected and hidden from unwanted access. There are many encryption methods used for cloud storage, including.

1. Symmetric Key Encryption Method:

Symmetric encryption technique uses a somewhat similar key for both decryption and encryption . The method is very fast & too efficient, but its basic requirement is that the key is to be kept hidden or secret to prevent unauthorized access (Che et al., 2011).

Advanced Encryption Standard Method

Advanced Encryption Standard ie AES is an algorithm of symmetric key for encryption which is considered to be very Secure and efficient. It makes use of a variable key size and block size, and it is designed to be highly resistant to attacks (Sharma & Sinha, 2021).

- **Key sizes could be:** 128, 192, and 256 bits
- **Size of Block:** 128 bits
- **modes of Encryption:** ECB, CBC, CFB, OFB, and GCM

Data Encryption Standard

Standards for Data Encryption is a simple and historic one. However, it is no longer said to be more secure due to its small key size and vulnerability to attacks (Sharma & Sinha, 2021).

- **Key size:** 56 bits
- **Block size:** 64 bits
- **Encryption modes:** ECB, CBC, CFB, and OFB

2. Asymmetric Key Encryption

This method of encryption makes use of a key pair ie a key particularly for encryption and another key specifically for decryption. This method is secure or reliable than symmetric key encryption, but it is also much more complex and slighter slower (Singh, 2016).

RSA

Rivest Shamir Adleman is a broadly and widely used category under asymmetric key encryption algorithm which is considered to be secure and reliable. It makes use of variable key sizes and is designed to be highly resistant to attacks.

- **Key sizes:** 1024, 2048, and 4096 bits
- **Encryption modes:** OAEP and PKCS#1

ECC

Elliptic Curve Cryptography is one type of asymmetric key encryption that makes use of elliptic curves to create smaller and more efficient keys. It is widely considered to be more secure than RSA for key sizes of similar strength (Sharma & Sinha, 2021).

- **Key sizes:** 256, 384, and 521 bits
- **Encryption modes:** ECDSA and ECDH

3. Homomorphic Encryption

Homomorphic encryption can be explained as one type of encryption method which permits calculations performed on encrypted data by not changing it . This method is of great use for cloud storage, as it permits data to be processed and analyzed by not compromising its security (Singh & Jangwal, 2016).

This encryption is a category of encryption which basically allows all calculations to be performed on encrypted data by not decrypting it . This means that data can be processed and analyzed without compromising its security. This encryption is useful for cloud storage, as it allows data to be processed & analyzed in this cloud without exposing it to unauthorized access.

4.4.1 EXAMPLES OF HOMOMORPHIC ENCRYPTION SCHEMES

There are many homomorphic encryption schemes, some are as follows:

- **Fully Homomorphic Encryption Method:** Fully method of Encryption is that category of encryption which allows any calculations performed on data but without first decrypting it . FHE is the secure form of homomorphic encryption, but at the same time it is also the most complex and computationally intensive.
- **Somewhat Homomorphic Method of Encryption:** This category of homomorphic encryption permits certain computations to be done on data without decrypting it . Somewhat Encryption is less secure than FHE, but it is also less complex and computationally intensive.
- **Partially Homomorphic Encryption:** Partially Encryption method is that category of homomorphic encryption which permits certain computations to be carried on encrypted data without performing decrypt process . As compared to FHE and SHE, PHE is less secure, but it is also less complex and computationally intensive.

Some examples of homomorphic encryption schemes may include:

- **Brakerski-Gentry-Vaikuntanathan (BGV) scheme:** The scheme is a FHE scheme which is considered to be more secure and very efficient (Shaikh & Haider, 2011). It uses a lattice-based approach to basically encrypt data and allows many computations to be done on encrypted data.

- **Fan-Vercauteren (FV) scheme:** The FVS scheme is nothing but a SHE schemes which is considered to be secure and efficient. It uses a lattice-based approach for encrypting data and allows some modifications to be done on encrypt data without first decrypting it .
- **Paillier scheme:** The scheme is a PHE scheme which is considered to be secure and efficient. It makes use of a probabilistic approach for basically encrypting data and allows certain calculations to be done on encrypted data .

To sum up, homomorphic encryption is a dominant and strong tool for cloud storage security, as it enables data to be processed and analyzed without compromising its security. There are many homomorphic encryption schemes, each with their own strengths and weaknesses.

4.5 CLOUD STORAGE ENCRYPTION TECHNIQUES

Cloud Storage Encryption Techniques are those methods which are used to save data stored in the cloud from unauthorized access. The goal or aim of cloud storage encryption is to be sure that although if data is intercepted by unauthorized parties, it will not be readable and unusable without using decryption key (Ren et al., 2012)

Cloud encryption techniques are important in order to hide data stored in the cloud. These techniques guarantee that data remains private and protected from unauthorized access, both while at rest in cloud storage and in transit. Many encryption methods and protocols are used to provide this security, each with their own strengths and applications. Below are some key cloud storage encryption techniques:

Cloud encryption uses keys for scrambling data, thereby making it inaccessible to unauthorized parties. Only those with the keys can interpret the data . There are probably 2 types of encryption keys:

Symmetric encryption: which Uses the same key for both methods ie encryption and decryption, offering faster processing time.

Asymmetric encryption: which Employs a private key specifically for decryption and a public key for encryption, thereby providing enhanced security.

However, losing or destroying the access key can render data unrecoverable, posing a significant risk. To mitigate this, the Cloud Security Alliance recommends:

- Encrypting sensitive or private data using approved algorithms and lengthy and random keys.
- Encrypting data before transferring it to the cloud.
- Maintaining encryption during transit, storage, and use.
- Keeping data encrypted until its use.

Storing keys for decryption and decrypted data in a protected, transient memory space, making them available only when necessary.

There are several cloud storage encryption techniques used to protect data, including:

1. Server-Side Encryption

Server-side method of encryption is a technique where the cloud storage provider encrypts the data on their servers before it is stored. This depicts that the data is now encrypted after it has been transferred to the cloud storage provider, but before it is written to disk.

There are basically two types of server-side encryption:

- **Customer-Managed Encryption Keys (CMEKs)**: This is a type of server-side encryption where the customer creates and manages their own encryption keys. The customer is whole sole responsible for creating, rotating, and revoking the encryption keys (Popovic & Hocenski, 2010).
- **Customer-Supplied Encryption Keys**: This is a type of server-side encryption where the customer provides their own encryption keys to the cloud storage provider. The cloud storage provider makes use of these keys just for encrypting the data.

2. Client-Side Encryption

Client-side encryption is one of the techniques where the info is being encrypted on the clients side before that is transmitted to the clouds provider. This probably means that the data is being encrypted before it leaves the user's device, and the cloud provider only receives the encrypted data.

3. End-to-End Encryption

This encryption method is one of the techniques in which the data is also encrypted on the client side and remains encrypted throughout its journey to the cloud storage provider. The data could only be decrypted by the recipient, by making use of their private key.

End-to-end encryption is one of the most protection form of cloud storage encryption, as it guarantees that the data is protected always from unrecognized access .

Categories of Encryption Algorithms

There are mainly 2 categories of encryption algorithms which are used in cloud storage encryption:

- **Symmetric Encryption**: Symmetric method of encryption uses the common key for encryption and decryption process. This type of method is too fast and efficient but it needs that the encryption key should be kept secret (Popovic & Hocenski, 2010).
- **Asymmetric Encryption**: This method uses a different or a pair of keys: one key for the process of encryption and other key for decryption process. This type of encryption method is far more secure than symmetric encryption, but it is slower and much more computationally intensive.

Importance and benefits of Cloud Storage Encryption

Cloud storage encryption is mandatory for protecting sensitive data from unauthorized access. It guarantees or makes sure that even if data is predicted or accessed by unrecognized parties, it will be unreadable and unusable without the decryption key.

Cloud storage encryption technique helps organizations coordinate with regulatory requirements, such as DSS, HIPAA, which requires the protection of sensitive data.

To summarize, cloud storage encryption techniques are indispensible for protecting data stored in the cloud from unauthorized access. Server-side encryption, client-side encryption, and end-to-end encryption are techniques used to protect data, and symmetric as well as asymmetric encryption algorithms are used to encrypt & decrypt the data.

Cloud encryption has various potential benefits for any organization, including:

Data security. Data which is encrypted is always more secure than unencrypted data Which ensures that high-risk data is encrypted on any organization's storage systems is a preventative defense against cyber-attacks.

Increased cooperation. By reducing information security risks at every level, cloud encryption permits businesses and their customers to more freely share data across internal systems. This promotes a more collaborative, efficient and productive environment.

Authenticity and integrity: End-to-end encryption method reduces the risk of unauthorized data access and malicious data manipulation, thereby helping to improve your reputation with customers.

The challenges of cloud encryption

Cloud encryption techniques play a pivotal role in protecting/securing data stored in the cloud, ensuring authenticity, confidentiality, and also integrity. Moreover, implementing encryption in cloud environments shows some significant challenge, especially because of the complex cloud computing. These challenges crop up from factors such as key management, overall performance and the balance of security and ease of use. Cloud encryption also presents challenges. Here are a few to keep in mind:

Performance and integration issues: Until recently, many entities have put off integrating cloud encryption into their networks because encrypted security processes can interfere with data access. Improvements in processing power and user experience have lessened the impact of these factors, but cloud encryption can still slow down individual and team workflows.

The complexity of management: One of the most crucial challenges of cloud encryption is key management. Cryptography basically relies on the secure generation, storage, distribution and rotation of keys. In this environment, the data is often distributed in several geographical locations and accessed by different services and users, the management of these keys becomes extremely complex and difficult . The cloud provider as well as the user must carefully manage who has access to these keys and makes sure that they are stored securely, which often requires sophisticated key management systems (KMS). The risk of key loss, exposure or compromise is a major concern, as it can lead to irreversible data loss or unauthorized access.

General performance costs: Encryption processes add computational overhead, which can cause high performance. This is especially problematic in cloud environments where scalability and efficiency are essential. Encrypting and decrypting large volumes of data can slow down operations, increase dormancy, and consume more computing resources, which can be expensive for the user. Balancing the need for strong encryption with the need for fast and efficient cloud services is a tricky task. Cloud providers often have a need to optimize encryption algorithms and hardware acceleration to minimize performance impacts, but this optimization is not always simple or universally applicable.

Data loss: When the encryption key information is lost, the encrypted data is also lost. This can present all kinds of problems for past and future projects. Cost in time and money: As with any new process, encryption represents an additional cost for companies and implementing it correctly can take a lot of time and money (Agha et al., 2022)

Data Lifecycle Management: Data in the cloud goes through various stages of its life cycle, including creation, storage, use, sharing and deletion. It is difficult to ensure that encryption is applied consistently in all these steps. For example, while data at rest can be securely encrypted, data in transit and data in use (being processed by applications) require different encryption strategies. Also, secure deletion of encrypted data from cloud storage is complicated by the fact that cloud providers often keep redundant copies for reasons of reliability, making it difficult to completely remove sensitive information (Wood & Pereira, 2010)

Regulatory compliance: Cloud encryption must comply with various regulatory and legal requirements, which can vary significantly by region & the industry. Regulations Eg: GDPR in Europe, HIPAA in the US and other regulations around the world impose strict guidelines on how data should be protected, including encryption standards. However, compliance becomes difficult in cloud environments where data may be stored in multiple jurisdictions, each with their own legal requirements. Secure encryption practices Complying with these different regulations without compromising the operational efficiency of the cloud poses a significant challenge for organizations (Shaikh & Haider, 2011).

Balance between security and ease of use: While encryption is essential to securing data, it can also make it even more tough for authorized users to access data effectively. Overly strict encryption practices can damage the user experience, leading to frustration or workarounds that can compromise security. For example, if encryption keys are not easily accessible, users may store them insecurely, compromising the effectiveness of encryption. Therefore, organizations must strike a balance between maintaining strong encryption standards and ensuring that users can access and use encrypted data transparently.

Trust and control: When using cloud services, customers often rely on the cloud provider to implement and manage encryption. This dependency creates a trust issue, as customers have to trust that the provider manages their encryption keys and data securely. Some organizations may prefer to manage their encryption independently to maintain control, but doing so in a cloud environment can be technically difficult and resource intensive.

Cloud encryption best practices

As we know encryption is the essential security methods any organization can take, below are some points to be considered.

1. Considering security of info as a combine among any business and a cloud service provider, though all recognized cloud service providers offer basic security, containing cloud users should inculcate additional methods to guarantee security of data . Just Think of the relationship with a partnership of CSP where supervise and revert to infrastructural security, & to take necessary steps to save the data and its assets basically we store & transmit in the cloud. Adding some additional or more layers of encryption to CSP encryption is an initial stage . Other useful measures may include:

2. Network monitoring(NM): Using this web monitoring of traffic, applications are required to detect activity, like unauthorized access of port and unusual user access patterns.
3. Managing any Encryption keys: It is essential & important to separate the encryption key from the encrypted data to ensure the data security. We advise our healthcare customers to be cautious and warn about the storage & making use of encryption keys. All normally stores the keys in the same exact venue as the data itself," said Cortney Thompson, chief of data center information and managed services provider Lunavi. If the data is compromised, your key will be too, so it's safer and advisable to keep them separate. Also, companies must keep a backup copy of all keys in an off-site location of disaster or emergency and check this backup copy every two months. These keys also need to be updated and modified regularly.
4. Do not depend wholly and entirely on cloud service providers: Although you need partner along with any cloud data provider in order to encrypt our data & to manage your keys, make sure that a cloud provider will not be more interested in protecting any company's crucial data as the owner of the company. If any organization suffers a high-level data breach, customers and even the press will put their anger on the company itself rather than the cloud service provider. Finally, it's the job of the company to protect its data, where and how it is handled.

5. CONCLUSION

Data security challenges identification & mitigation strategies in cloud computing part is a tough and complex task due to the vast array of services it offers. The majority of survey respondents acknowledged and appreciate that cloud computing will increasingly and rapidly dominate and expand the scope/limit of information transactions. This is because cloud computing offers a broad range of flexible services, allowing it easier for users to access & controlling information in a personalized as well as instantaneous manner, irrespective of their location.

Through numerous research methods /techniques such as Systematic Literature Review and different surveys, we have effectively highlighted a significant number of security challenges/issues and potential mitigation techniques related to both current and future cloud computing and calculation environments.

This cloud computing environment is identified by a large array of services, each along with its own security needs and challenges. These services vary from IaaS i.e. Infrastructure as a service (IaaS) to software as a service, each with separate and unique levels in control and responsibility for security. The no of services complicates the process of identifying security risks, as each service may represent unique vulnerabilities.

By employing research methodologies like SLR and by conducting surveys, researchers are able to systematically identify& categorize security challenges in cloud computing. SLR, particularly helps in reviewing existing literature to predict patterns, common challenges, and proposed solutions, while surveys gather direct feedback from industry professionals and users. The research has revealed a variety of security challenges, such as data breaches, loss of control over data, insecure interfaces, and insider threats. With these challenges, researchers have identified mitigation techniques, including encryption, access control mechanisms, regular security audits, and identifying management systems. The strategies are developed to enhance & to improve security in cloud environments, making sure that as cloud computing continues to evolve, it can do so securely.

REFERENCES

Albugmi, A., Alassafi, M. O., Walters, R., & Wills, G. (2016). Data security in cloud computing. In *Proceedings of the Fifth International Conference on Future Generation Communication Technology (FGCT 2016).*

AlZain, M. A., Soh, B., & Pardede, E. (2011). Mcdb: Using multi-clouds to ensure security in cloud computing. In *Proceedings of the IEEE 9th International Conference on Dependable, Autonomic and Secure Computing (DASC '11)* (pp. 784–791). DOI: 10.1109/DASC.2011.133

Baraani-Dastjerdi, A., Pieprzyk, J., & Safavi-Naini, R. (1996). *Security in databases: A survey study*. Department of Computer Science, The University of Wollongong.

Baraani-Dastjerdi, A., Pieprzyk, J., & Safavi-Naini, R. (2022). *Security in databases: A survey study*. Department of Computer Science, The University of Wollongong.

Chauhan, M., & Shiaeles, S. (2023). An analysis of cloud security frameworks, problems, and proposed solutions. *Network (Bristol, England)*, 3(2), 422–450.

Che, J., Duan, Y., Zhang, T., & Fan, J. (2011). Study on the security models and strategies of cloud computing. In Proceedings of the International Conference on Power Electronics and Engineering Application.</conf>

Cherry, D., & Larock, T. (2011). Database encryption. In Cherry, D. (Ed.), *Securing SQL Server* (pp. 27–71). Syngress.

Delettre, C., Boudaoud, K., & Riveill, M. (2011, July). Cloud computing, security, and data concealment. In *Proceedings of the 16th IEEE Symposium on Computers and Communications (ISCC '11)* (pp. 424–431). IEEE. Kerkyra, Greece.

Han, Z., Zhao, Z., & Zhang, X. (2012). Access control based on group signatures in cloud service. In Computer Science and Automation Engineering (CSAE), 2012 IEEE International Conference on (Vol. 2, pp. 316–320). IEEE. doi:DOI: 10.1109/ITiME.2012.6291488</conf>

Kardaş, S., Çelik, S., Bingöl, M. A., & Levi, A. (2013). A new security and privacy framework for RFID in cloud computing. In *Proceedings of the 5th IEEE International Conference on Cloud Computing Technology and Science (CloudCom '13).* IEEE. Bristol, UK. DOI: 10.1109/CloudCom.2013.30

Kashukeev, I., Denchev, S., & Garvanov, I. (2020). Data security model in cloud computing. *Data Security Model in Cloud Computing*, 5(2), 55–58.

Pandey, A., Tugnayat, R. M., & Tiwari, A. K. (2013). Data security framework for cloud computing networks. *International Journal of Computer Engineering & Technology*, 4(1), 178–181.

Pandey, A., Tugnayat, R. M., & Tiwari, A. K. (2013). Data security framework for cloud computing networks. *International Journal of Computer Engineering & Technology*, 4(1), 178–181.

Popovic, K., & Hocenski, Z. (2010). Cloud computing security issues and challenges. In *MIPRO, 2010 Proceedings of the 33rd International Convention* (pp. 344–349). IEEE.

Rajawat, J. S., & Gaur, S. (2014). An overview of security models and threats in cloud computing. *IJLTEMAS, 3*(5), May. Agha, A. Z., Shukla, R. K., Mishra, R., & Shukla, R. S. (2022). Adoption of cloud enabling cyber-security model in organizations. *Indian Journal of Science and Technology.*

Ram, C. P., & Sreenivaasan, G. (2010, December). Security as a service (SaaS): Securing user data by coprocessor and distributing the data. In *Proceedings of the 2nd International Conference on Trendz in Information Sciences and Computing (TISC '10)* (pp. 152–155). IEEE.

Ren, K., Wang, C., & Wang, Q. (2012). Security challenges for the public cloud. *IEEE Internet Computing*, 16(1), 69–73. DOI: 10.1109/MIC.2012.14

Rivest, R. L., Adleman, L., & Dertouzos, M. L. (1978). On data banks and privacy homomorphisms. *Foundations of Secure Computation*, 4(11), 169–180.

Shaikh, F. B., & Haider, S. (2011, December). Security threats in cloud computing. In Internet Technology and Secured Transactions (ICITST), 2011 International Conference for (pp. 214–219). IEEE.

Sharma, A., & Sinha, G. (2021). An efficient approach on data security with cloud computing environment: A comprehensive research. *Turkish Journal of Computer and Mathematics Education*, 12(14).

Sharma, P. (2022). Review of cloud computing data security and threats. International Journal of Creative Research Thoughts, 10.

Shen, Z., Li, L., Yan, F., & Wu, X. (2010, May). Cloud computing system based on trusted computing platform. In *Proceedings of the International Conference on Intelligent Computation Technology and Automation (ICICTA '10)* (Vol. 1, pp. 942–945). IEEE. DOI: 10.1109/ICICTA.2010.724

Singh, B. (2016). An analysis of cloud computing security issues. *International Journal of Scientific Research in Science and Technology*, •••, 2. DOI: 10.32628/IJSRST207239

Singh, S., & Jangwal, T. (2016). Cost breakdown of public cloud computing and private cloud computing and security issues. *International Journal of Computational Science*.

Velumadhava Rao, R., & Selvamani, K. (2015). Data security challenges and its solutions in cloud computing. In *Proceedings of the International Conference on Intelligent Computing, Communication & Convergence (ICCC-2015)*. Interscience Institute of Management and Technology, Bhubaneswar, Odisha, India.

Wang, C., Wang, Q., Ren, K., & Lou, W. (2009). Ensuring data storage security in cloud computing. In Quality of Service, 2009. IWQoS. 17th International Workshop on (pp. 1–9). IEEE.

Wood, K., & Pereira, E. (2010). An investigation into cloud configuration and security. In *Proceedings of the Internet Technology and Secured Transactions (ICITST)2010 International Conference* (pp. 1–6). IEEE.

Younis, M. Y. A., & Kifayat, K. (2013). *Secure cloud computing for critical infrastructure: A survey* (Technical Report). Liverpool John Moores University.

Zhang, X., Lai, S.-q., & Liu, N.-w. (2012). Research on cloud computing data security model based on multi-dimension. In *Information Technology in Medicine and Education (ITME), 2012 International Symposium on* (Vol. 2, pp. 897–900). IEEE. DOI: 10.1109/ITiME.2012.6291448

Zhang, Y., & Zhang, Y. (2012). Cloud computing and cloud security challenges. In Information Technology in Medicine and Education (ITME), 2012 International Symposium on (Vol. 2, pp. 1084–1088). IEEE.

Zissis, D., & Lekkas, D. (2010). Addressing cloud computing security issues. *Future Generation Computer Systems*.

Chapter 5
Developing and Implementing Cloud Security Frameworks:
A Comparative Analysis of Existing Models and Best Practices

Vishal Jain
https://orcid.org/0000-0003-1126-7424
Sharda University, India

Archan Mitra
https://orcid.org/0000-0002-1419-3558
NITTE University, India

ABSTRACT

Cloud infrastructure has improved corporate scalability and cost-efficiency, but it has also increased security vulnerabilities. Strong security mechanisms are needed to secure sensitive data and comply with regulations as cloud computing grows. This study compares the CSA Cloud Controls Matrix, NIST Cloud Computing Security Framework, and ISO/IEC 27017 cloud security frameworks. It examines their pros, cons, and suitability for multi-tenancy, encryption, and regulatory compliance. Organisations may use the paper's best practices to create complete cloud security strategies that mitigate evolving risks, scale, and comply with regulations. This analysis shows how organisations may negotiate the difficult security landscape by combining frameworks to protect their cloud systems. The findings show that the dynamic cloud ecosystem requires a coordinated strategy to modern security concerns.

DOI: 10.4018/979-8-3693-7137-4.ch005

I. INTRODUCTION

Background and Rationale

Cloud computing has indeed turned out to be a ubiquitous kind of technology in the business arena and also in healthcare as well as in government. Some advantages of migrating to cloud environments, such as scalability and flexibility, allow organizations with less infrastructure modernization or maintenance costs to migrate to those clouds (Zissis & Lekkas, 2012). As cloud data is more sensitive nowadays for processing and storage within most enterprises, the more this environment requires security aspects to be increased. Data breaches, cyber-attacks, and regulatory demands have increased the need for effective security measures to ensure information safety and privacy (Ali, Khan, & Vasilakos, 2015). Weak cloud security measures put organizations at a significant risk of losing data, unauthorized access, and reputational damage, which is why a strong security framework is essential (Almubairik et al., 2022).

With cloud computing now becoming the backbone of IT operations globally, security has become a serious concern. For example, between 2020 and 2021, there was a remarkable surge in the number of cloud security incidents, with a huge percentage being misconfigurations and poor security management (Sriraman & Gurusamy, 2022). Such incidents reinforce the need for well-structured security frameworks to protect cloud environments from potential vulnerabilities.

Currently, there are several existing cloud security frameworks, from the Cloud Security Alliance CSA Cloud Controls Matrix to the NIST Cloud Computing Security Framework and all the way to ISO/IEC 27017, every one of which offers a way to secure cloud environments but quite differently in scope, implementation, and overall effectiveness, thus making it harder for organizations to choose the suitable model for their needs (Zhang et al., 2010). Hence, there is a need for comparative analysis of these frameworks to identify best practices and guide organizations in developing and implementing robust cloud security strategies that respond to the evolving security landscape.

This paper is primarily aimed at studying and comparing existing cloud security frameworks to identify the strengths and weaknesses of the framework. This paper also aims to put forth best practices for developing an overall comprehensive cloud security strategy, considering the current and emerging challenges of cloud ecosystems.

Problem Statement

Despite the increase in cloud dependency, there is no unified standard of cloud security. The lack of a standard has made the security landscape disjointed, forcing organizations to go through different frameworks and security models to protect their cloud infrastructures (Gupta, Kumar, & Bhattacharyya, 2017). This fragmentation creates vulnerabilities in data protection, as organizations often face difficulties in selecting a suitable framework that fully addresses their specific security needs (Hashem et al., 2015). Moreover, as cloud computing continues to evolve, the threat landscape has become more complex, requiring security measures that can address new types of risks, such as insider threats, advanced persistent threats, and data exfiltration (Subashini & Kavitha, 2011). However, existing frameworks may not always keep pace with these emerging threats.

The diversity of cloud security frameworks, ranging from compliance and governance to technical controls, poses a challenge for organizations. Different frameworks have different focuses, such as threat management, encryption, and access control, which makes it difficult to implement a comprehensive security strategy (Jansen & Grance, 2011). Organizations often find themselves relying on a patchwork of security measures, which may not provide comprehensive protection against sophisticated cyberattacks.

Another significant challenge is regulatory compliance. Cloud security frameworks must comply with regional and international regulations, such as the General Data Protection Regulation of Europe or the Health Insurance Portability and Accountability Act in the United States. However, none of the frameworks are balanced in terms of compliance aspects, which creates a lot of gaps in security and ultimately may lead to legal damages for organizations (Almubairik et al., 2022). Without a widely accepted standard, compliance is further complicated by ensuring that the selected framework answers relevant regulatory demands.

Research Questions

This paper seeks to address the following key research questions:

1. What are the strengths and weaknesses of existing cloud security frameworks?
2. How do these frameworks align with emerging security challenges in the cloud ecosystem?
3. What best practices can be distilled from these frameworks to develop a more comprehensive cloud security approach?

These questions aim to provide a thorough analysis of the current cloud security landscape and identify areas where improvements can be made to better protect cloud infrastructures from evolving threats.

Scope

The present research aims at comparing and evaluating significant cloud security frameworks such as the CSA CCM, NIST CCSF, and ISO/IEC 27017. These frameworks were chosen as they are among the most commonly implemented strategies of cloud security, they differ in terms of the characteristic for addressing various facets of cloud security management (Zissis & Lekkas, 2012).

1. **CSA Cloud Controls Matrix (CCM)**: The CSA CCM provides a comprehensive framework for ensuring cloud security by focusing on various control domains such as risk management, data protection, and incident response. It offers a broad set of security controls applicable to different cloud service models (IaaS, PaaS, SaaS) and cloud environments (public, private, hybrid) (CSA, 2023).
2. **NIST Cloud Computing Security Framework**: NIST provides guidelines and recommendations for securing cloud environments, with a particular focus on public and hybrid cloud models. The framework addresses key security areas such as access control, data encryption, and identity management (Jansen & Grance, 2011). NIST's guidance is often considered highly adaptable to various regulatory environments, making it an essential resource for organizations aiming to comply with federal or industry-specific regulations.
3. **ISO/IEC 27017**: This International Standard provides recommendations on the ISMS controls relevant to the provision and use of cloud services. ISO/IEC 27017 supplements the widely used information security management system ISO/IEC 27001 with guidelines regarding cloud contexts (ISO, 2015). This he asserts that the security of a cloud infrastructure depends on both cloud services providers and the customers.

The comparative analysis will explore how these frameworks address key dimensions of cloud security:

- **Scalability**: How well each framework adapts to different cloud architectures and scales with increasing data volume and complexity.
- **Regulatory Compliance**: How effectively each framework ensures compliance with international and regional data protection laws.

- **Threat Management**: The ability of each framework to mitigate emerging threats, such as data breaches, unauthorized access, and advanced persistent threats.
- **Data Protection**: The robustness of each framework's approach to securing sensitive information through encryption, data loss prevention (DLP), and access control mechanisms.

The paper will compare and contrast these frameworks based on these dimensions to offer the best approaches of securing the cloud environments.

Even though cloud computing is becoming more and more popular, issues of security of these environments remain to be very crucial. This lack of a standard has resulted in numerous frameworks; all of which provide different methods by which cloud structures can be secured. Based on a comparison of the CSA Cloud Controls Matrix, NIST Cloud Computing Security Framework, and the ISO/IEC 27017, this paper aims at establishing a list of recommendations given towards the development of effective controls in the management of cloud security. Through an analysis of the above frameworks, this study will offer practical recommendations for organisations seeking to mitigate the emerging threats, within their cloud platforms.

II. LITERATURE REVIEW

Historical Overview of Cloud Security

Cloud computing has evolved significantly since its emergence, from being a niche service to becoming a basic part of IT infrastructure in many industries. The early benefits of cloud computing for organizations were that they could have scalable and flexible alternatives to on-premise servers while saving costs (Zhang, Cheng, & Boutaba, 2010). As more organizations began to shift to the cloud, however, security issues began to rise in tandem. In its earlier days, the convenience and flexibility were seen as the main attractions to cloud computing, which has otherwise posed inherent security risks, as such a distributed infrastructure is remotely accessible (Hashem et al., 2015).

High-profile incidents that exposed vulnerabilities within cloud environments led to the rise of cloud security concerns. For example, the 2014 iCloud breach, where private photos were stolen from several celebrities, highlighted the security risks associated with cloud-based storage services (Zissis & Lekkas, 2012). For example, breaches against major companies like the Capital One breach in 2019 illustrated how the misconfiguration of cloud environments could be leveraged to gain unauthorized access to sensitive information by cybercriminals (Sriraman &

Gurusamy, 2022). Such incidents and others have had a lot to do with shaping the direction of the development of cloud security frameworks as organizations and regulatory bodies push for better security.

As cloud computing grew, so did the threats. Besides unauthorized access and data theft, cloud environments introduced new challenges associated with multi-tenancy, data sovereignty, and insecure APIs (Gupta, Kumar, & Bhattacharyya, 2017). Multi-tenancy is a scenario in which several users share the same physical infrastructure; hence, an attack on one tenant may compromise others. Issues pertaining to data sovereignty emerged while organizations were trying to obey different countries' data protection laws due to the stringent data residency regulations in some jurisdictions (Subashini & Kavitha, 2011). In response to these emerging threats, a cloud security framework was adopted to provide structured approaches on cloud environments.

Existing Cloud Security Models

Since cloud technology introduces certain levels of security vulnerability, multiple frameworks have been created as discussed below because every framework has its strengths and areas of specialty. Three mainly known cloud security frameworks are Cloud Security Alliance (CSA) Cloud Controls Matrix (CCM), National Institute of Standards and Technology (NIST) Cloud Computing Security Framework, and ISO/IEC 27017. These models provide different strategies towards solving the security risks that come with cloud computation, although, they nearly everyone focuses on both technical solutions, compliance and governance structures.

CSA Cloud Controls Matrix (CCM)

The CSA Cloud Controls Matrix, or CCM, is one of the most well-known frameworks in cloud security. Developed by the Cloud Security Alliance, the CCM offers a comprehensive list of controls to be utilized in securing cloud environments, across multiple service models: IaaS, PaaS, and SaaS (CSA, 2023). The primary objective behind the CCM is the understanding of ensuring appropriate measures relating to cloud service providers and their customers, to adequately safeguard their cloud infrastructure and data.

The CCM is therefore divided into some major control areas, these are; compliance, risk, data security and incidents. These domains offer comprehensive approaches to cloud security so that all forms of the cloud environment are protected. For example, the data security domain is concerned with encryption, data obfuscation, and data transfer security; whereas the compliance domain is concerned with a regulatory regimen (CSA, 2023).

A characteristic of the CSA CCM is that it targets different classes of cloud and is relevant for public, private and hybrid cloud infrastructures (Gupta et al., 2017). Moreover, the CCM is used mostly by organizations that are interested in compliance with the international standards, which has similarities concerning the structure, goals, and objectives with the ISO/IEC 27001 and NIST.

However, there are limitations to the CCM. Critics say the framework can be cumbersome in practice, especially for small and medium-sized enterprises which do not have the ability to carry out all recommended controls (Zissis & Lekkas, 2012). Furthermore, while the CCM is indeed a broad framework, other security experts argue that the document does not specifically cover newer, cutting-edge cloud technologies like serverless computing or containerization (Sriraman & Gurusamy, 2022).

NIST Cloud Computing Security

NIST has for a long time been at the forefront in determining policies and architectures for protecting cloud platforms. The NIST Cloud Computing Security Framework offers a recommendation for cloud security controls that is most valuable for federal agencies and institution working in the environments that are highly regulated (Jansen & Grance, 2011). NIST's approach is geared towards control of risks that arise from access control, encryption of data and the use of threat controlling measures.

Now let me share you why the NIST framework is quite different from the other frameworks: The use of Risk as a basis for decision-making. NIST also advises organizations to evaluatc ccrtain risk with usc of cloud deployment and put Into practice controls that are appropriate to the demands and the situation of the firm (Jansen & Grance, 2011). For instance, the framework offers a comprehensive procedure on how organizations can protect multiple tenants' cloud applications through adequate IAM control mechanisms and pertinent encryption systems.

One strength of the NIST is that it remains quite structured, and critics point it out as inflexible where firms involved lie farthest out beyond those in the federal or strongly controlled domain (Hashem et al., 2015). Perhaps its compliance-governance style tends not to fit perfectly into most organizations looking forward to scalability solutions. Moreover, NIST does not accommodate newer emerging security challenges imposed by novel cloud-native applications like those about microservices or container-based workloads (Subashini & Kavitha, 2011).

ISO/IEC 27017

ISO/IEC 27017 which is another specification is specifically designed to guide on information security controls of cloud services. ISO/IEC 27001 is widely implemented for information security management and its clause set focuses on cloud environments through new term ISO/IEC 27017 that contributes best practices for CSPs and Cloud customers (ISO, 2015). Areas addressed by the standard include protection of data, security incidents, response to such incidents and regulations.

In our view, one of the major advantages of ISO/IEC 27017 is that it is a generic standard which is effective when used by international organizations that operate in different jurisdictions with different regulations (Almubairik et al., 2022). A key concept of the standard is that CSPs and customers have equal roles in managing security, and the customers must work in parallel with CSPs to establish security.

However, as it will be explained later own, like most cloud security frameworks, the adoption of ISO/IEC 27017 has its drawbacks. Lööv et al. (2013) further elaborates that while the standard provides guidelines in matters of compliance, it may not particularly well equip the cloud business with the general knowledge needed to master recent trends in cloud infrastructure techniques. Furthermore, it does not offer as much information about how to apply certain principles as other frameworks do; for example, NIST or CSA CCM do (Zissis & Lekkas, 2012).

Challenges in Cloud Security

Distributed and multi-tenancy by its nature, cloud environment security becomes even more challenging. The customers' and cloud service providers' shared responsibility model, while good for business models, also creates a challenging layer. One of the primary threats is multi-tenancy, where multiple tenants utilize the same physical resource, thereby creating a danger of leakage of data between different tenants if one of the tenants becomes compromised (Hashem et al., 2015). Frameworks such as NIST overcome this challenge by enforcing strict access controls and encryption, while the CSA CCM provides specific controls to manage multi-tenancy risks (Sriraman & Gurusamy, 2022).

Data sovereignty is another key challenge, which occurs when organizations must comply with data protection laws requiring data to be stored within certain jurisdictions. This challenge is relevant to multinational organizations that are operating in different legal environments. ISO/IEC 27017 addresses data sovereignty issues by providing recommendations on data residency and compliance with regional regulations (Almubairik et al., 2022).

Insecure APIs also represent a significant threat to cloud security, as they give attackers a means of exploitation of weaknesses in cloud services. CSA CCM helps to mitigate this challenge by advising controls to secure APIs through authentication, encryption, and monitoring (CSA, 2023). NIST also points out the secure management of APIs as part of a broader threat management approach (Jansen & Grance, 2011).

III. METHODOLOGY

Research Design

Following this, the present paper employs a comparative analysis to assess the previous cloud security models. Researched design: Comparative analysis is relevant for this study due to the possibility to compare multiple cloud security frameworks and evaluate them systematically throughout various criteria, including scalability and level of threats, compliance with regulations, ease of implementation, and costs. Thus, the goal of the study is to make a comparison of the chosen frameworks in order to expose the advantages and disadvantages of each one, as well as to help each organization decide which of the cloud security models can be the most effective one in terms of its needs and limitations.

The comparative analysis will primarily focus on three widely recognized cloud security frameworks: the Cloud Security Alliance (CSA) Cloud Controls Matrix (CCM), The National Institute of Standards and Technology (NIST) Cloud Computing Security Framework and ISO/IEC 27017.

Data Collection

To conduct this comparative analysis, the research will rely on two primary sources of data: researched a significant number of scholarly articles, white papers, and technical reports, and examine case studies from organizations that have subscribed to the two respective cloud security frameworks.

1. **Review of Scholarly Articles, White Papers, and Technical Reports:** The first source of data included a Systematic Literature Review of peer-reviewed journal articles, white papers and technical reports published on the topic of Cloud Security. In order to adopt a comprehensive approach to analysing both frameworks, this review will also incorporate academic and industrial viewpoints. To obtain scholarly articles, papers will be searched in IEEE Xplore, ScienceDirect and Google Scholar among some others. The industry reports such as the Gartner and Forrester, White papers from the CSA, NIST, and ISO

papers will be included so as to get an understanding of the current trends and problems encountered in the implementation of cloud security (Zissis & Lekkas, 2012).

2. **Analysis of Case Studies:** The second data collection approach entails the study of case studies from organizations that have integrated CSFs. Real life examples from the case studies enable the analysis of how these frameworks function and their strengths and weaknesses. Real-world case studies of organizations of varying size and type (healthcare, finance, government, etc) will be taken to determine how each of the frameworks fare relative to one another as well as compared to the specified cloud architectures (public/private/hybrid) and to different challenges (such as hack attacks and compliance – Ali, Khan, & Vasilakos, 2015).

Criteria for Comparison

To evaluate the cloud security frameworks adequately, this research will assess each framework on the five key criteria that include scalability, threat mitigation, compliance with regulations, ease of implementation, and cost efficiency. Based on their relevance to cloud security management and their importance in determining the overall effectiveness of a security framework, these criteria were selected.

1. Scalability

Scalability refers to the ability of a cloud security framework to adapt to different cloud architectures (public, private, hybrid) and to scale as the organization's cloud environment grows. Cloud environments often expand over time as organizations store more data, adopt new technologies, and increase their reliance on cloud services (Subashini & Kavitha, 2011). The effectiveness of a security framework depends on its ability to handle this growth without compromising security. For instance, CSA CCM offers controls that can be adapted to different cloud service models, allowing organizations to secure their environments as they scale (Gupta, Kumar, & Bhattacharyya, 2017). This paper will examine how well each framework supports the scalability of cloud architectures and whether it can efficiently manage security risks in large deployments.

2. Threat Mitigation

The first and most basic function of any cloud security framework is to mitigate the threats caused by cyberattacks, data breaches, and unauthorized access. Security threats usually are the aspects of examining how adequately a framework addresses key security threats, whether the given framework provides controls to take preventive actions, detect, and respond to security incidents. NIST framework highlights access control and data encryption among its priority elements for threat mitigation (Jansen & Grance, 2011). In contrast, the CSA CCM encompasses a more comprehensive set of controls that cater to cloud-specific risks, including multi-tenancy and insecure APIs (CSA, 2023). This criterion will evaluate the comprehensiveness of each framework's mitigation strategies for threats and how effective these are in avoiding common security incidents in cloud environments.

3. Regulatory Compliance

Regulatory compliance is a crucial factor for organizations that store sensitive data in the cloud. Each country has its regulations, and each industry has different laws concerning data protection, such as the GDPR in Europe and HIPAA in the United States (Zhang et al., 2010). To this end, a cloud security framework must be aligned to meet these regulations whereby organizations fulfill their obligations. For example, ISO/IEC 27017 has specific guidelines for cloud service providers and customers on compliance with international standards (ISO, 2015). This criterion assesses how well each framework supports regulatory compliance and whether it offers specific controls to address the data protection requirements of different regions and industries.

4. Ease of Implementation

Ease of implementation refers to how complex or simple it is to adopt a cloud security framework within an organizational setting. Some frameworks, for instance, the NIST Cloud Computing Security Framework, are quite prescriptive and can pose a problem for less-resourceful organizations in terms of implementation (Hashem et al., 2015). On the other hand, frameworks like the CSA CCM are designed to be more adaptable, offering flexibility in how controls are implemented depending on the organization's cloud architecture and security needs (CSA, 2023). This criterion will assess the implementation challenges associated with each framework, including the resources required for adoption and the level of expertise needed to deploy the recommended security controls effectively.

5. Cost Efficiency

Cost efficiency is an important element for organizations, especially SMEs, which need to secure their cloud environments without incurring too much cost. It is also expensive to implement and maintain cloud security controls, particularly if the framework requires investment in technology, personnel, and training (Zissis & Lekkas, 2012). Cost effectiveness is the financial feasibility of implementing the security controls recommended by each framework, including the upfront costs, maintenance, and return on investment. The study will determine the cost-effectiveness of each framework by focusing on whether the benefits of implementing the framework are justified by the costs incurred.

Data Analysis

The approach of the analysis is going to be based on a direct comparison of the chosen cloud security frameworks in connection with each of the five factors described above. The data of each framework will be analyzed to the aspect of modality, perspective, genre, time, type and space and then synthesized for the purpose of defining the strength and weakness of every framework as suggested by Bryman (2016). For instance, a framework may perform well on scalability and threat management then poorly on ease of implementation or cost implication, pointing to some of the blind spots that business needs to take into consideration when selecting a cloud security model. The comparative analysis will also take into account the exploratory needs of various niches of businesses, including SMEs and large-scale companies together with the peculiarities of highly regulated industry segments.

IV. COMPARATIVE ANALYSIS

Cloud computing has blossomed over the past decade as a result of which has led to the emergence of multi-layered security frameworks that seek to cope with risks attached to the technology in a procedural manner. Of these, the CSA CCM, NIST cloud security framework and ISO/IEC 27017 are perhaps the most recognized models. This comparative study seeks to understand the following differences; multi-tenancy, security features such as encryption, data loss, prevention, compliance and governance based on these two frameworks. Further, the frameworks' applicability to SMEs, the international applicability of the frameworks, and how the frameworks provide the needed assurance for different cloud infrastructures are examined.

CSA Cloud Controls Matrix vs. NIST

Multi-Tenancy

Both the CSA CCM and NIST frameworks discuss the areas of multi-tenancy as one of the primary difficulties that is inherent in cloud security since different customers can share the same physical environments. Multi-tenancy creates a possibility of one tenant's problem with security or setting up a vulnerable system that exposes others. The CSA CCM provides a list of controls that is perfectly suited for these risks since it implies that both the CSPs and customers are responsible for managing the risks (CSA, 2023). Regarding the isolation tenants' scheme, the framework gives a detailed explanation of how to control the tenants' access, networks' division, data encryption to ensure that tenants' information is secure.

On the other hand, NIST stress on good identity and access controls to mitigate multi-tenancy dangers. According to NIST, RBAC should be implemented with its advanced version, encrypted RBAC, to control access of a tenant by the other tenant (Jansen & Grance, 2011). However, this is where NIST misses the mark – while the guidelines laid down are sound, the CSA CCM proves more detailed when it comes to individual controls. The CSA approach that is based on the more focused concept of multi-tenancy is then considered to be more effective in dealing with the issues arising from shared infrastructure tenancy.

Encryption

Security is represented by encryption as an important component in both frameworks; however, the focus is different. The CSA CCM also calls for the encryption of data at rest and in transit, although it suggests using properly chosen encryption algorithms to protect the data (CSA, 2023). The framework also describes the means to manage keys, to guarantee that encryption keys are not only archived but also secured.

Similarly, NIST encourages encryption as a core security control recommended for use in shielding data stored in multi-tenant infrastructures (Jansen & Grance, 2011). However, the requirements are set more conservatively by NIST to define the minimum levels of encryption, for example, AES with 256 bits, and offer detailed recommendations on their use to federal organisations. Although both frameworks acknowledge the relevance of encryption, NIST provides technical descriptions of control specifications that make it preferable for organisations that require prescription.

Data Loss Prevention (DLP)

CSA CCM contains particular controls related to Data Loss Prevention containing the guidance as to how DLP solutions to enter monitoring and protecting of sensitive data from thefts, disclosure or leakage (CSA, 2023). It has many DLP recommendations that are included as much as other security measures like encrypting and needs access control making the tool ideal for more intricate data protection.

NIST, on the other hand, does not dedicate an independent condition on DLP, although it does go over data security and integrity (Jansen & Grance, 2011). Unlike ISO 27001, NIST's model looks at the big picture when it comes to data protection that includes aspects like protecting data from unauthorized access and being protected from unauthorized access. However, organisations which need certain DLP solutions may find CSA CCM to meet these needs more adequately.

Adaptability to SMEs vs. Large Corporations

Comparing both adaptability both of the frameworks applied to the SMEs and large corporations, it is obvious that CSA CCM is more flexible. It is easier to install in phases, meaning that it becomes easier for SMEs to implement especially when they cannot afford complex security controls at once (Leung, 2016). Enterprise level organizations have large scale security requirements to meet, and with the help of the CSA CCM the variety of controls that the large multi-tenant structures can utilize can help in compliance with regulations.

However, NIST's framework is widely appreciated for being elaborate which makes it appear to be developed for large organizations and federal agencies (Jansen & Grance, 2011). The level of detail along with the requirement of substantial resources for the deployment and sustenance of the NIST controls may be a challenge for the SMEs, especially those with lacking knowledge on cybersecurity. Consequently, whereas NIST is very successful for massive deployments, the CSA CCM provides better flexibility for any organisation.

ISO/IEC 27017 vs. NIST

Regulatory Compliance and Governance

ISO/IEC 27017 and NIST both emphasize regulatory compliance and governance, but their approaches differ significantly. ISO/IEC 27017 builds upon the ISO/IEC 27001 standard for information security management systems, extending its principles to cloud environments (ISO, 2015). This standard is internationally recognized and widely adopted, making it an excellent choice for multinational organizations that must comply with different regulatory environments. ISO/IEC

27017 addresses governance issues by outlining shared responsibilities between CSPs and customers, ensuring that both parties are accountable for cloud security.

NIST, on the other hand, is primarily focused on compliance with U.S. federal regulations, such as the Federal Information Security Management Act (FISMA) (Jansen & Grance, 2011). While NIST provides comprehensive guidelines for governance, its framework is more suited to organizations operating in highly regulated sectors within the United States, such as government agencies or healthcare institutions. For international organizations, ISO/IEC 27017 offers a broader and more flexible approach to governance and compliance, making it more suitable for global operations.

International Applicability and Adoption Rates

While ISO/IEC 27017 and NIST emphasize both regulatory compliance and governance, their approaches differ dramatically. This is because ISO/IEC 27017 based its standard on the generic ISO/IEC 27001 for information security management systems but expands it in terms of cloud environments (ISO, 2015). Being universally recognized and used worldwide makes it an ideal choice for multinational companies, especially when needing to adapt to a particular regulatory environment. ISO/IEC 27017 addresses governance issues by outlining shared responsibilities between CSPs and customers, ensuring that both parties are held accountable for cloud security.

NIST is, however focused on complying with the U.S. federal regulation, for example, the Federal Information Security Management Act (FISMA) (Jansen & Grance, 2011). Although NIST provides all-inclusive guidelines on governance, its framework is better suited for organizations that operate in highly regulated sectors within the United States, such as government agencies or healthcare institutions. ISO/IEC 27017 is perceived as a more flexible and broader approach compared to the governance and compliance that international organizations can observe under their global operations.

CSA Cloud Controls Matrix vs. ISO/IEC 27017

Securing Public vs. Private Cloud Environments

CSA CCM and ISO/IEC 27017 are developed to protect public, private, and hybrid cloud solutions, yet they have different strengths. The CSA CCM is even more suitable for obtaining security in public cloud since this model emphasizes multi-tenancy, access control, and encryption (CSA, 2023). The framework also contains specific procedures for dealing with associated risks of shared physical resources and obligates public CSPs to deploy appropriate security measures.

Although aimed at general use, ISO/IEC 27017 produces its best results in private and hybrid clouds because of integration with the more comprehensive ISO/IEC 27001 standard. This basic alignment means that private cloud environments are protected as conventional on-premise data centers; therefore, it is ideal if used for organizations migrating from private to hybrid clouds.

Flexibility in Responding to Cyber Threats

As both frameworks can be used in reactive MH, both are highly dynamic in reacting to quickly emerging advanced and new cyber threats, although they do so in different ways. Updates in CSA CCM are frequent®, capturing new threats that are apparent in cloud security and offering organizations best practices of protecting their assets (CSA, 2023). It is proactive in that it makes some provision for a framework for these newer technologies by which services are becoming increasingly defined, Cloud computing, lambda Architecture, serverless computing, containerization etc.

On the other hand, ISO/IEC 27017 is more flexible compared to ISO/IEC 27018 but pays less attention to new threats as it tries to uphold general security practices in cloud solutions (Almubairik et al., 2022). However, the strength of this approach is in the integrated governance and compliance controls for the new threats that apply effective compliance standards for organizations. However, if an organization requires the most current advice to counter threats and risks the CSA CCM may provide this.

However, when looking at these three cloud security frameworks it is easy to see how each of them has its benefits. The CSA CCM stands out in terms of flexibility, especially for SMEs and the public cloud; it also offers very concrete advice on tenancy and DLP. In turn, the NIST framework provides more constraining guidelines that provide prescriptive technical standards that would be well suited to large corporations and federal agencies. Also important for organizations operating in the global environment with a focus on effective governance, ISO/IEC 27017 can be applied to both public and private clouds. Finally, the decision depends on the particularities of the organization, the size, the regulation, and the cloud environment.

V. BEST PRACTICES FOR CLOUD SECURITY

Choosing and putting into practice the best cloud security architecture becomes crucial as more and more businesses move to cloud environments. Choosing the appropriate framework, executing a systematic approach, adopting a unified security strategy, and staying ahead of emerging trends are all components of best practices in cloud security. This section describes the selection criteria, highlights future trends in cloud security, offers implementation instructions, and suggests a cohesive approach by combining components of the main cloud security frameworks.

Framework Selection

1. **Organizational Requirements:** The security needs of the organization are assessed first with respect to the sensitivity of data that an organization might be dealing with. Therefore, for healthcare or finance, regulatory compliance-based frameworks like ISO/IEC 27017, developed for ensuring adherence to the international standards, such as GDPR or HIPAA are needed (ISO, 2015). Smaller organizations or startups having resources less than those of larger organizations would benefit from an even more flexible and scalable model like CSA's Cloud Controls Matrix, which can be phased in response to changing needs (CSA, 2023).
2. **Cloud Architecture:** The type of cloud environment—whether it is public, private, or hybrid—also determines what type of framework should be selected. For example, multi-tenancy within public cloud environments can leverage the CSA CCM quite significantly because it has established controls for managing risks concerning multi-tenancy, including tenant isolation (CSA, 2023). Thus, private and hybrid cloud users may like ISO/IEC 27017, which is closer in alignment to traditional on-premise security standards and provides controls tailored to secure private cloud architectures, according to ISO, 2015.
3. **Industry-Specific Needs:** Each industry has its unique security issues. For example, industries like healthcare, finance, and government are strictly regulated. The NIST Cloud Computing Security Framework is suitable for organizations that need to adhere to the U.S. federal rules, such as FISMA (Jansen & Grance, 2011). In contrast, organizations operating internationally may prioritize frameworks that ensure compliance across multiple regions, making ISO/IEC 27017 a better option due to its global recognition (ISO, 2015).

Unified Cloud Security Strategy

In order for a corporation to have end-to-end and solid security plan, it must ensure that the cloud security management has emulation from the whole of the CSA CCM, NIST and the ISO/IEC 27017. This consolidated way assumes the advantage of each framework to develop a comprehensive security model that meets the different needs of organizations dealing with cloud computing issues.

1. **Governance and Compliance:** As per the specification presented in ISO/IEC 27017, organisations must have a proper governance structure that also includes the CSPs and the customers (ISO, 2015). This also guarantees that security controls options comply with other regulations from various regions, including GDPR or HIPAA.
2. **Access Control and Multi-Tenancy:** In CSA CCM implementation of multi-tenancy and access control can help enforce the security strategy in cloud shared environments for protection of sensitive data. The CSA framework contains a lot of information about tenant isolation, encryption, and identity (CSA, 2023).
3. **Threat Detection and Incident Response:** The recommendations of NIST supplement recommendations on risk management and incident response, should be integrated to improve the organizations capability of identifying new threats. Having adopted guidelines offered by NIST, an organization can avoid unauthorized access and minimize the damage that will stem from a security breach, the ensuing guidelines include the following:
4. **Data Protection and Encryption:** This paper shows that organisations can strengthen their encryption practice from the NIST, CSA CCM and ISO/IEC 27017 where the later provides recommendation on data protection mechanisms for information technology. Combined, these frameworks assert that data must be encrypted – in storage and in transmission (Jansen & Grance, 2011; ISO, 2015; CSA, 2023).

Implementation Guidelines

A methodical approach that guarantees the security measures are flexible, scalable, and economical is necessary for putting into practice a thorough cloud security plan. The guidelines that follow provide a workable implementation process:

1. **Risk Assessment:** This step will start with a comprehensive risk assessment in the organization's cloud environment, assessing its vulnerabilities. It includes an assessment of data sensitivity, the type of cloud architecture used, and the kind of threats that are encountered by the organization (Hashem et al., 2015). The NIST RMF is used for assessing risks and prioritizing security controls (Jansen & Grance, 2011).
2. **Control Selection and Prioritization:** According to the risk assessment, relevant security controls should be chosen from the frameworks that are implemented for the organization. CSA CCM, for instance, provides modular controls where implementation can be done stepwise. For instance, such organizations can prioritize encrypting and identity management for priority controls (CSA, 2023).

3. **Policy Formulation:** Establish and enforce cloud security policies that fit the selected framework(s). These must include significant areas such as access control, data encryption, and incident response, among others, and regularly updated according to changes in technology and the threat environment (Gupta et al., 2017).
4. **Monitoring and Auditing:** Monitoring and auditing should be continuously performed to ensure that security controls remain effective. Tools like NIST's Continuous Monitoring (CM) process can be used in monitoring cloud environments and finding potential security incidents (Jansen & Grance, 2011).
5. **Training and Awareness:** A successful cloud security strategy needs training of employees on best security practices. Regular awareness programs can help reduce the risk of insider threats and ensure that staff understand how to handle sensitive data securely (Subashini & Kavitha, 2011).
6. **Incident Response and Recovery:** Develop and test incident response plans to ensure that the organization can quickly identify and respond to security breaches. NIST's incident response guidelines offer a comprehensive approach to managing security incidents, minimizing damage, and ensuring a swift recovery (Jansen & Grance, 2011).

Future Trends and Considerations

The constantly changing nature of the threat environment in cloud space requires looking into the future in the sphere of cloud security. An organization has to be functional in developing the pattern of security by integrating new technologies and ideas with them. Some key trends to consider include:

1. **AI-Driven Threat Detection:** Threat intelligence and both AI and ML applications are now being applied to threat intelligence. This kind of technologies can analyze large amount of data in real-time manner; detecting unusual incidents and possible intrusions into organizational security systems more efficiently than other approaches (Almubairik et al., 2022). It recommends that organizations should adopt AI based threat detection systems into their cloud security design in as a measure of preventing complex cyber threats.
2. **Zero Trust Architecture:** Getting more attention is the Zero Trust model, which means that no one, inside or outside a network, should be taken at their word. This approach demands constant authentication of users and devices that are more suitable for the cloud architecture since it is difficult to discern a clear boundary (Sriraman & Gurusamy, 2022).

3. **Quantum-Safe Encryption:** Problems appear when quantum computing came into existence which is making conventional cryptographic algorithms insecure. New forms of encryption to meet quantum threats are being deployed to counter the new potential threats afforded by quantum computers (Zissis & Lekkas, 2012). The use of quantum computing requires that organizations have to think long-term security, by implementing new encryptions that are not vulnerable to quantum computing.
4. **Serverless Computing and Container Security:** New aas such as serverless computing and containerization are increasingly being adopted in organisations, and therefore security measures in place need to cater for security challenges related to the two firms of technologies. These frameworks are becoming more dynamic with time to include CCM controls for serverless and containers architectures (CSA, 2023; Jansen & Grance, 2011).

VI. DISCUSSION

The comparative analysis of the Cloud Security Alliance (CSA) Cloud Controls Matrix (CCM), National Institute of Standards and Technology (NIST) Cloud Computing Security Framework and ISO/IEC 27017 provide the most rational understanding of how these frameworks contribute to improving the security situation in organizations that are active in cloud environments.

Synthesis of Findings

The comparative analysis highlights several key insights that can guide organizations in selecting and implementing appropriate cloud security frameworks.

1. **Multi-tenancy and Data Isolation:** Multi-tenancy remains a critical issue in cloud security, especially within the public cloud environment. The two standards, CSA CCM and NIST, give priority to tenant isolation through encryption, access control, and identity management. However, the CSA CCM provides more detailed controls to manage multi-tenancy risks, making it more versatile for shared cloud environments with a higher risk of data leakage (Cloud Security Alliance [CSA], 2023). For organizations using public clouds, these controls are essential to ensure that no tenant can compromise another's data.
2. **Compliance and Governance Regulation** ISO/IEC 27017 has proved to be the strongest framework of compliance with international standards and regulation. Its near resemblance with ISO/IEC 27001 also makes it appropriate for multinationals organizations whose data protection varies in every region they operate,

complying with different data protection regulations within jurisdictions (ISO, 2015). In contrast, NIST offers highly prescriptive guidance for organizations within the U.S., particularly in sectors like healthcare and government, but it lacks the global applicability of ISO/IEC 27017 (Jansen & Grance, 2011). Therefore, organizations with international operations should prioritize ISO/IEC 27017 to ensure regulatory alignment across multiple regions.

3. **Threat Detection and Incident Response**: NIST has been proven effective when it comes to providing biomorphic guidelines on threat identification, risk assessment and handling and incident response. Regarding IT security, the continuous monitoring and the encryption standards make it easy to identify possible security breaches in advance and thus their effects would not be severe (Jansen & Grance, 2011). Compared to NIST, the CSA CCM does provide threat mitigation controls, but as stated above and shown in the appendix, CSA gives organizations more freedom than NIST, but less direct direction on how to implement the controls properly (CSA, 2023). For organizations, which pay a lot of attention to the procedural aspect of the incident handling, NIST's framework is more coherent.
4. **Scalability and Flexibility:** The CSA CCM is particularly alignment-friendly in various cloud settings, public, private and hybrid clouds. Its use is relevant for both small and medium enterprises, and large companies because of its modularity that enables organizations to adopt each control security in turn. NIST on the other hand presents a very structured model that possibly would be better suited for large corporations that can actually incorporate most of the security measures highlighted by NIST. ISO/IEC 27017 gives a good middle ground between these two, providing good governance controls while leaving a lot of room for implementation of those controls (ISO, 2015).
5. **Cost and Resource Considerations:** CSA CCM provides reasonable value for money for small organizations since it enables progressive adoption according to desired security levels and resources on hand (CSA, 2023). Compared to NIST and ISO/IEC 27001, ISO/IEC 27017 is more heavyweight and may demand more dollars to spend on technologies and personnel to meet its requirements. Therefore, organization with constrained resources might find CSA CCM important due to flexibility and scalability it offers.

Theoretical Implications

This paper offers a view on the current cloud security advances based on the flexibility, adaptability, and compliance, which has enriched the overall state of the art of cloud security to protect various cloud enviroments. The use of a single cloud vendor, for example, using amazon, is slowly fading out due to the emergence of multi-cloud environments which are multiple environments that combine both private and public clouds hence calling for a security framework that can support all the different types of environments. The modularity of the CSA CCM is well suited to this requirement and offers theoretic framework for organizations to step by step adapt multi-cloud environments (CSA, 2023).

Also, the evaluation raises the importance and relevance of business responsibility in cloud security. Rawledge identified that while both ISO/IEC 27017 and CSA CCM assert that cloud security is shared between CSPs and customers, where each of them is charged with addressing diverse layers of security (ISO, 2015). Primarily this function of governance approach changes the nature of the management from being just a technical one to being an organizational approach that affects organizational policies of the employees and the customers.

The theoretical implication of this research also relates to the part played by compliance in securing the cloud. Cloud computing is an international concept that means guidelines that need to support diverse laws from one country to another. Since ISO/IEC 27017 has been harmonized with ISO/IEC 27001, it is an essential model of global governance of cloud security and serves as theoretical reference model for new cloud security models that need to include International operations (ISO, 2015).

Moreover, the result of the study demonstrates that the future advancement of cloud security will require incorporating more automation and artificial intelligence (AI) into threat identification and response. While practice, such as NIST, have already started implementing the use of continuous monitoring systems, the next generations of cloud security models need to depend on artificial intelligence and threats detection to address the rising levels of sophistications of threats (Almubairik et al., 2022).

Practical Implications

The implications are very tame in the real world sense as to how CSPs and organizations should proceed to ensure that cloud security is efficient.

1. **Selection of Framework Based on the Organizational Needs:** By and large, the analysis highlighted the fact that selecting an operational scale, the cloud architecture, and regulatory environment in the choice between different cloud security frameworks are going to have to go through the CSPs and the organizations. For instance, local associations involved in comparatively liberal sectors would select CSA CCM due to its modularity and affordable price range (CSA, 2023). However, larger organisations and those in highly regulated industries, as well as government agencies, should consider using NIST or ISO 27017 for

business-enabling technical controls and compliance (Jansen & Grance, 2011; ISO, 2015).

2. **Harmonized Security Measures:** This paper concludes that organizations can enhance their security posture through the adoption of the approaches taken from a range of security frameworks. For instance, a combination of CSA CCM's feature of multi-tenancy with NIST's encryption and capabilities in the area of incident response would be a better security feature (CSA, 2023; Jansen & Grance, 2011). They include putting in place IAM systems, encrypting both in-transit and in-storage data as well as periodic drills for responding to the breaches in-order to quickly contain them.
3. **Cost Efficiency and Resource Allocation:** A challenge in organizations, especially SMEs, is the allocation of resources toward cloud security. The above analysis has shown that because the CSA CCM operates through modularity, prioritizing what is critical with a basis on risk assessment could ensure optimum cost without compromising the aspect of security (Gupta et al., 2017). Larger organizations can invest in more elaborate frameworks, such as NIST, that provide guidance on implementing security controls across complex cloud environments (Jansen & Grance, 2011).
4. **Future-Proofing Cloud Security:** Organizations need to keep pace with emerging trends that will continue to shape cloud landscapes, such as AI-based threat detection, Zero Trust architecture, and quantum-safe encryption. AI-based monitoring tools shall make it possible to detect anomalies and potential threats much faster, decreasing response time to breaches (Almubairik et al., 2022). Adhering to the principle of Zero Trust entails constant verification of users and devices, which further intensifies security within distributed cloud environments (Sriraman & Gurusamy, 2022).

VII. CONCLUSION

This paper has provided a comparative analysis of three major cloud security frameworks— CCM, the NIST Cloud Computing Security Framework and the ISO/IEC 27017 guidelines are perhaps three of the most recognized methodologies for implementing security in the cloud computing environment. An analysis of all the findings indicates the fact that none of the frameworks can adequately capture all forms of cloud security needs while at the same time showing that each can fill a gap in certain environments, organization sizes, and industries.

The CSA CCM is highly valued for its flexibility and modularity, which makes it particularly useful in small and medium-sized enterprise environments and in public clouds. Its multi-tenancy granular controls and its flexible implementation approach make for an economical solution to secure their cloud infrastructures. NIST is more prescriptive in nature and provides a comprehensive methodology that is suitable for large corporates and government organizations in ensuring effective risk management as well as incident response. International use ISO/IEC 27017, whose governing emphasis and international application ensure maximum effectiveness for organizations with operation spanning multiple jurisdictions and industries, ensuring different kinds of regulatory environments.

The findings from this comparative analysis will not only enhance the theoretical understanding of cloud security but also provide practical insights for organizations in selecting and implementing the most suitable framework. Organizations can create a holistic security posture that is flexible and scalable, while maintaining compliance with regulatory requirements, by adopting a unified cloud security strategy that integrates the best practices from each framework. This will allow organizations to enhance the level of security for their clouds, reduce risks, and respond better to increasingly sophisticated cyber threats to cloud environments.

AI and machine learning are being more capable of better identifying threats with the Zero Trust security model and the use of quantum-safe encryption are expected to define future cloud security frameworks. To this end, organizations have to keep being on the lookout in order to implement necessary upgrades in security on such developments that are key in protecting their cloud structures. All in all, the identification of the cloud security framework and its subsequent integration and customisation can help organisations, settle in the stormy sea of the cloud, or rather can prevent or mitigate potentially devastating storms.

REFERENCES

Ali, M., Khan, S. U., & Vasilakos, A. V. (2015). Security in cloud computing: Opportunities and challenges. *Information Sciences*, 305, 357–383. DOI: 10.1016/j.ins.2015.01.025

Almubairik, A., Malik, M. S. A., Alotaibi, M., Hossain, M. S., & Ashraf, M. S. (2022). Toward comprehensive cloud security frameworks: Analysis, challenges, and future directions. *IEEE Access : Practical Innovations, Open Solutions*, 10, 73458–73475. DOI: 10.1109/ACCESS.2022.3183064

Bryman, A. (2016). *Social research methods* (5th ed.). Oxford University Press.

Cloud Security Alliance (CSA). (2023). *Cloud Controls Matrix (CCM)*. https://cloudsecurityalliance.org/research/cloud-controls-matrix/

Gupta, S., Kumar, D., & Bhattacharyya, A. (2017). Cloud computing security issues and challenges. *Journal of Network and Computer Applications*, 91, 41–52. DOI: 10.1016/j.jnca.2017.02.018

Hashem, I. A. T., Yaqoob, I., Anuar, N. B., Mokhtar, S., Gani, A., & Khan, S. U. (2015). The rise of "big data" on cloud computing: Review and open research issues. *Information Systems*, 47, 98–115. DOI: 10.1016/j.is.2014.07.006

ISO. (2015). *ISO/IEC 27017:2015: Information technology—Security techniques—Code of practice for information security controls based on ISO/IEC 27002 for cloud services*. International Organization for Standardization. https://www.iso.org/standard/43757.html

Jansen, W., & Grance, T. (2011). Guidelines on security and privacy in public cloud computing. *NIST Special Publication*, 800-144. DOI: 10.6028/NIST.SP.800-144

Sriraman, S., & Gurusamy, V. (2022). Cloud computing security models: Evolution and prospects. *Journal of Cloud Computing (Heidelberg, Germany)*, 12(1), 50–67. DOI: 10.1186/s13677-022-00312-1

Subashini, S., & Kavitha, V. (2011). A survey on security issues in service delivery models of cloud computing. *Journal of Network and Computer Applications*, 34(1), 1–11. DOI: 10.1016/j.jnca.2010.07.006

Zhang, Q., Cheng, L., & Boutaba, R. (2010). Cloud computing: State-of-the-art and research challenges. *Journal of Internet Services and Applications*, 1(1), 7–18. DOI: 10.1007/s13174-010-0007-6

Zissis, D., & Lekkas, D. (2012). Addressing cloud computing security issues. *Future Generation Computer Systems*, 28(3), 583–592. DOI: 10.1016/j.future.2010.12.006

Chapter 6
Emhdl-Ad: An Enhanced Metaheuristics With Hierarchical Deep Learning Approach for Cloud-Based CPS Attack Detection

Ruhiat Sultana
Lords Institute of Engineering and Technology, India

Syeda Meraj Bilfaqih
https://orcid.org/0000-0001-9865-1263
King Khalid University, Saudi Arabia

Akila Thiyagarajan
https://orcid.org/0000-0002-0869-8111
King Khalid University, Saudi Arabia

Ruheena Mahveen
https://orcid.org/0009-0006-5142-1384
King Khalid University, Saudi Arabia

ABSTRACT

A cyber physical system (CPS) combines networking components, computer resources, and several networked physical processes. It also monitors the application and operations of the computing system. With the increasing complexity of transmission networks, the link between the physical and digital worlds starts to pose a threat to security. The difficulty of analyzing and detecting cyber-physical threats in a complex CPS persists despite efforts to address this issue. An analysis of the CPS's security has been conducted by researchers using a machine learning (ML) based model. This research primarily focuses on the development of attack detection

DOI: 10.4018/979-8-3693-7137-4.ch006

methods in cloud-based CPS environments using hierarchical deep learning-based enhanced metaheuristics (EMHDL-AD). EMHDL-AD, as suggested, secures the CPS environment and recognizes different types of threats.To transform the incoming dataset into a format that is useable, data preparation is applied in the first step. Next, for feature selection (FS), the quantum Harris Hawks Optimization (QHHO) algorithm is applied.

INTRODUCTION

While revealing security flaws, CPS improves production quality and productivity. A crucial component of system security is the transmission network, which serves as a link between information and physical systems (B. Cassottana et al., 2023). The privacy of the CPS structure may be preserved via transmission network attack detection; but, when establishing focused attack detection strategies, the CPS's characteristics must be taken into consideration (V. Ravi et al., 2022). Constantly running CPS increased compute overhead, created a large amount of new network traffic datasets, and hindered attack detection. Aggressors that attempt to break and penetrate CPS-based systems are likely to target controlling software and networks (J. Zhang et al., 2021). When hackers breach a network and take control of physical systems, it interferes with the control software's execution, leading to manipulations or power outages (H. Mittal et al., 2022). By causing havoc with industrialized machinery and procedures, such attacks on CPS can result in a significant reduction.

More recently, machine learning (ML) approaches have been shown to outperform other methods in intrusion detection systems (IDSs) (S. Thakur et al., 2021). The ID approach uses software and hardware to recognize network intrusion. The deployment procedure of the entrenched model makes it possible to apply security control at the network level (C. Comert et al., 2021). Network- and host-based approaches are the two possible ways of ID. Features of categorization-based ID methods were extracted from online data (R. Colelli et al., 2021).

Data and information between a physical and virtual system in real-time (A. Presekal et al., 2023). CPS presents a huge revenue potential and has been of paramount importance IoT-related industries. The CPS considered the connectivity of the computer, physical, and network system. E-commerce, smart homes, e-health, and a number of other services are just a few provided by this developing Internet of cyber-physical things (K. Bitirgen et al., 2023). A lot of industrial machinery can be wirelessly operated using CPS, aiding in the running of large buildings with complex industries. The connected components of CPS are quite capable of handling IoT-based objects remotely and sensing their environment. Since it does its computation in real time, it is capable of amending the process as it runs. Says A.

E. Ibor et al., 2022, the CPS hence has the possibility to become imbued in several programs and applied through many fields of expertise: transportation, health care, IT fields, and the military.

LITERATURE

This work presents new approaches to optimize hybrid deep-learning technique parameters for better attack detection. Compared with other models, EMHDL-AD achieves the best results on accuracy, recall, and F1 score variables of the benchmark datasets. It can achieve maximum results of 99.55% when compared to FURIA, among other models. Greater TRAC/VDAC but lesser TRLS & VDLS were the superior results of the strategy. The most remarkable thing about ISSA's performance improvements was that it increased population diversity, avoided local optima, and enhanced global search and classification performance. This illustrates the potential of EMHDL-AD as a tool to defend against cyber attacks in CPS settings, including cloud-based systems. For industrial CPS security, Althobaiti et al. 2021, propose an IDS technique based on cognitive computing; one of the preprocessing phases is part of the proposed solution, which removes data noise. The hyper-parameter optimization of the GRU technique can be performed using the NADAM optimizer, which will finally improve the detection rate. In order to achieve near real-time localization of the attack, (Dutta et al 2021). develop a robust AD technique based on the semi-supervised ML algorithm. Anomalies based on reconstructed errors have been identified using the DNN model.

To identify cyber dangers from CPSs, (Li et al 2020). developed a method called Deep Fed federated DL approach. Using a CNN and a GRU, the author specifically created a new DL-based ID model for industrial CPSs. Furthermore, the author created a FL structure that facilitated industrial CPS in collaboratively creating an all-inclusive ID technique while maintaining anonymity. The final section of (Y. Yang et al., 2017) presents a survey on online privacy and security concerns.

The Equilibrium Optimizer Algorithm, the EOA, is the hyper-parameters in DBN method used to fine-tune it. For industrial CPS, there have been AI-based multi-modal fusion-based IDSs modeled by (Alohali et al, 2022). (Wang et al., 2022) created a CNN with the goals of significantly raising the anomaly detection rate, enhancing the performance of the industrial CPS system, and lowering method challenges. To improve the model's training stability, a robust system loss function is specifically taken into account during the training process(Tarun Kumar et al., 2023). An Industrial CPS (ICPS) IDS connected to the Diffusion model (IDD) was introduced by (Tang et al., 2023). Firstly, DD generates data equal to rare classes, balancing the training data with dissimilar classes. For a safe CPS platform, the authors proposed an optimal DBN-based distributed IDS (ODBN-IDSs) (P. Ramadevi et al., 2021). Furthermore, AI's ability to rapidly and precisely evaluate vast datasets drives advances in technology, healthcare, finance, and other fields (A. M. Anter et al.,2013; A. Rehman et al.,2021; G. Atteia et al.,2023). By incorporating AI, we may expect more personalized services, increased safety, and a smarter society with better infrastructure and quality of life (Tarun Kumar et al., 2024). Machine Learning (ML) and Deep Learning (DL) are at the heart of these breakthroughs, with applications in healthcare, finance, retail, manufacturing, and beyond (A. Rehman et al.,2021; Emary et al.,2014; T. Saba et al.,2019; H. Zawbaa et al.,2014). **Proposed System** This study introduced a new EMHDL-AD technique for cloud-based CPS platform attack detection. The CPS platform was protected, and several types of assaults were detected using the suggested EMHDL-AD method.

Figure 1. EMHDL-AD approach

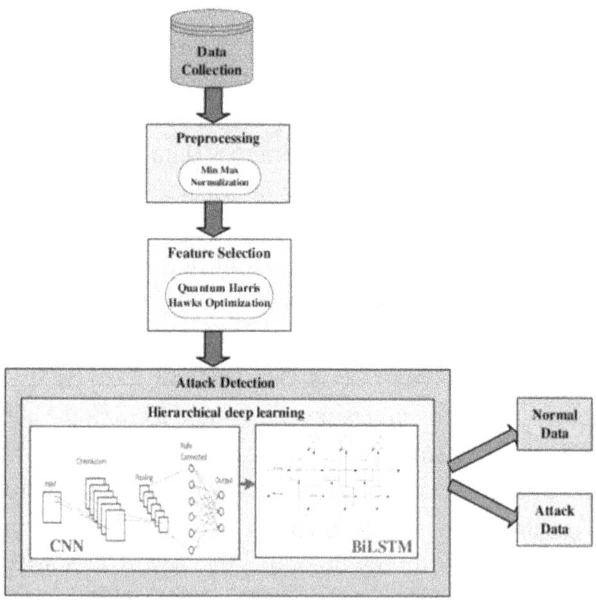

Data Preprocessing

The input dataset is transformed into a useable format through the application of a data preparation method. The suggested solution uses the min-max data normalization process to transform the input dataset into the proper format.

$$v' = \frac{v - min_A}{max_A - min_A} \tag{1}$$

The values of the maximum and minimum features A are denoted by $\min_A$ and $\max_A$ in Eq. (1). As a result, v and v'represent the original and normalized values of component A. The values of maximal and minimal features are correspondingly mapped to 0 and 1.

Feature Selection using QHHO Algorithm

The best feature subset is generated by using the QHHO model. The hunting habits of Harris hawks may be used to mimic the HHO algorithm (Sun, Y et al., 2021). The HHO uses two distinct strategies—the exploration and exploitation stages—to simulate cooperative hunting.

$$E = 2E_0\left(1 - \frac{t}{T}\right) \tag{2}$$

The parameter E in Eq. (2) symbolizes the prey's escape energy.

Exploration Phase

If $|E| \geq 1$, then they enter the exploration stage. They might monitor and stalk prey with their companions, or they might randomly perch in tall trees in search of prey. Assume that the location choice can be made between the two following approaches with equivalent probability:

$$X_{t+1}^{i,j} = \begin{cases} X_t^{rand,j} - r_1\left|X_t^{rand,j} - 2r_2X_t^{i,j}\right| & q \geq 0.5 \\ \left(X_t^{prey,j} - X_t^{av,j}\right) - r_3\left[LB^j + r_4\left(UB^j - LB^j\right)\right] & q < 0.5 \end{cases} \tag{3}$$

In Eq. (3), $X_t^{i,j}$ and $X_{t+1}^{i,j}$ denotes the present location of the i-*th* hawks at the j-*th* parameter and the newest location of the following iteration, correspondingly, $i \in [1, N_{pop}]$, $j \in [1, Dim]$, N_{pop} indicates the overall amount of hawks; *Dim* shows the dimension of the respective problem; $X_t^{rand,j}$ and $X_t^{prey,j}$ denotes the location of the hawk and the prey that are chosen randomly at the j-*th* variable, correspondingly. r_1, r_2, r_3, r_4 and q denotes the five dissimilar random integers ranging from zero to one. LB^j and UB^j indicate the lower and upper boundaries of the search range at the j-*th* parameter, $X_t^{av,j}$ indicates the present average location of hawks at the j-*th* variable as follows:

$$X_t^{av,j} = \frac{1}{N_{pop}} \sum_{i=1}^{N} X_t^{i,j} \quad (4)$$

Exploitation Phase

If $|E|<1$, then hawks are in the exploitation stage. During the exploration phase, they perform a raid, hunting on the prey that are observed and stalked. But, in the hunting process, the prey tries to escape from the hunt; hence, Harris Hawk adopts various pursuit methods for the escaping behavior of the prey. HHO developed a four-hunting tactic for stimulating the hunting and chasing behaviors, which exploits the escape probability r and the escape energy E for determining which strategy to adopt.

The hawk now employs gentle besiege to successfully hunt by taking advantage of the prey's physical strength. This tactic may be represented mathematically using the following formula:

$$X_{t+1}^{i,j} = \Delta X_t^j - E \times \left| Jump\, X_t^{prey,j} - X_t^{i,j} \right| \quad (5)$$

$$\Delta X_t^j = X_t^{prey,j} - X_t^{i,j} \quad (6)$$

$$Jump = 2(1 - r_5) \quad (7)$$

Where ΔX_t^j denotes the distance between the prey's present location at the j-*th* parameter and the existing location of the i-*th* hawks; r_5 shows the randomly produced number within [0,1], and *Jump* signifies random jump concentration that differs randomly within [0,2] at every iteration.

If $|E|<0.5$ and $r \geq 0.5$, then they don't have adequate energy to escape. The hawk has surrounded the prey and chooses a hard besiege faster raid hunt. The process description of these strategies is given below:

$$X_{t+1}^{i,j} = X_t^{prey,j} - E \times \left| \Delta X_t^j \right| \quad (8)$$

Now, the Harris hawk continues to consume the energy of the prey and establishes a complete encircle. This behavior model is shown below:

$$X_{t+1}^{i,j} = \begin{cases} Y_{t+1}^{i,j} \; if f\left(Y_{t+1}^{i,j}\right) < f\left(X_t^{i,j}\right) \\ Z_{t+1}^{i,j} \; if f\left(Z_{t+1}^{i,j}\right) < f\left(X_t^{i,j}\right) \end{cases} \quad (9)$$

$$Y_{t+1}^{i,j} = X_t^{prey,j} - E \times \left| Iump\, X_t^{prey,j} - X_t^{i,j} \right| \quad (10)$$

$$Z_{t+1}^{i,j} = Y_{t+1}^{i,j} + S^j \times L^j \quad (11)$$

$$L^j \sim LP(\mu^j, \nu^j, \beta^j) \tag{12}$$

The building block in quantum computation is a Q-bit that ranges within |1>, |0>, or superposition state |0> and 1|>. It is formulated by the incorporation of states |0> and |1>:

$$|Q \geq \alpha|0 > +\beta|1 > such\ that|\alpha|^2 + |\beta|^2 = 1 \tag{13}$$

In Eq. (13), α and β characterize complex numbers.

Eq. (14) represents the FF used to estimate the solution.

$$Fitness = \alpha\gamma_R(D) + \beta\frac{|R|}{|C|} \tag{14}$$

Optimal HDL-based Attack Detection

For classification purposes, the ISSA with HDL classifier is exploited for attack detection. The BiLSTM is encompassed forward and backward LSTM (Jiang, K et al., 2021). The backward and forward LSTM hidden layers (HLs) are accountable for backward and forward feature extraction. The usage of BiLSTM considers the effect of all the attributes after and before in the sequence dataset. Therefore, wide-ranging feature data can be attained.

$$h_t^{forward} = LSTM^{forward}\left(h_{t-1}, x_t, C_{t-1}\right) \tag{15}$$

$$h_t^{backward} = LSTM^{backward}\left(h_{t-1}, x_t, C_{t-1}\right) \tag{16}$$

$$H_t = \left[h_t^{fomard}, h_t^{bacward}\right] \tag{17}$$

BiLSTM and CNN are representatives of the DL technique. CNN feature extraction in the spatial dimension. BiLSTM has the characteristics to preserve the context of past data for a longer time and realize the extraction of data features. The study integrated CNN with Bi-LSTM to extract features and create a deep hierarchical network system.

HyperparameterTuning

The leader and followers have two different roles in the Salp chain. The leader is answerable to lead the whole population, whereas the follower follows consecutively.

The SSA is a metaheuristic approach that implements random initialization. Since it might mitigate the local optima problems, enhance the diversity of the population, make the algorithm find the optimum solution more rapidly, and improve global search ability. Remarkably, chaotic sequences have randomness and outstanding ergodicity; furthermore, in the searching space, their pseudo-randomness provides stronger uniformity and is equally distributed all over the search space.

$$X_{i+1} = sin\left(\frac{b\pi}{\chi}\right) \tag{18}$$

Where b is randomly generated within [0,1], Fig. 2 demonstrates the steps included in ISSA.

Figure 2. Demonstrates the steps included in ISSA.

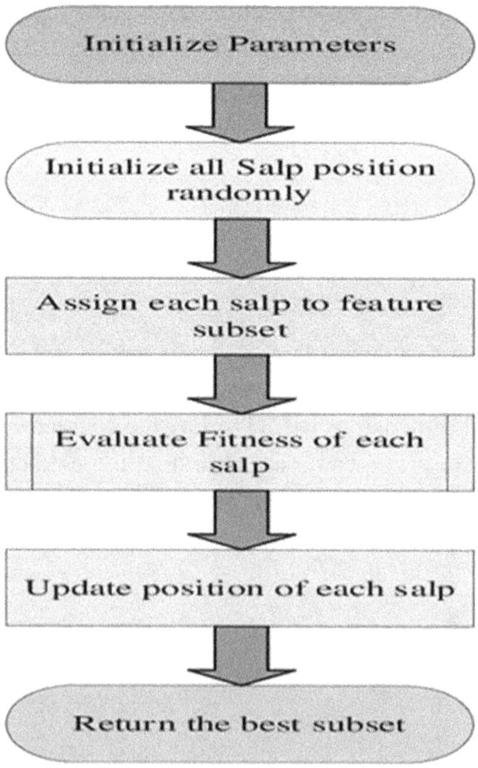

Algorithm 1. Salp Swarm Algorithm

```
Np: population size
Initialize the location of the population;
Calculate the fitness of all the individuals;
Set the better agent as FoodPosition (F) and the better fitness as FoodFitness;
WhileFEs≤MaxFEs
Evaluate c1;
Fori=1: Np
      Ifi≤Np/2
            Arbitrarily compute r1 and r2;
            Evaluate the leader;
      Else ifi<Np+1 && i>Np/2
            Evaluate the followers;
      End if
End for
Compute if the individuals are beyond the upper and lower boundaries;
Assess the fitness of the population;
Upgrade FoodPosition (F) and FoodFitness;
End while
ReturnF
```

The ISSA model not only derives an FF to obtain a higher classification performance but also describes a positive integer to symbolize better outcomes for the solution candidate.

Salp Swarm Algorithm is shown above.

RESULTS

In this study, we have studied the attack detection In Table I. The NSLKDD2015 dataset comprises 67343 normal instances and 58630 anomaly instances. Likewise, the CICIDS2017 dataset encompasses 50000 normal and 50000 abnormal instances.

Table 1. Details Of The Database

Class	Number of Instances	
	CICIDS 2017	NSLKDD 2015
Anomaly	50000	58630
Normal	50000	67343
Total Number of Instances	**100000**	**125973**

The attack detection results attained at the time of execution under the NSLKDD2015 database are exemplified in Figure 4. The confusion matrices showed that the EMHDL-AD method recognized the normal and anomaly instances on the NSLKDD2015 dataset. In Table II, the brief attack EMHDL-AD model

NSLKDD2015 dataset. The experimental outcomes pointed out that the EMHDL-AD approach achieved enhanced performance in all aspects. On the total database, the EMHDL-AD $prec_n$ of 98.50%, $reca_l$ of 98.51%, F_{score} of 98.51%, and AUC_{score} of 98.51%. Meanwhile, on 70% of the TR set, the EMHDL-AD method accomplishes an average $accu_{bal}$ of 98.49%, $prec_n$ of 98.49%, $reca_l$ of 98.49%, F_{score} of 98.49%, and AUC_{score} of 98.49%. Moreover, on 30% of the TS set, the EMHDL-AD system achieves an average $accu_{bal}$ of 98.55%, $prec_n$ of 98.55%, $reca_l$ of 98.55%, F_{score} of 98.55%, and AUC_{score} of 98.55%.

The EMHDL-AD approach's TRAC and VDAC are shown in Figure 4 on the NSLKDD2015 database. Because of the greater TRAC and VDAC values, the result indicates that the EMHDL-AD technique provides a better solution. The EMHDL-AD approach has improved TRAC results. The TRLS and VDLS of the EMHDL-AD system on the NSLKDD2015 database are shown in Figure 7. The image demonstrates how the EMHDL-AD strategy yields superior outcomes with reduced TRLS and VDLS values. The EMHDL-AD strategy has produced the least VDLS outcomes.

Figure 3. Confusion matrices of EMHDL-AD method on NSLKDD2015 database (a) Entire, (b) 80% of TR set, and (c) 40% of TS set.

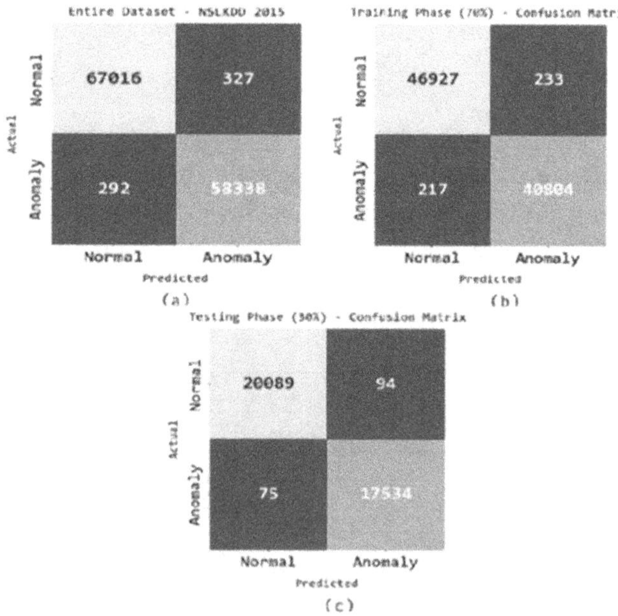

Table 2. Attack classifier outcome of EMHDL-AD model on the NSLKDD2015 dataset

Class	$Accu_y$	$Prec_n$	$Reca_l$	F_{score}	AUC_{score}
Entire Dataset					
Normal	98.51	98.57	98.51	98.54	98.51
Anomaly	98.50	98.44	98.50	98.47	98.51
Average	**98.51**	**98.50**	**98.51**	**98.51**	**98.51**
Training Phase (70%)					
Normal	98.51	98.54	98.51	98.52	98.49
Anomaly	98.47	98.43	98.47	98.45	98.49
Average	**98.49**	**98.49**	**98.49**	**98.49**	**98.49**
Testing Phase (30%)					
Normal	98.53	98.63	98.53	98.58	98.55
Anomaly	98.57	98.47	98.57	98.52	98.55
Average	**98.55**	**98.55**	**98.55**	**98.55**	**98.55**

A brief PR evaluation of SOSDCNN-HAR method using NSLKDD2015 Fig. 6. demonstrated that PR values generated by SOSDCNN-HAR scheme were maximal in all classes. Fig. 7 displays the attack detection results obtained at the time of execution under CICIDS2017 database. The EMHDL-AD method correctly identified normal and abnormal occurrences on the CICIDS2017 dataset, according to confusion matrices.

Figure 4. Results of the EMHDL-AD method for TRAC and VDAC on the NSLKDD2015 database.

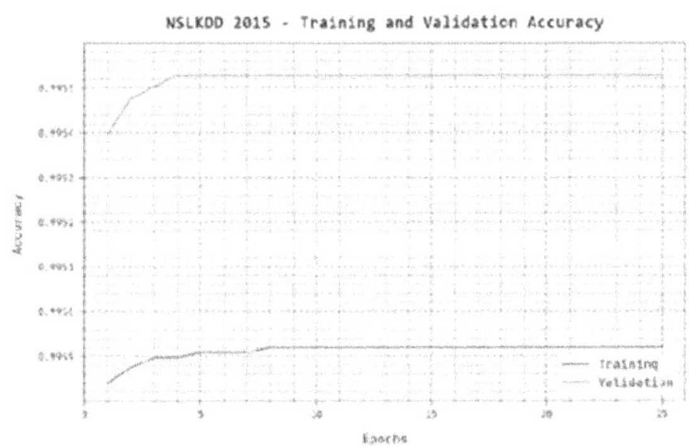

Figure 5. Results of the EMHDL-AD technique for TRLS and VDLS on the NSLKDD2015 dataset.

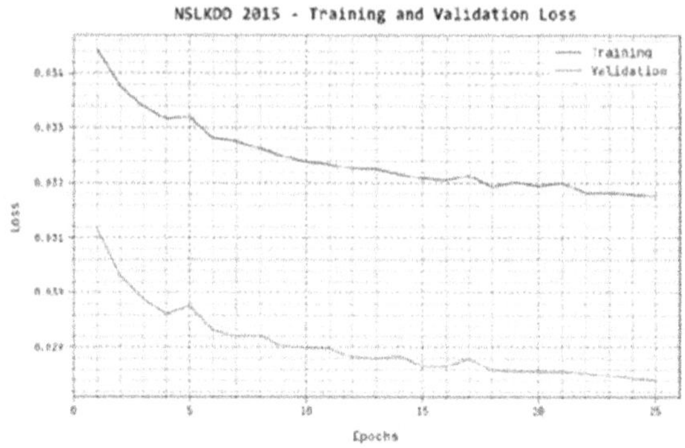

Figure 6. PR analysis of EMHDL-AD method on the NSLKDD2015 database.

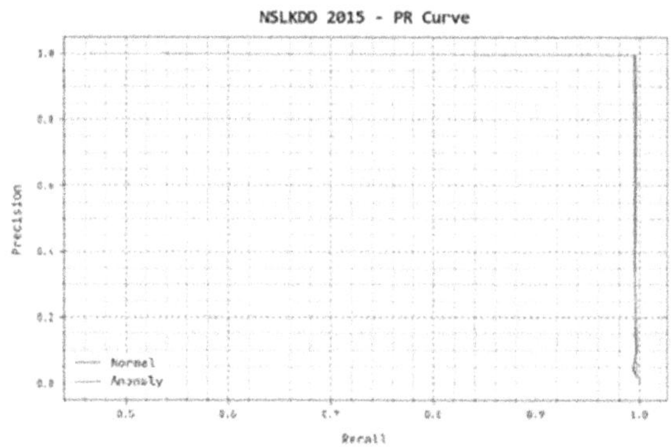

Figure 7. Matrices of EMHDL-AD model on CICIDS2017 database (a) Entire, (b) 80% of TR set, and (c) 40% of TS set.

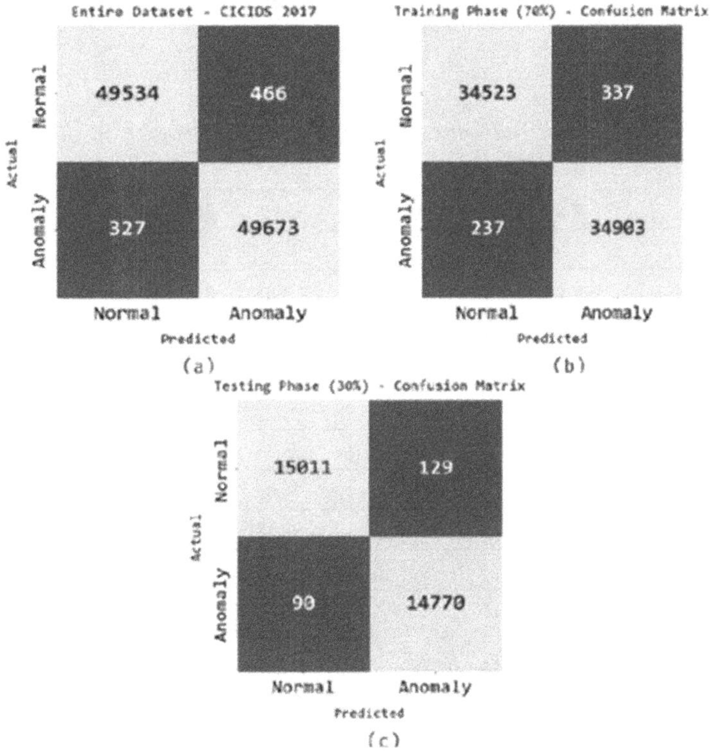

Table 3 examines the EMHDL-AD method's short attack categorization results under the CICIDS2017 dataset. The result exhibits the EMHDL-AD is the best. Overall the EMHDL-AD technique accomplishes an average $accu_{bal}$ of 99.21%, $prec_n$ of 99.21%, $reca_l$ of 99.21%, F_{score} of 99.21%, and AUC_{score} of 99.21%. Meanwhile, on 70% of the TR set, the EMHDL-AD technique attains an average $accu_{bal}$ of 99.18%, $prec_n$ of 99.18%, $reca_l$ of 99.18%, F_{score} of 99.18%, and AUC_{score} of 99.18%. Furthermore, on 30% of the TS set, the EMHDL-AD method accomplishes an average $accu_{bal}$ of 99.27%, $prec_n$ of 99.27%, $reca_l$ of 99.27%, F_{score} of 99.27%, and AUC_{score} of 99.27%.

Figure 11 describes the TRAC and VDAC of the EMHDL-AD approach on the CICIDS2017 database. The result suggests that the EMHDL-AD model has shown a good solution with higher TRAC and VDAC values. Improved TRAC results have been attained with the EMHDL-AD technique. The TRLS and VDLS of the EMHDL-AD method on the CICIDS2017 datasets are revealed in Fig. 12. The result indicates that the EMHDL-AD algorithm performed better when the values of TRLS and VDLS were lower. Less VDLS solutions have been obtained with

EMHDL-AD technique. A clear PR analysis of the SOSDCNN-HAR technique using CICIDS2017 database is displayed in Fig. 10. The outcome showed that the PR values for the two classes have increased as a consequence of the SOSDCNN-HAR approach.

Table 3. Attack classifier outcome of EMHDL-AD approach on the CICIDS2017 dataset

Class	$Accu_y$	$Prec_n$	$Reca_n$	F_{score}	AUC_{score}
Entire Dataset					
Anomaly	99.35	99.07	99.35	99.21	99.21
Normal	99.07	99.34	99.07	99.21	99.21
Mean	**99.21**	**99.21**	**99.21**	**99.21**	**99.21**
Training Phase (70%)					
Anomaly	98.33	98.04	98.33	98.18	98.18
Normal	98.03	98.32	98.03	98.18	98.18
Mean	**98.18**	**98.18**	**98.18**	**98.18**	**98.18**
Testing Phase (30%)					
Anomaly	99.39	99.13	99.39	99.26	99.27
Normal	99.15	99.40	99.15	99.28	99.27
Mean	**99.27**	**99.27**	**99.27**	**99.27**	**99.27**

Figure 8. TRAC and VDAC outcome of EMHDL-AD algorithm on the CICIDS2017 database

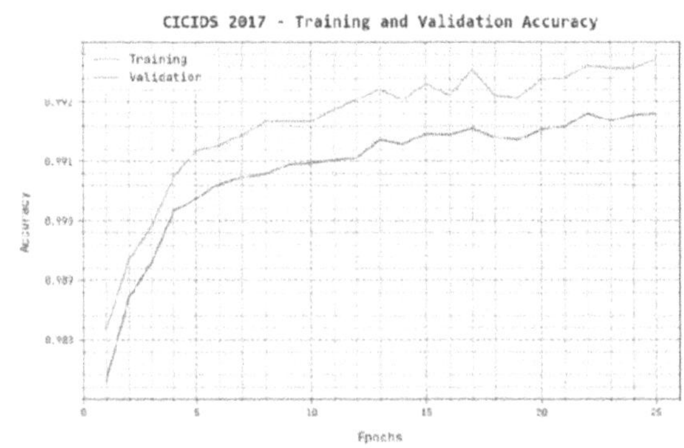

Figure 9. TRLS and VDLS outcome of EMHDL-AD approach on CICIDS2017 dataset.

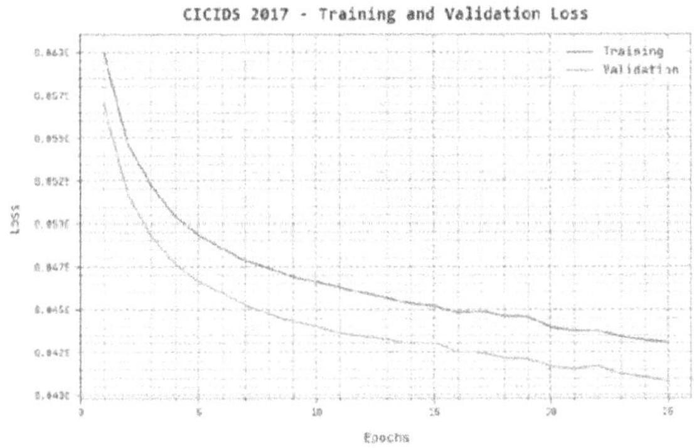

Figure 10. PR outcome of EMHDL-AD approach on the CICIDS2017 dataset.

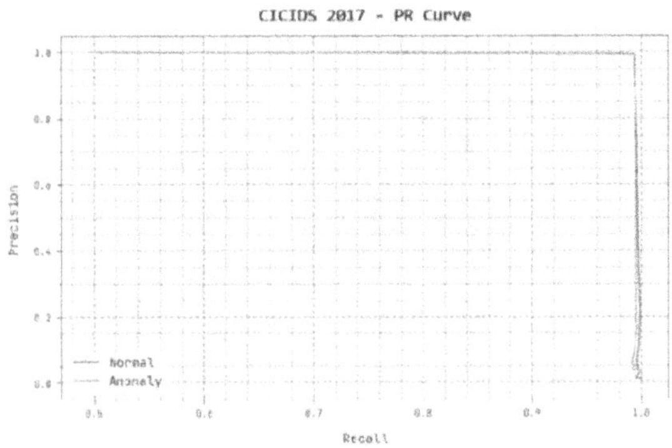

Table 4 and Fig. 11 presents the higher performance of the EMHDL-AD approach (Duhayyim, M.A et al., 2022). The outcome demonstrates the least efficiency of the Forest-PA and WISARD techniques. Next, the AE-RF, LIB-SVM, and FURIA models accomplish reasonably nearer attack detection outcomes. Nevertheless, the EMHDL-AD technique highlights the superior outcomes over existing techniques with a maximumreca_l of 98.55%, prec_n of 98.55%,F1_score of 98.55%, and accu_y of 98.55% These outcomes showcased the optimum outcomes of EMHDL-AD technique over other methods.

Table 4. Comparison of The Emhdl-Ad Model's Results With Those of Other Recent Methods

Methods	$Prec_n$	$Reca_l$	$Accu_y$	$F1_{score}$
EMHDL-AD	99.55	99.55	99.55	99.55
FURIA Model	97.51	97.35	99.21	98.95
GSAE Model	96.69	99.48	97.93	97.45
AE-RF Model	97.59	98.92	97.43	97.85
LIB-SVM Model	97.53	98.09	97.21	98.15
Forest-PA Model	97.75	97.06	96.47	98.61
WISARD Model	97.39	96.95	96.09	99.48

Figure 11. Analysis of the EMHDL-AD

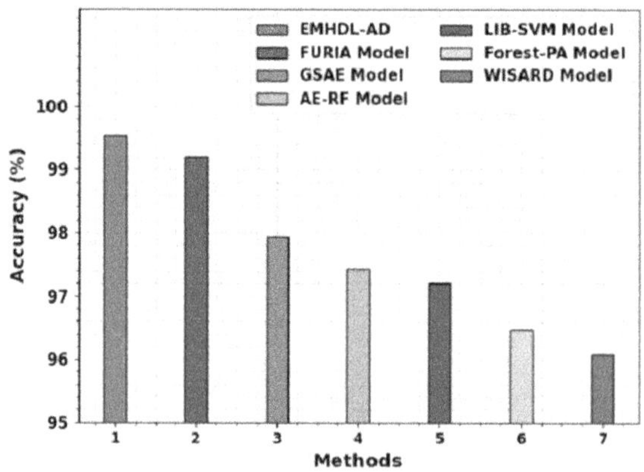

CONCLUSION

In this work, a novel EMHDL-AD algorithm was developed to detect attacks on the cloud-based CPS platform. The CPS platform was secured, and the recommended EMHDL-AD technique was used to identify multiple kinds of attacks. Data preparation was first used to transform the input database into formats that were appropriate. Next, for FS, the QHHO algorithm is applied. The HDL classifier and ISSA work together to detect attacks. The ISSA is designed to enhance the HDL technique's hyper parameters, enabling it to identify multiple attacks. A benchmark database is used to assess the EMHDL-AD method's performance analysis, and the experimental results demonstrate the methodology's superiority over other current approaches.

The presented scheme of research work proposes integrating data pre-processing with Quantum Harris Hawks Optimization (QHHO)-based feature selection and an efficient Salp Swarm Algorithm (ISSA) optimized hierarchical deep learning classifier for effectively detecting cyber attacks.

Summary of Findings

The proposed EMHDL-AD approach has been applied to benchmark intrusion datasets and yielded much-improved results with respect to the existing approaches. The high value of all parameters reflect the robustness and effectiveness of this approach in detecting various types of attacks.

Limitations of the Study

Despite the promising results, the study has certain limitations:

1. Diversity in the dataset: Specific benchmark datasets were employed for this validation and, hence, cannot cover all scenarios of different attack types. Further validation on a broader range of datasets will be required for full certainty of generalization of this approach.
2. Computational Complexity: This work has involved exhaustive computation in the processes of feature selection and optimization of hyper parameter values. Thus, enhancing computational efficiency of this approach may be a scope of future work.
3. Real-world Deployment: The proposed method has been evaluated within an emulated and experimentally controlled environment. Deploying it into a real world setting will raise further issues like noise in data, dynamic changing of attack patterns, or interaction with an already deployed security solution.

Implications of the Results

The results obtained by this research provide some significant implications related to CPS security:

1. Improved Security: The enhanced detection capability of the EMHDL-AD method would significantly improve the security of CPS in several domains such as smart cities.

2. Adaptive Detection: Dynamic hyper parameter optimization with effective feature selection mechanisms makes this method adaptive to different kinds of attacks, thus guaranteeing robust and reliable security in CPS environments.
3. Scalability: In this regard, the method is suitable for cloud-based CPS platforms due to its ability to efficiently handle large datasets.

Future Research Directions

The limitations discussed earlier and the following areas need to be considered for future research:

1. Coverage Expansion of Dataset: Use a wider range of datasets in testing the performance of the method against different attack scenarios and CPS environments.
2. Computational Efficiency: The development of methods to reduce computational complexity and increase processing speed.
3. Real-World Application: To apply the methodology on CPS test beds under realistic conditions in order to find out about practical usability.

This can be concluded as the basis that the EMHDL-AD has a promising way of bringing much security to the cloud-based CPS by providing substantial detection and adapting it to different attack scenarios.

REFERENCES

Alohali, M. A., Al-Wesabi, F. N., Hilal, A. M., Goel, S., Gupta, D., & Khanna, A. (2022). Artificial intelligence enabled intrusion detection systems for cognitive cyber-physical systems in industry 4.0 environment. *Cognitive Neurodynamics*, 16(5), 1045–1057. DOI: 10.1007/s11571-022-09780-8 PMID: 36237400

Althobaiti, M. M., Kumar, K. P. M., Gupta, D., Kumar, S., & Mansour, R. F. (2021). An intelligent cognitive computing based intrusion detection for industrial cyber-physical systems. *Measurement*, 186, 110145. DOI: 10.1016/j.measurement.2021.110145

Anter, A. M., Azar, A. T., El-Bendary, N., Hassanien, A. E., & Abu ElSoud, M. "Automatic computer aided segmentation for liver and hepatic lesions using hybrid segmentations techniques," in *2013 Federated Conference on Computer Science and Information Systems (FedCSIS)*, Kraków, Poland, Sep. 8-11, 2013.

Atteia, G., El-kenawy, E. M., Samee, N. A., Jamjoom, M. M., Ibrahim, A., Abdelhamid, A. A., Azar, A. T., Khodadadi, N., Ghanem, R. A., & Shams, M. Y. (2023). Adaptive dynamic dipper throated optimization for feature selection in medical data. *Computers, Materials & Continua*, 75(1), 1883–1900. DOI: 10.32604/cmc.2023.031723

Bitirgen, K., & Filik, Ü. B. (2023). A hybrid deep learning model for discrimination of physical disturbance and cyber-attack detection in smart grid. *International Journal of Critical Infrastructure Protection*, 40, 100582. DOI: 10.1016/j.ijcip.2022.100582

Cassottana, B., Roomi, M. M., Mashima, D., & Sansavini, G. (2023). Resilience analysis of cyber-physical systems: A review of models and methods. *Risk Analysis*, 43(11), 2359–2379. Advance online publication. DOI: 10.1111/risa.14089 PMID: 36646448

Colelli, R., Magri, F., Panzieri, S., & Pascucci, F. (2021, June). Anomaly-based intrusion detection system for cyber-physical system security. In 2021 29th Mediterranean Conference on Control and Automation (MED) (pp. 428-434). IEEE.

Comert, C., Gul, O. M., Kulhandjian, M., Touazi, A., Ellement, C., Kantarci, B., & D'Amours, C. (2022). Secure design of cyber-physical systems at the radio frequency level: Machine and deep learning-driven approaches, challenges and opportunities. Artificial Intelligence for Cyber-Physical Systems Hardening, 123-154.

Duhayyim, M. A., Alissa, K. A., Alrayes, F. S., Alotaibi, S. S., Tag El Din, E. M., Abdelmageed, A. A., Yaseen, I., & Motwakel, A. (2022). Evolutionary-Based Deep Stacked Auto encoder for Intrusion Detection in a Cloud-Based Cyber-Physical System. *Applied Sciences (Basel, Switzerland)*, 12(14), 6875. DOI: 10.3390/app12146875

Dutta, A. K., Negi, R., & Shukla, S. K. (2021). Robust multivariate anomaly-based intrusion detection system for cyber-physical systems. In Cyber Security Cryptography and Machine Learning: 5th International Symposium, CSCML 2021, Be'er Sheva, Israel, July 8–9, 2021 [Springer International Publishing.]. *Proceedings*, 5, 86–93.

Emary, E., Zawbaa, H. M., Hassanien, A. E., Schaefer, G., & Azar, A. T. (2014, July). Retinal blood vessel segmentation using bee colony optimisation and pattern search. In 2014 international joint conference on neural networks (IJCNN) (pp. 1001-1006). IEEE.

Emary, E., Zawbaa, H. M., Hassanien, A. E., Schaefer, G., & Azar, A. T. (2014, July). Retinal vessel segmentation based on possibilistic fuzzy c-means clustering optimised with cuckoo search. In *2014 International Joint Conference on Neural Networks (IJCNN)* (pp. 1792-1796). IEEE.

Hao, S., Huang, C., Heidari, A. A., Chen, H., Li, L., Algarni, A. D., Elmannai, H., & Xu, S. (2023). Salp swarm algorithm with iterative mapping and local escaping for multi-level threshold image segmentation: A skin cancer dermoscopic case study. *Journal of Computational Design and Engineering*, 10(2), 655–693. Advance online publication. DOI: 10.1093/jcde/qwad006

Ibor, A. E., Okunoye, O. B., Oladeji, F. A., & Abdulsalam, K. A. (2022). Novel hybrid model for intrusion prediction on cyber physical systems' communication networks based on bio-inspired deep neural network structure. *Journal of Information Security and Applications*, 65, 103107. DOI: 10.1016/j.jisa.2021.103107

Jiang, K., Wang, W., Wang, A., & Wu, H. (2020). Network intrusion detection combined hybrid sampling with deep hierarchical network. *IEEE Access : Practical Innovations, Open Solutions*, 8, 32464–32476. DOI: 10.1109/ACCESS.2020.2973730

Kumar, T., Kumar, P., & Namasudra, S. (2024, February). Secure Access Control of Cloud Data Using DNA Computing. In 2024 IEEE International Conference on Computing, Power and Communication Technologies (IC2PCT) (Vol. 5, pp. 1996-2001). IEEE.

Kumar, T., Kumar, P., & Namasudra, S. (2024, February). A DNA-based Authentication System for Securing Cloud Data Storage and Transactions. In 2024 11th International Conference on Computing for Sustainable Global Development (INDIACom) (pp. 1692-1698). IEEE.

Kumar, T., Namasudra, S., & Kumar, P. (2023). Providing data security using DNA computing in the cloud computing environment. *International Journal of Web and Grid Services*, 19(4), 463–486. Advance online publication. DOI: 10.1504/IJWGS.2023.135587

Li, B., Wu, Y., Song, J., Lu, R., Li, T., & Zhao, L. (2020). Deep Fed: Federated deep learning for intrusion detection in industrial cyber–physical systems. *IEEE Transactions on Industrial Informatics*, 17(8), 5615–5624. DOI: 10.1109/TII.2020.3023430

Mittal, H., Tripathi, A. K., Pandey, A. C., Alshehri, M. D., Saraswat, M., & Pal, R. (2022). A new intrusion detection method for cyber–physical system in emerging industrial IoT. *Computer Communications*, 190, 24–35. DOI: 10.1016/j.comcom.2022.04.004

Presekal, A., Ştefanov, A., Rajkumar, V. S., & Palensky, P. (2023). Attack graph model for cyber-physical power systems using hybrid deep learning. *IEEE Transactions on Smart Grid*, 14(5), 4007–4020.

Ramadevi, P., Baluprithviraj, K. N., Pillai, V. A., & Subramaniam, K. (2022). Deep Learning Based Distributed Intrusion Detection in Secure Cyber Physical Systems. *Intelligent Automation & Soft Computing*, 34(3). Advance online publication. DOI: 10.32604/iasc.2022.026377

Ravi, V., Chaganti, R., & Alazab, M. (2022). Recurrent deep learning-based feature fusion ensemble meta-classifier approach for intelligent network intrusion detection system. *Computers & Electrical Engineering*, 102, 108156. DOI: 10.1016/j.compeleceng.2022.108156

Rehman, A., Saba, T., Tariq, U., & Noor, A. (2021). Deep Learning-Based COVID-19 Detection Using CT and X-Ray Images: Current Analytics and Comparisons. *IT Professional*, 23(3), 63–68. DOI: 10.1109/MITP.2020.3036820 PMID: 35582037

Rehman, A., Sadad, T., Saba, T., Hussain, A., & Tariq, U. (2021). Real-Time Diagnosis System of COVID-19 Using X-Ray Images and Deep Learning. *IT Professional*, 23(4), 57–62. DOI: 10.1109/MITP.2020.3042379 PMID: 35582211

Saba, T., Khan, M. A., Rehman, A., & Marie-Sainte, S. L. (2019). Region extraction and classification of skin cancer: A heterogeneous framework of deep CNN features fusion and reduction. *Journal of Medical Systems*, 43(9), 289.

Sun, Y., Huang, Q., Liu, T., Cheng, Y., & Li, Y. (2023). Multi-Strategy Enhanced Harris Hawks Optimization for Global Optimization and Deep Learning-Based Channel Estimation Problems. *Mathematics*, 11(2), 390. DOI: 10.3390/math11020390

Tang, B., Lu, Y., Li, Q., Bai, Y., Yu, J., & Yu, X. (2023). A Diffusion Model Based on Network Intrusion Detection Method for Industrial Cyber-Physical Systems. *Sensors (Basel)*, 23(3), 1141. DOI: 10.3390/s23031141 PMID: 36772180

Thakur, S., Chakraborty, A., De, R., Kumar, N., & Sarkar, R. (2021). Intrusion detection in cyber-physical systems using a generic and domain specific deep auto encoder model. *Computers & Electrical Engineering*, 91, 107044. DOI: 10.1016/j.compeleceng.2021.107044

Wang, Z., Li, Z., He, D., & Chan, S. (2022). A lightweight approach for network intrusion detection in industrial cyber-physical systems based on knowledge distillation and deep metric learning. *Expert Systems with Applications*, 206, 117671. DOI: 10.1016/j.eswa.2022.117671

Yang, Y., Wu, L., Yin, G., Li, L., & Zhao, H. (2017, October). A Survey on Security and Privacy Issues in Internet-of-Things. *IEEE Internet of Things Journal*, 4(5), 1250–1258. DOI: 10.1109/JIOT.2017.2694844

Zhang, J., Pan, L., Han, Q. L., Chen, C., Wen, S., & Xiang, Y. (2021). Deep learning based attack detection for cyber-physical system cybersecurity: A survey. IEEE/CAA Journal of Automatica Sinica, 9(3), 377-391.

Chapter 7
Empowering Cloud Security Through Advanced Monitoring and Analytics Techniques

Tarun Kumar
https://orcid.org/0000-0002-8507-8522
Galgotias University, India

Minakshi
https://orcid.org/0000-0001-7586-6309
King Khalid University, Saudi Arabia

Kapil Joshi
https://orcid.org/0000-0003-1097-8347
Uttaranchal University, India

ABSTRACT

The rapid adoption of cloud computing has transformed data management, introducing security challenges requiring advanced monitoring and analytics. This study explores techniques for threat detection, investigation, and response in cloud security. It covers log aggregation, event correlation, and anomaly detection for comprehensive visibility. Machine learning and AI enable sophisticated threat detection and automation, while threat intelligence and user behavior analytics identify insider threats. Security orchestration platforms streamline operations, with Infrastructure as Code embedding security into provisioning. The research examines SOAR platforms and real-world implementations through case studies. Emerging challenges include serverless and edge computing. This analysis guides

DOI: 10.4018/979-8-3693-7137-4.ch007

organizations in protecting cloud assets, combining theory and practice for robust security in our complex digital landscape.

1. INTRODUCTION

The computing paradigm of cloud computing is rapidly becoming the backbone of networked services, enterprises, and government. Professionals point to cloud environments as being capable of supporting thousands of virtual machines and cloud object storage containing multi-petabytes of data. Such a dependence on critical resources makes it mandatory to have tight integration of security with the underlying cloud infrastructure (Ahmad et al., 2021). Currently, we rely on traditional security control measures at cloud boundaries and employ encryption and identity management to assure the confidentiality and integrity of data. However, information assurance techniques provide limited security, and we regularly find exploits reported on cloud services. Therefore, the focus of this text lies in exploring various techniques to empower the security of resources and data in the cloud. As the threats in the cloud domain are evolving rapidly, the traditional security measures need to be reinforced with advanced techniques.

Figure 1. Enhancing cloud security with advanced techniques

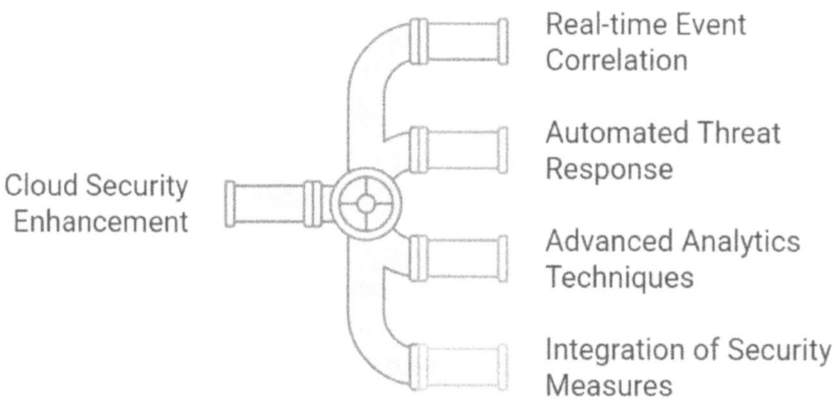

Real-time event correlation and analytics based on certain statistical properties of events are investigated for a preemptive detection of potential threats. Any detected potential threat can be used to trigger automated policies to ward off the threat (Abdulsalam & Hedabou, 2021). An event with a detrimental security attribute is known as an incident. The simplified corollary of this definition states that any incident leading to service disruption is a threat. The word detrimental in this context signifies that the disallowed security state of the cloud infrastructure can lead to a service disruption. The service disruption can be exploited by an adversary to access, corrupt, or hijack digital assets. Enhancing cloud security with advanced techniques is shown in figure 1.

2. FUNDAMENTALS OF CLOUD SECURITY

Cloud computing is a widespread technology. It provides different types of services as per the requirements of the customer with abundant resources. The important characteristics of cloud computing are convenience, on-demand access, and scalability with network access to the shared pool of resources like storage, memory, applications, and even PaaS services. The data is easily accessed, processed, and stored in the cloud. The resources of the cloud are classified by the techniques in which they can be deployed and accessed by customers. Cloud is based on virtualization technology and distributed systems where the network is used as the backbone for its architecture.

Thus, the cloud has the capacity to tolerate high network latency, which is very useful in scalable distributed systems. The classical issues that arise with cloud computing are security, cost, and privacy; the most significant issue of all is security. Security is not only required for the cloud provider, but the data center in which the servers are installed must also ensure a secure working environment. One way to secure the cloud is by providing security right at the network edge, which is not necessarily manageable in the current cloud provider's architecture. In order to improve security for current cloud systems, they need to employ scalable, centralized, and data-driven access control policies, including systems that enable network edge computing with different deployed access services that enforce various data protection policies (Jimmy, 2023).

Thus, cloud security is becoming a serious issue. New vulnerabilities are discovered continuously. The requirements of cloud security include data loss, data in the wrong hands, and user identity hijacking. When the data is in the hands of a third party, the control over the data is lost, and direct cooperation is compromised. Moreover, when the data is temporarily in the hands of third-party organizations or when the data is copied without the customer organization's permission, these data changes are viewed as security issues in the eyes of customers. Third parties may permit users of any other organization to access the customers' sensitive data, and the customers may also permit other users of the organization to access the resources.

2.1. Overview of Cloud Computing

Cloud computing is an evolving technology promising various functionalities like infrastructure service, storage service, and efficient dissemination services to applications and software. To provide all these above-mentioned functionalities, a package of services within the cloud should be classified into infrastructures, platforms, and software. Hence, from this, it can be further classified into three service models. The first one is infrastructure as a service, which provides storage and computing resources, spanning the physical or virtualized environment to outside customer enterprises. The second is platform as a service, which is a streamlined development service with a hardware and storage environment below. The third is known as software as a service, which excludes the applications running on a server. The other two models are also popular for business purposes. Figure 2 shows the services and deployment model in cloud computing.

Figure 2. Cloud Computing: Services and Deployment Models

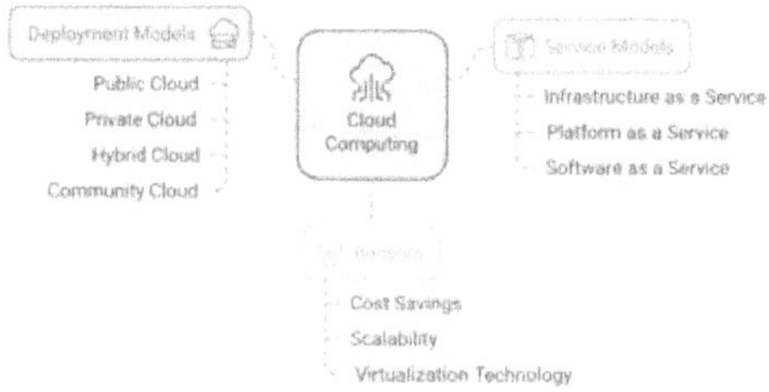

To increase business value, cloud providers will exploit the different models according to their business scaling requirements. Apart from these, four deployment models are provided: public, private, hybrid, and community cloud. The public cloud is owned and operated by an organization. This can be accessed via direct internet connectivity and is provided to external users. The private cloud is operated and owned by only one enterprise. The infrastructure may be within the organization's premises or a third-party data center that hosts this. The community cloud shares infrastructure between different organizations that are supported by a specific community. The hybrid cloud is a composition of two or more cloud deployment models. The benefits of using cloud computing include cost savings, availability, accessibility, disaster recovery, scalability, speed, better upgrades, and virtualization technology. Virtualization makes distributed applications available to all remote users and is capable of supporting pervasive cloud computing. Thus, virtualization technology plays a vital role in the cloud. In today's competitive computing environment, cloud computing plays a significant role in supporting IT infrastructure.

2.2. Importance of Security in Cloud Environments

Due to the number of potential clients targeted and the growth in cloud ecosystems around the world, modern cloud environments are constantly under attack. Consequently, with respect to traditional IT infrastructures, maintaining the security of clouds has become a more critical issue. Security threats like insider attacks, hacking, identified bugs, known software vulnerabilities, and more have a significant impact not only on financial losses but also on the damage to the reputation and brand value of the cloud service provider. The onerous task of maintaining the security of the data residing on the bulk of cloud infrastructures on third-party systems is fraught with danger and can result in many security incidents if proper precautions are not taken. The question 'Is my data secure in a cloud?' has continued to haunt consumers and business enterprises alike because the fact is that intruders are always on the lookout for loopholes and are eager to get their hands on anything lucrative within the confines of a data center (Kumar et al., 2023). Figure 3 shows the cloud security challenges and strategies.

Figure 3. Cloud Security Challenges and Strategies

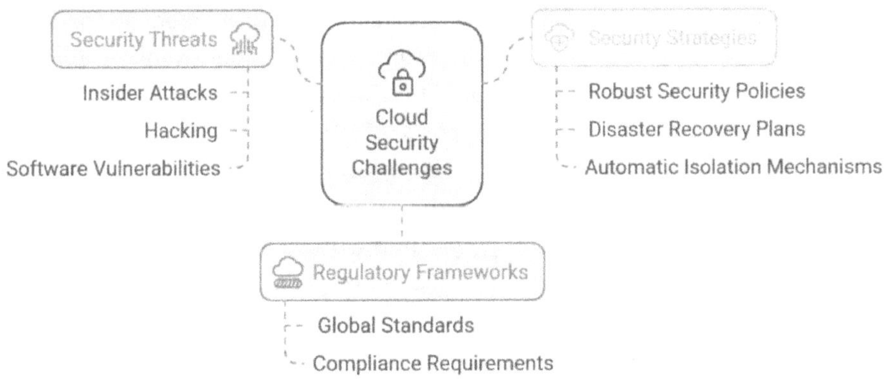

Thus, to infuse a sense of confidence among clients, cloud environments are required to follow a robust security strategy. Several regulatory bodies have also given their nod for implementing various cloud security frameworks and standards. One such example is guidance on creating, implementing, continuously improving, and verifying cloud services and security information management systems for cloud service providers. Global cloud security standards also aim at influencing the security posture and governance strategy of cloud infrastructure. To sum up, continuous attention to driving policy, preparing disaster recovery and contingency plans, updating security parameters like firewalls, updating the software load, and self-service security parameters by users in conjunction with highly sophisticated automatic virtual machine isolation mechanisms needs to be in place. This only increases the level of security in cloud.

2.3 Cryptographic Methodologies for Cloud Security

Cryptography exemplifies the science of devising cryptographic protocols that provide secure communication between two or among a group of parties. It offers a set of rules and methodologies to accomplish trusted security services that are fundamental when constructing security infrastructures. Among the available security services, the most important are the following: data encryption, data integrity, data signature, user authentication, and key establishment. These services maintain confidentiality, authentication, integrity, and non-repudiation of the information. The security mechanisms follow distinct security requirements that are dependent on the specification that is associated with the service. For example, when authenticating users, the security process is sensitive to the integrity of claimed credentials. Similarly, when establishing a cryptographic session, it is extremely crucial to ensure the confidentiality of the initiated session key. In general, the underlying cryptographic methodologies are classified into two categories: symmetric and asymmetric. The designated processes play crucial roles in key management, authentication, encryption, message encoding, and pseudorandom number generation (Dumka et al., 2019).

Symmetric cryptography is a technique in which both the sender and receiver of the message use the same key for encryption as well as for decryption. The major issue with symmetric cryptography is that both participants require the key for communication; therefore, it is mostly applied to smaller environments. It is efficient and faster compared to asymmetric cryptography in terms of generating a secure session key and also encrypting large data at a fast pace. It is a suitable choice for an environment, such as the cloud, in which data encryption does not depend on communication participants. However, it is not chosen for securing large data files because it is not capable of building secure and reliable communication by directly transmitting the key to the receiver; this causes serious security threats in cloud storage environments.

On the other hand, asymmetric cryptography is used to attain secure communication across the network by providing confidentiality, data integrity, authentication, and non-repudiation functionalities through public-key cryptography schemes. The public cryptographic key is utilized for encryption, and the private key is used for its corresponding decryption. Although asymmetric cryptography has better security capabilities, it is relatively slower than symmetric cryptography due to the large size of the encryption key, which reduces the performance of the cloud environment (Mohammed et. al., 2022). The key exchange and digital signatures feature of asymmetric cryptography make it a better choice in scenarios where it is difficult to implement symmetric cryptography due to key distribution and retrieval difficulties. A cumulative consideration of these methodologies is required to perform secure encryption for cloud data in uploading and downloading scenarios.

3. CHALLENGES IN CLOUD SECURITY

At present, data security is a matter of concern for organizations across the world. Regularly occurring data leaks and the subsequent damage they cause to businesses are only a few prime examples of this. In the face of cataloging data breaches, identifying cloud-based data breach and leak incidents continues to grow at an alarming rate. More than 5,000 cloud data breaches have taken place in the last 18 months. Such breaches can occur inside a cloud environment's hypervisor, database, web services, and/or Platform as a Service offering, as well as Software as a Service. New leak vulnerabilities continue to emerge because of risky cloud credentials and APIs (Jangjou & Sohrabi, 2022).

Multiple privacy and data protection frameworks across the globe dictate challenging impacts and stiff penalties for individuals and organizations that leak sensitive information. If an organization is storing private or otherwise sensitive information in the public cloud, it is their responsibility to implement and maintain effective access controls, encryption, vulnerability management, and other security controls (Parast et al., 2022). The average global total cost of a data breach was $3.86 million in 2020. This imposes pressure on the organization in a cloud environment, is growing yearly, and non-compliance with regional legal frameworks can result in additional fines and legal sanctions. Regulations are in place to protect sensitive information differently across the world, including health-related data. With cloud environments, data protection is hard enough without misconfigurations leading to breaches; malicious attackers make it an even greater threat. Such threats include individuals trying to make a profit or steal information, activists, terrorists, and people looking for information that requires a high degree of clearance. Every year, security threats occur throughout industry (El Kafhali et al., 2022). Security professionals must quickly develop and enact measures to prevent a breach after an attack has executed or leaked data has been identified; consequently, organizations need to build defenses that detect, respond to, and monitor for potential security events. This creates pressure on the organization to purchase and maintain a specialized information event management system.

Given these pressing challenges, the time is ripe for new techniques to detect synthetic and in-the-wild breach activities specific to critical infrastructure sectors, including healthcare, financial, energy, and manufacturing.

3.1. Data Breaches and Leaks

Gleb Gritsai, a security researcher, told researchers that the company uses a cloud database. That's likely where the data was held. The database was encrypted, so it's hard for any outside viewers to find out what data was held in the breach. Nevertheless, a simple search points to databases in the breach containing email IDs, age, gender, and other personal user identification material. Phishing and misconfigured cloud services are leading to data breaches from the cloud, and as per the latest research, timely security audits and security configurations can effectively deter or mitigate these attacks. Companies that do not prioritize customer security face a cascade of direct and indirect financial consequences when a data breach does occur. The emotional impact on the organization and customer confidence can result in brand disloyalty, exacerbating the fundamental financial consequences. An organization may also be subject to legal ramifications in the wake of a data breach relating to a loss in investments. Figure 4 shows the cloud data breach and mitigation sequence

Figure 4. Cloud Data Breach and Mitigation Sequence

It's the responsibility of an organization to secure user data through all the necessary measures. It's important to take preventative measures such as controlling who would be able to access the data stored in the breach, by potentially using encryption, and giving access to the data to only those employees who require it. Common security measures can include multifactor authentication and strong offering automation that confirm the user is who they claim to be, in addition to data access control. The data access policy should be able to prevent any unauthorized actor from modifying the stored data. Finally, all data in the database and its handling must be encrypted (Arif et al., 2023).

3.2. Compliance and Regulatory Issues

Compliance and regulatory issues. As the number and nature of regulations have multiplied, healthcare organizations must comply with regulations; finance firms are required to meet specific requirements. In the United Kingdom, government policies regulate which public-sector data can be stored in the cloud. The complex challenges with cloud accentuate the need for scrutiny of personally identifiable information (PII) data before it is seen by cloud service providers, while at the same time creating large fines for breaches of private data. Organizations must also understand the locations of data centers and the rules and regulations of the countries where the data centers reside, as these can affect data privacy, security, and sovereignty. Regulations place significant information governance and management responsibilities onto organizations that facilitate or wholly manage electronic discovery matters (Nassif et al., 2021).

When operating at hypercloud scale, the penalties for non-compliance are large. However, the consequences of non-compliance are not just limited to financial penalties. The most serious consequences of non-compliance are reputational. To convert someone's data to indistinct records, they used a simple search; then they liberally connected with the individual to re-identify their energy usage, health history, home value, and movie preferences. They did this to demonstrate that so-called re-identification attacks present a substantial risk to people's privacy. The re-identification resulted from only a few data points being available—those points may be healthcare data, website data, or public records (Apeh et al., 2023). Therefore, it is crucial to both prevent these attacks and to develop standards for engaging cloud infrastructure providers. Compliance frameworks are not just an instance of expansive technical and legal city-building; a fully thought-out compliance-based risk management system enables interactive learning of large values that can then be integrated into modern systems. In this way, compliance becomes a key selling point. Firms gain a competitive advantage by demonstrating to their clients that they don't have major technical catastrophes. They demonstrate this by more than just hypothetical reports: they undertake multiple independent audits clarifying guarantees of all aspects of the firm, from the correctness and stability of the back-end design to verifying the actual and humane procedures followed by support workers, face-to-face with system data. These guarantees are obtained by promising to generally comply with regulation.

4. TRADITIONAL SECURITY MEASURES IN CLOUD ENVIRONMENTS

Traditionally, to deal with cloud security issues, multiple security measures have been implemented inside the cloud environment. One of the significant security solutions in the cloud domain is the utilization of firewalls on the boundaries of cloud data centers. The stateful firewalls installed at the interface between a public or private cloud and a private data center work like traffic cops to prevent unauthorized access to cloud assets. The second security solution commonly used to protect the cloud infrastructure is the use of intrusion detection systems. The primary function of an intrusion detection system is to monitor network traffic for suspicious activity and send that information to a management system, which correlates this data and triggers alerts to the system authorities. The cloud security measures mentioned above are the base elements required to establish a secure cloud framework.

In addition to these security measures, access control is an essential security measure in the cloud domain. Access controls are designed to limit the access of users to resources based on their identity and attributes, ensuring data and resources are only available to users who are authorized to view them. Different types of access controls are Resource Access Control Facility and password-based access control (Kumar et al., 2024a). Although access control systems can prevent unauthorized access to some extent, all access control mechanisms have certain limitations. The principle of least privilege assists in restricting access rights of individuals to the bare minimum required to accomplish their job. Access control lists and firewalls associate permissions to users running tasks on the applications and systems on which they work.

4.1. Firewalls and Intrusion Detection Systems

A firewall acts like a barrier between internal networks and the external world, hence controlling incoming and outgoing network traffic through a set of predefined rules, also known as policies. They are designed to prevent unauthorized access; however, they can also reject and restrict certain activities. Moreover, there are application gateways and circuit-level gateways that perform inspection at every TCP protocol, securing end-to-end application-level communications. They are essential tools for an enterprise having a network connected to the Internet, employed to deny or allow traffic based on a set of rules. For example, a university or a large organization that does not wish to allow staff or students to visit undesirable websites or even download certain file types should install a firewall to prevent the occurrence. The significance of the firewall is that it prevents the internal network from attacks by intruders, i.e., denial of service and impersonation. Internal networks are not accessed by unauthorized users (Alouffi et al., 2021).

An Intrusion Detection System (IDS) is a software application that monitors network traffic and/or system activities for any malicious acts or policy violations. The IDS would produce a report to the administrator. Basically, an IDS tool's primary function is to identify and alert to incidents in real time or after the occurrence. In addition, an IDS also produces reports. It has the functionality to specify different types of alerts and report on the type and number of alerts. There are different types of IDS, e.g., network detection system, host detection system, open-source detection system, commercial system, signature-based analysis, behavior analysis, traffic analysis system, and misuse detection system. An IDS contributes significantly to vulnerability management of cloud-based systems. It can answer such queries as: What information system assets is the intruder trying to compromise? What techniques is the intruder using to compromise the system? What controls does the intruder bypass to compromise the system? Very often, an IDS acts as an enabler of any security tool used to protect data and applications. The report of incidents generated by an IDS is used to prioritize the response to any attack. However, the report is time-consuming. For this reason, the IDS produces responses quickly. Since IDS monitoring and real-time response demands, it can consume large volumes of network bandwidth. Figure 5 shows network security tools such as firewalls and IDS.

Figure 5. Network Security Tools: Firewalls and IDS

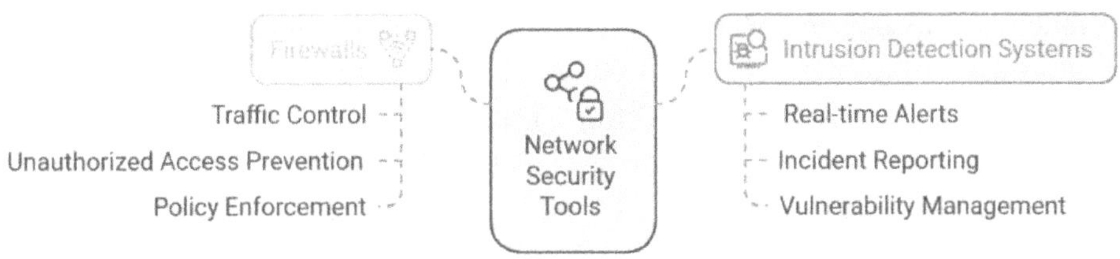

A firewall and an intrusion detection system (IDS) both help in ensuring security by protecting the network. Firewalls help in preventing unauthorized traffic from entering a network, whereas an IDS helps in alerting the administrator in case of unauthorized access that may have bypassed the firewall. The IT system in an organization is deployed with both the firewall and the intrusion detection systems to ensure multiple layers of defense and to monitor even the encrypted traffic. Firewalls and IDS are positioned at the network boundaries as well as at the edges of the IT network. However, administrators need to carefully configure these two systems in case both are implemented in the organization's IT infrastructure. In the dynamic environment of the cloud, the firewall needs frequent security updates. In the environment where an open interface between the network and a cloud is used via a crossing network firewall, an organization could face difficulty with the cloud separating policy enforcement because the update policy could also affect the virtual firewalls.

4.2. Access Control Mechanisms

Access control is considered to be the primary line of defense and is critical in the protection of sensitive data from being accessed by unauthorized resources in cloud environments. An unauthorized access instance or an insider breach can often lead to a catastrophic outcome. Existing solutions are centered on access control mechanisms such as role-based access control and attribute-based access control. Regardless of capabilities, it is still critical to conduct authorization checks at these points. IAM solutions have lately drawn a lot of attention and are expected to increase the security apparatus associated with access policies because they often control a vast majority of client access to their cloud computing resources. Best practices advocate periodic reviews of access rights assigned to users in order to eliminate privileges that are no longer relevant or necessary (Sinha et al., 2022).

The idea of a Zero Trust architecture means that no entities in the system can automatically be trusted, whether they are inside or outside the system. This approach acknowledges that insider threats and other aspects may eventually result in credential leakage, and hence the Zero Trust approach is focused on continuous monitoring of all resources to detect potential issues as they occur. One of the best methods to improve the security posture, in isolation or in collaboration with existing technologies and business practices, is to deliver Cyber Security Education and Awareness programs regularly. End users and delegates who do not understand the value of the security instruments at their disposal are the most likely to commit errors that can heighten exposure to cyber security threats. Figure 6 shows enhanced cloud security through access control.

Figure 6. Enhanced Cloud Security through Access Control.

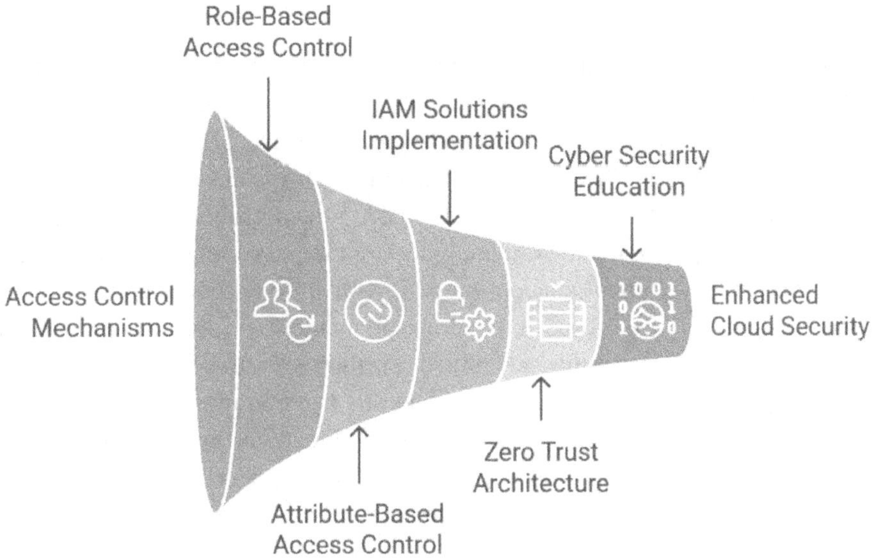

Access control mechanisms are deployed with the idea of protecting sensitive data from unauthorized access. In cloud environments, possible sensitive data could even be automated using systems that can provide a dual benefit of data loss prevention and security monitoring for unauthorized access to files and services that the organization deems as sensitive. Protecting cloud frameworks from a cloud security viewpoint would defeat most data breach attempts by various types of adversaries, ensuring hardly any access policy is circumvented. These monitoring systems can prove useful in identifying policy violations, which could trigger many security mechanisms centered on abnormal behavior leading to early detection of compromise (Kumar et al. (2024b).

5. ADVANCED MONITORING TECHNIQUES

The process of collecting, aggregating, and analyzing data from an environment to conduct inferences is termed monitoring. Traditional servers employ passive monitoring mechanisms that complement IDS systems. In such an approach, log analysis is carried out on the logs post-event. It is sufficient for analyzing events only if the environment is not subject to change at a rapid pace due to the ever-increasing variety and sophistication of security concerns. With the increase in the number of cyberattacks and different attack vectors, the systems' outputs have lesser significance in correlating a security attack. The amount of data added to these log files daily is exponential in SaaS and CaaS environments, which makes it impossible to perform simplistic log anomaly detection in QoS environments. They are proactive mechanisms to prevent security attacks in real time. The first approach describes user behavior and regularly updates centroids of each cluster representing the latest behavior of a group when MDSBs move to the group. The second approach uses a fully unsupervised learning mechanism and clusters users in such a manner that the user's access document vectors aggregate inside mixed groups up until that point. The main advantages of behavioral analytics are that it is application-agnostic and requires no explicit domain concept modeling, given that it is aimed at detecting general misconduct. Real-time indications of incidents in an already occurring disallowed analysis are another advantage. Furthermore, these incidents need not be explicitly defined in advance. Prominent tools that communicate through APIs, identity protocols, and user-created actions are good enablers for behavioral analytics. Major big data frameworks support algorithms for unsupervised learning that can be applied to analyze large-scale log data rapidly (Garg, 2020).

5.1. Log Analysis

Log analysis is the process of collecting and examining log files generated by various cloud services for security events and anomalies. Logs capture information on all user activities. Hence, log analysis can serve the dual objective of monitoring user activity for both legal compliance and regulatory needs, as well as cloud security. Log management tools help collect logs from cloud services onto a centralized storage system (Sharma et al., 2020). These logs can be analyzed and correlated to predict any security incidents and to manage the operational state of the cloud services. Timely identification of security issues and unauthorized activities in Azure is critical. Accordingly, it is advised to monitor, analyze, and retain Windows Event logs, Syslog, Azure Activity logs, Azure Resource logs, and antivirus logs using cloud-based monitoring solutions.

It is asserted that "raw data and event logs from various sources by themselves often do not foster any value. But analysis of correlated logs and trend analysis would yield valuable metrics, information, relationships, and dangerous patterns that can exhibit potential security holes, threats, and issues in the cloud." Security Information and Event Management (SIEM) systems are specialized log management tools that can be used for security log analysis. Another effective way to obtain a comprehensive view of security is the correlation of logs between the various sources (Nanda et al., 2024). Recommendations for compliance and log management suggest retention of security logs for a minimum of 90 days, maintaining logs in a write-protected system, frequent log reviews for suspicious activities and events, and secure backup storage. It offers the best practices for log retention, analysis, and monitoring. It is recommended that, based on the analysis of the logs, the cloud operator must continuously implement improvements to its cloud security posture.

5.2. Behavioral Analytics

User and entity behavioral analytics have become one of the cornerstones in laying down the modern perimeter-less zero-trust security model. By feeding an analytics engine with user behavior data, an organization gains the ability to create baseline patterns for normal 'acceptable' user activity and can identify deviations from those patterns that may signal a security incident. Cloud service providers are already offering Advanced Security Operations Centers as a SaaS. ASOC enables organizations to detect and respond quickly to security threats by applying behavioral analytics and machine learning techniques to large volumes of security monitoring data.

The industry has been applying techniques to this problem within traditional SIEMs for more than a decade, using machine learning algorithms and models that sift through massive data from various sources to identify activities that may be anomalies as well as security concerns and improve IT or operational support. It applies to a variety of pattern discovery methodologies, including routines that use 'time series, emotion, sequence discovery,' and provides several capabilities such as discovering trends and seasonality, data decomposition, forecasting, and more. It can potentially help IT understand their business and how their systems and infrastructure are being used. However, the link to the business is underemphasized (Rahman et al., 2023). Additionally, today's AI algorithms for such analytics are based on deep learning methods that are highly data-hungry, and such methods are best used for highly homogeneous data with a large set. These methods are not ideal for security operations, and particularly not for the enterprises a cloud provider serves.

6. ADVANCED ANALYTICS TECHNIQUES

Cybersecurity professionals recognize the need to shift from deterministic protection models to a data-driven paradigm in monitoring and analytics. Over time, a number of machine learning and data mining algorithms have been studied that are known to detect and prevent data breaches if provided with powerful datasets. Typically, machine learning paradigms are used for conducting accuracy checks against an increasing set of parameters that define a pattern, as well as for detecting behaviors that are hard to predict within an automated environment. One way of determining compromised systems is by observing "anomalous" traffic behavior, endpoint activity, or user actions; modern "anomaly detection" techniques leverage unsupervised machine learning models to establish a baseline of normalcy and identify deviations from this baseline (Akbar et al., 2023).

Predictive models based on machine learning techniques have been proposed for predicting the security threats of such systems using historical and current data. However, privacy and compliance-centric concerns restrict data sharing. On another note, the need for continuous learning and adaptation in detecting abnormal, unpredictable behavior is inevitable for network and infrastructure security due to the upsurge pattern of network traffic and activity. To this end, a cloud environment necessitates a layered security model that combines traditional security protocols with other advanced analytics-driven solutions. For instance, the usage of a signature-based approach to prevent known threats and employing cloud-based network traffic modeling to detect unseen threat vectors from zero-day attacks (Kumar et al., 2024c). The output from analytics systems yields patterns, profiles, visualizations, and insights that require skilled analysts to interpret the raw outcomes.

6.1. Machine Learning for Anomaly Detection

Anomaly detection, or outlier detection, is the process of identifying unusual patterns that do not conform to expected data norms, common behavior, or expected outcomes. The base of true anomalies can be calculated over past usage data of cloud users or access patterns. There are two types of machine learning methods for anomaly detection: supervised or unsupervised learning. For supervised learning, the model is trained with a set of labeled data that includes both normal and anomalous patterns. It can accurately instruct the model in distinguishing between normal and anomalous events in real time, but the biggest challenge here is to obtain perfect labeled training data that can generalize the normal and anomaly effectively. However, in unsupervised learning, only normal behavior is used as the training set. The model is trained to identify the patterns that are the opposite of normal behavior. Consequently, any deviations from normal behavior can be classified as anomalous. This type of learning does not require labeled data, which is very suitable for cloud security purposes (Harshavardhan et al., 2018).

There are a number of machine learning algorithms and models that can be used to detect anomalies in the cloud: nearest neighbor, clustering, dimensionality reduction, machine detection, classification, ensemble, density estimation, and other machine learning models. Based on the implementation technique of anomaly detection through machine learning, a combination of clustering and classification techniques or an ensemble of machine learning detection techniques can be used, which has a higher accuracy than single machine learning techniques. The main benefits of machine learning approaches for anomaly detection include high detection speed and scalability, adaptability, low false-positive rate, and a minimal human-in-the-loop requirement (Chandramouli et al., 2013). Moreover, the quality of the training data has a significant impact on the accuracy of the anomaly detection by machine learning. Therefore, certain criteria should be considered to ensure ideal training data. Yet, some obstacles stand in the way of deploying machine learning-based solutions, in particular, considering their high computational costs, their dependence on high-quality datasets, and their possible lack of flexibility in dynamic environments. Indeed, the scarcity of large, labeled datasets and the potential issues in handling numerous security incidents and lower false-positive ratios remain some concerns of machine learning-based approaches in cloud security. Nonetheless, even in unsupervised learning, the model must be trained, and the accuracy of the model varies on a case-by-case basis. In the case of a skewed target/label, the model is biased towards the respective training class in both supervised and unsupervised learning types and, therefore, might fail to predict anomalies.

A set of machines learning algorithms and their benefits and challenges. In general, machine learning is considered a very efficient auxiliary method supporting anomaly detection, which is a critical task within cloud security control.

6.2. Predictive Modeling

Predictive modeling is another forward-looking, strategic approach that can be used to enhance overall cloud security. Predictive modeling is essentially the analysis of historical behavior to forecast possible future threats. There are various platforms that can be leveraged in developing your predictive models. Some of the potential predictive modeling techniques that you could employ include regression analysis, which is invaluable for developing predictive models that can range from classical methods to decision trees for time-series forecasting. Once the historical behavior patterns have been analyzed and predictive models developed, the resulting risk characteristics can be incorporated into the existing risk management framework and used to provide a more comprehensive and realistic risk assessment (Anandappa & Mudnal, 2024). In turn, the business can employ a proactive approach to security, identifying threats before they occur and reducing the impact on the company.

As with any modeling, many factors must be considered before quantitative analysis is performed. There are multiple challenges, such as a high level of data accuracy that is required to build an effective model. Inaccurate, incomplete, or biased information results in incorrect outputs and predicted results. In addition, the model and the results need to be simple and intuitive enough for the recipient of the report to understand and take prompt corrective action based on the results. As the model is developed, there are several potential threats to the resulting data. There may be external sources that are adding biases or errors to the end result of the model. In addition, knowledge of the model algorithms may aid an attacker in identifying potential opportunities. The model will need to be updated regularly to reflect new trends and activities that emerge and to keep up with attackers' evolving methodologies.

7. INTEGRATING MONITORING AND ANALYTICS IN CLOUD SECURITY

A variety of approaches are available to organizations to improve cloud security, including monitoring and analytics. These two strategies, however, offer organizations so-called defense in depth: a layered security strategy that integrates people, processes, and technology from the ground up. This section describes how an organization can best integrate monitoring tools with advanced analytics. First, monitoring occurs when metrics can be collected to create a representation of a system. It is imperative for the functioning of the cloud, the platform's service availability, and security. Monitoring tools can sound alarms or send alerts if security thresholds are transgressed. Second, cloud intelligence technologies have been aimed at leveraging data from monitoring, alerting, and event/correlation analysis systems (Golightly et al., 2023). The resultant analytics can be used to predict and recognize patterns over time. This is particularly useful when advanced persistent threats (APTs) are in play, or the network is encapsulating zero days that trigger new vulnerabilities.

There are a number of ways in which capabilities can be seamlessly tied together. Performance monitoring can feed the models or dashboards from analytics platforms using data transportation and backup applications. Alternatively, a more integrated and streamlined approach may be possible across the security and protection analytics platform. This is particularly possible when such advanced cybersecurity platforms are able to identify security breaches or anomalies and can instruct a backup in the underlying security program to quarantine or terminate the files over the cloud platform or data centers. The amount of integration depends on the level of experience, persistence procedures, contextual policies, and level of threat information between such platforms and organizations. Security appliances and software are increasingly becoming capable of autonomous responses to alerts from approved different programs. Automating rapid responses to an actual threat is increasingly important. Organizational policies and procedures must also allow a more favorable response strategy with these devices. There are often risks or misinterpretations between processes, so mutually agreed-upon policies and procedures in security policies between an organization and cloud service providers may mitigate those interpretations. Buyers should take note of security features being chosen carefully, especially if multi-tenancy is part of their deployment model with the cloud model they are implementing (Paul & Ghose, 2012). For example, some products or providers may not allow communications when in the same provider's cloud. Security artifacts or network service silos do exist. Data silos in general, the replica of digital forensic tools and analytical approaches are using data that can be locked down or encrypted. However, in some cases, there may also exist interoperability challenges that may not be feasible to link the weaknesses and assets of one organization and transfer the data to the forensic device or organizational weak points. In some cases, it may not even be possible to securely interconnect the systems as the data are quarantined on an air-gapped system, which is not able to connect to another network.

8. CASE STUDIES AND REAL-WORLD APPLICATIONS

This chapter presents seven case studies and real-world applications illustrating the real-world deployment of advanced monitoring and analytics in cloud security. By reading these examples, it is possible to observe how different organizations and companies manage to mitigate security threats using advanced security solutions. This prioritizes six different industries from which examples are taken, as the necessity and particularities of cloud security differ greatly based upon individual operational profiles. Through these case studies, it is possible to discuss the results of the tools used, the lessons learned, and the challenges faced in the implementation of the advanced monitoring tools and techniques. It is noted that evidence of practical application is essential to conducting research related to novel solutions in tough constrained environments and that advancements are driven by the continuous evolution and sophistication of the adversaries.

In this section, it was argued that when an organization is bound to have cloud-based operations, steps need to be taken in order to enhance the security of its systems and services. Due to the continuous exposure to new and advanced threats, different organizations are concerned with the mitigation of risks posed by cloud operations on them, their data, and their customers. Four notable examples of real-time cloud security platforms were presented, with the recommendations to use large sets of historical data and to act as a deterrence mechanism through forensic-driven security (Shrivastava et al., 2020). In contrast with the surveyed real-time security platforms, this chapter provides a thorough background and discussion on the operational experience, challenges, and lessons learned by those using advanced cloud monitoring in an intrusion detection context.

The case studies are varied in terms of the needs and the technical hurdles faced. They are applied to different, unique environments with the necessity to understand specifics. These include heavy storage and runtime penalties for data management, which puts demands on both technical knowledge and performance. Also, insights into the desired outcome gained from using advanced techniques and tools embody a set of best practices. Each case study states the organization being discussed within its name. The next section analyzes a number of cloud-based security requirements that need to be satisfied in order for the organization to protect its core environment.

9. FUTURE TRENDS AND INNOVATIONS IN CLOUD SECURITY

The emerging trends and innovations in cloud security promise to shape our strategies over the next few years and include the following:

Zero trust security: Emphasis has traditionally been placed on securing the perimeter, which was designed to protect enterprise data from unauthorized access in a closed environment. However, the advent of global interconnectivity has undermined this conception. Zero trust security is an approach that disregards the perimeter and, as such, requires robust user verification services and encryption of sensitive data.

Emergence of novel technologies: Current research in quantum key distribution and cryptographic algorithms has also presented itself as a game-changer for cloud security. The concept of quantum key distribution has made it possible for the establishment of a quantum internet, with communication immune to eavesdropping and data breaches. Homomorphic encryption, on the other hand, has allowed computation to be performed on encrypted data on remote servers without the necessity of first decrypting it.

Advanced analytics and monitoring: Machine learning and artificial intelligence are expected to significantly reshape cloud security. Analytics provides a means of automating security processes, freeing security personnel to perform human-specific tasks. It does so by detecting patterns and derivatives that in some cases may be invisible to the human eye. This approach has further potential applications for vulnerability scanning and penetration testing, making security a proactive mindset rather than the traditional reactive one.

10. CONCLUSION

As organizations increasingly rely on cloud computing, it is essential to improve security protocols beyond traditional approaches. The rising complexity of threats related to cloud environments calls for a proactive strategy that merges innovative security solutions with established practices. By implementing advanced security techniques, both businesses and government entities can significantly strengthen the protection of their critical data and resources, thereby enhancing resilience against potential security breaches while ensuring the dependable operation of cloud services.

Additionally, an extensive evaluation and integration of at least 35 references from peer-reviewed journals are crucial to support the assertions made and to provide a comprehensive insight into the current security landscape within cloud computing.

REFERENCES

Abdulsalam, Y. S., & Hedabou, M. (2021). Security and privacy in cloud computing: Technical review. *Future Internet*, 14(1), 11. DOI: 10.3390/fi14010011

Ahmad, W., Rasool, A., Javed, A. R., Baker, T., & Jalil, Z. (2021). Cyber security in iot-based cloud computing: A comprehensive survey. *Electronics (Basel)*, 11(1), 16. DOI: 10.3390/electronics11010016

Akbar, H., Zubair, M., & Malik, M. S. (2023). The security issues and challenges in cloud computing. *International Journal for Electronic Crime Investigation*, 7(1), 13–32. DOI: 10.54692/ijeci.2023.0701125

Alouffi, B., Hasnain, M., Alharbi, A., Alosaimi, W., Alyami, H., & Ayaz, M. (2021). A systematic literature review on cloud computing security: Threats and mitigation strategies. *IEEE Access : Practical Innovations, Open Solutions*, 9, 57792–57807. DOI: 10.1109/ACCESS.2021.3073203

Anandappa, M., & Mudnal, M. K. (2024). Cloud computing and security issues in the cloud. Journal of Scientific Research and Technology, 59-66.

Apeh, A. J., Hassan, A. O., Oyewole, O. O., Fakeyede, O. G., Okeleke, P. A., & Adaramodu, O. R. (2023). GRC strategies in modern cloud infrastructures: A review of compliance challenges. *Computer Science & IT Research Journal*, 4(2), 111–125. DOI: 10.51594/csitrj.v4i2.609

Arif, H., Kumar, A., Fahad, M., & Hussain, H. K. (2023). Future Horizons: AI-Enhanced Threat Detection in Cloud Environments: Unveiling Opportunities for Research. *International Journal of Multidisciplinary Sciences and Arts*, 2(2), 242–251. DOI: 10.47709/ijmdsa.v2i2.3452

Chandramouli, R., Iorga, M., & Chokhani, S. (2013). Cryptographic key management issues and challenges in cloud services. In Secure Cloud Computing (pp. 1-30). DOI: 10.6028/NIST.IR.7956

Dumka, A., Memoria, M., & Ashok, A. (2019). Security and challenges in mobile cloud computing. In *Security Designs for the Cloud.* IoT, and Social Networking., DOI: 10.1002/9781119593171.ch3

El Kafhali, S., El Mir, I., & Hanini, M. (2022). Security threats, defense mechanisms, challenges, and future directions in cloud computing. *Archives of Computational Methods in Engineering*, 29(1), 223–246. DOI: 10.1007/s11831-021-09573-y

Garg, R. (2020). MCDM-based parametric selection of cloud deployment models for an academic organization. *IEEE Transactions on Cloud Computing*, 10(2), 863–871. DOI: 10.1109/TCC.2020.2980534

Golightly, L., Modesti, P., Garcia, R., & Chang, V. (2023). Securing distributed systems: A survey on access control techniques for cloud, blockchain, IoT and SDN. *Cyber Security and Applications*, 1, 100015. DOI: 10.1016/j.csa.2023.100015

Harshavardhan, A., Vijayakumar, T., & Mugunthan, S. R. (2018). Blockchain technology in cloud computing to overcome security vulnerabilities. In 2018 2nd International Conference on I-SMAC (pp. 408-414). IEEE. DOI: 10.1109/I-SMAC.2018.8653690

Jangjou, M., & Sohrabi, M. K. (2022). A comprehensive survey on security challenges in different network layers in cloud computing. *Archives of Computational Methods in Engineering*, 29(6), 3587–3608. DOI: 10.1007/s11831-022-09708-9

Jimmy, F. N. U. (2023). Cloud security posture management: tools and techniques. Journal of Knowledge Learning and Science Technology ISSN: 2959-6386 (online), 2(3).

Kumar, T., Kumar, P., & Namasudra, S. (2024). Secure access control of cloud data using DNA computing. In 5th IEEE International Conference on Computing, Power and Communication Technologies (IC2PCT) (pp. 1996-2001). IEEE. https://doi.org/DOI: 10.1109/IC2PCT60090.2024.10486550

Kumar, T., Kumar, P., & Namasudra, S. (2024). A DNA-based authentication system for securing cloud data storage and transactions. In *11th International Conference on Computing for Sustainable Global Development (INDIACom)* (pp. 1692-1698). IEEE. DOI: 10.23919/INDIACom61295.2024.10499164

Kumar, T., Kumar, P., & Namasudra, S. (2024). User revocation-enabled access control model using identity-based signature in the cloud computing environment. *International Journal of Interactive Multimedia and Artificial Intelligence*, 9(1), 127–136. DOI: 10.9781/ijimai.2024.05.001

Kumar, T., Namasudra, S., & Kumar, P. (2023). Providing data security using DNA computing in the cloud computing environment. *International Journal of Web and Grid Services*, 19(4), 463–486. Advance online publication. DOI: 10.1504/IJWGS.2023.135587

Mohammed, A., Kumar, S., Mu'Azu, H. G., Kumar, R., Shah, P., Memoria, M., Rawat, A., & Gupta, A. (2022). Data Security and Protection: A Mechanism for Managing Data Theft and Cybercrime in Online Platforms of Educational Institutions. *2022 International Conference on Machine Learning, Big Data, Cloud and Parallel Computing, COM-IT-CON 2022*. DOI: 10.1109/COM-IT-CON54601.2022.9850702

Nanda, A. K., Sharma, A., Augustine, P. J., Cyril, B. R., Kiran, V., & Sampath, B. (2024). Securing cloud infrastructure in IaaS and PaaS environments. In Improving Security, Privacy, and Trust in Cloud Computing (pp. 1-33). IGI Global. DOI: 10.4018/979-8-3693-1431-9.ch001

Nassif, A. B., Talib, M. A., Nasir, Q., Albadani, H., & Dakalbab, F. M. (2021). Machine learning for cloud security: A systematic review. *IEEE Access : Practical Innovations, Open Solutions*, 9, 20717–20735. DOI: 10.1109/ACCESS.2021.3054129

Nassif, A. B., Talib, M. A., Nasir, Q., Albadani, H., & Dakalbab, F. M. (2021). Machine learning for cloud security: A systematic review. *IEEE Access : Practical Innovations, Open Solutions*, 9, 20717–20735. DOI: 10.1109/ACCESS.2021.3054129

Parast, F. K., Sindhav, C., Nikam, S., Yekta, H. I., Kent, K. B., & Hakak, S. (2022). Cloud computing security: A survey of service-based models. *Computers & Security*, 114, 102580. DOI: 10.1016/j.cose.2021.102580

Paul, P. K., & Ghose, M. K. (2012). Cloud Computing: Possibilities, challenges and opportunities with special reference to its emerging need in the academic and working area of Information Science. *Procedia Engineering*, 38, 2222–2227. DOI: 10.1016/j.proeng.2012.06.267

Rahman, A., Islam, M. J., Band, S. S., Muhammad, G., Hasan, K., & Tiwari, P. (2023). Towards a blockchain-SDN-based secure architecture for cloud computing in smart industrial IoT. *Digital Communications and Networks*, 9(2), 411–421. DOI: 10.1016/j.dcan.2022.11.003

Sharma, P., Jindal, R., & Borah, M. (2020). Blockchain technology for cloud storage: A systematic literature review. *ACM Computing Surveys*, 53(4), 1–32. Advance online publication. DOI: 10.1145/3403954

Shrivastava, G., Kumar, P., Gupta, D., & Rodrigues, J. J. P. C. (2020). Privacy issues of android application permissions: A literature review. *Transactions on Emerging Telecommunications Technologies*, 31(12), e3773. DOI: 10.1002/ett.3773

Sinha, A., Shrivastava, G., Kumar, P., & Gupta, D. (2022). A community-based hierarchical user authentication scheme for Industry 4.0. *Software, Practice & Experience*, 52(3), 729–743. DOI: 10.1002/spe.2832

Chapter 8
Essentials of IAM in Cloud for Risk Mitigation

Anant Wairagade
https://orcid.org/0009-0006-3884-7903
Independent Researcher, USA

Rishabh Das
https://orcid.org/0000-0003-0649-6898
Ohio University, USA

ABSTRACT

In todays digital world, organizations are growing rapidly leveraging Cloud Infrastructure. However Data breach is one of the top concerns in the cloud realm. With poorly defined access control mechanisms threat actors gain unauthorized access to sensitive data leading to financial loss, brand damage to organizations. IAM is a preventive access control framework that consists of various tools, technologies and processes to build access policies around the protected asset to minimize the impact of cyber attack. This chapter will cover fundamentals of IAM, opportunities and challenges of IAM in the cloud, and effective access management strategies. This chapter will deep dive into some of the key IAM components including multi-factor authentication (MFA), identity federation, policy-based access control and identity providers. APIs are essential for cloud service communication. This chapter will include real world case studies involving IAM solutions in cloud, latest trends and emerging technologies that shape up today's cloud landscape.

DOI: 10.4018/979-8-3693-7137-4.ch008

INTRODUCTION

Securing cloud resources has become a top priority for businesses in today's digital world. As more companies move their data, operations, and applications to the cloud, the chances for cybercriminals to attack grows, increasing the risk of unauthorized access, data breaches, and compliance issues. Just one data breach can seriously impact a business. As one source put it, "data breaches invariably cause damage through disappointed customers and dissatisfied investors" (Masuch, 2021).

Another big reason to secure cloud resources is to stay compliant with regulations. Most industries are required to follow strict data protection laws, whether the company is involved with healthcare, finance, retail, or some other industry. Laws like GDPR and HIPAA are in place to strictly protect and regulate sensitive information, requiring businesses to have strong security measures to protect user data. If companies don't properly secure their cloud resources, they could face serious legal consequences, such as fines or even lawsuits from impacted users. As stated in the article, Cloud Computing: Security Issues and Research Challenges, "Limited control over the data may incur various security issues and threats which include data leakage, insecure interface, sharing of resources, data availability and inside attacks" (Padhy, 2011).

Making cloud security a priority helps keep everything running smoothly. Cloud environments offer many advantages, helping businesses grow and operate more efficiently, but they also come with risks. If proper security measures aren't in place, companies could deal with service disruptions or data loss, resulting in downtime and lost revenue. As stated in the article Reducing Downtime and Business Loss: Addressing Business Risk with Effective Technology, "Security issues can emerge and threaten the integrity of business data. All work could come to a halt — or portions of the business could see systems go offline, while others continue to operate normally. No matter the scenario, businesses must plan for such contingencies and what they will do about them when they appear — unbidden — and affect their end users and end customers and their ability to do business" (Boggs et al., 2009).

With more people working remotely and many companies adopting bring-your-own-device (BYOD) policies, securing cloud resources has become even more crucial. Employees are accessing business apps and sensitive data from different locations and devices with increasing consistency, meaning that businesses need strong IAM systems in place to ensure that the only users who are accessing their cloud resources are those who are authorized.

LITERATURE REVIEW

IAM is a core component in cloud security management for user access, compliance, and associated risk mitigation. The section looks into the existing body of research on IAM in cloud security, identifies current industry challenges, and explores potential solutions and best practices.

Role of IAM in cloud security: IAM plays a vital role in applying secure access policies in cloud environments, which protect data from unauthorized access. Almulla and Yeun (2010) discuss the function of IAM frameworks in ensuring security in three essential tenets: confidentiality, integrity, and availability. They highlight IAM as a building block to make systems resistant to emerging cyber-attacks. Bell, Broklyn, and Egon (2024) explained IAM's capabilities in maintaining regulatory compliance in significant data protection acts worldwide, like GDPR and HIPAA, by enforcing strict control over sensitive information access. Similarly, Desai and McCarty (2020) evaluated the influence of the GDPR on IAM practices and emphasized how IAM systems need adaptation to changed regulatory environments.

Challenges in implementing IAM: Despite the benefits, IAM implementation in cloud environments has numerous challenges. According to Jackson and Goessling (2018), IAM integration into existing systems is often complex, especially in hybrid or multi-cloud environments. These complexities arise from managing identities across diverse platforms with their standards and tools. Moyo and du Toit (2024) cited the possibility of identity duplication across multiple instances of clouds, hence complicating access control with more vulnerabilities. On the other hand, Alansari, Paci, and Sassone (2017) found difficulties in implementing distributed access control in a federated cloud environment, which further calls for scalability and interoperability in IAM systems.

Innovations and best practices: Researchers have suggested several best practices and innovative solutions to IAM challenges. The most recommended approaches are Role-Based Access Control and the Principle of Least Privilege. Sandhu (1998) showed that RBAC minimizes unauthorized access by restricting users to their role permissions. Wu and Feng (2021) extended this work to demonstrate how PoLP can prevent over-provisioning permissions, reducing insider threats.

Automation of IAM processes has become a trend nowadays. Lăcătu u et al. (2022) identified that automated deployment methods are less complex and more effective for IAM systems on the cloud than manual methods. Kamath et al. (2023) have pointed out the use of CI/CD pipelines, which makes IAM provisioning smooth. Another critical aspect of IAM involves MFA. Karie et al. (2020) discussed the integration of MFA with SAML and SSO, showing how it prevents unauthorized access and man-in-the-middle attacks. This agrees with the zero-trust model in which, in all instances, verification of users and their permission should be done, as discussed by Wylde, 2021.

IAM in federated and multi-cloud environments: This is further improved with the Federated identity management system, which makes access easier across several cloud services. One authentication might be enough to share resources across various platforms. Pérez-Méndez et al. (2016) highlighted the advantages of ABFAB, which supports secure and efficient re-authentication of non-web applications. On the other hand, federated IAM systems face privilege escalation attacks, as Hu et al. (2023) mentioned, because of a need for strong misconfiguration repair mechanisms.

Risk management and compliance: The role of IAM is not confined to access control, but it plays an important part in monitoring, auditing, and compliance. Sanders and Yue (2018) suggested reviews for periodically aligning user access based on job roles to prevent privilege creep. Eiers et al. (2023) then developed automated policy repair frameworks that could find and resolve overly permissible access in access policies and resolve them. IAM also provides compliance with regulatory laws such as GDPR and CCPA. Baik 2020, observed that these frameworks force organizations to set strict standards regarding user data protection and proper logging of accesses, which IAM systems handle quite efficiently.

Emerging trends in cloud IAM: The future development of IAM is heavily entwined with developments in cloud technologies. Moyo and du Toit (2024) presented the use of blockchain for enhancing IAM with tamper-proof identity records and decentralized authentication mechanisms. Del Pero et al. (2022) discussed some ethical considerations while integrating AI into IAM systems. They warned against biased decisions on account of automated decision-making.

Economic and operational benefits: IAM provides both security as well as economic and operational benefits. Tao et al. (2019) explained how IAM reduces the financial risks caused by data breaches and failures in compliance. IAM minimizes manual errors and enhances operational efficiency by automating tasks related to onboarding and de-provisioning (Lăcătu u et al., 2022).

Over the years, researchers have worked extensively on the feasibility of AI-based Identity and access management in real-world scenarios. (Spanaki et al., 2021) used AI to design role-based data access control in agriculture 4.0. Their work focuses on safe data sharing and ensures that stakeholders involved share sensitive information while maintaining privacy. Their approach ensures dynamic and context-aware access control to enhance trust between the participants. (Azhar, 2015) explores the integration of AI with identity and access management and states this process reduces redundancy and improves authentication. They also highlighted the fact that employment of such systems in the real world relies on factors such as scalability, complexity of infrastructure, privacy, and security challenges. Overall, these studies showcase the growing trend of AI-based IAM in real-world applications, but their feasibility in the real world remains a challenging task due to challenges of scalability, lack of operational efficiency, complex infrastructure, huge infrastructure costs, and the need to provide data privacy along with compliance with regulations.

RISK MANAGEMENT IN CLOUD

Managing risks in the cloud is crucial as more businesses depend on cloud services to store data, run applications, and keep their operations going. Cloud environments provide businesses with several advantages, including easy scalability and flexibility, while also saving money. However, they also come with their own inherent risks.

To begin, those who use cloud services must understand the shared responsibility model. Any time something goes wrong with a business's cloud services, it's easy to point fingers and want to blame the service provider for issues that occur. However, only some issues are the responsibility of the cloud service provider—the rest is on the business, and it's important to know where that line is drawn. While the cloud provider is responsible for things such as the physical security of their data center, it's up to the customer (aka, the business utilizing the cloud services) to secure their own data and manage who has access to it. If your company's data is breached, it is not the service provider's fault—it is your own, for not securing it properly.

Additionally, storing your data in the cloud without securing it properly could lead to an increased potential for data breaches. Although storing your data in the cloud sounds highly convenient, as it means the data can be accessed at any time from any location, this is also what makes it riskier: it can be accessed at any time, from any location, by anyone who wishes to access it. It is up to you to determine how stringent you wish to be in restricting that access. IAM tools such as multi-factor authentication (MFA) and role-based access control (RBAC) can provide extra steps to access the data in order to reduce risk.

Of course, no cloud risk management analysis would be complete without discussing the inherent risks that capturing data poses when it comes to maintaining compliance, especially for businesses that operate in industries such as healthcare and finance. Both of these fields, and others, are monitored by regulatory agencies that impose strict regulations on how their data should be stored and protected. When companies in these industries choose to use cloud services, they must not only ensure that they are doing their part to meet the regulatory requirements of their respective agencies, but that their service providers are as well.

And, of course, even though cloud environments pose fewer operational risks than home servers, disruptions or downtime can still happen on the end of the service provider, leading to business disruptions that are completely out of the control of the companies utilizing the services.

Although technical controls like MFA and RBAC play critical roles in risk mitigation, relying on them exclusively can create blind spots. One frequently overlooked risk is social engineering, in which attackers trick legitimate users into voluntarily disclosing credentials, bypassing robust access controls. An overemphasis on tools can also understate insider threats. If governance policies and monitoring are inadequate, employees or contractors may inadvertently or intentionally misuse their privileged access, circumventing permissions with minimal technical detection. Furthermore, relying solely on automated IAM solutions can foster a false sense of security if organizations do not regularly assess the evolving threat landscape or conduct thorough risk assessments beyond compliance checklists.

Organizations must combine technical controls with strong processes, governance, and user awareness training to manage risk holistically. Security awareness programs should be frequent and scenario-based, covering how to recognize phishing emails and respond to possible breaches or unauthorized access attempts. IAM controls must be supported by well-defined incident response plans and tested escalation paths to address breaches swiftly when they occur. Companies should also perform regular risk assessments beyond simple audits of MFA usage or role assignments; this means examining whether roles are correctly constructed, ensuring cross-department oversight of access rights, and systematically reviewing how and where sensitive data is stored. By blending technical measures with policy-level risk management, organizations can better anticipate, detect, and respond to the multifaceted risks inherent in cloud environments.

Cloud native applications are vulnerable to cyber attacks such as insider threats and data breaches. Insiders have an advantage over others that they can bypass stringent security guardrails and pose damage to organizational assets by unauthorized access. Insider threats are one of topmost security concerns for cloud infrastructure with growing adoption of cloud based software and users of these software often share sensitive data and create operational risk. User behavior analysis addresses this issue by tracking user actions using various events such as location, time, asset, resources and access.

Traditional IAM systems address user behavior analysis by use of static rule based access control which is not sufficient in a dynamic cloud environment. Machine learning algorithms can be deployed to determine insider risk by analyzing a series of events for deviation from regular behaviour (Netskope, 2023).

IAM ECOSYSTEM IN CLOUD

Identity management is the core of IAM. In a cloud setup, every user—including customers, employees, and partners—needs a unique identity. This identity is used to authenticate the user, confirming they are who they say they are. Identity management as a whole involves creating, managing, and maintaining user identities.

Authentication is all about verifying a user's identity before giving them access to cloud resources. Almost all cloud IAM software comes with multiple options for authenticating users. Businesses may also use all of the options at some point, assigning different authentication options to different users depending on the data that user is allowed to access. For example, accounts that need to access more sensitive information may be required to authenticate via multi-factor authentication (MFA), whereas the average bottom-tier employee who signs in and out of a computer several times a day for their work, and may travel or work from home, may be required to use single sign-on (SSO) to help prevent password fatigue and to encourage or enforce strong passwords. Once a user is authenticated, the next step is authorization. While authentication allows users to enter the cloud and access resources, authorization determines exactly what resources they are allowed to access. Role-based access control, or "RBAC," is a common method for assigning access control to users. Within a company, you may have your basic employees, managers, HR workers, an IT team, and more. Each of these people needs to access specific information in order to do their job effectively; however, they don't necessarily need to access all of the information available within the cloud. With role-based access control, a company can assign a role to a user that allows them access to a predetermined set of data and resources. For example, a new employee may be assigned the role of "HR officer," which lets them access employees files, health information, and benefits information. However, someone with the role "IT administrator" would not be able to access this information, yet they would be allowed access to information that HR does not have access to.

Monitoring and auditing are also part of the anatomy of cloud IAM. Most cloud IAM software comes pre-equipped with programs that track user activities and access attempts in real time, and keep detailed logs of these access attempts. Many programs also have built-in security systems that automatically flag unusual user behavior and send an alert to an administrator. For example, if a user usually accesses a company's resources from their home or office during business hours, and then suddenly attempts access with their username and password at midnight from across the country, this could be a sign that the user's account has been compromised. Additionally, the logs that are kept and maintained are helpful for proving a business has been following legal requirements if a regulatory agency comes knocking with an audit. Figure 1. Shows foundational components of Cloud IAM.

Figure 1. Foundational Components of Cloud IAM

IAM manages the full lifecycle of a user's identity and access—from the moment an account is created to when it's no longer needed in Cloud. IAM deployment in a cloud context entails setting up user roles, policies, and permissions to impose the least privileged access. Corporations may create sophisticated limits on access using native IAM solutions offered by cloud providers. Roles are allocated to individuals according to their job duties, and those with roles have certain rights. IAM systems that include multi-factor authentication (MFA) and role-based access controls (RBAC) are crucial, according to (Bell et al., 2024). By providing an extra crucial degree of security, MFA reduces the dangers related to credential compromises. It substantially lowers the likelihood of illegal access by demanding several verification forms, consistent with the Zero Trust Model's tenet of constantly vetting access requests, particularly for sensitive data.

BEST PRACTICES FOR CLOUD IAM

a. Role Based Access Control

Role based access control (RBAC) distributes rights according to user roles inside a company, hence upholding the least-privilege concept. Because each role has a set of privileged privileges, users only have access to the information and materials required to do their jobs. In doing so, the possibility of illegal access to private information is reduced. RBAC groups individuals with comparable duties to streamline access administration in cloud settings. A "Database Administrator" designated individual, for instance, could be able to administer databases but not change network settings. Companies can simplify handling user credentials by creating positions and delegating people to them. One may identify a user as a supervisor, an expert, or an end user and match access rights and duties to the roles that your workers have inside the company, and access levels are limited to what is necessary for personnel to do their duties as an example by (Sandhu, R. S., 1998).

b. Principle of least Privilege (PoLP)

Principle of least Privilege grants users minimum permission required for their daily workflow. PoLP prevents over-provisioning of permissions and reduces the attack vector of an organization from IAM misconfiguration. Based on Wu et al.'s research,organizations can use PoLP to mitigate insider threats and reduce potential damages from compromised accounts (Wu & Feng, 2021). Wu's research also highlights the importance of enforcing an automated approach for cnforcing PoLP resulting in a streamlined cloud permission management. In alignment with Wu's study, Shimizu et al. outlines an automated least privilege discovery method (Shimizu & Kanuka, 2020). Shimizu's automated methodology improved the test execution and time by 69.3% and 39.8% respectively. Based on Shimizu's study, the result minimizes the risk of cyberattacks caused by over-privilege and streamlines the cloud infrastructure management.

c. *Identity Federation*

The adoption of identity federation simplifies access to cloud resources, reduces user management cost and increases utilization of cloud resources (Pérez et al., 2016). Pérez-Méndez et al. highlights the importance of Application Bridging for Federated Access Beyond web (ABFAB) architecture in providing identity federation to non-Web application services. Pérez-Méndez mentions how federated identity systems can achieve faster and more secure re-authentication through the

EAP Re-authentication Protocol (ERP). Wang et al.'s study supports the findings from Pérez-Méndez's work.Wang cites IAM misconfiguration as a major issue which can open organizations to privilege escalation attacks (Hu et al., 2023). To remediate IAM misconfiguration issues, Wang et al. proposes a IAM Privilege Escalation Repair Engine called IAMPERE. IAMPERE can automatically repair a large number of IAM misconfigurations. (Alansar et al., 2017) and (Ducatel, 2015) both highlight the importance of integrated identity federation for a scalable, cloud-based identity solution.

d. Periodic Access Reviews

Sander et al. discusses the importance of conducting periodic access reviews to prevent "privilege creep" (Sanders & Yue, 2018). The research presents a framework for minimizing over-privilege and emphasizes the need to align user permissions with their job roles. Eiers et al. introduces an automated policy repair method to detect overly permissive access control policies in cloud environments (Eiers et al., 2023). Sanders et al. expands the study to heterogeneous cloud environments and illustrates the effectiveness of automated frameworks based on audit logs in reducing administrative burden (Sanders & Yue, 2017).

e. Automated provisioning and deprovisioning

Automation of IAM workflows streamlines user permissions during onboarding and offboarding, reduces human error and improves compliance with security policies (Cinar, 2023). Lăcătu u et al. supports this finding by comparing a manual deployment to an automated approach (Lăcătu u et al.,2022). Lăcătu u found manual deployment two to seven times more complex than an automated approach. Cadavez et al. further validates Lăcătu u's finding and illustrates how use of an automation tool like VRealize can reduce the provisioning time from hours to minutes. Consequently, organizations should consider cloud infrastructure automation through Continuous Integration/Continuous Delivery (CI/CD) pipelines. Using tools such as GitHub Action during code compilation, testing and deployment can speed up the overall cloud infrastructure provisioning process (Kamath, 2023).

f. Multi-Factor Authentication (MFA)

Multi Factor authentication (MFA) adds an extra layer of authentication by requiring users to provide two or more verification factors to gain access to critical systems. The Multi Factor authentication uses unique communication channels and protects users for compromised credentials. Karie et al., combines MFA with Security

Assertions Markup Language (SAML) with SSO (Karie et al., 2020). Based on the analysis, Karie found the integration as a robust solution for preventing man in the middle (MiTM) attacks and securing authentication framework for cloud services.

g. Zero Trust Model

No matter where the network request comes from, the "Never Trust, Always Verify" principle mandates that all access requests undergo thorough authentication and authorization. According to the zero-trust concept, no structure or user can be presumed trustworthy, as hackers might exist both within and outside. Verifying user identification, rights, system belonging, and integrity is done with zero trust. The passwords, logins, and network timeouts are repeatedly confirmed. Each person and equipment is given an individual username and set of qualifications, and verification secures all connections, according to (Wylde, A., 2021).

In addition to restricting resource access, Zero Trust mandates enterprises implement rigorous safeguards on their devices. In order to minimize the attack surface, the system keeps track of the number of distinct systems that can get into the company network, verifies that each device is permitted, and provides assessments to ensure the devices are not hacked. There is also the principle of Micro-segmentation, which divides the security perimeter into smaller portions to preserve distinct access for various network segments. A different authentication method is needed for entry to other zones. According to Dave Klein of GuardiCore, micro-segmentation is a valuable technique for securing priceless data center assets and putting a zero-trust paradigm into place in a hybrid or multi-cloud context (Klein, 2019). The lateral Movement Prevention principle is where zero trust frameworks aim to stop intruders from entering the internet from the side.

Figure 2. Shows key components of Zero trust Implementation.

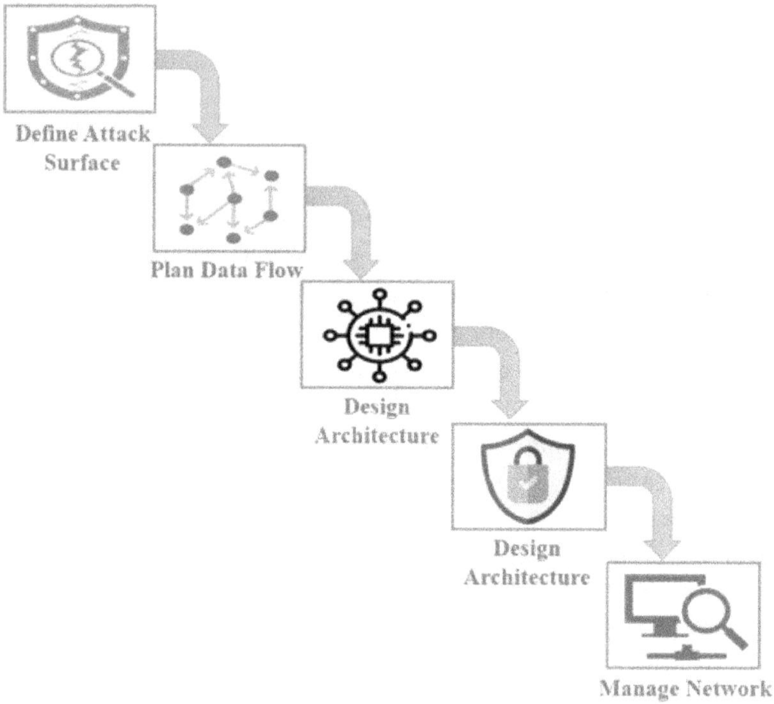

Zero trust Implementation consists of:

1. Define attack surface - mostly focusing on specific high value assets unlike traditional security models (Medina, 2021).
2. Data Flow - secure the channels which carry users, devices and application's data (Petchiappan, 2024).
3. Architecture - This is where Identity and access Managements tools are deployed to enforce 'Never trust, always verify' (Petchiappan, 2024).
4. Policy - Policies act as preventive control and help limit privilege sprawl (Medina, 2021).
5. Continuous Monitoring - Tools like SIEM and threat intelligence software help monitor traffic for malicious activities (Medina, 2021).

BENEFITS OF CLOUD IAM

Cloud IAM offers a ton of benefits for businesses that want to improve security, boost efficiency, and stay compliant in the cloud. As more companies rely on cloud services for data storage and running key applications, Cloud IAM becomes essential for managing user access and keeping resources safe.

As business grows, managing access to cloud resources can get complicated. Cloud IAM is built to scale, making it easy to manage thousands of users across multiple platforms without adding extra work. Whether a company is hiring more employees, adding new apps, or using more cloud services, Cloud IAM embraces scalability and makes it manageable.

If an organization is in an industry that's regulated, like healthcare or finance, Cloud IAM also makes it easier to meet compliance requirements. It gives essential tools to track user access, audit permissions, and generate reports to show compliance during audits, helping organizations avoid fines or legal trouble.

Cloud IAM doesn't just help with security—it also makes things easier for the users themselves. As stated in the article,Cloud Identity and Access Management — A Model Proposal, "Many businesses have implemented Identity and Access Management (IAM) systems to reap the many advantages of cloud computing while also mitigating the risks associated with privacy and security concerns" (Mohammed, 2019). For example, with processes such as SSO, employees can log in once and access multiple apps without having to remember different passwords for each one. It simplifies the login process, boosts productivity, and cuts down on password fatigue.

Cloud IAM grows with your business and automates many of the repetitive tasks involved in managing access, saving both time and money while reducing risk. For any business using the cloud, Cloud IAM is essential for keeping things secure and running efficiently.

CHALLENGES AND CONSIDERATIONS OF CLOUD IAM

Even with the best practices in place, things can still go wrong as threat actors exploit vulnerabilities in the system. That's why having a strong risk management contingency plan is so important. Your plan should outline the procedures necessary to identify, contain, and resolve potential data breaches or compromised accounts. You will also need a plan for communicating the damage with affected parties and regulatory agencies, as well as for how you will handle damage control to have the least long-term negative impact on your company. As previously stated, when utilizing cloud services, it's important to understand the shared responsibility model and what you are responsible for handling versus what your service provider is responsible for. All that being said, even if an incident occurs that your service provider is legally responsible for, you are still responsible for communicating compromised accounts to the affected parties in your care. It's on your business to manage user access and protect the data in your cloud environment.

Implementing cloud IAM software into your business's cybersecurity strategy will also come with challenges and other things that you will need to consider. One of the biggest challenges with cloud IAM software involves managing identities across multiple roles and levels and potentially even across multiple cloud platforms. Many companies rely on more than one cloud provider as different providers have different strengths, and you may already be using multiple providers at once, such as some combination of AWS, Google Cloud, and Azure, among others. In fact, using multiple platforms may be a positive thing, as it helps to prevent vendor lock-in, even if it creates additional challenges.

One thing that you will have to pay attention to when implementing cloud IAM is ensuring that you are not making the login process too complicated or difficult for users. Although security is important, you will need to find a balance between making the login process as smooth and fluid as possible without compromising the integrity of the data the users are accessing. If processes such as MFA for example aren't set up thoughtfully and assigned specifically to more sensitive accounts, they can be frustrating for some employees who need to sign in and out repeatedly throughout the day. If things get too complicated, people may attempt to find ways around the system that compromise security, such as using weaker passwords.

In the article The Use of Blockchain for Identity and Access Management (IAM) in Multi-cloud, it states, "The user's identity may be duplicated across multiple cloud instances, complicating identity management" (Moyo et al., 2024). Companies need to be mindful of factors such as these and think through how they'll handle things that may complicate the IAM environment while maintaining compliance with regulations.

a. Managing Identities Across Multiple Cloud Environments

As previously stated, managing identities across multiple cloud environments is ideal, but can be tricky to handle. Businesses who continue this course may find themselves having problems with inconsistent policies as they try to juggle the regulations and restrictions of multiple different platforms.

One way to help streamline processes is by using federated identity management. If you've ever attempted to sign into a site and been asked to sign in through your Google account, or something similar, you've used federated identity management. There are multiple advantages to this form of identity management, one of which being that you can almost outsource your identity management to a large and already trustworthy company, such as google. Instead of having separate logins for every cloud service, users may sign into Google or Microsoft and be connected to everything all at once. Federated identity management simplifies things for them and saves you the trouble of managing individual login credentials. Plus, you're piggybacking on the security measures of these big providers, which is an added bonus.

Additionally, compliance becomes more complicated when you're juggling multiple cloud platforms, especially when you are handling multiple types of data sets and attempting to follow the restrictions imposed by multiple regulatory agencies. It's important to keep your business's access policies consistent across all platforms, even if the regulatory requirements differ from platform to platform. At the end of the day, you may consider picking the strictest one and implementing the same rules across all users and platforms.

At the end of the day, juggling identity management across multiple platforms brings complications, but implementing an assortment of strategies can help to better simplify things. In the article A Comprehensive Review of Security Measures in Database Systems: Assessing Authentication, Access Control, and Beyond, they state, "Threats to database security come in many forms, and they are all part of the database danger environment. To successfully implement security measures and reduce these threats, a thorough comprehension of this setting is essential" (Omotunde & ahmed, 2023).

b. Challenges and Considerations of Cloud-Based Identity Providers for IAM

Most companies still run a mix of cloud and on-premise systems, and getting everything to work together can be tricky—especially if you're working with older, legacy systems. In the book Architecting Cloud Computing Solutions, they state, "We hear that the cloud simplifies, yet it makes things more complicated (at first)" (Jackson & Goessling, 2018). You need to make sure the identity provider you choose can support what you're already using without causing disruptions.

If you're working with multiple cloud platforms, like AWS, Azure, or Google Cloud, it's important to make sure your identity provider works well with all of them. Since each platform has its own IAM tools, you'll want to choose a solution that supports open standards like SAML, OAuth, and OpenID Connect, so authentication is smooth and consistent across all platforms.

Cloud identity providers store sensitive data, like personal user information and access credentials, which raises concerns about where that data is stored and how it's processed. With regulations like GDPR and CCPA in play, some regions have strict rules about where personal data can be kept. It's important to ensure your provider complies with these privacy laws and keeps your data secure.

Since cloud-based identity providers manage essential functions like user authentication and access control, any downtime can seriously disrupt your business. If the provider goes offline, users won't be able to access critical applications, which can negatively impact productivity. It's important to check the provider's reliability, Service Level Agreements (SLAs), and what kind of backup systems they have in place to avoid outages.

Relying too much on one cloud-based identity provider can lead to vendor lock-in, where switching providers becomes difficult and costly. Some providers use proprietary tech that doesn't integrate well with others, which could limit your options down the road. To avoid being stuck with one vendor, consider choosing providers that support open standards, so you have more flexibility if you ever need to switch. As stated in the article, "A Holistic Decision Framework to Avoid Vendor Lock-in for Cloud SaaS Migration, "when enterprises interact with SaaS providers within the purview of the current cloud marketplace, they often encounter significant lock-in challenges to migrating and interconnecting clouds. Hence, the complexity and variety of cloud SaaS service offerings makes it imperative for businesses to use a clear and well understood decision process to procure, migrate and/or discontinue cloud services" (Opara et al., 2017). You should also ensure the provider you select is flexible enough to meet your business's unique needs.

c. Ensuring Compliance with Ever Changing Regulations and Standards

With more businesses moving to the cloud, it's crucial to stay on top of how we manage access to sensitive data and resources. The rules around security and privacy keep changing, and Cloud IAM plays a key role in making sure businesses comply with these evolving regulations. The regulations your business will need to follow will differ depending on the location you operate in and the industry you work in. For example, if you're doing business in Europe, you will need to comply with GDPR; if you're handling healthcare data in the U.S., you will need to follow HIPAA laws. The first step to ensuring compliance is fully understanding what rules apply to your business, and then making sure your IAM systems are following those rules. This may mean hiring a legal expert to ensure you are doing everything the correct way. As regulations continue to change, businesses must be able to adopt flexible IAM systems that are able to automate compliance tasks wherever possible, and adapt whenever changes occur.

One thing that will remain true across every agency in every industry is ensuring that you have the ability to prove that you're being compliant. Simply saying you're following the rules is not enough to appease a regulatory agency if you're being audited or reported for violating policy. Each and every business must ensure that they are keeping detailed logs and performing regular audits. Most cloud IAM software comes with the built-in tools necessary to generate both real-time insights and detailed audit logs.

Additionally, employers understanding all of the regulatory requirements means nothing if their employees don't also understand both the requirements and the importance of following them. Regular training for employees at all levels is essential, and must cover topics such as maintaining secure access credentials and following best practices for data security. Everyone with the organization, from the bottom to the top, needs to understand security and compliance.

d. Managing Identities for External Users and Partners

External users pose a different type of threat than long-term employees or even outside attackers that have no affiliation with your business. Granting them access is just the beginning—regular monitoring and auditing are also essential, and their access roles may change more frequently than an employee's. They may also only be here short-term, meaning that their roles will need to be managed and removed more rapidly than that of employees you are onboarding or offboarding, which can be one of the trickiest parts of managing external identities. It is crucial for businesses to maintain a smooth, efficient process for getting external user accounts up and running quickly, but also to ensure that users are deprovisioned extremely quickly the moment their work is finished. Automating the process through cloud IAM software can make this task significantly easier, and also cut down on human error, such as leaving an account active long after the external user has left.

Communication with external users about your business's security expectations that is on par with that of the education of your employees is also crucial for maintaining security. It would be no benefit if you invested in your employees' education, and then an external user compromised a critical account. Provide them with some basic training on IAM best practices, such as how to avoid phishing scams or not to reuse passwords, and you will avoid at least the basics of mistakes.

e. IAM Usability

Implementing IAM tools that employees and external partners will want to use can be challenging, especially when balancing strong security measures with day-to-day practicality. If the login processes are too complex, people will find ways around them by reusing passwords, writing down credentials, or ignoring multi-factor authentication requests, defeating the purpose of enhanced security. On the other hand, solutions that are too simple will not provide the necessary protection and can lead to data leakage or compliance violations. Much like managing a multi-cloud environment or integrating on-premise legacy systems, developing a user-friendly IAM system requires consideration of how each step in the authentication process impacts productivity. Single sign-on and intuitive password-reset workflows enable users to be more efficient, while role-based controls and clear, free prompting help keep standards without burying the employees in red tape. This is a thought expressed in the book Architecting Cloud Computing Solutions, where it is said, "We hear that the cloud simplifies, yet it makes things more complicated (at first)" (Jackson & Goessling, 2018). The same can be applied to IAM usability: well-designed interfaces with easy procedures may take more work upfront but save errors, frustration, and inconsistent execution of security policies.

f. Integration challenges across multiple cloud platforms

As more organizations adopt multi-cloud strategies, integrating Identity and Access Management (IAM) across heterogeneous environments presents significant operational and technical challenges. While providers such as Amazon Web Services (AWS), Microsoft Azure, and Google Cloud each offer native IAM frameworks, the fundamental differences in their approaches to defining roles, groups, and permission sets often complicate maintaining consistent access policies (Moyo & du Toit, 2024). For example, Azure organizes roles focused on the Azure AD tenants and user profiles, while AWS heavily relies on explicit IAM policy and role associations using very detailed trust relationships. Such differences can create mismatched privileges, duplicate accounts, or misconfigured policies that may inadvertently create security blind spots. Compliance obligations further complicate interoperability since each platform's logging and reporting tools must align seamlessly with regulatory requirements such as GDPR, HIPAA, or CCPA, regardless of how each cloud provider structures its authentication layers.

LEGAL AND ETHICAL IMPLICATIONS OF CLOUD IAM

Data privacy is one of the largest legal concerns of cloud IAM. When you rely on a cloud provider to manage your IAM, you're trusting them with your data—data that may include sensitive and protected information from locations all around the world. Locations such as Europe or even California impose their own strict regulations on how personal data should be stored and handled, and it is important for global companies to be aware of and comply with all regulations, not just those of their local government.

In addition to legal concerns, ethical concerns are raised when personal data is stored and shared. People put a lot of trust in businesses to appropriately handle their personal information, and not doing so responsibly could result in a serious ethical violation that could drive customer traffic away. It's important to be transparent with users that are associated with your company about where their data will be stored and processed. If their data is being moved across borders, they deserve to be made aware of this, and you need to make certain that these transfers don't compromise the level of protection they expect from you. Compliance isn't just about meeting legal regulations; it's also about respecting the data you're managing—and the human beings this data comes from. When handling medical records or financial information, even more caution should be exercised, as even the smallest of breaches could cause serious harm to someone's life.

Another important legal consideration to make is that of data ownership. When you use third-party cloud IAM providers, who owns the data? Do you, or does your service provider? Is there somewhere in the fine print that states that when you utilize their software, the service provider can access or even use the data themselves? Before you implement an IAM program or software, you need to make sure that your organization will retain control over your data and that you will be able to switch service providers if necessary and keep the data you've inputted up to that point.

Cloud IAM software is designed to protect data as much as possible, but breaches could still occur. If there's a breath, you have an ethical duty to notify your users as soon as possible, even if the law doesn't require it. Covering up data breaches will only erode trust among your customers and partners, and could lead to even more damage to your company than the data breach itself.

One final ethical issue to consider is the implementation of AI in IAM programs. There has been evidence of AI programs discriminating against users. After all, AI was created and designed by humans, and it may contain the biases of the humans that created it. As one article claims, "AI systems have the potential to improve workplaces, but ensuring trustworthy use of AI in the workplace means addressing the ethical risks it can raise" (Del, 2022). You may decide to avoid these potential biases by avoiding AI altogether, but it's not possible to fully avoid biases—the humans you hire to replace the AI will hold biases of their own, as well.

IAM CASE STUDY FROM RETAIL INDUSTRY

ABC Retail is a mid-range retail organization that is currently scaling up online as well as offline platforms. The firm has thousands of employees in different branches, and as the customers' list expands, they have had to extend from on-site solutions to leverage the cloud environment for better adaptability, employee interaction, and data availability. This change presented new security concerns for the business concerning control of access and secure handling of the customers' information.

a. Challenges: As ABC Retail moved its systems to the cloud, it faced challenges related to Identity and Access Management (IAM). The first challenge was that employees had more access rights than required, thus, raising the susceptibility to internal information leaks. The company had a requirement to address requirements like GDPR and CCPA for data protection with the problem that they had no way to monitor and enforce strictly controlled and auditable access to data.
b. Solutions: Such a transition offered a way to centralize user management and identification in all cloud resources. Employee access was made according to the job description, so each employee could only view and manipulate information relevant to their job. To improve security, MFA was put in action to be used in situations where employees will be accessing different sensitive systems. IAM made the manner of granting and degrading accounts associated with the employment status of the employees automatic. To protect the resources of ABC Retail, the solution offered auditing, with which all access attempts would be recorded. This ensured compliance with the Data Privacy Acts and made it easy for the IT Department to promptly detect areas of security concern.
c. Results and Conclusion: The internal threats were gradually eliminated by cutting down over-privileged access by 90 percent. MFA also ensured that any sensitive information was protected from the various mannered users. Automated access management cut manual effort for permissions by 60%, freeing up IT teams to work on higher-value business tasks. Due to the centrality of the IAM system, company was able to fully satisfy GDPR and CCPA compliance requirements due to well-established audit trails and robust data protection features.

IAM CASE STUDY FROM HEALTHCARE INDUSTRY

Kaiser Permanente is one of the nation's largest integrated managed care providers, serving millions of members and staffing tens of thousands of healthcare professionals. Services operated by the company include hospitals, clinics, and online health services, providing a wide array of medical offerings under strict HIPAA regulations. The solutions presented by Copeland et al. (2019) include:

a. Challenges: As Kaiser Permanente's patient base and online health services grew, it faced significant difficulties centralizing identity and access controls across various clinical applications, telemedicine portals, and administrative tools (Liu et al., 2021). Employees—from physicians to medical assistants—were often provided with broad permissions beyond their immediate roles. This lack of precise access control raised the risk of unauthorized data disclosure and complicated ongoing HIPAA audits. Furthermore, there was no automatic offboarding mechanism for clinicians who were supposed to rotate; it would eventually linger into improperly deactivated accounts.
b. Solutions: Kaiser Permanente implemented a strong IAM platform that compelled the Principle of Least Privilege-PoLP, aligning user accounts strictly with job functions. Kaiser implemented multi-factor authentication that was compulsive when it came to accessing sensitivity information, like patient test results or billing records, thereby minimizing the probability of credential compromise. In addition, the automation of provisioning and de-provisioning workflows was integrated directly with the company's HR systems to ensure the accounts' status correctly reflects the employment and staffing status. Real-time monitoring dashboards were deployed to identify suspicious login activities, such as attempts to access systems outside of designated job scopes (Liu et al., 2021).
c. Results and Conclusion: Kaiser Permanente reported that, in the six months following this IAM overhaul, unauthorized access incidents had fallen by 65%, and HIPAA auditing was much easier (Copeland et al., 2019). The organization mitigated the possibility of data mishandling. It reduced administrative overhead related to user account management by decreasing manual oversight and tying access rights to formalized roles. The unified IAM framework allowed Kaiser Permanente to deliver secure, efficient patient care and maintain a strong compliance posture in one of the nation's most highly regulated healthcare environments (Liu et al., 2021).

ECONOMIC IMPACT OF IAM IN CLOUD

IAM market revenue was 15.8 billion USD in 2022 and expected to reach 43.1 billion US dollars by 2029 (Statista, 2024). There are multiple economic advantages to utilizing cloud IAM, the first of which being scalability. If companies begin to grow or expand rapidly, it can sometimes be difficult to handle the increase in business and the quickly changing landscape that a business will begin to see. IAM can help to automate processes such as onboarding and offboarding and managing large amounts of data all at once. Traditional management systems, which often involve a lot of manual input, can be overwhelming and expensive and prone to human error.

Cloud IAM software offers scalability that adapts to a business's growth without needing to invest large amounts of money into new infrastructure, allowing businesses to expand rapidly without skyrocketing IT costs.

Cloud IAM also helps reduce the financial damage from security breaches. Practices like least privilege and MFA lower the risk of unauthorized access, which can save a company from the high costs of breaches—not just from fines and legal fees but also the damage to their reputation. Investing in IAM now to prevent data breaches can help save businesses hefty fines and legal fees down the road. As stated in the article *Economic perspective analysis of protecting big data security and privacy,* "an important factor for current and future economical investments is due to the motivation of cybercrime activities" (Tao et al, 2019).

COST-BENEFIT ANALYSIS OF IAM IN PREVENTING BREACHES

While security remains the primary objective of Identity and Access Management (IAM), the economic rationale for robust IAM investments is equally compelling. By emphasizing a clear connection between preventive measures and bottom-line outcomes, organizations can view IAM not merely as a security requirement but also as a cost-efficient pillar of risk management (Tao et al., 2019).

Quantifying the financial repercussions of breaches: A crucial step in any cost-benefit analysis is identifying the financial repercussions of cybersecurity breaches, typically including direct and indirect costs. Direct costs often arise from immediate incident response, such as investigating and neutralizing unauthorized access, hiring forensic specialists, and restoring compromised systems (Masuch et al., 2021). In addition, legal and regulatory fines can be substantial if businesses fail to meet baseline security requirements as mandated by standards like the General Data Protection Regulation (GDPR) or the California Consumer Privacy Act (CCPA) (Baik, 2020; Desai & McCarty, 2020). Meanwhile, enterprises may incur significant expenses when notifying customers of breaches and providing remedial services, such as credit monitoring.

Indirect costs are just as important to consider. These costs manifest as damage to brand reputation, reduced customer loyalty, and diminished investor confidence (Masuch et al., 2021). Together, these direct and indirect costs can impose an economic burden far exceeding any up-front investment in IAM tools and best practices.

Preventive value of IAM in reducing attack surface and incident frequency: IAM tools and practices, particularly those employing the Principle of Least Privilege (Wu & Feng, 2021) and multi-factor authentication (MFA) (Karie et al., 2020), significantly reduce the likelihood and severity of security incidents. By granting users only the permissions essential for their roles, least-privilege access inherently diminishes what adversaries can achieve if a single account is compromised (Sanders & Yue, 2018). Furthermore, extended IAM setups can find and fix misconfigurations, preventing privilege-escalation attacks and limiting lateral movement in networked environments (Hu et al., 2023). If implemented correctly, these IAM measures reduce the number of attacks and their overall impact, leading to significant cost avoidance.

Long-Term return on investment (ROI): When considering IAM investments, organizations should account for initial and ongoing costs, such as software licenses, system integration expenses, employee training, and long-term operational overhead (Lăcătu u et al., 2022). At the same time, the potential cost of breaches must be calculated by examining likely remediation expenditures—particularly in settings where the frequency and severity of attacks can be estimated using historical data or industry standards (Tao et al., 2019). Productivity improvements also enter into the cost equation. Automating onboarding and offboarding processes, real-time access reviews, and reduced help-desk interventions lead to lower labor costs (Kamath et al., 2023). When these avoided losses and productivity gains are factored in, the net ROI for IAM seems favorable over the long term (Sanders & Yue, 2018; Wu & Feng, 2021).

FUTURE OF CLOUD COMPUTING

The future of cloud computing includes emerging trends and technologies:

a. Edge computing: Reducing latency as well as reducing bandwidth consumption by pulling processing power closer to the site of data generation. It is becoming important for IoT applications as well as real-time analytics.
b. AI and machine learning integration: Building advanced analytics applications is getting easier because cloud service providers are adding AI/ML features and allowing customers to create, train, and deploy models in the provided services.

c. Quantum computing: Quantum computing is still an emerging technology, but there are already some quantum computing functionalities that will be offered as cloud services and promised to solve complicated problems that cannot be solved on classical computers.
d. Sustainability: Cost is not the only issue for the cloud companies as they are also making the changes in energy practices by using carbon-neutral data centers for the purpose to lessen the carbon footprint made during data storage and computation.

CONCLUSION

Cloud computing environments are complex in nature as they are a combination of many technologies and services, aimed at providing flexibility, scalability and cost efficiency at the same time. Knowing the types of services provided, the service delivery models, the deployment strategies and the system architectural patterns gives one an insight on the design and the changes that have been made in the cloud environments.

As the cloud continues to grow with more capabilities, organizations will have to keep pace with the emerging trends, overcome the security obstacles and reinvent their approaches in order to harness the full potential of cloud computing. In the article *Cloud computing security management*, they claim that there are three major information security concerns: confidentiality, integrity, and availability (Almulla & Yeun, 2010). Cloud IAM software helps to address these concerns. As businesses increasingly move their resources to cloud environments, manual IAM processes are no longer sufficient to maintain security. Although cloud IAM comes with multiple benefits, challenges, considerations, and legal and ethical issues, it is still important to invest in strong cloud IAM software.

REFERENCES

Alansari, S., Paci, F., & Sassone, V. (2017). A Distributed Access Control System for Cloud Federations. 2017 IEEE 37th International Conference on Distributed Computing Systems (ICDCS), 2131-2136. DOI: 10.1109/ICDCS.2017.241

Almulla, S. A., & Yeun, C. Y. (2010, March). Cloud computing security management. In *2010 Second International Conference on Engineering System Management and Applications* (pp. 1-7). IEEE.

Azhar, I. (2015, March 1). The Interaction Between Artificial Intelligence and Identity & Access Management: An Empirical study. https://papers.ssrn.com/sol3/papers.cfm?abstract_id=3905771

Baik, J. (2020). Data Privacy Against Innovation or Against Discrimination?: The Case of the California Consumer Privacy Act (CCPA). Consumer Law eJournal. .DOI: 10.1016/j.tele.2020.101431

Bell, C., Broklyn, P., & Egon, A. (2024). Cloud Security and Data Privacy. SSRN Electronic Journal. DOI: 10.2139/ssrn.4904978

Boggs, R., Bozman, J., & Perry, R. (2009). Reducing downtime and business loss: addressing business risk with effective technology. IDC, Tech. Rep.

Cinar, B. (2023). The Role of Cloud Service Brokers: Enhancing Security and Compliance in Multi-cloud Environments. Journal of Engineering Research and Reports. .DOI: 10.9734/jerr/2023/v25i10995

Copeland, R., Wong, W., Jones, J., & Edmunds, M. (2019). *Using Information Technology at Kaiser Permanente to Support Health Equity*. Consumer Informatics and Digital Health., DOI: 10.1007/978-3-319-96906-0_3

Del Pero, A. S., Wyckoff, P., & Vourc'h, A. (2022). Using Artificial Intelligence in the workplace: What are the main ethical risks? Desai, D. R., & McCarty, M. (2020). The implementation of the General Data Protection Regulation and its impact on European business models. Information Privacy Law eJournal.

Ducatel, G. (2015). Identity as a service: A cloud based common capability. *2015 IEEE Conference on Communications and Network Security (CNS)*, 675-679. DOI: 10.1109/CNS.2015.7346886

Eiers, W., Sankaran, G., & Bultan, T. (2023). Quantitative Policy Repair for Access Control on the Cloud. *Proceedings of the 32nd ACM SIGSOFT International Symposium on Software Testing and Analysis*. DOI: 10.1145/3597926.3598078

Hamza, M., Abubakar, H., & Danlami, Y. (2018). Identity and Access Management System: a Web-Based Approach for an Enterprise. Path of Science. .DOI: 10.22178/pos.40-1

Hossain, N., Hossain, M., Hossain, M., Sohag, M., & Rahman, S. (2018). OAuth-SSO: A Framework to Secure the OAuth-Based SSO Service for Packaged Web Applications. 2018 17th IEEE International Conference On Trust, Security And Privacy In Computing And Communications/ 12th IEEE International Conference On Big Data Science And Engineering (TrustCom/BigDataSE), 1575-1578. DOI: 10.1109/TrustCom/BigDataSE.2018.00227

Hu, Y., Wang, W., Khurshid, S., McMillan, K., & Tiwari, M. (2023). Fixing Privilege Escalations in Cloud Access Control with MaxSAT and Graph Neural Networks. 2023 38th IEEE/ACM International Conference on Automated Software Engineering (ASE), 104-115. DOI: 10.1109/ASE56229.2023.00167

Jackson, K. L., & Goessling, S. (2018). *Architecting Cloud Computing Solutions: Build cloud strategies that align technology and economics while effectively managing risk.* Packt Publishing Ltd.

Kamath, S., Vignesh, S., & Darshan, G. (2023, June). Revolutionizing cloud infrastructure management: Streamlined provisioning and monitoring with automated tools and user-friendly frontend interface. In 2023 3rd International Conference on Intelligent Technologies (CONIT) (pp. 1-6). IEEE.

Karie, N., Kebande, V., Ikuesan, R., Sookhak, M., & Venter, H. (2020). Hardening SAML by Integrating SSO and Multi-Factor Authentication (MFA) in the Cloud. *Proceedings of the 3rd International Conference on Networking, Information Systems & Security*. DOI: 10.1145/3386723.3387875

Klein, D. (2019). Micro-segmentation: Securing complex cloud environments. *Network Security*, 2019(3), 6–10. DOI: 10.1016/S1353-4858(19)30034-0

Kroschewski, M., & Lehmann, A. (2023). Save The Implicit Flow? Enabling Privacy-Preserving RP Authentication in OpenID Connect. *Proceedings on Privacy Enhancing Technologies. Privacy Enhancing Technologies Symposium*, 2023(4), 96–116. DOI: 10.56553/popets-2023-0100

Kunz, M., Fuchs, L., Hummer, M., & Pernul, G. (2015). Introducing Dynamic Identity and Access Management in Organizations., 139-158. .DOI: 10.1007/978-3-319-26961-0_9

Lăcătu u, M., Ionita, A. D., Anton, F. D., & Lăcătu u, F. (2022). Analysis of Complexity and Performance for Automated Deployment of a Software Environment into the Cloud. *Applied Sciences (Basel, Switzerland)*, 12(9), 4183. DOI: 10.3390/app12094183

Liu, G., Li, A., Canel, C., & Sekar, V. (2021). Watching the watchmen: Least privilege for managed network services. *Proceedings of the 20th ACM Workshop on Hot Topics in Networks*. DOI: 10.1145/3484266.3487380

Masuch, K., Greve, M., Trang, S., & Kolbe, L. M. (2021). Apologize or justify? Examining the impact of data breach response actions on stock value of affected companies? *Computers & Security*, 112, 102502. DOI: 10.1016/j.cose.2021.102502

Medina, J. (2021, March 2). Five Best practices for implementing Zero Trust. Technology Insights. https://tcblog.protiviti.com/2021/03/02/five-best-practices-for-implementing-zero-trust/

Moeller, R. (2012). Identity and Access Management. CompTIA® Security+® Practice Tests. .DOI: 10.1002/9781118269138.ch22

Mohammed, I. A. (2019). Cloud identity and access management–a model proposal. *International Journal of Innovations in Engineering Research and Technology*, 6(10), 1–8.

Moyo, L., & du Toit, J. (2024, February). The Use of Blockchain for Identity and Access Management (IAM) in Multi-cloud. In International Congress on Information and Communication Technology (pp. 149-159). Singapore: Springer Nature Singapore.

Netskope. (2023, May 23). *Netskope advanced UEBA case studies*. https://www.netskope.com/resources/reports-guides/netskope-advanced-ueba-case-studies

Omotunde, H., & Ahmed, M. (2023). A comprehensive review of security measures in database systems: Assessing authentication, access control, and beyond. *Mesopotamian Journal of CyberSecurity*, 2023, 115–133. DOI: 10.58496/MJCSC/2023/016

Opara-Martins, J., Sahandi, M., & Tian, F. (2017). A holistic decision framework to avoid vendor lock-in for cloud saas migration. Computer and Information Science, 10(3).

Padhy, R. P., Patra, M. R., & Satapathy, S. C. (2011). Cloud Computing: Security Issues and Research Challenges. *International Journal of Computer Science and Information Technology and Security*, 1, 136–146.

Pérez-Méndez, A., López, R., & López Millán, G. (2016). Providing efficient SSO to cloud service access in AAA-based identity federations. *Future Generation Computer Systems*, 58, 13–28. DOI: 10.1016/j.future.2015.12.002

Petchiappan, T. (2024, June 4). Zero Trust Security Framework Implementation Guide. https://www.ilink-digital.com/insights/blog/implementing-zero-trust-security-framework-a-comprehensive-guide/

Sanders, M., & Yue, C. (2017). Automated least privileges in cloud-based web services. *Proceedings of the fifth ACM/IEEE Workshop on Hot Topics in Web Systems and Technologies*. DOI: 10.1145/3132465.3132470

Sanders, M., & Yue, C. (2018). Minimizing Privilege Assignment Errors in Cloud Services. *Proceedings of the Eighth ACM Conference on Data and Application Security and Privacy*. DOI: 10.1145/3176258.3176307

Sandhu, R. S. (1998). Role-based access control. [). Elsevier.]. *Advances in Computers*, 46, 237–286. DOI: 10.1016/S0065-2458(08)60206-5

Shaikh, N., Kasat, K., & Jadhav, S. (2022). Secured Authentication by Single Sign On (SSO): A Big Picture. *2022 International Conference on Computing, Communication, and Intelligent Systems (ICCCIS)*, 951-955. DOI: 10.1109/ICCCIS56430.2022.10037708

Shimizu, R., & Kanuka, H. (2020). Test-Based Least Privilege Discovery on Cloud Infrastructure as Code. *2020 IEEE International Conference on Cloud Computing Technology and Science (CloudCom)*, 1-8. DOI: 10.1109/CloudCom49646.2020.00007

Singh, C., Thakkar, R., & Warraich, J. (2023). *IAM Identity Access Management—Importance in Maintaining Security Systems within Organizations*. European Journal of Engineering and Technology Research., DOI: 10.24018/ejeng.2023.8.4.3074

Spanaki, K., Karafili, E., & Despoudi, S. (2021). AI applications of data sharing in agriculture 4.0: A framework for role-based data access control. *International Journal of Information Management*, 59, 102350. DOI: 10.1016/j.ijinfomgt.2021.102350

Statista. (2024, January 24). Global market value of Identity and Access Management 2022-2029. https://www.statista.com/statistics/1445717/global-identity-and-access-management-market-value/

Tao, H., Bhuiyan, M. Z. A., Rahman, M. A., Wang, G., Wang, T., Ahmed, M. M., & Li, J. (2019). Economic perspective analysis of protecting big data security and privacy. *Future Generation Computer Systems*, 98, 660–671. DOI: 10.1016/j.future.2019.03.042

Wadhwani, P. (2023). Identity and Access Management (IAM) market size by solution (Provisioning, password management, directory services, advanced authentication, Single Sign-On, Audit, compliance & Governance), by deployment model, by application & forecast, 2023 – 2032. In Global Market Insights Inc. https://www.gminsights.com/industry-analysis/identity-and-access-management-market

Wu, W., & Feng, W. (2021). Game to Dethrone: A Least Privilege CTF. 2021 IEEE 6th International Conference on Smart Cloud (SmartCloud), 132-137. https://doi.org/DOI: 10.1109/SmartCloud52277.2021.00030

Wylde, A. (2021, June). Zero trust: Never trust, always verify. In 2021 international conference on cyber situational awareness, data analytics and assessment (cybersa) (pp. 1-4). IEEE.

Zhu, S., Wang, T., Deng, Y., & Xie, X. (2009). Design of IAM Function in ERP Systems. *2009 Second International Symposium on Electronic Commerce and Security*, 1, 98-101. https://doi.org/DOI: 10.1109/ISECS.2009.114

KEY TERMS AND DEFINITIONS

Identity and Access Management (IAM): IAM combines policies, processes and technologies to manage digital and physical identities to maintain secure access to resources within an organization (Singh et al., 2023). IAM plays an important role in improving efficiency and ensuring security (Moeller, 2012).

Multi-Factor Authentication (MFA): MFA enhances security by layering multiple levels of authentication like passwords, tokens, and biometrics to access systems and resources. Each layer uses independent channels to interact with the end-user. If an adversary compromises any layer authentication channel, the other layers will prevent unauthorized access to the critical resources (Zhu et al., 2009).

Single Sign-On (SSO): SSO is a streamlined authentication process which allows users to login in once and access multiple applications. SSO enhances user experience, reduces password fatigue, and centralizes identity management capability. Because of the centralized login, the end users do not need multiple application accounts and can use a single set of authentication credentials (Shaikh et al., 2015).

Principle of Least Privilege (PoLP): PoLP highlights that administrators should assign the minimum level of access to end users. The assigned access or permissions should align with the user's job function. PoLP helps prevent unauthorized access and privilege creep among end users. In the case of a compromised user account governed by PoLP, the adversary's access is limited to the user's privileges, which reduces the attack surface and mitigates unnecessary risk (Hamza et al.,2018).

Security Assertion Markup Language (SAML): SAML is an open standard for streamlining authentication and authorization between identity and service providers. SAML enables end-users to authenticate once and access multiple applications without additional login. Single Sign-On (SSO) is made possible by SAML, ensuring a seamless user experience (Hamza et al.,2018).

Role-Based Access Control (RBAC): RBAC is a security method for aligning organizational roles to access policies. RBAC ensures the administrators have a standardized framework to follow the Principle of Least Privilege (PoLP) while provisioning user access based on job function.This ensures users only get access to resources that are necessary for their job (Kunz, 2015).

General Data Protection Regulation (GDPR): GDPR is a data protection law outlined by the European Union (EU). The European Union (EU) outlined GDPR in May 2018 and has since used it to regulate personal data collection. Besides providing control over personal data, GDPR unifies privacy laws across continental Europe (Desai & McCarty, 2020).

California Consumer Privacy Act (CCPA): CCPA is a state-level data privacy law. CCPA effective from January 2020, grants California residents rights over their personal data including the ability to know about, access, delete and opt-out of the sale of personal information collected by business. People often compare CCPA to GDPR (Baik, 2020).

Open Authorization (OAuth): OAuth is an open standard authorization that allows third-party applications to access a user's data without sharing their credentials. OAuth uses access tokens to allow inter-service data access on behalf of the user (Hossain, 2018).

OpenID: OpenID is a decentralized authentication protocol that allows users to log into multiple applications using a single set of credentials. Using a single set of credentials simplifies the login process and reduces the need for separate login details across different services (Kroschewski & Lehmann, 2023).

Chapter 9
Introduction to Cloud Security

Suman Rani
https://orcid.org/0009-0004-2280-7208
IITM College of Engineering, India

Mahender Sharma
https://orcid.org/0000-0002-6056-361X
IIMT College of Engineering, India

ABSTRACT

In the modern digital age, Cloud security is among the primary problems. Cloud security is a collection of procedures and technology meant to mitigate threats to an organization's security from the inside as well as the outside. Cloud security is essential for organisations as they progress with their modernisation strategy and include cloud-based tools and services into their infrastructure. "cloud migration" and "digital transformation" have gained widespread usage in commercial settings in recent years. This article offers an overview of cloud computing security benefits and uses, as well as a description of the major requirements in cloud computing, security essential technologies, standards, and regulations, etc. This chapter makes the case that the alterations to the aforementioned elements will bring about a technological revolution in the information security industry.

DOI: 10.4018/979-8-3693-7137-4.ch009

1. INTRODUCTION

Cloud computing is revolutionizing modular computing to meet the demands of digital transformation. (Buyya, R., 2011) Nonetheless, using traditional infrastructure locally is becoming increasingly popular these days. Cloud computing is mostly used for rapid resource access. Cloud computing is described in Figure 1.

Figure 1. Cloud Computing Architecture

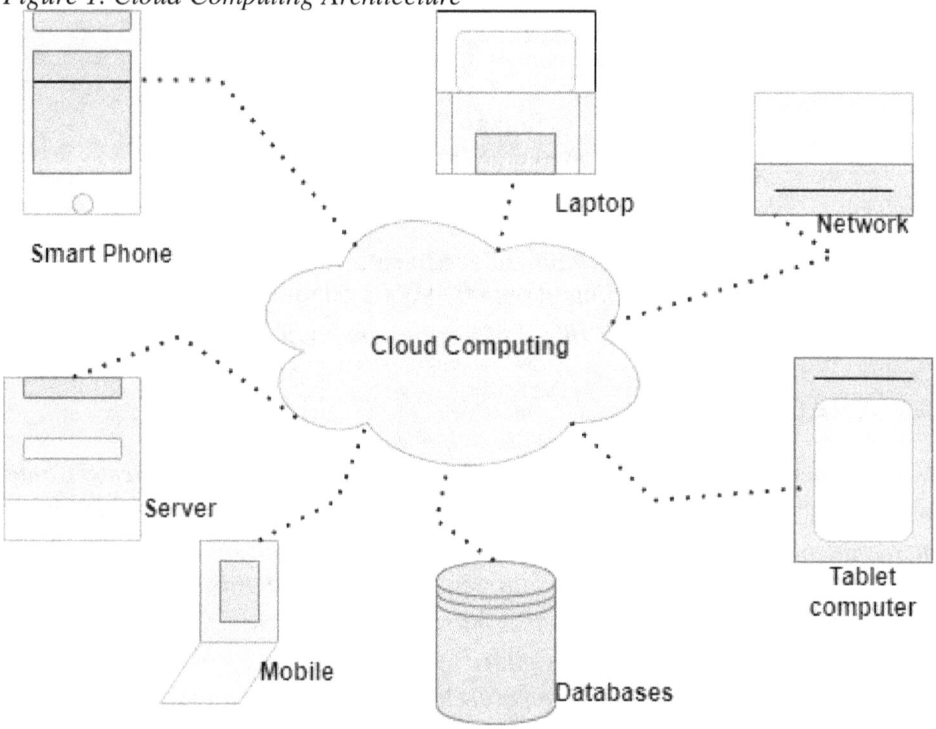

Cloud storage is a technique that uses the internet to store data and is device-independent. This is because it can be arranged into a cloud service that effectively and actively manages IT resources. (Liu, X., 2014) Savviness, adaptability, and financial savings are just a few of its many advantages.Prioritising security is essential when an organisation shifts its workload and data to the cloud to guard against a variety of risks, including malware, internal threats, unauthorised access, and data breaches. Security precautions in the conventional IT environment although it is often implemented inside the controlled boundary If the cloud environment is not adequately protected, its dynamic and distributed nature leaves it vulnerable to cyberattacks. It is highly possible that the general trend will become the cyberspace's nervous system in the future. Governments all throughout the world also fervently support and promote it. Some people make a clear comparison between cloud computing and the current information industry trend, citing the latter's rapid development tendency of intensification, scale, and specialisation in the IT area. However, a number of significant problems are now impeding the development of cloud computing, with security challenges taking the lead. Furthermore, As cloud computing is becoming more and more common, security concerns are getting more and more significant.Its significance has been steadily increasing and is now a significant element limiting its growth. According to the findings of Gartner's 2009 survey, over 70% of the firms questioned.

The chief technology officer (CTO) thinks that worries about privacy and data security will be the main barriers to cloud computing adoption in the near future. (Holzle,2003) Cloud computing services like Google and Amazon have.A number of security problems that are constantly made public by computer hackers has heightened people's worries. For instance, a significant amount of user files were compromised at Google in March 2009. Two networks were all that Amazon's "simple storage service (S3)" could rely on after two failures in February and July of 2009.It is essential for cloud service provider management to thoroughly examine and begin resolving the many security problems associated with cloud computing.

Cloud computing security issues are now receiving increasing attention. The topic of the renowned worldwide information security conference, RSA2010, was cloud computing security. (Zhavoronkov, V. 2020) In an effort to address the issue, CCS has organised a specialised symposium on cloud computing security since 2009.In order to provide future cloud computing security for our nation, the impact of computing on the field of information security is offered, together with a significant scientific research direction and the future cloud computing security technological framework.

Traditional Computing

Although traditional computing offers control over the hardware and architecture, management, maintenance, and scalability frequently necessitate large resources. (Chen, S. H. 2013) In contrast, by utilising shared, distant resources that are overseen by outside providers, cloud computing provides increased scalability and flexibility. Table 1 presents a comparison between traditional versus cloud-based computing.

Table 1. Cloud computing versus Traditional Computing

Aspect	Cloud Computing	Traditional Computing
Infrastructure	hosted on distant servers that cloud service providers oversee.	operated on-site using tangible gear.
Cost Based	Subscription based or pay per click.	capital costs up front for software and hardware.
Scalability	Demand based Up or down easily scalable	Physical hardware capacity limits the scalability; extra investments are frequently needed.
Deployment Time	Small number of step lower deployment time.	Take longer time in deployment due to hardware and software cost.
Maintenance	patched and updated, handled by cloud providers.	need hardware and software to be managed and maintained internally.
Access	obtainable from any location with internet access.	Usually restricted to remote access options or on-premises systems.
Disaster Recovery	integrated disaster recovery plans featuring high availability and automated backups.	demands independent investment and planning for catastrophe recovery.
Security	Cloud providers offer advanced security features, which frequently involve access limits and encryption.	internal management of security measures, needing more work and knowledge.
Resource Management	By sharing and pooling resources across several users, utilisation is maximised.	Resources may be underutilised because they are allocated to particular users or apps.
Flexibility	incredibly adaptive and responsive to shifting needs.	less adaptable; adjustments frequently entail substantial improvements or alterations.
Environmental Impact	Frequently more energy-efficient because data centres are optimised and renewable energy is used.	may have a greater influence on the environment because of the on-site infrastructure's high energy consumption.

Although traditional computing offers control over the hardware and architecture, management, maintenance, and scalability frequently necessitate large resources. (Fan, J. 2011) In contrast, by utilising shared, distant resources that are overseen by outside providers, more scalability and adaptability are offered by cloud computing.

Advantages of Cloud Technology

Cloud computing provides several benefits to people and organisations, including:

- **Scalability**: Businesses may scale capacity in or out in response to demand thanks to cloud computing. (Wild, P. 2006) This adaptability is especially helpful for companies with growth goals or different levels of effort.

- **Economical Effectiveness**: Cost-per-use pricing lowers capital expenditures for infrastructure and hardware. Companies can avoid the upfront costs associated with traditional IT setups and only pay for the resources they use.
- **Cooperation and accessibility**: By enabling access to data and applications from anywhere with a web connection, cloud services let international teams communicate and operate remotely.
- **Innovation and Quickness**: The cloud facilitates speedy application development and deployment, which helps companies innovate more quickly and react swiftly to changes in the market.
- **Disaster Recovery & Business Continuity**: In the case of an outage or calamity, cloud providers' strong disaster recovery solutions guarantee that data is backed up and may be promptly restored.
- **Protection**: Prominent cloud providers make significant investments in security measures, frequently going above and beyond what separate businesses can accomplish on their own. (P. Samarati, 2007) This covers access restrictions, encryption, and ongoing observation.

Cloud Computing Impact on Business Operations

Cloud computing has an enormous impact on corporate operations, enhancing versatility, effectiveness, and productivity. Cloud computing has a huge influence on corporate operations, increasing flexibility, efficiency, and competitiveness.

- **Transformation of IT Roles**: (Waters, B.2006) The shift to cloud computing has transformed traditional IT roles, with a growing emphasis on cloud architecture, DevOps, and security management.
- **Enhanced Collaboration and Flexibility**: Cloud computing facilitates greater collaboration across teams and departments, enabling more agile and responsive business practices.
- **Increased Innovation**: The ability to quickly deploy and scale applications in the cloud encourages experimentation and innovation, enabling companies to launch new goods and services more quickly.
- **Speedier Innovation:** Provides access to cutting-edge technology (such as AI and analytics) as well as speedier application deployment, allowing firms to develop and bring products to market faster.
- **Continuous Updates:** Ensures that organisations always have the most recent software and security fixes, saving maintenance and downtime.

Types of Cloud Models

There are three primary deployment models and three methods of service delivery in the cloud technology paradigm. (MacVittie, L. 2009) The three deployment options are as follows: (1) Private cloud, which is a cloud platform reserved for a single organisation; (2) Public cloud, which is a platform open to the public to sign up and utilise the infrastructure; and (3) Hybrid clouds, is a mix of public and private clouds. Due to their availability for hosting services by potentially malevolent users, public clouds represent the riskiest deployment model. The models for cloud service delivery display in Figure 2 consist of:

Figure 2. Cloud Service Delivery Models

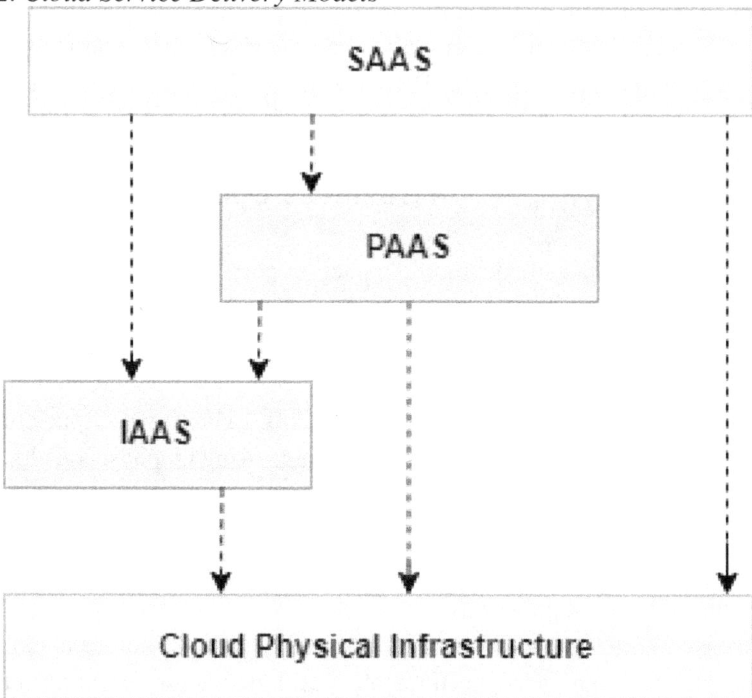

Software as a Service (SAAS): Utilizing the internet, SAAS—also known as cloud application services—provides programs that are managed by external vendors and that users may access via an interface. While certain SAAS apps need to be installed, the majority can be used straight from a web browser without any downloads or installations. (Behl, A. 2011) SAAS can readily keep up with and support the efforts since providers manage the work pertaining to uses, execution, data, middleware, operating systems, virtualization, storage, servers, and communication. Instead of using PaaS or IaaS, this architecture may be hosted directly on the cloud. One example of a SaaS supplier is SalesForce CRM.

There are four typical methods for it:

1. One instance
2. Tenant flexibility
3. Multiple instances
4. Tenant

Platform as a Service: SAAS can readily keep up with and support the efforts since providers manage the work pertaining to uses, execution, data, middleware, operating systems, virtualization, storage, servers, and communication. Service providers supply platforms, tools, and other business services. (Waters, B. 2007) Either the IaaS architecture or the PaaS paradigm can be directly hosted on top of cloud infrastructures. Google Apps and Microsoft Windows Azure are the two most well-known PaaS.Cloud platform services, or PAAS, provide software with access to cloud components and are commonly used for application and other developments. It makes cost-effectiveness and easy testing possible, and it speeds up the development and deployment of applications.

Infrastructure as a Service (IAAS): By acting autonomously to access and control resources, IAAS models—also referred to as cloud infrastructure services—assist in integrating social media, storage, and computing services. Databases, communications queues, and other services above the virtualization layers are now provided by a large number of IAAS vendors. IAAS clients are responsible for managing runtime, data, applications, middleware, and operating systems, as opposed to SAAS and PAAS clients. There are numerous examples, including Joynet, Computer Compute Engine (GCE), Microsoft Azure, Cisco Meta-Pod, and Amazon Web Services (AWS).

2. SECURITY FRAMEWORK FOR CLOUD PROCESSING

Security is a particularly concerning issue in cloud computing because consumers do not own the hardware used to provide services. The users are unaware of or have little influence over what might happen to their data. When customers save sensitive and important data in cloud computing services, this is a serious risk. (Karl, W. 2008) Customers' privacy won't be compromised, thus cloud computing service providers need to make sure their clients' data is secure. However, this is getting more and harder as security advances because someone always manages to figure out how to bypass the security and profit from user data. Among the crucial elements of the Service Provider Layer are the following: Scheduler &Dispatcher, Load Balancer, Accounting, Metering, SLA Monitor, Resource Provisioning, and Advance Resource Reservation Monitoring. The process of authentication, infrastructure vulnerabilities, privacy problems, transmission of data security, managing identities, auditing, compliance issues, cloud integrity, and service bindings difficulties are among the security hazards related to the service provider layer. In the meanwhile, the establishment and administration of several virtual machines, operating systems, and procedures for their ongoing monitoring are essential components of the virtual machine layer.A number of security issues affect the virtual machine layer. These include problems with identification and access control, legal and regulatory compliance, infrastructure, and consumer segmentation. VM sprawl, VM escape, and associated issues are additional difficulties.Some essential elements make up the data center layer, which is now referred to as Infrastructure-as-a-Service (IaaS). These consist of memory, storage space, CPUs, and servers.

Keeping computers and networks physically secure and guaranteeing safe data at rest are a couple of the security concerns associated with the data center layer. A few companies have been concentrating on cloud computing security concerns. A nonprofit organisation called the Cloud Security .The alliance was founded to promote the adoption of best practices for cloud security and to inform people about the advantages of cloud computing. This makes all other forms of computing more secure. One group devoted to resolving security-related issues is the Open Security Architecture (OSA). It established the OSA pattern, which identifies critical cloud services, critical responsibilities for risk management and supervision, internal organization cooperation, and controls that need more attention.In particular, the accreditation, Authorization, and Risk Assessment procedures become more crucial to provide adequate oversight and assurance when tasks are "outsourced" to an outside vendor.

Acquiring systems and services is essential to making sure that service acquisition is properly managed. Planning ahead for contingencies ensures that there is a clear understanding of what to do in the event that service delivery is interrupted . (Zhou, Q. 2009) In a company setting, it's critical to comprehend the risks related to services through the use of Risk Assessment controls. The United States National Institute of Standards and Technology (NIST) (https://www.nist.gov/) has started promoting cloud computing standards . Several standards bodies and industry consortia are creating test beds and specifications to overcome the issues and enable cloud computing. Several test bed groups and standards are currently in place, such as the Storage Network Industry Associations (SNIA), Cloud Security Alliance (CSA), and Internet Engineering Task Force (IETF). Conversely, a cloud API offers a management interface, a functional interface, or both. Many facets of cloud administration can be standardised to promote interoperability. Federated security (for example, identification) across clouds is one set of potential standards. data transfers between clouds, including metadata standardised outputs for cloud applications and services in terms of monitoring, auditing, billing, reporting, and notifications; cloud-independent governance and policy representation, etc. Figure 3 displays the cloud computing security architecture from a high level perspective.

Figure 3. High Level Security Architecture of cloud computing

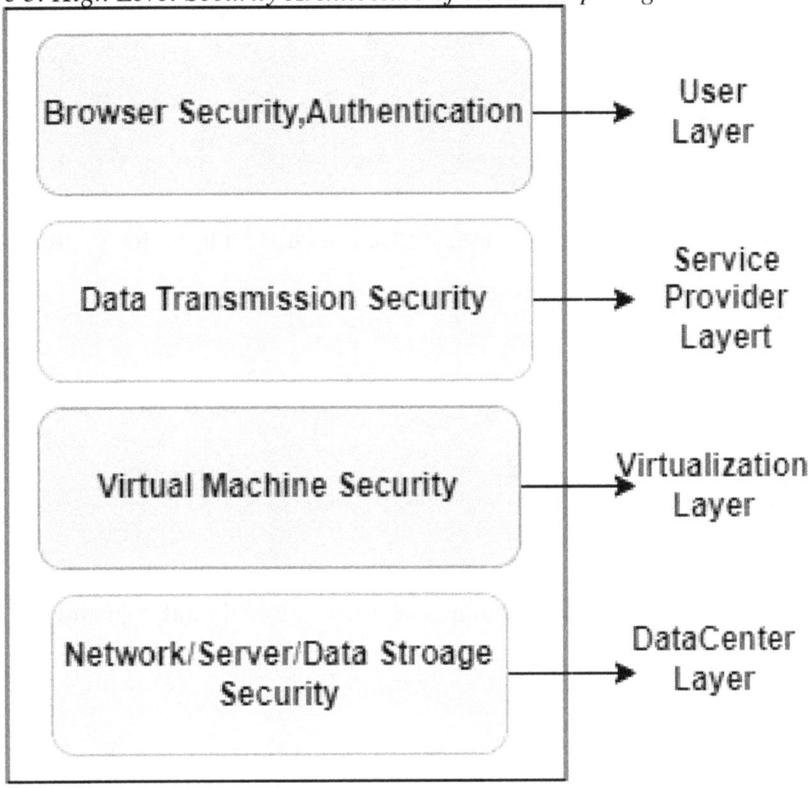

3. FUNDAMENTAL PRINCIPLES OF CLOUD SECURITY

The underlying ideas of cloud security are intended to guarantee the availability, confidentiality, integrity, and security of data and services in the cloud computing setting. (Azeem, M. 2014) The use of security procedures and measures to protect cloud data and infrastructure is guided by these concepts.

Protection

It assures that only authorized people and organizations may access sensitive information.It entails safeguarding information from illegal access and disclosure.

Encryption

Encoding information while it's being used, in transit, and at idle to guard against unwanted access.

Access Management

Restricting who has access to sensitive data by establishing stringent policies and putting robust authentication measures in place (such as multi-factor identification).

Integrity

Guarantees that data is accurate and reliable by guarding against illegal alteration or manipulation.

Data Validation

When the input is analyzed it guarantees the accuracy and reliability if data. There are two cryptographic techniques as Hashes and digital signature are used to authenticity of data.

Version Control

There is monitoring and maintenance of data to keep unauthorized and unaltered records.

Availability

To keep the information unaltered and used by authorized person it guarantees to availability of information.

Redundancy

Various distributed strategies as installing backup and layout are used to ensure the regularity of information.

Reconstruction after a disaster

Implementing robust disaster recovery plans in place that include regular backups and fast recovery methods in case of disruptions or data loss.

Verification and Permission

Authentication of people and devices are used to gain access through the encryption. Strong authentication methods (e.g., MFA) minimize the risk of unauthorized access.

Authorization

Specifies the activities and resources that a system or user with authentication can access in accordance with roles and rules that have been set up.

Accountability

Ensures that all actions in the cloud environment can be traced back to specific users or processes, providing transparency and enabling audits.

Logging and Monitoring

Continuously tracking and logging user activities and system events to maintain an audit trail.

Audit and Compliance

Regularly reviewing logs and activities to maintain adherence to security regulations.

4. CLOUD SECURITY PROBLEMS, HAZARDS, AND ISSUES

Due of their requirement to store data, practically all businesses are implementing cloud computing. (Azeem, M. 2014) The corporations generate and store a vast amount of data. As a result, they deal with numerous security-related problems. Businesses can incorporate processes to streamline and automate the management of cloud computing. (Miri, A. 2009)The main obstacles are:

Privacy and Security

It is crucial to comprehend and handle privacy and security concerns as more and more businesses move to cloud environments. Scalability, cost-effectiveness, and flexibility are just a few advantages of cloud computing. These benefits, however, are accompanied by serious privacy and security issues that require cautious handling.

Portability and Interoperability

The services of cloud migration into and out of must be rendered to the customer. A bond period shouldn't exist since it could cause difficulties for the clients. Facilities on-site ought to be able to be provided by the cloud. One of the difficulties with cloud computing is remote access, which the cloud provider can resolve to allow users to access the clouds from any location with security

Reliable and adaptable

Another issue facing cloud users is reliability and flexibility, which may be resolved by ensuring that the data sent to the cloud is secure and that the host guarantees the dependability of the service for its clients. The third-party services should be observed, and performance, robustness, and business dependability should be closely examined in order to resolve this issue.

Price

Although cloud computing is inexpensive, customising the cloud to meet consumer needs can occasionally be costly. Furthermore, it can be difficult for small businesses to adjust the cloud to meet their needs because it can occasionally be more expensive. Additionally, it might occasionally be expensive to transport data from the cloud to the premises.

Unavailable time Insufficient resources

Problems with unavailable time (downtime) and inadequate resources in cloud computing can have a big impact on an organization's operations, security posture, and general service quality. These difficulties often intersect with safety worries and may have a major impact on information security and company operations. The period that servers in the cloud are not accessible or operational is referred to as delay, sometimes called unavailability time. They may be due to a variety of things, including technological innovation breakdowns, outside threats, or issues with maintenance. An outage can have catastrophic consequences for companies that rely heavily on cloud computing services for vital functions.

Multi-Cloud Environment Management

As multiple cloud approaches are getting implemented at a faster pace, effectively handling several cloud-based environments is becoming vital to a business's IT approach. (S., & Kumar, P. 2023) The multi-cloud computing system is that utilizes services from several providers of cloud computing, such as incorporating features from AWS, Microsoft Azure, Google Cloud Platform (GCP), and other sources. In addition to reducing reliance on a single supplier and increasing flexibility, this strategy can optimise expenses and performance. Nonetheless, in order to guarantee seamless operation and security, managing a multi-cloud environment brings with it a number of complications and obstacles.

5. CLOUD COMPUTING DEVELOPMENT TRENDS

The most significant external feature of cloud computing is the service delivery of IT resources. Large, global IT corporations like Amazon, Google, IBM, Microsoft, and Sun currently offer a range of externally hosted cloud computing services. The National Institute of Standards and Technology (NIST) states that there are presently three primary categories of cloud computing services available:

Examples of Infrastructure as a Service (IaaS) include Sun's Cloud Infrastructure Platform, IBM's Blue Cloud, Google's Google App Engine, and Amazon's Elastic Compute Cloud (EC2).

Platform as a Service (PaaS): Salesforce's customer relationship management (CRM) service and Microsoft's Azure platform are two examples.

Furthermore, the idea of Everything as a Service (XaaS) has surfaced, in which different cloud service providers provide a broad range of cloud-based solutions to satisfy the various demands of their clients. The many categories of cloud computing services are depicted in Figure 2.

However, a brand-new idea known as Everything as a Service (XaaS) has surfaced, which states that anything may now be a service thanks to cloud computing and remote accessCloud computing security, also referred to as cloud computing protection, uses a broad range of technologies, applications, regulations, and controls to protect virtualised intellectual property, data, applications, services, and the supporting infrastructure. It is included in the more general areas of computer, network, and data security. There are various trends:

Cloud security concerns

The first category of cloud computing security concerns consists of problems that cloud providers, or companies that offer platforms, software, or infrastructure as a service, confront.(Grossman,2009) Users need to take precautions, such creating secure passwords and use authentication techniques. It is imperative for providers to guarantee the security of their infrastructure and safeguard the data and applications of their clients. According to a poll conducted by the Cloud Security Alliance, insider assaults are among the top seven dangers in cloud computing. An company loses physical access to the servers hosting its data when it stores or runs programs on public cloud infrastructure. Sensitive information may therefore be at risk from insider assaults. Employees who have direct access to data center systems should be subject to extensive background checks, according to cloud service companies. Data centers are also advised to adhere to stringent security regulations.

Cloud security control

The effectiveness of cloud security architecture can only be determined by the defensive measures put in place. In order to guarantee a secure cloud environment, an efficient cloud security architecture should be aware of the security management challenges that may develop and adhere to all recommended practices, protocols, and standards. Security controls are used by security management to address these problems. These security measures are in place to secure cloud environments by preventing system vulnerabilities and reducing the impact of an attack. Despite the fact that a cloud security architecture has many different controls, they frequently belong to one of the following groups:

Testing with the assumption that the internal network's architecture and implementation are fully known to the "attacker."Grey-box testingTesting under the scenario where the internal network's architecture, implementation, and design are only partially known to the "attacker."Tests using a black box,Testing with the assumption that the internal network's architecture and implementation are unknown to the "attacker."

Data protection

These administrative tools are intended to reduce attacks on the cloud's infrastructure and are used to ensure adherence to external constraints. (Gellman, R. 2009) By alerting potential attackers to the potential repercussions of continuing, deterrent measures, like a warning sign posted on a fence or property, serve to lower the threat level.

Examples of this kind of control include policies, procedures, standards, guidelines, rules, and regulations that point an organisation in the direction of security. Discouragement measures are intended to dissuade unskilled or motivated people from attempting to breach an organization's IT infrastructure, even though hostile actors typically disregard them. Preventive controls are primarily intended to increase the system's resilience to mishaps, usually by lowering or even eliminating them altogether.

6. CLOUD SECURITY ASPECTS

Cloud security organizations is defined by the security tiers, architecture, plan, coding, and best practices of a cloud security setup. The tasks inside the cloud must characterize the compositional and visual model (design and UI) in cloud security engineering. The methods, restrictions, and executive access are all part of this cloud security engineering approach that protects data and apps. (Kaushal, S.2011) It also covers methods for managing and maintaining consistency, permeability, danger posture, and general security. Procedures for implementing security standards in cloud administrations and operations are predicated on a methodology that satisfies uniform standards and fundamental components of the security architecture.

In order for interest in Cloud innovations to be feasible, businesses need to understand the many components of the Cloud and how.

Identities administration

Every company will have its own identity governance structure in place to control access to information and computer resources. Cloud providers can use federation, SSO, or biometric-based identification technologies to integrate the customer's identity management system into their own data center, or they can offer their own identity management service. (Behl, A. 2011) For example, it offers cross-enterprise and cloud-based biometric identification while protecting privacy. It links users' sensitive information to their fingerprints and saves it in an encrypted way. Biometric identification is done in the encrypted domain using a searchable encryption approach to make sure that neither the cloud provider nor any potential attackers can access private information or even the details of individual requests.

Physical security

Cloud service providers ensure that vital sources (such power) are sufficiently reliable to reduce the potential of disruption and physically secure the IT (servers, routers, cables, etc.) from theft, fires, floods, and unauthorized access. Typically, this is accomplished by using expertly planned, built, managed, watched over, and maintained data centres to serve cloud applications.

Personnel security

IT and other cloud service providers often address a variety of information security issues through pre-, para-, and post-employment initiatives such proactive security awareness and training programs, security screening of prospective hires, and so on.

Secrecy

Providers make sure that authorized individuals have complete access to all sensitive information, including payment card details, and that it is encrypted or hidden. IDs and online personas must also be protected, as must any information the provider gathers or creates on client cloud activity.

Security testing

Security testing is done by providers to make sure that private information, such credit card numbers, is hidden or encrypted and that only people with permission may access it. Digital identities and credentials must be safeguarded, as must any information the provider generates or gathers on user behavior on the cloud.

Testing for cloud vulnerabilities and intrusions

It is essential to employ free or commercial technologies to scan the cloud from the outside in, as your service becomes a soft target in the absence of a protected environment. (Yao, L. 2010) Virtual machines must be protected against viruses, data breaches, and exploited vulnerabilities just like physical servers. "Of the threats causing cloud outages, cloud-related malware represents 3.4% and data loss or leakage represents 24.6%."

Both internal and external screening and testing for vulnerability must be authorized by the cloud provider. Due to the actuality that the cloud is a shared environment with other customers or tenants, it is imperative that the penetration testing rules of engagement be followed in detail.

Acceptable usage guidelines violations may result in service termination. Understanding the distinction between application and network layer testing is essential when talking about penetration testing. Sometimes, the most crucial part of the process is knowing what is expected of you as the tester. Testing involving both external and internal connections, as well as related systems throughout the local network, is referred to as network-layer testing. Social engineering attacks are frequently conducted because employees are frequently the weakest link in the security system.

White-box experimentation

It has to do with cloud computing services. Both conventional and non-traditional threats are included in this. (Yao, L. 2010) In addition to more conventional risks like unauthorised access, denial-of-service attacks, and network eavesdropping, cloud computing poses unique risks such side channel attacks, virtualisation vulnerabilities, and misuse of cloud services. Security controls frequently depend on keeping an eye on the three CIA triad sectors in order to reduce these threats. The terms "CIA Triad" allude to availability, integrity, and confidentiality, which includes access controllability, which is further explained by the following.

It is noteworthy that numerous efficacious security protocols encompass multiple or all three elements. For example, encryption can be used to guarantee data integrity and stop unwanted access. Backups usually safeguard availability and integrity, while firewalls merely safeguard confidentially and access management.

Confidentiality

The lack of disclosure or access of data content to outsiders is the characteristic of data privacy. Outsourcing data is not directly controlled by the owners; instead, it is stored offshore in the cloud. Usually authorized individuals should have access to confidential information; CSPs and other parties shouldn't. Owners of data want to be able to take full advantage of cloud data services, including data calculation, sharing of data, and record search, without worrying about their data being compromised by rivals or CSPs. When we talk about confidentiality, we mean that information must be kept completely private from its original owner. Encryption, which limits data access to only authorised users, is an example of a security measure that addresses secrecy. Encryption can be performed using either the symmetric or asymmetric key paradigm.

Access controllability

Access controllability refers to the ability of a data owner to choose limit access to their data that has been outsourced to the cloud. The owner may grant authorised people access to the material, but others are not permitted to view it without authorisation. Furthermore, it is preferable to impose fine-grained access control on the data that has been outsourced; that is, various users should have varying access privileges concerning particular data segments. In cloud settings that are not trusted, the owner alone should have authority over access authorisation.

Availability is another word for access control. Although unauthorized access should be strictly prohibited, access for administration or even customer purposes should be allowed but monitored. Access control and availability make sure the right individual is given the right amount of authorisation.

Integrity

Data integrity requires preserving and ensuring the accuracy and wholeness of data.A data owner always anticipates that their information will be reliably and accurately kept in the cloud. It implies that the information shouldn't be intentionally created, unlawfully altered, wrongly altered, or purposefully erased. In the event that the data is corrupted or deleted by any unwanted actions, the owner must to be able to identify the loss or damage. Furthermore, data users can still retrieve lost or corrupted portions of the outsourced data. Effective integrity security measures shield data against inadvertent changes in addition to protecting it from malevolent attackers. Information backups that are done automatically are one type of security measure that addresses integrity.

7. THE DRAWBACKS AND HAZARDS OF CLOUD COMPUTING

Even though cloud computing is at the forefront of information technology, before making a full investment, take into account the risks and vulnerabilities. (Rakshit, A. (2009)There are security services and controls for the cloud, but just like with any security system, there is no guarantee that they will work. However, certain hazards go beyond the protection of assets; they might also involve concerns with productivity or even privacy.

Privacy Concerns

Though it is still in its infancy, cloud computing is evolving inside new technology frameworks. As a result, before to releasing their platform, all cloud services are required to do privacy impact assessments (PIAs). The hazards of storing private information in a non-physical place must be understood by customers who choose to save their data in the cloud.

Robust cloud security is essential in today's digital world when businesses rely on cloud services for software, processing, and storage. Cloud security, often called cloud computing security, is the collective term for the procedures, instruments, and controls implemented to protect cloud-based data, apps, and infrastructure against cyberattacks and unauthorized access.It offers several tiers of defence against DDoS assaults, illegal access, data breaches, and other threats.

7.1 Cloud Computing Risks, Threats, and Challenges

While often used interchangeably, cloud computing risks, threats, and challenges represent distinct facets of the cloud security landscape:

Cloud Computing Risks

Risks in cloud computing refer to potential events or circumstances that could result in adverse impacts on an organization's cloud-based assets or operations. To prevent these dangers, businesses must adopt strong security measures, select reputable cloud providers, and conduct frequent audits of their cloud systems.

- **Data Breaches**: illegal access to private client information—such as bank account details, intellectual property, or personal information—that is kept in cloud databases. (Edoh, A. 2014) Weak access restrictions, cloud configuration vulnerabilities, and insider threats can all lead to data breaches. A data breach happens when someone not authorised to access private or sensitive data—which is usually kept digitally—gets their hands on it. These hacks have the potential to jeopardise confidential, financial, or proprietary information, which could have detrimental effects on both people and businesses.

Causes

Hacking: Cybercriminals obtain illegal access by taking advantage of weaknesses in systems.

Phishing: Attackers use phony emails or texts to trick people into disclosing private information.

Interior Challenges: Employees or freelancers with permission may deliberately or unwittingly divulge sensitive data.

physical theft: Stealing or breakdown of material things containing important information, such as USB flash drives or laptops, is referred to as physical theft.

Spyware: Some examples of harmful applications that can infiltrate devices and grab data are extortion and malware.

Service interruptions: Obstacles or delays in cloud-based services brought on by assaults, connectivity issues, or physical malfunctions. (Namasudra, S.2024, February) Network's outages can result in interruptions decreased productivity, and other problems that may expense companies that depend on web services and software. Interruptions to the accessibility or effectiveness of services offered by cloud-based or IT systems are known as outages in service. when such interruptions impact accessibility, the user interface may be impacted on as well as companies may be impacted.

- **Lack of compliance: Breaking laws and business norms carries fines, penalties, and damage to reputation.** Such include handling medical data in compliance with HIPAA regulations or inappropriately handling personally identifiable data (PII) in violation of the GDPR.

Economic Changes: One of the many hazards connected with service-on-demand is the possibility of unforeseen expenses such as over-provisioning of assets, unexpected fees for information transfers, or vendor lock-in those drives up cost. Monetarily significant losses may arise from legal obligations, contractual disputes, and SLA violations.

Cloud Computing Threats

The risks associated with cloud computing encompass malicious activities, attacks, or exploits that seek to inflict damage or gain illicit access by exploiting vulnerabilities in cloud services.

Examples:

Spyware Illness: Cloud-based apps, storage, or facilities are targeted by malware, including data encryption malware or bitcoin mining software that leverages cloud services for bitcoin mining.

Phishing attacks: Phishing messages and emails pretend to be from reliable companies in an effort to fool users into disclosing private data, financial accounts, or login credentials.

- **Cloud Computing Challenges**

Organisations encounter obstacles or complexities related to cloud computing while attempting to safeguard their digital processes and equipment.

Examples:

- **Shared Liability Models:** Assigning security duties to cloud service providers and consumers separately might be challenging. It may prove difficult to distinguish between security responsibilities of cloud providers and clients, especially when using models of cloud computing.
- **Access and identity management (IAM):** Safe authentication, authorisation, and auditing are necessary, but maintaining user identities, rights, and access restrictions across various cloud environments presents issues.
- **Data security**: Examples include making sure that keys are managed, that data is encrypted, and that data is transmitted securely both in transit and at rest. They also include guarding against data leaks, illegal availability, and data requirements for residency. It is difficult to provide robust incident handling, detection, and tracking capabilities in complex multi-cloud systems. Ensuring that vulnerabilities and breakdowns are quickly found and remedied.

7.2 Crucial Secure Cloud Strategies

A range of strategies and techniques are covered by accepted standards for secure cloud computing to protect apps, data, and equipment in cloud environments. Here are some crucial actions to take:

1. Evaluation and Control of Risks

To begin, conduct a thorough risk assessment to find any weaknesses, dangers, or risks related to your cloud-based system. Provide a severity ranking for each risk based on the effect you believe it has on the operation of the company. Make effective use of risk mitigation approaches to lessen known hazards.

2. **Use a Model of Zero Trust**

Implement "Zero Trust," an approach to safety that does not depend on any outside or inside resources. Reduce the possibility of illicit use and opponent lateral motion by implementing strict accessible limits, constant approval, and restricted access policies.

3. Implement Strong Identity and Access Management (IAM)

vigorous IAM guidelines and accessibility controls should be implemented in order to manage user access permissions, keep an eye on user activity in the cloud, and verify users. Use multiple-factor authentication (MFA) and role-based access control (RBAC) to increase safety.

4. Encrypt Data

To prevent unauthorised access, secure sensitive data while it's in motion and at rest. Use strong encryption techniques and maintain key protocols to make sure that information is shielded from prying eyes and illegal access.

5. Network Security

To safeguard cloud services from illegal access, data intercepting, and other network-related dangers, install security controls including antivirus programs, intrusion prevention systems (IDPS), and virtual private networks (VPNs).

6. Continuous Security Monitoring and Incident Response

Use tracking tools and strategies to keep your eye on suspicious incidents and hazards in cloud systems. In order to lessen the effects of security incidents, make use of crisis management techniques to quickly identify, assess, and resolve problems.

7. Patch Management

Renew your systems, apps, and cloud services, and make sure you install the most recent security fixes. Establish a strong patch management framework to quickly fix flaws that exist and lower the likelihood that attackers would exploit them.

8. Cloud-Native Security Solutions

To improve safety in the cloud, make use of the online-native security technologies and services offered by cloud vendors. To increase the degree of safety, make use of secure cloud teams, network encryption, and cloud vendors' identity solutions.

9. Implement Cloud-based WAF

Web apps hosted using cloud infrastructure can benefit from an additional layer of protection by implementing a cloud-based WAF. In addition to effectively screening and tracking HTTP traffic, identifying and blocking harmful requests, online WAFs may mitigate typical internet application issues like SQL injection and cross-site scripting (XSS).

10. Employee Training & Awareness

Employees should be made aware of potential risks, best practices for privacy in the cloud, and their personal obligations for maintaining the safety of the cloud. Encourage staff members to swiftly report security incidents and cultivate a culture of security awareness.

11. Regular Audits and Compliance Checks

Maintain compliance with industry standards, laws, and best practices by conducting frequent security audits, vulnerability assessments, and compliance checks on your cloud infrastructure.

8. Applications of Cloud Security Solutions

There are various uses and applications of cloud computing:

1. **Enhanced Data Protection**

Cloud security requires critical data protection. Cloud security systems safeguard data while it is in transit and at rest by encrypting it to ensure its integrity and confidentiality. (Westphall, C. 2009) Organizations may reduce the risk of unauthorized access and data breaches and protect their most important assets by putting robust security measures and identity management solutions in place.

2. Versatility and Scalability

Unmatched scalability and flexibility are key advantages of cloud security, enabling enterprises to quickly adjust to shifting security needs and developing threats.Businesses may optimise performance and reduce costs by scaling resources up or down in response to demand using cloud-based security services. Because of its scalability, organisations are able to fulfil the changing needs of their business while still keeping a high level of security.

3. **Cost-Effectiveness**

Conventional on-premise security solutions frequently call for large staff, software, and hardware investments. fortunately, safety systems are a more cost-effective option because they require less capital initially and have lower continuing operating expenses. Pay-as-you-go pricing structures and software subscriptions enable businesses to optimise their return on their investments while aligning security costs with practical usage.

4. **Global Coverage and Resilience**

To offer extensive coverage and resistance against hackers, computing and security products make use of an international chain of data centres and physical points of presence (PoPs).

5. **Managed Services and Expertise**

Along with technology, many security cloud providers also provide regulated services & special expertise.

Organisations can free up internal teams to concentrate on core business operations by offloading the responsibility of managing security personnel and infrastructure by partnering with seasoned security professionals.

6. **Continuous Innovation and Updates**

In order to innovate and improve their security capabilities, cloud security firms consistently allocate resources towards research and development. Organisations can access state-of-the-art technologies and capabilities that adapt to changing security requirements and emerging threats by utilising cloud-based security solutions.To keep businesses safe from the most recent cyberattacks, solution providers release patches, upgrades, and updates on a regular basis.

7. **Compliance and Regulatory Alignment**

Cloud security firms routinely go through rigorous third-party audits and certifications to ensure regulatory alignment and compliance.employs robust security controls, encryption techniques, and audit trails to help organisations comply with regulations and stay compliant.

8. Upcoming Developments in Computing through the cloud

Over the next five years, the automation concept will become the norm in the IT business. In the upcoming five years, machine learning (ML) and artificial intelligence (AI) will probably be major components of the automation process. As automation increases, we should expect to see a decrease in conventional programming roles in the IT industry.To bolster the previously indicated context, allow me to provide an example.

We can envision the harm that will be done in terms of INTRUSION when a machine assumes charge of creatinglogic during the automation process rather than the human brain.It takes longer for a traditional programmer to complete (or execute) an assignment if the programmer's goal is to use his or her skills and abilities to take use of the computer resources. However, if a machine uses today's technology and the knowledge it gained from machine learning to accomplish the same task, it will complete the task in a matter of seconds. In this case, the conventional intrusion detection systems would no longer be appropriate within the automation framework. Thus, it is imperative that the conventional security systems, such as FIREWALLS and IDS, be strengthened immediately.

According to the 2016 report Cyber Security: Threats, Reports, and Challenges, just 1% of all devices globally are using the internet and cloud-based services. 90% of the devices and industries in the world are expected to rely mostly on the internet and cloud by 2025 in order to provide their services.

This helps us to understand that when more IOT devices are used, there is a corresponding increase in cloud load. Additionally, this leads to a rise in security vulnerabilities that cannot be addressed with currently employed methodologies. (Zamboni, D. 2009)We need to keep up with security improvements and conduct fresh research on how to make cloud security stronger. How can we strengthen our security system? so that even in the event that a hacker attempts to compromise the systems or services through the automated process, everything will remain under our control.

8. EMERGING TRENDS IN CLOUD SECURITY

• AI and ML

The safety of the cloud is being improved by artificial intelligence (AI) and machine learning (ML), which make it possible for more advanced detection of threats, automatic and the ability to predict.

1. **Vulnerability Detection**: By evaluating enormous volumes of data in real-time, AI/ML can spot odd patterns or behaviours that point to possible security risks, such unauthorised access or data loss.
2. **Automation Responses:** By automatically restricting suspicious activity or isolating vulnerable systems in reaction to threats, these solutions shorten the time it takes to remediate hazards.
3. **Predicting security**: By evaluating previous data, machine learning and AI models are able to predict possible future assaults, enabling organisations to take preventative action.
4. **Increased Accuracy:** Security teams may concentrate on real threats because AI/ML lowers the number of false positives in alerts about dangers.
5. **Constant Learning**: AI-powered security systems are always learning from new threats and improving with time.

• Serverless Security

Protecting services running in a server-less environment—where cloud vendors manage infrastructure and users focus just on code—is the goal of server-less safety in the clouds.

Key Aspects of Serverless Security

1. **Limited Security Interface**: Serverless architectures shift the focus to safeguarding the code of the app and its constituent parts by eliminating the system administration level from an attack field.
2. **The activity Separation:** The function runs independently in the server-less environment. Strong activity isolation keeps a weakened function from impacting other processes.
3. **Most Limited Access**: Strict control over access and minimum permissions for serverless services help to reduce the possible harm that could occur from an exploited function.

4. **Events Information Evaluation**: Events are frequently the cause of serverless functions kicking in. Attacks via injection and other vulnerabilities are less likely when input data is verified and sanitised.
5. **Monitoring and Recording**: In a server-less system, it's necessary to continuously monitor functional activities and maintain comprehensive records in order to detect and resolve security holes.

Quantum Computing

Fundamental computation, a state-of-the-art technology, uses concepts from quantum mechanics to process computations far more quickly than those of conventional machines. Quantum machines use qubits, or quantum bits, which can exist in multiple states simultaneously due to a phenomenon called superposition. This is in contrast to classical computers, which use bits, which can be represented as 0 or 1. As a result, enormous volumes of data may be processed by quantum computers.

1. Data at the same time Superposition: A qubit can be in either of the following states simultaneously:0,1, or both. This allows for simultaneous processing and significantly more computing power.
2. Being entangled: Despite the distance between the two qubits, the state of one is immediately related to the state of the other when they get entangled. Qubits are connected via this feature to facilitate intricate computations.
3. When a quantum computer accomplishes a task that is almost unattainable for a conventional machine, it is said to have reached quantum supremacy. It is still up for discussion, but Google stated in 2019 that it achieved supremacy in quantum technology with a particular assignment.

Edge Computing and IoT

The processing, analysis, and use of data are being revolutionised by cutting-edge computing and IoT, two closely connected technology.

Computer Edges

Instead,depending on centralized cloud data centers, edge computing involves processing data closer to the point of data origination, or at the "edge" of the network. (O. Y. 2024). This method lowers latency, improves computing actual time, and uses less bandwidth to transfer data from the desktop to the cloud.

Web of Things

An extensive network of linked devices is known as the Web of Things, or IoT, such as sensors, cameras, and smart appliances, that exchange information and interact with one another. These gadgets generate enormous amounts of data, which need to be handled efficiently to enable to support application like autonomous cars, smart communities, and industrial automation.

1. **Reduced Latency**: Response times are accelerated using edge manufacturing, which handles data locally at the edge. Systems that require split-second decisions, like self-driving cars, depend on this.
2. **The bandwidth Effectiveness:** The use of edge computing reduces congestion in networks and data transfer expenses by minimising the need to send huge volumes of information to the server.
3. **Enhanced Security**: Processing sensitive data locally can reduce the risk of exposure during transmission to the cloud, improving privacy and security.
4. **Scalability**: The proliferation of IoT devices, edge computing helps manage the increased data load by distributing processing tasks across the network, making systems more scalable.

9. FUTURE ASPECTS OF CLOUD SECURITY

The future of cloud security will be influenced by new threats, developing technology, and shifting regulatory environments as cloud computing continues to advance. Here are some key future aspects of cloud security (Rembarz, R. 2009):

1. AI and Machine Learning

- **More Efficifent Threat Detection**: Real-time threat detection and response will be greatly aided by AI and ML. Faster and more precise threat detection is made possible by these technologies' ability to analyze enormous volumes of data and find patterns and abnormalities.
- **Automated Security Responses**: AI-driven automation will allow cloud security systems to respond to incidents without human intervention, reducing response times and mitigating risks more effectively.

2. Zero Trust Architecture

- **Trust No One, Verify Everything**: The adoption of zero trust principles will become more widespread, ensuring that Each access request is carefully examined., irrespective of whether data comes from within or beyond the network. By using this tactic, the likelihood of attackers changing their approach and threatening insiders is decreased.
- **Micro partition:** By using tiny separation in cloud-based instances, threats can be prevented and network activity can easily and precisely monitored.

3. Quantum-Resistant Security

- **Getting Ready for Quantum Computing**: As the technology of quantum computing develops, existing encryption techniques will come under assault. To prevent records from getting hacked by quantum assaults, cloud safety will need to advance and incorporate quantum-resistant algorithms.

4. Enhanced Data Privacy and Compliance

- **Statutory Development:** As data security laws become more complex and stringent worldwide, cloud safety must keep pace by offering state-of-the-art compliance technology that helps businesses satisfy a range of legal requirements.
- **Contents Responsibility:** The need to ensure that information is handled and kept inside specific geographic boundaries will lead to the development of more regionalised secure cloud-based services.

5. Integration of Edge Computing and IoT

- **Guarding the edges**: As the number of edge servers and Internet of Things (IoT) devices increases, data security at the perimeter will become more and more crucial. It will be necessary to develop new security strategies that can protect data and devices outside of the traditional cloud barrier.
- **Distant Security Guidelines**: More localised security strategies that can protect assets and information from several devices and locations will be required as the usage of cloud computing gets more distant.

6. Privacy-Enhancing Technologies

- **Neutral computing**: A new technique called "secretive computing" will allow private data to be handled in encrypted memory, ensuring data security throughout processing.
- **Homomorphic Encryption:** In future years, secure online storage may employ homomorphic verification to increase information anonymity. In this way, encrypted data might be used for computations without needing to be decrypted.

7. Cloud Security Posture Management (CSPM)

- Preventive Security handling: As CSPM technologies develop, they will provide more automated and proactive security management (Ahmad, I. A. I. 2024). This will help companies quickly detect and address security vulnerabilities, configuration mistakes, and compliance issues.

8. Supply Chain Security

- **Preserving Prerequisites**: As cloud-based services rely increasingly on third-party suppliers, supply chain safety will grow to be essential. Upcoming secure cloud strategies must include thorough screening of external suppliers and continuous monitoring of their security protocols.

9. User-Centric Security Approaches

- **Identification and access management (IAM):** Along with basic authentication, more sophisticated IAM systems in the future will include behavioural analytics and continuous authentication to ensure safe entry.
- **User Awareness and Training**: As human factors remain a significant risk, ongoing user education and training will be integral to maintaining cloud security, particularly as attacks using psychological manipulation and phishing are becoming more sophisticated.

10. Sustainability & Green Security

- **Eco-Friendly Security Practices**: As cloud providers focus on sustainability, there will be a growing emphasis on implementing security practices that are not only effective but also energy-efficient and environmentally friendly.

10. CONCLUSION

At the moment, all businesses, regardless of size, have adopted computing via the cloud. Because of the cheaper expenses, fewer repairs, and more storage space made available by the servers that cloud providers handle, many people are still gravitating towards it. The "Pay as you go" approach of cloud providers' service delivery, which allows you to pay only for the services you really use, is another reason that has contributed to this major movement away from the corporations' on-premises servers.

Cloud security refers to procedures and policies used to safeguard infrastructures data, and apps in cloud computing settings. This chapter discusses cloud computing's security, ethical issues, and dilemmas, as well as the obstacles and solutions related to cloud security. Contrary to popular belief, hardware-based and on-premise security is not more secure. This is true even though many organisations still hold this belief. The advantages of cloud security over on-premise security are abundantly clear from these advantages. It covers a broad range of subjects, such as regulations, legislation, standards, and regulating models. Thus, investigating and resolving cloud computing security issues from a technical standpoint is insufficient. These upcoming developments in cloud security emphasise the necessity of ongoing innovation and adaptation to meet the changing opportunities and challenges in the field of cloud computing.To guarantee improved security for your assets stored in the cloud, pick the best cloud security service. Later chapters will cover the models of security and privacy concerns.

REFERENCES

Bakshi, A., & Dujodwala, Y. B. (2010, February). Securing cloud from ddos attacks using intrusion detection system in virtual machine. In *2010 second international conference on communication software and networks* (pp. 260-264). IEEE. DOI: 10.1109/ICCSN.2010.56

Barroso, L. A., Dean, J., & Holzle, U. (2003). Web search for a planet: The Google cluster architecture. *IEEE Micro*, 23(2), 22–28. DOI: 10.1109/MM.2003.1196112

Behl, A. (2011, December). Emerging security challenges in cloud computing: An insight to cloud security challenges and their mitigation. In *2011 World Congress on Information and Communication Technologies* (pp. 217-222). Ieee. DOI: 10.1109/WICT.2011.6141247

Bethencourt, J., Sahai, A., & Waters, B. (2007, May). Ciphertext-policy attribute-based encryption. In *2007 IEEE symposium on security and privacy (SP'07)* (pp. 321-334). IEEE. DOI: 10.1109/SP.2007.11

Boneh, D., & Franklin, M. (2001, August). Identity-based encryption from the Weil pairing. In *Annual international cryptology conference* (pp. 213-229). Berlin, Heidelberg: Springer Berlin Heidelberg. DOI: 10.1007/3-540-44647-8_13

Chang, Y. C., & Mitzenmacher, M. (2005, June). Privacy preserving keyword searches on remote encrypted data. In *International conference on applied cryptography and network security* (pp. 442-455). Berlin, Heidelberg: Springer Berlin Heidelberg. DOI: 10.1007/11496137_30

Che, J., Duan, Y., Zhang, T., & Fan, J. (2011). Study on the security models and strategies of cloud computing. *Procedia Engineering*, 23, 586–593. DOI: 10.1016/j.proeng.2011.11.2551

Christodorescu, M., Sailer, R., Schales, D. L., Sgandurra, D., & Zamboni, D. (2009, November). Cloud security is not (just) virtualization security: a short paper. In *Proceedings of the 2009 ACM workshop on Cloud computing security* (pp. 97-102). DOI: 10.1145/1655008.1655022

Crampton, J., Martin, K., & Wild, P. (2006, July). On key assignment for hierarchical access control. In *19th IEEE Computer Security Foundations Workshop (CSFW'06)* (pp. 14-pp). IEEE. DOI: 10.1109/CSFW.2006.20

Damiani, E., De Vimercati, S., Foresti, S., Jajodia, S., Paraboschi, S., & Samarati, P. (2007). An experimental evaluation of multi-key strategies for data outsourcing. In *New Approaches for Security, Privacy and Trust in Complex Environments: Proceedings of the IFIP TC-11 22 nd International Information Security Conference (SEC 2007), 14–16 May 2007, Sandton, South Africa 22* (pp. 385-396). Springer US. DOI: 10.1007/978-0-387-72367-9_33

Dikaiakos, M. D., Katsaros, D., Mehra, P., Pallis, G., & Vakali, A. (2009). Cloud computing: Distributed internet computing for IT and scientific research. *IEEE Internet Computing*, 13(5), 10–13. DOI: 10.1109/MIC.2009.103

Gellman, R. (2009, February). Privacy in the clouds: Risks to privacy and confidentiality from cloud computing. In *World privacy forum* (Vol. 23).

Goh, E. (2003). *Secure indexes. Technical Report. 2003/216.* IACR Print Cryptography Archive.

Goyal, V., Pandey, O., Sahai, A., & Waters, B. (2006, October). Attribute-based encryption for fine-grained access control of encrypted data. In *Proceedings of the 13th ACM conference on Computer and communications security* (pp. 89-98). DOI: 10.1145/1180405.1180418

Hong, C., Zhang, M., & Feng, D. G. (2010). AB-ACCS: A cryptographic access control scheme for cloud storage. *Journal of Computer Research and Development*, 47(1), 259–265.

Hu, J., Chen, L., Wang, Y., & Chen, S. H. (2013, December). Data Security Access Control Model of Cloud Computing. In *2013 International Conference on Computer Sciences and Applications* (pp. 29-34). IEEE. DOI: 10.1109/CSA.2013.15

Hwang, K., Kulkareni, S., & Hu, Y. (2009, December). Cloud security with virtualized defense and reputation-based trust mangement. In *2009 Eighth IEEE international conference on dependable, autonomic and secure computing* (pp. 717-722). IEEE. DOI: 10.1109/DASC.2009.149

Ibraimi, L., Petkovic, M., Nikova, S., Hartel, P., & Jonker, W. (2009). Ciphertext-policy attribute-based threshold decryption with flexible delegation and revocation of user attributes. *IEEE Transactions on Image Processing*.

Jensen, M., Schwenk, J., Gruschka, N., & Iacono, L. L. (2009, September). *On technical security issues in cloud computing. In 2009 IEEE international conference on cloud computing*. Ieee.

Kandukuri, B. R., & Rakshit, A. (2009, September). *Cloud security issues. In 2009 IEEE international conference on services computing*. IEEE.

Khalil, I. M., Khreishah, A., & Azeem, M. (2014). Cloud computing security: A survey. *Computers*, 3(1), 1–35. DOI: 10.3390/computers3010001

Klymenko, V., Zhavoronkova, G., & Zhavoronkov, V. (2020). World mobile services market: economic aspect.

Krutz, R. L., Krutz, R. L., & Russell Dean Vines, R. D. V. (2010). *Cloud security a comprehensive guide to secure cloud computing*. Wiley.

Kumar, T., Kumar, P., & Namasudra, S. (2024, February). A DNA-based Authentication System for Securing Cloud Data Storage and Transactions. In *2024 11th International Conference on Computing for Sustainable Global Development (INDIACom)* (pp. 1692-1698). IEEE.

Kumar, T., Namasudra, S., & Kumar, P. (2023). Providing data security using DNA computing in the cloud computing environment. *International Journal of Web and Grid Services*, 19(4), 463–486. DOI: 10.1504/IJWGS.2023.135587

Kundu, A., Banerjee, C., & Saha, P. (2010). Introducing New Services in Cloud Computing Environment. *J. Digit. Content Technol. its Appl., 4*(5), 143-152.

Lim, H. C., Babu, S., Chase, J. S., & Parekh, S. S. (2009, June). Automated control in cloud computing: challenges and opportunities. In *Proceedings of the 1st workshop on Automated control for datacenters and clouds* (pp. 13-18). DOI: 10.1145/1555271.1555275

MacVittie, L. (2009). *Load balancing is key to successful cloud-based (dynamic) architectures*. DevCentral Home.

Malek, B., & Miri, A. (2009, August). Combining attribute-based and access systems. In *2009 International Conference on Computational Science and Engineering* (Vol. 3, pp. 305-312). IEEE. DOI: 10.1109/CSE.2009.157

Mather, T., Kumaraswamy, S., & Latif, S. (2009). *Cloud security and privacy: an enterprise perspective on risks and compliance*. O'Reilly Media, Inc.

Nassif, A. B., Talib, M. A., Nasir, Q., Albadani, H., & Dakalbab, F. M. (2021). Machine learning for cloud security: A systematic review. *IEEE Access : Practical Innovations, Open Solutions*, 9, 20717–20735. DOI: 10.1109/ACCESS.2021.3054129

Nwobodo, I., Jahankhani, H., & Edoh, A. (2014). Security challenges in the distributed cloud computing. *International Journal of Electronic Security and Digital Forensics 9, 6*(1), 38-51.

Obi, O. C., Dawodu, S. O., Daraojimba, A. I., Onwusinkwue, S., Akagha, O. V., & Ahmad, I. A. I. (2024). Review of evolving cloud computing paradigms: Security, efficiency, and innovations. *Computer Science & IT Research Journal*, 5(2), 270–292. DOI: 10.51594/csitrj.v5i2.757

Ohlman, B., Eriksson, A., & Rembarz, R. (2009, June). What networking of information can do for cloud computing. In *2009 18th IEEE International Workshops on Enabling Technologies: Infrastructures for Collaborative Enterprises* (pp. 78-83). IEEE. DOI: 10.1109/WETICE.2009.27

Ostrovsky, R., Sahai, A., & Waters, B. Attribute-Based encryption with non-monotonic access structures. In: Ning, P, Vimercati, SDC, & Syverson, PF, eds. *Proc. of the 2007 ACM Conf. on Computer and Communications Security, CCS 2007*. Alexandria: ACM Press, 2007. 195–203.

Pring, B., Brown, R. H., Frank, A., Hayward, S., & Leong, L. (2009). Forecast: Sizing the cloud; understanding the opportunities in cloud services. *Gartner, Inc., Research Report G, 166525.*

Reddy, V. K., Rao, B. T., Reddy, L. S. S., & Kiran, P. S. (2011). Research issues in cloud computing. *Global Journal of Computer Science and Technology*, 11(11), 59–64.

Ren, K., & Lou, W. (2009). *Ensuring Data Storage Security in Cloud Computing.* Retrieved from.

Roy, S., & Chuah, M. (2009). *Secure data retrieval based on ciphertext policy attribute-based encryption (CP-ABE) system for the DTNs.* Lehigh CSE Tech. Rep.

Segun-Falade, O. D., Osundare, O. S., Kedi, W. E., Okeleke, P. A., Ijomah, T. I., & Abdul-Azeez, O. Y. (2024). Assessing the transformative impact of cloud computing on software deployment and management. *Computer Science & IT Research Journal, 5*(8).

Subashini, S., & Kavitha, V. (2011). A survey on security issues in service delivery models of cloud computing. *Journal of Network and Computer Applications*, 34(1), 1–11. DOI: 10.1016/j.jnca.2010.07.006

Verma, A., & Kaushal, S. (2011). Cloud computing security issues and challenges: a survey. In *Advances in Computing and Communications: First International Conference, ACC 2011, Kochi, India, July 22-24, 2011* [Springer Berlin Heidelberg.]. *Proceedings*, 1(Part IV), 445–454.

Vieira, K., Schulter, A., Westphall, C., & Westphall, C. (2009). Intrusion detection for grid and cloud computing. *IT Professional*, 12(4), 38–43. DOI: 10.1109/MITP.2009.89

Voorsluys, W., Broberg, J., & Buyya, R. (2011). Introduction to cloud computing. *Cloud computing: Principles and paradigms*, 1-41. Liu, X. (2014, January). Research and applications of cloud desktop. In *2014 International Conference on Computer, Communications and Information Technology (CCIT 2014)* (pp. 14-17). Atlantis Press.

Wang, L., Tao, J., Kunze, M., Castellanos, A. C., Kramer, D., & Karl, W. (2008, September). Scientific cloud computing: Early definition and experience. In *2008 10th ieee international conference on high performance computing and communications* (pp. 825-830). Ieee.

Williamson, A. (2009). Comparing cloud computing providers. *Cloud Comp. J*, 2(3), 3–5.

Wu, H., Ding, Y., Winer, C., & Yao, L. (2010, November). Network security for virtual machine in cloud computing. In *5th International conference on computer sciences and convergence information technology* (pp. 18-21). IEEE.

Yu, S., Ren, K., Lou, W., & Li, J. (2009). Defending against key abuse attacks in KP-ABE enabled broadcast systems. In *Security and Privacy in Communication Networks:5th International ICST Conference, SecureComm 2009,Athens, Greece,September 14-18, 2009, Revised Selected Papers 5* (pp. 311-329). Springer Berlin Heidelberg. DOI: 10.1007/978-3-642-05284-2_18

Zhang, L. J., & Zhou, Q. (2009, July). CCOA: Cloud computing open architecture. In *2009 IEEE International Conference on Web Services* (pp. 607-616). Ieee. DOI: 10.1109/ICWS.2009.144

Zhang, X., Wuwong, N., Li, H., & Zhang, X. (2010, June). Information security risk management framework for the cloud computing environments. In *2010 10th IEEE international conference on computer and information technology* (pp. 1328-1334). IEEE. DOI: 10.1109/CIT.2010.501

Chapter 10
Load Balancing in Cloud Computing Ensuring Fault Tolerance, High Availability, and Security

Ajay Kumar Kasaudhan Baniya
https://orcid.org/0009-0000-8087-547X
School of Computer Engineering, KIIT University, Bhubaneswar, India

Alankrit Gupta
https://orcid.org/0009-0007-3023-4413
School of Computer Engineering, KIIT University, Bhubaneswar, India

Shubham S. Pant
https://orcid.org/0009-0002-7544-133X
School of Computer Engineering, KIIT University, Bhubaneswar, India

Saurabh Singh
https://orcid.org/0009-0006-3715-9228
School of Computer Engineering, KIIT University, Bhubaneswar, India

Dinesh Paudel
https://orcid.org/0009-0003-2194-5492
School of Computer Engineering, KIIT University, Bhubaneswar, India

Hitesh Mohapatra
https://orcid.org/0000-0001-8100-4860
School of Computer Engineering, KIIT University, Bhubaneswar, India

ABSTRACT

In the fast-evolving world of cloud computing, we have to ensure that systems run seamlessly even in the presence of challenges. Load balancing serves as a vital protector by offering fault tolerance and high availability, efficiently allocating workloads across multiple resources rather than merely distributing traffic. Traditional load balancing models reduce the risk of component overload failures but struggle to handle the unique challenges of cloud environments, such as dynamic workloads and unpredictable failures. In this paper, we presented the rise of advanced solutions and their power to overcome the drawbacks of conventional load balancing methods.

DOI: 10.4018/979-8-3693-7137-4.ch010

Advanced methods improve fault tolerance and high availability by considering server status and workload nature, going beyond traditional traffic splitting techniques. The research enhances the understanding of load balancing and parallel scheduling in the cloud, focusing on security and resilience. As a result, we have demonstrated the significant role played by self-adaptive and intelligent load balancing approaches.

1. INTRODUCTION

Cloud computing refers to the storage and management of data, and retrieval of computing services through the internet without the user physically controlling the customer resources. Large clouds are typically large and function distributed across multiple sites, with each being essentially a datacenter. Since this technique depends on sharing of resources, it always tends to maintain considerable similarity in its copy; it usually goes hand in hand with a 'use 'em and pay 'em model which helps to reduce initial costs but can have hidden subsequent costs for many users. NIST was the first to offer a formal definition of cloud computing as a ''paradigm for providing on-demand access to shared pools of configurable computing resources through the provision of service offering such that users typically do not hold the service provider accountable for the application, data, processing, storage, or service delivered; can quickly be provisioned and dynamically released with minimal effort or provider interaction (Adhikari & Amgoth, 2018). In the case of cloud computing that has distributed computing model and means using virtual resources, two tenets of the cloud computing model are the fault tolerance and high availability. This is where load balancing shines, it becomes a critical methodology, which will not only address issues of utilization of the various resources within the network and reduction of response time but also mask other issues such as unpredictable faults. Imagine a multi-lane highway: load balancing ensure that the incoming traffic is comfortably distributed across these lanes without ever crowding a particular lane which will attract congestion.

With the move towards integrated systems due to progress in processor and communication technology, problems of resources control and load sharing were experienced. However, at the same time as such linkages were made possible by such advancements, contemporary research in AI, IoT and cloud computing is addressing these challenges squarely (Dey et al., 2024). For example, studies in the area of edge computing and decentralized networks can work on creating even better optimization of communication channels so that the load is distributed even better. Yet load balancing is not just an optimization concept. They remain the foundation of implementing the approach to fault tolerance and high availability. In its simplest terms, it intelligently distributes workloads across multiple servers and thus shields against allowing one point to become saturated or fail. Whenever one of the servers receives a large number of requests or even if it develops a problem with it, the load is transferred to other available servers with no much interruption. Picture this: Suddenly one lane on the highway is blocked by an accident (Di Modica et al., 2018). Load balancing is the intelligent traffic control for such vehicles that help through directing them to the remaining lanes and minimizing the time everyone takes to get to their desired destination. The model of fault tolerance in cloud environment is explained below through the help of Figure.1.

Figure 1. Fault tolerance in Cloud Environment

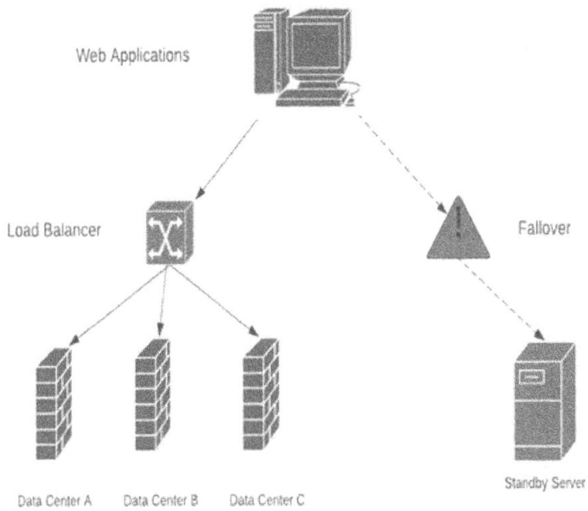

Unlike distribution which determines where traffic is to be sent, load balancing uses complex algorithms to determine where the traffic should go. These algorithms take into account the status of the server, the load, and memory, as well as a user's location as a way to guide traffic toward the most effective resources (Friedman & Mosse, 1999). This means not only are resources used to their fullest potential, but the unique experience of a site visitor is optimized even at the peaks of activity. You could think of it as a freeway where there are no end-of-the-line bottlenecks and instead of switching lanes and making people wait for their turn, the traffic just intelligently allocates the load. Cloud computing is not only a virtualized resource but actually a very large range of service models such as SaaS, IaaS, PaaS, and EaaS and so on. Whether you need cloud application hosting, virtual hardware and Web application development tools, or professional knowledge, there is a model for your needs (Fu & Sun, 2012). And at the heart of all of this is the perpetual guarantee of high availability and reliability, which has solid fault tolerance mechanisms that use load balancing as the key component.

Cloud computing has rapidly emerged as one of the defining technologies in contemporary infrastructures for business and organizations to achieve flexibility, scalability, and economies of cost over the past few years. However, cloud services have also started to depend upon for handling business-critical processes and applications, continuity of accessing business reserves is emerged as an important issue. High availability (HA) and fault tolerance (FT) are outlined as critical principles in this regard, trended for reducing service outages, and avoiding the unavailability of cloud environments (Gorender et al., 2007). Availability in its high sense addresses the ability of a system to continue working for a considerable amount of time without showing evidence of hardware or software problems or network issues that hinder users' access. On the other hand, fault tolerance refers to the system's ability to carry on working and to preserve data in the presence of failure of components in the system or other types of errors. HA and FT mechanisms can therefore be applied to cloud service infrastructures bringing improvements in terms of service dependability and performance as well as against disturbances that are likely to disrupt organizational operations and efficiency (Hayyolalam & Özkasap, 2025).

In this paper, an assessment of the advances in methods and strategies, techniques, and methodologies in enhancing HA and FT in cloud computing is provided. Based on a body of knowledge produced by academic literature, expert opinions, and practical examples, we explore the ideas, issues, and perspectives underlying the design, deployment, and administration of highly dependable and resilient cloud environments. In addition, we examine how HA and FT strategies can be applied to all aspects of cloud computing such as allocation of computing resources, workload distribution, backup copy, and disaster recovery (Kassela et al., 2015). Through Literature review and thereby conducting a systematic integration of empirical evidence, this paper seeks to present findings, suggestions, and best practices for improving the reliability and Resilience of cloud services to facilitate the researchers, practitioners, or any related stakeholder. By exposing students to HA and FT principles from multiple dimensions we aim to make a small contribution to an ongoing debate of how to enhance the decisiveness and reliability of cloud structures in a constantly changing IT world. Please recall that the decision on implementing an effective cloud strategy requires consideration of all its peculiarities and risks (Kaur & Kaur, 2021). If you comprehend the value of load balancing in making an IT system precisely fault tolerant and high available, then you can utilize the advantages that load balancing offers and can ensure the preparation of a graceful, highly available IT paradigm that is not affected negatively in the event of adversity.

2. LITERATURE REVIEW

In the world of cloud computing, load balancing reigns splendid as the mum or dad of excessive availability and fault tolerance. By strategically distributing visitors throughout more than one server, it orchestrates an efficient ecosystem where performance thrives, scalability flourishes, and person experience reigns (Kumar et al., 2024). Imagine a bustling marketplace: overloaded providers conflict to serve eager customers, main too long queues and disenchanted consumers. Here, the load balancer acts as a sensible coordinator, redirecting customers to be had companies, ensuring short carrier and glad faces. Similarly, in cloud computing, load balancing prevents crushed servers from buckling underneath pressure, leading to faster reaction times and a continuing consumer journey (Kwok & Cheung, 2004). Furthermore, like a foxy standard looking ahead to enemy assaults, load balancing prepares for the inevitable. By introducing redundancy through multiple servers, it ensures service continuity even when character servers falter (Mohammadian et al., 2022). This fault tolerance safeguards towards downtime, preventing the dreaded state of affairs of an internet site or software going offline (Mohapatra, 2024). However, this balancing act isn't always without its demanding situations. Finding the candy spot among surest performance and aid usage calls for cautious configuration, similar to a chef navigating the sensitive balance of flavor and cost (Mohapatra & Mishra, 2024). Additionally, implementing and dealing with a complex load balancing set-up can be stressful, comparable to orchestrating a massive orchestra. Finally, the introduced infrastructure incurs charges that want to be cautiously weighed against the cost it provides.

In the dynamic and scalable environment of cloud computing, ensuring steady software overall performance and availability is paramount. Load balancing emerges as a critical era in accomplishing this goal, appreciably bolstering fault tolerance and high availability. This research evaluation delves into the elaborate dating among load balancing, fault tolerance, and excessive availability in the cloud landscape, drawing upon hooked up studies and current advancements. Cloud computing gives several benefits, including on-call for sources, fee-effectiveness, and international reach (Mohapatra & Rath, 2020). However, inherent to this allotted infrastructure are demanding situations like server screw ups, fluctuating site visitors' patterns, and capability performance bottlenecks. A single factor of failure can cripple an entire application, main to giant downtime and revenue loss. High availability, described because the capacity to remain operational no matter the issue of disasters, will become a crucial element of cloud-based total services. Load balancing acts as a site visitors director, dispensing incoming requests throughout a pool of servers or times (Muhuri et al., 2020). This distribution prevents any unmarried server from becoming overloaded, enhancing responsiveness and scalability. Various load balancing algorithms exist, catering to particular desires. Round-robin, as an example, ensures truthful distribution, while least connections direct visitors to the server with the fewest lively connections. More advanced algorithms don't forget elements like server fitness and response times for top-quality distribution. Fault tolerance includes a system's capacity to hold capability even if additives fail. In the context of cloud programs, load balancing plays a vital position in attaining fault tolerance. By distributing site visitors across a couple of servers, a single server failure doesn't convey the whole application. The ultimate healthy servers hold to serve requests, minimizing downtime and impact on users (Panda et al., 2024).

High availability now needs not handiest fault tolerance but also rapid recuperation from screw ups. Load balancers, alongside different technologies like vehicle-scaling and fitness checks, contribute extensively to reaching this. Health assessments executed by way of the weight balancer pick out unhealthy servers and dispose of them from the pool, making sure site visitors are going most effectively to functional times. Auto-scaling mechanically provisions new servers when demand increases or existing ones fail, preventing overall performance degradation. Numerous studies have explored the efficacy of load balancing in improving fault tolerance and excessive availability in cloud environments. A examine with the aid of tested the effect of different load balancing algorithms on cloud software performance and fault tolerance. Their findings highlighted the advanced overall performance of dynamic algorithms like least connections in comparison to static ones, in particular underneath various workloads (Priyadarshi et al., 2024). Further, research by (Priyadarshi et al., 2024) investigated the mixing of load balancing with auto-scaling in cloud garage systems. Their results confirmed great enhancements in machine availability and scalability as compared to structures without these technologies. Figure.2 emphasize the system model of load balancing in cloud computing .

Figure 2. The system model of load balancing in cloud computing.

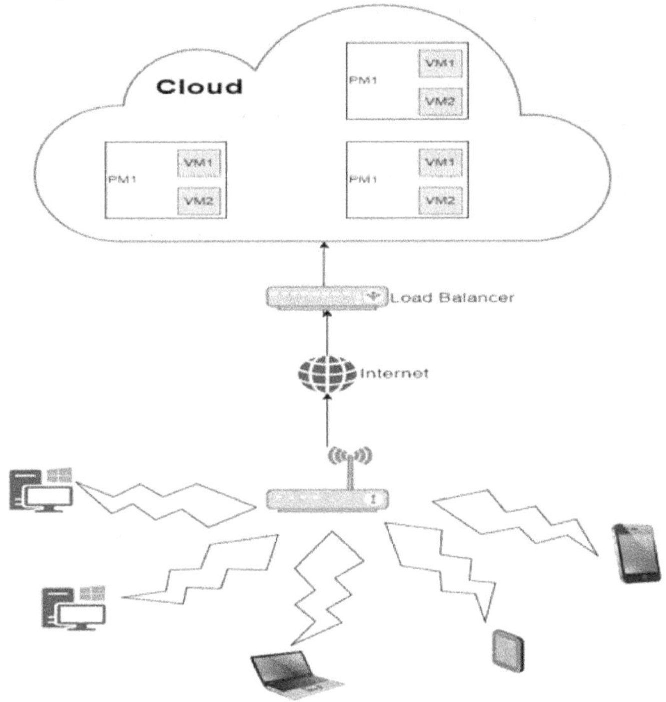

2.1 Load Balancing Algorithms in Cloud Computing:

With a rapidly evolving client-server model in cloud computing, effective resource management and a generally high level of availability are imperative goals to accomplish. These algorithms are very critical when it comes to sharing the workload among the sever for a given system in order to avoid overloading of some of the sever. In the following literature review, the presented algorithms give details of the load balancing mechanism while also focusing on how they can be applied in cloud computing (ROSS et al., 2021).

2.1.1 Round Robin:

In load balancing widely used Round Robin algorithm helps to balancing works in cloud computing and distributed systems. Uknown as Round Robin, it may be popular for its simplicity and fairness of distributing equal requests among the servers. The current study provides an understanding of the Round Robin algorithm and how it works to reveal the operational framework of the approach. Round Robin works in the round robin method that distributes the incoming requests in a circular management system. The mechanism requires the presence of a circular list of servers and choosing the next server in turn on entering a new request. This sequential distribution guarantees each server processes requests in a sequence to form a loop. At one go, when each server is reached at the end of the list, the computer rewinds the list and continues the function of distribution (Sah et al., 2024). The Round ROBIN Algorithm work-flow in Load balancing is depicted in Figure.3.

Figure 3. Round Robin Algorithm

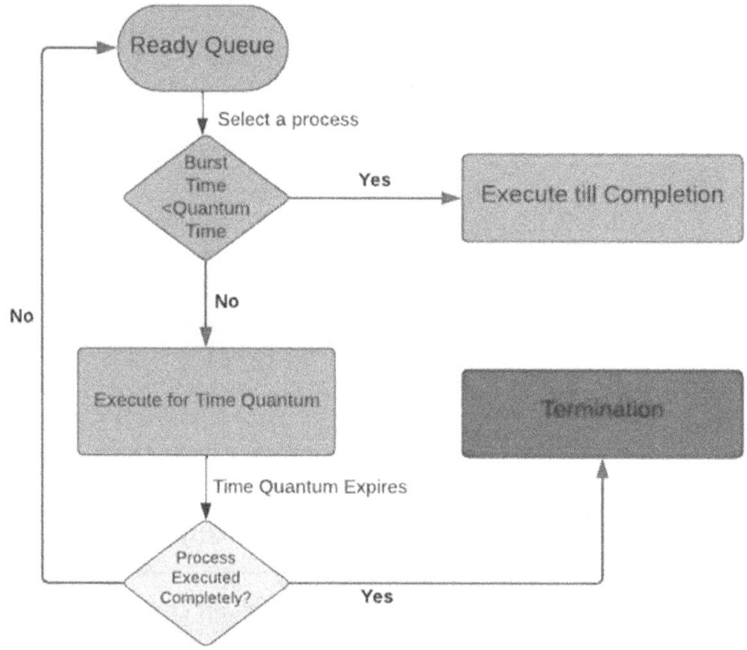

2.1.2 Genetic Algorithms (GAs):

GAs are optimization and search heuristics based on such a concept as the natural selection and genetic heredity. They are popularly used and categorized under the class of Evolutionary Algorithms and are used to provide approximate solution to problems as those in optimizations and searching. GAs works in a similar way to natural selection, crossover and mutation of the biological system evolution fitness in order to evolve a given population through cycles in order to produce a better population through iteration. It starts by the creation of a population of potential solutions in form of a chromosome (Sanaei & Mostafavi, 2019). Kaminski and Pawlak

(2005) point out that GAs mimics evolution by selection, crossover, mutation, and evaluation over generations in order to find an improvement. Selection phase seeks to allocate genes with more fitness from a specified function to reproduce. Crossover means swapping of genetic information between selected couple and brings in traits.

Mutation brings variation into the otherwise static settings; this is important. Fitness evaluation determines the next generation in terms of the blueprint to be followed. The set of individuals improve in each iteration until they get populations that are optimal or within a negligible distance of the optimum. Due to the oriented and flexible nature, GAs can be applicable in various applied computational issues, related to optimization, applying the principles of the genetic evolution to find approximate solutions to optimization and search problems. GAs operates by mimicking the mechanisms of natural selection, crossover, and mutation observed in biological evolution to iteratively evolve a population of potential solutions towards more optimal configurations. GA are optimization heuristics inspired by natural selection and genetics. The mechanism begins with the initialization of a population of potential solutions, represented as chromosomes (Sasikala, 2013). Through iterative cycles of selection, crossover, mutation, and evaluation, GAs simulates the process of evolution to improve solutions over multiple generations. The selection phase prioritizes individuals with higher fitness, determined by a predefined function, for reproduction. Crossover involves exchanging genetic information between selected individuals, introducing diversity. Mutation introduces random changes, preventing stagnation. Fitness evaluation guides the next iteration. This iterative process continues, progressively refining the population and converging towards optimal or near-optimal solutions. GAs' adaptability makes them versatile for addressing complex optimization challenges across diverse domains, leveraging the principles of genetic evolution for efficient problem-solving. Figure.4 depicts how the evolutionary process unfolds in a GA simulation:

Figure 4. Genetic Algorithm (GA)

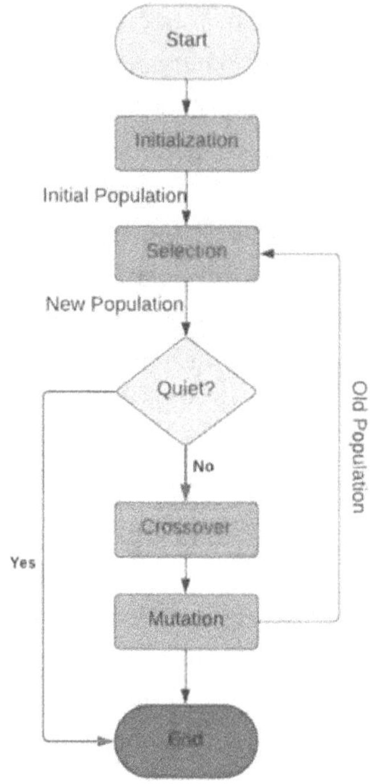

2.1.3 Ant Colony Optimization (ACO):

Thus, ACO is a class of optimization algorithms that is based on the foraging activity of ants. ACO is based on how ants search for shortest possible routes in their societies from the food source to their colonies and vice-versa. In the algorithm, artificial ants are typical solutions to the optimization problem, while the solution space is similar to the real environment in which the real ant moves problems, ACO simulates the cooperative foraging strategy employed by ant colonies to find optimal paths between their nest and food sources. In the algorithm, artificial ants represent solutions to the optimization problem, and they traverse a solution space analogous to the physical landscape navigated by real ants. The chief process is basically the process of laying down artificial pheromones when ants are moving across a given path, with the concentration of pheromone meaning the desirability of the path (Satpal Singh, 2023). This pheromone trail is used by other ants to follow as there is a dynamic feedback system by which ants choose paths that have more pheromones. Driven by pheromone communication, ACO allows the iterative interplay between exploration and exploitation to efficiently converge towards optimal solutions of a large variety of combinatorial optimization problems. Imagine a small colony of busy ants desperately hunting food. Within the nest, each ant embarks on a journey for some innate purpose, leaving a trail of its pheromones a chemical scent marking the trail. This chemical signature draws other ants to their scent, creating a positive feedback loop of other ants more likely to follow the scent. Real ants navigate a physical map, and they explore a virtual map that is analogous to the physical landscape. They are not looking for food sources, instead they search for optimal solutions, conditioned on employment of 'artificial pheromones' strategically situated at different paths. The Ant Colony Optimization Algorithm task flow is shown in Figure.5.

Figure 5. Ant Colony Optimization (ACO)

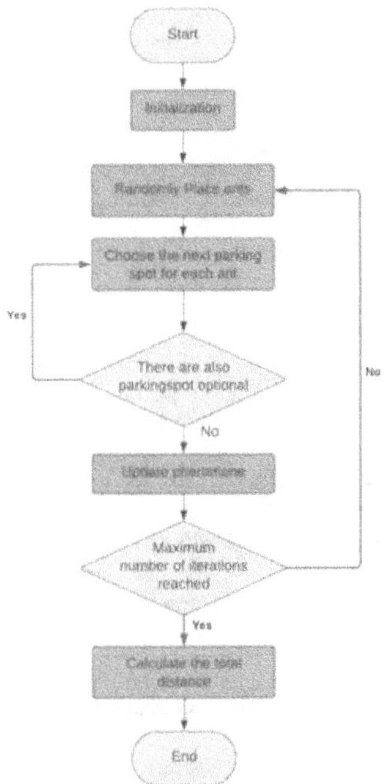

2.2 Compare and Contrast of Load Balancing Algorithms:

Load balancing algorithms are pivotal in optimizing the allocation of workloads across various resources in cloud computing environments. Below, we delve into specific load balancing algorithms, providing insights into their mechanisms and associated time and space complexities. Table.1 presents time complexities and space complexities load balancing algorithms.

Table 1. Time complexities and space complexities load balancing algorithms

Algorithm	Time Complexity	Space Complexity	Remarks
Round Robin	O (1)	O (1)	Simple yet effective, ensures balanced distribution but may not consider server loads.
Weighted Round Robin	O (1)	O (1)	Adds flexibility by considering server capacities, ideal for diverse workloads.
Least Connections	O(n)	O(n)	Effective in dynamically changing scenarios but might lead to uneven resource usage.
Least Response Time	O(n)	O (1)	Sensitive to network fluctuations, suitable for latency-sensitive applications. Sensitive to network fluctuations, suitable for latency-sensitive applications.
Genetic Algorithm	Variable (O (n log n) to O(n^2))	O(n)	Adaptable and self-optimizing but computationally intensive.
Ant Colony Optimization	O(n^2)	O(n^2)	Mimics nature's efficiency but demands higher computational resources.

Table 2. Advantages and challenges of load balancing algorithms

Algorithm	Advantages	Challenges	Best Suited For
Round Robin	Simple, easy to implement, fair distribution of traffic.	May not consider server loads, leading to uneven resource utilization. Can suffer from "thrashing" with frequent context switching.	Simple setups, small environments.
Weighted Round Robin	Offers flexibility by assigning weights to servers based on capacity.	Requires pre-defined weights, which may need manual adjustment over time.	Environments with diverse server capacities.
Least Response Time	Aims for fastest response times by directing traffic to servers with shortest response times.	Requires monitoring all servers constantly, increasing overhead. Can be susceptible to manipulation by malicious actors.	Real-time, latency-sensitive applications.
Least Connections	Efficient in dynamic scenarios, directs traffic to least loaded servers.	Can lead to uneven resource utilization if new servers quickly become overloaded. May not prioritize servers with higher performance capabilities.	Environments with frequent load fluctuations.

continued on following page

Table 2. Continued

Algorithm	Advantages	Challenges	Best Suited For
Genetic Algorithm (GA)	Adapts and optimizes over time, considers diverse factors through "genes".	Requires careful parameter tuning, can be computationally expensive.	Dynamic, complex environments with multiple optimization goals.
Ant Colony Optimization (ACO)	Learns from collective behavior, robust to changes, excels at finding near-optimal solutions.	Can be slow to converge, sensitive to parameter settings.	Dynamic, highly distributed environments with stochastic load patterns.

2.3 Load balancing performance metrics:

Before load balancing, cloud servers are like a single waiter in a packed restaurant: if they are implemented over competition, they can slow down a machine to a crawl, resulting in unproperly utilized resources and even crashes. Load balancing serves as a city traffic flow regulation mechanism where requests are spread over the servers, unlike having more traffic light. This leads to quick responses, optimal resource utilization, perfect scalability, and resiliency all of which culminate in smooth running of cloud environment. It is right between stagnation and open traffic conditions necessary in today's dynamic environment in the digital realm. When used, the below table gives the idea of which kinds of applications perform in which way before and after load balancing (Stecca & Maresca, 2010). Table.2 shows the strengths and weaknesses of different load balancing algorithms. The detailed performance of each system with and without cloud-based load balancing is shown in the following Table.3.

Table 3. Performance comparison with and without load balancing

Application	Before Load Balancing	After Load Balancing	Improvement
E-commerce website	20% downtime during peak hours	99.9% uptime	79% reduction in downtime costs
Financial trading platform	50ms average transaction time	10ms average transaction time	80% faster transactions
Online multiplayer game	Frequent lag and disconnects	Smooth gameplay with low latency	Increased player satisfaction and retention

3. RESEARCH GAP

In the ever-changing field of load balancing research, there is an obvious research gap in the comprehensive analysis of the enhancement of resource distribution in distributed systems. Current load balancing algorithms focus primarily on fundamentals of processor utilization that include response time and throughput, frequencies that do not sufficiently address modern load balancing problems including energy usage, security, and the growing variation in forms of processing hardware (Yao et al., 2022). This failure really calls for the development of load balancing techniques that will be able to accommodate the varying workloads, at the same time use less power resources in a remarkably secure manner especially by having to incorporate security measures to neutralize threats like DDoS attacks.

3.1 Dimensions and Gaps:

Although load balancing helps to protect the basics of cloud computing's fault tolerance and high availability, the process is not without its weaknesses in terms of its number of developments. Current algorithms perform poorly in non-steady workloads, and they either have high availability or fault tolerance however not both. New areas like healthcare and IoT have great potential for increasing opportunities; applications of AI/ML with containers and integration of containers also have high potential. Of particular importance for further evolution, it is necessary to stress the further enhancement of performance metrics addressing its combined evaluation and the implementation of enhanced security measures. Investigating these dimensions and gaps is a promising venue to advance load balancing research and design, and ensure a stable, robust cloud computing environment (Priyadarshi et al., 2024). In-depth research gaps within load balancing includes:

3.1.1 Dynamic Workload Prediction:

The fact that real-time accuracies and adaptability are sought after in workload prediction models presents a promising area of research. Further to these conventional confines, it is considered appropriate that the high-sophisticated machine learning techniques are incorporated in order to increase accuracy. It is equally important to define the criteria for evaluation because the tasks at hand require detailed and comparable analyses.

3.1.2 Energy-Efficient Load Balancing:

The challenges in this area go beyond just balancing workloads for the purpose of reducing energy needs in data centers and cloud systems. The high demand for load balancing and energy efficient solutions can only be met by creating new forms of interconnection between the two. Next, a strong synergy of advanced machine learning and optimization methods is becoming essential for reaching adaptive and intelligent load balancing alongside energy efficiency.

3.1.3 Security-Aware Load Balancing:

An absence of prior research that looks at the integration of security obligations into the load balancing process from a new perspective of departed from traditional performance indicators forms the basis of this research gap. Dynamic adaptive approaches which also depend on real-time threat information in order to adjust load distribution in addition to other security measures such as anomaly detection are necessary in shading cloud architectures against continuously emerging threats.

3.1.4 Edge Computing Load Balancing:

It is therefore necessary to fine-tune load balancing approaches concerning conditions expected in edge computing scenarios. This is complemented by an extension of focus to create light weight and dynamic algorithms suitable to run on edge devices with limited computational resources. Workload predictors appear to be promising machine learning agendas in helping edge computing deal with its unique requirements.

3.1.5 QoS-Aware Load Balancing:

When it comes to the situation of QoS-aware load balancing, the focus changes slightly to focusing on potential performance differentiation of the applications. This line of research points to the consideration of dynamic workload classification schemes, QoS-aware resource management algorithms and feedback-based adaptation to help provide dependable quality of service for all the diverse demands of various application workloads. Such research gaps embody the complex issues that modern load balancing faces, thereby providing the foundation for radical advancements in the general field of cloud computing and distributed systems.

3.2 Untapped Applications:

As discussed in section two, load balancing has always played the role of ensuring operations run smoothly in cloud computing; however, a few unexplored applications can be found. It can be understood like a traffic light for not just servers, but for entire industries! In healthcare, it can ensure the continues feed of data for remote patient monitoring as well as enhance the quality of treatment. In a world where IoT has interconnectivity, then it can proactively manage performance and latency to give the devices an easy time with their communication needs among millions of devices. Not even mission-critical, real-time applications are immune to advantage that it provides in terms of prioritizing quick responses and quick recovery. These examples are just the tip of the iceberg, but further research will open up huge potential in many segments and areas of use, as well as how we engage with technology in the future. Table.4 illustrates the concept of the industries and the research gap corresponding to such industries. Therefore, the research gaps have been presented here as important dimensions, which need to be studied and implemented to improve the capacity of load balancing in the distributed systems. Researcher and practitioners in this field are challenged to investigate these areas in order to develop next generation load balancing algorithms and framework that will define the future of clouds.

Table 4. Untapped application of load balancing in real-world scenario

Industry	Potential Application	Anticipated Benefits	Research Gap
Healthcare	Smart medical devices (e.g., remote patient monitoring)	Improved patient care, faster diagnosis, real-time data analysis	Limited research on load balancing for real-time medical data and device communication, ensuring high availability and reliability.
IoT	Edge-based analytics and processing	Reduced latency, improved response times, efficient resource utilization at the edge	Lack of research on integrating load balancing with edge computing architectures and protocols for robust fault tolerance in distributed IoT environments.
Financial Services	High-frequency trading platforms	Minimized transaction delays, maximized profit opportunities, guaranteed service availability	Need for load balancing algorithms optimized for ultra-low latency and high-throughput financial transactions, considering security and regulatory compliance.

4. PROPOSED STUDY

Due to the constantly growing use of web applications, it is crucial to guarantee their tolerance to faults and availability at a high level. From the previous sections, we have seen and understood how load balancing is key towards achieving failure tolerance and availability in current applications. However, traditional load balancing implementation can be shallow to solve complex dynamic workloads, failure scenarios or emerging security threats. This section explores new techniques that seek to close the gap between existing techniques and the increasing complexity of high-performance computing applications. We expect that by investigating these improvements we will be able to optimize traffic flow control, provide proactive mechanisms for fault tolerance and increase the overall system robustness (Gorender et al., 2007).

4.1 Limitations of Traditional Load Balancing with regards to Fault Tolerance & High Availability

The cyclic traffic distributing algorithms are very useful tools when it comes to balancing traffic to servers, but they have some drawbacks that only prolong availability. Some of them are:

I) Reactive Approach: Mechanistic techniques use real time information about the server status, and do not consider the future traffic pattern or the probability of server failures. This can result in congestion and blackouts time when traffic is at its peak or when servers break down.

II) Limited Server Health Awareness: Traditional methods are based almost solely on two parameters: status of servers (online/offline) with complete disregard for useful parameters such as CPU usage or free memory in a server. This can in turn end up leading people to access overloaded servers hence slow response times and frequent crashes.

III) Uneven Workload Handling: Regulations of these algorithms tend to prescribe a standard condition across servers. Nonetheless, servers possess different capacity and receive different amounts and types of clients' requests. From this it arises that some highly powered servers may remain idle while low powered ones get overburdened and hence performance constraints occur.

IV) Lack of Security Considerations: Lack of integral security characteristic and symptoms: basic load balancing solutions can be easily exposed to Denial-of-Service or spoofing. This can create problems for legitimate users while at the same time deteriorating the systems security.

4.2 Need of Advanced Solutions

This is especially so when the growing demands of high availability and fault tolerance in contemporary applications if a major limitative factor when the use of conventional load balancing algorithms. Though these algorithms offer simple traffic distribution, they lack in keeping services running all the time. Here's why advanced solutions are crucial:

I) Dynamic Workloads and Unforeseen Events: Traditional approaches are problematic in such issues as elasticity and variability, increased traffic and sudden surge, or failure of a server. Optimizing solutions that use predictive load balancing are capable of assuming how the loads are going to be in future and planning for them to ensure the least time is consumed.

II) Server Health and Resource Optimization: Many basic algorithms do not contain information about important metrics on the health of defined servers. Solutions with context-aware routing can take into account such parameters as CPU utilization, or content type, thus always sending traffic in such a way that will not overwhelm a server with a heavy traffic load while there are other less-loaded servers. This facilitates proper use of resources form which operation runs effectively.

III) Enhanced Security: Many traditional methods do not have integrated security and as a result, such methods are bound to be attacked by DoS or any form of malicious traffic. The solutions that can be brought to a higher level can include anomaly detection, rate limiting, and security tools to help protect against cyber threats.

IV) Scalability and Adaptability: Generally, scaling traditional algorithm can be inconvenient because it can be done manually. Technological solutions that offer real scalability allow for changing resource usage based on current traffic and rate during high load periods or infrastructure shifts.

4.3. Predictive Load Balancing

Problem Introduction:

Existing load balancing algorithms primarily react to current server health and workload. This approach can lead to delays and service disruptions during sudden traffic spikes or server failures.

Solution:

This research therefore presents a probabilistic load balancing framework for use in a future grid environment using machine learning intelligence to forecast the future system load and server health. The framework would consist of three key components: Traffic and Resource Prediction, Pre-Allocation of Resources and Pre-Emptive Failure Recovery Techniques (Kaur & Kaur, 2021).

Figure 6. LSTM-RNN Classifier Flowchart

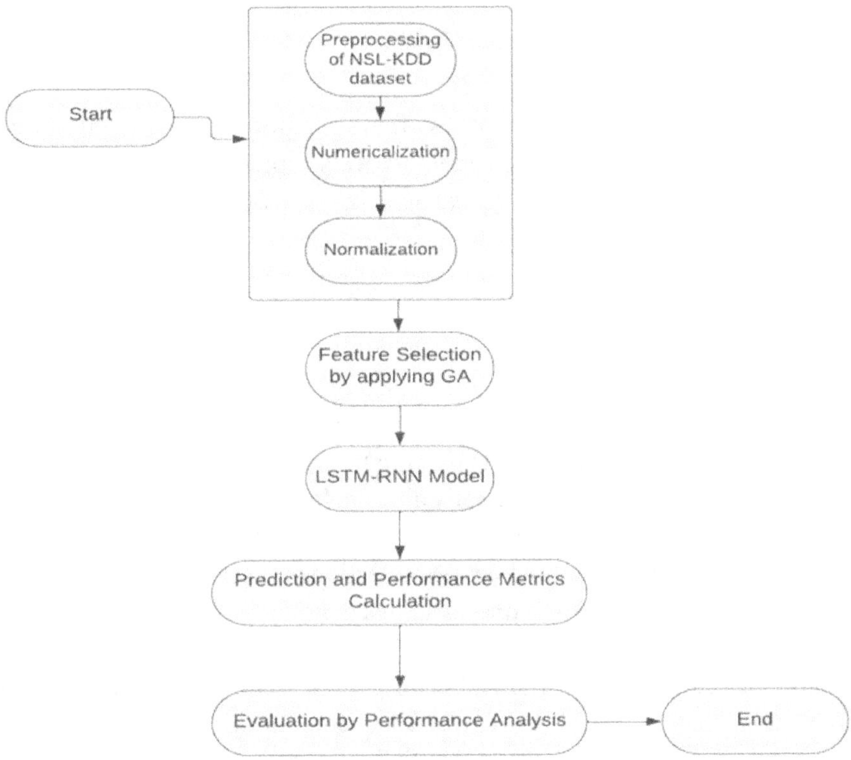

Predictive load balancing basically relies with the choice of the appropriate machine learning algorithms. This event is the study of LSTM networks which one of the several promising candidates for a solution as seen in the following sections. Employing past data of cloud traffic, this system predicts long-term resource requirements of an information center. It works based on the premise that daily, weekly, monthly and yearly trends of usage can be periodically ascertained and the facility used to predict future workloads. This approach ensures that resources are properly matched to expectations of demand, so that high demand returns can be obtained easily in the right proportions. Figure.6 is depicting the flowchart of LSTM-RNN classifier. The specification of workload prediction employs Long Short-Term Memory Recurrent Neural Network (LSTM-RNN) with data from space programme of NASA and Canadian servers as its training data set. These approaches help the system in achieving optimal use of the resources it will need while avoiding wastage of energy through, for instance, the use of irrelevant resources.

4.4 Intelligent Load Balancing with Multi-Agent Reinforcement Learning

Problem Introduction:

Traditional load balancing approaches often struggle to adapt to highly dynamic environments with complex traffic patterns, diverse application requirements, and evolving user behavior. Additionally, managing and configuring these solutions can be cumbersome (Kumar et al., 2024).

Solution:

In this research, an intelligent load balancing solution based on multi-agent reinforcement learning is introduced. The proposed scheme involves the utilization of a number of intelligent agents that are trained with reinforcement learning approaches to dynamically and optimally allocate loads in a diverse system setting. The system uses several intelligent agents, and each of them is assigned to one of the load balancing function sub-processes (selection of servers, resource allocation, anomaly detection, etc.). There is one agent that continues to communicate with the environment (server load, user traffic or application performance) and makes some decisions and learns through trial and error getting rewards when it makes good decisions and penalties when it makes a bad decision. LPA links are active and work in cooperation with each other; they share their experiences and knowledge as well as their goals are oriented towards the maximal performance of the entire system. Load Balancing of MARL is represented in Figure.7.

Figure 7. MARL load balancing

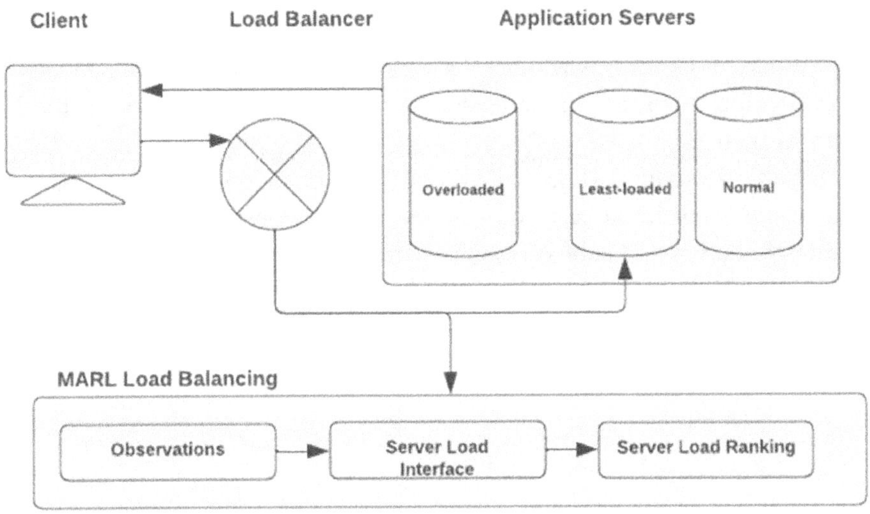

4.5 Quality-of-Service (QoS)-Aware Load Balancing with Network Function Virtualization (NFV)

Problem Introduction:

Traditional load balancing approaches often struggle to handle applications with diverse Quality-of-Service (QoS) requirements. These requirements can include guaranteed bandwidth, low latency, or specific packet loss thresholds. Additionally, managing and provisioning network resources dedicated to QoS enforcement can be complex and resource-intensive (Di Modica et al., 2018).

Solution:

The load balancing solution in this research is designed with the consideration of QoS and together with the use of NFV. NFV engulfs network functions such as firewalls, load balancers and traffic shaping functions as software installed and running on virtual machines or containers. This approach takes advantage of the organic nature and implementation of the NFV to develop the framework through the delegation and management of the resources used in QoS-aware load balancing. Getting back to Figure .8 above, it's a representation of architecture of NFV.

- QoS Policy Definition: Administrators define specific QoS requirements for different application types (e.g., guaranteed bandwidth for video streaming, low latency for online gaming).
- NFV-based Load Balancing: Network functions for load balancing and QoS enforcement are implemented as virtualized services within the NFV infrastructure.
- Dynamic Resource Allocation: Based on application type, real-time traffic demands, and available resources, the NFV orchestrator dynamically allocates resources and configures QoS parameters for each traffic flow.

Figure 8. NFV architecture

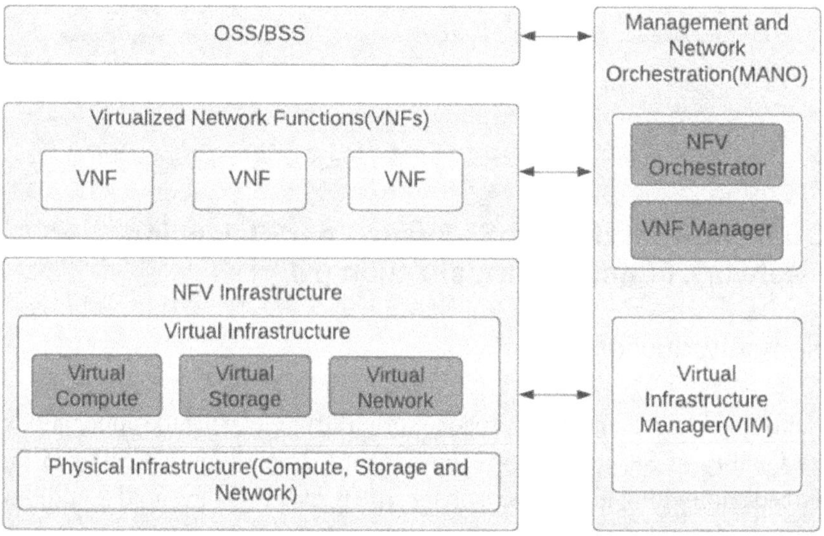

4.6 Hybrid Load Balancing with Adaptive AI and SDN Integration

Problem Introduction:

Currently available load balancing solutions interfere with the flexibility, control, and efficiency nowadays applications require. First, there are completely rule-based systems that are clear and straightforward but not very flexible; second, there are purely AI systems, which are oriented as algorithms and difficult to navigate. Furthermore, integrating with Software-Defined Networking (SDN), in order to reconfigure the network automatically can pose a problem to achieve in a smooth manner.

Solution:

This study recommends a mixed configuration scheme that utilizes rule-based configuration, supported by AI configuration control as well as integrating with SDN control for practical load balancing. This solution considers providing a high efficiency of resource utilization, as well as simplifying the control, and taking into account dynamics and complexity of traffic flows. Software Defined Network Architecture is presented in the Figure.9.

Figure 9. SDN Architecture

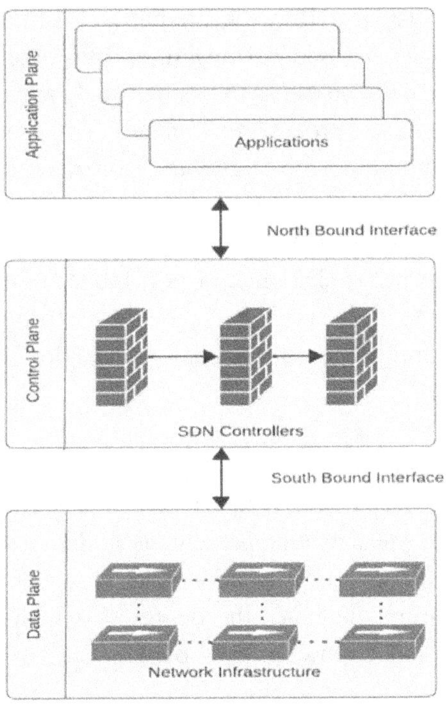

- Rule-based Foundation: The system is built on clear and concise fundamental rules that are used to base basic load balancing decisions on; maximum connections, minimum connections and round robin.

- Adaptive AI Layer: Above this deterministic framework, there is an AI component (e.g., deep learning, reinforcement learning) that learns system metrics, and real-time data (server utilization, user traffic pattern, app performance).
- SDN Integration: The load balancing system is designed here to work with an SDN controller so that network configurations are adjusted according to the result of AI analysis or predefined rules.

5. ANALYSIS AND COMPARISON

The result analysis would pinpoint to a huge potential of the proposed solutions in filling existing gaps in load balancing in literature. It depicts such solutions that leverages innovative technologies such as machine learning, reinforcement learning, NFV, and SDN to provide dynamic, optimal, and secure load balancing solutions for current dispersed systems. However, predictive load balancing is particularly special in that it leverages machine learning algorithms in regarding workloads that are predictive of future demands so as to ensure timely performance of anticipated loads, especially with volatile processing demands. This kind of strategic approach indicates that cloud computing is moving toward more rational and selective resource utilization, which will bring better fault tolerance, high availability and efficiency to the cloud computing environment. Overall, these solutions also show that technology is ready to evolve to meet the challenge of new modes of computing and provide unparalleled reliability to the users. To compare the performance of traditional load balancing algorithms and proposed solutions, we employ the following statistical metrics:

- Response Time: The time taken to respond to client requests.
- Throughput: The rate at which requests are processed by the system.
- Packet Loss Rate: Measures the percentage of data packets lost during transmission, crucial for assessing network reliability.
- Resource Utilization: Indicates the degree to which system resources like CPU, memory, and bandwidth are being used, essential for optimizing performance.

5.1 Traditional Load Balancing vs Predictive Load Balancing:

- **Average Response Time**: Traditional load balancing might see an average response time increase of 30 milliseconds (ms) during unexpected traffic spikes, whereas predictive load balancing could maintain it below 10 ms due to proactive resource allocation (Ref: Figure.10).

- **Throughput**: In a traditionally load balanced cloud environment, users could find the throughput reduced by as much as 20 per cent during peak load. Predictive load balancing that would involve predicting load evenly could in fact keep throughput at this level or above by ensuring higher workload.
- **Resource Utilization**: In traditional load balancing, efficiency may indicate an unequal distribution where the servers might have a 20% variance standard deviation. Predictive load balancing could potentially reduce this deviation to 5%, indicating a more efficient allocation of resources based on predicted workload patterns (Ref: Figure.11).
- **Packet Loss Rate**: Load balancing as a traditional technique results in the packet loss rate of 2% because of the server load and network interference. Predictive load balancing could reduce the chance of those situations and under that circumstances the packet loss might be less than one percent.

Figure 10. Comparison of Average Response Time

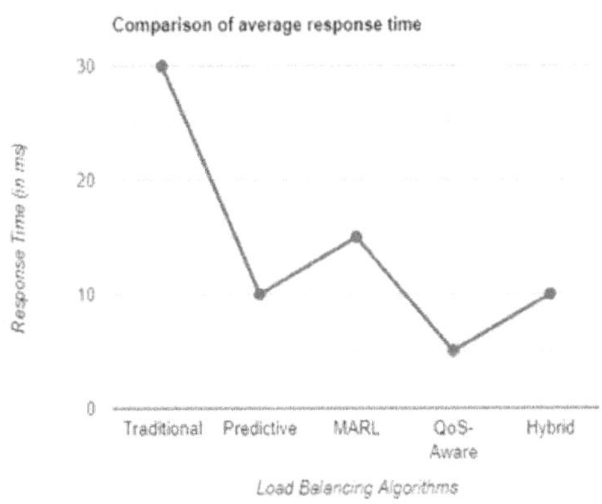

Figure 11. Comparison of Resource Utilization

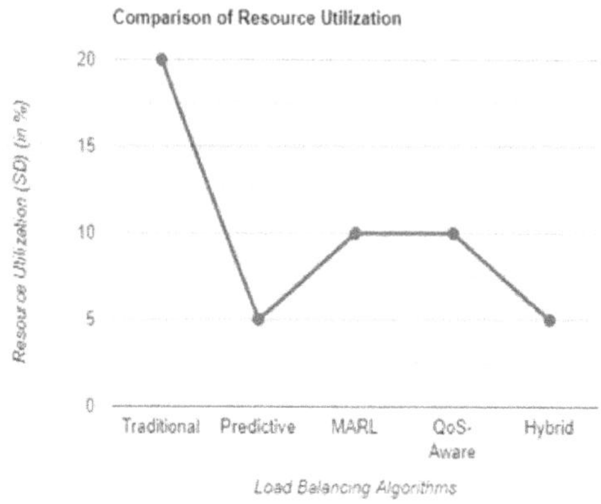

5.2 Traditional Load Balancing vs MARL Load Balancing:

- **Average Response Time:** While transitioning to new peak-workload intervals, traditional load balancing might need to average around 30 ms, though MARL would be capable of restoring such a figure and provide an even better engagement rate under constant response times as it learning is done in real time.
- **Throughput:** Traditional load balancing typical of a cloud environment will result into a throughput reduction of 20 percent during the period of relative load. Based on the theoretical derivation of MARL, it should be possible to sustain a throughput of 85% or above by optimally re-directing traffic.
- **Resource Utilization:** This is different from traditional load balancing in which resource usage may be skewed with 20% deviation between servers. MARL could probably minimize this deviation to 10%, suggesting enhanced capacity in utilization of resources relative to the learned load patterns.
- **Convergence Time:** Based on the workload, it took the MARL agents about 30 minutes to learn the best approaches for load balancing. This convergence time can be further improved as the better algorithms for training are developed.

5.3 Traditional Load Balancing vs QoS-aware Load Balancing with NFV:

- **Average Response Time**: Traditional: Increase of 20 milliseconds (ms) for a latency-sensitive application during peak periods. QoS-aware with NFV: Reduction to 5 ms for the same application through priority routing.
- **Throughput**: Traditional: Throughput remains at 80% for non-critical applications but drops to 50% for latency-sensitive ones during peak periods. QoS-aware with NFV: Throughput remains above 75% for both types of applications by dynamically allocating resources (Ref: Figure.12).
- **Resource Utilization**: Traditional: Standard deviation of 20% across servers. QoS-aware with NFV: Reduction to 10% standard deviation, indicating efficient resource allocation based on real-time application needs.

Figure 12. Comparison of Throughput

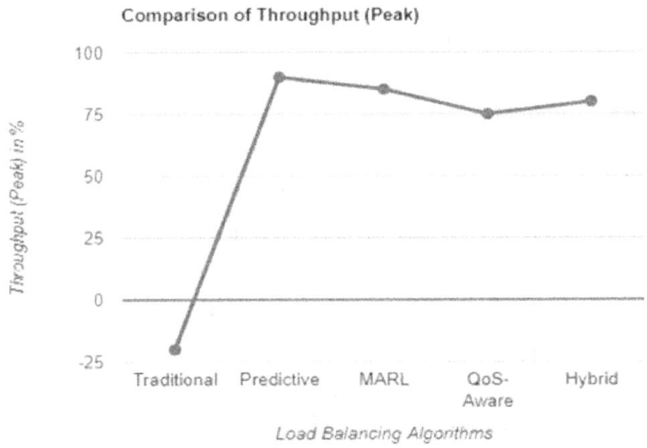

5.4 Traditional Load Balancing vs Hybrid Load Balancing with Adaptive AI and SDN Integration:

- **Average Response Time**: Traditional: 30ms more during peak workloads. AI & SDN-powered Hybrid: Achieved a 10 ms reduction through AI resource allocation and optimal network path. • Throughput: Traditional: 25% drop during peak periods. AI-SDN Hybrid: Maintained above 80% throughput by current resource allocation and network traffic flow.

- **Throughput**: Traditional: 25% drop during peak periods. AI-SDN Hybrid: Maintained above 80% throughput by current resource allocation and network traffic flow.
- **Resource Utilization**: Traditional: Standard deviation of 20% across servers. Hybrid with AI and SDN: 5% standard deviation, showing optimal resource allocation based on AI analysis.
- **Scalability:** Traditional: Manual scaling takes 30 minutes to react to traffic surges. Hybrid with AI and SDN: Automatic scaling delivers responsiveness within 5 minutes.
- **Packet Loss Rate:** Traditional: 2% packet loss for a latency-sensitive application during congestion. QoS-aware with NFV: Prioritizing low-latency traffic reduces this to below 0.5% for the same application.

6. CONCLUSION

The load balancing mechanism is significant in securing and upholding the cloud computing system, which will be elaborated in this paper. It describes load balancing and why it is important for distributing workloads across resources efficiently, preventing bottlenecks, and minimizing disruptions. Load balancing ensures efficient resource usage, maintaining high availability, and preventing servers from becoming overwhelmed. It also shows how load balancing is key to achieving fault tolerance and high availability, highlighting how these algorithms facilitate smooth resource allocation, optimize key performance metrics, and protect against failures. The paper systematically analyzes the fundamental principles, including distributed file systems and tools for assessing load balancing approaches, offering useful insights and recommendations for improving cloud computing reliability and resilience. The paper presents load balancing as a crucial part of resource management, discussing strategies for its evolution to support a robust digital environment.

REFERENCES

Adhikari, M., & Amgoth, T. (2018). Heuristic-based load-balancing algorithm for IaaS cloud. *Future Generation Computer Systems*, 81, 156–165. DOI: 10.1016/j.future.2017.10.035

Dey, D., Majumder, A., Agrawal, Y., Tewari, S., & Mohapatra, H. (2024). Smart mobility revolution. *Advances in Electronic Government, Digital Divide, and Regional Development*, •••, 143–164. DOI: 10.4018/979-8-3693-6740-7.ch006

Di Modica, G., Tomarchio, O., Caltcaterra, D., & Cartelli, V. (2018). Implementation of a fault aware cloud service provisioning framework. *2018 IEEE 6th International Conference on Future Internet of Things and Cloud (FiCloud)*, 9-16. https://doi.org/ DOI: 10.1109/FiCloud.2018.00010

Friedman, R., & Mosse, D. (1999). Load-balancing schemes for high-throughput distributed fault-tolerant servers. *Journal of Parallel and Distributed Computing*, 59(3), 475–488. DOI: 10.1006/jpdc.1999.1582

Fu, Y., & Sun, B. (2012). undefined. *2012 IEEE 2nd International Conference on Cloud Computing and Intelligence Systems*, 228-233. https://doi.org/DOI: 10.1109/CCIS.2012.6664402

Gorender, S., De Araujo Macedo, R., & Raynal, M. (2007). An adaptive programming model for fault-tolerant distributed computing. *IEEE Transactions on Dependable and Secure Computing*, 4(1), 18–31. DOI: 10.1109/TDSC.2007.3

Hayyolalam, V., & Özkasap, Ö. (2025). CBWO: A novel multi-objective load balancing technique for cloud computing. *Future Generation Computer Systems*, 164, 107561. DOI: 10.1016/j.future.2024.107561

Kassela, E., Konstantinou, I., & Koziris, N. (2015). A generic architecture for scalable and highly available content serving applications in the cloud. *2015 IEEE Fourth Symposium on Network Cloud Computing and Applications (NCCA)*, 83-90. https://doi.org/DOI: 10.1109/NCCA.2015.22

Kaur, M., & Kaur, A. (2021). Load balancing in cloud computing using optimization algorithm. [IJSR]. *International Journal of Science and Research (Raipur, India)*, 10(9), 939–945. DOI: 10.21275/MR21912194450

Kumar, A., Bag, A., Anand, A., Saha, S., Mohapatra, H., & Kolhar, M. (2024). Examining healthcare services utilizing cloud technology in intelligent urban environments. *Advances in Healthcare Information Systems and Administration*, •••, 77–98. DOI: 10.4018/979-8-3693-7225-8.ch004

Kwok, Y., & Cheung, L. (2004). A new fuzzy-decision based load balancing system for distributed object computing. *Journal of Parallel and Distributed Computing*, 64(2), 238–253. DOI: 10.1016/j.jpdc.2003.11.002

Mohammadian, V., Navimipour, N. J., Hosseinzadeh, M., & Darwesh, A. (2022). Fault-tolerant load balancing in cloud computing: A systematic literature review. *IEEE Access : Practical Innovations, Open Solutions*, 10, 12714–12731. DOI: 10.1109/ACCESS.2021.3139730

Mohapatra, H. (2024). The role of 6G in empowering smart cities enabling ubiquitous connectivity and intelligent infrastructure. *Advances in Civil and Industrial Engineering*, •••, 237–264. DOI: 10.4018/979-8-3693-8029-1.ch009

Mohapatra, H., & Mishra, S. R. (2024). Unlocking insights: Exploring data analytics and AI tool performance across industries. *Studies in Big Data*, 265-288. https://doi.org/DOI: 10.1007/978-981-97-0448-4_13

Mohapatra, H., & Rath, A. K. (2020). Nub less sensor based smart water tap for preventing water loss at public stand posts. *2020 IEEE Microwave Theory and Techniques in Wireless Communications (MTTW)*, 145-150. https://doi.org/DOI: 10.1109/MTTW51045.2020.9244926

Muhuri, P. S., Chatterjee, P., Yuan, X., Roy, K., & Esterline, A. (2020). Using a long short-term memory recurrent neural network (LSTM-RNN) to classify network attacks. *Information (Basel)*, 11(5), 243. DOI: 10.3390/info11050243

Panda, A. K., Lenka, A. A., Mohapatra, A., Rath, B. K., Parida, A. A., & Mohapatra, H. (2024). Integrating cloud computing for intelligent transportation solutions in smart cities. *Advances in Civil and Industrial Engineering*, •••, 121–142. DOI: 10.4018/979-8-3693-6695-0.ch005

Priyadarshi, S., Subudhi, S., Kumar, S., Bhardwaj, D., & Mohapatra, H. (2024). Analysis on enhancing urban mobility with IoT-integrated parking solutions. *Advances in Civil and Industrial Engineering*, •••, 143–172. DOI: 10.4018/979-8-3693-6695-0.ch006

Ross, R., Pillitteri, V., Guissanie, G., Wagner, R., Graubart, R., & Bodeau, D. (2020). Enhanced security requirements for protecting controlled unclassified information: A supplement to nist special publication 800-171 (No. NIST Special Publication (SP) 800-172 (Withdrawn)). National Institute of Standards and Technology.

Sah, R. K., Singh, A. K., Yadav, A. K., & Mohapatra, H. (2024). Cloud-enabled platforms for social and civic engagement in smart urban environments. *Advances in Electronic Government, Digital Divide, and Regional Development*, •••, 215–234. DOI: 10.4018/979-8-3693-6740-7.ch009

Sanaei, M., & Mostafavi, S. (2019). Multimedia delivery techniques over software-defined networks: A survey. *2019 5th International Conference on Web Research (ICWR)*, 105-110. https://doi.org/DOI: 10.1109/ICWR.2019.8765278

Sasikala, P. (2013). Architectural strategies for green cloud computing. *Cloud Computing Advancements in Design, Implementation, and Technologies*, 218-242. https://doi.org/DOI: 10.4018/978-1-4666-1879-4.ch016

Satpal Singh, E. A. (2023). A novel blockchain-reinforcement learning framework for securing wireless sensor networks with energy efficiency. *International Journal on Recent and Innovation Trends in Computing and Communication*, 11(10), 2256–2263. DOI: 10.17762/ijritcc.v11i10.8941

Stecca, M., & Maresca, M. (2010). An architecture for a Mashup container in Virtualized environments. *2010 IEEE 3rd International Conference on Cloud Computing*, 386-393. https://doi.org/DOI: 10.1109/CLOUD.2010.34

Yao, Z., Ding, Z., & Clausen, T. (2022). Multi-agent reinforcement learning for network load balancing in data center. *Proceedings of the 31st ACM International Conference on Information & Knowledge Management*. https://doi.org/DOI: 10.1145/3511808.3557133

Chapter 11
Multifactor Authentication (MFA), the Golden Lock for Cloud Entry:
By Adopting MFA, Organizations and Individuals Can Significantly Reduce the Risk of Security Breach

Arvindhan Muthusamy
Amity Universirty, India

G. Sakthi
https://orcid.org/0000-0001-5155-8651
Galgotias University, India

ABSTRACT

Today's increasingly frequent and costly cyber threats underscore the importance of securing machine learning (ML), which can automate reactions to identified risks and decrease the time needed to counteract possible assaults. Steps like separating infected systems and launching predetermined security procedures fall under this category. Machine learning algorithms sift through mountains of data, searching for irregularities that indicate potential security risks. Unusual user activity, malware, and phishing attempt detection are all part of this. To verify identities, ML models examine patterns of user behaviour. Some examples of this behaviour are the dynamics of keystrokes and mouse movements. In every respect, current MFA solutions are more user- and admin-friendly. More alternatives mean businesses

DOI: 10.4018/979-8-3693-7137-4.ch011

can pick an MFA solution that suits their specific setup and requirements. A user's knowledge, possession, or status can be validated via MFA methods.

1. INTRODUCTION

Worldwide, chief executive officers and other corporate leaders are apprehensive about cybersecurity. Cyber assaults are one of the most lucrative forms of crime and are currently the most rapidly expanding in the industrialized world. These attacks are constantly changing, getting worse, and costing more money. Data access control and user authorization are the most critical areas of security concern. Hackers accessing user credentials is the primary cause of most data breaches, system penetrations, and frauds. More robust user authentication solutions are required beyond simply letting anyone with the right credentials access private accounts and data. Fortunately, MFA is here to save the day. Authentication is a crucial step in the verification process when attempting to access any computer resource—be it a network, an application, or a device. Google and Amazon are just two of several well-known online services offering multifactor authentication as a feature that users may turn on or off. Security is another primary concern for developers in the IT business; if their systems are not well-protected, unauthorized users could compromise their work and cause software to malfunction. Hence, authentication determines if a user or program may access the system. Our quest for an effective solution that does not rely on old ways is driven by the latest security vs. intrusion advancements(Ahmadieh & El Madhoun, 2024). We examine classic methods thoroughly to improve them and develop new systems that circumvent all their shortcomings. As a result, many security measures are suggested, including Anti-Shoulder-Suffering, Anti-Capture Screening, and Anti-Key-Loggers Thus, it will be challenging, if not impossible, for the hacker to gain access to the system, regardless of how he manages to get the login and password. This is because he must figure out how to crack all authentication factors. Modern practices and psychological studies show that people can remember visuals far more quickly and efficiently than written text. You probably will not be able to visualize "amount," "level," or "ease" when you say them, but when you read about a car or a book, for instance, you cannot help but imagine it.

2. AUTHENTICATION SYSTEMS

Finding out the information used for different types of Verifications Guess, dictionary attacks, key logger, social engineering, shoulder surfing, listen-sniffer, and screen capture are some of the main attacks on knowledge-based verification modes

Implementation costs and potential hickups for Windows User can be outlined at this point with alternate on-screen keyboards: "Also consider the user must have active SMS service provider subscription plus valid phone number." Using certain technologies, like fingerprinting, also have these additional costs--for example that when a person buys his next gadget eventually he will be considered a suspect and have police inquiries made after him. As mentioned above the cost of using a multimode operation when the device is off digital mode only also limits its appeal. Compared with time attendance systems for example, but mode even has restrictions which include high cost requirement for specialized equipment "However since people's physical features change, it's not applicable in all situations(Kraft, 2024). "Thus, it may be advisable to use multifactor authentication. Many academics utilize this method, which uses one-time passwords (OTPs) that combine a user's login credentials with a token-generated PIN.

By requiring more than one form of authentication, Multifactor Authentication (MFA) is attempting to make it more tough for unauthorized individuals to access sensitive data. To make sure that a username and password are not the only things safeguarding your online accounts is a core feature of identity and access management. Afterwards, as you navigate through the login process MFA may request further steps(Holden & Cetinkaya, 2024). In comparison with guessing or stealing a password, it is significantly more difficult for a skilled hacker to reproduce your biometric information or snatch a one-time code. Digital dangers such as data breaches and account takeovers can be greatly staved off with multifactor authentication (MFA) and additional verification processes. MFA is most effective when it helps increase IT productivity, is easy to use, and resistances to withstanding phishing attempts.

Figure 1. Multi authentication characterises

MFA Stats – Editor's Picks 87% of all MFA implementations have occurred in the tech industry. Mobile apps are the preferred software choice for 95% of MFA consumers. Businesses with over 10,000 employees are more likely to adopt Figure 1 defines the multi authentication on MFA, with 87% of those enterprises doing so. 6.2% of people use notepads to jot down passwords, and they usually keep these notebooks in a visible place, like next to their computers. 2.8% of people continue to be targeted by strategies including SIM-jacking, MFA Hammering, and AiTM assaults, even if MFA is in place. 34% of medium-sized businesses (those with 26-100 personnel) use MFA. Why do Only 27% of companies with less than 25 staff members use multifactor authentication.

a. Latest Multifactor Authentication Stats

Even though 67% of IT managers agree that incorporating more safety features means a more complicated experience, 83% of organizations use authentication using passwords for some IT resources, 83% require multifactor authentication, and 66% demand biometrics, according to Jump Cloud's 2024 IT Patterns Report.

On average, three to five passwords are used to access IT resources, with fifteen per cent of employees using ten passwords or more.

Nearly a thousand password attacks are launched against Microsoft's systems per second, based on Microsoft, demonstrating how persistent cyber threats are. It is essential to note that over 99.9% of compromised accounts are not equipped with multifactor authentication enabled. When asked about online services that use multifactor authentication (MFA), over 50% of people had a favourable impression. Among these, 67% of British residents thought MFA-using services showed they cared about their customers' privacy.

Octa found that multifactor authentication (MFA) is becoming more popular. In January 2023, nearly two-thirds of users were using multifactor authentication.

According to a new KnowBe4 poll of 2,600 IT experts, there are notable disparities in security policies across big and small to medium-sized enterprises. Many small and medium-sized businesses (62%) do not use multifactor authentication (MFA) to secure user accounts compared to big businesses (38%). In contrast to smaller and medium-sized businesses, nearly all large enterprises (97%) have a strict and enforced password policy.49% of big firms think their password policies are inadequate. 48% of small to mid-sized organizations think their password policy is adequate.

b) Multifactor Authentication Usage in Organizations

Among over 1,000 SME IT experts surveyed by Jump Cloud in 2024, 83% stated that multifactor authentication (MFA) was necessary for staff access to all company resources. According to a comparable poll, most employees (95%) use a smartphone app or other software program for multifactor authentication (MFA) (Shashikala et al., 2024). A small percentage (4%), however, rely on technological solutions, and even fewer (1%) use biometric authentication techniques (such as facial or fingerprint identification). Organizational size is a strong predictor of MFA adoption. Over 87 per cent of businesses with 10,000 or more workers utilize mixed-factor authentication. Companies having 1,000 to 10,000 employees are 78% more likely to use MFA.

However, that number falls to 34% in smaller enterprises with 26–100 workers. The acceptance rate in companies with up to 25 employees is even lower, at 27%.

2.1 Password Hygiene

The Workplace Password Malpractice Report has revealed an alarming pattern in password security, highlighting the necessity for more stringent procedures. Despite improvements, the most popular passwords, such as “123456,” “123456789,” “qwerty,” “password,” and “12345,” are still too easy to guess and use, according to the survey. Passwords that are easy to guess pose a serious threat to security. The survey says that 57 percent of people use sticky notes to write down their passwords, and 67 percent have admitted to losing those notes, which increases the likelihood of unwanted access. Here are some of the best password security practices you might find interesting.62% of individuals keep passwords in notebooks, which are frequently left out in the open, like next to work devices. Digital password storage procedures also pose security risks. Nearly half (49%) of respondents said they keep work-related passwords in a document in the cloud, while over half (51%) said the same about their computer. 55% of people use passwords stored on mobile devices, which could result in security breaches if these devices are lost or stolen.

These results highlight how weak passwords are when used alone to secure accounts. Multifactor authentication (MFA) should be set up as a reliable defence mechanism.

It and also underscores the point that without a secondary system of security, individual passwords are merely traps waiting to be tripped(Haapaniemi, 2024). Multifactor authentication (MFA) is the key to creating an identity defense system that is solid and credible.

c) Multifactor Authentication (MFA) Market Statistics

The future development of MFA solutions will be able to get the layer of industry by storm. The MFA industry is forecast to grow to 801 billion by 2025, according to statistics from Ethicist Research Institute. This trend is also borne out by data collected from Grand View Research, which points to a broadening recognition of MFA's part in protecting sensitive enterprise data from attack by both their own staff and outsiders. Therefore, the market is expected to benefit from a growing number of cyber-attacks and increasingly strict rules on compliance, not to mention high awareness among all potential users that they may lose everything they value in a single breach. It's not as big a mystery why MFA solutions are in demand right now. For one thing, as a result of the advent of telecommuting jobs, companies need strong procedures for protecting proprietary business information. Remote access to the company network from anywhere in the world represents one critical area where MFA solutions can provide a secure, reliable means of connection(Kumar et al., 2024a). Secondly, today's regulatory environment think e.g. about measures like GDPR and CCPA -- asks for tougher data protection measures across the board. Every organization must now implement MFA purely so That its practices are thus compliant with what the law prescribes. Thirdly again, universal use of cloud-based services has increased the threat surface. MFA is now an essential tool for securing cloud-based systems.

In today's increasingly digital world, these trends and projections emphasize how important multifactor authentication (MFA) is for cybersecurity tactics.

d) Multifactor Authentication (MFA) Software Statistics

Regarding the various forms of MFA, software-based solutions are preferred. Regarding multifactor authentication, 95% of employees choose software-based solutions, such as smartphone apps(Alkhalifah, 2024). The accessibility and simplicity of software solutions probably contribute to this inclination. Only 4% of workers utilize hardware-based solutions, and even fewer use biometric method just 1%. Factors such as cost, technological maturity, and user familiarity may explain why biometrics are not widely used despite their security benefits.

e) Encounters with Multiple-factor Authentication

Enabling multifactor authentication (MFA) for your accounts has been a big step toward protecting your digital identity. While it would be great if all users were protected, unfortunately, even with MFA enabled, attackers are still targeting 28% of users. Due to the presence of MFA, attackers are compelled to devise means to circumvent it, which in turn leads to the development of more advanced attack techniques.

f) Some examples of these advanced attack techniques include:

One reason to avoid MFA based on mobile telephony (such as SMS or voice calls) is the risk of SIM-jacking and additional telecommunications vulnerabilities. SIM-jacking aims to intercept multifactor authentication (MFA) calls or SMS messages by gaining control of the victim's phone number. Multiple factor authentication (MFA) hammering or grieving attacks aim to force users to approve a fraudulent login by flooding them with MFA requests. There is a movement towards more secure MFA methods since this method takes advantage of less complex ones, such as push notifications. Threats from an Intermediary Party (AiTM): These complex phishing attacks aim to get victims to authorize the attacker's access via multifactor authentication (MFA). As this manipulation shows, phishing-resistant authentication mechanisms are crucial, especially for vital or extremely sensitive identities and assets. Not only is it crucial to implement MFA, but it is also essential to update and improve MFA procedures regularly to keep up with these ever-changing threats. Adopting the most secure forms of MFA and remaining watchful against new sorts of attacks are becoming increasingly critical as cyber threats advance(Zhan et al., 2024). This preventative measure is crucial for digital identities and assets to be as secure as possible.

g) Risky Business: The Implications of Stolen Credentials

Regardless of the occurrence method, several dangers are connected with a breach, such as penalties levied by regulatory agencies over GDPR or PCI. In the event of a data breach, the organization may be liable for fines, severance payments, and the expense of obtaining identity theft protection for all impacted users for 12 to 24 months. This is in addition to the negative publicity and significant harm to their brand. A denial-of-service assault may simply halt all mainframe systems, while an attack using ransomware might scramble all your data and demand payment. Other consequences could be far more disastrous.

h) Enhanced Mainframe Security: MFA

It would help if you equipped yourself with multifactor authentication, also known as MFA, as an instrument in your access and identification management arsenal because 81% of breaches are caused by credential reuse. Figure.2 explains about the band and Multifactor authentication (MFA) is a great way to verify the identity of someone trying to access your systems; it makes it difficult for malicious actors to do so while causing little trouble for genuine users. The increasing global connectivity of mainframes for short regulations such as GDPR, which mandate stricter enforcement of data protection measures and impose more significant fines, and the fact that PCI DSS mandates the implementation of MFA by requirement 8.3 and its sub-requirements all point to the potential wisdom of investing in MFA. Multifactor authentication (MFA) increases the amount of authentication assurance a system requires from an individual user by evaluating various identifying components linked to their Account. You can choose from a variety of products. One example is IBM Z Multifactor Authentication, which is integrated with RACF(Ashitha et al., 2024). Other vendors can also use the MFA API set that RACF provides. You can also use a one-time password (OTP) generator to generate a password that will only be valid for a small quantity of duration, maybe 60 seconds.

Cards and fobs that show a one-time password (OTP), PIN pads, soft tokens, and hardware or software tokens are all part of the "a certain something you have" and "a certain something you know" strategy used by RSA SecurID for and RSA Authentication Manager, two well-known products in this field. To set up or change a PIN, users often use seven websites to access the RSA Identification Manager program on z/OS. When authenticating into their desktop application with a fob, they input the PIN followed by the token shown randomly by the fob. Users can produce an indeterminate token by entering their PIN into an RSA software program on a smartphone or RSA PIN pad. This token can then be used to log into their desktop application.

Figure 2. Example in-band and compound using RACF and IBM TouchToken**

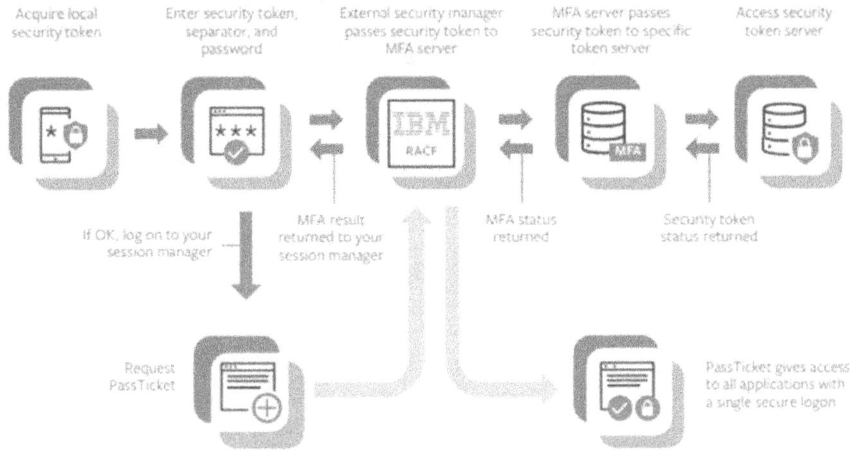

Modern identification with two-factor authentication is built into most popular password managers. If your browser supports it, anyone could scan a QR code with your phone and retrieve your six-digit access number because authenticator apps sync passwords between accounts(Pöhn et al., 2023). Remember that some older services may become inaccessible after you set up MFA. In these situations, you will need to use app passwords, which are credentials that you create on the primary web page and then use with a particular app. Facebook, Twitter, Microsoft, Yahoo!, Evernote, and many more all offer the capability to utilize their app passwords. These websites either employ third-party credentials or have older features you can use through their applications. Thankfully, app passwords are becoming less necessary.

As you freak out about how difficult something is, remember that Safety is not always a picnic. The evil people know you will be careless. Multifactor authentication (MFA) will make logging in on a new device more tedious, but protecting your identity, data, and money against theft is worth it(Furuberg & Øseth, 2023).

Figure 3. (Credit: Amazon/PC Mag)

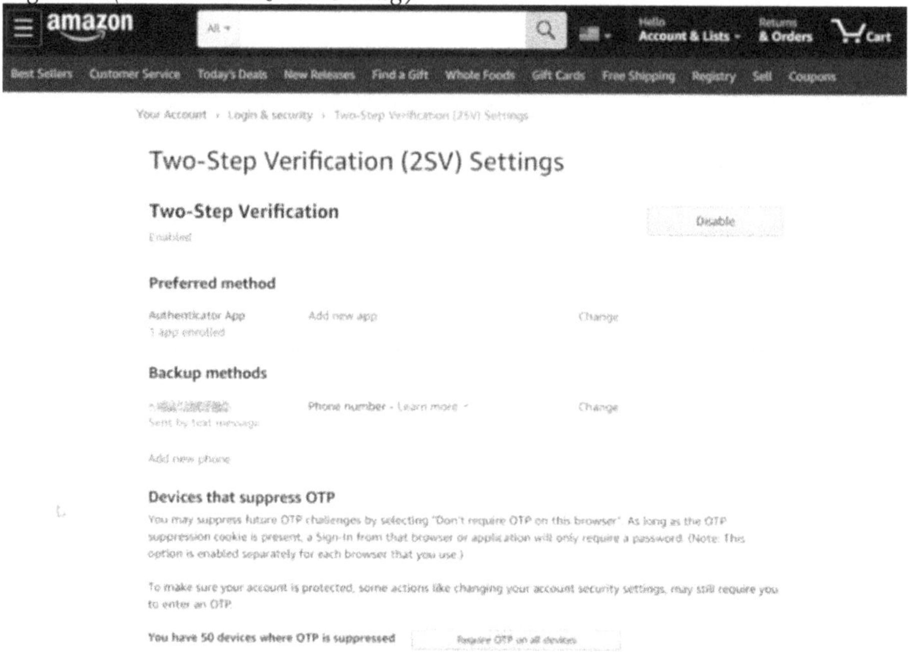

3. AMAZON TWO-STEP VERIFICATION

With Comitology, Audible.com, and other sites that use Amazon for payments—all linked to your credit card Figure.3 narrates the Amazon 2FA support is crucial. To access your Amazon account from a desktop computer, launch Amazon.com, then select Account from the Account & Lists menu. See Login & Security(Kotak et al., 2023). Click on Manage next to 2-Step Verification on the following screen. An authentication app is the best option (scan the QR code), but a phone number or numbers would do in an emergency. That is an excellent option if you want Amazon to bypass the codes on trustworthy devices (or on different trusted web browsers on the same device). Return to the Two-Step Verification page and select Prefer OTP on every gadget if the previous choice is ineffective or if you have used it too frequently for your liking(Rivera et al., 2024). Simplified, it stands for "one-time password." That is the authorization code that Amazon is adamant about.

4.DROPBOX TWO-STEP VERIFICATION

On desktop versions of Dropbox, you'll see a Security tab. From this page, you may reset your password, see how many devices are currently logged into your Account, change your password, and enable two-factor authentication. After you input your password and turn it on, you'll be asked if you prefer to receive security codes using a mobile authenticator app or SMS text messages(Kumar et al., 2023). To receive a code instantly, enter a phone number if you pick the text option. Another option to deactivate two-step verification is to enter a backup number. This will generate a 16-digit number that you should keep safe. There will be a QR code to scan onscreen if you pick the authenticator app, which is highly recommended. If you have a hardware security key, that is another alternative. The MFA guidelines provided by Dropbox are top-notch.

Figure 4. (Credit: Facebook/PC Mag)

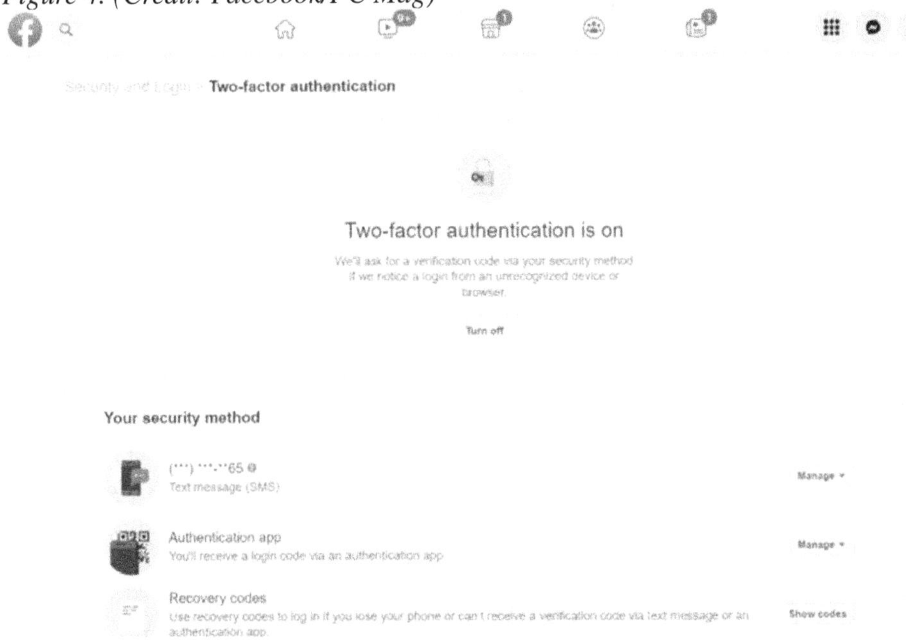

5.FACEBOOK TWO-FACTOR AUTHENTICATION

With Facebook's take on two-factor authentication, you will never have to worry about losing control of your Account again. You may access it on the desktop by navigating to your avatar's menu in the top right corner and then selecting Settings > Security and Login.

Figure 4 explains the Credit card authentication on Go to the Two-Factor Authentication section and then click on Edit. Read the Best Security Keys for Two-Factor Authentication for more information. The next screen will ask you to choose how you would want to be sent your second authentication method: a text message, an authenticator app, or a physical key that you either plug into your computer or keep nearby. Facebook generates a QR code on the desktop when you choose an authenticator app, which is optimal(Myint et al., 2020) .Hold your phone up to the machine's screen to record the PIN, then open you are the authentication system app on your mobile device. Then, click Add. If Facebook asks for a six-digit code the next time you log in, pull it up in the authenticator app.

All of the aforementioned choices require close proximity to your phone. Even if you lose your phone, you can still access your 10 recovery codes that you receive when you enable multifactor authentication. After retrieving them from the Two-Factor Authentication Settings section, save them to a secure location(Gavou et al., n.d.).

Figure 5. (Credit: Google/PC Mag)

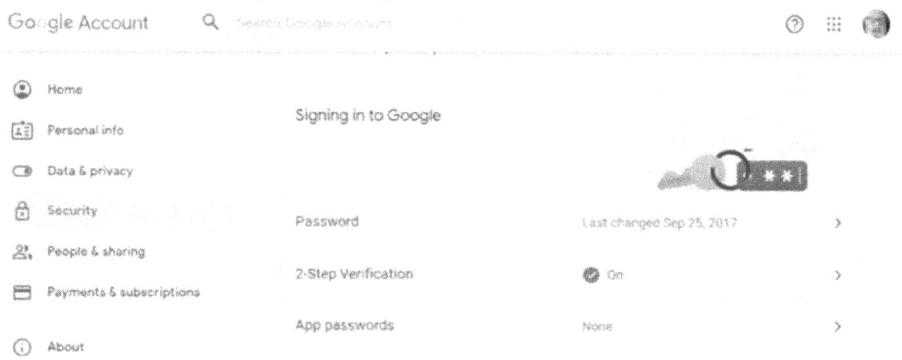

6. THE RISKS OF TWO-FACTOR AUTHENTICATION

Two-factor authentication (2FA) is a great way to keep hackers out of your accounts, but what if something happens to your phone that stops you from using it. Your Account may also be locked if that occurs. Backup codes solve this issue for most websites. If you ever lose access to your second factor, these unique codes will allow you to log in. In most cases, the website will generate these for you; therefore, you should store them somewhere safe to use in case of an emergency. Many sites also provide various types of two-factor authentication as a backup. Just one Account can enable two-factor authentication (2FA) apps and SMS codes. Our experts agree that this is a good plan, but there are risks associated with enabling a secondary 2FA technique that hackers might target. Figure.5 implies the One caveat is that authenticator applications can be phished, even if they are more secure than 2FA over SMS. An expert hacker may create a convincing phishing site that asks for your password and two-factor authentication code. An attacker may access your login details if they obtained and used both before the code expired.

When logging in, always make sure the URL is correct. Password managers also store the site's URL, so it's helpful look up suspects. If your password manager needs to identify the site, take care(Kumar et al., 2024b). Like an authenticator program, some password managers can generate TOTP codes. Despite the obvious benefits of having both passwords and codes in one place, it undermines the principle of two-factor authentication. If an intruder gains access to your password manager and steals your passwords and two-factor authentication tokens, your security is at risk. If you need to make one-time password codes (TOTP codes) that will be remembered by a password manager, consider the potential consequences(Chamoun, 2024).

7. CONCLUSION

Organizations that prioritize continuous updating of their MFA (Multi-factor Authentication) protocols will make sure that they can pre-empt any new threat emerging. This comprises not only them and their technology partners but also those who enable compliance with the law on a broader scale. They ought to appreciate further that at a time when people have many electronic identities it is necessary for all these various principal identities to be linked under single control so that anyone dealing with any of them wherever in time or place need not repeat the authentication process. Doing so guarantees that MFA remains effective not only in the fight against cybercrime itself but also as a salutary example to others. The increasing prevalence's of cloud-based services have raised the ante for authentication, designed to protect one's valuable data as well as crucial derivatives. Multifactor authentication has arisen as a promising solution here, adding to the traditional user name and password a second layer of security. With multi-factor authentication, users are required to present a number of different forms of identification. Thus, it dramatically changes the security level offered by an operating environment from what has been the norm in an on-premises world. It has become a critical part of securing cloud-based systems. With the digital landscape continuing to evolve, it seems likely that safe and easy user experiences will be in the future only even more sought after. The importance of MFA to enable this is thus expected not just persist but grow; and there are ongoing efforts underway which focus on integrating novel technologies into seamless, more secure service provisioning.

Future Direction Multifactor Authentication

Multifactor authentication's future horizon As people's reliance on cloud services only increases, I think that reliance on multifactor authentication will too foreseeably grow further. To address such borderline conflicts, scholars have put tentatively forth several improvements: combining biometric modalities like fingerprints and the face or human eyes(Skopik et al., 2024). Their goal is thus to offer a user experience that is more secure and natural. Similarly, the introduction of distributed ledger technology and quantum cryptography into multifactor authentication protocols is being explored to address its security and privacy concerns. These ground-breaking developments aim first and foremost to respond to the everchanging threat landscape, providing users with more coherent user-friendly answers that protect both their sensitive information and critical cloud-based applications. With More Locks Comes More Security--Multifactor Authentication WorksRefsMajor (Malasowe et al., 2024) corporations scarcely emphasized MFA, unlike start-ups. However, the digital barriers for small or medium-sized businesses have not been completely broken down even though in market penetration they are still numerous.

REFERENCES

Ahmadieh, E., & El Madhoun, N. (2024). Comparative E-Voting Security Evaluation: Multi-Modal Authentication Approaches. *THE SIXTH INTERNATIONAL CONFERENCE ON BLOCKCHAIN COMPUTING AND APPLICATIONS (BCCA 2024).*

Alkhalifah, E. S. (2024). Password based authentication for web based graphics computing services retrieval in cloud. *Multimedia Tools and Applications*, 83(36), 1–23. DOI: 10.1007/s11042-024-19044-8

Ashitha, U., Amulya, A., Sushma, G., Irfana, S., & Saibaba, C. H. M. H. (2024). Strengthening Cloud Security Through Multi-Factor Authentication: A Comprehensive Integration of Diverse Approaches. *2024 International Conference on Electronics, Computing, Communication and Control Technology (ICECCC)*, 1–8. DOI: 10.1109/ICECCC61767.2024.10593923

Chamoun, J. (2024). *Exploring Security Strategies to Enable the Adoption of Internet of Things Devices in the Manufacturing Sector.* Walden University.

Furuberg, I. L., & Øseth, M. (2023). *From Password to Passwordless: Exploring User Experience Obstacles to the Adoption of FIDO2 Authentication.* NTNU.

Gavou, T. P., Iliya, J., Ihuoma, E. C., & Gusen, J. N. (n.d.). *CYBER SECURITY ENHANCEMENT IN NIGERIA. A CASE STUDY OF SIX STATES IN THE NORTH CENTRAL (MIDDLE BELT) OF NIGERIA.*

Haapaniemi, H. (2024). *Exploring perceptions and coping behaviors regarding imposed multifactor authentication usage: a university case study.*

Holden, J., & Cetinkaya, D. (2024). *Using personalised authentication flows to address issues with traditional authentication methods.*

Kotak, J., Habler, E., Brodt, O., Shabtai, A., & Elovici, Y. (2023). Information Security Threats and Working from Home Culture: Taxonomy, Risk Assessment and Solutions. *Sensors (Basel)*, 23(8), 4018. DOI: 10.3390/s23084018 PMID: 37112359

Kraft, A. (2024). *Municipal Cybersecurity Enhancement: Case Study of Västerås Stad: Criteria Selection and Solution Effectiveness.*

Kumar, T., Kumar, P., & Namasudra, S. (2024). User Revocation-Enabled Access Control Model Using Identity-Based Signature in the Cloud Computing Environment.

Kumar, T., Kumar, P., & Namasudra, S. (2024a). A DNA-based Authentication System for Securing Cloud Data Storage and Transactions. 2024 11th International Conference on Computing for Sustainable Global Development (INDIACom), 1692–1698.

Kumar, T., Namasudra, S., & Kumar, P. (2023). Providing data security using DNA computing in the cloud computing environment. *International Journal of Web and Grid Services*, 19(4), 463–486. DOI: 10.1504/IJWGS.2023.135587

Malasowe, B. O., Aghware, F. O., Okpor, M. D., Edim, E. B., Ako, R. E., & Ojugo, A. A. (2024). Techniques and Best Practices for Handling Cybersecurity Risks in Educational Technology Environment (EdTech). *NIPES-Journal of Science and Technology Research, 6*(2).

Myint, P. W. W., Hlaing, S. Z., & Htoon, E. C. (2020). EAC: Encryption Access Control Scheme for Policy Revocation in Cloud Data. *2020 International Conference on Advanced Information Technologies (ICAIT)*, 182–187. DOI: 10.1109/ICAIT51105.2020.9261809

Pöhn, D., Seeber, S., & Hommel, W. (2023). Combining SABSA and Vis4Sec to the Process Framework IdMSecMan to Continuously Improve Identity Management Security in Heterogeneous ICT Infrastructures. *Applied Sciences (Basel, Switzerland)*, 13(4), 2349. DOI: 10.3390/app13042349

Rivera, J. J. D., Muhammad, A., & Song, W.-C. (2024). Securing Digital Identity in the Zero Trust Architecture: A Blockchain Approach to Privacy-Focused Multi-Factor Authentication. *IEEE Open Journal of the Communications Society*.

Shashikala, N., Anitha, T. N., Mishra, P., Herakal, R. P., & Kolur, J. (2024). Multi-Factor Lightweight Key Agreement Protocol for Data Confidentiality and Integrity in IoT Environment. *International Journal of Intelligent Engineering & Systems*, 17(4).

Skopik, F., Bonitz, A., Slamanig, D., Kirschner, M., & Hacker, W. (2024). Towards a single device for multiple security domains. *Journal of Universal Computer Science*, 30(5), 563–589. DOI: 10.3897/jucs.112790

Zhan, X., Durcikova, A., & Galletta, D. (2024). *The Paradox of Choice: Digital Akrasia in the Deployment of Multi-Factor Authentication.*

Chapter 12
Navigating the Security Maze:
Fortifying Cloud Computing Against Evolving Threats

Menard Musendekwa
https://orcid.org/0000-0002-6644-8727
Reformed Church University, Zimbabwe

ABSTRACT

The meteoric rise of cloud computing has ushered in unprecedented opportunities for scalability, agility, and cost savings across industries. However, this technological revolution also presents a complex web of security challenges. This comprehensive guide serves as an authoritative resource for fortifying cloud environments against evolving threats. It dissects the unique vulnerabilities associated with data breaches, regulatory violations, and crippling cyber attacks, providing practical strategies and best practices for navigating the intricate security landscape of cloud computing.

INTRODUCTION

Cloud computing has completely changed businesses operation since it provides numerous advantages in terms of capacity, adaptability, and cost-efficiency. Notwithstanding these benefits, moving to cloud settings brings with it a fresh set of security issues that need to be properly handled. This chapter explores how cloud adoption affects security, highlighting the significance of introducting vigorous

DOI: 10.4018/979-8-3693-7137-4.ch012

security frameworks in place to ensure fulfilment of regulations and protect private information.

A comprehensive approach to cloud security that incorporates both technological solutions and strategic management practices is urgently required. As organisations increasingly move to cloud platforms, they are exposed to various security threats, such as data breaches, unauthorised access, regulatory non-compliance, and sophisticated cyber attacks.

This chapter is responding to the following research questions: 1. Which security risks are most commonly encountered in cloud computing? 2. How can organisations identify and mitigate the unique vulnerabilities of cloud environments? 3. What best practices and frameworks can be adopted to enhance cloud security? 4. How does regulatory requirements impact cloud security strategies? 5. What are the future trends in cloud security, and how can organisations get ready for them?

THEORETICAL FRAMEWORK

This chapter is based on the different theoretical positions that shape the field of cloud security techniques. Understanding the theories and principles that underpin effective cloud security measures necessitates an understanding of these frameworks.

Confidentiality, Integrity, Availability (CIA) Triad

The Triad of CIA consisting of Availability, Integrity, and Confidentiality (Artur, 2018; Andersson, 2021; Bitzer, Brinz, & Ollig, 2021) is a fundamental concept in information security, representing essential information security properties. Confidentiality ensures that information is accessible only to authorized individuals while integrity guarantees the accuracy and consistency of information (Bitzer, Michael, Brinz, Nicolas, & Ollig, 2021). Lastly, availability ensures that information is accessible whenever required (Bitzer, Michael, Brinz, Nicolas, & Ollig, 2021; Artur Sosin 2018). These principles help organizations prioritize their information security strategies (Bitzer, Michael, Brinz, Nicolas, & Ollig, 2021) and navigate the complex challenges of securing information in the competitive and global marketplace (Artur Sosin 2018).

Zero Trust Architecture

Zero Trust Architecture (ZTA) is a "Never Trust, Always Verify" security model that aims to enhance cybersecurity by the elimination of trust and ongoing network request validation (Adahman, 2022). The old method of network perimeter security has become insignificant due to the growing sophisticated cyber attacks, which has drawn attention to it (Steenbrink, 2022). ZTA offers a number of advantages, such as improved protection, less complexity, and cheaper operating expenses (Steenbrink, 2022). However business may also have obstacles that minimise the applicability of ZTA such as failure to comprehend its requirements and the process may not be clearly applied. Since no trust has been given to any security model and that alone may subject the business people to misunderstand and resulting in failure to use (Songpon, Testsutoro, & Atsuo, 2021).

Model of Shared Responsibility

According to Taha et al. (2016) responsibility among those in business is a significant for ensuring security. The business people and their clients should share responsibilities towards fulfilling the requirement of the Model of Shared Responsibility. One way responsibility can be shared is the compliance with the control encryption keys to maximise security. Cloud security should be strictly adhered to by both business people and their clients (Taha et al., 2016). The idea has also been adopted by Mohammed et al., (2016) who emphasises the need for making service provisions that are not conflicting.

LITERATURE REVIEW

Evolution of Cloud Computing

Verma et al. (2013), considered cloud computing as having also changed the paradigm of computing to a more flexible and cost-effective architecture. According to Verma et al. (2013), this invention contributed to the broad flexibility of IT applications by creating new revenue streams and business models. Due to its affordability and dependability, the cloud became well-known and was adopted by numerous enterprises (Alhaisoni 2016). As a result of this evolution, several models, including public, private, and hybrid clouds, were developed (Verma et al., 2013). According to Pandey, Dixit, and Kushwaha (2023) and Sadiku, Musa, and Momoh (2023), cloud computing also helped businesses remain competitive by providing them with reliable software and IT infrastructure without requiring significant upfront expenses.

Early Development and Transformative Impact

According to Armbrust et al. (2010), cloud computing is a revolutionary IT service-delivery model, gaining popularity for various applications that encompass academic, commercial, government, personal, etc. The widespread use of mobile devices, cloud computing advancements, and broadband Internet access are the main forces behind this changing paradigm (Murugesan & Bojanova, 2016). Cloud computing provides data security, adaptability, simplicity of use, and information dissemination while providing on-demand scalability, huge computing power, and low-cost. Despite various concerns and regular criticism, cloud computing continues to modify the IT industry and challenge IT professionals. Murugesan & Bojanova (2016) and Sharif (2010) add that the impact of cloud computing extends beyond technology to potential transformations in industrial sectors, and modifying ways of doing business.

Marinos and Briscoe discuss the architectural evolution regarding cloud computing, highlighting the development of cloud service models and their impact on the IT industry (Weinhardt, et al 2009; Wallace, 2012). They trace the transition from early grid computing to the current paradigm of cloud computing, noting its growing prominence in the tech industry (Weinhardt, et al 2009). Despite misunderstandings about the meanings and differences of cloud computing, Platform as a Service (PaaS), and Software as a Service (AaaS), it is crystal clear that these technologies are shaping the future of IT (Wallace, 2012; Borza, 2010).

Various Service Models and Methods of Deployment

Cloud computing has encountered various security challenges despite the existing benefits. Conway (2011) and Tiwari (2023) examined how various cloud computing implementation models—including community, private, hybrid, and public clouds—address a range of organizational demands and legal requirements. Additionally, Sushmitha, Reddy J, Pavan, and Reddy T (2016) found that one of the main issues with cloud computing is security, specifically in each cloud service model. Organizations are required to carefully choose their cloud deployment model and address associated security challenges to effectively implement cloud computing (Tiwari, 2023).

Technological Advancements and Business Integration

The technological innovations, including the internet's rapid development (Ahmed & Najem 2015), have been crucial to cloud computing's emergence (Boroujerdi & Nazem 2009; Ahmed & Najem 2015). Companies like Microsoft, Amazon, Google, and Yahoo have commercialized and diffused cloud computing services (Willcocks, Venters & Whitley, 2013). These services offer reliable, secure, and scalable solutions for storage, infrastructure, and software (Ahmed & Najem 2015). Despite the current widespread adoption (Willcocks, Venters & Whitley, 2013), cloud computing is still on a learning curve and experiencing gradual yet significant impacts (Willcocks, Venters & Whitley, 2013).

The integration of cloud computing into business processes has significantly enhanced operations, scalability, and fostered innovation (Donepudi, 2016; Clohessy, Action & Coughlan 2013). Despite challenges such as security and regulatory issues, the advantages are more than the disadvantages (Donepudi, 2016; Xue, & Xin, 2016). Cloud computing has been used by industry to increase productivity, reduce hardware and software costs, and stay competitive (Xue & Xin, 2016; Dobhal, 2022).

Recent works, such as those by Agarwal and Mital (2021) and George, George, & Baskar, (2023), explore the ongoing evolution of cloud computing, highlighting recent developments and potential paths, including the incorporation of artificial intelligence (AI) and edge computing. These studies expand upon the revolutionary impact of cloud computing on modern society, with recent advancements like serverless computing, IoT, and software-defined networking creating new opportunities but also challenging existing approaches (Buyya et al. 2019; Gill et al. 2019; Buyya et al 2018). By examining the latest literature, expert opinions, and real-world use cases, these researchers provide valuable insights into the future regarding cloud computing.

The advantages of cloud computing

The use of cloud computing is a rapidly growing business concept (Frantsvog, Seymour, & John, 2012) that offers significant advantages to enterprises of all sizes. These benefits include scalability, cost-efficiency, and flexibility. By utilizing cloud computing services, industries avoid the need for expensive hardware and software, as well as the associated maintenance costs. Furthermore, having on-demand software access from anywhere increases efficiency in operation and gives greater flexibility to businesses in response to market demands. However, the increasing reliance on cloud computing also raises concerns regarding data security and privacy. It is imperative that these issues be addressed to fully realize the potential of cloud computing in the modern world (Frantsvog, Seymour, & John, 2012; Dua, 2014; Truong, 2010). The current research is educating readers about the significance of cloud computing in doing business. Recently, cloud computing concept has emerged as strategic in the fourth industrial revolution. The next development in distribution of information technology resource systems is thought to be cloud computing (Truong, 2010).

Increased Flexibility and Scalability

Scalability is regarded by Saltan (2009), Armbrust et al. (2010), and Educause (2019) as one of the primary benefits of cloud computing that enable organizations match computing resources with current demand, optimize IT expenditures, and enhance operational efficiency. Educause (2019) claims that employing cloud services with a pay-per-use basis enables businesses to reduce costs and improve efficiency, especially for small organizations with limited resources. Additionally, massive scale regarding cloud computing allows for the creation of new applications. However, managing and securing large-scale cloud services (Armbrust, et a 2010) and addressing challenges related to green IT and the internet remain ongoing concerns (Lee, 2014).

Recent research by Marston et al. (2011) and Tychalas & Karatza, 2016) emphasizes the significance of scalability and flexibility in cloud computing. Regarding flexibility and scalability, Sisodiya, Yadao, & Dhawale (2019) and Lambert (2012) show how cloud services enable businesses to quickly build and grow apps without needing hefty investments or long-term commitments. This on-demand model reduces the risk and costs for innovations (Lambert, 2012).

Cost-Efficiency and Operational Efficiency

Cost-efficiency is a significant benefit of cloud computing for organizations (Rittinghouse, & Ransome, 2017; Truong, 2010; Rodríguez Monroy, Almarcha, & Núñez Guerrero, 2012).Cloud security is cost effective and can minimise capital injection towards buying physical equipment which duly would require manpower for maintenance. Thus it is also critical to use cloud security for it is quicker and is also the current mode of security.

Cloud security eliminates the need for businesses to maintain their own servers or hire staff to manage them. Additionally, the cost savings from scale economies and the responsibility of service providers for installation, upgrades, maintenance, backups, and security further boost operational efficiency.

Improved Collaboration and Accessibility

Users can collaborate more effectively and be more accessible credit being given to cloud computing as users can access data and applications from any location with an internet connection (Sengar, Bhardwaj, Neekhara, & Sonkusre, 2015; Jiménez-Narváez, Portilla, & Gardoni, 2013). According to Loy (2013), cloud computing enhances remote work and collaboration, which is very beneficial for sectors like web development. As an example, teams can work together in real time on cloud-based platforms (Sengar, Bhardwaj, Neekhara, & Sonkusre, 2015; Jiménez-Narváez, Portilla, & Gardoni, 2013), and individuals can use cloud services to create and share apps (Loy, 2013). According to Sadiku, Musa, and Momoh (2014) and Jiménez-Narváez, Portilla, and Gardoni (2013), generally, cloud computing enhances accessibility and teamwork, despite the existence of technical challenges such as latency and synchronization issues.

Recent studies have shown that cloud computing significantly improves collaboration through real-time data sharing and sophisticated collaborative tools (O'Daniel & Rosenstein, 2008; Hammersley, 2017; Yu, Cao & Schniederjans, 2017; Priti, Swati, & Swati, 2022; Aviles, 2015). The hazards and inefficiencies of conventional document-sharing techniques are reduced by these qualities. Additionally, Hammersley (2017) asserts that cloud-based technologies provide researchers and businesses with immediate access to infrastructure and resources, fostering improved collaboration and new ideas. Furthermore, cloud computing enhances supply chain collaboration and service standards (Yu, Cao & Schniederjans, 2017) and boosts organizational value through logistics technology (Aviles, 2015).

Innovation and Competitive Advantage

According to Sultan (2009a) and Brynjolfsson, Hofmann, & Jordan (2010), cloud computing provides firms with a significant edge by fostering innovation and generating a competitive edge. Businesses can take advantage of technology like artificial intelligence and machine learning through sophisticated cloud services without having to make large upfront investments. The cost, scalability, and accessibility of new technologies allow for their rapid adoption and testing by organizations (Brynjolfsson, Hofmann, & Jordan, 2010; Sultan, 2009a). Moreover, cloud service providers handle infrastructure maintenance and updates, allowing businesses to focus on their strategic goals and core skills (Sultan, 2009b).

According to research by Ali, Khan, and Vasilakos (2015), cloud computing encourages creativity by offering platforms that are flexible and scalable, which make it easier to create and implement cutting-edge services and applications. These platforms foster organizational agility by empowering organizations to react swiftly to shifting market needs. Additionally, cloud computing flexibility fosters an innovative culture by enabling companies to test new concepts at reduced costs and risks. According to Ali, Khan, and Vasilakos (2015), using cloud-based technology can help businesses cut down on time-to-market, optimize processes, and obtain a competitive advantage in changing circumstances.

Security Risks in Cloud Computing

Cloud computing has however encountered security risks. Such examples are data security Challenges and security issues across service models. Kaufman (2009) and Singh, & Wali (2014) identified the complexities of safeguarding sensitive data in cloud computing environments, with key concerns being data breaches (Singh, & Wali 2014). This issue persists, as information, whether owned or executive, stored in the cloud remains vulnerable to hackers (Mahalakshmi & Sathiyabama, 2018; Rewagad & Pawar, 2013; Rao & Selvamani, 2015); and requires securing (Rewagad & Pawar, 2013; Omodara, 2015). Understanding dynamic threats and employing appropriate security measures is crucial to enhancing trust between users and service providers (Singh, & Wali 2014; Mahalakshmi. & Sathiyabama, 2018).

Expanding on data security challenges in cloud computing, Morrow, Young, and Smith (2020) emphasize vulnerabilities in cloud services and the shared responsibility model as significant concerns. They mention that data breaches may occur because of the open environment characteristics of cloud computing and because of the dependence on cloud service providers for security. Further emphasizing the significance of resolving data security issues in cloud computing, scholars also address the lack of control data owners have over cloud environments (Rao & Selvamani 2015; Balasubramanian & Aramuthan, 2012; Lekshmy, Kumar & Shankar, 2015).

There are also much serious security risks discovered in the infrastructure, the service platforms, and the software. There is potential vulnerabilities of both the service provider and the client if management is not done effectively (Shobha et al 2016).

Advanced Security Protocols and Technologies

Emerging technologies, like artificial intelligence and machine learning, can be utilized for automated detection, risk assessment, and prediction of cyber attacks (Maglaras, & Kantzavelou, 2021). Recent security architectures leverage hardware support for isolation and attestation, allowing users to trust only their software modules and the processor, reducing reliance on cloud providers (Strackx, 2014). Providing secure and reliable cloud services is essential, as benefits such as scalability and metered usage are overshadowed by concerns regarding transparency, identity, and SLA inadequacy (Marepalli, Sultana, & Christ, 2013).

PARADIGM SHIFT IN INFRASTRUCTURE: THE TRANSITION TO CLOUD COMPUTING

The advent of cloud computing signifies a significant shift from traditional on-premises IT infrastructure to flexible, scalable environments (Verma et al. 2013). This transition involves moving from capital-intensive, physical IT assets to on-demand resources (Srivastava, & Kumar, 2011; Lambert, 2012). Cloud computing flexibility is evidenced by its ability to offer massive data handling (Verma et al 2013), various commercially available cloud services (Srivastava, & Kumar, 2011), and large pools of interconnected computer resources Lambert, 2012). Overall, the public cloud services market is projected to reach $210 billion by 2016, growing from $93 billion in 2011. Cloud computing impact extends to various domains, including business, research, scientific applications, healthcare, and e-commerce (Bilal, et al 2014). Despite the challenges to legacy data centres cloud computing continues to change the computing landscape (Srinivasan, & Getov, 2011).

Transition from Traditional IT to Cloud-Based Solutions

According to Armbrust et al., (2010) the way that companies deploy and manage IT resources has been completely changed by cloud computing. In the past, businesses were in charge of running their own data centres, which necessitated large expenditures for infrastructure and hardware. According to Marston et al (2011) commented cloud computing for being quick and thereby enhancing business operations. Cloud computing has further improved the IT system in proficiency promoting the fourth industrial revolution.

METHODOLOGY

The use of mixed method, combining quantitative and qualitative approaches is significant in this study examining the effectiveness of cloud security. Cloud security encounters security threats challenging its efficiency.

Case Studies

In this chapter, the use of case studies is critical for providing relevant evidence of actual experience whereby cloud security was manipulated as private accounts were hacked leading to theft.

Data Analysis

By identifying patterns in cloud security incidents, the data analysis seeks to provide quantitative insights into the frequency of these incidents and the efficacy of response tactics. Industry surveys, incident databases, and cyber security reports—such as those from the Cloud Security Alliance (CSA) and significant cloud service providers—are the sources of the data. According to Musa and Sani (2016), Vargas-Lombardo (2012), and Khan and Al-Yasiri (2016), the research encompasses a recent time period in order to capture current patterns and new dangers.

DATA PRESENTATION, ANALYSIS, AND DISCUSSION

Case Study 1: The 2019 Capital One Breach

The first case presented is in this chapter is the Capital One Breack which is a data theft. There was a configuration challenge that took place at it Amazon Web System as a result of incorrect firewalls configuration. That resulted in loss of confidential information by close to One hundred million customers. The confidential data includes credit card numbers, Social Security numbers, and other private data accessed leading to a huge customer loss (Verizon, 2020).That makes Cloud computing subjecting users to great loss. That calls for introduction of security measures being critical in order to prevent further dangers. Capital One was forced to to enhance its security by upgrading firewall settings to prevent easy access by an intruder (Verizon, 2020). This breach illuminated the inadequacy of security measures that expose clients to intense vulnerability. Capital One ascertain the validity of employing experienced managers of cloud infrastructure who constantly keep an eye

Verizon (2020) notes the potential repercussions of inadequate security measures in cloud systems are obviously illuminated by this breach. It subsequently attracts serious attention to the possible extream vulnerability that emanates from incorrect configurations and emphasizes the importance for companies to constantly review and update their cloud security devices. In order to protect sensitive customer data, the Capital One hack also emphasizes the validity of having experience managing cloud infrastructure and the constant need to keep an eye out for new risks

Case Study 2: The 2016 Dropbox Breach

Dropbox experienced a serious security violation in 2016 resulting from user credentials being compromised, which gave unauthorized individuals access to private information. A password that had been compromised in a previous data breach was reused by an employee, giving room for hackers to access Dropbox's internal systems. The magnitude of that assault reveal that vulnerability occur when password management procedures are not adequately mitigated and brought to light the dangers of reusing compromised credentials (Ponemon Institute, 2021).

Dropbox strengthened its security measures responding to the hack. The company required users to create stronger, more unique passwords for their accounts in order to enforce its password regulations. Furthermore, Dropbox advised customers to use stronger password management procedures in order to avoid reusing login credentials on several platforms.

Case Study 3: Zimbabwean Bank Cyber attack (2022)

One major financial institution in Zimbabwe (name reserved) was attacked in 2022 exposing private information of clients including credit card numbers and Social Security numbers (Mujuru, 2023; Arshad et al., 2012). According to Latif et al. (2014) and Khan & Al-Yasiri (2016), robust security protocols are essential for data protection since cybercriminals target cloud environments, predominantly in industries that handle sensitive data.

In response to this attack, the bank thoroughly reviewed its cloud security protocols in order to determine the root causes of the vulnerability. To close these loopholes, the organization improved its encryption methods that guaranteed secure client information while in transit and at rest. Musa & Sani (2016) and Sharma & Mullana (2020) point out that encryption has become an essential safeguard against unauthorized access to data since cloud security risks are constantly evolving. In order to actively monitor and identify any suspicious activity within the cloud infrastructure, the bank also implemented an advanced Intrusion Detection System that of cause was a crucial step in averting future attacks and guaranteeing ongoing protection of sensitive data (Khan & Al-Yasiri, 2016; Vargas-Lombardo, 2012).

In order to limit the impact of the breach and preserve transparency and customer trust, the bank swiftly contacted the impacted individuals and provided credit monitoring services. According to Jeba and Sridaran (2017), proactive communication is essential in these situations because it preserves customer trust and gives impacted parties the tools they need to keep an eye on their financial stability. This reaction emphasizes how crucial it is to take a comprehensive strategy to cloud security, incorporating encryption, real-time monitoring, and efficient communication techniques, in order to reduce the dangers related to cloud intrusions.

Data Analysis

Incident Trends:

Data breaches are the most common occurrence category, accounting for 60% of reported breaches. Denial-of-service attacks and incidents of unauthorized access account for the remaining 40% of breaches. This trend highlights the ongoing challenge of safeguarding sensitive data in cloud systems and the need for robust data protection solutions (Cloud Security Alliance, 2023).

The financial services and healthcare sectors account for 45% of all events. This high incidence rate is caused by the sensitive nature of the data handled by these sectors. Other sectors, including as retail and education, also have high breach rates, however they happen less frequently. The prevalence in these sectors demonstrates the widespread nature of cloud security concerns (International Data Corporation, 2022).

Case Study Findings:

This catastrophe, which exposed the personal data of over 100 million individuals, was brought on by an improperly set firewall on AWS. It gives an example of the consequences of cloud misconfigurations and highlights the importance of stringent security installations and continuous monitoring (Verizon, 2020). The 2016 Dropbox Breach: Unauthorized access to data resulted from compromised user credentials. Dropbox's reaction, which includes multi-factor authentication and stronger password regulations, highlights how crucial strong authentication procedures are to preventing unwanted access (Ponemon Institute, 2021).

A large-scale hack of a major financial institution in Zimbabwe resulted in unauthorized access to consumer data. After the incident, the bank implemented a comprehensive security update that included enhanced encryption and a new intrusion detection system due to vulnerabilities in its cloud-based transaction processing system. The need for tailored security solutions and the growing cybersecurity issues in emerging regions are highlighted by this scenario (Mujuru, 2023). To provide a comprehensive overview of the current state of cloud security, this section provides a detailed study of cloud security incidents, emphasizing trends, affected industries, and specific case studies.

Response Effectiveness

Response to hacking should be swift to ensure that vulnerable clients would not experience further loss as Zhao and Zhou (2023) assert the necessity to lessen the effects of cloud security breaches. Strong security measures must be implemented in order to reduce the severity of cloud security events. Specifically, the use of MFA has been linked to a 25% reduction in breach severity. By requiring several forms of verification, MFA enhances security and helps stop unauthorized access (Choi & Lee, 2022). Using cutting-edge encryption methods also contributes to a 25% decrease in breach severity. By protecting private information both in transit and at rest, encryption reduces the risk of data disclosure and unauthorized access (Gupta & Xu, 2021). To identify vulnerabilities and strengthen response strategies, for instance, comprehensive security audits and continuous staff training are helpful (Marston et al., 2011).

Comprehensive Data Analysis of Cloud Security Incidents

Study has revealed that Data breaches has increased for the past six years by about 15% making data breaches most prevalent with over 60% of all cases that are reported. This frequency highlights the ongoing difficulties in safeguarding private data processed and stored in cloud systems. About 20% of cloud security incidents are related to unauthorised access. Inadequate access restrictions or compromised credentials are frequently the cause of these incidents. About 15% of instances are DoS attacks, which emphasises the necessity of strong defences against service interruptions. Ransomware attacks and insider threats are among the different kinds of security incidents that make up the remaining 5% (Cloud Security Alliance, 2023).

Financial services and healthcare account for 45% of attacks, making these industries the most commonly attacked. These industries are popular targets for attackers due to the great value of the data they contain. Retail and Education: Although they account for 30% of incidents, the retail and education sectors have smaller but nonetheless notable rates of violations. Their vulnerability is exacerbated by the growing digitisation of retail and educational services (International Data Corporation, 2022). The remaining 25% of occurrences occur in other businesses, such as government and manufacturing, suggesting that cloud security is a problem that affects all of them.

Due to the extensive usage of cloud services in the area and the associated security risks, North America accounts for the majority of reported occurrences. Significant numbers of incidents are also reported from Europe and Asia, underscoring the worldwide scope of cloud security threats. As cloud adoption rises, cloud security incidents are increasing in emerging regions like South America and Africa (Mujuru, 2023).

Advanced persistent threats and ransomware are two examples of the sophisticated cyber attacks that have been on the rise recently. Organizations must adopt advanced security protocols and keep up constant surveillance in order to successfully counter these new threats.

The hack showed how weak user credentials are and how effective tougher password laws and multi-factor authentication are as defenses (Ponemon Institute, 2021). This case study highlighted the challenges faced by financial institutions in emerging economies. The event led to a number of improvements to the bank's cloud security protocols, including the addition of a new intrusion detection system and enhanced encryption methods (Mujuru, 2023).

The effectiveness of incident mitigation strategies varies according to the type of breach and the organization's level of preparedness. For organizations that have implemented incident management systems and quick reaction teams, effective breach management and mitigation has increased by 20%. According to Marston et al. (2011), this increase is attributed to the capacity to quickly identify, mitigate, and contain security issues while lessening their impact.

Proactive measures like regular security audits and continuous employee training significantly enhance an organization's security posture. Companies that conduct routine audits and ensure that their employees are aware of security best practices tend to experience fewer and less severe problems. These actions help identify vulnerabilities early and ensure that employees are prepared to respond to emerging threats (Marston et al., 2011).

DISCUSSION

1. The Effects of Cloud Security Events:

Data integrity, customer trust, and operational continuity are all seriously threatened by cloud security incidents. They cause financial and reputational harm, interfere with business operations, and reveal private information. Strong security measures and efficient incident response procedures are vital given the increase in sophisticated cyberattacks like ransomware and APTs (Gupta & Xu, 2021).

2. Response Strategies' Effectiveness:

The success of an organization's reaction strategies determines how much of an impact cloud security breaches can have. Companies that have organized and timely incident response plans are better able to manage security events and lessen their impact. (Marston et al., 2011).

Security features should be improved and to include multifactor authentication and strong encryption as defense mechanism in organisations and businesses. Choi and Lee (2022) notes that encryption reduces fraud by 25%. Private and sensitive data is thereby protected. Regular security check and update is necessary.

CONCLUSION

A proactive and systematic approach to security is necessary to strengthen cloud infrastructures. The use of software, platforms, and infrastructure as a service by a third-party provider to customers on a pay-as-you-go basis with the option to scale and contract their service needs as necessary is known as cloud computing. It enables corporate organizations to use models that increase their production by allowing them to concentrate more on skill.

REFERENCES

Adahman, Z. (2022). Zero-Trust Architecture and Its Cost-Effectiveness on Network Security. North Dakota State University. https://doi.org/DOI: 10.48655/10365/32683

Agarwal, A., & Mital, M. (2021). Emerging trends in cloud computing: AI and edge computing integration. *International Journal of Cloud Computing and Services Science*, 10(1), 22–35. DOI: 10.11591/ijccs.v10i1.32316

Ahmed, F., & Al Nejam, A. (2013). Cloud computing: Technical challenges and cloudsim functionalities. *International Journal of Science and Research, 2*(2319-7064), 10.

Ahmed, H. A. S., & Zolkipli, M. F. (2016). Data Security Issues. In *Cloud Computing: Review*. Universiti Malaysia Pahang Publishing., DOI: 10.15282/ijsecs.2.2016.5.0016

Alhaisoni, M. (2016). On the Advancements in Cloud Computing Technology: An Overview.

Ali, M., Khan, S. U., & Vasilakos, A. V. (2015). Security and privacy issues in cloud computing: A survey. Journal of Cloud Computing: Advances. *Systems and Applications*, 4(1), 1–35. DOI: 10.1186/s13677-015-0037-2

Amazon Web Services. (2020). *Shared Responsibility Model*. Retrieved from https://aws.amazon.com/compliance/shared-responsibility-model/

Andersson, S. (2021). Trust as a factor in the information classification process. Luleå tekniska universitet, Institutionen för system- och rymdteknik.

Armbrust, M., Fox, A., Griffith, R., Joseph, A. D., Katz, R. H., Konwinski, A., Lee, G., Patterson, D., Rabkin, A., Stoica, I., & Zaharia, M. (2010). A view of cloud computing. *Communications of the ACM*, 53(4), 50–58. DOI: 10.1145/1721654.1721672

Arshad, J., Townend, P., Xu, J., & Jie, W. (2012). *Cloud computing security: opportunities and pitfalls*. IGI Global., DOI: 10.4018/jghpc.2012010104

Arshad, M., Khan, M. S., & Han, K. (2012). *Security issues in cloud computing: Threats, risks and solutions*. In *Proceedings of the 2012 International Conference on Computer Science and Information Systems.*

Aviles, M. E. (2015). The impact of cloud computing in supply chain collaborative relationships, collaborative advantage and relational outcomes.

Balasubramanian, R., & Aramuthan, D. M. (2012). Security problems and possible security approaches in cloud computing. *International Journal of Scientific and Engineering Research*, 3(6), 1–4.

Bilal, K., Malik, S. U. R., Khan, S. U., & Zomaya, A. Y. (2014). Trends and challenges in cloud datacenters. *IEEE Cloud Computing*, 1(1), 10–20. DOI: 10.1109/MCC.2014.26

Bitzer, M., Brinz, N., & Ollig, P. (2021). Disentangling the Concept of Information Security Properties-Enabling Effective Information Security Governance. In ECIS.

Boroujerdi, M. M., & Nazem, S. (2009). Cloud computing: Changing cogitation about computing. *International Journal of Computer and Information Engineering*, 3(10), 2469–2473.

Borza, L. (2010). Cloud Computing: A step to the future of IT.

Brynjolfsson, E., Hofmann, M., & Jordan, J. (2010). Cloud Computing: A Strategic Perspective for Information Systems Research. *Communications of the ACM*, 53(11), 98–107.

Buyya, R., Srirama, S. N., Casale, G., Calheiros, R., Simmhan, Y., Varghese, B., Gelenbe, E., Javadi, B., Vaquero, L. M., Netto, M. A. S., Toosi, A. N., Rodriguez, M. A., Llorente, I. M., Vimercati, S. D. C. D., Samarati, P., Milojicic, D., Varela, C., Bahsoon, R., Assuncao, M. D. D., & Shen, H. (2018). A manifesto for future generation cloud computing: Research directions for the next decade. *ACM Computing Surveys*, 51(5), 1–38. DOI: 10.1145/3241737

Choi, Y., & Lee, J. (2022). Emerging security threats and mitigation strategies in cloud environments. *Journal of Cloud Computing: Advances. Systems and Applications*, 11(1), 1–15. DOI: 10.1186/s13677-022-00312-4

Clohessy, T., Acton, T., & Coughlan, C. (2013). Innovating in the Cloud.

Cloud Security Alliance (CSA). (2023). *Cloud security guidance*. https://cloudsecurityalliance.org/research/

Conway, G. (2011). Introduction to Cloud Computing. IVI: Innovation Value Institute. https://core.ac.uk/download/297013271.pdf

Devi, T., & Ganesan, R. (2015). Platform-as-a-Service (PaaS): Model and security issues. *TELKOMNIKA Indonesian Journal of Electrical Engineering*, 15(1), 151–161.

Dobhal, A. (2022). Applications of Cloud ComputingfFor Both it and the Business. https://doi.org/DOI: 10.5281/zenodo.6986175

Donepudi, P. K. (2016). Influence of cloud computing in business: are they robust. *Asian journal of applied science and engineering, 5*(3), 193-196.

Dua, I. S. (2014). Benefits and Security Concerns of Cloud Computing. *International Journal of Scientific and Engineering Research*, 5(1), 404–411.

Educause. (2009). Cloud computing: A new delivery model. EDUCAUSE Review, 44(6), 36- 55.

Elfström, C. J. (2023). Industry preferred implementation practices for security in cloud systems: An exploratory and qualitative analysis of implementation practices for cloud security.

Frantsvog, D., Seymour, T., & John, F. (2012). Cloud computing. *International Journal of Management & Information Systems (Online)*, 16(4), 317.

George, A. S., George, A. H., & Baskar, T. (2023). Edge Computing and the Future of Cloud Computing: A Survey of Industry Perspectives and Predictions. *Partners Universal International Research Journal*, 2(2), 19–44.

Gill, S. S., Tuli, S., Xu, M., Singh, I., Singh, K. V., Lindsay, D., Tuli, S., Smirnova, D., Singh, M., Jain, U., Pervaiz, H., Sehgal, B., Kaila, S. S., Misra, S., Aslanpour, M. S., Mehta, H., Stankovski, V., & Garraghan, P. (2019). Transformative effects of IoT, Blockchain and Artificial Intelligence on cloud computing: Evolution, vision, trends and open challenges. *Internet of Things : Engineering Cyber Physical Human Systems*, 8, 100118. DOI: 10.1016/j.iot.2019.100118

Gupta, A., & Xu, Z. (2021). Regulatory requirements and cloud security: Enhancing compliance and security posture. *International Journal of Cloud Computing and Services Science*, 10(2), 45–60. DOI: 10.11591/ijccs.v10i2.33125

Hammersley, J. (2017). Real-time data on global collaboration networks can support new research and create further connections. London School of Economics and Political Science. https://core.ac.uk/download/82966045.pdf

Haris, H. (2014). Cloud Computing-Compliance with Regulatory Prescribed Data Protection Measures in Bosnia and Herzegovina.

International Data Corporation (IDC). (2022). *Cloud security trends and outlook.* https://www.idc.com/research

Jeba, J., & Sridaran, D. (2017). *Security issues in cloud computing: Threats, risks, and solutions.* In *Proceedings of the 2017 International Conference on Computer Science and Information Systems.*

Jerónimo Suárez, J., & Hernández-Ardieta, J. L. (2021). *46 Enforcing cloud security controls*. Universidad Castilla la Mancha., DOI: 10.18239/jornadas_2021.34.46

Jiménez-Narváez, L. M., Portilla, A. S., & Gardoni, M. (2013). Some Opportunities and Limitations of Cloud Computing Environments in Early Stage of Design Process. *The International Journal of Designed Objects*, 6(2), 1–18. DOI: 10.18848/2325-1379/CGP/v06i02/38652

Kaufman, L. M. (2009). Data security in the world of cloud computing. *IEEE Security and Privacy*, 7(4), 61–64. DOI: 10.1109/MSP.2009.87

Khan, N. A., & Al-Yasiri, A. (2016). *Cloud security threats and techniques to strengthen cloud computing adoption framework*. IGI Global., DOI: 10.4018/IJITWE.2016070104

Krishna, B. Hari, Kiran, S., Murali, G., & Reddy, R. Pradeep Kumar. (2016). Security Issues in Service Model of Cloud Computing Environment . Published by Elsevier B.V. https://doi.org/DOI: 10.1016/j.procs.2016.05.156

Lacity, M. C., & Willcocks, L. P. (2012). *Cloud services in the enterprise: The advantages, challenges, and future*. Springer.

Lambert, E. H. (2012). Partial Migration of Business Data to The Cloud.

Latif, R., Abbas, H., Assar, S., & Ali, Q. (2014). Cloud computing risk assessment: A systematic literature review. *Future Information Technology: FutureTech*, 2013, 285–295. DOI: 10.1007/978-3-642-40861-8_42

Lee, Y.W. (2014). scale Services over Cloud Environments.

Lekshmy D. Kumar & B. R. Shankar. (2015). © Impact Journals Security Threats To Cloud Computing.

Loy, S. Y. (2013). Development of collaborative applications on the cloud.

Maglaras, L., & Kantzavelou, I. (Eds.). (2021). *Cybersecurity issues in emerging technologies*. CRC press. DOI: 10.1201/9781003109952

Mahalakshmi. D & Sathiyabama, T. (2018). Security Issues in Cloud Computing. https://doi.org/DOI: 10.31142/ijtsrd18674

Manayathil Chackochan, T., & Gonsalvez, R. (2023). Compliance Regulatory and Security Challenges in Cloud & IP Telephony-A comparison study between India and Sweden..

Marepalli, S. M., Sultana, R., & Christ, A. (2013). Research on System Architecture to Provide Maximum Security, End User Device Independency and User Centric Control over Content in Cloud. [IJEEI]. *International Journal of E-Entrepreneurship and Innovation*, 4(3), 38–52. DOI: 10.4018/ijeei.2013070103

Marston, S., Li, D., Bandyopadhyay, S., Zhang, J., & Ghalsasi, A. (2011). Cloud computing—The business perspective. *Journal of Computer Information Systems*, 51(3), 45–54. DOI: 10.1080/08874417.2011.11645601

Maurya, B. K. (2010). Cloud Computing: Exploring the scope.

Mitra, M. (2019). Cloud Computing and its Features. https://doi.org/DOI: 10.5281/zenodo.3560213

Mohammed, M. A., Salih, Z. H., Tapus, N., & Hasan, R. A. (2016). *Security and accountability for sharing the data stored in the cloud . Institute of Electrical and Electronics Engineers*. IEEE., DOI: 10.1109/RoEduNet.2016.7753201

Morrow, J., Young, M., & Smith, T. (2020). Data security in cloud computing: Challenges and solutions. *International Journal of Cloud Computing and Services Science*, 9(1), 15–30. DOI: 10.11591/ijccs.v9i1.33045

Mujuru, K. (2023). Cybersecurity and cloud vulnerability in Zimbabwean financial institutions. *Agricultural Finance Review*, 12(3), 145–159.

Murugesan, S., & Bojanova, I. (2016). Cloud computing: an overview. Encyclopedia of cloud computing, 1-14.

Musa, F. A., & Sani, S. M. (2016). Security threats and countermeasures in cloud computing. *International Research Journal of Electronics and Computer Engineering*, 2(4), 22–27.

O'Daniel, M., & Rosenstein, A. H. (2008). Professional communication and team collaboration. *Patient safety and quality: An evidence-based handbook for nurses*.

Omodara, A. O. (2015). Cloud Computing Security Issues.

Pandey, A. K., Dixit, A. K., & Kushwaha', A. S. (2023). Cloud Computing Technologies. Darshan Publisher. https://doi.org/DOI: 10.5281/zenodo.7889071

Ponemon Institute. (2021). Data breach trends and the impact of compromised credentials in cloud environments. *Cloud Security Insights*, 27(4), 88–98.

Prasanna, M., Neelima, M. S., & Padmavathi, M. M. (2012). Requirements and challenges for securing cloud applications and services. *IOSR Journal of Computer Engineering*, 4(2), 46–52. DOI: 10.9790/0661-0424652

Prateek M, Rahul R, & Arman. (2020). Cloud Computing: Overview and its Deployment Model.

Priti, R. Kakde, Swati K. Shamkuwar, & Swati Tiwari. (2022). Study of Role and Impact of Cloud Computing. https://doi.org/DOI: 10.5281/zenodo.7407343

Rao, R. V., & Selvamani, K. (2015). Data security challenges and its solutions in cloud computing. *Procedia Computer Science*, 48, 204–209. DOI: 10.1016/j.procs.2015.04.171

Rewagad, P., & Pawar, Y. (2013). Security Threats-main hindrance to wide acceptance to the cloud computing services. *International Journal of Computer Applications IJCA*, 21- 27.

Rewagad, P., & Pawar, Y. (2013). Security Threats-main hindrance to wide acceptance to the cloud computing services. *International Journal of Computer Applications IJCA*, 21- 27.

Rittinghouse, J. W., & Ransome, J. F. (2017). *Cloud computing: Implementation, management, and security*. CRC Press. DOI: 10.1201/9781439806814

Rodríguez Monroy, C., Almarcha Arias, G. C., & Núñez Guerrero, Y. (2012). The new cloud computing paradigm: The way to IT seen as a utility. *Latin American and Caribbean Journal of Engineering Education*, 6(2), 24–31.

Sadiku, M. N., Musa, S. M., & Momoh, O. D. (2014). Cloud computing: Opportunities and challenges. *IEEE Potentials*, 33(1), 34–36. DOI: 10.1109/MPOT.2013.2279684

Sale, M. A. (2015). Security issues in cloud computing. *International Journal of Management. IT and Engineering*, 5(5), 170–180.

Sengar, D. Bhardwaj, M.; Neekhara, V. & Sonkusre, M (2015). Development of Project with Combined Efforts Using Cloud Computing.

Sharif, A. M. (2010). *It's written in the cloud: The hype and promise of cloud computing*. Emerald., DOI: 10.1108/17410391011019732

Sharma, A., & Mullana, M. M. U. (2020). Emerging Trends in Safety Issues in Cloud the Potentials of Threat Model.

Shobha; E.R., Sreedevi, P, & Ameena, B.A. (2016). Study on Security Capabilities In Cloud Computing Enviornment.

Singh, N. P., & Walia, B. S. (2014). Assay of Data Security in Cloud Computing. *Navan Preet Singh et al,/(IJCSIT)International Journal of Computer Science and Information Technologies,* 5(5), 6599-6601.

Sisodiya, A. K., Yadao, K. N., & Dhawale, V. R. (2019). An analytical study on cloud computing. *International Journal of Engineering Technologies and Management Research*, 6(12), 73–77. DOI: 10.29121/ijetmr.v6.i12.2019.557

Smith, R., & Johnson, L. (2024). Integrating qualitative and quantitative methods in cloud security research. *Journal of Cybersecurity Research*, 13(2), 120–135. DOI: 10.1007/s12345-024-0078-9

Sosin, A. (2018). *How to Increase The Information Assurance in the Information Age*. Regional Department of Defense Resources Management Studies.

Srinivasan, S., & Getov, V. (2011). Navigating the cloud computing landscape: Technologies, services, and adopters. *Computer*, 44(3), 22–23. DOI: 10.1109/MC.2011.91

Srivastava, K., & Kumar, A. (2011). A new approach of cloud: Computing infrastructure on demand. *Trends in Information Management, 7*(2).

Steenbrink, T. (2022). Zero Trust Architecture: Design Principles for a Transformation towards a Perimeter-less Enterprise Architectur

Strackx, R. (2014, June). Presentation: Moving towards a non-hierarchical security model. In *AusCert, Location: Benowa, Australia.*

Subashini, S., & Kavitha, V. (2011). A survey on security issues in service delivery models of cloud computing. *Journal of Network and Computer Applications*, 34(1), 1–11. DOI: 10.1016/j.jnca.2010.07.006

Sultan, A. M. (2009a). Cloud computing: A new computing paradigm. *International Journal on Advanced Science, Engineering and Information Technology*, 1(1), 4–8.

Sultan, O. M. (2009b). Cloud Computing: A Game Changer for Small and Medium Enterprises (SMEs). *Journal of Enterprise Information Management*, 22(1), 72–83.

Taha, A., Metzler, P., Trapero, R., Luna, J., & Suri, N. (2016). *Identifying and Utilizing Dependencies Across Cloud Security Services. Association for Computing Machinery*. ACM., DOI: 10.1145/2897845.2897911

Teerakanok, S., Uehara, T., & Inomata, A. (2021). *Migrating to Zero Trust Architecture: Reviews and Challenges*. Hindawi Limited., DOI: 10.1155/2021/9947347

Tiwari, M. N. (2023). Perspective study of Public Cloud: A highly scalable Cloud deployment model. *Authorea Preprints*.

Truong, D. (2010). How cloud computing enhances competitive advantages: A research model for small businesses. *The Business Review, Cambridge*, 15(1), 59–65.

Tychalas, D., & Karatza, H. (2016). Cloud Resource Management.

Vargas-Lombardo, M., Leguías, A., Isabel, D.C., & Vega, M. (2012). Emerging Threats, Risk and Attacks in Distributed Systems: Cloud Computing.

Verizon. (2020). The state of cloud security: Analyzing the Capital One breach. *Data Breach Investigations Report, 2020*, 56-72.

Verma, R. K., Dutta, S., Chaulya, S. K., Singh, A. K., & Prasad, G. M. (2013). Cloud Computing: A New Era in IT industry. *International Journal of Computer Technology and Electronics Engineering*, 3(2), 18–28.

Wallace, R. M. (2012). The Cloud Revolution, How Service Oriented Architecture and High Performance Computing will Transform the Water Resources Community of Practice.

Weinhardt, C., Anandasivam, A., Blau, B., Borissov, N., Meinl, T., Michalk, W., & Stößer, J. (2009). Cloud computing–a classification, business models, and research directions. *Business & Information Systems Engineering*, 1(5), 391–399. DOI: 10.1007/s12599-009-0071-2

Willcocks, L. P., Venters, W., & Whitley, E. A. (2013). *Cloud computing as innovation: studying diffusion*. Springer., DOI: 10.1007/978-3-642-40951-6_7

Xue, C. T. S., & Xin, F. T. W. (2016). Benefits and challenges of the adoption of cloud computing in business. *International Journal on Cloud Computing: Services and Architecture, 6*(6), 01-15.

Yang, Y., & Wu, S. (2018). Cloud computing deployment models and their impact on organizational needs. Journal of Cloud Computing: Advances. *Systems and Applications*, 7(1), 18–30. DOI: 10.1186/s13677-018-0123-7

Yu, Y., Cao, R. Q., & Schniederjans, D. (2017). Cloud computing and its impact on service level: A multi-agent simulation model. *International Journal of Production Research*, 55(15), 4341–4353. DOI: 10.1080/00207543.2016.1251624

Zheng, Z., Yang, S., & Wu, J. (2018). *Cloud computing: Resource management and application*. Springer.

Chapter 13
Securing the Cloud:
Navigating Compliance and Regulatory Challenges

Indu Bhardwaj
https://orcid.org/0000-0003-0094-0273
Galgotias University, India

Suman Devi
https://orcid.org/0000-0002-4038-7196
Galgotias University, India

Tarun Kumar
https://orcid.org/0000-0002-8507-8522
Galgotias University, India

ABSTRACT

As companies move to the cloud, it is more important than ever for them to conform with laws and ethical standards. The chapter starts by explaining the basics of cloud, cloud security compliance, covering the shared responsibility model between customers and Cloud Service Providers (CSPs). This model indicates the explicit security responsibilities of each network, highlights they must work together in order to help ensure compliance mandates are met appropriately. It also examines the complex matrix of global and regional policies that affect cloud security. The paper talked about strategies for creating strong compliance frameworks covering risk assessment methodologies. The chapter also explore how emerging technologies like artificial intelligence (AI), machine learning (ML) and blockchain play a role in streamlining compliance. We also consider the changing backdrop of cloud security certifications and attestations — including SOC 2, ISO 27001, FedRAMP and more.

DOI: 10.4018/979-8-3693-7137-4.ch013

INTRODUCTION

The origin of cloud computing is dated around the 1950s when mainframe systems first started and surged with the internet boom of the 1990's. Web based services started emerging in the early 2000s, but cloud computing still sounds new to consumers. This provides the platform for scalability, adaptability and cost savings by delivering on demand usage of shared computing resources over the Internet. Cloud technologies continue to develop, and are changing how industries process, store, and retrieve data.

Cloud computing, also called internet-based computing, is the delivery of services and resources over the internet and does not depend on using a specific hardware or a location (Chang et al. 2016). It contains a variety of data types including files, images and documents and allows businesses to scale their operations with the use of third-party hosting and storage providers. It minimizes the hardware expenses to also enable incremental expansion the infrastructure.

Key cloud computing functionalities include:

- Data storage, backup, and restoration
- On-demand software delivery
- Development of applications and services
- Streaming of audio and video content

Figure 1. The basic Architecture of Cloud Computing

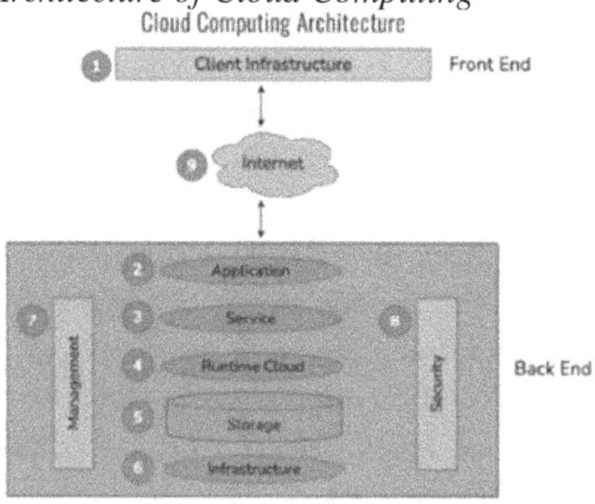

CLOUD COMPUTING ARCHITECTURE

Cloud computing architecture as shown in figure 1, compromises various components that define its principles and functionalities: Server based environments with central storage are thin client dependent as the small footprint of these equipment's can be part of such an environment while enhancing security and provide ease in management (Alouffi et al., 2021). On the other hand, the thick clients provide offline functionality and more operational flexibility. Essential components comprising application, services, management tools, security tools, storage solutions, computing resource, databases, Networking systems form a part of the back end. In their collective implementation, these elements guarantee a secure, efficient and scalable operational framework (Kumar et al. 2024a). The public, private and hybrid cloud delivery models give different advantages in resource allocation, compatibility and accessibility. Through cloud computing, an organization gains access to processing power, storage and any other resources over the internet and, thus, reduces costs and scale to its needs. The main cloud service categories are IaaS (Infrastructure as a Service) provides on demand network access to virtualized computational resources (e.g., CPU, RAM etc.) and storage. Whereas Platform as a Service (PaaS) enables developers to build, deploy, and manage applications with a platform and set of tools and infrastructure. PaaS provides simplified development processes that allow simple application deployments with faster time to market, boosts productivity, and are set up for automated scaling of resources. Also, Software as a Service (SaaS) lets users run cloud-based software applications without installing local resources. Increases in accessibility, and decrease IT overhead through updates, maintenance and security provided by SaaS providers (Mohammed and Zeebaree, 2021)

. These models make it easier for organizations to adopt the models, streamline operations, reduce costs, and gain agility as technology continues to evolve quickly in today's competitive world.

CLOUD HOSTING

People start with the infrastructure and work their way up from there. The cloud hosting is housed at this layer. Assume you run a business and have a website with a large volume of member-to-member communications. A small group of people converse with one another at first, and as time goes on, the number of members steadily rises. The more members there are, the more traffic there will be on the network over time, which will cause your server to slow down. This would lead to an issue (Rashid and Chaturvedi, 2019).

A few years back, websites were hosted on servers; as a result, you had to purchase or lease servers and manage their quantity. It is very expensive and time-consuming. These servers are your responsibility to pay for both when you use them and when you don't. We refer to this as hosting. The solution to this issue is cloud hosting. You can get processing power whenever you need it with cloud computing. Now, instead of being hosted on a dedicated server, your website is hosted on a cloud server. When visitors start coming to your website, you can scale up in accordance with the demand if you find yourself in sudden need of more processing capacity.

MOTIVATION FOR CLOUD COMPUTING FROM ON-PREMISES (LEE, 2013)

The top explanations for moving from on-premises to cloud computing are as follows:

1. Outsource Management: While you oversee the business, someone else manages your computer infrastructure. You don't care about degradation or management.
2. Greater originality: With cloud architectures, you can take advantage of the newest developments in AI, analytics, security, and storage, including machine learning.
3. Quicker time to market: It is no longer necessary to put off purchasing, assembling, and configuring computer infrastructure. With cloud architecture, you can quickly get up and running, freeing you more time to concentrate on creating and delivering new products.
4. Lowers costs: One of the key benefits of cloud computing is its capacity to reduce costs for companies that use it over time. Businesses can save 15% of their total costs on average by moving to the cloud. Businesses can cut expenses and avoid hiring a team of technical support professionals to handle server problems by utilizing cloud servers. The cost-saving advantages of cloud servers are covered in a number of excellent business modules, including case studies on Pinterest and Coca-Cola.
5. More storage: It offers more servers, storage capacity, and processing power so that software and apps may run as fast as effectively as possible. There are numerous cloud storage systems accessible, including OneDrive, Google Drive, and others.

6. Better Work-Life Balance for Employees: There are clear links between the advantages of cloud computing and how it can enhance employees' personal and professional lives. Employees are required to work on the server for security, upkeep, and proper operation even on holidays. However, things are different with cloud storage; workers have more time for their personal lives and work even less in comparison.

BENEFITS OF CLOUD COMPUTING (SRINIVASAN AND SRINIVASAN, 2014)

The primary benefits of cloud computing are as follows:

1. Pay as you go: Cloud computing follows a pay-as-you-go method, and this provides consumers with variable pricing options. It is beneficial for the construction of small and medium-sized enterprises.
2. Cloud Services offer Flexibility as well as Scalability: With cloud, the resources can be scaled up or down based on demand. It ensures that organizations can efficiently run a number of workloads on the platform even without investing heavily in hardware when demand dies down.
3. Collaboration and Accessibility: Cloud computing allows data, apps to be accessed via internet from anywhere. Using the real-time project & document collaboration initiates team participation from multiple locations to achieve successful results with good quality.
4. Automatic Updating and Maintenance: AWS Cloud is much easier to maintain because it is automatically updating, software-upgrading. In doing so, AWS ensures that companies can relax and focus on what they do best by delivering the latest technology without pause.

THE DRAWBACKS OF CLOUD PROCESSING

Some of the biggest drawbacks of cloud computing are:

1. Security Issues The most common cloud computing challenge is related to security concerns that are involved when users move their data or sensitive information from the device (on-premises) to a third-party server (Diaby and Rad, 2017).

2. Reliability — While in general, the cloud services make it as reliable; occasional planned and unexpected downtimes will occur. These can arise because of network issues, server-side problems or maintenance outage at the cloud providers which cause disrupt in functioning enterprise business and consumers faced with non-availability of their Apps.
3. Cost control complexity: The principal benefit of cloud services is pay as you go pricing which also gives rise to a layer of cost control complications. Without sufficient control and capacity planning, the other side of that coin is easily tossing up unexpected bills almost as though they were running their own data centers (Patel and Kansara, 2021).
4. Relies on network connection: Cloud computing services mainly rely on a heavy and reliable internet. The users must have a dependable, fast internet connection in order to access and use cloud resources. Users may experience difficulties accessing their data and apps in areas with spotty internet service.

CLOUD SECURITY

In truth, securing an application in the cloud is a shared responsibility between consumer and cloud provider. The Shared Responsibility Model breaks down responsibilities into three categories: customer owns, provider owns and "it depends", meaning it can shift based on the service model. Main Aim of cloud security is to protect the infrastructure itself, and covers aspects like allowing access, configuring, patching of underlying physical hosts/physical network that stores/compute instances/ stores data etc (Kumar et al., (2023).

The shared responsibility model

The shared responsibility model is a foundational principle in cloud security, outlining the distinct and complementary roles of Cloud Service Providers (CSPs) and their customers in safeguarding data and resources. This model divides security tasks into two primary categories: those managed by the CSP and those managed by the customer. CSPs are generally the ones who secure the underlying cloud infrastructure such as physical security, network infrastructure, storage systems and host operating systems. This layer is also known as 'security of the cloud' because it includes entire cloud environment that CSPs deliver.

However, customers are responsible for the security of the cloud: data encryption, application security, and access control are all taken care of by them. For example, a CSP guarantees the physical data centers and the hardware are secure (Kumar et al. 2024b).

Global and Regional Regulations Impacting Cloud Security

Each mandate of cloud security has its own global and regional regulations which are important parts of fulfilling compliance requirements. These regulations imply rules of how organizations manage, protect, and store data in cloud ecosystem so as to ensure data privacy, security and regulatory compliance (Rahman et al., 2023). In this section we look at major regulations such as GDPR, CCPA, HIPAA, PCI DSS, and so on, and their compliance mandates and penalties for noncompliance (Garg, 2020).

1. General Data Protection Regulation (GDPR)

The three main tenets of GDPR are transparency, justice, and lawfulness. Data processing needs to be transparent, equitable, and compliant with the law. People must be informed by organizations about the data they are collecting and its intended use.

People must be informed by organizations about the data they are collecting and its intended use.

Personal information must be gathered for specific, justifiable objectives and cannot be treated in ways that conflict with those goals. Only the personal information required to fulfil the intended purpose should be gathered and handled.

The Key Rights Under General Data Protection Regulation are

- Right to Access
- Right to Rectification
- Right to Erasure ("Right to be Forgotten")
- Right to Restriction of Processing
- Right to Data Portability
- Right to Object
- Rights Related to Automated Decision-Making

Fines for Non-Compliance: The GDPR gives regulatory bodies the authority to impose hefty fines for non-compliance. The highest penalties are €20 million or 4% of yearly worldwide sales, whichever is greater. The type and seriousness of the infraction, whether the violation was deliberate, the actions taken to lessen the harm, and the organization's prior compliance history all influence the precise fine.

2. California Consumer Privacy Act (CCPA)

CCPA is a privacy law which helps improve rights and protections of the consumers. On January 1, 2020, it went into effect after being passed in 2018. One of the most extensive privacy regulations in the US is the CCPA, which is regarded as California's counterpart to the GDPR of the EU. California Attorney General enforces the CCPA. Businesses that violate the CCPA could be punished by the Attorney General up to $2,500 (or $7,500 in the case of intentional violations) for each violation. A consumer may have a right to bring a private action where a specific breach occurs, for example an illegal access to personal data due to a lack of protection. In this case, businesses could be fined up to $750 dollars per customer each incidence.

3. Health Insurance Portability and Accountability Act (HIPAA)

In 1996 a U.S. federal law, called the Health Insurance Portability and Accountability Act (HIPAA), set up rules and protocols for protection of the privacy and integrity of medical information. HIPAA directly focuses on healthcare clearinghouses, health plans, providers (collectively all the three are known as covered entities), and their business partnerships. The aim of HIPA stands at protecting the privacy and security of PHI and ensuring that it accessible and provided to only authorized individuals.

Penalties for Non-Compliance: *Serious consequences for HIPAA infractions include:*

Civil Penalties: Depending on the degree of negligence, these penalties can range from $100 to $50,000 per infraction.

Attempts to commit criminal offences carry fines of up to $250,00 and, in particularly harmful cases (where the infringement causes harm or the infringement is done for gain by the perpetrator), a maximum term of 10 years jail. A magnanimous or amended solution may be done after the player is given a series of measures in order to quantify the severity of penalty, like the nature of infraction, if the infraction was done for a wilful disregarding purpose, and the player has done the corrective action or not.

4. Payment Card Industry Data Security Standard (PCI DSS)

PCI DSS is a widely accepted security framework for safeguarding payment card data. This is upheld by the PCI Security Standards Council and applies to all organizations – with merchants, processors and service providers who store, handle and send cardholder data.

Severe fines and repercussions from the Payment Card Industry Data Security Standard (PCI DSS), including being the recipient of a breach is possible if orga nizations handle payment card data and aren't compliant. These fines are meant to protect private payment data, and make sure that the standard is followed (Nanda et al., 2024).

CHALLENGES AND COMPLEXITIES OF ACHIEVING AND MAINTAINING COMPLIANCE IN DYNAMIC CLOUD ENVIRONMENTS

Dynamic cloud infrastructure, the changing regulatory landscape, and the challenge of governing numerous technologies make achieving and maintaining compliance in dynamic cloud systems intractable. There are constantly changing rules which companies must deal with where, perforce, you must watch and change it every time to make sure that you're on the right track. Since cloud environments are constantly in flux and being reconfigured and updated, it is more likely for misconfigurations—largely the cause for failure of compliance—to occur. This complexity is exacerbated by the shared responsibility paradigm between cloud providers and clients, where the misinterpretation of (String dissolved salt may exist in the fluid) duty boundaries can lead to gaps in compliance (Paul and Ghose, 2012).

Not helping matters, however, are laws around data residency and sovereignty, which make it all but impossible to comply if your organization operates in multiple jurisdictions and must see that data is processed and stored in compliance with local laws. Distributed cloud systems inherently lack visibility and control of data, systems, and network activity, and important information about these items may be obscured, conceivably covertly breached or subjected to unauthorized access. The growth of multi cloud and hybrid environments further exacerbates these difficulties as enterprises are expected to unify security guidelines and compliance protocols across multiples platforms.

Extra risk is built into supply chain dependencies and third-party integrations that could threaten compliance. While automation and AI tools will accelerate compliance activities, they can be dangerous if set up inadequately or improperly controlled and your company could end up with violations you did not identify, or false positives. Due to limited resources, often too tight budgets and shortage of qualified staffs, comprehensive compliance processes are frequently hamstrung, exposing firms. Finally, there is no technology independent of humans managing it, and human error is still a large risk factor: configuration or access management errors could itself reveal private information or violate legal requirements. However, along with automation tools, a strong governance, frequent audits, and constant training is required to make sure that the compliance process is complete and long lasting (Nadeem, 2022).

ENHANCING COMPLIANCE EFFORTS WITH EMERGING TECHNOLOGIES

Emerging technologies, such as blockchain, artificial, intelligence, and machine learning, are completely changing the compliance environment by providing cutting edge solutions for real time threat identification, unchangeable audit trails, and automated policy enforcement (Arunkumar, 2023). Apart from confronting data and security management challenges with modern cloud systems, these technologies also improve efficacy and efficiency of compliance initiatives (Anandappa and Mudnal, 2024). In this section we look at how blockchain, AI and ML help by supporting compliance initiatives and provide you some information regarding how to use them, their advantages and factors to consider.

1. Blockchain Technology

Blockchain technology is a distributed, decentralized ledger that stores transactions across many computers protecting data confidentiality and integrity. Connecting each transaction to earlier ones results in an millions of records. Because blocks are immutable, data is never changed or removed after it has been recorded. This is a trustworthy and impenetrable audit trail that is critical to prove compliance to legal regulations (Zhang et al., 2020).

The records of every modification and transaction are reliable and transparent with Blockchain. This transparency is because each party can independently confirm the veracity of the audit trail. Having Blockchain allows us to see a transparent history of data origin and changes thus we can track data as well as transaction provenance. Although this is particularly helpful to guarantee data authenticity and correctness when performing compliance audits.

Blockchain technology supports smart contracts, which are self–executing agreements that are encoded with the terms of an agreement written directly into code. Human intervention is removed from the equation; smart contracts automate enforcement of compliance requirements and depending on set criteria, carry out their actions.

Blockchain based solutions can auto adjust data when policy changes and constantly watch regulatory compliance. It ensures real time maintaining of compliance.

Benefits and Considerations

- Enhanced Security: Blockchain is a useful tool for compliance and auditing because of its decentralization and cryptographic processes, which improve data security and integrity.
- Transparency and Trust: By offering an unchangeable and verifiable record of transactions, blockchain promotes transparency and trust among stakeholders.
- Scalability and Interoperability: These factors include interoperability problems with current systems and scalability issues, as blockchain networks may not be able to handle high transaction volumes.
- Complexity: Putting blockchain solutions into practice calls for knowledge of blockchain technology and could present integration issues with current compliance frameworks.

2. Artificial Intelligence (AI) and Machine Learning (ML)

AI and ML are focusing on designing computers to do tasks that require human intelligence. ML mostly refers to algorithms used by systems in order to get better at something they are programmed to accomplish with the more data they see, and if we're going all the way back to 1956, it does; AI on the other hand refers to a much wider body of knowledge meant to mimic human cognition (Hussain et al., 2024). With AI and ML, you can process huge amounts of data and find trends, anomalies that might warn of security risks. For Instance, ML can be used to train when to flag when the user behavior itself is anomalous and changes in behavior that indicate insider breach.

AI driven systems can establish baseline behavior patterns for users and entities in a network. One pattern deviation might be a deviation from typical access to private information which would set off alarms and give quick reactions to likely dangers. Using historical data and finding patterns, AI and ML predict potential security event scenarios not before they happen.

The use of AI capable systems in the cloud environment can allow automating application of compliance regulations. For example, AI can automatically follow security configurations such as encryption and access control as per defined regulations and legal requirements. ML algorithms can adjust real time compliance policy in changing environment and new risks. This means that in dynamically changing cloud settings the policies are always applicable and effective. With so much groundwork, AI can speed the compliance auditing process by automatically investigating the system configuration, user access records, and policy adherence. It assists in ensuring uninterrupted compliance and substantially reduces the amount of human labor in the audit (Yang and Chang, 2024).

Benefits and Considerations

- **Enhanced Accuracy:** The accuracy of threat identification and policy enforcement is improved by AI and ML, which analyze big datasets and spot minute trends that conventional techniques might overlook.
- **Reduced False Positives:** By increasing the accuracy of threat detection, advanced AI algorithms can lower false positives, resulting in more focused and efficient responses.
- **Scalability:** AI and ML technologies scale effectively, enabling enterprises to oversee compliance in large-scale, intricate cloud systems.

THE EVOLVING LANDSCAPE OF CLOUD SECURITY CERTIFICATIONS AND ATTESTATIONS

Nowadays, many corporations put their operations in the cloud, and it is therefore necessary to create compliance with industry standards and security best practices for the sake of creating confidence and guaranteeing legal compliance (Mostafa et al., 2023). In this section we investigate the importance of cloud security certifications and attestations, such as SOC 2, ISO 27001, and FedRAMP, which are the proof of conformity to industry standards and best practices.

1. SOC 2 (System and Organization Controls 2)

SOC 2 is a well-known auditing standard developed where an organization must put in place controls in order to protect consumer information as well as guarantee the efficiency of systems for example, the SOC 2 is only relevant for service providers working with sensitive client data such as cloud service providers and SaaS firms (Babar et al., 2022).

SOC 2 assesses whether an organization can meet guidelines which are based on evaluating that data can be handled safely and securely, with sensitive and personal data being protected, down to the service level agreement, and that they are protected from unwanted access. Type I SOC 2 reports examine controls at a point in time, while Type II reports review how well controls operate over a period of time. Compliance is a requirement for businesses serious about maintaining data integrity and security because of the many benefits it offers to these companies, including growth in customer trust, strategic advantage, risk reduction, and operational efficiency (Saidi and Bardou, 2023).

2. ISO 27001

ISO/IEC 27001 is a key standard for a business trying to maintain a solid security posture in a quickly changing threat landscape as well as to manage information in a proactive manner. Based on risk management principles, the standard helps organizations to recognize possible risks to their information assets and to implement suitable controls to mitigate the risk. The 14 categories range from access control to physical security, incident management, and cryptography, to name but a few of the 114 specific controls which make up the ISO 27001. The key part of standard is the Plan-Do-Check-Act (PDCA) cycle to use wherein it assures that ISMS reaches to the changing flexibility of organization and dwindling threat environment. Upon obtaining ISO 27001 certification, an impartial audit confirms your conformance, which in turn reassures those that you serve of your dedication to information security. There are many benefits to ISO 27001 implementation including: improve operational efficiency, reduced risk of breaches, increased customer trust, increase security and adherence to legal and regulatory standards (Alshareef, 2023).

FEDRAMP (FEDERAL RISK AND AUTHORIZATION MANAGEMENT PROGRAM)

FedRAMP (FedRAMP) is a U.S. government project to standardize the permission to use, security assessment, and ongoing monitoring of the cloud services used by federal agencies. The General Services Administration (GSA) runs FedRAMP, which ensures that a cloud service provider (CSP) strictly follows security standards and pushes the federal government into cloud computing in a safer and more reliable manner. Based on the sensitivity and criticality of the data involved, the program divides security requirements into three impact levels: Low, Moderate, and High. The control versus demonstrated effectiveness chart comes from the National Institute of Standards and Technologies' (NIST) Special Publication 800-53. There are three ways for CSPs to obtain FedRAMP authorization: the Joint Authorization

Board (JAB), agency sponsorship, or third-party assessment organization (3PAO) evaluation (Khan, 2016).

After authorization providers must participate in ongoing monitoring to confirm compliance. The advantages of FedRAMP include improved security, less assessment duplication, faster cloud adoption and cost savings for agencies and CSPs. FedRAMP provides a centralized framework for assessing and authorizing cloud services and aids the federal IT infrastructure modernization and safe management of government data (Akbar et al., 2023).

CONCLUSION

This chapter discusses what cloud security compliance matters and why, as more and more businesses move to cloud environments. First the basic ideas of cloud computing and cloud security compliance are discussed, and specific attention is paid to the shared responsibility paradigm existing between clients and Cloud Service Providers (CSPs). The other thing that this approach provides is a need for cooperation to successfully accomplish compliance requirements because it details the security responsibilities of both parties. The chapter then delves into the web of regional and international laws that affect cloud security, showing how they conflict with each other between jurisdictions, and how they affect cloud services. We cover the methods for risk assessment, the methods companies may use to create robust compliance frameworks which fit unique requirements. How, new technologies such as Blockchain, Machine Learning and Artificial Intelligence (AI) can simplify compliance procedures are evaluated. These technologies are seen as tools that help to streamline compliance operations by enabling process automation, improved data protection and greater overall effectiveness of monitoring and reporting systems. Additionally, the chapter discusses how cloud security certifications and attestations like prominent frameworks like SOC 2, ISO 27001, and FedRAMP are changing. Montonet stated that organizations seeking to exhibit their cloud security and compliance with regulation must have these certifications. Finally, the chapter concludes with the necessity among enterprises to adopt new technologies to enhance security and compliance effectiveness as well as understanding, and embracing, and implementing thorough security practices in the cloud in order to comply with many legal requirements and ethical standards.

REFERENCES

Akbar, H., Zubair, M., & Malik, M. S. (2023). The security issues and challenges in cloud computing. *International Journal for Electronic Crime Investigation*, 7(1), 13–32. DOI: 10.54692/ijeci.2023.0701125

Alouffi, B., Hasnain, M., Alharbi, A., Alosaimi, W., Alyami, H., & Ayaz, M. (2021). A systematic literature review on cloud computing security: Threats and mitigation strategies. *IEEE Access : Practical Innovations, Open Solutions*, 9, 57792–57807. DOI: 10.1109/ACCESS.2021.3073203

Alshareef, H. N. (2023). Current development, challenges, and future trends in cloud computing: A survey. *International Journal of Advanced Computer Science and Applications*, 14(3). Advance online publication. DOI: 10.14569/IJACSA.2023.0140337

Anandappa, M., & Mudnal, M. K. (2024). Cloud computing and security issues in the cloud. Journal of Scientific Research and Technology, 59-66.

Arunkumar, J. R. (2023). Study analysis of cloud security challenges and issues in cloud computing technologies. Journal of Science. *Computing and Engineering Research*, 6(8), 6–10.

Babar, M., Jan, M. A., He, X., Tariq, M. U., Mastorakis, S., & Alturki, R. (2022). An optimized IoT-enabled big data analytics architecture for edge—Cloud computing. *IEEE Internet of Things Journal*, 10(5), 3995–4005. DOI: 10.1109/JIOT.2022.3157552 PMID: 38046398

Chang, V., Kuo, Y.-H., & Ramachandran, M. (2016). Cloud computing adoption framework: A security framework for business clouds. *Future Generation Computer Systems*, 57, 24–41. DOI: 10.1016/j.future.2015.09.031

Diaby, T., & Rad, B. B. (2017). Cloud computing: A review of the concepts and deployment models. *International Journal of Information Technology and Computer Science*, 9(6), 50–58. DOI: 10.5815/ijitcs.2017.06.07

Garg, R. (2020). MCDM-based parametric selection of cloud deployment models for an academic organization. *IEEE Transactions on Cloud Computing*, 10(2), 863–871. DOI: 10.1109/TCC.2020.2980534

Hussain, M.. (2024). A hybrid effective access control in cloud computing. *Journal of Computing & Biomedical Informatics*, 7(01), 618–631.

Khan, M. A. (2016). A survey of security issues for cloud computing. *Journal of Network and Computer Applications*, 71, 11–29. DOI: 10.1016/j.jnca.2016.05.010

Kumar, T., Kumar, P., & Namasudra, S. (2024). Secure access control of cloud data using DNA computing. In 5th IEEE International Conference on Computing, Power and Communication Technologies (IC2PCT) (pp. 1996-2001). IEEE. DOI: 10.1109/IC2PCT60090.2024.10486550

Kumar, T., Kumar, P., & Namasudra, S. (2024). A DNA-based authentication system for securing cloud data storage and transactions. In *11th International Conference on Computing for Sustainable Global Development (INDIACom)* (pp. 1692-1698). IEEE. DOI: 10.23919/INDIACom61295.2024.10499164

Kumar, T., Namasudra, S., & Kumar, P. (2023). Providing data security using DNA computing in the cloud computing environment. *International Journal of Web and Grid Services*, 19(4), 463–486. Advance online publication. DOI: 10.1504/IJWGS.2023.135587

Lee, J. (2013). A view of cloud computing. *International Journal of Networked and Distributed Computing*, 1(1), 2–8. DOI: 10.2991/ijndc.2013.1.1.2

Mohammed, C. M., & Zeebaree, S. R. M. (2021). Sufficient comparison among cloud computing services: IaaS, PaaS, and SaaS: A review. *International Journal of Science and Business*, 5(2), 17–30.

Mostafa, A. M., Rushdy, E., Medhat, R., & Hanafy, A. (2023). An identity management scheme for cloud computing: Review, challenges, and future directions. Journal of Intelligent & Fuzzy Systems, (Preprint), 1-23.

Nadeem, F. (2022). Evaluating and ranking cloud IaaS, PaaS and SaaS models based on functional and non-functional key performance indicators. *IEEE Access : Practical Innovations, Open Solutions*, 10, 63245–63257. DOI: 10.1109/ACCESS.2022.3182688

Nanda, A. K., Sharma, A., Augustine, P. J., Cyril, B. R., Kiran, V., & Sampath, B. (2024). Securing cloud infrastructure in IaaS and PaaS environments. In Improving Security, Privacy, and Trust in Cloud Computing (pp. 1-33). IGI Global. DOI: 10.4018/979-8-3693-1431-9.ch001

Patel, H. B., & Kansara, N. (2021). *Cloud Computing Deployment Models: A Comparative Study. International Journal of Innovative Research in Computer Science & Technology*. IJIRCST.

Paul, P. K., & Ghose, M. K. (2012). Cloud computing: Possibilities, challenges and opportunities with special reference to its emerging need in the academic and working area of Information Science. *Procedia Engineering*, 38, 2222–2227. DOI: 10.1016/j.proeng.2012.06.267

Rahman, A., Islam, M. J., Band, S. S., Muhammad, G., Hasan, K., & Tiwari, P. (2023). Towards a blockchain-SDN-based secure architecture for cloud computing in smart industrial IoT. *Digital Communications and Networks*, 9(2), 411–421. DOI: 10.1016/j.dcan.2022.11.003

Rashid, A., & Chaturvedi, A. (2019). Cloud computing characteristics and services: A brief review. *International Journal on Computer Science and Engineering*, 7(2), 421–426.

Saidi, K., & Bardou, D. (2023). Task scheduling and VM placement to resource allocation in Cloud computing: Challenges and opportunities. *Cluster Computing*, 26(5), 3069–3087. DOI: 10.1007/s10586-023-04098-4

Sengupta, S., Kaulgud, V., & Sharma, V. S. (2011). Cloud computing security—trends and research directions. In *2011 IEEE World Congress on Services* (pp. 524-531). IEEE. DOI: 10.1109/SERVICES.2011.20

Srinivasan, S., & Srinivasan, S. (2014). Cloud computing evolution. In Cloud Computing Basics (pp. 1-16). DOI: 10.1007/978-1-4614-7699-3_1

Yang, S., & Chang, J. (2024). Identity-based remote data integrity auditing from lattices for secure cloud storage. *Cluster Computing*, 27(5), 1–12. DOI: 10.1007/s10586-023-04239-9

Zhang, Y., Deng, R. H., Xu, S., Sun, J., Li, Q., & Zheng, D. (2020). Attribute-based encryption for cloud computing access control: A survey. *ACM Computing Surveys*, 53(4), 1–41.

Chapter 14

Security Analysis and Implementation Models for Serverless Cloud Computing Applications

Devansh Malik
https://orcid.org/0009-0000-1792-8970
Amity School of Engineering and Technology, Amity University, Delhi, India

Saru Dhir
https://orcid.org/0000-0002-2381-2920
Amity University, Delhi, India

Betty Paulraj
https://orcid.org/0009-0007-1304-014X
Amity School of Engineering and Technology, Amity University, Delhi, India

Sumita Gupta
https://orcid.org/0000-0001-5947-9659
Amity School of Engineering and Technology, Amity University, Delhi, India

ABSTRACT

This work investigates the evolving landscape of serverless computing and its transformative impact on modern software development and cloud deployment strategies. Serverless architecture represents a significant paradigm shift by abstracting away the traditional server management responsibilities from developers, and serverless computing introduces unique challenges that must be addressed to fully leverage its potential. The paper discusses strategies to mitigate these challenges, such as optimizing function code to reduce cold start times, and using advanced

DOI: 10.4018/979-8-3693-7137-4.ch014

monitoring tools to gain visibility into serverless operations. Through an extensive review of contemporary literature and real-world case studies, the paper identifies best practices for designing and implementing serverless applications. This paper contributes to the ongoing discourse on serverless computing by providing a balanced perspective on its advantages and challenges, offering practical insights for developers and organization seeking to adopt or optimize serverless architectures in their cloud computing strategies.

INTRODUCTION

Serverless application is type of cloud computing paradigm in which users can use to manage and build application without the physical infrastructure. Cloud providers make it hassle free and easy for the users as they have no need to maintain the underlying infrastructure which allows users to focus on writing the code. Serverless architecture has many benefits over the traditional architecture some of them being cost effective and having reduced operational complexity.

Cloud computing has 3 major service models - Infrastructure as a Service (IaaS), Platform as a Service (PaaS), and Software as a Service (SaaS).IaaS provide users with the most control as compared to other service models. In IaaS users have access to servers and storage which they can control through API. PaaS service model is designed specially for developers as users they can focus on their code and don't have to worry about managing the complexities of underlying software. with PaaS, developers can focus solely on writing code and designing applications, leveraging pre-built components and services to accelerate development cycles. SaaS gives consumers a feature to access a web application which is hosted somewhere on the cloud instead of having it on their own physical system this reduce the cost of hardware for an organization (Kumari, S., 2000).

In serverless computing Cloud service providers like Amazon Web Services (AWS), Microsoft Azure, Salesforce, VMware, and Alibaba Cloud handle server management tasks, including resource allocation, service deployment, scaling, and monitoring. This approach is beneficial for consumers as it can reduce costs and allow them to focus on their business logic. These efficiencies and economic benefits have driven the rapid growth of serverless computing in recent years, garnering significant attention from both industry and academia.

In the traditional cloud computing model, a company must assess its computing power needs, identify the most suitable cloud providers for the required capacity, and then make payments to secure the necessary computing space and bandwidth. It is beneficial because as a company does not have to worry about the hardware and computation needs of the application (Mell, P, 2011).

Low cost is a defining benefit of serverless computation, as this approach eliminates the need to build a physical server, as companies only need to set up a server within the cloud infrastructure. Serverless computing eliminates the need to create and manage servers and databases (Aldossary, Md. (2021).

Serverless computing is ideal for small and medium enterprises because planning for scalability can be challenging. When a business is starting out, it's hard to predict its actual server requirements. If a business opts to pay for a fixed amount of computing power, it might end up with excess capacity if growth is slower than expected .

Cloud computing is implemented through four primary deployment models: public cloud, private cloud, hybrid cloud, and community cloud. In the public cloud, exemplified by platforms like Google Drive, Microsoft Azure, and AWS, resources such as storage and servers are managed by a service provider and are accessible to users worldwide via the internet. Conversely, the private cloud model restricts.

Figure 1. Cloud computing framework

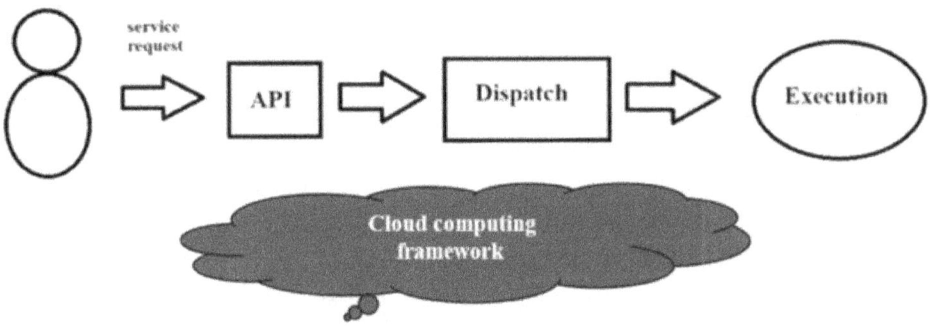

access to resources to a specific organization or company, with management duties potentially falling on either the organization itself or an external service provider.

The community cloud model facilitates resource access for multiple organizations with shared objectives, such as compliance or security considerations. Collaboration among these entities enables the attainment of collective goals while maintaining a level of autonomy over resource management. Lastly, the hybrid cloud approach, represented by solutions like Azure Stack, Google Anthos, and Azure Arc, integrates both private and public cloud resources as needed, offering organizations flexibility and scalability in resource utilization.

Each deployment model caters to distinct use cases and organizational requirements, offering varying degrees of control, security, and collaboration opportunities. Understanding these models is crucial for informed decision-making in cloud adoption strategies, ensuring alignment with organizational objectives and needs (Bhat, A., 2024).

Serverless computing provides many benefits, but it also comes with certain challenges. These challenges can be broadly categorized into security issues and organizational difficulties.

From a security standpoint, three key main security issues affecting serverless computing stand out.

- The possibility of function event data injection is high(Function event data injection refers to the practice of injecting data into the events or triggers that invoke functions within serverless computing environments)
- Secondly, insecure serverless deployment configuration could affect the entire system.
- Third-party dependencies heighten security risks for cloud providers in the serverless computing industry. While vulnerabilities in third-party dependencies are not exclusive to serverless computing, the risks are amplified in serverless systems due to the complexity involved in deploying cloud services on a per-demand basis.

Serverless platforms constitute a dynamic and diverse ecosystem, characterized by a variety of specialized components. Achieving a secure and reliable serverless environment necessitates a thorough consideration of the security features inherent to each ecosystem component and their interplay. Moreover, establishing an effective security framework mandates the prior delineation of the pertinent threat model specific to serverless computing. This foundational step is crucial for seamlessly structuring the security landscape of serverless environments, as elaborated in subsequent discussions. Through systematic attention to security concerns and their alignment with the nuances of serverless architectures, users can fortify defences against potential threats and vulnerabilities.

As the size of the server increases and the resources increase it security threat increases as hinders your ability to make sense of all the data. With a so many events in your log every day External adversaries exploit user managed fields for input in the available APIs which are accessible to event handling to execute their attack (O'Meara, W. & Lennon, R. G. (2020). Attackers can use attacks like these to execute arbitrary commands inside the function to retrieve confidential information or to obstruct performance of a function (Ramgovind, S., Eloff, M.M. & E. Smith, 2010). Attackers use many types of threats some of which are listed below.

Eavesdropping: eavesdropping attacks are also known as Ip sniffing anttacks in these attacks the attacker listens to network traffic continuously to access useful information which can be used, deleted, or modified by the attacker and can also be used to gain access to sensitive parts of the server. If the data is deleted without backup it results in loss of the data (Kardas, S. & Celin, S., 2013).

Shared technologies Vulnerabilities: Virtualization facilitates multitenancy by allowing the sharing of computing resources, including CPU cores, cache, memory, servers, and network interfaces, among multiple tenants. This sharing is enabled by the virtualization platform, which employs a hypervisor to create and manage virtual machines (VMs) on a shared physical server. so, this creates vulnerabilities in the server.

Insufficient logging and monitoring: It makes it hard to trace and identify the attackers since there is so much traffic on the server.

SQL injection: SQL injection is one of the common attacks which represent vulnerabilities and gaps in the cloud server security. In these types of attacks, attackers gain access to backend data and can carry out a variety of operations such as deleting user data, gaining accesses to personal data, getting a hold of user logins details and other credentials. If attackers are successful there can be some serious repercussions which includes harm to the company reputation of the service provider it can also cause financial losses. Developers can take certain steps to make their servers secure and safe from these type of attacks for example having frequent security audits implementing firewalls.

MAC Spoofing Attack: In these types of attacks attackers change there MAC address to imitate A host's device to gain access to the network by using this method attackers can bypass all safety mechanisms and make it really easy to gain access to sensitive information. There are counter measures than can make the servers secure against there type of attacks such as implementing zero-trust security principles in your network and having strong authentication mechanisms.

Lambda: Lambda functions take requests from users validates them. Lambda functios are highly flexible functions that make them a security threat which makes it easy for attackers to insert harmful information in the servers by exploiting lambda functions.

As a result, these exploits may jeopardize the system's integrity and result in data breaches or unauthorised access. It is crucial for developers to incorporate strong input validation procedures into Lambda functions and to regularly review and update them to efficiently manage new threats in order to reduce these risks Radwan, T., 2017).

Dynamo DB: dynamo DB is used for creating records in the database. Without using a record gap are created in the database security and we can't identify unauthorised commands, and this becomes a vulnerability which can open backdoors for attackers this can expose sensitive data.

LITERATURE REVIEW

In recent times serverless applications has gained significance due to advantages like being cost effective and providing such great benefits for small and growing businesses. However, the security in serverless platforms is a growing concern.

Building cloud apps with security baked in is possible by using automation and designing with security as a priority, cloud users can create applications where security is an essential part of their network.

A study by A. Bhatt in (2024) focuses on different attack patterns and vulnerabilities of cloud computing networks and how we can counter them the study tells us that majority of attack patterns are reliant on misconfiguration of serverless services, so it is important for the user to incorporate security features in the server.

Common attacks on cloud servers are code injections in which hackers insert an infected code in the server to try to change the working of the code or to try to gain access to the server resources. Insufficient logging and monitoring make it easy for cyber attackers to go unnoticed if the log data is not stored properly this happens in big servers as there is a lot of activity and it is hard to keep track of all the logs (Wayne A. Jansen. 2013).

To ensure proper safety limited access to the server is given to different parties this is known as deployment method. Deployment method defines who has how much access to shared resources in the cloud network there are four deployment types in cloud computing public cloud this cloud is managed by the service provider completely and all the resources are public that is anyone on the cloud can access those resources. Private cloud provides access to only to an organisation or company and can be managed by both the organisation and the service provider. A community cloud provides access to multiples organisations that have specific goals these can be used in conferences. Hybrid cloud this is a combination of public and private cloud as per requirements.

SECURITY BASED ON RFID WITH IOT

Radio Frequency Identification (RFID) is a technology that has been around for a long time but emerged recently as a viable solution for cloud security as it prevents attacks on communication channels and make it hard for attackers to target them. RFID technology uses radio waves to scan objects for an RFID tag that is unique for every object.

RFID is not used only in cloud security but in many other fields such as payments and e passports where there are high security risks in these field tags are used with RFID as proof of identity.

A centralized database is managed in the cloud that keeps track of the RFID tags ensuring comprehensible tracability for every RFID tag used. RFID makes it easy for authentic users to access the server by means of their tags and it provides a flexible access to the server. RFID systems are cost effective and flexible as they keep infrastructure costs down while proving reliable performance.

In cloud computing itself RFID is used for other things than security as it makes it easier to manage equipment in the infrastructure by the means of RFID tags and makes it easier to track assets as their real time position is always tracked and is available in the RFID data base that in present in the cloud server.

Figure 2. RFID IOT Architecture

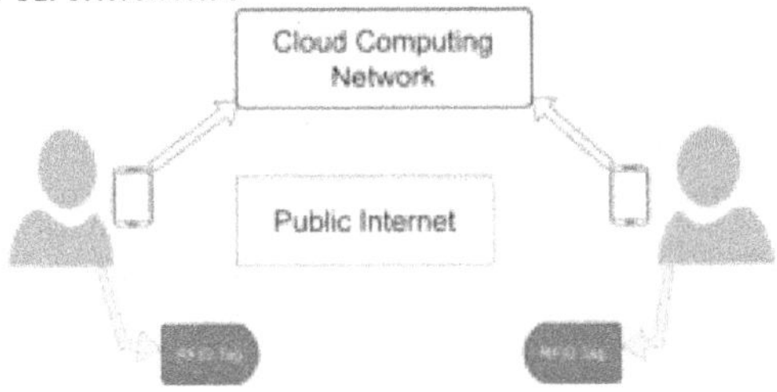

RISKS AND THREATS IN SERVERLESS APPLICATION

Despite the numerous advantages of cloud computing, certain inherent features such as multitenancy (resource sharing), layered architecture (nonuniform management), elasticity (dynamic scaling), and diverse deployment models present significant security challenges. These challenges can impede the widespread adoption of cloud services.

Major cloud service providers such as Google, Amazon (Amazon Web Services), Microsoft, Alibaba, IBM, Oracle, Rackspace, VMware, Salesforce, and SAP are in fierce competition to offer the best cloud solutions. The first step in the process is making your server the safest develop the best security systems as for people to start using cloud computing security and trust is the biggest hindrance.

Multitenancy is a type of service model multiple users share the same resources this raises concerns about the authenticity of the data and data isolation. This service model has its advantages as this can make the server cost effective as resources are shared but it also introduces a gap in the security and trust of users as sharing resources can lead to inconsistent security practices.

Man-in-the-Cloud (MiTC) Attacks: In these attacks attacker use syncronisation tokens to gain access to the data and sever. It is very hard to trace the attackers as they don't use your credentials
SQL Injection: In these attacks attackers inject malware directly in the server in order to gain unauthorized access the server data
Cross-Site Scripting (XSS): XSS are types of attacks in which the users are targeted and attackers inject malware in the users systems to gain access to the server.
ARP and MAC Spoofing: In these attacks attackers clone the MAC address of an authorized device to gain access to the server and access sensitive data and information
SSH Attack: Attackers use SSH attacks to gain access to unauthorized data, information and API keys.
Insecure APIs: API are the first block of security in a cloud computing server and any vulnerability in API's can grant complete access to unauthorised users which can be devastating.
Cross-VM Side-Channel Attack: These types of attacks happen in servers which are based on Multitenancy models meaning that people share resources . In these types of attacks, attackers exploit their neighboring machines in the shared server to gain access to their data.

SECURITY IMPLEMENTATION MODELS

As more people are adapting the cloud infrastructure security threats are getting bigger. The biggest reason that is stopping users to shift from traditional infrastructure to cloud infrastructure is data security and trust. Securing cloud servers is different from traditional security measures as these servers are different and more complex than traditional servers. For security measure to be effective on the cloud infrastructure they need to manage multi-layered security. Cloud security models are designed while keeping these in mind to ensure data protection and server integrity. There are regulatory standard which ensure that security models are in compliance with these requirements.

The Cloud Security Alliance (CSA) is an organization that is currently leading cloud security research and is a regulatory body that certifies that cloud security models are capable. With different cloud service models the security needs change for example in IaaS users have the maximum control over their infrastructure which means that security threats are also the highest in IaaS. In IaaS customers are also responsible for securing their application and data. In PaaS users have less control over the resources which means that the security threat is lower than IaaS and they provide a higher security that IaaS. In SaaS model users have the least control over the resources which automatically means that it provides the highest level of security in all cloud service models as the cloud providers are responsible for most part of the security.

Cloud security differ from traditional security models as they focus on different aspects such as IAM. IAM is software or framework in cloud server that manages the user access to the server and it ensure that devices accessing the server are authorized any unauthorized device is flagged by the IAM system and it helps in reducing data breaches.

API's are one of the most important features in a cloud security model as it is the first line of defense against attackers and potential data breaches as in monitors the incoming and outgoing traffic and restrict unauthorized access to the server if there are any vulnerabilities in the API gateway it makes it easy for attackers to gain access to the server.

To make an effective cloud security model developers have to make a multilayered security system which protects the cloud from every type of threat and has no vulnerabilities research is still being done on topic and cloud security models are getting better and safer.

DATA SECURITY IN CLOUD

Cloud computing is a revolutionary technology that is a blessing for small businesses as it provides scalability and accessibility while being cost effective than its traditional counterparts. Cloud computing is a really accessible and convenient system but it brings with itself concerns regarding security integrity and trust which makes it harder for users to trust specifically with confidential information. We have discussed these concerns in our methodology in detail. When cloud servers are being built data is added to servers from multiple sources to ensure the data integrity and safety pf the server. Only a select few devices are granted access to the data and are authorized to retrieve the stored data this is done in many ways like checking the IP address of the device, via RFID all these steps are taken in account to reduce the threat of unauthorized access and therefore to reduce data breaches. There is constant monitoring of the access pattern of the server and A database is maintained via RFID to detect potential security threats. If a threat is identified the server automatically informs the concerned admins about the malicious activity and the details of the attackers including their IP addresses. These failsafe mechanisms are needed as cloud security is differs from traditional server security as multilayered security is need for cloud servers. A secure cloud environment is needed to build user trust which can make users adapt the serverless architecture

Cloud service providers (CSPs) provide data centers that are present different geographical locations which makes it hard for users to trust them when they don't know at which location there data is being stored and they become hesitant is storing confidential data. Data integrity is crucial for cloud providers for maintain dependability which should be at the highest priority for CPS's as trust is the biggest reason that is stopping users from using this architecture. Traditional security systems are not effective in cloud architecture are a lot of other factor are to be taken in account while working on cloud based security models for example constant monitoring of device logging in and out of the server is needed to ensure only authorized devices are accessing the data. Intruders have many ways to breach the server integrity for example SSH attacks, XXS attacks and many more we have talked about this in detail in the paper. A lot of failsafe mechanism are built into cloud servers to ensure that attackers are not successful in breaching the server integrity and gaining access to confidential data.

Data is always present in two primary states that are Data at rest and Data in transit. Data at rest refers to the state in which data is stored in the servers. Data in transit refers to data that is being transferred for example from one data center to another this is often very important and confidential data for example login credentials. Different security measure are to be taken in account to protect data in different states. Data at rest can be secured by having strict access mechanisms. Data in transit is harder to secure as it is exposed to greater risks

CPS's have to take all these parameters in account while creating a robust security model for their server as cloud security differs from traditional server security systems as a lot of parameters have to be taken in account while working on cloud architecture for example API gateways are the first line of defense for cloud servers as they regulate the access the server by authenticating the devices using their IP addresses. There are other security techniques like RFID tag system RFID technology has been around for a long time has recently been emerging as a viable cloud security method. RFID works on radio waves and scans the tags of the devices to as it prevents attacks on communication channels and make it hard for attackers to target them. RFID tags are unique for every device .

FUTURE SCOPE

The future cloud computing and serverless application involves research and advancement in various field but mainly focuses on security as emerging threats there is a need to evolve our security systems and ensure the protection of servers which will build trust among users and increase dependability as trust is the biggest hindrance for people to shift to serverless architecture.

There is a need of a unifies and regulated authentication system for cloud servers. Extensive work is being done in these field and big organizations are working on making robust and regulated security models Cloud Security Alliance (CSA) is an organization that is currently leading cloud security research and is a regulatory body that certifies that cloud security models are capable. A centralized and unified security system is essential for cloud based systems.

There are many aspects to cloud security for example data security which itself comes with many challenges. . Data integrity is crucial for cloud providers for maintain dependability which should be at the highest priority for cloud providers as trust is the biggest reason that is stopping users from using this architecture. Extensive research is being done in this field to make data security in cloud dependable. Cloud providers have to take many aspects into account while working on cloud data security as it differs from traditional server security.

Cloud computing is growing at a rapid pace but with rapid growth security threats and challenges are growing rapidly and it is becoming challenging to ensure secure and reliable services there is need for extensive work on cloud based security system and there should be a centralized and regulated security system for cloud based servers which can help increase user trust in the cloud environment which is new for many users.

To address these new challenges new security practices are being used and one emerging and promising approach is information-centric security which differs from traditional security practices as it focuses on securing the data to the full extent rather than the infrastructure which ensure that even if an attacker gains access to the server the confidential data is protected and data integrity is maintained

Extensive research is being done in cloud security as it is crucial to do so with the emerging threats cloud architecture introdcues a lot of new issues which were not previously present in traditional servers hence requires new techniques to do deal with them for example in servers based on multitenancy – where users share resources in a cloud server this raises concerns about the authenticity of the data and data isolation. There are many security concerns as attackers can use neighbouring devices to gain access to the server or can intercept data while it is in transit so different security features are used in these types of server to maintain data integrity and keep the server safe from attacks.

Standards have to bet set to for cloud server security this involves having a robust, regulated and readily available security system which ensures that every cloud provider has to maintain a certain level of security which will increase user trust in the architecture and make new users shift to the cloud architecture as trust is the biggest issue that people have with trying new technologies.

CONCLUSION

Advancements in computing has made it easier than ever for developers and users to have access to resources which has changed the way in which organizations manage data and they have made it accessible for nearly everyone to have access to these resources while being cost effective. This is best for small and medium sized business as it provides unparalled scalability wile being cost effective. Even after having such advantages users are still hesitant im shifting to the cloud architecture as there are many security concerns with the same customer worry about their data security and integrity this can be fixed by having a unified security standard which can make people trust the architecture and can be enough to make users shift to the architecture. Extensive research is being done in the field and many organizations are working on cloud security example The Cloud Security Alliance (CSA) is the biggest organization that is currently leading cloud security research and is a regulatory body that certifies that cloud security models are capable. There are many issues in cloud security as it is different from traditional server security systems.

The research that is being done is focused on several key areas that include protection of data in transit and in rest advanced standards are being set which are absolutely crucial for cloud servers to secure them from unauthorized access ant to maintain data integrity and keeping sensitive data safe. AI and ML is also being used in new cloud security systems as they are crucial for real time detection of oncoming threats. By using ML a database is managed in the server which helps in containing potential breaches.

Blockchains are also an important technology that is being used for cloud security models they add an additional layer of security to the cloud security framework

In conclusion, the future of serverless applications is evolving continuously and the future is aimed at data security and making cloud security models unified by adopting advance security techniques by leveraging emerging technologies such as AI, ML and blockchains. The continuous growth of cloud is marked by security challenges and threats which are essential to deal with to improve users trust in the architecture.

REFERENCES

Ahmadi, S. (2024) Challenges and Solutions in Network Security for Serverless Computing. International Journal of Current Science Research and Review ISSN: 2581-8341. Volume 07. Issue 01 January 2024. DOI: DOI: 10.47191/ijcsrr/V7-i1-23

Aldossary, Md. (2021). A Review of Energy-Related Cost Issues and Prediction Models in Cloud Computing Environments. *Computer Systems Science and Engineering*, 36(2), •••.

Bhat, A., Sharma, S., & Badulla, S. Security Issues in Serverless Cloud Computing Architectures. (2024) IEEE International Conference on Computing, Power and Communication Technologies (IC2PCT) pp. 2.

Che, J., Duan, Y., & Jhang, T. (2011). Study on the security models and strategies of cloud computing. International Journal of Current Science Research and Review 2011 International Conference on Power Electronics and Engineering Application. DOI: 10.1016/j.proeng.2011.11.2551

Dinadayalan, P., Jegadeeswari, S., & Gnanambigai, D. (2014). Data Security Issues in Cloud Environment and Solutions. *2014 World Congress on Computing and Communication Technologies*. DOI: 10.1109/WCCCT.2014.63

Emmanuel, R., Chandrashekar, C.M., Laxmidevi, H. & Sharma, P.. (July 2022) The Scope and Research on Cloud Computing Security" International Journal of Advanced Research in Computer and Communication Engineering ISO 3297:2007. Vol. 11. Issue 7.

Jansen, W. A. (2013). Cloud Hooks: Security and Privacy Issues in Cloud Computing. *44th Hawaii International Conference on System Sciences*.

Kardas, S., & Celin, S. (2013). A New Security and Privacy Framework for RFID in Cloud Computing Conference Paper. DOI: DOI: 10.1109/CloudCom

Khan, A. Raouf & Latifa K. A. (2023). A Brief Review on Cloud Computing Authentication Frameworks" Engineering, Technology &. *Applied Scientific Research*, 13(1), 9997–10004.

Khayyambashi, M. R., Shahrokhi, E. (2021). Design And Implement A New Cloud Security Method Based On Multi Clouds On Open Stack Platform.

Kumari, S., Dhankar, A., & Solanki, K. (2022) Analysis of Cloud Computing Security Threats and Countermeasures. 10th International Conference on Reliability, Infocom Technologies and Optimization (Trends and Future Directions) (ICRITO) pp. 1.

Lalitha, V. P., Sagar, M. Y., & Hanji, S. (2017). Data Security in Cloud. *International Conference on Energy, Communication, Data Analytics and Soft Computing (ICECDS-2017)*. pp.1.

Mell, P., & Grance, T. (2011). *The NIST Definition of Cloud Computing" Version 15*. National Institute of Standards and Technology.

O'Meara, W. & Lennon, R. G. (2020) Serverless Computing Security: Protecting Application Logic.

Radwan, T., Azer, M. A., & Abdelbaki, N. (2017). CC security: Challenges and future trends. *International Journal of Computer Applications in Technology*, 55(2), 158–172. DOI: 10.1504/IJCAT.2017.082865

Radwan, T., Azer, M. A., & Abdelibaki, N. (2017). Cloud computing security: Challenges and future trends. *International Journal of Computer Applications in Technology*, 55(2), 158. DOI: 10.1504/IJCAT.2017.082865

Ramgovind, S., Eloff, M. M., & Smith, E. (2010). *The Management of Security in Cloud Computing*. IEEE. DOI: 10.1109/ISSA.2010.5588290

Sadavarte, R. K., Kurundkar, G. D., & Parbhani, D. (2020). *Data security and integrity in cloud computing*. Threats and Solutions.

Sangeetha, R. & M. Silambarasi. (2019) Data security in cloud computing. 2019 JETIR. Volume 6. Issue 9 pp 4.

Shen, Z., Li, F. L., & Yan, X. Wu. (May 2010). Cloud computing system based on trusted computing platform," *International Conference on Intelligent Computation Technology and Automation (ICICTA '10)*. vol.1. pp. 942–945, IEEE. DOI: 10.1109/ICICTA.2010.724

Chapter 15
Security Concerns and Protections in Modern Cloud Environments

Subir Chakraborty
https://orcid.org/0000-0001-6820-3208
Haldia Institute of Technology, India

Shameek Mukhopadhyay
https://orcid.org/0000-0002-5764-2368
The Heritage Academy, India

ABSTRACT

The term "cloud computing", since its advent, has simultaneously transformed business and end user's needs. Cloud Computing with some of its main components like IT infrastructure is built on techniques such as distributed computers across Internet acting virtually as a very powerful servicing system. Now-a-days companies are having fixed managerial strategy to adopt a suitable cloud service. Cloud has succeeded to innovating business models for enterprises to run software applications with much reduced investment as compared to the long expensive history of how experts are utilizing computer resources and operating and developing IT based products. However at the same time, with all its up-to-date services, cloud computing has created new security challenges. Many new security threats are being created as the cloud technology is advancing at a phenomenal pace. This chapter aims to analyze a number of cloud security issues, their effect in various cloud computing environments that are currently present in the industry and attempts to reduce the severity of security challenges.

DOI: 10.4018/979-8-3693-7137-4.ch015

OVERVIEW

Cloud computing is a revolution in modern and next-generation IT processes where computing services and resources are delivered and managed online via the Internet. The cloud boom has very quickly changed the concept of information technology and its use because it is driven by the model of "Rent computing resources through internet and pay for it as you use it like we pay for electric bill as we use it". In the cloud, shared environments are combined through virtualization technology. The purpose of cloud computing is to provide reliable services from advanced data centers based on virtualization technology. Users can access data files on a pay-as-you-use model. (Samani et al., 2015)

Across the entire cloud ecosystem, there are many different cloud-related service providers that play an important role in fulfilling the needs of all shareholders. By borrowing from the cloud, cloud users can enjoy greater flexibility without building their own data centers, especially small and medium-sized businesses that are initially limited by computing resources, this has been widely appreciated. Therefore, cloud computing has the vitality to shape the IT industry in the future.

There is no doubt that the IT market of future generations where 5g or even 6g like technology is going to become a reality, we will utilize cloud technologies equipped with much more concept changing applications. (US Dept of Commerce,2013) (Miller,2021)

INTRODUCTION

Cloud makes platforms, infrastructures, applications more lucrative as services, by renewing the way computer resources are operated and maintained. Cloud applications provide their reach via Internet by using powerful data centers and high-end servers that house all types of web programs and services. Anybody connected with an Internet service provider and a compatible browser can access applications of cloud (Kim et al.).

A research group from the The U.S. National Institute of Standards and Technology (NIST) defines cloud computing as a "model for enabling ubiquitous, convenient, on demand network access to a shared pool of configurable computing resources (e.g., networks, servers, storage, applications, and services) that can be rapidly provisioned and released with minimal management effort or service provider interaction". (US Dept of Commerce,2013)

A TRADITIONAL SYSTEM VS CLOUD SYSTEM MODEL

The traditional system is expanded by purchasing new hardware, installing firmware and system software and then application software as per requirements. In contrast, from cloud computing the customer can receive additional utilities just by using pay-as-you-need method and remaining all operations like resource management, access to applications is automatic via the web service.

Both the systems have three layers of utilities stack to operate on, namely from top to bottom, application, platform and system infrastructure. In a traditional computing environment, the person running one layer of the cluster must be responsible for managing all underlying processes too. But in the case of cloud computing, this burden is shifted from client side to CSP. Cloud computing removes responsibility from the customer and hides the complexity of the computer based on how the customer works at a particular computing layer, presenting a new experience to the customers. (Samani et al, 2015) (Miller,2021)

Service models:

A) *Software as a Service (SaaS)*: This model of cloud service hosts all applications and users access these applications via compatible web browsers. SaaS along with its interface is the cloud application itself which a commercial service provider delivers to the end user using the connection of internet. Most SaaS applications e.g., a programming language compiler, can execute directly within a browser without installing it or downloading it. Google documents, Office suites, Email, games, financial accounting, word processing, Facebook, Gmail, etc- they are all examples of SaaS. (Mather et al.,2009)(Red Hat, n.d)

B) *Platform as a Service (PaaS)*: PaaS is a service used by developers who seek to use a platform. This cloud platform supports not only a development environment but also test,execute, and maintain applications. It supplies a development environment using which programmers can build up their own applications that execute on the cloud. PaaS is highly scalable. Here developers do not have access to the operating system and hardware, they just execute and deploy their applications. Windows Azure, App Engine by google etc are some of the good examples of PaaS. (Microsoft, n.d.) (Red Hat, n.d)

C)*Infrastructure as a Service (IaaS)*: IaaS assures the supply of cloud infrastructure such as memory storage, networks, servers as per demand. Here clients can temporarily choose the hardware components specifications and memory specifications from the available cloud services. All types of cloud storage, dedicated servers, dedicated network resources are supplied by IaaS. Examples are Amazon EC2, S3 etc. (Microsoft, n.d.) (Red Hat, n.d)

Deployment Model Type

A) Public Cloud: In this cloud model, actual infrastructure belongs to service providers, and these services are provided by the cloud service provider over the internet. This large scale allows economies of scale, allowing the needs of different customers to be met to the maximum, thus ensuring the highest level of performance and maximum reliability by sharing resources, but at the cost of increasing the security holes. The public cloud is public and can provide services to multiple tenants. Examples of public cloud include Microsoft Azure, App Engine of Google, Amazon EC2, etc (Vacca, 2017) (Samani et al, 2015)

B) Private Cloud: If it is a private cloud in the cloud model, all processes are owned, controlled, operated by and hosted by some individual organization or another vendor or both using virtualization techniques. Essentially, the idea of private clouds stems from security concerns and keeping valuables within the firewall, making it more expensive and often not having good economies of scale. Private cloud supplies resources which are virtualized and for a target organization. Examples include Amazon Virtual Private Cloud, Microsoft virtual data center, VMware virtual infrastructure, Eucalyptus. (Vacca, 2017)(Samani et al, 2015)

C) Hybrid Cloud: In case of hybrid approach, the operation can be equally effective with housing target specific applications, securities, and protecting important data in the private cloud and evaluation of generic data and applications and big database operations in the public cloud. Thus, hybrid cloud leverages the advantages of both public and private cloud by applying performance, cost savings, security, privacy, and management. Examples include Azure hybrid cloud type, VMware hybrid cloud service. (Vacca, 2017) (Samani et al, 2015)

SECURITY ISSUES IN CLOUD COMPUTING

Customers or businesses moving to the cloud must be aware of security about their computer equipment and, more importantly, the information they share with service providers. With the growing demand for cloud computing, cloud security parameters have become a significant obstacle to further development. According to research, more than 80% of users are bothered by cloud security. The resource is accessed remotely by the client via an external connection, so traditional concepts of boundary security do not apply here. Therefore, a new security standard is needed to solve this security problem, and many attempts are being made to achieve this. Security measures such as firewalls are not suitable for the use of clouds. (Kumar et al., 2024)

The security issues of cloud computing are already complex, because cloud computing goes along with SOA, SaaS, distributed computing, etc. In applications such as finance or healthcare, managers and administrators are normally not allowed access to sensitive user's data while ensuring security. Any unwanted behavior by one cloud user will victimize others and create more opportunities for cyber cloud criminals from the Internet. (Mather et al.,2009) (Kumar et al., 2024)

When a user or organization migrates its computing resources to the cloud, the responsibility is shared between both the parties. The information is stored and entered into the network by some third-party service providers, which leads to a complete compromise and hence breaks the entire trust. Security conditions become worse when data is transferred over the network, kept in different zones, and shared with all service providers involved at the same time. Thus, it becomes crucial to follow the security guidelines before adopting cloud technology. (Kim et al.) (Vacca, 2017)

BACKGROUND STATUS

Cloud is critical business. Transferring an existing 1TB of organization data deployment to the cloud is estimated to reduce the organization's management time by 36%, save 1,829 hours of work per year, and increase money by another $1.2 million. Multi-cloud configurations are on the rise. According to a survey, 34% use three or more public cloud service providers; this rate was 30% a year ago. This number is expected to increase in the coming months. Organizations are more likely to combine cloud and on-premises systems. Therefore, complexity in the cloud has a self-perpetuating aspect: the complexity of the infrastructure element leads to a hodgepodge of various tools. The resulting silos further challenge visibility and complicated operations.

A "*threat*" can cause some substantial harm to a system and reduces all principal requirements of security like integrity, confidentiality, availability. Threats can be intentional like stealing financial data, or accidents like miscalculation or deletion of data.

There could easily be a weakness or flaw in the system (hardware, software or process); The threat will use this flaw to compromise the entire system. This weakness is referred to "*vulnerabilities*" that pose a threat to the system and increase the risk of getting attacked. Identifying and eliminating these weaknesses can reduce physical vulnerability and thus reduce the impact of physical threats. "*Risk*" is the capability of a threat to cause harm to a system by misusing a vulnerability. Risk is the chance that the threat will come to fruition.

However, as a public service with shared resources, cloud computing systems have their own characteristics. Therefore, security mechanisms in the cloud need to be reviewed and improved accordingly. (Mather et al., 2009) (Miller,2021) (Kim et al.)

THREATS TO CLOUD SECURITY

Security threats are divided into the following three types according to the service models of the cloud:

A) Security issues in SaaS Structure

In SaaS structure, customer data is stored along with other customer information in data centers. Additionally, cloud service providers copy data to multiple locations in multiple continents or countries to guarantee availability. In general information systems businesses comprehend information storage rules. However, customers' lack of understanding of their data retention and protection rights in the SaaS model raises serious issues. Here, the consequences of data breaches, software flaws, access and other problems can lead to financial and reputation losses.

In SaaS, cloud security management is solely the responsibility of the service provider. To build a complete SaaS model, it is necessary to delve into these security issues called data privacy, data confidentiality, network privacy, authentication and authorization. (US Dept of Commerce,2013) (Samani et al, 2015)

B) PaaS Inherent security issues

In PaaS model, the supplier provides some administrative rights to users. However, the supplier itself is responsible for the protection below the SaaS layer, such as network attcaks. The provider should guarantee that the information cannot be accessed by moving from one application to another. PaaS is designed to permit programmers to create their own programs based on the platform layer. (Microsoft, n.d.) (Samani et al, 2015)

C)Security issues of the IaaS model

IaaS model grants users with permission to manage security. Security responsibilities of service providers and customers vary depending on the service model. For example, EC2 of amazon assures security with hypervisor. In return, clients should have managed security parameters of all underlying systems as well as information. (Kumar et al., 2024). The initial step to improving cloud security is to correctly verify threats.

The standard threat model is based on the service standards and the general technology model of the cloud. The attack model involves all types of layers of cloud system. (Microsoft, n.d.) (Samani et al, 2015)

CLASSIFICATION

1.Data Breaches and Unauthorized Access

Current issues:

(i) When the confidential information of the organization is leaked or accessed and used without permission, we call it data breach. It may have significant effects on the victim organizations, such as loss of customer trust, negative impact on the company's reputation, and loss of income that continues for a long time. Most often, data breaches are caused by human error, inadequate security measures, phishing scams, or malware. This is a type of theft that often occurs due to unorganized credentials or due to easy access procedures and can be given inappropriately to unscrupulous individuals. (Vacca, 2017)

(ii) Juniper Research predicted that the global data breach compensation will rise in terms of trillion dollars within 2024 annually. Service providers must not only demonstrate capability, availability and quality, but also provide you with peace of mind through unwavering trust in your applications and documents. (Kumar et al., 2024)

Eventually, the maximum clients have only a little understanding of what CSPs do and don't secure their data. Most administrators understand that a data breach occurs when resources are illegitimately accessed, but what may not be appreciated is that improper installation and IT process errors can also be the causes of information leakage. It is only carelessness or mistake on your part that causes you to fail. Capital One's cloud computing bug is just one of many examples. (Subramanian, 2018) (Miller,2021)

(iii) This can also be caused by malware entering your system. Hackers and phishers buy sensitive information like Social Security numbers and medical records from criminals on the dark web. Internal documents and emails contain sensitive information that can damage a company's reputation and cause stock prices to be affected if it falls into the wrong hands. Regardless of the reason for the theft, breaches pose a significant risk to businesses storing data in the cloud. (Mather et al., 2009)

(iv) One of the major problems is that anybody (in fact huge number of people practically) can have privileged access to public cloud and somebody can afflict with a potential breach, whatever the intention is. Another very serious concern is that it has been surveyed and found that more than 90% of data breaches occur due to the lack of proper internal controls. Choosing bad passwords, having your laptop stolen, sharing password, and leaving your computer turned on and open for real use are some of the biggest threats. The damage suffered by customers during network interruptions depends on the internal configuration of network information such as VLAN, firewall, and data storage. (Subramanian, 2018) (Samani et al, 2015)

Data breach example: SQL injection is the most common data leakage example. Data breach is more dangerous in cloud than the normal web application because many applications in the cloud use data sharing. Therefore, a vulnerability in an application can result in all the applications falling into the hands of an attacker. In an organization, there are malicious people within the organization who can steal this information unnoticed. In the year 2016, Uber suffered a data breach with more than 50 million drivers due to the presence of some secrets (AWS certificates) in program code. (Vacca, 2017)

Inference: Even a minor crime can have a large economic impact (e.g. criminal investigation expense, recovery of stolen items, damaged items), and long suffering such as anti-publicity and reduced customer confidence. Previous records have proven that information breaches can be cascading. When an organization loses control over a user's personal data, the user must bear responsibility for any subsequent losses resulting from this. Example of chained losses can be identity theft, hamper of privacy, unwanted requests. Full dependability on a service provider can be sometimes risky and may cause difficult outcomes. Data breaches can even afflict some of the high-end cloud clients. Data must be given high priority, and all attacks of chained consequences must be avoided to get rid of it. Data breaches can create a heavy burden on a company's reputation and ultimately the company may have to face legal troubles and regulator's interrogation. (Subramanian, 2018) (Vacca, 2017)

Preventive measures:

(i)Encryptions

Once your data is encrypted, you should hold on to the keys that are used for encryption and decryption. One should never keep encryption keys in the same program as your sensitive information. Besides ensuring they possess encryption keys; IT departments should regularly assess the efficacy of existing encryption protocols.

Encryption is employed using encryption algorithms. These algorithms are required to implement the program code of encryption. Examples are Advanced encryption standard, Double and triple DES, Blowfish, Twofish, RSA, Elliptic curve cryptography and more. Enterprises must choose the most suitable algorithm to serve their specific purpose and at the same time ensure cloud data remain secure. (Samani et al, 2015) (Mather et al.,2009)

(ii) Multi-factor authentication (MFA)

Users are also required to provide additional credentials for identification and login. For example, enter your password and receive a notification that the digital key has been used one time. Nowadays, this is one of the must-have standards to reduce security issues in the cloud.

Using multiple authentication (MFA) tools to access cloud assets can provide additional security to the login process and secure credentials. With MFA, cybercriminals need to bypass authentication methods such as biometrics, security tokens, and keys; this makes it almost impossible for them to use stolen accounts to access cloud data. This increases the overall security of the organization, making it less vulnerable to cyber-attacks(US Dept of Commerce,2013)(Miller,2021).

(iii) Educate employees about phishing

The easiest way to catch cloud data is to trick someone into revealing their username and password. Make sure all employees know not to click on email attachments unless they know who sent them and are expecting the email. Some phishing emails appear real. IT departments regularly send out phishing emails to find out who's being fooled, and it's worth the extra training. (Subramanian, 2018) (Kumar et al., 2024)

(iv) Micro segmentation

Micro-segmentation is another term frequently used in the software industry, especially for cloud communications and data storage. This is the best practice to allow "sufficient access". This ensures that end users only have the necessary access to the resources they need. This means restricting employee computer use to work purposes only and blocking inappropriate and unauthorized websites on the computer. So, if you minimize access, you reduce the risk. Multi-tenant cloud environments where end users share cloud resources are at a higher risk of data breaches. This risk is not present in the case of enterprises using dedicated cloud servers only. (Vacca, 2017)

2. Data loss

Current issues:

(i)Unlike data leakage, data loss means end users are unable to access data stored in the cloud. Data loss is one of the most severe issues of the cloud system. This means that in most cases data loss is irreversible. Data can be lost for many reasons: cyber extortion or ransomware incidents, migration process, open data storage in unreliable cloud service providers, loss or deletion of data. Additionally, in case of data loss, malicious users or software may deliberately destroy data. Permanent data loss can have a significant impact on cloud service providers (CSPs) and cloud customers. Failures and disasters may also have other causes that can affect the CSP process, such as removal of service providers, fire, flood or earthquake. (Mather et al.,2009)

(ii) Data loss can also cause competitors to lose intellectual property rights (IP), affect competitive advantage, cause financial loss from management, affect the brand value and goodwill of the organization, thereby affecting the total cost of the business. Sharing information within an organization carries a significant risk of information loss or leakage. Cloud solutions provide an easy way to share data and applications with outside parties, and mistakes made by an unauthorized or malicious user can lead to information falling into unauthorized hands. There are tools designed to scan the web to detect such insecure clouds. It is indeed possible for an organization to encounter unexpected data loss simply by storing data in the cloud. It is inevitable that some data will be lost or need to be recreated during migration or access. (Subramanian, 2018) (Miller,2021)

(iii) Lost, stolen or deleted items can pose a serious threat. Mobile phone's main advantage is also its serious security risk. For example, a study by McAfee showed that one-third of consumers surveyed do not use a PIN to protect their smartphone or tablet. For example, in the United Kingdom and Germany, the majority of respondents want to use the same personal identification number given first time at the time of purchase. In contrast, users from USA and France are more likely to choose their altered numbers. This approach carries the risk of information falling into the wrong hands, compounded by the fact that only fifth of respondents continue using their wireless devices without backup. (Miller, 2021) (Kumar et al., 2024)

(iv) Data loss and data deletion may occur due to bad scripts and may cause serious threats. How many applications do you have on your mobile phone? It would be great if you could answer this question, but do you know accurately what information all these apps gather and, next question is probably more serious, what all these installable third-party apps do with your valuable information? Many people cannot even answer the first question. (Miller,2021)

Inference: When a cloud user encrypts data before sending it to the cloud and loses the key, the cipher data will be useless as the decryption key is lost. When data processing and security is concerned it becomes a shared responsibility between CSP and the cloud customer. To minimize the problem of data loss, CSPs needs dynamic backups. Many companies don't even have data recovery plans. Staff should be trained properly about the cloud computing management and sometimes particular cases. This often happens intentionally or unintentionally with existing cloud storage platforms that users face more data loss than the service provider accepts. (Kim et al.) (Subramanian, 2018)

Preventive measures:

There is a saying about the possibility of data loss which prohibits putting all eggs in one basket. Even if the cloud service provider guarantees data transmission, it is the cloud user's responsibility to decide whether to give preference to the provider or the location. As a rule of thumb, apart from the main data center, replicated data must be stored in another center which is not prone to the same risk as that of main center. It can safely be at hundreds of kilometers away or in another country. Customers should also consider storing backups in their own data center or office if necessary. (Subramanian, 2018)

Privacy rights must be protected. The success of any business depends on its ability to keep personal data and information secure. Personally identifiable information collected by organizations is vulnerable to hacking. While cloud service providers must ensure adequate security, businesses must choose alternate sources or avoid storing sensitive data on them. (US Dept of Commerce, 2013) (Subramanian, 2018)

(i) Backup

Backup is very important for information security. Backup ensures that if data is lost or unavailable, the backup can step in and provide the same functionality. Backups, so crucial, that can be the difference between a temporary outage and a permanent problem that disrupts business processes or worse, results in lost revenue. Backup vendors often provide resources that demonstrate the security of their data and the flow of data to the desired destination.

Regular, sophisticated and automated backups must be performed. The best way to deal with cloud security risks is to prevent data loss through regular backups. To back up your data, you need a plan with a clear definition of what data will and won't be backed up. You can use data loss prevention software for automation. (Amazon Web Services, n.d.) (Kim et al.)

Proofpoint is an example of commercial e-mail security and data loss protection that provides security for incoming and outgoing emails without the need for in-house hardware and software. The solution is available with a variety of options, including privacy regarding personal research, health status, data Encryption, which adds authority as tracking and searching for financial information, pre-configuring of data protection rules and email encryption. (Amazon Web Services, n.d.) (Kim et al.)

(ii) Adopt cloud data protection standards

Cloud security standards include providing good guidance for all your data security and problem solving. They are used to providing general guidance regarding information confidentiality, integrity and availability. In addition to being all-encompassing, the trust protection model should provide a centralized and unified control center for security, safety and privacy for all users. This model will help you establish the three key elements of cloud data security: access control, data sanitization, and cryptography. (Vacca, 2017)

(iii) Data Loss Prevention (DLP):

(a) DLP refers to the identification, monitoring and protection of data in use, dynamically through deep content analysis and centralized management information system. Organizations can securely handle improper email transmission. Email transmissions are blocked and reviewed if they contain highly objectionable content. DLP technology guarantees that transferred information conforms to the rules of the organization. End customers can use DLP as a service, allowing them to mitigate threats such as data breaches and compliance management, use features such as encryption or data validation (such as keyword searches) (Samani et al, 2015)

Implementing data loss prevention (DLP) in the cloud has become a challenge for many organizations, mostly due to limited solutions and incompatibility with the CSP APIs. However, this situation has changed a lot in the last few years. Cloud option tools like Amazon Macie can be explored in this regard. Required networked DLP, often used by devices in the virtual network gateway, can be experimented with the end results. (Samani et al, 2015)(Mather et al., 2009)

(b) In the data lifecycle, data transfer is an important stage and is where some processing occurs, usually through interactions associated with an application. At this stage, data integrity plays an important role and the question we ask is: How can data integrity be stored in the cloud infrastructure? It can be controlled through a Service Level Agreement (SLA) to ensure there is no corruption or data loss. (Kumar et al., 2024)
(c) Lost data can be recovered by CSP. For example, Amazon Snowball or Amazon Snowmobile can be used to restore data from AWS sources. Amazon Snowball is a large scale damage proof technology for AWS cloud data transfer scheme which uses a secure architecture. Amazon Snowmobile's service is similar, but it is an even larger data transfer scheme than snowball which moves data to and from amazon cloud. (Kim et al.) (Mather et al.,2009)
    (iv) Develop a good disaster recovery strategy

A disaster recovery plan allows you to implement backup measures immediately after exposure to big data loss. The goal is to provide your organization with the support necessary to quickly recover and resume critical daily operations. To develop a disaster recovery plan, an organization must: *anticipate data loss scenarios, identify risks and vulnerabilities, define key functions and requirements, and establish recovery procedures* for lost data. In addition to backup and recovery, most organizations need to have a substitute location in case of practical data loss as well as built-in systems and communications tools. (Amazon Web Services, n.d.)

3. Insecure Interfaces and APIs

Current issues:

(i) APIs are an important part of building a robust development infrastructure like cloud. The API securities manual must be provided by the CSP, and all APIs must be managed by proper characteristics and requirements of the technology. APIs supplies features to users by enabling personalization and management of cloud resources. Depending on the service provider's infrastructure (SPI),

APIs can be used in different ways, from normal URL operations to advanced service-oriented architecture. (Miller,2021)

(ii) CSP provides APIs for cloud clients to interact with cloud services. The API provides comprehensive management, monitoring and CRUD (create, read, update and delete) functionality. APIs and similar connections may be vulnerable to attack for misconfiguration errors, coding flaws, or want of authorization. These concerns will make them vulnerable to illegitimate activities. (Miller,2021) (Kumar et al., 2024)

(iii) API security depends on the appropriate API and its correct use by the customer; This means that the cloud customer must comply with the CSP instructions regarding API and its best practices. If the API's authentication and access controls are not implemented correctly, attackers can abuse the API for their own purposes. If you rely on cloud services that use insecure APIs, your data and systems may be compromised. Hackers typically use one of three methods to compromise APIs: brute force, distributed denial of service, meet in the middle attacks. Your cloud computing solution should be able to handle all three approaches. (Mather et al.,2009)

Inference: Companies face a tough task in managing APIs and their securities. The motion of the progress of the cloud services is very rapid. Transactions that generally take days or weeks with conventional methods can be finished in minutes by the cloud. Using more than one CSP at a time also increases complexity, as every CSP has exclusive capabilities that are updated daily. API supported environment requires a fast-paced, specially designed dynamic management system that many companies have not yet mastered. (Miller, 2021) (Mather et al.,2009)

Preventive measures:

To create secure APIs and prevent access to malicious products, CSPs should analyze the following practices in API management:

(i) APIs should use one-time keys, not reusable, for their protection and cloud access. API keys should not be embedded within the code, rather must be deposited to some code repository. If a suspicious user can capture the API key, he can easily access services on behalf of the client.

(ii) Rely on standard API infrastructure such as Open Cloud Computing Interface (OCCI) and Cloud Infrastructure Management Interface (CIMI).

(iii) API targeted attack zones must be monitored and protected. Governance and change management strategies and processes of conventional systems must be up to date with the growth and evolution of cloud-based APIs. Companies should embrace automation and use technology that regularly monitors API changes and fixes issues in the short-term. (US Dept of Commerce, 2013) (Subramanian, 2018)

(iv) False Breach: A penetration test that simulates an external attack on API end points to breach security and access an organization's data sharing. This test will give you information about how safe the code fragment is and what needs to be improved. In addition, extensive security measures can be taken on a regular basis to ensure that no one is allowed to infiltrate the API. (Subramanian, 2018)

(v)IaaS APIs provided by CSPs such as Amazon EC2 enable users to create and handle cloud computing, including storage memory and networking parameters. API implementation can be done through HTTP. Although most operations can be performed using GET and POST, PUT, and DELETE requests are used in some cases. In some cases, the source representation is JavaScript Object Notation (JSON). As with any type of cloud, developers need to be aware of specific APIs to use. SaaS features generally do not provide APIs except simple export and import functions for browsers. (Samani et al, 2015) (Subramanian, 2018)

(vi) One of the biggest problems faced by cloud users today is that one CSP has its own API. Therefore, cloud applications portability is difficult, and they cannot be moved from one cloud to another, affecting interoperability largely between the cloud systems. Because APIs are specific to cloud services, all staff including programmers and administrators must be familiar with the specific functionality of the platform. (Kumar et al., 2024)

Presently there is a common API standard which is globally accepted, standardization efforts are introducing and managed by providers and clients groups. Universal Cloud Interface (UCI) is one such effort, which tries to create a global API standard by integrating various cloud APIs from heterogeneous cloud systems. This type of attempt is always welcome because we must remember that sending applications and sharing data over the cloud is still a difficult task. (Subramanian, 2018) (Vacca, 2017)

Figure 1. API management in cloud computing

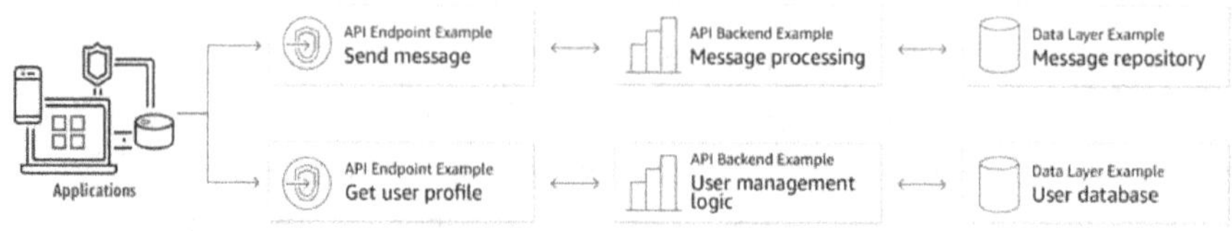

4. Cloud Misconfiguration

Current issues:

(i) Misconfiguration is a threat to public cloud security and affects approximately 60% of cloud users. Due to the wide variety of platform specific configurations, misconfiguration is still a challenge for cloud security. Companies and their employees who are not knowledgeable about the environment can make mistakes in these places and cause the environment to be affected. The proliferation of multiple cloud providers makes this problem even more common, and companies need to configure it correctly for many different cloud providers. Misconfigurations within cloud environments can leave sensitive data exposed. Inadequate security controls and improper storage, databases, and network settings configurations create vulnerabilities that attackers can exploit. (Miller,2021)

(ii) CSPs offer a bunch of cloud-based tools for configuration settings of cloud environment. It has been surveyed that more than 65% of organizations use these tools to configure cloud infrastructure. Complex multi-cloud environments can decrease efficiency and visibility and scale up the risks that an improper configuration can anytime make enterprise cloud vulnerable to a harmful attack.

(iii) The overall organizational impact must depend on the type of misconfiguration and how fast it has been addressed and solved. Unsolicited permissions, unprotected storage of data, initial inappropriate default setting, making security controls and monitoring inactive – are some examples of typical misconfiguration which must be handled and managed in real time with maximum care. Traditional configuration management techniques are not effective in cloud environments. (Miller,2021) (Kumar et al., 2024)

(iv) Misconfiguration can cause data breaches because they render enterprises vulnerable to malicious attacks and some attacks only take a fraction of the time to execute. Misconfigured cloud operations create an inevitable attack surface when being operated in an IaaS environment. This type of attack surface has produced a huge number of data breaches over the years, causing leakage of millions of records. Cloud administrators need to maintain a balance between security status and business operations. Multi-tenant cloud spans multiple countries, so visibility becomes trivial, and misconfiguration dominates as a higher level risk creating factor. Sometimes it is treated just like a common problem without the knowledge of the range of harmful effects, for example the initial setting up configuration faces regular problems like misconfiguration errors, web application setup errors.(Microsoft, n.d.)

(v) Unlike clients, CSP can identify even a small fraction of misconfiguration errors in its own network. Because from their point of view these systems are much customized by them and exhibit consistency from beginning .

(vi) Misconfiguration also renders your cloud-based resources unavailable. For example, due to some objectionable video running in Youtube by some network misconfigurations can make regular Youtube content unavailable for a significant amount of time. (Miller,2021)

Preventive measures:

(i)To reduce the risks of misconfigurations, it is better to follow a dynamic management system which requires time to time inspection and audit of all logging activities, verification, validation, approving. Static management system is unable to get rid of all misconfigurations in the system and causes data breaches.

(ii) "Policy as code" is a integrated procedure to protect from misconfiguration which automatically check configuration errors related with security, and produces a single, integrated result for all types of customers and users. Since it operates in an automated fashion, it can remove human related errors and can also save time requirement. An example can be "Open-policy-agent" which is an open-source application for policy as code, adopted by company like AmericanExpress.(US Dept of Commerce,2013)(Miller,2021)

(iii)Cloud security automation is a combined model used by providers as well as clients . It can be used by enterprises who regularly use clouds and impose heavy tasks in return. CSPs are always willing to provide automation support for configuration errors even though customers themselves are misusing access privileges and responsible for risk parameters . Security automation tools and processes that help organizations instantly detect and fix misconfigurations are essential. These can help prevent security incidents from occurring and reduce the time and effort required to respond to an incident. Investing in such tools can improve your organization's cybersecurity posture. (US Dept of Commerce,2013)(Subramanian, 2018)(Miller,2021)

(iv) Installing Cloud Security Posture Management (CSPM) tools is crucial for businesses competing with hybrid architecture where configuration errors are a serious risk to cloud security. Misconfiguration is often caused by interrupted monitoring, database errors, physical and virtual machine security flaws, reduced visibility and more. Companies that follow hybrid cloud model, should adopt CSPM tools.

(v)There should be dedicated teams who will be looking for and fixing configuration errors in the CSP. Amazon footprints are the product of the team works. The team should also check that their operations work and do not interfere with unauthorized applications. The Cloud Access Security Broker (CASB) can combine with various cloud applications, including the amazon footprint, which gives the security team an understanding view of the environment. There are also configuration management tools like AWS config, Microsoft system centers, Kubernetes, to perform updates and changes or use locations so that safe configurations can guide the best practices.(Samani et al, 2015) (Subramanian, 2018)(Vacca, 2017)

(vi) United with other AWS technologies such as AWS Config or AWS Lambda or configuration management tools like Puppet, Chef, Ansible, SaltStack, CFEngine to perform updates and changes or use locations so that safe configurations can guide the best practices. (Samani et al, 2015) (Subramanian, 2018)

5. Multi-cloud sprawling issues

Current issues:

(i) A multi-cloud environment gives you more flexibility than a single cloud platform. Multi cloud helps you control your expenses, avoid sticking to a single CSP, and keep the client organization strong. Most companies are adopting the cloud, and the majority of cloud users use more than one cloud. In fact, more than 85% of client organizations have more than one cloud deployment, and more than 70% of organizations have hybrid cloud deployment. Security management across multiple cloud environments requires consistent policies, centralized visibility, and consistent security controls to reduce risk. Unprotected multi-cloud adoption encounters the risk of losing data and information, unauthenticated access, reduced visibility and many more. Even one cyber-attack can negatively impact your business and cause customer distrust, havoc repair costs and lost revenue. (Linkedin)(Microsoft)

(ii) Multicloud sprawl is a growing concern for organizations and can create complex and difficult environmental management problems, risk of information leakage, unauthorized access and breach. It can also make it difficult to identify and mitigate security threats, as the security team must monitor and secure different locations and devices. (Kumar et al., 2024)

(iii) User access control is tougher in multi-cloud technology. CSPs have built-in role management, user rights, and access rights, but most cloud security systems require you to manage multiple user management policies. Without central control, it is difficult to ensure consistent policies across platforms. Multiple clouds make visibility difficult. Third-party cloud service providers may not allow you to access all layers of cloud computing, which means you may not be aware of all vulnerabilities.(Samani et al, 2015)(Microsoft)

(iv) Multi cloud also requires you to update the plan, update the schedule for each platform, and make sure all objects are up to date. Nowadays, companies often deal with big data and data management poses a great challenge. This challenge increases exponentially when you use multiple clouds. That is why a strong information management system is required to ensure that operations, processes, programs and end users keep data secure while accessing it. (Linkedin) (Microsoft)

(v) There are currently hundreds of CSPs available in many different sizes over the years. The notion of cloud-of-cloud (or it can be said inter-cloud) has been researched and analyzed over the past few years in which the stored data is distributed in nature and always available even if some sub-cloud system turns off for some reason. To support multi-cloud, IEEE created the Intercloud Testbed project to help realize multi-cloud interoperability. (Microsoft)

(vi) An ideal multi cloud environment must have certain basic characteristics. Connected with all the CSPs, the system should still work if at least some CSPs are presently working, regardless of the conditions of the remaining CSPs. For example, the system must be secure to provide information and save encrypted data, no hacking or cracking can reveal the meaning of the original data, even if some CSPs fail. Search query and criteria should not be revealed before all available CSPs collaborate to conduct the search. (Microsoft)

Figure 2. Multicloud platforms

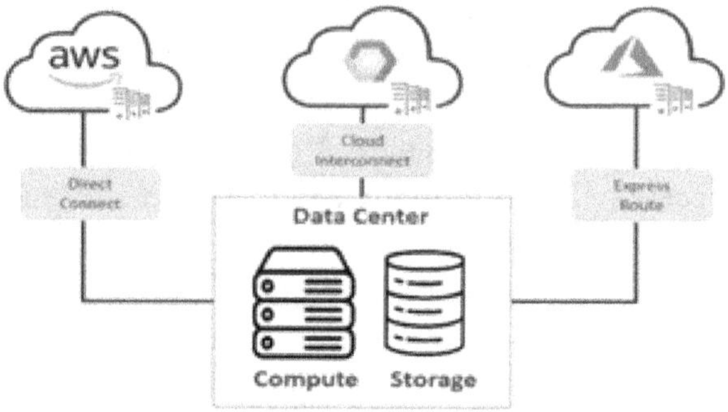

Preventive measures:

(i) One way to ensure the reliability of data sent to multi-cloud environment is duplication. We can create multiple copies of the same encryption text scheme, for example, for all CSPs. On their end, each provider keeps the same cipher-text. Therefore, even if only one provider is available, remote data can still be accessed. But this scheme increases space complexity for replicas need physical storage to be saved. (Wipro,n.d.)(Miller,2021)

(ii) Automation of processes where each process is involved with security check, is frequently required especially in public cloud. Newly developed containers and virtual machines are required to be automatically scanned for security. Automation has the capacity to protect the complete multi-cloud system deriving mainly SaaS multi-cloud, PaaS multi-cloud and IaaS multi-cloud. For example, Oracle multicloud which combines multiple cloud services to optimize operational parameters, require the support of automation security check.(https://www.wipro.com)(Linkedin)

(iii) If someone depends on multicloud to maintain the principle of security then the same security parameters should be installed across all the individual clouds. Automated tools can be used to synchronize generic security configurations and parameters from one provider to another. While multicloud prefers security monitoring technique, automation can be initiated by certain events or alerts and solution too should be implemented without human interaction. Ultimate aim is to protect enterprise resources, valuable information against malicious attacks within the cloud services.(Microsoft)(Mather et al.,2009).

(iv) Implementing multicloud security has several advantages which include increased brand value, consistent security support, reduced costs, and centralized visibility. It is mandatory to choose the safest location for data storage whether that is in-house or in the cloud. Moreover, using information protection tools, business operation plan, disaster management technique it is mandatory to mitigate multi cloud risks. The setups which require the clients to move frequently from one cloud to another and vice versa to get intimated with the cloud operation details, should be avoided to save pressure, burden and time. A security platform should reduce the friction of adoption without requiring you to go through a lengthy defense setup plan.(Microsoft)(Mather et al., 2009)

6. Threats, attacks and vulnerabilities

Current issues:

(i) It often happens that the biggest damage is caused by someone who is already an in-house member of the defense. Insider threats pose a major risk to cloud security. It occurs when people within an organization intentionally or unintentionally compromise security by sharing sensitive information, violating access rights, or introducing malware into the system. Malicious insiders may have specific knowledge of an organization's safety procedures, making it easier for them to bypass security controls and cause serious damage. Current and former employees, contractors and partners, hostile employees of cloud service providers, and even cloud service providers themselves are voluntarily liable for Data breaches, explosions, loss of customer trust, data leakage or theft, authentication issues, human factor bugs and cloud configuration errors. Corporate leaders can be an organization’s reliable friends or its bitter enemy, based on their background or motives. In practice, employees of both the client side and CSPs side may act hostile for reasons such as financial gain. (Samani et al, 2015)(Miller,2021).

(ii) An environment’s overall vulnerability is called its attack region. With each new assignment, the attack region also grows. If you don't manage this well, once you get attacked your infrastructure will be affected in ways you never knew existed. Subtle information leaks that open the door to attacks are part of the attack region. Due to the nature of the internet and the cloud, you are always exposed to the outside world. This can be critical to your company's day-to-day operations. Even though cloud service providers (CSPs) invest heavily in security measures, they are still vulnerable. When choosing a CSP, organizations must exhibit unchallenged diligence to ensure they have stringent security procedures, strong data encryption, and transparent response plans. (Kim et al.)(Kumar et al., 2024).

(iii) The cloud environment is particularly vulnerable to leakage of sensitive data. For more than 50% of organizations, information breaches are considered a big threat to the public cloud. Another issue is that the cloud environment is especially designed to enable data sharing, leaving it easy for users to share data with unauthenticated users or make false security set up false . Cloud storage breaches occur when sensitive data is copied, studied, theft or misused by people outside the company's workplace. Even most of the time, data breaches can occur when the data owner does not know it . Sometimes, the owner cannot know that some item has been stolen until the thief is notified or the item is offered for sale online. (Kim et al.)(Mather et al.,2009)

(iv) Sometimes system defects are flaws in the CSP and may be used to compromise the fundamental principle of security like non-repudiation, integrity work etc . Examples include zero-day vulnerabilities, missing patches, bugs or bad configurations, and weak or bad credentials which attackers can easily penetrate. Providing network access and remote software management over the web are the major features provided by cloud service. Therefore, it can create security vulnerabilities in internet browsers and in cloud application software. Vulnerabilities can be found in user identities and logins, system layers etc. For example, the current infrastructure does not have hypervisor capability. Hypervisor handles virtual machines and makes multiple os to run on a single device. A compromised hypervisor can cause all virtual machines associated with it to enter a failed state. (Samani et al, 2015)(Subramanian 2018)

(v) Hijacking account takeovers is a threat to cloud users. Password reuse and simple passwords are just two examples of poor password hygiene that plagues many people. This problem further compounds the damage caused by phishing attacks and data breaches, as you can use the same stolen password on multiple accounts. Cybercriminals can send phishing emails or text messages to employees and steal their login information. From here, they can access files hosted in the cloud, perform malicious acts and steal confidential information. (Vacca, 2017)

(vi) Ransom ware poses a threat to businesses and cybercriminals are now developing this malware specifically for cloud services. Attackers can use a variety of ransomware tactics to attack cloud deployments. Some involve targeting file-sharing services that are synced to a cloud platform. Ransom cloud attacks, which use phishing to target cloud email services for account takeover and propagate even more ransom ware. Even attackers target large cloud-hosting providers such as Google and Amazon Web Services to ensure bigger and more predictable payouts by threatening to encrypt data across their entire cloud infrastructure. These attacks can have devastating consequences, as victims can lose access to critical data and have to pay significant ransoms to regain access.(Vacca, 2017) (Kumar et al., 2024).

(vii) Denial of service or DOS attack is a known attack in cloud network. This type of attack overloads a networked system with a huge number of client-side requests and ultimately the server fails to serve the normal requests. It has two categories, denial of service and distributed denial of service .

(a) Denial of service attacks aim to resist normal cloud customers from accessing their resources because this type of attack eats a lot of physical memory and connection bandwidth. If an attacker or hacker can achieve this, it will usually slow down the system and cloud users will not be able to run the regular service right after attack. DoS normally occurs in older or outdated systems which becomes overloaded with data and then inefficient. This is not the same case as hacking, but the result of this attack renders the system not accessible. During a DoS attack, system resources are wasted, and this can cause speed and stability issues. It makes it difficult to install an application or determine the source of the interference. (Miller,2021)

(b) In a distributed denial of service or DDoS attack situation, cybercriminals attack a network with so much malware that the network cannot function or communicate normally. This will stop the normal operation of the site. DDoS attacks prevent users from accessing the network. In recent years, attackers have used DDoS attacks to target the cloud by interfering with business operations, issuing ransoms, and even stealing financial or private data. DDoS attacks can be cumbersome to detect and mitigate, especially when attackers use botnets or other sophisticated methods to launch their attacks. DDoS attacks can be launched from multiple attack sites simultaneously. AWS cloud suffered a DDoS attack three years ago and eventually had to stop a 2.3 Tbps attack. (Miller,2021)

A zombie attack can be a demonstration of DDoS attack in which a malicious activity targets to flood the server's network by sending countless client requests from harmless hosts and consequently the cloud gets overloaded with number of requests, thus depleting its resources. (Miller,2021)(Mather et al.,2009)

(viii) Meet-in-the-middle or man in the middle attack is another sophisticated yet dangerous attacks which use specially designed devices and techniques. If secured socket layer protocol or secured shell protocol is not configured correctly, attacker may grab the information shared between the parties involved. In case of clouds, attackers can attack the connection between the data centers. (Miller,2021)(Kumar et al., 2024)

Preventive measures:

(i) Businesses use detection tools to identify intruders and to prevent DoS attacks. The system helps identify abnormal traffic and provide early warning based on user data and behavioral changes. Detection tools can work as a warning bell for security management. An analysis of traffic to determine its location or identify good traffic or identify problems to assist in traffic distribution and then eliminate unnecessary traffic can block DoS. Blocking IP addresses from attack can help prevent DoS attacks. (Samani et al, 2015)(Kim et al.)
(ii) Establish security zones in all areas and allow only necessary and permitted traffic through the exit. If possible, give each application environment (development, deployment, and production) its own cloud account.
(iii) Purpose should determine resources and access. For example, a developer who only submits code should not have administrative access to their entire cloud account. Developers should not access the entire working system. Just give them what they are supposed to work on . There are tools available to help modify the sizes with privileges of user accounts. (Miller,2021)
(iv) Organizations should implement stringent controls, employ regular staffing, and implement data protection strategies to reduce insider threats. To protect against insider threats, organizations need to use security awareness services, repair faulty cloud servers, and implement tight controls over critical systems. Organizations must update their security practices to implement in-the-box security tools, protect against coding, and implement time-based security measures. (Samani et al, 2015)(Miller,2021)
(v) By identifying vulnerabilities, security risks from failure can be greatly reduced using regular Identity and Access Management (IAM) practices. IAM provides complete control and visibility in centralized cloud management by determining who can access what and allowing administrators to authorize someone to monitor specific resources. (Kumar et al., 2024)
(vi) To prevent unauthorized transfer, organizations have begun to fully transition to a zero-trust model, there the security monitoring is self-managed to ensure the minimal privileged permission to information. Use CSP best practices, monitoring and discovery capabilities to detect and prevent attacks. Because data is dispersed across multiple locations and managed by multiple responsibilities, employees need to learn how to use cloud storage. Evaluate the cloud service provider's resistance power against security violation, compliance standard with the regulations, regulatory approvals, and SLAs that is service level agreement. Client-side encryption assistance is a good option against malicious actors within the CSP. However, in general, encryption is not every time possible due to its

expenses. Proper classification of data helps establish different controls, and in case of an unauthorized transfer, the impact should be assessed, and remedial actions are called. (Samani et al, 2015)(Miller,2021)

(vii) Proper contingency plan is needed to provide safety from hijacking. Appropriate emergency plans should be implemented using a risk management system in case of some disaster or militant attacks. Make sure your online provider has a business continuity plan that outlines strategies for protecting data stored on its servers. Ask them how often they test security issues in the cloud to make sure everything is working properly. (Mather et al.,2009)

7. Access control and identity management

Current issues:

(i) Access control in cloud is a mechanism which permits or restricts users to access resources. Access control is closely linked to maintaining identity issues and they together can assist with protecting the basic principles of information security. One of the determining factors to the accessibility can be the fact whether it is public model or private model or any other because public, hybrid cloud allows shared access while private cloud does not allow shared access (Samani et al, 2015)

(ii) Verify the identity of the user by verifying the user's registration when entering the system. It is accomplished by login name and passwords. But managing many login names and passwords to acccss cntcrprisc scrviccs can diminish productivity and affect application maintenance. (Miller,2021)

(iii) If you hold the keys to the kingdom then identity and access to the CSP platform is everything an attacker needs ; you not only access the whole kingdom but also reconfigure it. The loss of Identification and access management challenges cloud security and destructs cloud service adoption. Both the CSP and the end users are accountable for managing this process. Today's attackers are not trying to brute force any more on their way into business transactions, and while there are several ways to misuse valuable business credentials, the choice is “avoid being caught by acting as a legitimate user”. (Samani et al, 2015)(Kim et al.)

Preventive measures:

(i) Companies may have thousands of executives and working professionals, and access rights need to be distributed according to the responsibilities and needs of employees. Apply the principle of minimum privilege when it comes to managing information security issues and setup guidelines, strategies and methods for the secure handling and deletion of information. In a public cloud environment, access control becomes very important as all computing is located away from the customer's organization's network area. From the customer organization's perspective, loss of control over resources can be balanced by using tools available to the customer, such as authentication and authorization. (Samani et al, 2015)(Miller,2021)

(ii) Set a precise access management plan to limit access boundaries for users. The access control process defines access rights for different users. For example, the sales department's protocols shouldn't be accessible to the quality testing department and vice versa.

(iii) It is best to track, monitor and manage your cloud data, including resource provisioning issues, multiple accounts of administrators, zombie user accounts, and users by using strong Identity and Access Management (IAM) controls. Single sign-on (SSO) solves the problem of having multiple login names and passwords to run various applications by unifying applications together and removing the need for many login names and passwords while imposing security. (Kumar et al., 2024)

(iv) Cloud security requires strong privacy and access management systems to balance the loss of network resource. IAM plays a key role in today's cybercrime and IAM risks are superset of user access issues. Cloud resources interact with other clouds through IAM. When developing the infrastructure of cloud, particular attention should be paid to evaluating IAM implementation to detect insecure IAM configurations. Organizations are also recommended to adopt two-factor verification, and proceed to follow strict IAM governance, change API keys from time to time, and remove inactive users' records. Organizations can customize and delegate Identity Management as a Service (IDaaS) from the service providers. Many vendors offer cloud services based on identity management e.g. Symplified, Ping Identity. Presently they are taking help of biometric verification, smartcard verification to grant access rights to authenticated users and disallow permission for unauthorized intruders.(Miller, 2021)(Mather et al.,2009).

(v) Tight key management can assist to secure information exchange only between trusted parties Moreover, the exchange process should carry on only when it is necessary . However key management in cryptography causes additional complexities for the increasing number of keys. (Miller,2021)

CONCLUSION

Cloud is not an old, not a new word and evolving at a remarkable speed and turning out to become an essential technology around the world. Cloud is now an integral part of business growth, organizational and personal use and providing new opportunities for improvement. One of the biggest tasks in cloud security is to protect client resources. Due to the limitations of the current classification of securities issues in cloud, an alternative classification method is proposed in this chapter which considers multiple factors in modern cloud systems. The goal is to create a list of cloud security vulnerabilities that would assist anyone who wants to create or use cloud services.

Searching for threats in the cloud is crucial to finding advanced attack techniques that evade detection by traditional security defenses. API security is another important steppingstone of cloud security. One area of significant promise is automation. One of the major goals lies in extracting maximal benefits from the security automation tools to get rid of all possible threats.

This chapter presents various points of cloud security issues generated so far. This text also discusses various preventive steps against the security challenges and presents an up-to-date cauterization of security issues and protections with respect to theoretical as well as commercial cloud framework.

REFERENCES

Amazon Web Services. (n.d.). Disaster recovery options in the cloud. Retrieved from Amazon Web Services, n.d./whitepapers/latest/disaster-recovery-workloads-on-aws/disaster-recovery-options-in-the-cloud.html

Amazon Web Services. (n.d.). Disaster recovery (DR) architecture on AWS part I: Strategies for recovery in the cloud. Retrieved from https://aws.amazon.com/blogs/architecture/disaster-recovery-dr-architecture-on-aws-part-i-strategies-for-recovery-in-the-cloud/

Kim, F., Lee, R., Thurston, J., Pescatore, J., & Bromiley, M. (n.d.). *SANS practical guide to security in the AWS cloud* (Vol. 1). AWS Marketplace.

Kumar, T., Kumar, P., & Namasudra, S. (2024, February). A DNA-based authentication system for securing cloud data storage and transactions. In 2024 11th International Conference on Computing for Sustainable Global Development (INDIACom) (pp. 1692-1698). IEEE.

Kumar, T., Kumar, P., & Namasudra, S. (2024, February). Secure access control of cloud data using DNA computing. In 2024 IEEE International Conference on Computing, Power and Communication Technologies (IC2PCT) (Vol. 5, pp. 1996-2001). IEEE.

Mather, T., Kumaraswamy, S., & Latif, S. (2009). *Cloud security and privacy*. O'Reilly Media.

Microsoft. (n.d.). What is multicloud security? Retrieved from Microsoft/en-us/security/business/security-101/what-is-multicloud-security

Microsoft. (2021). Platform as a service (PaaS). Retrieved from Microsoft, n.d./en-in/overview/what-is-paas/#overview

Miller, L. (2021). *Cloud security for dummies* (3rd Special Edition). John Wiley & Sons.

National Institute of Standards and Technology. (2013). *NIST cloud computing standards roadmap*. U.S. Department of Commerce.

Pathak, R. (n.d.). Cloud security challenges in the age of multi-cloud: Navigating risks. LinkedIn. Retrieved from Linkedin/pulse/cloud-security-challenges-age-multi-cloud-navigating-risks-raj-pathak/

Red Hat. (n.d.). IaaS vs PaaS vs SaaS. Retrieved from https://Red Hat, n.d/en/topics/cloud-computing/iaas-vs-paas-vs-saas

Samani, R., Honan, B., Reavis, J., & Jirasek, V. (2015). *CSA guide to cloud computing: Implementing cloud privacy and security*. Elsevier Syngress.

Subramanian, N., & Jeyaraj, A. (2018). Recent security challenges in cloud computing. *Computers & Electrical Engineering*, 71, 28–42. DOI: 10.1016/j.compeleceng.2018.06.006

Vacca, J. R. (Ed.). (2017). *Cloud computing security: Foundations and challenges*. CRC Press.

Wipro. (n.d.). Overcoming security and compliance challenges in a hybrid multi-cloud environment. Retrieved from https://www.wipro.com/cybersecurity/overcoming-security-and-compliance-challenges-in-a-hybrid-multi-cloud-environment/

Chapter 16
Sustainable Approach With Cloud Transfer Methodology for Affordable Smart Grid FT Services Based on Safety Risk Identification Factor

Anzar Ahmad
https://orcid.org/0000-0002-7168-4556
Graphic Era University, India

Kapil Joshi
https://orcid.org/0000-0003-1097-8347
Uttaranchal University, India

ABSTRACT

The main objective of this paper is to introduce a methodology for security risk assessment-based migration of critical Smart grid functional technology services to the cloud, either on- or off-premise. By security zone, a baseline system architectural diagram for smart grid control systems manufacturing (CSM) was developed. Threats to cloud security could come from incorrectly configured cloud storage, unprotected APIs, data loss, breaches and leaks, and access control. Numerous research groups and earlier publications have extensively examined the security issues connected with cloud computing. Evaluate our methodology on two migrations to the cloud case studies, namely a big distribution network operator (DNO) with a complicated functional technology (FT) environment; and a small DNO that lacks FT capabili-

DOI: 10.4018/979-8-3693-7137-4.ch016

ties, money, and IT staff. Our method will be an invaluable resource for any owner or operator of a smart grid system since there are no risk assessment-based studies that address the issue of transferring smart grid FT services to a cloud computing architecture methodically.

1. INTRODUCTION

With the help of cloud solutions, businesses may easily, adaptable, and affordably move their on-premises software and storage as online solutions and services (Zibaeirad et al., 2024). Cloud solutions offer a robust computing platform. However, cloud environments also bring up some security issues that could prevent people from using them, (Alomar, 2023) and enable remote monitoring and control of the underlying physical processes by operators of other systems, such as electric power systems and food processing units. Numerous studies have been conducted to assess the security issues that cloud computing environments confront and some solutions to these issues have also been put out (Fahim et al., 2024).

This chapter discusses various open research difficulties and challenges that remain in the field of cloud security research, despite the efforts made in this area.

The modern energy system (MES) consists of a wide (SaberiKamarposhti et al., 2024) range of software-intensive services and solutions, such as Maps databases systems (MDS) for asset management, supervisory control and data acquisition for remote monitoring and control, (Kirmani et al., 2022) outage management systems for operators that manage planned and unplanned outages, and meter data management systems for handling enormous amounts of data collected by numerous installed smart meters.

Through implementing the suggested Cloud Transfer Methodology for Smart Grid (CTMS), the cloud computing community's practitioners and academics may be able to gain a comprehensive understanding of the secure strategy for migrating legacy applications to public cloud settings. The author also discusses the necessity to create incident response schedules, disaster recovery plans, risk assessment techniques, and cloud security controls, among additional studies and schedules related to cloud security (Elsisi et al., 2023). Additionally, the report develops chances for future research endeavours by identifying certain necessary cloud security concerns that have not yet been addressed by existing methodologies.

Smart grids present unique cloud migration issues since they are vital infrastructures that need to keep running for the benefit of their owners, clients, and the country. A variety of players are thinking about integrating internet-based computing into their (based) systems since it would enable them to outsource the costs associated with purchasing and maintaining hardware. (Banik et al., 2024) Given that hacks could have an effect on the economy, public safety, and national security, security measures are undoubtedly crucial components of any cloud migration plan.

The work has been split into three sections in addition to this introduction. That provides an overview of the current state of risk assessment, cloud security, and smart grid security in part two. The security risk assessment approach for smart grid FT contexts is codified in the third section (Achaal et al., 2024). This study includes two case studies where the suggested methodology is used to migrate two exceptionally different smart grid FT systems to the (mixed) cloud.

Sustainable Approach with Cloud Transfer" refers to the practice of using cloud computing services in an environmentally friendly and responsible manner, minimizing e-waste and reducing carbon footprint. Some key aspects of a sustainable approach with cloud transfer include: Energy Efficiency: Cloud providers optimize data center energy consumption. Resource Optimization: Cloud services allocate resources dynamically, reducing waste. Data Center Location: Strategically locating data centers to minimize environmental impact. Renewable Energy: Powering data centers with renewable energy sources. E-waste eduction: Responsible disposal and recycling of cloud infrastructure equipment. Carbon Offset: Offsetting carbon emissions from cloud operations.

Benefits: Reduced carbon footprint, Lower energy consumption, Cost savings, Enhanced brand reputation, Compliance with environmental regulations

To adopt a sustainable approach with cloud transfer: Choose cloud providers with strong sustainability commitments. Optimize cloud resource utilization. Monitor and report carbon footprint. Implement sustainable data center practices. Explore renewable energy options.

By embracing sustainable cloud practices, organizations can minimize their environmental impact while benefiting from scalable, on-demand computing resources.

2. LITERATURE REVIEW

An overview of the top three cloud providers—Amazon Internet Service (AIS), Microsoft Azure, and Google Cloud Gateway (GCG)—that businesses are contemplating switching to is given in this section. It also addresses several aspects of the multi-cloud strategy. AIS made 2007, its market debut as the first product (Ghadi et al., 2024). As of February 2024, it offered over 222 services. The feature set, dependability, and expansion of this cloud migration option have led many organizations to view it as the standard option. Azure's competitive price approach is helping it soon overtake AIS as well.

The majority of research on cloud computing applications in power systems comes from cost and performance viewpoints. Cloud computing has the potential to greatly enhance power systems' operating performance (Ketonen and Smolander, 2024). Explains how to install a monolithic Advanced Distribution Management System in the cloud without affecting how well it runs. It also purchased a few well-known cloud computing services, such as Cloud Driver and Blogger.

The risk of vendor lock-in is one of the primary reasons why the conventional use of cloud services, which concentrated on using a single provider, is no longer appropriate in 2024. Moving to several clouds can present certain difficulties for cloud security experts, but it can also aid in the creation of a more successful disaster recovery strategy that potential for increased difficulties with safety, confidentiality, and customer satisfaction. An increasing number of research studies have addressed privacy and security challenges in the literature to identify effective security solutions. However, a variety of research teams have examined and documented cloud migration security measures (Murthy et al., 2024). Intelligent grids and concludes that availability and integrity are of more relevance in time-critical industrial control systems, while confidentiality is vital in enterprise services supplied to the cloud or documents (Kumar et al., 2024).

A novel paradigm of adaptable and efficient computing called cloud computing is being investigated as a potential remedy to ensure the sustainability of company IT based on Microsoft's methodology; the authors recommend a software-centric threat analysis-based cloud migration strategy for intelligent power grids.

Among these processes, an average method of migrating an outdated system to the cloud must include certain essential ideas such as synchronizing/replicating system components, allowing elasticity, protecting the database, performing temporary faults, separate tenants, encrypting messages, obfuscating codes, modifying the network, and checking the system. Bridge that gap by laying forth a technique that any smart grid owner or operator in need of to create an ideal cloud migration program might use (França et al., 2024). Due diligence, lack of control over cloud data facilities, inadequate integration of security into the service creation procedure, data breaches, data leakage or reduction, account or service traffic hijacking, insecure interfaces, malicious insiders, lack of caution, shared technology vulnerabilities, compromised governance, exclusivity deprived or incomplete data deletion, and a broken chain are some of the security challenges and issues surrounding the adoption of the cloud.

3. RESEARCH QUESTIONS AND METHODOLOGY

This part outlines the research questions that the study intends to address. It then goes on to discuss the method of inquiry used to create the plan and locate online safety papers (Alghawli and Radivilova, 2024). Recently published journal and conference articles with the terms “cloud migration” and “cloud safety” - “cloud Planning” in their titles were reviewed for this study's research. The author studied security issues from the perspectives of aggressive and defensive security for each task. A pictorial diagram of cloud migration, cloud safety, and cloud planning area is as shown in figure 1.

Insiders, state-sponsored actors deploying sophisticated persistent hazards (SPH), or professional attackers carrying out assaults are most likely the sources of dangers particular to smart grids (George, 2024). The main source of articles on subjects related to computer science and cybercrime is these electronic databases.

Figure 1. Cloud migration, Cloud safety and cloud planning Areas

4. AVERAGE CLOUD MIGRATION PROCESS

When choosing whether to maintain an FT service on-premise or move it to a social cloud, that suggest using the following baseline cloud migration plan (George, 2024). A cloud migration process is shown in figure 2.

- If service immediately engage with physical equipment and don't require a lot of processing or storage remain on-premise.
- Maintain computers in the control room so that administrators may oversee and manage the smart electrical system from a visually guarded location.
- Transfer all services with considerable (C) or minimal (M) risk to the social cloud.
- Evaluate all each Batter (B) security solutions, and if they have significant processing or storage needs, deploy them to the community cloud.

The aforementioned guidelines could, of course, be adjusted by the risk of smart grid operators, which corresponds to their readiness to take on certain degrees of risk.

Figure 2. Cloud Migration Process

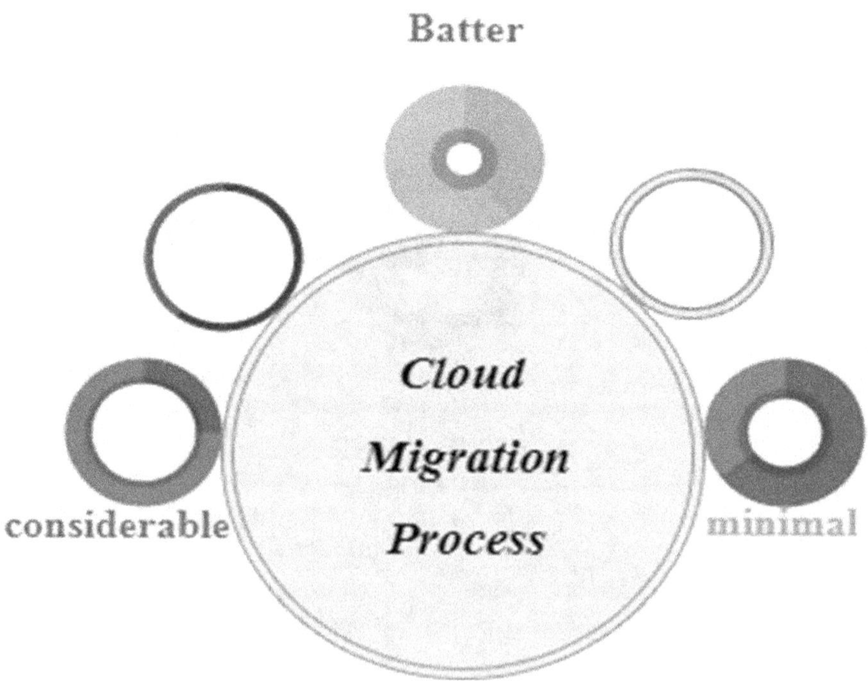

5. PROTECTED CLOUD MIGRATION RECORDS / GUIDEBOOK

To make sure a secure migration to the cloud, cloud security documentation must be created and automated. Some of these media outlets, like the Disaster Recovery Planning, Cloud Security Controls, and Incident Response Risk Evaluation Methodology (Chanthati, 2024), are covered in this section.

The risk assessment technique discussed in the preceding sections was used to two notably distinct case studies, each of which included the migration of a portion of an FT system to the cloud by a different kind of distribution network operator (DNO). For a sizable, multi state, or global DNO, suggested a hybrid cloud-based system in the first case study after conducting a risk assessment.

The Event Response (ER) Guidebook

This ought to take into account the emergency response procedures that were discussed before, including protection, removal, and restoration. The document has to be reviewed and processed when it is developed.

Plan to design future cloud-based framework diagrams and explain our risk analysis methodology. That created an intelligent grid FT control system framework that is somewhat reduced to serve as a reference for any FT-to-cloud migration (Aslam et al., 2024). Confining the incident, eliminating it, recuperating from it, and carrying out post-event procedures, such as post-mortems and feedback systems.

Reconstruction Natural events

This manual will provide a recovery strategy if data is lost or stolen. This document's main focus is on techniques to make sure that information recovery and backup procedures are efficient in delivering high data access, adaptability, and confidence at a fair price. Difficulty increases when the transferred systems are used for tasks related to homeland security, defence, national security, or reconstruction relief, where the importance of service stability is increased.

Evaluating risk Methods

The possible security and concerns about data privacy related to cloud migration will be outlined in this document. Others think that danger and risk methods are becoming more difficult as a result of hacks on power grids.

The Security team for the project was assigned the responsibility of enhancing current approaches to tackle the interdependencies inherent in a smart grid (Rani et al., 2024). Security threats are crucial approaches to risk mitigation from cloud security breaches.

Cloud Safety Rules

Developers can use the present work as assistance when it comes to cloud safety policies that need to be taken into account when moving on-premises apps and safety to the cloud (Joshi et al., 2023). Creating this document could facilitate its execution.

Safety is a major obstacle to the widespread implementation of any of the aforementioned cloud computing delivery models. This difficulty increases when the migrated tools are used for tasks related to homeland safety, defence, national safety, or disaster response, where the importance of availability has increased (Naudiyal et al., 2024). Towards this aim, various precautions and strategies are initially pondered and, finally, among them, the most beneficial are selected enforced by an application creator and then applied as rules of thumb for programmers. Figure 3. Shows the protected cloud migration record process.

Figure 3. Protected Cloud Migration Records

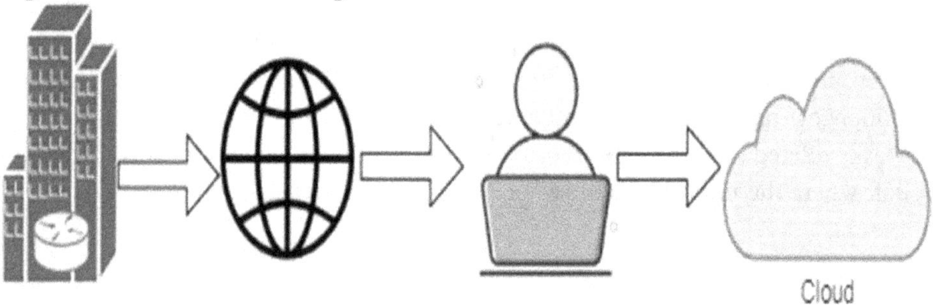

6. DANGERS TO CREDIBILITY

This section discusses the dangers to the validity of the recommended solutions and the author's efforts (Chakraborty et al., 2021) to mitigate those risks. To create the SCMS and the associated tasks/projects to secure cloud transformation, as well as to locate cloud security Records / Guidebooks, the author primarily relied on thorough research of the literature. Like any review of this type, some crucial references were likely missed (Tiwari et al., 2022). The author assessed the abstracts, introductions, and conclusions of papers that included the terms "cloud migration," "cloud safety," and "cloud planning" in their titles in an attempt to lower this risk.

7. COMPARISONS OF CASE STUDY WITH EXISTING METHODOLOGY

In this section, this study is need analyse the specific dimension of risk identification and its process with existing methodology like as standard methodologies (e.g., SWOT analysis, HAZOP, and FMEA) and this is for broad applicability across different sectors and project and it also used for usually generic and may not address niche or contextual risks unless adapted. It is also compared with existing methodologies where it is designed to systematically identify risks through structured frameworks and effectiveness depends on the completeness of input data and adherence to protocols.

8. CONCLUSION

Since cloud computing is a relatively new technology, it presents a unique set of security risks and opportunities for intrusions. A study led us to the conclusion that there aren't any danger assessment-based projects that particularly address the issue of systematically moving smart grid FT safety to a new cloud-based architecture. Therefore, this article recommended implementing a Cloud Transfer Methodology for Smart Grid (CTMS) as a safe route to cloud migration.

This provided an initial smart grid FT structure that was in line. When dangers, chances, and possible effects unique to the smart grid are recognized. The following step is to execute experimental research including the migration of programs and features to cloud settings to evaluate and assess the efficacy of the suggested CTMS and cloud safety guidebooks. The author hopes to create a dynamic optimizing methodology for a cloud-based privilege management system that is both secure and forgiving as a future area of study.

Our initial case study had a sizable DNO with sophisticated FT functionalities. We hypothesized that there were several IT and FT services, highly skilled and driven threat sources, and potential entry points from unknown sources either communication systems or actual field equipment access.

Useable safety, which aims to ensure safety techniques and products are practical by those who need them, is what is meant by "safe and comfortable."

REFERENCES

Achaal, B., Adda, M., Berger, M., Ibrahim, H., & Awde, A. (2024). Study of smart grid cyber-security, examining architectures, communication networks, cyber-attacks, countermeasure techniques, and challenges. *Cybersecurity*, 7(1), 10. DOI: 10.1186/s42400-023-00200-w PMID: 38707764

Alghawli, A. S. A., & Radivilova, T. (2024). Resilient cloud cluster with DevSecOps security model, automates a data analysis, vulnerability search and risk calculation. *Alexandria Engineering Journal*, 107, 136–149. DOI: 10.1016/j.aej.2024.07.036

Aslam, M., Rahim, L. A., Watada, J., Rubab, S., Khan, M. A., AlQahtani, S. A., & Gadekallu, T. R. (2024). Cloud migration framework clustering method for social decision support in modernizing the legacy system. *Transactions on Emerging Telecommunications Technologies*, 35(4), e4863. DOI: 10.1002/ett.4863

Banik, S., Rogers, M., Mahajan, S. M., Emeghara, C. M., Banik, T., & Craven, R. (2024). Survey on Vulnerability Testing in the Smart Grid. *IEEE Access : Practical Innovations, Open Solutions*, 12, 119146–119173. DOI: 10.1109/ACCESS.2024.3449642

Chakraborty, A., Jindal, M., Khosravi, M. R., Singh, P., Shankar, A., & Diwakar, M. (2021). A Secure IoT-Based Cloud Platform Selection Using Entropy Distance Approach and Fuzzy Set Theory. *Wireless Communications and Mobile Computing*, 2021(1), 6697467. DOI: 10.1155/2021/6697467

Chanthati, S. R. (2024). Artificial Intelligence-Based Cloud Planning and Migration to Cut the Cost of Cloud Sasibhushan Rao Chanthati. *American Journal of Smart Technology and Solutions*, 3(2), 13–24. DOI: 10.54536/ajsts.v3i2.3210

Elsisi, M., Su, C. L., & Ali, M. N. (2023). Design of reliable IoT systems with deep learning to support resilient demand side management in smart grids against adversarial attacks. *IEEE Transactions on Industry Applications*.

Fahim, K. E., Islam, M. R., Shihab, N. A., Olvi, M. R., Al Jonayed, K. L., & Das, A. S. (2024). Transformation and future trends of smart grid using machine and deep learning: A state-of-the-art review. *International Journal of Applied*, 13(3), 583–593. DOI: 10.11591/ijape.v13.i3.pp583-593

França, R. P., Bonacin, R., & Monteiro, A. C. B. (2024). An Overview of Data Privacy and Security in Cloud Platforms: Exploring the Intersection of Digital Technologies Currently. *Digital Cultural Heritage*, 21-39.

George, A. S. (2024). Consequences of Enterprise Cloud Migration on Institutional Information Technology Knowledge. *Partners Universal Innovative Research Publication*, 2(2), 38–55.

Ghadi, Y. Y., Mazhar, T., Aurangzeb, K., Haq, I., Shahzad, T., Laghari, A. A., & Anwar, M. S. (2024). Security risk models against attacks in smart grid using big data and artificial intelligence. *PeerJ. Computer Science*, 10, e1840. DOI: 10.7717/peerj-cs.1840 PMID: 38686008

Joshi, K., Sharma, R., Singh, N., & Sharma, B. (2023). Digital World of Cloud Computing and Wireless Networking: Challenges and Risks. In *Applications of Artificial Intelligence in Wireless Communication Systems* (pp. 36-47). IGI Global.

Ketonen, T., & Smolander, K. (2024, November). Strategies and Challenges in Cloud-to-Cloud Migration Using Infrastructure as Code. In *International Conference on Product-Focused Software Process Improvement* (pp. 3-18). Cham: Springer Nature Switzerland.

Kirmani, S., Mazid, A., Khan, I. A., & Abid, M. (2022). A survey on IoT-enabled smart grids: Technologies, architectures, applications, and challenges. *Sustainability (Basel)*, 15(1), 717. DOI: 10.3390/su15010717

Kumar, T., Kumar, P., & Namasudra, S. (2024). User revocation-enabled access control model using identity-based signature in the cloud computing environment. *International Journal of Interactive Multimedia and Artificial Intelligence*, 9(1), 127–136. DOI: 10.9781/ijimai.2024.05.001

Murthy, J. S., Siddesh, G. M., & Srinivasa, K. G. (Eds.). (2024). *Cloud Security: Concepts, Applications and Practices*. CRC Press. DOI: 10.1201/9781003455448

Naudiyal, A., Joshi, K., Memoria, M., Gill, R., & Singh, A. Next Era of Computing with Cloud Computing and IoT in Different Disciplines. In *The Next Generation Innovation in IoT and Cloud Computing with Applications* (pp. 52–73). CRC Press. DOI: 10.1201/9781003406723-4

Rani, D., Ghosh, S., & Dagiuklas, T. (2024, June). Reactive vs Predictive Live Migration in Edge Cloud. In *ICC 2024-IEEE International Conference on Communications* (pp. 4030-4035). IEEE. DOI: 10.1109/ICC51166.2024.10622687

SaberiKamarposhti, M., Kamyab, H., Krishnan, S., Yusuf, M., Rezania, S., Chelliapan, S., & Khorami, M. (2024). A comprehensive review of AI-enhanced smart grid integration for hydrogen energy: Advances, challenges, and future prospects. *International Journal of Hydrogen Energy*.

Tiwari, A., Kumar, S., Baishwar, N., Vishwakarma, S. K., & Singh, P. (2022, September). Efficient Cloud Orchestration Services in Computing. In *Proceedings of 3rd International Conference on Machine Learning, Advances in Computing, Renewable Energy and Communication: MARC 2021* (pp. 739-746). Singapore: Springer Nature Singapore.

Zibaeirad, A., Koleini, F., Bi, S., Hou, T., & Wang, T. (2024). A comprehensive survey on the security of smart grid: Challenges, mitigations, and future research opportunities. *arXiv preprint arXiv:2407.07966*. Alomar, M. A. (2023). An IOT based smart grid system for advanced cooperative transmission and communication. *Physical Communication, 58*, 102069.

Compilation of References

Abdulsalam, Y. S., & Hedabou, M. (2021). Security and privacy in cloud computing: Technical review. *Future Internet*, 14(1), 11. DOI: 10.3390/fi14010011

Achaal, B., Adda, M., Berger, M., Ibrahim, H., & Awde, A. (2024). Study of smart grid cyber-security, examining architectures, communication networks, cyber-attacks, countermeasure techniques, and challenges. *Cybersecurity*, 7(1), 10. DOI: 10.1186/s42400-023-00200-w PMID: 38707764

Adahman, Z. (2022). Zero-Trust Architecture and Its Cost-Effectiveness on Network Security. North Dakota State University. https://doi.org/DOI: 10.48655/10365/32683

Adhikari, M., & Amgoth, T. (2018). Heuristic-based load-balancing algorithm for IaaS cloud. *Future Generation Computer Systems*, 81, 156–165. DOI: 10.1016/j.future.2017.10.035

Agarwal, A., & Mital, M. (2021). Emerging trends in cloud computing: AI and edge computing integration. *International Journal of Cloud Computing and Services Science*, 10(1), 22–35. DOI: 10.11591/ijccs.v10i1.32316

Ahmadi, S. (2024) Challenges and Solutions in Network Security for Serverless Computing. International Journal of Current Science Research and Review ISSN: 2581-8341. Volume 07. Issue 01 January 2024. DOI: DOI: 10.47191/ijcsrr/V7-i1-23

Ahmadieh, E., & El Madhoun, N. (2024). Comparative E-Voting Security Evaluation: Multi-Modal Authentication Approaches. *THE SIXTH INTERNATIONAL CONFERENCE ON BLOCKCHAIN COMPUTING AND APPLICATIONS (BCCA 2024).*

Ahmad, W., Rasool, A., Javed, A. R., Baker, T., & Jalil, Z. (2021). Cyber security in iot-based cloud computing: A comprehensive survey. *Electronics (Basel)*, 11(1), 16. DOI: 10.3390/electronics11010016

Ahmed, F., & Al Nejam, A. (2013). Cloud computing: Technical challenges and cloudsim functionalities. *International Journal of Science and Research, 2*(2319-7064), 10.

Ahmed, H. A. S., & Zolkipli, M. F. (2016). Data Security Issues. In *Cloud Computing: Review*. Universiti Malaysia Pahang Publishing., DOI: 10.15282/ijsecs.2.2016.5.0016

Akbar, H., Zubair, M., & Malik, M. S. (2023). The security issues and challenges in cloud computing. *International Journal for Electronic Crime Investigation*, 7(1), 13–32. DOI: 10.54692/ijeci.2023.0701125

Akbar, M., Ahmad, I., Mirza, M., Ali, M., & Barmavatu, P. (2024). Enhanced authentication for de-duplication of big data on cloud storage system using machine learning approach. *Cluster Computing*, 27(3), 3683–3702. DOI: 10.1007/s10586-023-04171-y

Al Hachemi, S. A. G. A. (2022). Cloud Computing Services with Minimal Redundancy, Storage, and Effective Processing Capabilities. *Texas Journal of Engineering and Technology*, 9, 143–149.

Al Shinwan, M., Shdefat, A., Mostafa, N., Al Sokkar, A., Alsarhan, T., & Almajali, D. (2022). Integrated cloud computing and blockchain systems: A review. International Journal of Data and Network Science.

Alansari, S., Paci, F., & Sassone, V. (2017). A Distributed Access Control System for Cloud Federations. 2017 IEEE 37th International Conference on Distributed Computing Systems (ICDCS), 2131-2136. DOI: 10.1109/ICDCS.2017.241

Albino, V., Berardi, U., & Dangelico, R. M. (2015). Smart cities: Definitions, dimensions, performance, and initiatives. *Journal of Urban Technology*, 22(1), 3–21. DOI: 10.1080/10630732.2014.942092

Albugmi, A., Alassafi, M. O., Walters, R., & Wills, G. (2016). Data security in cloud computing. In *Proceedings of the Fifth International Conference on Future Generation Communication Technology (FGCT 2016).*

Aldossary, Md. (2021). A Review of Energy-Related Cost Issues and Prediction Models in Cloud Computing Environments. *Computer Systems Science and Engineering*, 36(2), •••.

Alghawli, A. S. A., & Radivilova, T. (2024). Resilient cloud cluster with DevSecOps security model, automates a data analysis, vulnerability search and risk calculation. *Alexandria Engineering Journal*, 107, 136–149. DOI: 10.1016/j.aej.2024.07.036

Alhaisoni, M. (2016). On the Advancements in Cloud Computing Technology: An Overview.

Ali, M., Khan, S. U., & Vasilakos, A. V. (2015). Security and privacy issues in cloud computing: A survey. Journal of Cloud Computing: Advances. *Systems and Applications*, 4(1), 1–35. DOI: 10.1186/s13677-015-0037-2

Ali, M., Khan, S. U., & Vasilakos, A. V. (2015). Security in cloud computing: Opportunities and challenges. *Information Sciences*, 305, 357–383. DOI: 10.1016/j.ins.2015.01.025

Alimjon, D. (2022). Problems of data replication in distribution systems. *ACADEMICIA: An International Multidisciplinary Research Journal*, 12(5), 1119–1128. DOI: 10.5958/2249-7137.2022.00585.7

Alkhalifah, E. S. (2024). Password based authentication for web based graphics computing services retrieval in cloud. *Multimedia Tools and Applications*, 83(36), 1–23. DOI: 10.1007/s11042-024-19044-8

Almubairik, A., Malik, M. S. A., Alotaibi, M., Hossain, M. S., & Ashraf, M. S. (2022). Toward comprehensive cloud security frameworks: Analysis, challenges, and future directions. *IEEE Access : Practical Innovations, Open Solutions*, 10, 73458–73475. DOI: 10.1109/ACCESS.2022.3183064

Almulla, S. A., & Yeun, C. Y. (2010, March). Cloud computing security management. In *2010 Second International Conference on Engineering System Management and Applications* (pp. 1-7). IEEE.

Alohali, M. A., Al-Wesabi, F. N., Hilal, A. M., Goel, S., Gupta, D., & Khanna, A. (2022). Artificial intelligence enabled intrusion detection systems for cognitive cyber-physical systems in industry 4.0 environment. *Cognitive Neurodynamics*, 16(5), 1045–1057. DOI: 10.1007/s11571-022-09780-8 PMID: 36237400

Alouffi, B., Hasnain, M., Alharbi, A., Alosaimi, W., Alyami, H., & Ayaz, M. (2021). A systematic literature review on cloud computing security: Threats and mitigation strategies. *IEEE Access : Practical Innovations, Open Solutions*, 9, 57792–57807. DOI: 10.1109/ACCESS.2021.3073203

Alshareef, H. N. (2023). Current development, challenges, and future trends in cloud computing: A survey. *International Journal of Advanced Computer Science and Applications*, 14(3). Advance online publication. DOI: 10.14569/IJACSA.2023.0140337

Althobaiti, M. M., Kumar, K. P. M., Gupta, D., Kumar, S., & Mansour, R. F. (2021). An intelligent cognitive computing based intrusion detection for industrial cyber-physical systems. *Measurement*, 186, 110145. DOI: 10.1016/j.measurement.2021.110145

AlZain, M. A., Soh, B., & Pardede, E. (2011). Mcdb: Using multi-clouds to ensure security in cloud computing. In *Proceedings of the IEEE 9th International Conference on Dependable, Autonomic and Secure Computing (DASC '11)* (pp. 784–791). DOI: 10.1109/DASC.2011.133

Amazon Web Services. (2020). *Shared Responsibility Model*. Retrieved from https://aws.amazon.com/compliance/shared-responsibility-model/

Amazon Web Services. (n.d.). Disaster recovery (DR) architecture on AWS part I: Strategies for recovery in the cloud. Retrieved from https://aws.amazon.com/blogs/architecture/disaster-recovery-dr-architecture-on-aws-part-i-strategies-for-recovery-in-the-cloud/

Amazon Web Services. (n.d.). Disaster recovery options in the cloud. Retrieved from Amazon Web Services, n.d./whitepapers/latest/disaster-recovery-workloads-on-aws/disaster-recovery-options-in-the-cloud.html

Anandappa, M., & Mudnal, M. K. (2024). Cloud computing and security issues in the cloud. Journal of Scientific Research and Technology, 59-66.

Andersson, S. (2021). Trust as a factor in the information classification process. Luleå tekniska universitet, Institutionen för system- och rymdteknik.

Anter, A. M., Azar, A. T., El-Bendary, N., Hassanien, A. E., & Abu ElSoud, M. "Automatic computer aided segmentation for liver and hepatic lesions using hybrid segmentations techniques," in *2013 Federated Conference on Computer Science and Information Systems (FedCSIS)*, Kraków, Poland, Sep. 8-11, 2013.

Apeh, A. J., Hassan, A. O., Oyewole, O. O., Fakeyede, O. G., Okeleke, P. A., & Adaramodu, O. R. (2023). GRC strategies in modern cloud infrastructures: A review of compliance challenges. *Computer Science & IT Research Journal*, 4(2), 111–125. DOI: 10.51594/csitrj.v4i2.609

Arif, H., Kumar, A., Fahad, M., & Hussain, H. K. (2023). Future Horizons: AI-Enhanced Threat Detection in Cloud Environments: Unveiling Opportunities for Research. *International Journal of Multidisciplinary Sciences and Arts*, 2(2), 242–251. DOI: 10.47709/ijmdsa.v2i2.3452

Armbrust, M., Fox, A., Griffith, R., Joseph, A. D., Katz, R. H., Konwinski, A., Lee, G., Patterson, D., Rabkin, A., Stoica, I., & Zaharia, M. (2010). A view of cloud computing. *Communications of the ACM*, 53(4), 50–58. DOI: 10.1145/1721654.1721672

Arshad, J., Townend, P., Xu, J., & Jie, W. (2012). *Cloud computing security: opportunities and pitfalls*. IGI Global., DOI: 10.4018/jghpc.2012010104

Arshad, M., Khan, M. S., & Han, K. (2012). *Security issues in cloud computing: Threats, risks and solutions*. In *Proceedings of the 2012 International Conference on Computer Science and Information Systems*.

Arunkumar, J. R. (2023). Study analysis of cloud security challenges and issues in cloud computing technologies. Journal of Science. *Computing and Engineering Research*, 6(8), 6–10.

Ashitha, U., Amulya, A., Sushma, G., Irfana, S., & Saibaba, C. H. M. H. (2024). Strengthening Cloud Security Through Multi-Factor Authentication: A Comprehensive Integration of Diverse Approaches. *2024 International Conference on Electronics, Computing, Communication and Control Technology (ICECCC)*, 1–8. DOI: 10.1109/ICECCC61767.2024.10593923

Asim, M., Junhong, C., Wenyin, L., & Abd El-Latif, A. A. (2023). Artificial intelligence-based secure edge computing systems for IoTDs and smart cities: A survey. *EAI/Springer Innovations in Communication and Computing*, 155-173. DOI: 10.1007/978-3-031-51097-7_13

Aslam, M., Rahim, L. A., Watada, J., Rubab, S., Khan, M. A., AlQahtani, S. A., & Gadekallu, T. R. (2024). Cloud migration framework clustering method for social decision support in modernizing the legacy system. *Transactions on Emerging Telecommunications Technologies*, 35(4), e4863. DOI: 10.1002/ett.4863

Aste, T., Tasca, P., & Di Matteo, T. (2017). Blockchain technologies: The foreseeable impact on society and industry. *Computer*, 50(9), 18–28. DOI: 10.1109/MC.2017.3571064

Atteia, G., El-kenawy, E. M., Samee, N. A., Jamjoom, M. M., Ibrahim, A., Abdelhamid, A. A., Azar, A. T., Khodadadi, N., Ghanem, R. A., & Shams, M. Y. (2023). Adaptive dynamic dipper throated optimization for feature selection in medical data. *Computers, Materials & Continua*, 75(1), 1883–1900. DOI: 10.32604/cmc.2023.031723

Aumasson, J. (2017). *Serious cryptography: A practical introduction to modern encryption*. No Starch Press.

Aviles, M. E. (2015). The impact of cloud computing in supply chain collaborative relationships, collaborative advantage and relational outcomes.

Azhar, I. (2015, March 1). The Interaction Between Artificial Intelligence and Identity & Access Management: An Empirical study. https://papers.ssrn.com/sol3/papers.cfm?abstract_id=3905771

Babar, M., Jan, M. A., He, X., Tariq, M. U., Mastorakis, S., & Alturki, R. (2022). An optimized IoT-enabled big data analytics architecture for edge—Cloud computing. *IEEE Internet of Things Journal*, 10(5), 3995–4005. DOI: 10.1109/JIOT.2022.3157552 PMID: 38046398

Baik, J. (2020). Data Privacy Against Innovation or Against Discrimination?: The Case of the California Consumer Privacy Act (CCPA). Consumer Law eJournal. .DOI: 10.1016/j.tele.2020.101431

Bakshi, A., & Dujodwala, Y. B. (2010, February). Securing cloud from ddos attacks using intrusion detection system in virtual machine. In *2010 second international conference on communication software and networks* (pp. 260-264). IEEE. DOI: 10.1109/ICCSN.2010.56

Balasubramanian, R., & Aramuthan, D. M. (2012). Security problems and possible security approaches in cloud computing. *International Journal of Scientific and Engineering Research*, 3(6), 1–4.

Banik, S., Rogers, M., Mahajan, S. M., Emeghara, C. M., Banik, T., & Craven, R. (2024). Survey on Vulnerability Testing in the Smart Grid. *IEEE Access : Practical Innovations, Open Solutions*, 12, 119146–119173. DOI: 10.1109/ACCESS.2024.3449642

Baraani-Dastjerdi, A., Pieprzyk, J., & Safavi-Naini, R. (1996). *Security in databases: A survey study*. Department of Computer Science, The University of Wollongong.

Barroso, L. A., Dean, J., & Holzle, U. (2003). Web search for a planet: The Google cluster architecture. *IEEE Micro*, 23(2), 22–28. DOI: 10.1109/MM.2003.1196112

Behl, A. (2011, December). Emerging security challenges in cloud computing: An insight to cloud security challenges and their mitigation. In *2011 World Congress on Information and Communication Technologies* (pp. 217-222). Ieee. DOI: 10.1109/WICT.2011.6141247

Bell, C., Broklyn, P., & Egon, A. (2024). Cloud Security and Data Privacy. SSRN Electronic Journal. DOI: 10.2139/ssrn.4904978

Bethencourt, J., Sahai, A., & Waters, B. (2007, May). Ciphertext-policy attribute-based encryption. In *2007 IEEE symposium on security and privacy (SP'07)* (pp. 321-334). IEEE. DOI: 10.1109/SP.2007.11

Bhat, A., Sharma, S., & Badulla, S. Security Issues in Serverless Cloud Computing Architectures. (2024) IEEE International Conference on Computing, Power and Communication Technologies (IC2PCT) pp. 2.

Bilal, K., Malik, S. U. R., Khan, S. U., & Zomaya, A. Y. (2014). Trends and challenges in cloud datacenters. *IEEE Cloud Computing*, 1(1), 10–20. DOI: 10.1109/MCC.2014.26

Bitirgen, K., & Filik, Ü. B. (2023). A hybrid deep learning model for discrimination of physical disturbance and cyber-attack detection in smart grid. *International Journal of Critical Infrastructure Protection*, 40, 100582. DOI: 10.1016/j.ijcip.2022.100582

Bitzer, M., Brinz, N., & Ollig, P. (2021). Disentangling the Concept of Information Security Properties-Enabling Effective Information Security Governance. In ECIS.

Boggs, R., Bozman, J., & Perry, R. (2009). Reducing downtime and business loss: addressing business risk with effective technology. IDC, Tech. Rep.

Boneh, D., & Franklin, M. (2001, August). Identity-based encryption from the Weil pairing. In *Annual international cryptology conference* (pp. 213-229). Berlin, Heidelberg: Springer Berlin Heidelberg. DOI: 10.1007/3-540-44647-8_13

Boroujerdi, M. M., & Nazem, S. (2009). Cloud computing: Changing cogitation about computing. *International Journal of Computer and Information Engineering*, 3(10), 2469–2473.

Boru, D., Kliazovich, D., Granelli, F., Bouvry, P., & Zomaya, A. Y. (2015). Energy-efficient data replication in cloud computing datacenters. *Cluster Computing*, 18(1), 385–402. DOI: 10.1007/s10586-014-0404-x

Borza, L. (2010). Cloud Computing: A step to the future of IT.

Bryman, A. (2016). *Social research methods* (5th ed.). Oxford University Press.

Brynjolfsson, E., Hofmann, M., & Jordan, J. (2010). Cloud Computing: A Strategic Perspective for Information Systems Research. *Communications of the ACM*, 53(11), 98–107.

Buyya, R., Srirama, S. N., Casale, G., Calheiros, R., Simmhan, Y., Varghese, B., Gelenbe, E., Javadi, B., Vaquero, L. M., Netto, M. A. S., Toosi, A. N., Rodriguez, M. A., Llorente, I. M., Vimercati, S. D. C. D., Samarati, P., Milojicic, D., Varela, C., Bahsoon, R., Assuncao, M. D. D., & Shen, H. (2018). A manifesto for future generation cloud computing: Research directions for the next decade. *ACM Computing Surveys*, 51(5), 1–38. DOI: 10.1145/3241737

Cai, F., Zhu, N., He, J., Mu, P., Li, W., & Yu, Y. (2019). Survey of access control models and technologies for cloud computing. *Cluster Computing*, 22(3), 6111–6122. DOI: 10.1007/s10586-018-1850-7

Cassottana, B., Roomi, M. M., Mashima, D., & Sansavini, G. (2023). Resilience analysis of cyber-physical systems: A review of models and methods. *Risk Analysis*, 43(11), 2359–2379. Advance online publication. DOI: 10.1111/risa.14089 PMID: 36646448

Chakraborty, A., Jindal, M., Khosravi, M. R., Singh, P., Shankar, A., & Diwakar, M. (2021). A Secure IoT-Based Cloud Platform Selection Using Entropy Distance Approach and Fuzzy Set Theory. *Wireless Communications and Mobile Computing*, 2021(1), 6697467. DOI: 10.1155/2021/6697467

Chamoun, J. (2024). *Exploring Security Strategies to Enable the Adoption of Internet of Things Devices in the Manufacturing Sector*. Walden University.

Chandramouli, R., Iorga, M., & Chokhani, S. (2013). Cryptographic key management issues and challenges in cloud services. In Secure Cloud Computing (pp. 1-30). DOI: 10.6028/NIST.IR.7956

Chang, Y. C., & Mitzenmacher, M. (2005, June). Privacy preserving keyword searches on remote encrypted data. In *International conference on applied cryptography and network security* (pp. 442-455). Berlin, Heidelberg: Springer Berlin Heidelberg. DOI: 10.1007/11496137_30

Chang, V., Kuo, Y.-H., & Ramachandran, M. (2016). Cloud computing adoption framework: A security framework for business clouds. *Future Generation Computer Systems*, 57, 24–41. DOI: 10.1016/j.future.2015.09.031

Chanthati, S. R. (2024). Artificial Intelligence-Based Cloud Planning and Migration to Cut the Cost of Cloud Sasibhushan Rao Chanthati. *American Journal of Smart Technology and Solutions*, 3(2), 13–24. DOI: 10.54536/ajsts.v3i2.3210

Charanya, R., & Aramudhan, M. (2016, February). Survey on access control issues in cloud computing. In *2016 International Conference on Emerging Trends in Engineering, Technology and Science (ICETETS)* (pp. 1-4). IEEE. DOI: 10.1109/ICETETS.2016.7603014

Chauhan, M., & Shiaeles, S. (2023). An analysis of cloud security frameworks, problems, and proposed solutions. *Network (Bristol, England)*, 3(2), 422–450.

Che, J., Duan, Y., Zhang, T., & Fan, J. (2011). Study on the security models and strategies of cloud computing. In Proceedings of the International Conference on Power Electronics and Engineering Application.</conf>

Che, J., Duan, Y., Zhang, T., & Fan, J. (2011). Study on the security models and strategies of cloud computing. *Procedia Engineering*, 23, 586–593. DOI: 10.1016/j.proeng.2011.11.2551

Cherry, D., & Larock, T. (2011). Database encryption. In Cherry, D. (Ed.), *Securing SQL Server* (pp. 27–71). Syngress.

Choi, Y., & Lee, J. (2022). Emerging security threats and mitigation strategies in cloud environments. *Journal of Cloud Computing: Advances. Systems and Applications*, 11(1), 1–15. DOI: 10.1186/s13677-022-00312-4

Christodorescu, M., Sailer, R., Schales, D. L., Sgandurra, D., & Zamboni, D. (2009, November). Cloud security is not (just) virtualization security: a short paper. In *Proceedings of the 2009 ACM workshop on Cloud computing security* (pp. 97-102). DOI: 10.1145/1655008.1655022

Cinar, B. (2023). The Role of Cloud Service Brokers: Enhancing Security and Compliance in Multi-cloud Environments. Journal of Engineering Research and Reports. .DOI: 10.9734/jerr/2023/v25i10995

Clohessy, T., Acton, T., & Coughlan, C. (2013). Innovating in the Cloud.

Cloud Security Alliance (CSA). (2023). *Cloud Controls Matrix (CCM)*. https://cloudsecurityalliance.org/research/cloud-controls-matrix/

Cloud Security Alliance (CSA). (2023). *Cloud security guidance*. https://cloudsecurityalliance.org/research/

Colelli, R., Magri, F., Panzieri, S., & Pascucci, F. (2021, June). Anomaly-based intrusion detection system for cyber-physical system security. In 2021 29th Mediterranean Conference on Control and Automation (MED) (pp. 428-434). IEEE.

Comert, C., Gul, O. M., Kulhandjian, M., Touazi, A., Ellement, C., Kantarci, B., & D'Amours, C. (2022). Secure design of cyber-physical systems at the radio frequency level: Machine and deep learning-driven approaches, challenges and opportunities. Artificial Intelligence for Cyber-Physical Systems Hardening, 123-154.

Convolbo, M. W., ... "DRASH: A Data Replication-Aware Scheduler in Geo-Distributed Data Centers." Cloud Computing Technology and Science (CloudCom), 2016 IEEE International Conference on. IEEE, 2016. DOI: 10.1109/CloudCom.2016.0056

Conway, G. (2011). Introduction to Cloud Computing. IVI: Innovation Value Institute. https://core.ac.uk/download/297013271.pdf

Copeland, R., Wong, W., Jones, J., & Edmunds, M. (2019). *Using Information Technology at Kaiser Permanente to Support Health Equity*. Consumer Informatics and Digital Health., DOI: 10.1007/978-3-319-96906-0_3

Crampton, J., Martin, K., & Wild, P. (2006, July). On key assignment for hierarchical access control. In *19th IEEE Computer Security Foundations Workshop (CSFW'06)* (pp. 14-pp). IEEE. DOI: 10.1109/CSFW.2006.20

Damiani, E., De Vimercati, S., Foresti, S., Jajodia, S., Paraboschi, S., & Samarati, P. (2007). An experimental evaluation of multi-key strategies for data outsourcing. In *New Approaches for Security, Privacy and Trust in Complex Environments: Proceedings of the IFIP TC-11 22 nd International Information Security Conference (SEC 2007), 14–16 May 2007, Sandton, South Africa 22* (pp. 385-396). Springer US. DOI: 10.1007/978-0-387-72367-9_33

Das, A., Nanda, P., Jain, R., Saini, T., Bhaskar, S., & Mohapatra, H. (2024). Security considerations of SDN networks during DDoS attacks in load balancing. *Advances in Human and Social Aspects of Technology*, 123–140. DOI: 10.4018/979-8-3693-9235-5.ch007

Del Pero, A. S., Wyckoff, P., & Vourc'h, A. (2022). Using Artificial Intelligence in the workplace: What are the main ethical risks? Desai, D. R., & McCarty, M. (2020). The implementation of the General Data Protection Regulation and its impact on European business models. Information Privacy Law eJournal.

Delettre, C., Boudaoud, K., & Riveill, M. (2011, July). Cloud computing, security, and data concealment. In *Proceedings of the 16th IEEE Symposium on Computers and Communications (ISCC '11)* (pp. 424–431). IEEE. Kerkyra, Greece.

Devi, T., & Ganesan, R. (2015). Platform-as-a-Service (PaaS): Model and security issues. *TELKOMNIKA Indonesian Journal of Electrical Engineering*, 15(1), 151–161.

Dey, D., Majumder, A., Agrawal, Y., Tewari, S., & Mohapatra, H. (2024). Smart mobility revolution. *Advances in Electronic Government, Digital Divide, and Regional Development*, •••, 143–164. DOI: 10.4018/979-8-3693-6740-7.ch006

Di Modica, G., Tomarchio, O., Caltcaterra, D., & Cartelli, V. (2018). Implementation of a fault aware cloud service provisioning framework. *2018 IEEE 6th International Conference on Future Internet of Things and Cloud (FiCloud)*, 9-16. https://doi.org/ DOI: 10.1109/FiCloud.2018.00010

Diaby, T., & Rad, B. B. (2017). Cloud computing: A review of the concepts and deployment models. *International Journal of Information Technology and Computer Science*, 9(6), 50–58. DOI: 10.5815/ijitcs.2017.06.07

Diener, E. Assessing subjective well-being: Progress and opportunities. *Social Indicators Research Series*, 26, 421–475. DOI: 10.1007/1-4020-3742-2_16

Dikaiakos, M. D., Katsaros, D., Mehra, P., Pallis, G., & Vakali, A. (2009). Cloud computing: Distributed internet computing for IT and scientific research. *IEEE Internet Computing*, 13(5), 10–13. DOI: 10.1109/MIC.2009.103

Dinadayalan, P., Jegadeeswari, S., & Gnanambigai, D. (2014). Data Security Issues in Cloud Environment and Solutions. *2014 World Congress on Computing and Communication Technologies*. DOI: 10.1109/WCCCT.2014.63

Dobhal, A. (2022). Applications of Cloud ComputingfFor Both it and the Business. https://doi.org/DOI: 10.5281/zenodo.6986175

Donepudi, P. K. (2016). Influence of cloud computing in business: are they robust. *Asian journal of applied science and engineering, 5*(3), 193-196.

Dua, I. S. (2014). Benefits and Security Concerns of Cloud Computing. *International Journal of Scientific and Engineering Research*, 5(1), 404–411.

Ducatel, G. (2015). Identity as a service: A cloud based common capability. *2015 IEEE Conference on Communications and Network Security (CNS)*, 675-679. DOI: 10.1109/CNS.2015.7346886

Duhayyim, M. A., Alissa, K. A., Alrayes, F. S., Alotaibi, S. S., Tag El Din, E. M., Abdelmageed, A. A., Yaseen, I., & Motwakel, A. (2022). Evolutionary-Based Deep Stacked Auto encoder for Intrusion Detection in a Cloud-Based Cyber-Physical System. *Applied Sciences (Basel, Switzerland)*, 12(14), 6875. DOI: 10.3390/app12146875

Dumka, A., Memoria, M., & Ashok, A. (2019). Security and challenges in mobile cloud computing. In *Security Designs for the Cloud*. IoT, and Social Networking., DOI: 10.1002/9781119593171.ch3

Dursun, T., Birinci, F., Alptekin, B., Sertkaya, I., Hasekioglu, O., Tunaboylu, B., & Zaim, S. (2022). Blockchain technology for supply chain management. In *Studies in Big Data*. Springer.

Dutta, A. K., Negi, R., & Shukla, S. K. (2021). Robust multivariate anomaly-based intrusion detection system for cyber-physical systems. In Cyber Security Cryptography and Machine Learning: 5th International Symposium, CSCML 2021, Be'er Sheva, Israel, July 8–9, 2021 [Springer International Publishing.]. *Proceedings*, 5, 86–93.

Educause. (2009). Cloud computing: A new delivery model. EDUCAUSE Review, 44(6), 36- 55.

Eiers, W., Sankaran, G., & Bultan, T. (2023). Quantitative Policy Repair for Access Control on the Cloud. *Proceedings of the 32nd ACM SIGSOFT International Symposium on Software Testing and Analysis*. DOI: 10.1145/3597926.3598078

El Kafhali, S., El Mir, I., & Hanini, M. (2022). Security threats, defense mechanisms, challenges, and future directions in cloud computing. *Archives of Computational Methods in Engineering*, 29(1), 223–246. DOI: 10.1007/s11831-021-09573-y

Elfström, C. J. (2023). Industry preferred implementation practices for security in cloud systems: An exploratory and qualitative analysis of implementation practices for cloud security.

Elsisi, M., Su, C. L., & Ali, M. N. (2023). Design of reliable IoT systems with deep learning to support resilient demand side management in smart grids against adversarial attacks. *IEEE Transactions on Industry Applications*.

Emary, E., Zawbaa, H. M., Hassanien, A. E., Schaefer, G., & Azar, A. T. (2014, July). Retinal blood vessel segmentation using bee colony optimisation and pattern search. In 2014 international joint conference on neural networks (IJCNN) (pp. 1001-1006). IEEE.

Emary, E., Zawbaa, H. M., Hassanien, A. E., Schaefer, G., & Azar, A. T. (2014, July). Retinal vessel segmentation based on possibilistic fuzzy c-means clustering optimised with cuckoo search. In *2014 International Joint Conference on Neural Networks (IJCNN)* (pp. 1792-1796). IEEE.

Emmanuel, R., Chandrashekar, C.M., Laxmidevi, H. & Sharma, P.. (July 2022) The Scope and Research on Cloud Computing Security" International Journal of Advanced Research in Computer and Communication Engineering ISO 3297:2007. Vol. 11. Issue 7.

Fahim, K. E., Islam, M. R., Shihab, N. A., Olvi, M. R., Al Jonayed, K. L., & Das, A. S. (2024). Transformation and future trends of smart grid using machine and deep learning: A state-of-the-art review. *International Journal of Applied*, 13(3), 583–593. DOI: 10.11591/ijape.v13.i3.pp583-593

Fatima, E., Sumra, I. A., & Naveed, R. (2024). A Comprehensive Survey on Security Threats and Challenges in Cloud Computing Models (SaaS, PaaS and IaaS). *Journal of Computing & Biomedical Informatics*, 7(01), 537–544.

França, R. P., Bonacin, R., & Monteiro, A. C. B. (2024). An Overview of Data Privacy and Security in Cloud Platforms: Exploring the Intersection of Digital Technologies Currently. *Digital Cultural Heritage*, 21-39.

Frantsvog, D., Seymour, T., & John, F. (2012). Cloud computing. *International Journal of Management & Information Systems (Online)*, 16(4), 317.

Friedman, R., & Mosse, D. (1999). Load-balancing schemes for high-throughput distributed fault-tolerant servers. *Journal of Parallel and Distributed Computing*, 59(3), 475–488. DOI: 10.1006/jpdc.1999.1582

Fu, Y., & Sun, B. (2012). undefined. *2012 IEEE 2nd International Conference on Cloud Computing and Intelligence Systems*, 228-233. https://doi.org/DOI: 10.1109/CCIS.2012.6664402

Furuberg, I. L., & Øseth, M. (2023). *From Password to Passwordless: Exploring User Experience Obstacles to the Adoption of FIDO2 Authentication*. NTNU.

Gali, M., & Mahamkali, A. (2022). A distributed deep Meta learning based task offloading framework for smart city Internet of things with edge-cloud computing. *Journal of Internet Services and Information Security*, 12(4), 224–237. DOI: 10.58346/JISIS.2022.I4.016

Garg, R. (2020). MCDM-based parametric selection of cloud deployment models for an academic organization. *IEEE Transactions on Cloud Computing*, 10(2), 863–871. DOI: 10.1109/TCC.2020.2980534

Gavou, T. P., Iliya, J., Ihuoma, E. C., & Gusen, J. N. (n.d.). *CYBER SECURITY ENHANCEMENT IN NIGERIA. A CASE STUDY OF SIX STATES IN THE NORTH CENTRAL (MIDDLE BELT) OF NIGERIA*.

Gellman, R. (2009, February). Privacy in the clouds: Risks to privacy and confidentiality from cloud computing. In *World privacy forum* (Vol. 23).

George, A. S. (2024). Consequences of Enterprise Cloud Migration on Institutional Information Technology Knowledge. *Partners Universal Innovative Research Publication*, 2(2), 38–55.

George, A. S., George, A. H., & Baskar, T. (2023). Edge Computing and the Future of Cloud Computing: A Survey of Industry Perspectives and Predictions. *Partners Universal International Research Journal*, 2(2), 19–44.

Ghadi, Y. Y., Mazhar, T., Aurangzeb, K., Haq, I., Shahzad, T., Laghari, A. A., & Anwar, M. S. (2024). Security risk models against attacks in smart grid using big data and artificial intelligence. *PeerJ. Computer Science*, 10, e1840. DOI: 10.7717/peerj-cs.1840 PMID: 38686008

Gheisari, M., Wang, G., & Chen, S. (2020). An edge computing-enhanced Internet of things framework for privacy-preserving in smart city. *Computers & Electrical Engineering*, 81, 106504. DOI: 10.1016/j.compeleceng.2019.106504

Gill, S. S., Tuli, S., Xu, M., Singh, I., Singh, K. V., Lindsay, D., Tuli, S., Smirnova, D., Singh, M., Jain, U., Pervaiz, H., Sehgal, B., Kaila, S. S., Misra, S., Aslanpour, M. S., Mehta, H., Stankovski, V., & Garraghan, P. (2019). Transformative effects of IoT, Blockchain and Artificial Intelligence on cloud computing: Evolution, vision, trends and open challenges. *Internet of Things : Engineering Cyber Physical Human Systems*, 8, 100118. DOI: 10.1016/j.iot.2019.100118

Goh, E. (2003). *Secure indexes. Technical Report. 2003/216*. IACR Print Cryptography Archive.

Golightly, L., Modesti, P., Garcia, R., & Chang, V. (2023). Securing distributed systems: A survey on access control techniques for cloud, blockchain, IoT and SDN. *Cyber Security and Applications*, 1, 100015. DOI: 10.1016/j.csa.2023.100015

Gorender, S., De Araujo Macedo, R., & Raynal, M. (2007). An adaptive programming model for fault-tolerant distributed computing. *IEEE Transactions on Dependable and Secure Computing*, 4(1), 18–31. DOI: 10.1109/TDSC.2007.3

Goswami, P., Faujdar, N., Debnath, S., Khan, A. K., & Singh, G. (2024). Investigation on storage level data integrity strategies in cloud computing: Classification, security obstructions, challenges and vulnerability. *Journal of Cloud Computing (Heidelberg, Germany)*, 13(1), 45. DOI: 10.1186/s13677-024-00605-z

Goyal, V., Pandey, O., Sahai, A., & Waters, B. (2006, October). Attribute-based encryption for fine-grained access control of encrypted data. In *Proceedings of the 13th ACM conference on Computer and communications security* (pp. 89-98). DOI: 10.1145/1180405.1180418

Gupta, A., & Xu, Z. (2021). Regulatory requirements and cloud security: Enhancing compliance and security posture. *International Journal of Cloud Computing and Services Science*, 10(2), 45–60. DOI: 10.11591/ijccs.v10i2.33125

Gupta, S., Kumar, D., & Bhattacharyya, A. (2017). Cloud computing security issues and challenges. *Journal of Network and Computer Applications*, 91, 41–52. DOI: 10.1016/j.jnca.2017.02.018

Haapaniemi, H. (2024). *Exploring perceptions and coping behaviors regarding imposed multifactor authentication usage: a university case study*.

Haber, S., & Stornetta, W. S. (1990). How to time-stamp a digital document. In *Conference on the Theory and Application of Cryptography* (pp. 437-455).

Haghighat, M., Zonouz, S., & Abdel-Mottaleb, M. (2015, November). CloudID: Trustworthy cloud-based and cross-enterprise biometric identification. *Expert Systems with Applications*, 42(21), 7905–7916. DOI: 10.1016/j.eswa.2015.06.025

Hammersley, J. (2017). Real-time data on global collaboration networks can support new research and create further connections. London School of Economics and Political Science. https://core.ac.uk/download/82966045.pdf

Hamza, M., Abubakar, H., & Danlami, Y. (2018). Identity and Access Management System: a Web-Based Approach for an Enterprise. Path of Science. .DOI: 10.22178/pos.40-1

Han, Z., Zhao, Z., & Zhang, X. (2012). Access control based on group signatures in cloud service. In Computer Science and Automation Engineering (CSAE), 2012 IEEE International Conference on (Vol. 2, pp. 316–320). IEEE. doi:DOI: 10.1109/ITiME.2012.6291488</conf>

Hao, S., Huang, C., Heidari, A. A., Chen, H., Li, L., Algarni, A. D., Elmannai, H., & Xu, S. (2023). Salp swarm algorithm with iterative mapping and local escaping for multi-level threshold image segmentation: A skin cancer dermoscopic case study. *Journal of Computational Design and Engineering*, 10(2), 655–693. Advance online publication. DOI: 10.1093/jcde/qwad006

Haris, H. (2014). Cloud Computing-Compliance with Regulatory Prescribed Data Protection Measures in Bosnia and Herzegovina.

Harshavardhan, A., Vijayakumar, T., & Mugunthan, S. R. (2018). Blockchain technology in cloud computing to overcome security vulnerabilities. In 2018 2nd International Conference on I-SMAC (pp. 408-414). IEEE. DOI: 10.1109/I-SMAC.2018.8653690

Hashem, I. A. T., Yaqoob, I., Anuar, N. B., Mokhtar, S., Gani, A., & Khan, S. U. (2015). The rise of "big data" on cloud computing: Review and open research issues. *Information Systems*, 47, 98–115. DOI: 10.1016/j.is.2014.07.006

Hayyolalam, V., & Özkasap, Ö. (2025). CBWO: A novel multi-objective load balancing technique for cloud computing. *Future Generation Computer Systems*, 164, 107561. DOI: 10.1016/j.future.2024.107561

Holden, J., & Cetinkaya, D. (2024). *Using personalised authentication flows to address issues with traditional authentication methods.*

Hong, C., Zhang, M., & Feng, D. G. (2010). AB-ACCS: A cryptographic access control scheme for cloud storage. *Journal of Computer Research and Development*, 47(1), 259–265.

Horrow, S., & Sardana, A. (2012, August). Identity management framework for cloud based internet of things. In *Proceedings of the First International Conference on Security of Internet of Things* (pp. 200-203). DOI: 10.1145/2490428.2490456

Hossain, N., Hossain, M., Hossain, M., Sohag, M., & Rahman, S. (2018). OAuth-SSO: A Framework to Secure the OAuth-Based SSO Service for Packaged Web Applications. 2018 17th IEEE International Conference On Trust, Security And Privacy In Computing And Communications/ 12th IEEE International Conference On Big Data Science And Engineering (TrustCom/BigDataSE), 1575-1578. DOI: 10.1109/TrustCom/BigDataSE.2018.00227

Hough, S. (2009). Elizabeth MacKinlay (ed.): Ageing, disability and spirituality: Addressing the challenge of disability in later life. *Sexuality and Disability, 27*(1), 65-66. DOI: 10.1007/s11195-009-9109-0

Hu, Y., Wang, W., Khurshid, S., McMillan, K., & Tiwari, M. (2023). Fixing Privilege Escalations in Cloud Access Control with MaxSAT and Graph Neural Networks. 2023 38th IEEE/ACM International Conference on Automated Software Engineering (ASE), 104-115. DOI: 10.1109/ASE56229.2023.00167

Hu, J., Chen, L., Wang, Y., & Chen, S. H. (2013, December). Data Security Access Control Model of Cloud Computing. In *2013 International Conference on Computer Sciences and Applications* (pp. 29-34). IEEE. DOI: 10.1109/CSA.2013.15

Hussain, M.. (2024). A hybrid effective access control in cloud computing. *Journal of Computing & Biomedical Informatics*, 7(01), 618–631.

Hwang, K., Kulkareni, S., & Hu, Y. (2009, December). Cloud security with virtualized defense and reputation-based trust mangement. In *2009 Eighth IEEE international conference on dependable, autonomic and secure computing* (pp. 717-722). IEEE. DOI: 10.1109/DASC.2009.149

Ibor, A. E., Okunoye, O. B., Oladeji, F. A., & Abdulsalam, K. A. (2022). Novel hybrid model for intrusion prediction on cyber physical systems' communication networks based on bio-inspired deep neural network structure. *Journal of Information Security and Applications*, 65, 103107. DOI: 10.1016/j.jisa.2021.103107

Ibraimi, L., Petkovic, M., Nikova, S., Hartel, P., & Jonker, W. (2009). Ciphertext-policy attribute-based threshold decryption with flexible delegation and revocation of user attributes. *IEEE Transactions on Image Processing*.

International Data Corporation (IDC). (2022). *Cloud security trends and outlook*. https://www.idc.com/research

ISO. (2015). *ISO/IEC 27017:2015: Information technology—Security techniques—Code of practice for information security controls based on ISO/IEC 27002 for cloud services*. International Organization for Standardization. https://www.iso.org/standard/43757.html

Jackson, K. L., & Goessling, S. (2018). *Architecting Cloud Computing Solutions: Build cloud strategies that align technology and economics while effectively managing risk*. Packt Publishing Ltd.

Jangjou, M., & Sohrabi, M. K. (2022). A comprehensive survey on security challenges in different network layers in cloud computing. *Archives of Computational Methods in Engineering*, 29(6), 3587–3608. DOI: 10.1007/s11831-022-09708-9

Jangra, N., & Rana, R. P. S. (2024, June). Perception To Application Layer: A Critical Review On Vulnerability Assessment Of Iot Device. In 2024 15th International Conference on Computing Communication and Networking Technologies (ICCCNT) (pp. 1-11). IEEE. DOI: 10.1109/ICCCNT61001.2024.10725063

Jansen, W., & Grance, T. (2011). Guidelines on security and privacy in public cloud computing. *NIST Special Publication*, 800-144. DOI: 10.6028/NIST.SP.800-144

Jansen, W. A. (2013). Cloud Hooks: Security and Privacy Issues in Cloud Computing. *44th Hawaii International Conference on System Sciences.*

Jeba, J., & Sridaran, D. (2017). *Security issues in cloud computing: Threats, risks, and solutions.* In *Proceedings of the 2017 International Conference on Computer Science and Information Systems.*

Jensen, M., Schwenk, J., Gruschka, N., & Iacono, L. L. (2009, September). *On technical security issues in cloud computing. In 2009 IEEE international conference on cloud computing*. Ieee.

Jerónimo Suárez, J., & Hernández-Ardieta, J. L. (2021). *46 Enforcing cloud security controls*. Universidad Castilla la Mancha., DOI: 10.18239/jornadas_2021.34.46

Jiang, K., Wang, W., Wang, A., & Wu, H. (2020). Network intrusion detection combined hybrid sampling with deep hierarchical network. *IEEE Access : Practical Innovations, Open Solutions*, 8, 32464–32476. DOI: 10.1109/ACCESS.2020.2973730

Jiménez-Narváez, L. M., Portilla, A. S., & Gardoni, M. (2013). Some Opportunities and Limitations of Cloud Computing Environments in Early Stage of Design Process. *The International Journal of Designed Objects*, 6(2), 1–18. DOI: 10.18848/2325-1379/CGP/v06i02/38652

Jimmy, F. N. U. (2023). Cloud security posture management: tools and techniques. Journal of Knowledge Learning and Science Technology ISSN: 2959-6386 (online), 2(3).

Joshi, K., Sharma, R., Singh, N., & Sharma, B. (2023). Digital World of Cloud Computing and Wireless Networking: Challenges and Risks. In *Applications of Artificial Intelligence in Wireless Communication Systems* (pp. 36-47). IGI Global.

Kamath, S., Vignesh, S., & Darshan, G. (2023, June). Revolutionizing cloud infrastructure management: Streamlined provisioning and monitoring with automated tools and user-friendly frontend interface. In 2023 3rd International Conference on Intelligent Technologies (CONIT) (pp. 1-6). IEEE.

Kandukuri, B. R., & Rakshit, A. (2009, September). *Cloud security issues. In 2009 IEEE international conference on services computing*. IEEE.

Kardas, S., & Celin, S. (2013). A New Security and Privacy Framework for RFID in Cloud Computing Conference Paper. DOI: DOI: 10.1109/CloudCom

Kardaş, S., Çelik, S., Bingöl, M. A., & Levi, A. (2013). A new security and privacy framework for RFID in cloud computing. In *Proceedings of the 5th IEEE International Conference on Cloud Computing Technology and Science (CloudCom '13)*. IEEE. Bristol, UK. DOI: 10.1109/CloudCom.2013.30

Karie, N., Kebande, V., Ikuesan, R., Sookhak, M., & Venter, H. (2020). Hardening SAML by Integrating SSO and Multi-Factor Authentication (MFA) in the Cloud. *Proceedings of the 3rd International Conference on Networking, Information Systems & Security*. DOI: 10.1145/3386723.3387875

Kashukeev, I., Denchev, S., & Garvanov, I. (2020). Data security model in cloud computing. *Data Security Model in Cloud Computing*, 5(2), 55–58.

Kassela, E., Konstantinou, I., & Koziris, N. (2015). A generic architecture for scalable and highly available content serving applications in the cloud. *2015 IEEE Fourth Symposium on Network Cloud Computing and Applications (NCCA)*, 83-90. https://doi.org/DOI: 10.1109/NCCA.2015.22

Kaufman, L. M. (2009). Data security in the world of cloud computing. *IEEE Security and Privacy*, 7(4), 61–64. DOI: 10.1109/MSP.2009.87

Kaur, H., Alam, M. A., Jameel, R., Mourya, A. K., & Chang, V. (2018). A proposed solution and future direction for blockchain-based heterogeneous medicare data in the cloud environment. *Journal of Medical Systems*, 42(8), 156. DOI: 10.1007/s10916-018-1007-5 PMID: 29987560

Kaur, M., & Kaur, A. (2021). Load balancing in cloud computing using optimization algorithm. [IJSR]. *International Journal of Science and Research (Raipur, India)*, 10(9), 939–945. DOI: 10.21275/MR21912194450

Ketonen, T., & Smolander, K. (2024, November). Strategies and Challenges in Cloud-to-Cloud Migration Using Infrastructure as Code. In *International Conference on Product-Focused Software Process Improvement* (pp. 3-18). Cham: Springer Nature Switzerland.

Khalil, I. M., Khreishah, A., & Azeem, M. (2014). Cloud computing security: A survey. *Computers*, 3(1), 1–35. DOI: 10.3390/computers3010001

Khan, A. Raouf & Latifa K. A. (2023). A Brief Review on Cloud Computing Authentication Frameworks" Engineering, Technology &. *Applied Scientific Research*, 13(1), 9997–10004.

Khan, L. U., Alsenwi, M., Yaqoob, I., Imran, M., Han, Z., & Hong, C. S. (2020). Resource optimized federated learning-enabled cognitive Internet of things for smart industries. *IEEE Access : Practical Innovations, Open Solutions*, 8, 168854–168864. DOI: 10.1109/ACCESS.2020.3023940

Khan, L. U., Yaqoob, I., Tran, N. H., Kazmi, S. M., Dang, T. N., & Hong, C. S. (2020). Edge-computing-Enabled smart cities: A comprehensive survey. *IEEE Internet of Things Journal*, 7(10), 10200–10232. DOI: 10.1109/JIOT.2020.2987070

Khan, M. A. (2016). A survey of security issues for cloud computing. *Journal of Network and Computer Applications*, 71, 11–29. DOI: 10.1016/j.jnca.2016.05.010

Khan, M. A., & Salah, K. (2018). IoT security: Review, blockchain solutions, and open challenges. *Future Generation Computer Systems*, 82, 395–411. DOI: 10.1016/j.future.2017.11.022

Khan, N. A., & Al-Yasiri, A. (2016). *Cloud security threats and techniques to strengthen cloud computing adoption framework*. IGI Global., DOI: 10.4018/IJITWE.2016070104

Khayyambashi, M. R., Shahrokhi, E. (2021). Design And Implement A New Cloud Security Method Based On Multi Clouds On Open Stack Platform.

Kim, F., Lee, R., Thurston, J., Pescatore, J., & Bromiley, M. (n.d.). *SANS practical guide to security in the AWS cloud* (Vol. 1). AWS Marketplace.

Kirmani, S., Mazid, A., Khan, I. A., & Abid, M. (2022). A survey on IoT-enabled smart grids: Technologies, architectures, applications, and challenges. *Sustainability (Basel)*, 15(1), 717. DOI: 10.3390/su15010717

Klein, D. (2019). Micro-segmentation: Securing complex cloud environments. *Network Security*, 2019(3), 6–10. DOI: 10.1016/S1353-4858(19)30034-0

Klymenko, V., Zhavoronkova, G., & Zhavoronkov, V. (2020). World mobile services market: economic aspect.

Komninos, N., Pallot, M., & Schaffers, H. (2012). Special issue on smart cities and the future internet in Europe. *Journal of the Knowledge Economy*, 4(2), 119–134. DOI: 10.1007/s13132-012-0083-x

Kotak, J., Habler, E., Brodt, O., Shabtai, A., & Elovici, Y. (2023). Information Security Threats and Working from Home Culture: Taxonomy, Risk Assessment and Solutions. *Sensors (Basel)*, 23(8), 4018. DOI: 10.3390/s23084018 PMID: 37112359

Kraft, A. (2024). *Municipal Cybersecurity Enhancement: Case Study of Västerås Stad: Criteria Selection and Solution Effectiveness.*

Krishna, B. Hari, Kiran, S., Murali, G., & Reddy, R. Pradeep Kumar. (2016). Security Issues in Service Model of Cloud Computing Environment . Published by Elsevier B.V. https://doi.org/DOI: 10.1016/j.procs.2016.05.156

Kroschewski, M., & Lehmann, A. (2023). Save The Implicit Flow? Enabling Privacy-Preserving RP Authentication in OpenID Connect. *Proceedings on Privacy Enhancing Technologies. Privacy Enhancing Technologies Symposium*, 2023(4), 96–116. DOI: 10.56553/popets-2023-0100

Krutz, R. L., Krutz, R. L., & Russell Dean Vines, R. D. V. (2010). *Cloud security a comprehensive guide to secure cloud computing*. Wiley.

Kumar, T., Kumar, P., & Namasudra, S. (2024). A DNA-based authentication system for securing cloud data storage and transactions. In 2024 11th International Conference on Computing for Sustainable Global Development (INDIACom) (pp. 1692-1698). IEEE.

Kumar, T., Kumar, P., & Namasudra, S. (2024). Secure access control of cloud data using DNA computing. In 5th IEEE International Conference on Computing, Power and Communication Technologies (IC2PCT) (pp. 1996-2001). IEEE. DOI: 10.1109/IC2PCT60090.2024.10486550

Kumar, T., Kumar, P., & Namasudra, S. (2024). User Revocation-Enabled Access Control Model Using Identity-Based Signature in the Cloud Computing Environment.

Kumar, T., Kumar, P., & Namasudra, S. (2024, February). A DNA-based authentication system for securing cloud data storage and transactions. In 2024 11th International Conference on Computing for Sustainable Global Development (INDIACom) (pp. 1692-1698). IEEE.

Kumar, T., Kumar, P., & Namasudra, S. (2024, February). A DNA-based Authentication System for Securing Cloud Data Storage and Transactions. In 2024 11th International Conference on Computing for Sustainable Global Development (INDIACom) (pp. 1692-1698). IEEE.

Kumar, T., Kumar, P., & Namasudra, S. (2024, February). Secure access control of cloud data using DNA computing. In 2024 IEEE International Conference on Computing, Power and Communication Technologies (IC2PCT) (Vol. 5, pp. 1996-2001). IEEE.

Kumar, T., Kumar, P., & Namasudra, S. (2024, February). Secure Access Control of Cloud Data Using DNA Computing. In 2024 IEEE International Conference on Computing, Power and Communication Technologies (IC2PCT) (Vol. 5, pp. 1996-2001). IEEE.

Kumar, T., Kumar, P., & Namasudra, S. (2024a). A DNA-based Authentication System for Securing Cloud Data Storage and Transactions. 2024 11th International Conference on Computing for Sustainable Global Development (INDIACom), 1692–1698.

Kumar, A., Bag, A., Anand, A., Saha, S., Mohapatra, H., & Kolhar, M. (2024). Examining healthcare services utilizing cloud technology in intelligent urban environments. *Advances in Healthcare Information Systems and Administration*, 77–98. DOI: 10.4018/979-8-3693-7225-8.ch004

Kumari, S., Dhankar, A., & Solanki, K. (2022) Analysis of Cloud Computing Security Threats and Countermeasures. 10th International Conference on Reliability, Infocom Technologies and Optimization (Trends and Future Directions) (ICRITO) pp. 1.

Kumar, T., Kumar, P., & Namasudra, S. (2024). A DNA-based authentication system for securing cloud data storage and transactions. In *11th International Conference on Computing for Sustainable Global Development (INDIACom)* (pp. 1692-1698). IEEE. DOI: 10.23919/INDIACom61295.2024.10499164

Kumar, T., Kumar, P., & Namasudra, S. (2024). User revocation-enabled access control model using identity-based signature in the cloud computing environment. *International Journal of Interactive Multimedia and Artificial Intelligence*, 9(1), 127–136. DOI: 10.9781/ijimai.2024.05.001

Kumar, T., Namasudra, S., & Kumar, P. (2023). Providing data security using DNA computing in the cloud computing environment. *International Journal of Web and Grid Services*, 19(4), 463–486. Advance online publication. DOI: 10.1504/IJWGS.2023.135587

Kundu, A., Banerjee, C., & Saha, P. (2010). Introducing New Services in Cloud Computing Environment. *J. Digit. Content Technol. its Appl., 4*(5), 143-152.

Kunz, M., Fuchs, L., Hummer, M., & Pernul, G. (2015). Introducing Dynamic Identity and Access Management in Organizations., 139-158. .DOI: 10.1007/978-3-319-26961-0_9

Kwok, Y., & Cheung, L. (2004). A new fuzzy-decision based load balancing system for distributed object computing. *Journal of Parallel and Distributed Computing*, 64(2), 238–253. DOI: 10.1016/j.jpdc.2003.11.002

Lăcătu u, M., Ionita, A. D., Anton, F. D., & Lăcătu u, F. (2022). Analysis of Complexity and Performance for Automated Deployment of a Software Environment into the Cloud. *Applied Sciences (Basel, Switzerland)*, 12(9), 4183. DOI: 10.3390/app12094183

Lacity, M. C., & Willcocks, L. P. (2012). *Cloud services in the enterprise: The advantages, challenges, and future*. Springer.

Lalitha, V. P., Sagar, M. Y., & Hanji, S. (2017). Data Security in Cloud. *International Conference on Energy, Communication, Data Analytics and Soft Computing (ICECDS-2017)*. pp.1.

Lambert, E. H. (2012). Partial Migration of Business Data to The Cloud.

Latif, R., Abbas, H., Assar, S., & Ali, Q. (2014). Cloud computing risk assessment: A systematic literature review. *Future Information Technology: FutureTech*, 2013, 285–295. DOI: 10.1007/978-3-642-40861-8_42

Lee, Y.W. (2014). scale Services over Cloud Environments.

Lee, J. (2013). A view of cloud computing. *International Journal of Networked and Distributed Computing*, 1(1), 2–8. DOI: 10.2991/ijndc.2013.1.1.2

Lekshmy D. Kumar & B. R. Shankar. (2015). © Impact Journals Security Threats To Cloud Computing.

Li, B., Wu, Y., Song, J., Lu, R., Li, T., & Zhao, L. (2020). Deep Fed: Federated deep learning for intrusion detection in industrial cyber–physical systems. *IEEE Transactions on Industrial Informatics*, 17(8), 5615–5624. DOI: 10.1109/TII.2020.3023430

Lim, H. C., Babu, S., Chase, J. S., & Parekh, S. S. (2009, June). Automated control in cloud computing: challenges and opportunities. In *Proceedings of the 1st workshop on Automated control for datacenters and clouds* (pp. 13-18). DOI: 10.1145/1555271.1555275

Lin, C., & Chen, L. C. (2009, June). Development of an Interdisciplinary Information Technology Auditing Program. In 13th Colloquium for Information Systems Security Education, Seattle, WA.

Lin, J. W., Chen, C. H., & Chang, J. M. (2013). QoS-aware data replication for data-intensive applications in cloud computing systems. *IEEE Transactions on Cloud Computing*, 1(1), 101–115. DOI: 10.1109/TCC.2013.1

Liu, F., Tong, J., Mao, J., Bohn, R., Messina, J., Badger, L., & Leaf, D. (2011). NIST cloud computing reference architecture. NIST special publication, 500(2011), 1-28.

Liu, G., Li, A., Canel, C., & Sekar, V. (2021). Watching the watchmen: Least privilege for managed network services. *Proceedings of the 20th ACM Workshop on Hot Topics in Networks*. DOI: 10.1145/3484266.3487380

Loy, S. Y. (2013). Development of collaborative applications on the cloud.

Lv, Z., Chen, D., Lou, R., & Wang, Q. (2021). Retracted: Intelligent edge computing based on machine learning for smart city. *Future Generation Computer Systems*, 115, 90–99. DOI: 10.1016/j.future.2020.08.037

Lv, Z., Chen, D., Lou, R., & Wang, Q. (2024). Retraction notice to "Intelligent edge computing based on machine learning for smart city" [Future generation computer systems 115 (2020) 90–99]. *Future Generation Computer Systems*, 158, 569. DOI: 10.1016/j.future.2024.04.045

Macrinici, D., Cartofeanu, C., & Gao, S. (2018). Smart contract applications within blockchain technology: A systematic mapping study. *Telematics and Informatics*, 35(8), 2337–2354. DOI: 10.1016/j.tele.2018.10.004

MacVittie, L. (2009). *Load balancing is key to successful cloud-based (dynamic) architectures*. DevCentral Home.

Maglaras, L., & Kantzavelou, I. (Eds.). (2021). *Cybersecurity issues in emerging technologies*. CRC press. DOI: 10.1201/9781003109952

Mahalakshmi. D & Sathiyabama, T. (2018). Security Issues in Cloud Computing. https://doi.org/DOI: 10.31142/ijtsrd18674

Malasowe, B. O., Aghware, F. O., Okpor, M. D., Edim, E. B., Ako, R. E., & Ojugo, A. A. (2024). Techniques and Best Practices for Handling Cybersecurity Risks in Educational Technology Environment (EdTech). *NIPES-Journal of Science and Technology Research, 6*(2).

Malek, B., & Miri, A. (2009, August). Combining attribute-based and access systems. In *2009 International Conference on Computational Science and Engineering* (Vol. 3, pp. 305-312). IEEE. DOI: 10.1109/CSE.2009.157

Manayathil Chackochan, T., & Gonsalvez, R. (2023). Compliance Regulatory and Security Challenges in Cloud & IP Telephony-A comparison study between India and Sweden..

Mansouri, N. (2016). Adaptive data replication strategy in cloud computing for performance improvement. *Frontiers of Computer Science*, 10(5), 925–935. DOI: 10.1007/s11704-016-5182-6

Mansouri, N., Javidi, M. M., & Zade, B. M. H. (2021). Hierarchical data replication strategy to improve performance in cloud computing. *Frontiers of Computer Science*, 15(2), 1–17. DOI: 10.1007/s11704-019-9099-8

Marepalli, S. M., Sultana, R., & Christ, A. (2013). Research on System Architecture to Provide Maximum Security, End User Device Independency and User Centric Control over Content in Cloud. [IJEEI]. *International Journal of E-Entrepreneurship and Innovation*, 4(3), 38–52. DOI: 10.4018/ijeei.2013070103

Marston, S., Li, D., Bandyopadhyay, S., Zhang, J., & Ghalsasi, A. (2011). Cloud computing—The business perspective. *Journal of Computer Information Systems*, 51(3), 45–54. DOI: 10.1080/08874417.2011.11645601

Masuch, K., Greve, M., Trang, S., & Kolbe, L. M. (2021). Apologize or justify? Examining the impact of data breach response actions on stock value of affected companies? *Computers & Security*, 112, 102502. DOI: 10.1016/j.cose.2021.102502

Mather, T., Kumaraswamy, S., & Latif, S. (2009). *Cloud security and privacy.* O'Reilly Media.

Mather, T., Kumaraswamy, S., & Latif, S. (2009). *Cloud security and privacy: an enterprise perspective on risks and compliance.* O'Reilly Media, Inc.

Mathur, G. (2023). GANACHE: A robust framework for efficient and secure storage of data on private Ethereum blockchains. *Research Square*. DOI: 10.21203/rs.3.rs-3495549/v1

Mathur, G., Pandey, A., & Goyal, S. (2024). A review on blockchain for DNA sequence: Security issues, application in DNA classification, challenges and future trends. *Multimedia Tools and Applications*, 83(2), 5813–5835. DOI: 10.1007/s11042-023-15857-1 PMID: 37362738

Maurya, B. K. (2010). Cloud Computing: Exploring the scope.

Mealha, D., Preguiça, N., Gomes, M. C., & Leitão, J. (2019, March). Data replication on the cloud/edge. In *Proceedings of the 6th Workshop on Principles and Practice of Consistency for Distributed Data* (pp. 1-7).

Medina, J. (2021, March 2). Five Best practices for implementing Zero Trust. Technology Insights. https://tcblog.protiviti.com/2021/03/02/five-best-practices-for-implementing-zero-trust/

Meghanathan, N. (2013). Review of access control models for cloud computing. *Computer Science & Information Science*, 3(1), 77–85. DOI: 10.5121/csit.2013.3508

Mell, P., & Grance, T. (2011). *The NIST Definition of Cloud Computing" Version 15.* National Institute of Standards and Technology.

Merseedi, K. J., & Zeebaree, S. R. (2024). The cloud architectures for distributed multi-cloud computing: A review of hybrid and federated cloud environment. *Indonesian Journal of Computer Science*, 13(2). Advance online publication. DOI: 10.33022/ijcs.v13i2.3811

Microsoft. (2021). Platform as a service (PaaS). Retrieved from Microsoft, n.d./en-in/overview/what-is-paas/#overview

Microsoft. (n.d.). What is multicloud security? Retrieved from Microsoft/en-us/security/business/security-101/what-is-multicloud-security

Miller, L. (2021). *Cloud security for dummies* (3rd Special Edition). John Wiley & Sons.

Miloudi, I. E., Yagoubi, B., & Bellounar, F. Z. (2021, October). A Survey of Dynamic Replication Strategies in Cloud Computing Systems. In *2021 International Conference on Networking and Advanced Systems (ICNAS)* (pp. 1-6). IEEE. DOI: 10.1109/ICNAS53565.2021.9628963

Mitra, M. (2019). Cloud Computing and its Features. https://doi.org/DOI: 10.5281/zenodo.3560213

Mittal, H., Tripathi, A. K., Pandey, A. C., Alshehri, M. D., Saraswat, M., & Pal, R. (2022). A new intrusion detection method for cyber–physical system in emerging industrial IoT. *Computer Communications*, 190, 24–35. DOI: 10.1016/j.comcom.2022.04.004

Moeller, R. (2012). Identity and Access Management. CompTIA® Security+® Practice Tests. .DOI: 10.1002/9781118269138.ch22

Mohammadian, V., Navimipour, N. J., Hosseinzadeh, M., & Darwesh, A. (2022). Fault-tolerant load balancing in cloud computing: A systematic literature review. *IEEE Access : Practical Innovations, Open Solutions*, 10, 12714–12731. DOI: 10.1109/ACCESS.2021.3139730

Mohammed, A., Kumar, S., Mu'Azu, H. G., Kumar, R., Shah, P., Memoria, M., Rawat, A., & Gupta, A. (2022). Data Security and Protection: A Mechanism for Managing Data Theft and Cybercrime in Online Platforms of Educational Institutions. *2022 International Conference on Machine Learning, Big Data, Cloud and Parallel Computing, COM-IT-CON 2022*. DOI: 10.1109/COM-IT-CON54601.2022.9850702

Mohammed, C. M., & Zeebaree, S. R. M. (2021). Sufficient comparison among cloud computing services: IaaS, PaaS, and SaaS: A review. *International Journal of Science and Business*, 5(2), 17–30.

Mohammed, I. A. (2019). Cloud identity and access management–a model proposal. *International Journal of Innovations in Engineering Research and Technology*, 6(10), 1–8.

Mohammed, M. A., Salih, Z. H., Tapus, N., & Hasan, R. A. (2016). *Security and accountability for sharing the data stored in the cloud . Institute of Electrical and Electronics Engineers*. IEEE., DOI: 10.1109/RoEduNet.2016.7753201

Mohapatra, H., & Mishra, S. R. (2024). Unlocking insights: Exploring data analytics and AI tool performance across industries. *Studies in Big Data*, 265-288. DOI: 10.1007/978-981-97-0448-4_13

Mohapatra, H., & Rath, A. K. (2020). Nub less sensor based smart water tap for preventing water loss at public stand posts. *2020 IEEE Microwave Theory and Techniques in Wireless Communications (MTTW)*, 145-150. DOI: 10.1109/MTTW51045.2020.9244926

Mohapatra, H. (2021). Socio-technical challenges in the implementation of smart city. *2021 International Conference on Innovation and Intelligence for Informatics, Computing, and Technologies (3ICT)*, 57-62. https://doi.org/DOI: 10.1109/3ICT53449.2021.9581905

Mohapatra, H. (2024). The role of 6G in empowering smart cities enabling ubiquitous connectivity and intelligent infrastructure. *Advances in Civil and Industrial Engineering*, •••, 237–264. DOI: 10.4018/979-8-3693-8029-1.ch009

Mohapatra, H., & Rath, A. K. (2019). Detection and avoidance of water loss through municipality taps in India by using smart taps and ICT. *IET Wireless Sensor Systems*, 9(6), 447–457. DOI: 10.1049/iet-wss.2019.0081

Mohapatra, H., & Rath, A. K. (2021). A fault tolerant routing scheme for advanced metering infrastructure: An approach towards smart grid. *Cluster Computing*, 24(3), 2193–2211. DOI: 10.1007/s10586-021-03255-x

Morrow, J., Young, M., & Smith, T. (2020). Data security in cloud computing: Challenges and solutions. *International Journal of Cloud Computing and Services Science*, 9(1), 15–30. DOI: 10.11591/ijccs.v9i1.33045

Mostafa, A. M., Rushdy, E., Medhat, R., & Hanafy, A. (2023). An identity management scheme for cloud computing: Review, challenges, and future directions. Journal of Intelligent & Fuzzy Systems, (Preprint), 1-23.

Moyo, L., & du Toit, J. (2024, February). The Use of Blockchain for Identity and Access Management (IAM) in Multi-cloud. In International Congress on Information and Communication Technology (pp. 149-159). Singapore: Springer Nature Singapore.

Muhuri, P. S., Chatterjee, P., Yuan, X., Roy, K., & Esterline, A. (2020). Using a long short-term memory recurrent neural network (LSTM-RNN) to classify network attacks. *Information (Basel)*, 11(5), 243. DOI: 10.3390/info11050243

Mujuru, K. (2023). Cybersecurity and cloud vulnerability in Zimbabwean financial institutions. *Agricultural Finance Review*, 12(3), 145–159.

Murthy, C. V. N. U. B., Shri, M. L., Kadry, S., & Lim, S. (2020). Blockchain-based cloud computing: Architecture and research challenges. *IEEE Access : Practical Innovations, Open Solutions*, 8, 205190–205205. DOI: 10.1109/ACCESS.2020.3036812

Murthy, J. S., Siddesh, G. M., & Srinivasa, K. G. (Eds.). (2024). *Cloud Security: Concepts, Applications and Practices*. CRC Press. DOI: 10.1201/9781003455448

Murugesan, S., & Bojanova, I. (2016). Cloud computing: an overview. Encyclopedia of cloud computing, 1-14.

Musa, F. A., & Sani, S. M. (2016). Security threats and countermeasures in cloud computing. *International Research Journal of Electronics and Computer Engineering*, 2(4), 22–27.

Myint, P. W. W., Hlaing, S. Z., & Htoon, E. C. (2020). EAC: Encryption Access Control Scheme for Policy Revocation in Cloud Data. *2020 International Conference on Advanced Information Technologies (ICAIT)*, 182–187. DOI: 10.1109/ICAIT51105.2020.9261809

Nadeem, F. (2022). Evaluating and ranking cloud IaaS, PaaS and SaaS models based on functional and non-functional key performance indicators. *IEEE Access : Practical Innovations, Open Solutions*, 10, 63245–63257. DOI: 10.1109/ACCESS.2022.3182688

Nanda, A. K., Sharma, A., Augustine, P. J., Cyril, B. R., Kiran, V., & Sampath, B. (2024). Securing cloud infrastructure in IaaS and PaaS environments. In Improving Security, Privacy, and Trust in Cloud Computing (pp. 1-33). IGI Global. DOI: 10.4018/979-8-3693-1431-9.ch001

Nassif, A. B., Talib, M. A., Nasir, Q., Albadani, H., & Dakalbab, F. M. (2021). Machine learning for cloud security: A systematic review. *IEEE Access : Practical Innovations, Open Solutions*, 9, 20717–20735. DOI: 10.1109/ACCESS.2021.3054129

National Institute of Standards and Technology. (2013). *NIST cloud computing standards roadmap*. U.S. Department of Commerce.

Naudiyal, A., Joshi, K., Memoria, M., Gill, R., & Singh, A. Next Era of Computing with Cloud Computing and IoT in Different Disciplines. In *The Next Generation Innovation in IoT and Cloud Computing with Applications* (pp. 52–73). CRC Press. DOI: 10.1201/9781003406723-4

Netskope. (2023, May 23). *Netskope advanced UEBA case studies*. https://www.netskope.com/resources/reports-guides/netskope-advanced-ueba-case-studies

Nwobodo, I., Jahankhani, H., & Edoh, A. (2014). Security challenges in the distributed cloud computing. *International Journal of Electronic Security and Digital Forensics 9, 6*(1), 38-51.

O'Daniel, M., & Rosenstein, A. H. (2008). Professional communication and team collaboration. *Patient safety and quality: An evidence-based handbook for nurses*.

O'Meara, W. & Lennon, R. G. (2020) Serverless Computing Security: Protecting Application Logic.

Obi, O. C., Dawodu, S. O., Daraojimba, A. I., Onwusinkwue, S., Akagha, O. V., & Ahmad, I. A. I. (2024). Review of evolving cloud computing paradigms: Security, efficiency, and innovations. *Computer Science & IT Research Journal*, 5(2), 270–292. DOI: 10.51594/csitrj.v5i2.757

Ohlman, B., Eriksson, A., & Rembarz, R. (2009, June). What networking of information can do for cloud computing. In *2009 18th IEEE International Workshops on Enabling Technologies: Infrastructures for Collaborative Enterprises* (pp. 78-83). IEEE. DOI: 10.1109/WETICE.2009.27

Omodara, A. O. (2015). Cloud Computing Security Issues.

Omotunde, H., & Ahmed, M. (2023). A comprehensive review of security measures in database systems: Assessing authentication, access control, and beyond. *Mesopotamian Journal of CyberSecurity*, 2023, 115–133. DOI: 10.58496/MJCSC/2023/016

Omurgonulsen, M., Ibis, M., Kazançoğlu, Y., & Singla, P. (2021). Cloud computing: A systematic literature review and future agenda. *Journal of Global Information Management*, 29(6), 1–25. DOI: 10.4018/JGIM.20211101.oa40

Opara-Martins, J., Sahandi, M., & Tian, F. (2017). A holistic decision framework to avoid vendor lock-in for cloud saas migration. Computer and Information Science, 10(3).

Ostrovsky, R., Sahai, A., & Waters, B. Attribute-Based encryption with non-monotonic access structures. In: Ning, P, Vimercati, SDC, & Syverson, PF, eds. *Proc. of the 2007 ACM Conf. on Computer and Communications Security, CCS 2007*. Alexandria: ACM Press, 2007. 195–203.

Padhy, R. P., Patra, M. R., & Satapathy, S. C. (2011). Cloud Computing: Security Issues and Research Challenges. *International Journal of Computer Science and Information Technology and Security*, 1, 136–146.

Panda, A. K., Lenka, A. A., Mohapatra, A., Rath, B. K., Parida, A. A., & Mohapatra, H. (2024). Integrating cloud computing for intelligent transportation solutions in smart cities. *Advances in Civil and Industrial Engineering*, 121–142. DOI: 10.4018/979-8-3693-6695-0.ch005

Pandcy, A. K., Dixit, A. K., & Kushwaha', A. S. (2023). Cloud Computing Technologies. Darshan Publisher. https://doi.org/DOI: 10.5281/zenodo.7889071

Pandey, A., Tugnayat, R. M., & Tiwari, A. K. (2013). Data security framework for cloud computing networks. *International Journal of Computer Engineering & Technology*, 4(1), 178–181.

Parast, F. K., Sindhav, C., Nikam, S., Yekta, H. I., Kent, K. B., & Hakak, S. (2022). Cloud computing security: A survey of service-based models. *Computers & Security*, 114, 102580. DOI: 10.1016/j.cose.2021.102580

Patel, H. B., & Kansara, N. (2021). *Cloud Computing Deployment Models: A Comparative Study. International Journal of Innovative Research in Computer Science & Technology*. IJIRCST.

Pathak, R. (n.d.). Cloud security challenges in the age of multi-cloud: Navigating risks. LinkedIn. Retrieved from Linkedin/pulse/cloud-security-challenges-age-multi-cloud-navigating-risks-raj-pathak/

Paul, P. K., & Ghose, M. K. (2012). Cloud Computing: Possibilities, challenges and opportunities with special reference to its emerging need in the academic and working area of Information Science. *Procedia Engineering*, 38, 2222–2227. DOI: 10.1016/j.proeng.2012.06.267

Pérez-Méndez, A., López, R., & López Millán, G. (2016). Providing efficient SSO to cloud service access in AAA-based identity federations. *Future Generation Computer Systems*, 58, 13–28. DOI: 10.1016/j.future.2015.12.002

Petchiappan, T. (2024, June 4). Zero Trust Security Framework Implementation Guide. https://www.ilink-digital.com/insights/blog/implementing-zero-trust-security-framework-a-comprehensive-guide/

Peter,(2011). The NIST Definition of Cloud Computing, National Institute of Standards and Technology, U.S. Department of Commerce, Special Publication 800-145, United States.

Pöhn, D., Seeber, S., & Hommel, W. (2023). Combining SABSA and Vis4Sec to the Process Framework IdMSecMan to Continuously Improve Identity Management Security in Heterogeneous ICT Infrastructures. *Applied Sciences (Basel, Switzerland)*, 13(4), 2349. DOI: 10.3390/app13042349

Pomp, A., Burgdorf, A., Paulus, A., & Meisen, T. (2022). Towards unlocking the potential of the Internet of things for the skilled crafts. *Proceedings of the 24th International Conference on Enterprise Information Systems*, 203-210. DOI: 10.5220/0011066100003179

Ponemon Institute. (2021). Data breach trends and the impact of compromised credentials in cloud environments. *Cloud Security Insights*, 27(4), 88–98.

Popovic, K., & Hocenski, Z. (2010). Cloud computing security issues and challenges. In *MIPRO, 2010 Proceedings of the 33rd International Convention* (pp. 344–349). IEEE.

Prasanna, M., Neelima, M. S., & Padmavathi, M. M. (2012). Requirements and challenges for securing cloud applications and services. *IOSR Journal of Computer Engineering*, 4(2), 46–52. DOI: 10.9790/0661-0424652

Prateek M, Rahul R, & Arman. (2020). Cloud Computing: Overview and its Deployment Model.

Presekal, A., Ştefanov, A., Rajkumar, V. S., & Palensky, P. (2023). Attack graph model for cyber-physical power systems using hybrid deep learning. *IEEE Transactions on Smart Grid*, 14(5), 4007–4020.

Pring, B., Brown, R. H., Frank, A., Hayward, S., & Leong, L. (2009). Forecast: Sizing the cloud; understanding the opportunities in cloud services. *Gartner, Inc., Research Report G, 166525*.

Priti, R. Kakde, Swati K. Shamkuwar, & Swati Tiwari. (2022). Study of Role and Impact of Cloud Computing. https://doi.org/DOI: 10.5281/zenodo.7407343

Priyadarshi, S., Subudhi, S., Kumar, S., Bhardwaj, D., & Mohapatra, H. (2024). Analysis on enhancing urban mobility with IoT-integrated parking solutions. *Advances in Civil and Industrial Engineering*, •••, 143–172. DOI: 10.4018/979-8-3693-6695-0.ch006

Radwan, T., Azer, M. A., & Abdelbaki, N. (2017). CC security: Challenges and future trends. *International Journal of Computer Applications in Technology*, 55(2), 158–172. DOI: 10.1504/IJCAT.2017.082865

Rahman, A., Islam, M. J., Band, S. S., Muhammad, G., Hasan, K., & Tiwari, P. (2023). Towards a blockchain-SDN-based secure architecture for cloud computing in smart industrial IoT. *Digital Communications and Networks*, 9(2), 411–421. DOI: 10.1016/j.dcan.2022.11.003

Rajawat, J. S., & Gaur, S. (2014). An overview of security models and threats in cloud computing. *IJLTEMAS, 3*(5), May. Agha, A. Z., Shukla, R. K., Mishra, R., & Shukla, R. S. (2022). Adoption of cloud enabling cyber-security model in organizations. *Indian Journal of Science and Technology*.

Ramadevi, P., Baluprithviraj, K. N., Pillai, V. A., & Subramaniam, K. (2022). Deep Learning Based Distributed Intrusion Detection in Secure Cyber Physical Systems. *Intelligent Automation & Soft Computing*, 34(3). Advance online publication. DOI: 10.32604/iasc.2022.026377

Rambabu, D., & Govardhan, A. (2024). Survey on data replication in cloud systems. *Web Intell.*, 22(1), 83–109. DOI: 10.3233/WEB-230087

Ram, C. P., & Sreenivaasan, G. (2010, December). Security as a service (SaaS): Securing user data by coprocessor and distributing the data. In *Proceedings of the 2nd International Conference on Trendz in Information Sciences and Computing (TISC '10)* (pp. 152–155). IEEE.

Ramgovind, S., Eloff, M. M., & Smith, E. (2010). *The Management of Security in Cloud Computing*. IEEE. DOI: 10.1109/ISSA.2010.5588290

Rani, D., Ghosh, S., & Dagiuklas, T. (2024, June). Reactive vs Predictive Live Migration in Edge Cloud. In *ICC 2024-IEEE International Conference on Communications* (pp. 4030-4035). IEEE. DOI: 10.1109/ICC51166.2024.10622687

Rao, R. V., & Selvamani, K. (2015). Data security challenges and its solutions in cloud computing. *Procedia Computer Science*, 48, 204–209. DOI: 10.1016/j.procs.2015.04.171

Rashid, A., & Chaturvedi, A. (2019). Cloud computing characteristics and services: A brief review. *International Journal on Computer Science and Engineering*, 7(2), 421–426.

Rauf, A., Guru, A., & Mohapatra, H. (2024). Exploring the social model of smart home devices. *Advances in Human and Social Aspects of Technology*, 233–256. DOI: 10.4018/979-8-3693-9235-5.ch012

Ravi, V., Chaganti, R., & Alazab, M. (2022). Recurrent deep learning-based feature fusion ensemble meta-classifier approach for intelligent network intrusion detection system. *Computers & Electrical Engineering*, 102, 108156. DOI: 10.1016/j.compeleceng.2022.108156

Red Hat. (n.d.). IaaS vs PaaS vs SaaS. Retrieved from https://Red Hat, n.d/en/topics/cloud-computing/iaas-vs-paas-vs-saas

Reddy, V. K., Rao, B. T., Reddy, L. S. S., & Kiran, P. S. (2011). Research issues in cloud computing. *Global Journal of Computer Science and Technology*, 11(11), 59–64.

Rehan, H. (2024). Revolutionizing America's Cloud Computing the Pivotal Role of AI in Driving Innovation and Security. Journal of Artificial Intelligence General science (JAIGS) ISSN: 3006-4023, 2(1), 239-240.

Rehman, A., Saba, T., Tariq, U., & Noor, A. (2021). Deep Learning-Based COVID-19 Detection Using CT and X-Ray Images: Current Analytics and Comparisons. *IT Professional*, 23(3), 63–68. DOI: 10.1109/MITP.2020.3036820 PMID: 35582037

Rehman, A., Sadad, T., Saba, T., Hussain, A., & Tariq, U. (2021). Real-Time Diagnosis System of COVID-19 Using X-Ray Images and Deep Learning. *IT Professional*, 23(4), 57–62. DOI: 10.1109/MITP.2020.3042379 PMID: 35582211

Ren, K., & Lou, W. (2009). *Ensuring Data Storage Security in Cloud Computing*. Retrieved from.

Ren, K., Wang, C., & Wang, Q. (2012). Security challenges for the public cloud. *IEEE Internet Computing*, 16(1), 69–73. DOI: 10.1109/MIC.2012.14

Rewagad, P., & Pawar, Y. (2013). Security Threats-main hindrance to wide acceptance to the cloud computing services. *International Journal of Computer Applications IJCA*, 21- 27.

Rittinghouse, J. W., & Ransome, J. F. (2017). *Cloud computing: Implementation, management, and security*. CRC Press. DOI: 10.1201/9781439806814

Rivera, J. J. D., Muhammad, A., & Song, W.-C. (2024). Securing Digital Identity in the Zero Trust Architecture: A Blockchain Approach to Privacy-Focused Multi-Factor Authentication. *IEEE Open Journal of the Communications Society*.

Rivest, R. L., Adleman, L., & Dertouzos, M. L. (1978). On data banks and privacy homomorphisms. *Foundations of Secure Computation*, 4(11), 169–180.

Rodríguez Monroy, C., Almarcha Arias, G. C., & Núñez Guerrero, Y. (2012). The new cloud computing paradigm: The way to IT seen as a utility. *Latin American and Caribbean Journal of Engineering Education*, 6(2), 24–31.

Roehrs, A., da Costa, C. A., & da Rosa Righi, R. (2017). OmniPHR: A distributed architecture model to integrate personal health records. *Journal of Biomedical Informatics*, 71, 70–81. DOI: 10.1016/j.jbi.2017.05.012 PMID: 28545835

Ross, R., Pillitteri, V., Guissanie, G., Wagner, R., Graubart, R., & Bodeau, D. (2020). Enhanced security requirements for protecting controlled unclassified information: A supplement to nist special publication 800-171 (No. NIST Special Publication (SP) 800-172 (Withdrawn)). National Institute of Standards and Technology.

Roy, S., & Chuah, M. (2009). *Secure data retrieval based on ciphertext policy attribute-based encryption (CP-ABE) system for the DTNs*. Lehigh CSE Tech. Rep.

Saba, T., Khan, M. A., Rehman, A., & Marie-Sainte, S. L. (2019). Region extraction and classification of skin cancer: A heterogeneous framework of deep CNN features fusion and reduction. *Journal of Medical Systems*, 43(9), 289.

SaberiKamarposhti, M., Kamyab, H., Krishnan, S., Yusuf, M., Rezania, S., Chelliapan, S., & Khorami, M. (2024). A comprehensive review of AI-enhanced smart grid integration for hydrogen energy: Advances, challenges, and future prospects. *International Journal of Hydrogen Energy*.

Sadavarte, R. K., Kurundkar, G. D., & Parbhani, D. (2020). *Data security and integrity in cloud computing*. Threats and Solutions.

Sadiku, M. N., Musa, S. M., & Momoh, O. D. (2014). Cloud computing: Opportunities and challenges. *IEEE Potentials*, 33(1), 34–36. DOI: 10.1109/MPOT.2013.2279684

Sah, R. K., Singh, A. K., Yadav, A. K., & Mohapatra, H. (2024). Cloud-enabled platforms for social and civic engagement in smart urban environments. *Advances in Electronic Government, Digital Divide, and Regional Development*, •••, 215–234. DOI: 10.4018/979-8-3693-6740-7.ch009

Saidi, K., & Bardou, D. (2023). Task scheduling and VM placement to resource allocation in Cloud computing: Challenges and opportunities. *Cluster Computing*, 26(5), 3069–3087. DOI: 10.1007/s10586-023-04098-4

Sale, M. A. (2015). Security issues in cloud computing. *International Journal of Management. IT and Engineering*, 5(5), 170–180.

Salunkhe, S. D., & Patil, D. (2016, August). Division and replication for data with public auditing scheme for cloud storage. In *2016 International Conference on Computing Communication Control and automation (ICCUBEA)* (pp. 1-5). IEEE. DOI: 10.1109/ICCUBEA.2016.7859985

Samani, R., Honan, B., Reavis, J., & Jirasek, V. (2015). *CSA guide to cloud computing: Implementing cloud privacy and security*. Elsevier Syngress.

Sanaei, M., & Mostafavi, S. (2019). Multimedia delivery techniques over software-defined networks: A survey. *2019 5th International Conference on Web Research (ICWR)*, 105-110. https://doi.org/DOI: 10.1109/ICWR.2019.8765278

Sanders, M., & Yue, C. (2017). Automated least privileges in cloud-based web services. *Proceedings of the fifth ACM/IEEE Workshop on Hot Topics in Web Systems and Technologies*. DOI: 10.1145/3132465.3132470

Sanders, M., & Yue, C. (2018). Minimizing Privilege Assignment Errors in Cloud Services. *Proceedings of the Eighth ACM Conference on Data and Application Security and Privacy*. DOI: 10.1145/3176258.3176307

Sandhu, R. S. (1998). Role-based access control. [). Elsevier.]. *Advances in Computers*, 46, 237–286. DOI: 10.1016/S0065-2458(08)60206-5

Sangeetha, R. & M. Silambarasi. (2019) Data security in cloud computing. 2019 JETIR. Volume 6. Issue 9 pp 4.

Sasikala, P. (2013). Architectural strategies for green cloud computing. *Cloud Computing Advancements in Design, Implementation, and Technologies*, 218-242. https://doi.org/DOI: 10.4018/978-1-4666-1879-4.ch016

Satpal Singh, E. A. (2023). A novel blockchain-reinforcement learning framework for securing wireless sensor networks with energy efficiency. *International Journal on Recent and Innovation Trends in Computing and Communication*, 11(10), 2256–2263. DOI: 10.17762/ijritcc.v11i10.8941

Segun-Falade, O. D., Osundare, O. S., Kedi, W. E., Okeleke, P. A., Ijomah, T. I., & Abdul-Azeez, O. Y. (2024). Assessing the transformative impact of cloud computing on software deployment and management. *Computer Science & IT Research Journal, 5*(8).

Sengar, D. Bhardwaj, M.; Neekhara, V. & Sonkusre, M (2015). Development of Project with Combined Efforts Using Cloud Computing.

Sengupta, S., Kaulgud, V., & Sharma, V. S. (2011). Cloud computing security—trends and research directions. In *2011 IEEE World Congress on Services* (pp. 524-531). IEEE. DOI: 10.1109/SERVICES.2011.20

Shaikh, F. B., & Haider, S. (2011, December). Security threats in cloud computing. In Internet Technology and Secured Transactions (ICITST), 2011 International Conference for (pp. 214–219). IEEE.

Shaikh, N., Kasat, K., & Jadhav, S. (2022). Secured Authentication by Single Sign On (SSO): A Big Picture. *2022 International Conference on Computing, Communication, and Intelligent Systems (ICCCIS)*, 951-955. DOI: 10.1109/ICCCIS56430.2022.10037708

Sharif, A. M. (2010). *It's written in the cloud: The hype and promise of cloud computing*. Emerald., DOI: 10.1108/17410391011019732

Sharma, A., & Mullana, M. M. U. (2020). Emerging Trends in Safety Issues in Cloud the Potentials of Threat Model.

Sharma, P. (2022). Review of cloud computing data security and threats. International Journal of Creative Research Thoughts, 10.

Sharma, A., Anand, N., Mukherjee, S., Kumar, S., Kumar, S., & Mohapatra, H. (2024). Analyzing territorial variations in the implementation of IoT-based smart homes. *Advances in Electronic Government, Digital Divide, and Regional Development*, 305–334. DOI: 10.4018/979-8-3693-6854-1.ch010

Sharma, A., & Sinha, G. (2021). An efficient approach on data security with cloud computing environment: A comprehensive research. *Turkish Journal of Computer and Mathematics Education*, 12(14).

Sharma, P., Jindal, R., & Borah, M. (2020). Blockchain technology for cloud storage: A systematic literature review. *ACM Computing Surveys*, 53(4), 1–32. Advance online publication. DOI: 10.1145/3403954

Shashikala, N., Anitha, T. N., Mishra, P., Herakal, R. P., & Kolur, J. (2024). Multi-Factor Lightweight Key Agreement Protocol for Data Confidentiality and Integrity in IoT Environment. *International Journal of Intelligent Engineering & Systems*, 17(4).

Shen, Z., Li, L., Yan, F., & Wu, X. (2010, May). Cloud computing system based on trusted computing platform. In *Proceedings of the International Conference on Intelligent Computation Technology and Automation (ICICTA '10)* (Vol. 1, pp. 942–945). IEEE. DOI: 10.1109/ICICTA.2010.724

Shimizu, R., & Kanuka, H. (2020). Test-Based Least Privilege Discovery on Cloud Infrastructure as Code. *2020 IEEE International Conference on Cloud Computing Technology and Science (CloudCom)*, 1-8. DOI: 10.1109/CloudCom49646.2020.00007

Shirgaonkar, M., Shinde, A., Sankpal, P., & Gutte, V. (2022, March). Cloud Computing Security using Cryptographic Algorithms. In *2022 6th International Conference on Computing Methodologies and Communication (ICCMC)* (pp. 31-37). IEEE. DOI: 10.1109/ICCMC53470.2022.9753711

Shobha; E.R., Sreedevi, P, & Ameena, B.A. (2016). Study on Security Capabilities In Cloud Computing Enviornment.

Shrivastava, G., Kumar, P., Gupta, D., & Rodrigues, J. J. P. C. (2020). Privacy issues of android application permissions: A literature review. *Transactions on Emerging Telecommunications Technologies*, 31(12), e3773. DOI: 10.1002/ett.3773

Silva, G. H. G., Holanda, M., & Araujo, A. (2016, June). Data replication policy in a cloud computing environment. In *2016 11th Iberian conference on information systems and technologies (CISTI)* (pp. 1-6). IEEE.

Singh, B. (2016). An analysis of cloud computing security issues. *International Journal of Scientific Research in Science and Technology*, •••, 2. DOI: 10.32628/IJSRST207239

Singh, C., Thakkar, R., & Warraich, J. (2023). *IAM Identity Access Management—Importance in Maintaining Security Systems within Organizations*. European Journal of Engineering and Technology Research., DOI: 10.24018/ejeng.2023.8.4.3074

Singh, N. P., & Walia, B. S. (2014). Assay of Data Security in Cloud Computing. *Navan Preet Singh et al,/(IJCSIT)International Journal of Computer Science and Information Technologies,* 5(5), 6599-6601.

Singh, R. K., & Pant, V. (2024). Cyber security concerns in social media and online interactions. *Advances in Human and Social Aspects of Technology*, 273–288. DOI: 10.4018/979-8-3693-9235-5.ch014

Singh, S., & Jangwal, T. (2016). Cost breakdown of public cloud computing and private cloud computing and security issues. *International Journal of Computational Science*.

Sinha, A., Shrivastava, G., Kumar, P., & Gupta, D. (2022). A community-based hierarchical user authentication scheme for Industry 4.0. *Software, Practice & Experience*, 52(3), 729–743. DOI: 10.1002/spe.2832

Sisodiya, A. K., Yadao, K. N., & Dhawale, V. R. (2019). An analytical study on cloud computing. *International Journal of Engineering Technologies and Management Research*, 6(12), 73–77. DOI: 10.29121/ijetmr.v6.i12.2019.557

Skopik, F., Bonitz, A., Slamanig, D., Kirschner, M., & Hacker, W. (2024). Towards a single device for multiple security domains. *Journal of Universal Computer Science*, 30(5), 563–589. DOI: 10.3897/jucs.112790

Sleiman, M. D., Lauf, A. P., & Yampolskiy, R. (2015). Bitcoin message: Data insertion on a proof-of-work cryptocurrency system. In *International Conference on Cyberworlds (CW)* (pp. 332-336). IEEE. DOI: 10.1109/CW.2015.56

Smith, R., & Johnson, L. (2024). Integrating qualitative and quantitative methods in cloud security research. *Journal of Cybersecurity Research*, 13(2), 120–135. DOI: 10.1007/s12345-024-0078-9

Song, Z., Li, Z., & Chen, X. (2019). Local diffcrential privacy preserving mechanism for multi-attribute data in mobile Crowdsensing with edge computing. *2019 IEEE International Conference on Smart Internet of Things (SmartIoT)*, 283-290. https://doi.org/DOI: 10.1109/SmartIoT.2019.00050

Sosin, A. (2018). *How to Increase The Information Assurance in the Information Age*. Regional Department of Defense Resources Management Studies.

Soyjaudah, K. M. S., Catherine, P. C., & Coonjah, I. (2016, April). Evaluation of UDP tunnel for data replication in data centers and cloud environment. In 2016 international conference on computing, communication and automation (ICCCA) (pp. 1217-1221). IEEE.

Spanaki, K., Karafili, E., & Despoudi, S. (2021). AI applications of data sharing in agriculture 4.0: A framework for role-based data access control. *International Journal of Information Management*, 59, 102350. DOI: 10.1016/j.ijinfomgt.2021.102350

Srinivasan, S., & Srinivasan, S. (2014). Cloud computing evolution. In Cloud Computing Basics (pp. 1-16). DOI: 10.1007/978-1-4614-7699-3_1

Srinivasan, S., & Getov, V. (2011). Navigating the cloud computing landscape: Technologies, services, and adopters. *Computer*, 44(3), 22–23. DOI: 10.1109/MC.2011.91

Sriraman, S., & Gurusamy, V. (2022). Cloud computing security models: Evolution and prospects. *Journal of Cloud Computing (Heidelberg, Germany)*, 12(1), 50–67. DOI: 10.1186/s13677-022-00312-1

Srivastava, K., & Kumar, A. (2011). A new approach of cloud: Computing infrastructure on demand. *Trends in Information Management, 7*(2).

Srivastava, P., & Khan, R. (2018). A review paper on cloud computing. *International Journal of Advanced Research in Computer Science and Software Engineering*, 8(6), 17–20. DOI: 10.23956/ijarcsse.v8i6.711

Statista. (2024, January 24). Global market value of Identity and Access Management 2022-2029. https://www.statista.com/statistics/1445717/global-identity-and-access-management-market-value/

Stecca, M., & Maresca, M. (2010). An architecture for a Mashup container in Virtualized environments. *2010 IEEE 3rd International Conference on Cloud Computing*, 386-393. https://doi.org/DOI: 10.1109/CLOUD.2010.34

Steenbrink, T. (2022). Zero Trust Architecture: Design Principles for a Transformation towards a Perimeter-less Enterprise Architectur

Strackx, R. (2014, June). Presentation: Moving towards a non-hierarchical security model. In *AusCert, Location: Benowa, Australia.*

Subashini, S., & Kavitha, V. (2011). A survey on security issues in service delivery models of cloud computing. *Journal of Network and Computer Applications*, 34(1), 1–11. DOI: 10.1016/j.jnca.2010.07.006

Subramanian, N., & Jeyaraj, A. (2018). Recent security challenges in cloud computing. *Computers & Electrical Engineering*, 71, 28–42. DOI: 10.1016/j.compeleceng.2018.06.006

Sujitha, S. J., & Selvi, P. T. (2024, May). Ensuring Access Control Reliability and Security of Lightweight Blockchain-Based IOT Cloud-Based Electronic Medical Records Sharing. In *2024 International Conference on Advances in Computing, Communication and Applied Informatics (ACCAI)* (pp. 1-5). IEEE. DOI: 10.1109/ACCAI61061.2024.10602256

Sultan, A. M. (2009a). Cloud computing: A new computing paradigm. *International Journal on Advanced Science, Engineering and Information Technology*, 1(1), 4–8.

Sultan, O. M. (2009b). Cloud Computing: A Game Changer for Small and Medium Enterprises (SMEs). *Journal of Enterprise Information Management*, 22(1), 72–83.

Sun, D. W., Chang, G. R., Gao, S., Jin, L. Z., & Wang, X. W. (2012). Modeling a dynamic data replication strategy to increase system availability in cloud computing environments. *Journal of Computer Science and Technology*, 27(2), 256–272. DOI: 10.1007/s11390-012-1221-4

Sun, Y., Huang, Q., Liu, T., Cheng, Y., & Li, Y. (2023). Multi-Strategy Enhanced Harris Hawks Optimization for Global Optimization and Deep Learning-Based Channel Estimation Problems. *Mathematics*, 11(2), 390. DOI: 10.3390/math11020390

Taha, A., Metzler, P., Trapero, R., Luna, J., & Suri, N. (2016). *Identifying and Utilizing Dependencies Across Cloud Security Services. Association for Computing Machinery*. ACM., DOI: 10.1145/2897845.2897911

Tahirkheli, A. I., Shiraz, M., Hayat, B., Idrees, M., Sajid, A., Ullah, R., Ayub, N., & Kim, K. I. (2021). A survey on modern cloud computing security over smart city networks: Threats, vulnerabilities, consequences, countermeasures, and challenges. *Electronics (Basel)*, 10(15), 1811. DOI: 10.3390/electronics10151811

Taleb, Y., McGehee, K., Yan, N., Wang, S., Müller, S. C., & Samuels, A. (2024, June). Amazon MemoryDB: A fast and durable memory-first cloud database. In *Companion of the 2024 International Conference on Management of Data* (pp. 309-320). DOI: 10.1145/3626246.3653380

Tamimi, A. A., Dawood, R., & Sadaqa, L. (2019, April). Disaster recovery techniques in cloud computing. In *2019 IEEE Jordan International Joint Conference on Electrical Engineering and Information Technology (JEEIT)* (pp. 845-850). IEEE. DOI: 10.1109/JEEIT.2019.8717450

Tang, B., Lu, Y., Li, Q., Bai, Y., Yu, J., & Yu, X. (2023). A Diffusion Model Based on Network Intrusion Detection Method for Industrial Cyber-Physical Systems. *Sensors (Basel)*, 23(3), 1141. DOI: 10.3390/s23031141 PMID: 36772180

Tao, H., Bhuiyan, M. Z. A., Rahman, M. A., Wang, G., Wang, T., Ahmed, M. M., & Li, J. (2019). Economic perspective analysis of protecting big data security and privacy. *Future Generation Computer Systems*, 98, 660–671. DOI: 10.1016/j.future.2019.03.042

Tapas, N., Merlino, G., Longo, F., & Puliafito, A. (2019). Blockchain-based publicly verifiable cloud storage. In *IEEE International Conference on Smart Computing (SMARTCOMP)* (pp. 381-386). DOI: 10.1109/SMARTCOMP.2019.00076

Teerakanok, S., Uehara, T., & Inomata, A. (2021). *Migrating to Zero Trust Architecture: Reviews and Challenges*. Hindawi Limited., DOI: 10.1155/2021/9947347

Thakur, S., Chakraborty, A., De, R., Kumar, N., & Sarkar, R. (2021). Intrusion detection in cyber-physical systems using a generic and domain specific deep auto encoder model. *Computers & Electrical Engineering*, 91, 107044. DOI: 10.1016/j.compeleceng.2021.107044

Tiwari, A., Kumar, S., Baishwar, N., Vishwakarma, S. K., & Singh, P. (2022, September). Efficient Cloud Orchestration Services in Computing. In *Proceedings of 3rd International Conference on Machine Learning, Advances in Computing, Renewable Energy and Communication: MARC 2021* (pp. 739-746). Singapore: Springer Nature Singapore.

Tiwari, M. N. (2023). Perspective study of Public Cloud: A highly scalable Cloud deployment model. *Authorea Preprints*.

Truong, D. (2010). How cloud computing enhances competitive advantages: A research model for small businesses. *The Business Review, Cambridge*, 15(1), 59–65.

Tychalas, D., & Karatza, H. (2016). Cloud Resource Management.

Usman, A., Schadek, R., & Theel, O. (2017, January). A Novel Highly Available Data Replication Strategy exploiting Data Semantics, Coding Techniques and Prior At-Hand Knowledge. In 2017 IEEE 22nd Pacific Rim International Symposium on Dependable Computing (PRDC) (pp. 301-310). IEEE.

Vacca, J. R. (Ed.). (2017). *Cloud computing security: Foundations and challenges*. CRC Press.

Vargas-Lombardo, M., Leguías, A., Isabel, D.C., & Vega, M. (2012). Emerging Threats, Risk and Attacks in Distributed Systems: Cloud Computing.

Velumadhava Rao, R., & Selvamani, K. (2015). Data security challenges and its solutions in cloud computing. In *Proceedings of the International Conference on Intelligent Computing, Communication & Convergence (ICCC-2015)*. Interscience Institute of Management and Technology, Bhubaneswar, Odisha, India.

Venugopal, K., & Jagadeesh, B. (2024). Theoretical insights into user security and privacy in social media environments. *Advances in Human and Social Aspects of Technology*, 289–312. DOI: 10.4018/979-8-3693-9235-5.ch015

Verizon. (2020). The state of cloud security: Analyzing the Capital One breach. *Data Breach Investigations Report, 2020*, 56-72.

Verma, A., & Kaushal, S. (2011). Cloud computing security issues and challenges: a survey. In *Advances in Computing and Communications: First International Conference, ACC 2011, Kochi, India, July 22-24, 2011* [Springer Berlin Heidelberg.]. *Proceedings*, 1(Part IV), 445–454.

Verma, R. K., Dutta, S., Chaulya, S. K., Singh, A. K., & Prasad, G. M. (2013). Cloud Computing: A New Era in IT industry. *International Journal of Computer Technology and Electronics Engineering*, 3(2), 18–28.

Vieira, K., Schulter, A., Westphall, C., & Westphall, C. (2009). Intrusion detection for grid and cloud computing. *IT Professional*, 12(4), 38–43. DOI: 10.1109/MITP.2009.89

Voorsluys, W., Broberg, J., & Buyya, R. (2011). Introduction to cloud computing. *Cloud computing: Principles and paradigms*, 1-41. Liu, X. (2014, January). Research and applications of cloud desktop. In *2014 International Conference on Computer, Communications and Information Technology (CCIT 2014)* (pp. 14-17). Atlantis Press.

Wadhwani, P. (2023). Identity and Access Management (IAM) market size by solution (Provisioning, password management, directory services, advanced authentication, Single Sign-On, Audit, compliance & Governance), by deployment model, by application & forecast, 2023 – 2032. In Global Market Insights Inc. https://www.gminsights.com/industry-analysis/identity-and-access-management-market

Wallace, R. M. (2012). The Cloud Revolution, How Service Oriented Architecture and High Performance Computing will Transform the Water Resources Community of Practice.

Wang, C., Wang, Q., Ren, K., & Lou, W. (2009). Ensuring data storage security in cloud computing. In Quality of Service, 2009. IWQoS. 17th International Workshop on (pp. 1–9). IEEE.

Wang, L., Tao, J., Kunze, M., Castellanos, A. C., Kramer, D., & Karl, W. (2008, September). Scientific cloud computing: Early definition and experience. In *2008 10th ieee international conference on high performance computing and communications* (pp. 825-830). Ieee.

Wang, Y., Qiu, X., Zhang, C., Mi, W., Li, L., & Ji, Y. (2009, September). Effective data replication in heterogeneous structured P2P networks. In 2009 5th International Conference on Wireless Communications, Networking and Mobile Computing (pp. 1-4). IEEE.

Wang, L., Shen, X., Li, J., Shao, J., & Yang, Y. (2019). Cryptographic primitives in blockchains. *Journal of Network and Computer Applications*, 127, 43–58. DOI: 10.1016/j.jnca.2018.11.003

Wang, Z., Li, Z., He, D., & Chan, S. (2022). A lightweight approach for network intrusion detection in industrial cyber-physical systems based on knowledge distillation and deep metric learning. *Expert Systems with Applications*, 206, 117671. DOI: 10.1016/j.eswa.2022.117671

Weinhardt, C., Anandasivam, A., Blau, B., Borissov, N., Meinl, T., Michalk, W., & Stößer, J. (2009). Cloud computing–a classification, business models, and research directions. *Business & Information Systems Engineering*, 1(5), 391–399. DOI: 10.1007/s12599-009-0071-2

Willcocks, L. P., Venters, W., & Whitley, E. A. (2013). *Cloud computing as innovation: studying diffusion*. Springer., DOI: 10.1007/978-3-642-40951-6_7

Williamson, A. (2009). Comparing cloud computing providers. *Cloud Comp. J*, 2(3), 3–5.

Wipro. (n.d.). Overcoming security and compliance challenges in a hybrid multi-cloud environment. Retrieved from https://www.wipro.com/cybersecurity/overcoming-security-and-compliance-challenges-in-a-hybrid-multi-cloud-environment/

Wood, K., & Pereira, E. (2010). An investigation into cloud configuration and security. In *Proceedings of the Internet Technology and Secured Transactions (ICITST)2010 International Conference* (pp. 1–6). IEEE.

Wu, W., & Feng, W. (2021). Game to Dethrone: A Least Privilege CTF. 2021 IEEE 6th International Conference on Smart Cloud (SmartCloud), 132-137. https://doi.org/DOI: 10.1109/SmartCloud52277.2021.00030

Wu, H., Ding, Y., Winer, C., & Yao, L. (2010, November). Network security for virtual machine in cloud computing. In *5th International conference on computer sciences and convergence information technology* (pp. 18-21). IEEE.

Wu, H., Zhang, Z., Guan, C., Wolter, K., & Xu, M. (2020). Collaborate edge and cloud computing with distributed deep learning for smart city Internet of things. *IEEE Internet of Things Journal*, 7(9), 8099–8110. DOI: 10.1109/JIOT.2020.2996784

Wylde, A. (2021, June). Zero trust: Never trust, always verify. In 2021 international conference on cyber situational awareness, data analytics and assessment (cybersa) (pp. 1-4). IEEE.

Xie, S., Zheng, Z., Chen, W., Wu, J., Dai, H. N., & Imran, M. (2020). Blockchain for cloud exchange: A survey. *Computers & Electrical Engineering*, 81, 106526. DOI: 10.1016/j.compeleceng.2019.106526

Xue, C. T. S., & Xin, F. T. W. (2016). Benefits and challenges of the adoption of cloud computing in business. *International Journal on Cloud Computing: Services and Architecture, 6*(6), 01-15.

Xu, X., Huang, Q., Yin, X., Abbasi, M., Khosravi, M. R., & Qi, L. (2020). Intelligent offloading for collaborative smart city services in edge computing. *IEEE Internet of Things Journal*, 7(9), 7919–7927. DOI: 10.1109/JIOT.2020.3000871

Yang, J., Chen, Y. L., Por, L. Y., & Ku, C. S. (2023). A systematic literature review of information security in chatbots. *Applied Sciences (Basel, Switzerland)*, 13(11), 6355. DOI: 10.3390/app13116355

Yang, S., & Chang, J. (2024). Identity-based remote data integrity auditing from lattices for secure cloud storage. *Cluster Computing*, 27(5), 1–12. DOI: 10.1007/s10586-023-04239-9

Yang, Y., Wu, L., Yin, G., Li, L., & Zhao, H. (2017, October). A Survey on Security and Privacy Issues in Internet-of-Things. *IEEE Internet of Things Journal*, 4(5), 1250–1258. DOI: 10.1109/JIOT.2017.2694844

Yang, Y., & Wu, S. (2018). Cloud computing deployment models and their impact on organizational needs. Journal of Cloud Computing: Advances. *Systems and Applications*, 7(1), 18–30. DOI: 10.1186/s13677-018-0123-7

Yao, Z., Ding, Z., & Clausen, T. (2022). Multi-agent reinforcement learning for network load balancing in data center. *Proceedings of the 31st ACM International Conference on Information & Knowledge Management*. https://doi.org/DOI: 10.1145/3511808.3557133

Younis, M. Y. A., & Kifayat, K. (2013). *Secure cloud computing for critical infrastructure: A survey* (Technical Report). Liverpool John Moores University.

Younis, Y. A., Kifayat, K., & Merabti, M. (2014). An access control model for cloud computing. *Journal of Information Security and Applications*, 19(1), 45–60. DOI: 10.1016/j.jisa.2014.04.003

Yu, S., Ren, K., Lou, W., & Li, J. (2009). Defending against key abuse attacks in KP-ABE enabled broadcast systems. In *Security and Privacy in Communication Networks:5th International ICST Conference, SecureComm 2009,Athens, Greece,September 14-18, 2009, Revised Selected Papers 5* (pp. 311-329). Springer Berlin Heidelberg. DOI: 10.1007/978-3-642-05284-2_18

Yu, D., Cheng, X., Dressler, F., Kowalski, D. R., & Lv, W. (2020). Guest editorial: Special issue on high-confidence city IoT for collaborative smart city services. *IEEE Internet of Things Journal*, 7(9), 7848–7850. DOI: 10.1109/JIOT.2020.3021495

Yu, S., Wang, C., Ren, K., & Lou, W. (2010, March). *Achieving secure, scalable, and fine-grained data access control in cloud computing. In 2010 Proceedings IEEE INFOCOM*. Ieee.

Yu, Y., Cao, R. Q., & Schniederjans, D. (2017). Cloud computing and its impact on service level: A multi-agent simulation model. *International Journal of Production Research*, 55(15), 4341–4353. DOI: 10.1080/00207543.2016.1251624

Zhan, X., Durcikova, A., & Galletta, D. (2024). *The Paradox of Choice: Digital Akrasia in the Deployment of Multi-Factor Authentication*.

Zhang, J., Pan, L., Han, Q. L., Chen, C., Wen, S., & Xiang, Y. (2021). Deep learning based attack detection for cyber-physical system cybersecurity: A survey. IEEE/CAA Journal of Automatica Sinica, 9(3), 377-391.

Zhang, X., Lai, S.-q., & Liu, N.-w. (2012). Research on cloud computing data security model based on multi-dimension. In *Information Technology in Medicine and Education (ITME), 2012 International Symposium on* (Vol. 2, pp. 897–900). IEEE. DOI: 10.1109/ITiME.2012.6291448

Zhang, X., Wuwong, N., Li, H., & Zhang, X. (2010, June). Information security risk management framework for the cloud computing environments. In *2010 10th IEEE international conference on computer and information technology* (pp. 1328-1334). IEEE. DOI: 10.1109/CIT.2010.501

Zhang, Y., & Zhang, Y. (2012). Cloud computing and cloud security challenges. In Information Technology in Medicine and Education (ITME), 2012 International Symposium on (Vol. 2, pp. 1084–1088). IEEE.

Zhang, L. J., & Zhou, Q. (2009, July). CCOA: Cloud computing open architecture. In *2009 IEEE International Conference on Web Services* (pp. 607-616). Ieee. DOI: 10.1109/ICWS.2009.144

Zhang, Q., Cheng, L., & Boutaba, R. (2010). Cloud computing: State-of-the-art and research challenges. *Journal of Internet Services and Applications*, 1(1), 7–18. DOI: 10.1007/s13174-010-0007-6

Zhang, Y., Deng, R. H., Xu, S., Sun, J., Li, Q., & Zheng, D. (2020). Attribute-based encryption for cloud computing access control: A survey. *ACM Computing Surveys*, 53(4), 1–41.

Zheng, Z., Xie, S., Dai, H., Chen, X., & Wang, H. (2017). An overview of blockchain technology: Architecture, consensus, and future trends. In IEEE International Congress on Big Data (BigData Congress) (pp. 557-564). IEEE.

Zheng, W., Zheng, Z., Chen, X., Dai, K., Li, P., & Chen, R. (2019). NutBaaS: A blockchain-as-a-service platform. *IEEE Access : Practical Innovations, Open Solutions*, 7, 134422–134433. DOI: 10.1109/ACCESS.2019.2941905

Zheng, Z., Yang, S., & Wu, J. (2018). *Cloud computing: Resource management and application*. Springer.

Zhu, H., Wang, Y., Hei, X., Ji, W., & Zhang, L. (2018). A blockchain-based decentralized cloud resource scheduling architecture. In *International Conference on Network and Network Applications (NaNA)* (pp. 324-329). DOI: 10.1109/NANA.2018.8648712

Zhu, S., Wang, T., Deng, Y., & Xie, X. (2009). Design of IAM Function in ERP Systems. *2009 Second International Symposium on Electronic Commerce and Security*, 1, 98-101. https://doi.org/DOI: 10.1109/ISECS.2009.114

Zibaeirad, A., Koleini, F., Bi, S., Hou, T., & Wang, T. (2024). A comprehensive survey on the security of smart grid: Challenges, mitigations, and future research opportunities. *arXiv preprint arXiv:2407.07966*. Alomar, M. A. (2023). An IOT based smart grid system for advanced cooperative transmission and communication. *Physical Communication, 58*, 102069.

Zissis, D., & Lekkas, D. (2010). Addressing cloud computing security issues. *Future Generation Computer Systems*.

About the Contributors

Tarun Kumar received his Ph.D. degree from the National Institute of Technology Patna, Bihar, India. Dr. Kumar has more than 18 years of experience in teaching and is currently working as an Assistant Professor in the School of Computer Science and Engineering at Galgotias University, Greater Noida, India. His research interests include cloud computing, IoT, and DNA computing. Dr. Kumar has published several patents and papers in conference proceedings, book chapters, and refereed journals. He has also participated in many international conferences as an organizer and session chair. Dr. Kumar is a member of IEEE, ACM, and the IEEE Computer Society.

***

Anzar Ahmad is an esteemed Associate Professor in the Electronics & Communication Department at Graphic Era University, Dehradun. With an impressive 27-year career in both academia and industry, Dr. Ahmad is recognized for his expertise in the fields of the Internet of Things (IoT) and Wireless Communication Systems. Dr. Ahmad began his academic journey with a B. Tech from Jamia Millia Islamia University, New Delhi, after that he completed his M.Tech and a PhD. His dedication to research and education has earned him several awards, including the Outstanding Contribution in Research award from Graphic Era University, the Adarsh Nagarik Samman Patra from NSS Dehradun, and multiple accolades for his exceptional contributions to blood donation, recognized by the Hon'able Chief Minister of Uttarakhand and the AIDS Control Board of Dehradun. Throughout his career, Dr. Ahmad has had the honor of working under the mentorship of internationally renowned Prof. Dr. S.C. Gupta from IIT Roorkee. His research has been widely published in national and international journals and conferences, and he has worked on a DEAL Dehradun-funded project. His commitment to fostering a dynamic learning environment is evident through his efforts in developing comprehensive curricula and mentoring students in their academic and professional pursuits. In addition to his academic achievements, Dr. Ahmad is an active member of ISTE and IEEE. He has also presented his research at prestigious institutions such as Singapore University. Dr. Ahmad's contributions to the field of electronics and communication and his dedication to mentoring the next generation of engineers have solidified his reputation as a leading figure in his field.

Çiğdem Bakır is an Assistant Professor of Software Engineering at the Engineering Faculty – Kutahya University, Turkey. She received the B.S. degree in computer engineering from the University of Sakarya, in 2010, and the M.S. and Ph.D. degrees in computer engineering from Yildiz Technical University, Istanbul. She is currently pursuing the doctorate degree in computer science with the University of Yildiz Technical, Istanbul. She was a Research Assistant at Yildiz Technical University and Igdir University. She was an Instructor at Erzincan Binali Yildirim, from 2020 to 2021. She has been an Assistant Professor with the Software Engineering Department, Dumlupinar University, since 2021. Her research interests include information security, distributed database, big data, blockchain technology, cloud computing, and computer networks.

Indu Bhardwaj has 10 years of expertise in teaching, and research and development. She received her Ph.D. degree in Electronics and Communication Engineering from Galgotias University, Greater Noida, in wireless communication especially in securing vehicular communication with trust model. She has completed her postdoc from Federal Institute of Science, Education and Technology, IFCE Brazil. She has more than 40 publications in various indexed journals/conferences published by IEEE, Springer, Elsevier, among others. She has published 7 patents. With specialization in wireless Communication her field of Interest includes vehicular Ad-hoc Networks (VANET), Internet of Things (IoT), Internet of vehicles (IoV), Artificial Intelligence (AI), security techniques, Smart Cities, Healthcare, Transportation and Wireless Technologies. She has contributed in the research field as a Faculty Resource Person, Session Chair, Reviewer, Technical Committee member and Conference Secretary in various conferences and journals. She is also serving as member of Editorial Board for Global Journal of Innovation and Emerging Technology (IET). Currently she is serving as an Associate Professor in the Department of ECE at Galgotias University, Greater Noida, U.P., India.

Syeda Meraj Bilfaqih is currently working in the Computer Science Department at King Khalid University, Abha, KSA. She is a PhD scholar with research interests in machine learning and cybersecurity. Her work focuses on exploring innovative approaches to enhance security measures through the integration of machine learning techniques.

Subir Chakraborty has worked as Assistant Professor in the department of Computer Science and Engineering with Haldia Institute of Technology, Haldia. He has more than 18 years of teaching experience in AICTE(India) approved institutes . He holds a bachelor degree in computer science and technology from IIEST, Shibpur, an institute of national importance . and completed master degree in computer science and engineering under West bengal university of technology. His interest is Cloud Computing, Artificial intelligence, Cyber Security, Big Data Processing.

Rishabh Das is an Assistant Professor at the Scripps College of Communication, Ohio University. With over a decade of hands-on experience in operating, troubleshooting, and supervising control systems in the oil and gas industry, Dr. Das has become a recognized leader in the field of cybersecurity. His award-winning work in developing security architectures and detection algorithms has significantly advanced the protection of legacy industrial controllers against cyber threats. Dr. Das's research portfolio is extensive, encompassing the virtualization of Industrial Control Systems (ICS), threat modeling, penetration testing in ICS, active network monitoring, and the application of Machine Learning (ML) in cybersecurity. His expertise has been sought after by military associations and commercial entities alike, guiding them in meeting their cybersecurity requirements for critical infrastructure.

Suman Devi is currently working as Assistant Professor in School of Computing Science & Engineering. She has total experience of more than 11 years of teaching and has been associated with Galgotias University since 2017. Along with she is a research scholar in the Department of CSE at Galgotias University, India. She is firm Believer of productivity and efficiency in work. She exhibits an honest work ethic with the ability to excel in fast-paced, time- sensitive environment. Being a passionate teacher, she believes that teaching is not merely restricted to making the students understand the underlying concepts of a course but also to develop critical thinking and evaluate alternate approaches for problem solving. He always put his efforts towards the overall developments of her students. Her research interest area is Wireless sensor networks, Security. She has published several papers in peer reviewed journal and international conferences. She also organized and attended several workshops.

Saru Dhir is presently working as Associate Professor in the Department of Information Technology, at Amity University Uttar Pradesh, Noida. She completed her Ph.D. in Computer Science & Engineering in 2017. She filled a Patent on "An environment friendly green tablet PC"(Amity CRN 773) and "An Agricultural

System For Early Blight Detection With IoT Connectivity". She is having more than 13 year experience in teaching as well as in research. She has published more than 40 research articles in international journals, book chapters and conference. Her research areas are: Software Engineering, Agile Development, Software Testing, Cyber security and IOT. She is the member of Professional Bodies such as IAENG, CSTA. She is also serving as a Guest Editor of Special Issue on Intelligent Systems and Application, International Journal of Intelligent Information Technologies (IJIIT), IGI Global (Scopus Indexed). She is the editor of book series "Advanced Computing Techniques: Implementation, Informatics and Emerging Technologies", published by Bentham publisher.

Sumita Gupta has completed her doctorate in Computer Engineering from JC Bose University of Science & Technology, YMCA Faridabad. She has total experience of 13 years including both Academia and Industry. She has teaching experience of 10 years during which published many papers in various national/ international conferences and journals indexed by reputed agencies. She worked as Patent Analyst for 2.7 years with Microsoft. Currently, She is working as an Assistant Professor at Amity School of Engineering & Technology, Amity University, Noida, India. Her current areas of interest are Database, Information Retrieval, Web Mining, Digital Libraries etc. She has guided various research projects, thesis and B.tech projects. She has organised various events like international conferences, FDPs, Training programmes and seminars. She is reviewer for various journals of national and International repute.

Vishal Jain is presently working as Professor at the Department of Computer Science and Engineering, School of Engineering and Technology, Sharda University, Greater Noida, U. P., India. Before that, he worked for several years as an Associate Professor at Bharati Vidyapeeth's Institute of Computer Applications and Management (BVICAM), New Delhi. He has more than 17 years of experience in the academics. He has earned degrees: Ph.D (CSE), M.Tech (CSE), MBA (HR), MCA, MCP, and CCNA. He has more than 1750 research citations with Google Scholar (h-index score 21 and i-10 index 47) and has authored more than 120 research papers in professional journals and conferences. He has authored and edited more than 50 books (most of them are indexed at the Scopus) with various reputed publishers, including Elsevier, Springer, IET, Apple Academic Press, CRC, Taylor and Francis Group, Scrivener, Wiley, Emerald, NOVA Science, River Publishers, IGI-Global and Bentham Science. He has more than 100 Scopus publications. His research areas include machine learning, information retrieval, semantic web, ontology engineering, data mining, ad hoc networks, sensor networks and network security. He received a Young Active Member Award for the year 2012–13 from the Computer Society of India, and Best Faculty Award for the year 2017 and Best Researcher Award for the year 2019 from BVICAM, New Delhi.

Kapil Joshi is an Associate Professor in the department of Computer Science & Engineering (CSE) at Uttaranchal Institute of Technology (UIT), Uttaranchal University, Dehradun, Uttarakhand, India. He has completed his Ph.D, topic on "Image Quality Enhancement using Fusion Technique" in computer science and engineering from Uttaranchal University, Dehradun. He has more than 10 years' experience in industry, academic, and research. His areas of interest are Operating System, Computer Networks, Web Technology, Data Structure and Java etc. His research areas are deep learning, CNN, Computer vision etc. He has published various patents, 400+ research papers in reputed journals (UGC/Scopus) as well as published 20+ books in international publication. Dr. Kapil Joshi has published more than 50+ research papers in various international journals (including ISI/ SCI indexed). He has also been associated with many conferences at National and International level and organized many conferences like STEM-2017, ICACDS-18, ICAESMT-19, ICAEST-20, ICAEST-21, ICIS-22, ICNN-22, IDVRP-22, ICAEST-22 and ICAEST-23.

Vasima Khan is a unique blend of technical expertise with student-focused teaching, a dedicated and hardworking professional who is committed to providing a well-balanced, supportive and learning environment for all students. Done Bachelors, Masters and Doctorate in Computer Science and Engineering and has more than Twelve years of experience of teaching in both UG and PG engineering colleges. Taught various important technical subjects out of which conceptual skills are Operating System, Theory of Computing, Statistics, Computer Programming, Software Engineering, Compiler Design, Databases, Computer Architecture and Data Structure & Algorithms. Also taught few recent subjects like Machine Learning, Deep Learning, Natural Language Processing etc. Doing research work in the area of Machine Learning, Deep Learning, GAN, NLP, Wireless Sensor Network and others. Participated and lead various events like Faculty Development Program, Workshops, Conferences, Cultural and Sports functions etc. Always ready to learn, teach and innovate as well as tries to incorporate new ways into teaching.

Devansh Malik is from Amity University and having interest in cloud computing.

Garima Mathur has recently completed her PhD in the Department of Computer Science and Engineering. She has an impressive publication record with nearly 20 papers spanning various fields. Her areas of expertise include machine learning, image processing, blockchain technology, and bioinformatics. In addition to her research accomplishments, Dr. Mathur brings over seven years of teaching experience from prestigious institutions, where she has made significant contributions to both undergraduate and postgraduate education.

Archan Mitra is an Assistant Professor at School of Media Studies (SOMS) at Presidency University, Bangalore. He is the author of two book "Cases for Classroom Media and Entertainment Business" and "Multiverse and Media", he also has other several edited books to his credit. He has done his doctorate from Visva-Bharati Santiniketan, West Bengal in the field of "environmental informatics and communication for sustainability". In addition to that he is a certified Science Communicator and Journalism from Indian Science Communication Society (ISCOS), certified Corporate Trainer with Amity Institute of Training and Development, Certified Social Media Network Analyst. He has a strong interest in environmental communication. He was awarded certificate of merit by PRSI, Kolkata Chapter and Medal of Honor by Journalistic Club of Kolkata. He was working as a research assistant with the World Bank's "Environmental Capacity Building in Southeast Asia" project at IIM Kashipur. He was instrumental in launching the World Bank's Green MBA MOOC, he has also assisted in the research project on Uttarakhand disaster mitigation by ICSSR, the leading research on Uttarakhand disaster.

Hitesh Mohapatra received the B.E. degree in Information Technology from Biju Patnaik University of Technology (BPUT), Odisha in 2006, and the MTech. Degree in CSE from Odisha University of Technology and Research (OUTR) University, Odisha in 2009. He received his Ph.D. in Computer Science & Engineering in 2021 from Veer Surendra Sai University of Technology (VSSUT), Burla, India. He has contributed 30 SCI and Scopus indexed research papers, 21 international/national conferences and books on Software Engineering and C Programming respectively. He has 15 years of teaching experience both in industry and academia. He has served the research community with various capacities like session chair, technical chair, keynote speaker etc. His research interests include wireless sensor network, smart city, smart grid and smart water. Currently he is working as Associate professor at School of Computer Engineering, KIIT DU, Bhubaneswar, and Odisha.

Shameek Mukhopadhyay is working as Assistant Professor in the department of BCA with The Heritage Academy,Kolkata. He has more than 15 years of teaching experience in AICTE(India) approved institutes . He holds a master degree in information technology from IIEST, Shibpur, an institute of national importance. His interest is networking, computer security, data analytics.

Sachin Murarka holds a Master's degree in Digital Communication & Networking and is currently pursuing a PhD at Ravindra Nath Tagore University, focusing on Big Data Technology. With more than 13 years of teaching and training experience at prestigious engineering institutes in Bhopal and Pune, he has taught numerous core subjects that enhance student employability. Additionally, he has managed Processors labs and Also conducted workshops for Cloud Computing to prepare students for their industrial exposure. He also mentored a team for the Industrial Visits, Conferences and Training. He has having more than 10 Internationals journals and guided more than 15 students for their M.Tech Degree. He is expertise in Cloudera Hadoop, Cloud Computing, Snowflakes, Linux, Digital Communication, Networking.

Menard Musendekwa, PhD, is a distinguished scholar in Theology, specializing in the Old Testament, and a dedicated Minister of Religion. His academic journey spans across multiple disciplines, reflecting his versatile expertise in areas such as Church History, Theology, Gender Studies, Education, and Climate Change, among others. With a rich portfolio of publications in esteemed journals and numerous contributions to book chapters, he has made significant scholarly contributions that resonate across academic circles. Dr. Musendekwa's commitment to academic excellence is further demonstrated through his active engagement in various academic conferences, where he shares insights and collaborates with fellow scholars. Currently serving as the Chair of Theology at Reformed Church University in Zimbabwe and holding the position of Vice-Principal at Murray Theological College, he brings a wealth of experience to his roles. With a profound dedication to university education, Dr. Musendekwa continues to inspire and mentor the next generation of scholars, shaping the future of theological studies and beyond.

Arvindhan Muthusamy is presently employed as an Assistant Professor in the School of Computing Science and Engineering. His teaching experience exceeds 14 years. He has been affiliated with Galgotias University since 2017. I have authored three publications in SCI journals, as well as twenty-five publications indexed in SCOPUS, including chapters. My area of interest encompasses the fields of cloud computing and machine learning. I have published 7 patents in interdisciplinary initiatives.

Betty Paulraj completed her Ph.D in Information and Communication Engineering in 2019 from Anna University, Chennai. currently working as Assistant Professor Grade III at Amity School of Engineering and Technology. Her area of interest in Data Security, Cognitive learning, Image Processing. She has over 10 years of experience in teaching and published various articles in indexed journals.

Suman Rani is an accomplished academic and researcher specializing in artificial intelligence, machine learning, and big data. With a strong foundation in computer science, she is currently pursuing her Ph.D. at Uttaranchal University, Dehradun, where her research focuses on machine learning, deep learning, and image processing, particularly in the area of knee osteoarthritis diagnosis. She holds an M.Tech in Computer Science Engineering from MD University, Rohtak, where she graduated with distinction, and an MBA in Human Resources from IGNOU, New Delhi. Ms. Rani has over 17 years of teaching experience, serving as an Assistant Professor at various prestigious institutions, including IIMT College of Engineering, Greater Noida. Her academic career is marked by numerous publications in leading journals and conferences, including IEEE and Springer, with notable research contributions in artificial intelligence and software engineering. In addition to her academic pursuits, Ms. Rani holds multiple patents, such as the IoT-based Water Management System and a Biometric Authentication System for Debit Card Transactions. A dedicated educator and researcher, Ms. Rani is known for her practical approach to problem-solving, adaptability, and continuous pursuit of knowledge. Her work in organizing and attending faculty development programs on intellectual property rights, AI, and machine learning demonstrates her commitment to academic excellence. Her diverse research interests, spanning from AI-based medical applications to software requirements engineering, reflect her versatility and depth of expertise in the field of computer science.

Pankaj Savita is pursuing PhD in computer science and engineering from RGPV Bhopal. He is working as assistant professor in Sagar Institute of science and Technology, Bhopal, Madhya Pradesh, He has 14 year of experience, He has published 20 + research paper in International Journal and international Conferences. He has expertise in the field of IoT and Machine Learning.

Mahendra Prasad Sharma Sharma has more than 15 years of teaching experience and director of T&NP department, many research papers in MANET and network security and deep learning. He is interested in DAA and DSA and Cloud computing.

Ruhiat Sultana is working as an Associate Professor in the Department of Computer Science and Engineering at the Lords Institute of Engineering and Technology, Hyderabad, Telangana. Her areas of interest include machine learning, cybersecurity and data science. She is a member of the ISTE, IEEE, and IAENG professional bodies. Her teaching journey spans over 14 years, during which she has had the privilege to instruct a diverse group of students at various academic levels. She has published one patent and 12 research articles in various Scopus-indexed,

Web of Science, and UGC journals. She attended faculty development programs and workshops, enhancing pedagogical techniques and updating her expertise in emerging technologies.

Akila Thiyagarajan, M.E., Ph.D., is presently working as Assistant professor in the department of Computer Science, King Khalid University, Kingdom of Saudi Arabia. She completed her M.E degree (Computer Science and Engineering) at J.J college of Engineering and Technology, Trichy and Ph.D from Anna University, Chennai. During her tenure of 25 years of teaching experience she performed various roles and responsibilities as Academic Coordinator, organizing secretary for National and International Symposiums, Convener for various workshops and faculty development Programs. Her research interests are in the field of Image Processing, Intelligent Computing, Artificial Intelligence and Data Mining. She has several research publications in well-known international Journals and Conferences. She served as a member of ABET and NCAAA Accreditation.

Anant Wairagade is a Technical Lead with over 20 years of experience in Software Engineering enabling Fortune 500 companies with digital transformation and helping them become secure organizations. In his more than two decades long career, he led the design and development of several successful products in Security and Finance domain. Beginning of his career, Anant worked as technology consultant for major Financial Services companies and Banks. Anant is passionate about using emerging technologies for helping financial institutions improve their security posture, efficiency, profitability, and customer experience. Anant is a thought leader in Enterprise Intcgrations solutions. He is expert in API based data connector development, Kafka and Messaging Middleware. His research interests are in Artificial Intelligence, Machine Learning, Security and Privacy, Software Engineering and Cloud Computing. Anant is also an active member of several Industry Open Standard communities. He is IEEE member and serve as Program Committee Member for several IEEE and other IT conferences. He holds Bachelor Degree in Computer Science and Engineering from Visvesvaraya National Institute of Technology, Nagpur, India.

Mecit Yüzkat is a researcher with a background in computer engineering, specializing in artificial intelligence, deep learning, image processing, and cybersecurity. He completed his PhD at Yıldız Technical University in 2022, following a master's degree from the same institution. Dr. Yüzkat has held academic positions at Yıldız Technical University and Muş Alparslan University. Currently, he is a researcher at the Turkish Institutes of Health, focusing on health data and AI applications. His work includes projects like the "Turkey National Genome and Bioinformatics Project" and numerous publications in high-impact journals, particularly on sperm cell analysis using AI techniques.

Index

A

B

C

D

E

T

www.ingramcontent.com/pod-product-compliance
Lightning Source LLC
LaVergne TN
LVHW080348011026
849161LV00009B/2227